WYOMING
HANDBOOK
SECOND EDITION

WYOMING
HANDBOOK
SECOND EDITION

DON PITCHER

MOON
PUBLICATIONS INC.

WYOMING HANDBOOK
SECOND EDITION

Please send all comments, corrections, additions, amendments, and critiques to:

**WYOMING HANDBOOK
C/o MOON PUBLICATIONS
P.O. BOX 3040
CHICO, CA 95927~3040, USA**

Published by
Moon Publications, Inc.
P.O. Box 3040
Chico, California 95927, USA

Printed by
Colorcraft Ltd.

Printing History
1st edition—July 1991
2nd edition—August 1993

Library of Congress Cataloging in Publications Data
Pitcher, Don 1953—
Wyoming Handbook / Don Pitcher. —2nd ed.
p. cm.
Includes bibliographical references and index.
ISBN 0-918373-98-0
1. Wyoming—Guidebooks. I. Title.
F759.3P58 1993 92-42315
917.8704'33—dc20 CIP

Printed in Hong Kong

Editor: Elizabeth Rhudy
Copy Editors: Mark Arends, Deana Corbitt
Layout and Production: Aaron Yamaguchi
Cartographers: Bob Race, Brian Bardwell
Index: Mark Arends

Front cover and all color photos by Don Pitcher

Wyoming seems to be the doing of a mad architect—tumbled and twisted, ribboned with faded, deathbed colors, thrust up and pulled down as if the place had been startled out of a deep sleep and thrown into a pure light.
—Gretel Ehrlich in *The Solace of Open Spaces*

God bless Wyoming and keep it wild.
—last entry in the diary of a girl
who died in the Tetons

ACKNOWLEDGMENTS

The detailed information in this book did not simply fall from heaven into the publisher's computer files. Nor did it come solely because of my own labor. The words are mine, but many individuals assisted along the way. As I traveled around Wyoming researching this new edition, I was inundated with suggestions for changes. I especially appreciate those who offered insights gleaned from a life's experience in their hometown: the chamber of commerce volunteers who graciously endured a barrage of questions, the motel employees who offered tips on the best local eateries, the convenience store clerks who knew when the movie stars were in town (and how fast they were going when the cops stopped them for speeding), the waitresses who told of wonderful country roads to nowhere, the government officials who offered tips on the most scenic backcountry trails, and the many others whose advice ended up in this guide. The book itself is the product of the staff at Moon who herded it through editing, layout, production, shipping, marketing, and a thousand other steps that I only half understand.

It would be impossible to list everyone in Wyoming who helped out, but the following folks provided invaluable assistance: Vince Arbour, Larry Armstrong, Dan Brecht, Eleanor Carrigen, Michael Devine, Alice Eddy, Tamra Dereemer, Anne Carey, Dawn Hill, Paul Hoffman, Nancy and Marvin Jacobs, Jim Joseph, Betty Macon, Dave McGinnis, Edre Maier, Carole Perkins, Patricia Robbins, Carl Schrier, Mark Setright, Alice Smith, Dave Taylor, Diane Tjenos, Judy Walton, Carol Waller, and Timothy White. This book represents my own perceptions of Wyoming, views that are not necessarily in congruence with those of any of these individuals. A special tip of the hat to those kind readers of the first edition who took the time to write me with comments and pointers. Johan Bakker, Dennis Crawford, Lawrence Marcott, and Tawnya Michie all contributed ideas that made it into this book in one form or another.

Perhaps my biggest IOUs go out to friends and relatives in Wyoming, Maine, Nebraska, and California who put me up—and put up with me—while I wrote various portions of this edition: Bob Boyer, Marian Huber, Dave Hurst, Holly and Doug Miner, Charlie Otto, Betty and Lawrence Pitcher, Dale Pitcher, Gary Richards, Glenn Ryburn, Bill Trush, and Sheri Woo. Happy trails to all.

CONTENTS

MAPS

MAP SYMBOLS

FREEWAY	INTERSTATE HIGHWAY
MAIN HIGHWAY	
SECONDARY ROAD	U.S. HIGHWAY
UNPAVED ROAD	
FOOT PATH, TRAIL	STATE HIGHWAY
STATE BORDER	
OTHER BORDER	O LARGE CITY
TUNNEL	o SMALL CITIES & TOWNS
PASS	▲ MOUNTAIN
RAILROAD	▲ CAMPGROUND
BRIDGE	■ POINT OF INTEREST

 WATERFALL

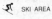 WATER

PICNIC AREA

SKI AREA

N.W.R. NATIONAL WILDLIFE REFUGE
N.P. NATIONAL PARK
S.P. STATE PARK
CG. CAMPGROUND

CHARTS

ABBREVIATIONS

a/c—air conditioned
B&B—bed and breakfast
CG—campground
d—double occupancy

I—interstate highway
mph—miles per hour
OW—one way
pp—per person

RT—roundtrip
RV—recreational vehicle
s—single occupancy

IS THIS BOOK OUT OF DATE?

Although this travel guide is updated every two years, it is always surprising to discover how much can change in that time. Wyoming is not a static place; prices rise, businesses fail, and new ones wait to be discovered. And, sometimes I simply miss the boat on an area that you may know better. This second edition contains extensive revisions and additions—a number of which were suggested by readers of the first edition. If you find any notable omissions, take offense at what is said, discover a new (or old) place worthy of mention, find inaccurate maps, or have any other comments, critiques, or compliments concerning this book, I would be happy to hear from you. All contributions will be acknowledged. Send your observations to:

Wyoming Handbook
Moon Publications
P.O. Box 3040
Chico, CA 95927-3040, USA

INTRODUCTION

It's kind of funny how you get used to the country. When I go to town, the noises keep me awake. The coal trains, the sirens going down the road, even if they are a long ways away. People get used to that. We've had people come out here who couldn't sleep because it was so quiet. No noise to lull them to sleep or whatever. My nearest neighbor is five miles away. It takes all kinds of people to make the world go around. If everybody in the world wanted to be a rancher, I probably wouldn't, because there wouldn't be anyplace to live.

—Ed Swartz, quoted in Steve Gardiner's **Rumblings from Razor City**

The expansively rugged land called Wyoming resonates with the spirit of the American West. For anyone who has spent time in Wyoming, the state evokes vivid images: cattle standing in the lee of snow fences; children riding horses along dusty dirt roads; weather-beaten ranches lit by the slanting light of late afternoon; oil-covered roustabouts struggling with the furious machinery of a drilling rig; the sounds of drumming and singing at a powwow; and cow towns where the area code is larger than the population. Here is the original "Wild West," the real-life inspiration for countless Western novels, movies, and songs.

A frontier spirit pervades both Wyoming's landscape and its people, mixing the past and present so completely that it sometimes seems as though around the next bend you might see Chief Washakie's braves circling a massive herd of bison, or Butch Cassidy and the Sundance Kid shooting it out with lawmen, or a party of fur trappers setting out for the mountains. Officially known as "the Equality State" because it was the first to allow women to vote, Wyoming actually revels in another title, "the Cowboy State." License plates carry the state emblem: a cowboy, hat in hand, atop a furiously bucking bronco. A cowboy hat and boots are acceptable dress anywhere, and the unpolished individuality embodied in the cowboy remains the state's heritage, even for those whose only connection is through country-western music.

The earliest Anglo explorers described Wyoming in less than flattering terms. The image that stuck was that of the "Great American

WYOMING ROADS AND HIGHWAYS

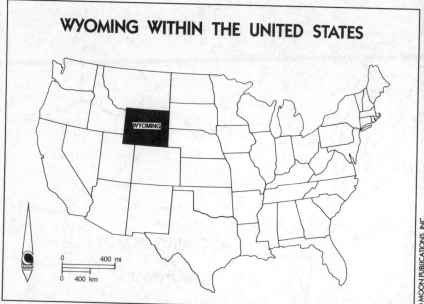

WYOMING WITHIN THE UNITED STATES

WYOMING

```
0        400 mi
0      400 km
```

Desert," a place where the native peoples flourished along with buffalo, antelope, jackrabbits, and rattlesnakes, but where homesteaders and ranchers struggled to survive. Hundreds of thousands of travelers pushed across Wyoming's basins and mountain ranges in the 19th century, bound for greener pastures and gold. Very few considered staying in such an unforgiving environment. Even today, the vast majority of those who enter Wyoming are en route to someplace else.

Seeing Wyoming

Although Wyoming is divided by three major interstate highways, the best way to see the state is from its smaller asphalt and gravel roads, where the pace slows and tumbleweeds pile against fences. From the freeways, the landscape is just a blur, but along the back roads this same land becomes transformed into a thing of raw-edged, surreal beauty. Old ranches hunker in the valleys, herds of deer and antelope glance up warily at passing cars, oddly colored rock pinnacles crown the crest of hills, and winding streams become glowing silver ribbons of light. The sense of stillness is broken only by the wind, the singing of birds, and the buzz of insects. Writer Gretel Ehrlich in *The Solace of Open Spaces* describes it best:

To live and work in this kind of open country, with its hundred-mile views, is to lose the distinction between background and foreground. When I asked an older ranch hand to describe Wyoming's openness, he said, "It's all a bunch of nothing—wind and rattlesnakes—and so much of it you can't tell where you're going or where you've been and it don't make much difference."

On the back roads you'll find folks lifting a hand to wave as you pass. Small-town cafes serve down-home food, friendly motel owners greet tired travelers, and the pace of living slows measurably. You can almost feel the stress of city life dissipating. People leave their homes, cars, and bikes unlocked; they load up wash in the laundromat and come back later to move it to the drier. They pull in at the drive-up liquor store for a six-pack. Unlike in big cities, where waiting in lines becomes a way of life, bank, grocery store, and post office queues are short or nonexistent. Try on a cowboy hat and boots, take a look around the local museum, or stop in for a beer at a country bar and joke with the locals. In a short while you'll gain an appreciation for Wyoming and the down-to-earth people who live here.

The Sky

In the vast open spaces of Wyoming, the sky takes on its own importance, sometimes making the land seem like an afterthought. The land changes slowly with the seasons—first a carpet of winter white, then the mud and first luminescent green buds of spring growth, followed by the verdant summer flowers, and finally the brilliance of fall cottonwood trees along a dry creek bed. But the sky follows the beat of another drummer, changing moment by moment throughout each day. Cottonball clouds float overhead, sending moving shadows across the landscape and coloring the sun's light. Storm clouds build on a summer afternoon, and in the distance a lightning bolt leaps to earth. Perhaps the most memorable times are the lingering sunsets, when colors seem to bounce back and forth across the sky, finally exiting as a fringe of color on the western horizon. At night, coyotes howl the same way they have for millennia, and an enormous panorama of stars arches above, undimmed by discordant city lights.

WYOMING COUNTIES

© MOON PUBLICATIONS, INC.

THE LAND

Covering nearly 98,000 square miles, Wyoming is the ninth-largest state. The states of Connecticut, Delaware, Hawaii, Maryland, Massachusetts, New Hampshire, New Jersey, Rhode Island, Vermont, and West Virginia would all fit within Wyoming's borders with room to spare. With just 456,000 inhabitants—the smallest population of any state—Wyoming remains a remarkably undeveloped and unsettled place. Cattle outnumber people by nearly three to one. The population density averages fewer than five people per square mile, and in some counties there is nearly a square mile of land for each person. With an average elevation of 6,700 feet (ranging from 3,125 feet to 13,804 feet), Wyoming is the second-highest state in the nation. Only Colorado is higher.

GEOGRAPHY

On the map, Wyoming is simply a gigantic trapezoidal chunk of earth. Its straight-line borders (375 miles from east to west and 276 miles north to south) are arbitrary human creations encompassing a surprising diversity of country. The **Continental Divide** wanders diagonally across the state from the northwest corner to south-central Wyoming. Two-thirds of Wyoming's lakes, rivers, and streams drain into tributaries of the Missouri River, eventually reaching the Atlantic Ocean; most of the rest flow into tributaries of the Colorado and Columbia rivers and hence to the Pacific Ocean. Small portions drop into the Great Basin (Salt Lake) or the Great Divide Basin (between Rock Springs and Rawlins), where the water evaporates or percolates into the ground

Wyoming's mountains generally trend in a northwest-to-southeast direction, but this gross overall pattern is broken up by smaller ranges. Northwestern Wyoming is dominated by a complex melange of mountains: the Absaroka, Teton, Gros Ventre, Wyoming, and Wind River ranges. North-central Wyoming is divided by the Big Horn Mountains, while the Laramie Range and the Medicine Bow Mountains dominate south-central Wyoming. The far northeast corner holds the Black Hills. In between these ranges, the land spreads out in broad basins, including Bighorn Basin and Powder River Basin in northern Wyoming, Wind River Basin in west-central Wyoming, and the Green River, Red Desert, and Washakie basins in the southwest. The eastern portion of Wyoming drops gently into the Great Plains.

CLIMATE

Sometimes I wish that Wyoming had more vegetation and less catarrh, more bloom and summer and fragrance and less Christmas and New Year's through the summer. I like the clear, bracing air of 7,500 feet above the civilized world, but I get weary of putting on and taking off my buffalo overcoat for meals all through dog days. I yearn for a land where a man can take off his ulster and overshoes while he delivers a Fourth of July oration, without flying into the face of Providence and dying of pneumonia. . . . As I write these lines I look out across the wide sweep of brownish gray plains dotted here and there with ranches and defunct buffalo craniums, and I see shutting down over the sides of the abrupt mountains, and meeting the foothills, a white mist which

---

Winter looks like a fictional place, an elaborate simplicity, a Nabokovian invention of rarefied detail. Winds howl all night and day, pushing litters of storm fronts from the Beartooth to the Big Horn Mountains. When it lets up, the mountains disappear. The hayfield that runs east from my house ends in a curl of clouds that have fallen like sails luffing from sky to ground. Snow returns across the field to me, and the cows, dusted with white, look like snowcapped continents drifting.

—*Gretel Ehrlich in*
The Solace of Open Spaces

WYOMING GEOGRAPHY

BEARTOOTH MOUNTAINS
YELLOWSTONE PLATEAU
BIGHORN BASIN
BIG HORN MOUNTAINS
BLACK HILLS
TETON MOUNTAINS
ABSAROKA MOUNTAINS
POWDER
RIVER
BASIN
GROS VENTRE MOUNTAINS
WIND RIVER MOUNTAINS
OWL CREEK MOUNTAINS
WIND RIVER BASIN
OVER THRUST BELT
GREEN MOUNTAINS
SHIRLEY BASIN
LARAMIE MOUNTAINS
HARTVILLE UPLIFT
GREEN RIVER BASIN
GREAT DIVIDE BASIN
HANNA BASIN
LARAMIE BASIN
DENVER - JULESBURG BASIN
CONTINENTAL DIVIDE
RED DESERT
MEDICINE BOW MOUNTAINS
WASHAKIE BASIN
SIERRA MADRE

melts into the gray sky. It is a snow storm in the mountains.

I saw this with wonder and admiration for the first two or three million times. When it became a matter of daily occurrence as a wonder or curiosity, it was below mediocrity. Last July a snow storm gathered one afternoon and fell among the foothills and whitened the whole line to within four or five miles of town, and it certainly was a peculiar freak of nature, but it convinced me that whatever enterprises I might launch into here I would not try to raise oranges and figs until the isothermal lines should meet with a change of heart.

—*Nineteenth-century humorist Bill Nye*

Wyoming's climate mirrors its diverse geography, ranging from arid deserts to cool mountain forests. The mountain ranges act as barriers to eastward-moving weather systems. Moist air is forced upward by the mountains, releasing rain or snow along the western slopes. By the time the clouds reach the east side, much of the water has been wrung out, creating a rain shadow. Because of this, midwinter finds Togwotee Pass smothered under many feet of snow while Dubois, in the lee of the Absaroka Range, may have only a dusting on the ground.

Visitors to Wyoming discover weather typical of the West's high plains and mountains: hot, dry summers punctuated by fierce thunderstorms, and cold winters with a fair amount of snow. Conditions vary greatly throughout the state, however, with cooler summers and heavy winter snows in the mountains.

Extremes

Wyoming has a reputation for extreme conditions. Wintertime blizzards periodically lash the land, and strong winds pile the snow into huge drifts. Summertime thunderstorms—particularly in the mountains—can occur almost daily in Southeastern Wyoming—with an average of nine hailstorms a year, is the hail capital of North America. Temperatures have been recorded from -66° F (Yellowstone National Park) to 114° F (the town of Basin). Precipitation shows a similar variation. In the high mountain ranges of northwestern Wyoming, as much as 60 inches (mostly snow) lands on the ground, while parched desert areas in Bighorn Basin and Great Divide Basin receive only six inches a year.

Wyoming is well-known for its wind. Through much of the state, the wind never seems to stop blowing, averaging more than 16 miles an hour along the eastern border. (Buffalo Bill Cody, a man who symbolizes the West in the American consciousness, once defended Wyoming when a friend complained of the wind: "You know where those winds come from? Well, this country up here is so close to paradise you can feel the breezes from heaven. That wind comes from the angels' wings. When they flap their wings the wind comes right down this valley.")

Basin Weather

In the expansive basins that cover much of Wyoming, typical midsummer daytime temperatures are in the 80s and 90s, with nights dropping into the 50s and 60s. Low relative humidity makes the heat easier to take. The wettest months are April and May, with lots of sun in the summer. Afternoon thunderheads often build up, temporarily blocking the sun, but generally dropping more lightning than rain. Fall can be a most pleasant time of year, with shirtsleeve weather in the day and cool evenings.

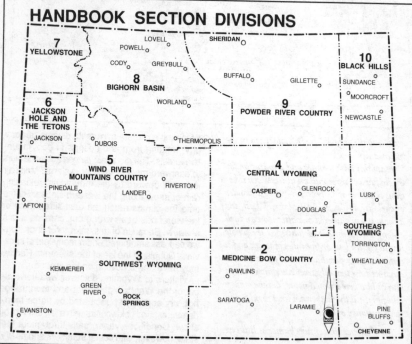

HANDBOOK SECTION DIVISIONS

7 YELLOWSTONE

POWELL
LOVELL
SHERIDAN
CODY
GREYBULL
BUFFALO
GILLETTE

10 BLACK HILLS
SUNDANCE

8 BIGHORN BASIN

MOORCROFT

6 JACKSON HOLE AND THE TETONS
JACKSON
WORLAND

9 POWDER RIVER COUNTRY
NEWCASTLE

DUBOIS
THERMOPOLIS

5 WIND RIVER MOUNTAINS COUNTRY
PINEDALE
LANDER
RIVERTON

4 CENTRAL WYOMING
CASPER
GLENROCK
LUSK
DOUGLAS

AFTON

1 SOUTHEAST WYOMING
TORRINGTON

3 SOUTHWEST WYOMING
KEMMERER

2 MEDICINE BOW COUNTRY
RAWLINS
WHEATLAND

GREEN RIVER
ROCK SPRINGS
SARATOGA
LARAMIE
PINE BLUFFS

EVANSTON
CHEYENNE

© MOON PUBLICATIONS, INC.

When winter arrives in November and December, it can do so with a vengeance, pushing the mercury well below zero. Snowfall is not great, totalling from 15 to 60 inches over the winter months, but when combined with winds pushing 50 mph it can look like a lot more. In places, snow fences extend for many miles beside the highways, attempting to blunt the blowing snow. Ground blizzards sometimes halt traffic along I-80 for days at a time. Locals joke that it only snows a couple of inches in December and then blows back and forth across the state the rest of the winter until the snow is finally worn out. Actually, winters are not all so bleak, and temperatures occasionally rise into the 50s. You can expect sun 60% of the time. Chinooks —warm downslope winds—are common in the winters along the eastern slopes of the mountains, particularly around Sheridan, Dubois, and Cody.

Mountain Weather

Many of the favorite sites in Wyoming—including Yellowstone and Grand Teton national parks—lie primarily above 7,000 feet. Here, the weather is considerably cooler than in the basins. Summertime temperatures rarely top 80° F, while nights often dip into the 40s. Snow is possible at any time of the

year. April and May are generally the wettest months. Spring comes late in the mountains, and high passes are often blocked by drifts until mid-July. Summer thunderstorms are common, especially in the northwestern mountains, where they gather over the high peaks most afternoons. Mid-September brings fall conditions as mountain temperatures often drop 20-30 degrees below summer readings, quickly turning the aspen leaves into a brilliant orange and sending most folks scurrying for warmer climes.

High-country winters are often severely cold and snowy, with temperatures below zero for days at a time. Snow depths often exceed six feet in the higher mountains. Grand Targhee Ski Resort, for example, receives some 42 feet of snow over a typical winter! Fortunately, the relative humidity is quite low, making the temperatures easier to tolerate and creating fluffy powder snow conditions. One surprising winter feature is the presence of temperature inversions in intermountain valleys such as Big Piney and Jackson Hole. These often occur on cold, clear nights when the cold air sinks into the valley floors. Skiers who leave the lodge bundled in down parkas and polypro are often surprised to find temperatures 30 degrees warmer on the mountaintop.

FLORA AND FAUNA

VEGETATION

Wyoming's topography and climate are reflected in its vegetation, with dense forests in the mountains and dry grasses and shrubs at lower elevations. The vegetation can be classified into six broad categories (see map): mixed-grass prairie, sagebrush steppe, desert shrublands, evergreen forests, deciduous forests, and alpine tundra. **Mixed-grass prairies** dominate the eastern third of Wyoming and contain such species as grama grass, wheatgrass, junegrass, bluegrass, and sage. The western two-thirds of Wyoming contains vast areas of **sagebrush steppe**, a threadbare carpet of big sagebrush, wheatgrass, needle-and-thread grass, grama grass, tumbleweed, and other plants. This is the country most folks associate with Wyoming—sagebrush extending

to the horizon. (An old cowboy saying goes, "I reckon the Lord done put tumbleweeds here to show which way the wind was a-blowin'.")

Wyoming also contains desert areas, notably the Red Desert and a large part of Bighorn Basin. Dominant plants in the **desert shrublands** include greasewood, saltbush, shadscale, and various kinds of sagebrush. At higher elevations where more moisture falls, the land is covered with **evergreen forests**. Ponderosa pines dominate forested parts of eastern Wyoming, while lodgepole pine, Douglas fir, Engelmann spruce, and subalpine fir exist in mountains to the west. A few areas also have pinyon pine and juniper trees. **Deciduous forests** are scattered in small patches around Wyoming, consisting of cottonwoods along riverbottoms, aspens in the middle elevations, and bur oak in the Black Hills. Treeline in much of Wyoming is around 9,500 feet. Above

SAGEBRUSH

Sagebrush is Wyoming's ubiquitous common denominator, a sweetly pungent bush found from the lowest deserts to 10,000-foot mountains. More sage grows here than anyplace else in North America. The volatile oils make it a last choice for cattle, and act as a natural herbicide, preventing competition from other plants. Ranchers consider the plant less than worthless, but native animals such as sage grouse, antelope, and mule deer depend upon sage for survival. You won't even find sage grouse where sage doesn't grow.

The terms sagebrush and sage are generally used interchangeably in the west. Note, however, that the spice on your kitchen shelf is not the same as the Wyoming plant *(Artemesia),* and any attempt to cook with sagebrush is likely to leave you gagging. Sage has been in the west for some 25 million years and is well adapted to the poor soils and arid conditions of the desert. Sage survives by using its network of shallow roots to draw moisture from the ground as it percolates down. Wyoming actually has at least seven different species of sage. Some of these exist only on very specific sites: black sagebrush grows on windy ridges between 5,000 and 8,000 feet where the soil is shallow and stony; alkali sagebrush indicates impermeable soils that are highly alkaline. The predominant species across much of Wyoming is big sagebrush, a bush that grows to three feet in height and often covers extensive areas.

this, one finds **alpine tundra**, where the dominant plants are low-growing herbs, grasses, and forbs.

WILDLIFE

When the first mountain men and explorers wandered into the vast land that became Wyoming, they found an incredible abundance of wildlife: herds of bison stretching to the horizon; antelope, elk, and deer grazing on the broad plains; as well as grizzly bears, wolves, coyotes, cottontails, and jackrabbits. Although wolves were poisoned to extinction, and only a few hundred bison and grizzlies remain, other animals fared better. Today, the two most common large mammals are mule deer and pronghorn antelope, both of which are found across much of Wyoming. The sagebrush lands also provide cover for sage grouse, a large chicken-like bird. The males perform an elaborate X-rated mating display. In the mountains, one often hears the early-summer drumming of ruffed grouse. Rarest of Wyoming's animals is the endangered black-footed ferret (see p. 75). Everyone's least favorite reptile is the prairie rattlesnake, found at low elevations throughout Wyoming. Watch your step!

Watchable Wildlife

Wyoming's undeveloped character makes it a mecca for those who enjoy watching wild animals. Yellowstone National Park is a favorite place to look for bison and elk, along with coyotes, moose, mule deer, bighorn sheep, river otters, and trumpeter swans. Both black and grizzly bears also live here, but are less commonly seen. Another popular place is the National Elk Refuge in Jackson Hole, the winter home for a herd of more than 7,500 elk. Excellent places to see bighorn sheep are the Dubois area and Bighorn National Recreation Area. Also watch for wild horses (Wyoming has around 3,500) at Bighorn National Recreation Area or in the Red Desert. Mountain goats live in the Beartooth Mountains along Wyoming's border with Montana. The high mountains of the Tetons and Wind River Range have such animals as pikas and yellow-bellied marmots, while the sagebrush country abounds with deer, antelope, coyotes, jackrabbits, cottontails, and prairie dogs. Certainly the most distinctive Wyoming critter is the jackalope (see p. 170).

Pronghorn Antelope

One of the most commonly seen Wyoming animals is the antelope (biologists prefer the name pronghorn). More than 360,000 live here, comprising half the world's pronghorn population. Antelope survive on plants that other animals avoid, notably sagebrush, perhaps Wyoming's most abundant plant. They are built for speed: oversized lungs and windpipe give them the ability to run for miles at a 30 mph pace and to

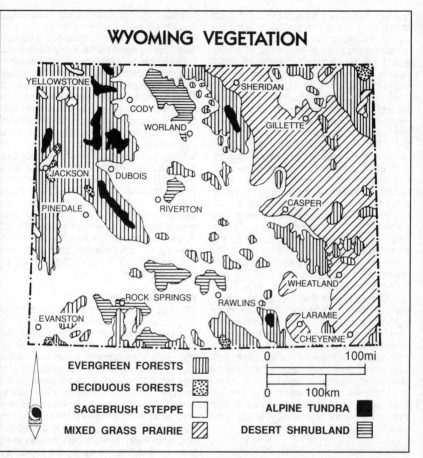

WYOMING VEGETATION

YELLOWSTONE
SHERIDAN
CODY
WORLAND
GILLETTE
JACKSON DUBOIS
CASPER
PINEDALE
RIVERTON
WHEATLAND
ROCK SPRINGS
RAWLINS
EVANSTON
LARAMIE
CHEYENNE

EVERGREEN FORESTS

DECIDUOUS FORESTS

SAGEBRUSH STEPPE

MIXED GRASS PRAIRIE

ALPINE TUNDRA

DESERT SHRUBLAND

0   100mi

0   100km

ADAPTED FROM WYOMING GEOMAPS BY SHEILA ROBERTS / GEOLOGICAL SURVEY OF WYOMING

accelerate to twice that for short bursts. To watch for predators, they have the largest eyes by body weight of any mammal. Despite this speed, pronghorn have an innate inquisitiveness that makes them relatively easy to hunt, an attribute that nearly drove them to extinction by market hunting early in this century. Strict laws and careful management have brought antelope populations back.

Deer

Wyoming has more deer than people. Two species can be seen along the state's roads:

white-tailed deer (common in the Black Hills) and the larger mule deer (found across the state). Be especially careful when driving after dusk during the fall breeding season, since the hormone-crazed bucks tend to leap out in front of cars. Nearly everyone who has lived in Wyoming has hit a deer under these circumstances. Slow down at night, especially in areas posted with Deer Crossing signs.

Elk

A majestic member of the deer family, elk (many biologists prefer the term wapiti) are a favorite both with tourists and hunters. Elk inhabit much of Wyoming, with the largest herds along the western mountains. More than 30,000 elk graze in Yellowstone National Park alone. With bulls weighing up to 900 pounds and cows up to 600 pounds, they are some of the largest antlered animals in the Americas.

Elk spend summers high in the mountains, feeding in alpine meadows and along forest edges. Mature bulls graze alone, but the cows and calves group into large herds for protection. When the fall rutting season arrives, bulls attempt to herd the cows and calves around, mating with cows when they come into estrus, and defending their harem from other bulls. During this time of year the bugling of bull elk is a common sound in the mountains, a challenge to any bull within earshot. When a competitor appears, a dominance display often follows—complete with bugling, stomping, and thrashing of the ground—to show who is the baddest bull around. In a fight, the bulls lock their massive antlers and try to push and twist until one finally gives in and retreats. These battles help ensure that the healthiest bulls produce the most offspring. Ironically, other bulls often wait in the wings for battles over the harem and rush in to mate with the cows while the larger bulls are sparring (when the cat's away . . .). The snows of late fall push elk to lower-elevation winter ranges, notably at the National Elk Refuge in Jackson Hole. When spring comes, the bulls drop their antlers and immediately begin to grow new ones. The elk head back into the high country, following the melting snowline.

BISON

The bison is the definitive frontier animal and Wyoming's state mammal. Its outline graces the Wyoming state flag. Weighing up to 3,000 pounds, they are also the largest land mammals in the New World. Bison live 45 years or more, with females bearing calves until they are in their 40s. The calves weigh 30 to 40 pounds at birth and within minutes are standing and able to graze. Two races of bison exist: the plains bison primarily east of the Rockies, and the mountain bison (sometimes called wood

bison) in the higher elevations. Technically, these huge, hairy beasts are bison—the only true buffalo are the water buffalo of Southeast Asia—but the name buffalo is commonly used.

With their massive heads, huge shoulder humps, heavy coats of fur, and small posteriors, buffalo are some of the strangest animals in North America. They look so front-heavy as to seem unstable, ready to topple forward onto their snout at any time. Despite this impression, buffalo are remarkably well adapted to life on the plains. A bison will use its strong sense of smell to find grass buried in a deep snowdrift and then sweep it away with a sideways motion of its head. The animals are also surprisingly fleet of foot, as careless Yellowstone photographers have discovered. In addition, the buffalo is one very tough critter. In 1907, a buffalo was pitted against four of the meanest Mexican bulls at a Juarez, Mexico, bullring. After knocking heads several times with the buffalo, the bulls fled and were saved only when bullfighters opened the chute gates to let them escape.

Blackening The Plains

When Europeans first reached the New World, they found massive herds of buffalo in the Appalachians and even more as they headed west. Daniel Boone hunted them in North Carolina in the 1750s; Pennsylvanians shot hundreds of buffalo that were invading their winter stores of hay. By 1820, settlers had nearly driven the buffalo to extinction in the East. But there were far more living to the west. As explorers, mountain men, and the first tentative settlers reached the "Great American Desert," they were awestruck by the numbers. Travelers told of slowly moving masses of buffalo blackening the plains, and they watched in astonishment as the herds stopped at rivers and literally drank them dry. A fair estimate of the original population of buffalo in North America is 75 million. Even in the middle 1860s, travelers through Wyoming's Wind River Valley reported seeing ten thousand bison at one time. A pioneer Kansas settler named William D. Street recalled a trip in which a herd roared past his camp for an entire night. The next morning, he climbed a nearby butte and saw buffalo covering the plains below. According to Street:

The herd was not less than twenty miles in width—we never saw the other side—at least sixty miles in length, maybe much longer; two counties of buffaloes! There might have been 100,000, or 1,000,000, or 100,000,000. I don't know. In the cowboy days in western Kansas we saw 7,000 head of cattle in one round-up. After gazing at them a few moments our thoughts turned to that buffalo herd. For a comparison, imagine a large pail of water; take from it or add to it a drop, and there you have it. Seven thousand head of cattle was not a drop in the bucket as compared with that herd of buffalo.

Indians And Buffalo

The Plains Indians depended heavily upon the buffalo for food, and—like the proverbial hot dog containing everything but the moo—they used every part of the animal. Hooves were carved into spoons, skins became buffalo robes and covers for boats and tipis, rawhide was used for drumheads, calf skins became storage sacks, hair was turned into earrings, and horns were formed into cups and arrow points. Everything that remained—including the muzzle, penis, eyes, and cartilage—was boiled down to use as glue for arrowheads. The ubiquitous buffalo chips became a cooking fuel on the treeless prairies.

Hunting techniques varied depending upon the terrain. When possible, Indians drove herds of bison into arroyos with no exit, over cliffs, or into deep sand or snow, making them easier to kill. When Spanish horses began arriving in the 16th century, they made it far easier to hunt bison. In the surround, mounted hunters attacked from at least two sides, creating chaos in the herd and allowing buffalo to be shot with arrows or guns.

When whites first spread across the plains, they found the bison a plentiful food source, but also viewed the massive herds as a hindrance to agriculture and cattle raising. These were not the only reasons whites wanted to destroy the buffalo; killing off the buffalo would starve the Indians into submission and force them to take a more "civilized" way of life. General Philip Sheridan, commenting in support of white buffalo hunters, said:

Instead of stopping the [white] hunters they ought to give them a hearty, unanimous vote of thanks, and appropriate a sufficient sum of money to strike and present to each one a medal of bronze, with a dead buffalo on one side and a discouraged Indian on the other. They are destroying the Indian's commissary, and it is a well-known fact that an army losing its base of supplies is placed at a great disadvantage. Send them powder and lead, if you will; for the sake of a lasting peace, let them kill, skin and sell until the buffaloes are exterminated.

This reckless slaughter did indeed endanger the Indians, but it also had an unwanted side effect: the Indians went on the warpath. The loss of their primary food source helped convince many Indians that their own extinction was next. The warriors who massacred Custer and his men at Little Big Horn had watched their people pushed to the brink of starvation by the destruction of the buffalo.

The Slaughter

Two factors propelled the slaughter to new heights in the 1870s: new railroads across the plains, and a sudden international demand for buffalo robes and hides. Buffalo meat proved to be a readily available food source for railway construction workers, and hunters such as "Buffalo Bill" Cody provided a steady supply, generally taking just the hindquarters and hump while leaving the rest on the plains. Hundreds of thousands were killed. Once the railroads were complete, a new "sport" appeared—shooting buffalo from the moving railcars and leaving them to rot on the prairie. Wealthy gentry from the East Coast and Europe also discovered the joys of killing. One Irish nobleman had an entourage of 40 servants, with an entire wagon just for firearms; he killed 2,000 buffalo in a three-year carnage.

Conservationists tried to halt the buffalo slaughter through legislation in 1874, but President Grant's corrupt secretary of the interior, Columbus Delano, said:

I would not seriously regret the total disappearance of the buffalo from our western prairies, in its effect upon the Indians. I would regard it rather as a means of hastening their sense of dependence upon the products of the soil and their own labors.

The legislation was pocket-vetoed by Grant.

In 1872, thousands of hide hunters spread through Kansas, Nebraska, and Colorado in search of buffalo. Over the next three years, they brought in more than three million buffalo hides, with Indians killing another 400,000 bison for meat and robes. Good hide hunters could bring down 25-100 buffalo in a typical day, keeping five skinners busy from sunup to sundown. One hunter, Jim White, killed at least 16,000 buffalo in his career. Only the hides, cured hams, and buffalo tongues (which could be salted and shipped in barrels) were saved. When Gen. Grenville M. Dodge toured Kansas in the fall of 1873, he noted that "the air was foul with a sickening stench, and the vast plain, which only a short twelvemonth before teemed with animal life, was a dead, solitary, putrid desert." Buffalo carcasses dotted the plains in such numbers that in later years bone pickers would collect massive piles of bones for knife handles, combs, and buttons, or to be ground up for sugar refining, fertilizer, or glue.

When the buffalo of the central states approached extinction, hunters turned their attention elsewhere, reaching Wyoming, Montana, and the Dakotas in 1880. In 1882, more than 200,000 hides were taken, and another 40,000 the following year. By 1884, only 300 hides were shipped. The slaughter was nearly over; only a few private herds and scattered individual bison

remained. The Indians who had once depended so heavily on buffalo for all the necessities of life were reduced to eating muskrats, gophers, and even grass. Some killed their horses, others stole settlers' cattle, and the rest had to beg the government for food. In only a couple of years, an entire culture had been decimated. But it was not just the buffalo that died or the Indians whose lives had been destroyed. Hide hunters often spiked buffalo carcasses with strychnine, returning later to skin the wolves that had come to feed on the meat. Coyotes, kit foxes, badgers, vultures, eagles, ravens, and anything else that ate the meat were also killed. With both the buffalo and the "vermin" out of the way, Wyoming and the West were safe for domestic sheep and cattle.

Protection

The first federal legislation protecting buffalo (only in Yellowstone National Park, however) did not pass until 1894. The following year, just 800 buffalo remained in all of North America, one-thousandth of one percent of their original numbers. Despite this dismal picture, the population has rebounded dramatically, and today an estimated 65,000 bison roam across America. In Wyoming, small populations can be seen in Hot Springs State Park and Grand Teton National Park, while one of the few large wild populations remains in Yellowstone National Park.

A strong demand for buffalo meat has led some Wyoming ranchers to raise bison. It's a highly specialized ranching endeavor, since the animals can flatten most fences and standard roundup techniques don't work. Durham Buffalo Ranch near Wright has one of the largest private buffalo herds in the country: 3,500 head. Ranchers have discovered that bison are more efficient grazers than cattle, making it possible to produce more meat per acre, and they are less susceptible to disease. Perhaps some day the vast herds of bison may return to Wyoming's rangelands in the form of bison ranches.

HISTORY

Although Wyoming is a young state—only reaching the century mark in 1990—it seems to have more history per square inch than just about any other place in America. This history is a mixture of Indians and cowboys, settlers and outlaws, schemers and dreamers, railroad magnates and cattle barons, and plain folks clinging to a plot of marginal farmland despite unbelievable odds. Wyoming's 19th-century frontier is a recurring theme in America's imagination, as revealed in countless books, songs, and movies. This rich treasure trove from the past is stored not just in the little-changed landscape where the ruts from wagon trains are still visible and emigrant names remain carved in rocky buttes, but also in the cattle drives and rodeos and the weather-etched faces of sheepherders and cowboys working the range. It is hard to imagine a place with a richer past.

NATIVE AMERICANS

Humans have been in Wyoming for perhaps 25,000 years. The Plains Indians—made up of 27 different tribes—were found from the Mississippi River to the Rockies, and from Texas to central Canada. The lives of these people revolved around the buffalo; they followed the vast herds, migrating where the buffalo led. Because of this nomadic life-style, everything they had was pared to the minimum. Pottery, so common in the southwestern deserts, was replaced by woven baskets on the plains. The tipi, an easily portable lodge, offered protection from the elements, and clothing was warm yet not burdensome.

Days Of Glory

Although many people view the Plains Indians as being in a state of balance with their environment, there is ample evidence that things were changing even before whites first pushed their way onto the plains. The arrival of horses and guns in the 17th and 18th centuries created a time of plenty that has rarely been known among nomadic hunting tribes. Horses made it easier to follow and hunt the huge bison herds, and tribes that had been at least partially farmers turned entirely to hunting. Native populations grew rapidly with the abundance of food. The warrior also gained importance with the changing culture, as raiding parties stole horses and attacked other tribes. Villages grew larger as families gathered for mutual protection from their enemies.

The turmoil that resulted led to a constantly changing situation in Wyoming during the 19th century, as the tribes each strove for control. It was this turbulent society that greeted the first Euro-American explorers. Whites were accustomed to well-defined land ownership, with definite boundaries in which one lived; here the territories were in a state of flux, with each tribe claiming overlapping areas.

During the 1700s, Indians from the Great Lakes and Canadian plains had moved into what would become Wyoming. By the 1850s, the Sioux were in Powder River Basin, the Crow in Bighorn Basin, and the Cheyenne and Arapaho south of the North Platte River. The Shoshones and Bannocks—originally from the Great Basin—had moved into the Green River and Wind River valleys, while their relatives, the Utes, held the Sierra Madre and desert land to the west. Communication between these diverse tribes was possible by a sophisticated sign language.

Treaties

During the first half of the 19th century, American explorers, fur trappers, traders, and settlers began to push across Wyoming. As emigration westward increased in the 1840s, so did conflicts with Indians. Whites complained of random attacks and stolen horses. Indians complained of trampled grass, polluted water, and wasteful killing of bison. To deal with these problems, a great council was called at Fort Laramie in 1851, attracting 10,000 Indians from many different tribes. Indian agent Thomas Fitzpatrick was anxious to gain permission for settlers to use the Oregon Trail across Indian lands in Wyoming. In exchange for gifts from the federal government in the form of annuities, the tribes agreed to stay within specified boundaries and to punish those who violated the accord or attacked white emigrants.

Father Pierre DeSmet drew up the boundaries, with allowances for hunting outside the "home" regions. The unstated long-term goal of the treaty was to transform the Indians from hunters into farmers. By developing a paternalistic system of dependency on the government combined with educational programs and settlement, the Indians would—in theory—become like the whites. Violence erupted almost immediately among the tribes and with Anglo emigrants. Soon, whites would be more concerned over how to dispossess the Indians of their land than how to get through it safely.

In 1861, the Fort Wise Treaty abrogated much of the Treaty of 1851, forcing the Arapaho and Cheyenne onto a desolate reservation at Sand Creek, Colorado, to get them away from the suddenly valuable land to the north. The treaty was signed by some leaders, but only after the starving individuals saw that they would not receive their annuities without affixing their X.

The Battle Begins

Colorado's Sand Creek Massacre of 1865 proved a turning point in the history of Indian-white relations. A small band of Arapaho attacked a family farm, brutally murdering the family. When the mutilated bodies were put on display in Denver, public outrage pushed Col. John M. Chivington—formerly a Methodist minister—to lead one of the most vicious and unwarranted attacks ever perpetrated by the Army. Two hundred Cheyenne and Arapaho died in the daybreak attack on Chief Black Kettle's peaceful village.

The Indians—not just the Cheyenne and Arapaho, but also the Sioux—quickly retaliated by striking throughout Colorado and Wyoming, killing some 75 settlers around the Rock Creek Station (northwest of present-day Laramie) and destroying stage stations all along the Oregon Trail. Over the next several years, hundreds died on both sides. The main focus of Indian attacks was the Bozeman Trail through the lush Powder River country of the Sioux (see p. 17). The Army responded with an alternating series of military campaigns and peace overtures as the national mood flip-flopped between war and accommodation.

The Sioux warrior Red Cloud proved a formidable military leader durng the Plains Indian wars.

A major cause of these conflicts was the hysteria that gold created. Each new gold rush—California in 1849, Colorado in 1859, Montana in 1864, and finally the Black Hills in 1874—led to new incursions onto Indian lands. When whites found Indians standing in the way of development, they attempted to renegotiate the treaties, or failing that, to find some excuse to set them aside. Once gold had been found, the end of Indian culture was almost a given. Senator John Sherman noted: "If the whole Army of the United States stood in the way, the wave of emigration would pass over it to seek the valley where gold was to be found."

Other factors also played critical roles in the destruction of the Indian way of life on the plains. Many tribes were devastated by diseases brought by contact with Europeans, especially smallpox, cholera, whooping cough, and venereal diseases. But perhaps the most crucial factor was the loss of their primary food source, the buffalo (see pp. 12-14).

Cultural Mistrust

Many whites viewed the Indians with deep distrust. Writer James Chisholm provided a typical frontier attitude, calling them "useless, strutting, ridiculous, pompous humbugs—lying, faithless, stealing, begging, cruel, hungry, howling vagabonds—cowardly, treacherous red devils." In 1869, Gen. Philip Sheridan took matters even further by claiming, "The only good Indian is a dead Indian."

The Indians themselves were not entirely innocent. Attacks on wagon trains were frequent, and many of the trappers, stagecoach drivers, and ranchers who settled in Wyoming were murdered and their bodies mutilated by the Sioux, Cheyenne, or Arapaho. Scalping—a practice introduced by white traders—became commonplace. Whites complained that the federal government was arming and feeding the Indians at the same time it was leading military campaigns against them.

Evicting The Indians

More than a thousand engagements were fought between Indians and whites in the late 19th century, killing at least 2,500 whites and twice as many Indians. On the plains, most of the battles involved the Sioux, Cheyenne, Arapaho, Kiowa, and Comanche tribes. The Shoshone under Chief Washakie always remained peaceful. The final drama came in the 1870s, beginning with the discovery of gold in the Black Hills of Dakota Territory. A flood of miners overwhelmed attempts by the government to keep them out of Sioux territory, and negotiations to purchase the land bogged down when Red Cloud demanded a $600 million payment.

In 1876, Gen. Sheridan led a three-pronged invasion to forcibly evict the Sioux from the Powder River region. He hadn't counted on two problems: the large numbers of Indians ready to do battle, and the rashness of junior officer Col. George A. Custer. At Little Big Horn on June 25, 1876, 225 of Custer's men were wiped out by a combined force of Indians led by Crazy Horse, Sitting Bull, and others. This massive Indian victory quickly became the rallying cry

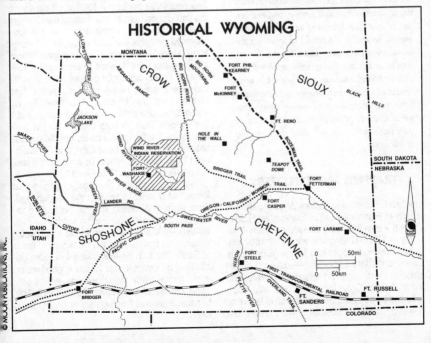

for whites anxious to "solve" the Indian problem by forcing them onto reservations. Within five years, the last of the tribes had given up the fight. The uprising that led to the infamous Wounded Knee Massacre of 1890 was a last dying gasp in the attempt to regain land that had once all belonged to Native Americans.

Those who had lived in this land for centuries had been evicted by new peoples from another world. Chief Washakie of the Shoshones described the painfulness of this change (quoted in *Chief Washakie*, by Mae Urbanek):

The white man, who possesses this whole vast country from sea to sea, who roams over it at pleasure, and lives where he likes, cannot know the cramp we feel in this little spot, with the undying remembrance of the fact, which you know as well as we, that every foot of what you proudly call America, not very long ago belonged to the red man. The Great Spirit gave it to us. There was room enough for all his many tribes, and all were happy in their freedom. But the white man had, in ways we know not of, superior tools and terrible weapons, better for war than bows and arrows; and there seemed no end to the hordes of men that followed them from other lands beyond the sea. And so, at last, our fathers were steadily driven out, or killed, and we, their sons, but sorry remnants of tribes once mighty, are cornered in little spots of the earth all ours of right—cornered like guilty prisoners, and watched by men with guns, who are more than anxious to kill us off.

TRAPPERS AND EXPLORERS

The first Europeans to explore Wyoming were in a party of Frenchmen led by François and Louis-Joseph Verendrye, who crossed northern Wyoming in 1743. During the winter of 1807-08, John Colter—a trapper and former guide for the Lewis and Clark Expedition—explored northwestern Wyoming in an attempt to develop the fur trade with Crow Indians. Colter was soon followed by other trappers in search of beavers. It was a hazardous business, with the constant threat of Indian attacks, along with the many natural hazards such as angry grizzlies, disease, and injuries. Help was hundreds of miles away. The mountain men era (see p. 257) lasted only until 1840 when demand for the furs plummeted, but the trappers' knowledge of the terrain proved invaluable. Many became guides for civilian and military expeditions, wealthy hunters, and government explorations of the West. The mountain passes they found (or more likely had been shown by Indians) provided a route for the exodus westward in the 1850s.

THE OREGON TRAIL

*When God made man,
He seemed to think it best
To make him in the East
And let him travel West.*

—from an Oregon Trail
pioneer's diary

The year 1993 marks the 150th anniversary of the first wagon train to travel along the Oregon Trail. To 19th-century emigrants this route represented perhaps the best example of "Manifest Destiny"—the idea of an American nation reaching from the Atlantic to the Pacific. The Oregon Trail is actually a general term used to describe a whole series of wagon roads that headed west from Missouri. At different times, and over various paths, this route encompassed the Oregon Trail (to both Oregon and Washington), the California Trail (to the gold fields), the Mormon Trail (to Salt Lake City), and the short-lived Pony Express route. To emigrants it was not a trail, but always "The Road."

Wyoming contains the least-changed and longest (487 miles) stretch of the Oregon Trail. From eastern Wyoming, the trail—actually a series of braided paths spreading across the river valleys—followed the North Platte and Sweetwater rivers upstream to the Continental Divide at South Pass. Travelers chose this route because of abundant forage for stock, good water, and a gentle grade over the divide. As the only route that met all three criteria, the Oregon Trail became a national thoroughfare to the Promised Land.

"Oregon Country" was not simply the area that would become the state of Oregon, but the entire region west of South Pass. Thus, the hills just beyond the Continental Divide in Wyoming became the "Oregon Buttes," and emigrants wrote of entering Oregon as they crossed the pass: "Today we entered Oregon. . . . We nooned beyond at a small spring and drank the waters of the Pacific!" (The vast land collectively called Oregon actually belonged to the British, but this legal nicety was quickly pushed aside by the influx of Americans.) West of South Pass, the route divided at the "Parting of the Ways." California- and Utah-bound travelers turned south to Fort Bridger, while those bound for Oregon and Washington headed due west on the Sublette or Lander cutoffs.

Origins

Americans emigrated west for a number of reasons: to escape a severe economic depression in the East, to get out of the crowded and polluted cities, to find religious freedom in Utah, to search for gold in the mountains of California, or simply to join in a great adventure in a new and undiscovered land. The first whites to cross the Continental Divide on what would become the Oregon Trail were a party of fur trappers known as the Astorians (see p. 181). They rode horses over South Pass in 1812, but it was not until a decade later that trappers really moved deeply into this country. The first freight wagons rolled over the pass in 1830, en route to a mountain men rendezvous on the Green River. By the early 1840s, emigration westward was getting easier and more inviting. Fort Laramie in eastern Wyoming and Fort Bridger in southwestern Wyoming provided valuable way stations where travelers could rest up, repair their wagons, trade worn-out stock for fresh animals, and purchase food, whiskey, and supplies.

The turning point in the history of the Oregon Trail came in 1843, when the Applegate Wagon Train left Independence, Missouri, with 1,000 people, 120 wagons, and 5,000 head of livestock. It was the largest wagon train ever assembled. Under the leadership of Marcus Whitman and guided by mountain man Bill Sub-

OREGON TRAIL

CANADA

WASHINGTON · COLUMBIA RIVER · FT. VANCOUVER · MT. HOOD · WHITMAN MISSION · OREGON CITY · THE DALLES · OREGON · IDAHO · FT. BOISE · FT. HALL · SODA SPRINGS · ICE SLOUGH · SOUTH PASS · FT. BRIDGER · MONTANA · NORTH DAKOTA · MISSOURI RIVER · SOUTH DAKOTA · MINNESOTA · WYOMING · INDEPENDENCE ROCK · FT. LARAMIE · SCOTTS BLUFF · CHIMNEY ROCK · COURTHOUSE ROCK · CALIFORNIA CROSSING · NEBRASKA · IOWA · FT. KEARNEY · NEVADA · UTAH · COLORADO · KANSAS · ALCOVE SPRING · ST. JOSEPH · INDEPENDENCE · MISSOURI · CALIFORNIA

0   200 mi
0   200 km

lette, they made it all the way to the Columbia and Willamette rivers by September. It had taken six long months to travel the 2,000 miles, but they had shown that the route was feasible. The gates of history had been cracked open, and they could never be closed again. Soon, the trickle westward turned into a flood tide.

Rolling West

Most travelers tried to depart Independence or St. Joseph, Missouri, in the spring, leaving as soon as the grass would support their stock. Typically, each evening found the emigrant just 15 miles farther down the trail, and it generally took five or six months to travel from Missouri to California or Oregon. They had to be over the mountains before the first snows of winter struck, and those who erred—such as the infamous Donner Party of 1846—paid a high price.

Emigrants were forced to travel as light as possible to lessen the burden on oxen. Some traders grew rich on the castoffs from overburdened wagon trains, while others profited by operating toll bridges and ferries across the North Platte and Green rivers. (Toll at the Green River crossing was sometimes a then unheard-of price: $16 per wagon!) Guidebooks—there were several; this was a big business even in the 19th century—described the crossings and camping places and suggested provisions for the 2,000-mile journey. A wagon, harness, and eight oxen cost travelers around $400.

Because of the scarcity of wood, Oregon Trail travelers used dry grass, sagebrush, or buffalo chips for fuel. Meals were simple but hearty, often consisting of a few staples, plus whatever game might be found along the trail. Today when you drive across the state, it is easy to see how trying an experience this must have been for the emigrants, as gale-force winds, dust, and lightning combine with the parched ground, deceptively long distances, and the lack of shade. Wyoming can be a harsh and unforgiving land; it is not a place to wander into unprepared. Perhaps a tenth of the people who set out on the Oregon Trail never made it to their destination. Many died from diseases such as cholera, or from accidents and drownings; others were killed by early winter storms and Indian attacks. Few of the graves are marked.

At the peak of migration in 1850 (when California gold fever had struck America), some 55,000 men, women, and children pressed their way across the plains and mountains. It is easy to imagine the impact these wagons could have had with their thousands of cattle, horses, and mules. The grass quickly became overgrazed under this onslaught, and the already-scarce water became badly polluted around popular campsites. Late-summer travelers were forced to range far and wide for better conditions, creating even more paths. The Indians who had lived here were shocked by the magnitude of the migration and began to realize not just what the whites were doing to their buffalo, but how overwhelmed they would be by the newcomers. (The entire Plains Indian population probably numbered 40,000 individuals at its peak, and disease and war greatly lessened these numbers.)

Finale

By 1870, perhaps 350,000 people had traveled across Wyoming by wagon train, stagecoach, horseback, and foot. It was the greatest peacetime migration in history. For most of them, this country seemed a worthless stretch of sagebrush, and a barrier to the green lands farther west. It took the railroad to change this. Completion of the transcontinental railroad in 1869 turned the Oregon Trail into an anachronism. Suddenly one could easily cross the nation within days instead of months. The trail continued to be used by freighters and some pioneers even as late as the turn of the century, but the vast majority of travelers turned to rail travel. An era had ended.

The mystique of the "great migration" continues to draw people from around the world. With the 150th anniversaries of the Oregon Trail in 1993 and the Mormon Trail in 1994, this interest will be focused on Wyoming, where the land has changed little over the decades. Much of the trail cuts across publicly owned land, and the tracks are readily visible in many places even after a century and a half. Explorers still discover artifacts strewn along the way. Visitors to Wyoming will enjoy delving into this rich past at such places as Fort Laramie, Oregon Trail Ruts, Register Cliff, Fort Caspar, Independence Rock, Devil's Gate, South Pass, Names Hill, and Fort Bridger. Hundreds of other lesser sights line the route, from the remains of old trading posts to the countless emigrant graves. Portions of the Oregon Trail are described in greater detail in the Southeast, Central, Wind River Mountains, and Southwest chapters of this book.

Contact the Wyoming Travel Commission at 777-7777 for information about festivities celebrating the 150th aniversery of the Oregon and Mormon trails. **Historic Trail Expeditions**, tel. 266-4868, and **Trails West**, tel. 332-7801 or (800) 327-4052, both offer wagon train and horse trips along the Oregon Trail in Wyoming. The city of Casper is in the process of developing a $10 million National Historic Trails Center near the Events Center.

THE PONY EXPRESS

On April 3, 1860, a lone rider galloped westward from the town of St. Joseph, Missouri. Nearly 2,000 miles away, another rider left the booming city of San Francisco, heading east. One of the most celebrated passages in American history had begun. Although it only lasted 18 months and was a financial disaster, the Pony Express caught the national imagination, proved that rapid mail service was possible even in the winter, and

helped keep California in the Union.

The Pony Express was the brainchild of William H. Russell, one of the great wheelers and dealers of the late 19th century and director of the Central Overland California and Pike's Peak Express Company. Russell, along with partners Alexander Majors and William Bradford Waddell, managed the largest freighting company in the West, a business that at one time owned 50,000 oxen for its 3,500 wagons and employed 4,000 workers.

In 1855, the firm of Russell, Majors, & Waddell secured a monopoly to supply all U.S. government military posts west of the Missouri River. Because of Mormon raids on the supply wagons and the failure of the War Department to pay the company for its services, it was soon in financial trouble. To escape, the company needed the contract for mail service between California and St. Louis, a route then held by the Butterfield Overland Mail Company. Butterfield's route took mail along a circuitous 25-day trek through Texas and Arizona into southern California. With the nation slipping rapidly toward the Civil War, and Texas on the side of the South, there were fears that mail service would be halted and that California might join the Confederacy.

PONY EXPRESSIONS

We had had a consuming desire from the beginning, to see a pony-rider, but somehow or other all that passed us and all that met us managed to streak by in the night, and so we heard only a whiz and a hail, and the swift phantom of the desert was gone before we could get our heads out of the windows. But now we were expecting one along every moment, and would see him in broad daylight. Presently the driver exclaims:

"HERE HE COMES!"

Every neck is stretched further, and every eye strained wider. Away across the endless dead level of the prairie a black speck appears against the sky, and it is plain that it moves. Well, I should think so! In a second or two it becomes a horse and rider, rising and falling, rising and falling—

sweeping toward us nearer and nearer—growing more and more distinct, more and more sharply defined—nearer and still nearer, and the flutter of the hoofs comes faintly to the ear—another instant a whoop and a hurrah from our upper deck, a wave of the rider's hand, but no reply, and man and horse burst past our excited faces, and go winging away like a belated fragment of a storm!

So sudden is it all, and so like a flash of unreal fancy, that for the flake of white foam left quivering and perishing on a mail-sack after the vision had flashed by and disappeared, we might have doubted whether we had seen any actual horse and man at all, maybe.

—Mark Twain in Roughing It

Express Mail

In 1859, the postmaster general signed a contract with Russell, Majors, & Waddell to operate coaches and horses along the central route to California. The Pony Express was born as a flamboyant symbol of the superiority of this route. Experienced young horsemen, some as young as 14 and none weighing more than 120 pounds, would ride the finest horses at a full gallop, carrying telegrams and mail through some of the most desolate land on earth. The trip was to take just 10 days.

Each horse had four mail pouches sewn into a leather *mochilla* that could be easily transferred between horses. (At $7.50 per half ounce, Pony Express mail was primarily urgent messages and newspapers.) Riders changed horses at relay stations—crude huts with a station keeper and stock tender—every 10 to 15 miles, continuing on for 75-100 miles before passing the precious package to another rider. After a short break, the rider would speed back to his home station with mail headed in the opposite direction. The whole operation required a military precision to keep the 119 relay and home stations stocked, make sure the horses were in good condition, and guard against attack. For their work, riders received $120 per month (including room and board).

The Demise

The threat of Indian hostilities became real when Nevada Piutes, angry after decades of abuse and the theft of their land, began attacking white settlements, killing 16 of the men working at the relay stations, taking 150 horses, and burning seven stations. A full-scale war was avoided, but it took more than a month to get the Express back into operation, at a cost of $75,000. Already a money loser, this helped ensure the collapse of the Pony Express. But it was not just money that brought down the Pony Express. Completion of the first continental telegraph line on October 24, 1861, contributed to its demise. The Pony Express, its mission replaced by a much more rapid means of communication, ended just two days later. Riders had delivered 34,753 pieces of mail, losing only one *mochilla* (both horse and rider were killed) out of 616 cross-country runs.

THE OVERLAND TRAIL

Lesser known and shorter-lived than the Oregon Trail, the Overland Trail was established by Ben Holladay, owner of the Overland Stage Company. Although the Oregon Trail had served for many years as the primary route west, by the 1860s a need was developing for a new path. Increasing Indian attacks made the Oregon Trail more dangerous, and the rapidly growing mining town of Denver was too far away. After Holladay was given the contract to deliver mail to the West, he quickly rerouted travel along a trail originally scouted by Jim Bridger.

The new route proved 60 miles shorter than the Oregon Trail, but it passed directly through the difficult desert country of western Wyoming, rather than along the relatively lush North Platte and Sweetwater rivers. Stage stations where teams could be changed were established every 10-15 miles, and home stations where travelers could stop for meals or primitive lodging were located every 50 miles. Conditions at these relay stations were primitive at best; one traveler described southwestern Wyomings' Sand Springs station as "roofless and chairless, filthy and squalid, with a smoky fire in one corner, and a table in the center of an impure floor, the walls open to every wind and the interior full of dust." But the stations were better than sitting outside in the blazing hot sun or the bitter winter winds.

The stages covered 100-125 miles in a 24-hour period but were extraordinarily expensive for the time: $500 from Atchison, Kansas, to San Francisco. Emigrants began using the new route instead of the Oregon Trail; in a single year (1864) some 17,584 men, women, and children used the Overland Trail, along with 50,000 stock and 4,264 wagons.

Although the new route remained relatively free from attacks for several years, the 1865 Sand Creek Massacre sent Indians on the warpath throughout the plains. Stage stations were destroyed, stagecoaches were attacked, and many died on both sides. The attacks continued sporadically for the next two years. With completion of the transcontinental railroad in 1869, the Overland Stage rapidly faded in importance, and stagecoach service ended. The *railroad building on the Great Plains, from* Harpers Weekly, *1875*

old Overland Trail continued to be used by wagons until the turn of the century.

CONNECTING THE COASTS

More than any other event, the completion of the transcontinental railroad led to the settlement and development of Wyoming. Most of its major towns and cities originated along the railroad lines. Not only did the railroad bring Wyoming within a couple of days of either coast, but it also led to the opening of coal mines to fuel the engines, hastened development of the logging industry (for railroad ties and mine props), and made it easy to ship cattle to market. Settlers could order most anything—Sears Roebuck even shipped prefabricated houses that filled two boxcars. It was no coincidence that Wyoming became a territory just as the railroad was being pushed across its southern border. An enduring impact from the railroad is a checkerboard pattern of public and private land ownership along the Union Pacific's route across Wyoming.

Surveying The Route

The Union Pacific's route was planned by Gen. Grenville M. Dodge, a veteran of battles with the Sioux in the Powder River country. The traditional Oregon Trail route ran too close to Sioux country, was too far from the gold-mining city of Denver, and didn't have the rich coal deposits of southwestern Wyoming. The course Dodge chose headed almost straight across southern Wyoming, climbing the Laramie Mountains west of Cheyenne, then cutting through the Laramie Plains and Red Desert before winding across the mountains of eastern Utah.

Despite Dodge's efforts to avoid direct confrontation with the Indians, and the government's diversionary tactic of building the Bozeman Trail through the Powder River country, the Arapaho did not take kindly to the presence of railroad survey and construction parties in their traditional hunting grounds. They pulled up survey stakes, stole horses, and killed surveyors and loggers, forcing Dodge to request military escorts. Three forts (Russell, Sanders, and Steele) were built in Wyoming to house these troops.

Working On The Railroad

To span the continent, the Union Pacific headed west from Omaha, while the Central Pacific worked east from Sacramento. By July 1867 tracklayers had reached the main division point, which would become Cheyenne, and they headed on west to found Laramie, Rawlins, Green River, and Evanston. Most of the Central Pacific's workers were Chinese contract laborers, while those on the Union Pacific were a mixture of Americans and emigrants, especially Irishmen. Great competition grew between the two groups, and a record was set as the tracklayers worked across the searing heat of Wyoming's Red Desert: the men laid 7$\frac{1}{2}$ miles of track in a single day. Laborers were paid an extraordinary $2.50 an hour, but the work was equally dangerous; it is said that the transcontinental railroad was built at the cost of 10 men's lives per mile of track! Many were buried right in the roadbed. The tracklayers finally pushed their way into Utah and met workers of the Central Pacific at Promontory Point on May 10, 1869.

The railroad brought with it a gang of men who seemed to thrive on corruption, thievery, prostitution, gambling, drunkenness, and murder. As construction moved westward, temporary towns sprang up along the way; many were gone as soon as the tracks were out of sight. The entire procession of construction workers and hangers-on quickly became known as Hell-on-Wheels.

Worst of the temporary frontier towns was Benton, located a few miles east of present-day Rawlins. Those who passed through called it "nearer a repetition of Sodom and Gomorrah than any other place in America," or a "congregation of scum and wickedness . . . by day disgusting, by night dangerous." There was no grass, little water, and the alkali dust stood eight inches deep. Murders were a nightly affair at the 25 saloons and five dance halls. The big attraction was gambling, with hundreds of men crowding the big tent each evening, paying for whiskey, dance-hall girls, or roulette wheels. Before the short-lived settlement could disappear in the alkali dust—just three months after its founding—more than 100 men lay buried in boot hill.

Newspaper reporter James Chisholm described these men in less than appealing terms:

I often speculate on what will finally become of all that rolling scum which the locomotive seems to blow onward as it presses westward. Will they get blown clean off the continent at last into the Pacific Ocean? One is gradually surrounded by the same faces in each successive town, the same gamblers, the same musicians playing the same old tunes to the same old dance, the same females getting always a little more dilapidated. As the excitement dies out of one town, and the railroad leaves it behind in a kind of exhausted repose, these old familiar faces die out to reappear in a new state of existence.

A rolling newspaper press tagged along with the flotsam and jetsam across Wyoming, printing the weekly *Frontier Index* in each new camp. Its editor, Legh Freeman, angered the primarily northern-born workers by constantly showing his support for the Confederacy; he once labeled Gen. Ulysses Grant "the whiskey bloated, squaw ravishing adulterer, nigger worshipping mogul rejoicing over his election to the presidency." In Bear River City (long gone, but near present-day Evanston), Freeman made the mistake of suggesting that several accused murderers then in jail should meet up with Judge Lynch. After a gang of vigilantes followed his suggestion by offering a necktie party for the three, other ruffians destroyed the *Frontier Index* office and chased its editor out of town.

STATEHOOD

Because of its difficult climate, a paucity of good agricultural lands, and the lack of major deposits of gold, Wyoming was one of the last states to be settled. At various times, portions of Wyoming were part of Indian country, Mexico, Louisiana, Missouri, Texas, Nebraska, Dakota, Idaho, Oregon, and Utah. In 1868, Wyoming Territory was carved out of Dakota Territory, a move primarily intended to keep the Democratic voters building the Union Pacific Railroad from overwhelming the Republican power base in distant Yankton. The folks out west were equally happy to gain independence from such a tenuous governmental link. It was not until May 19, 1869, that an organized government was established in the new territory. The first census of Wyoming in 1870 found just 9,000 people (Indians were not counted).

The word Wyoming comes from the Leni Lanape Indians of Pennsylvania, who used the word "Mecheweami-ing" to denote "At the Great Plains." The term was first applied to the land that would become Wyoming in 1865 when Ohio's J.M. Ashley introduced a bill to form a "temporary government for the territory of Wyoming." Newspaper editor Legh Freeman has been credited with popularizing the name and having it inserted in the bill that created Wyoming Territory in 1868.

A triumvirate of politicians—Francis E. Warren (see p. 57), John B. Kendrick, and Joseph M. Carey—governed Wyoming for much of its first half century. Carey, a Republican turned Democrat, was a founder of the powerful Wyoming Stock Growers Association and the Cheyenne Club. He was a strong proponent of Wyoming statehood and introduced the enabling legislation in the U.S. House. During the debate, he claimed a Wyoming population of something over 110,000 people, an exaggeration that helped sway enough House votes to pass the measure. (The U.S. census of the following year found just 62,555 people in Wyoming.) The act was signed into law by President Benjamin Harrison on July 10, 1890, making Wyoming the 44th state. Interestingly, this was the same year that the director of the U.S. Census Bureau declared that the "frontier of settlement" was no more.

The Equality State

Wyoming's first Territorial Legislature passed an act granting women the right to vote. The measure was signed into law by Gov. J.A. Campbell on Dec. 10, 1869, making this the first government in the world to grant women the right to vote. (Technically, Wyoming was not the first state to allow women suffrage; New Jersey widows already had limited voting rights.) The name "Equality State" comes from this bold step. It would be another 50 years before the 19th Amendment was finally passed, giving all women in America the right to vote. Not everyone looked upon women's suffrage as such a

BILL NYE ON WOMEN'S SUFFRAGE

There have been many reasons given, first and last, why women should not vote, but I desire to say, in the full light of a ripe experience, that some of them are fallacious. I refer more particularly to the argument that it will degrade women to go to the polls and vote like a little man. While I am not and have never been a howler for female suffrage, I must admit that it is much more of a success than prohibition and speculative science . . . In Wyoming, where female suffrage has raged for years, you meet quiet, courteous and gallant gentleman, and fair, quiet, sensible women at the polls, where there isn't a loud or

profane word, and where it is an infinitely more proper place to send a young lady unescorted than to the post office in any city in the Union. . . All these things look hopeful. We can't tell what the Territory would have been without female suffrage, but when they begin to hang men by law instead of by moonlight, the future begins to brighten up. When you have to get up in the night to hang a man every little while and don't get any per diem for it, you feel as though you were a good way from home.

—*Nineteenth-century humorist Bill Nye*

good step. In 1871, Democrats in the second territorial Legislature repealed the measure, then came within one vote of overriding Gov. Campbell's veto. (See p. 96 for more on women's suffrage.)

When the territory of Wyoming was seeking admission to the Union in 1890, the issue of giving women the right to vote—a measure included in Wyoming's new constitution—became a hotly contested topic. Alabama Senator John T. Morgan led the fight against admitting the new state, with the argument that the other half of the population would be polluted by politicians (such as himself?): "It is the immoral influences of the ballot upon women that I deprecate and would avoid. I do not want to see her drawn in contact with the rude things of this world where the delicacy of her senses and sensitivities would be constantly wounded by the attrition with bad and desperate and foul politicians and men."

Wyoming's status as the home for equal rights took another big step in 1925 after the death of Gov. William B. Ross. His wife, Nellie Tayloe Ross, was nominated to replace him, and she won the special election on a sympathy vote. She made no effort to get elected, noting, "I shall not make a campaign. My candidacy is in the hands of my friends. I shall not leave the house." She served ably as the nation's first woman governor and achieved considerable national attention. Despite a good record, Ross lost her bid for reelection, primarily because she was a Democrat in a heavily Republican state. In 1933, President Roosevelt appointed her as director of the U.S. Mint, a title she held for the next 20 years. She died in 1967 at the age of 101.

CATTLE COUNTRY

Hardly had the thunder of the Sioux ponies, along the Powder, the thunder of the cavalry died down, when over the southern horizon came a new army. An army of tossing horns, white in the sun; of lithe young men lolling in their saddles; riding at point, on the flanks, on the drag. The Cowboy was coming to Wyoming.

—Struthers Burt in
Powder River Let 'er Buck

Opening The Range
Once the bison herds had been decimated and the Indians evicted, cattlemen found what seemed like a Garden of Eden in Wyoming: land, grass, and water were essentially free for the taking. The cattle industry began innocently enough. In December 1863, Tom Alsop was returning to Omaha with a train of 50 wagons when a snowstorm pinned them down near present-day Cheyenne. Alsop abandoned the oxen and wagons on the plains and led his men safely home on horseback. The following spring, they rode back to recover the freight and were startled to discover that the cattle they had left to die of exposure had not only survived the winter but were thriving. The discovery soon attracted droves of ranchers.

The first cattle drive through Wyoming came in 1866, when a Montana merchant named Nelson Story decided that what the Virginia City miners needed was fresh beef. Heading south to Kansas with $10,000 sewn in the lining of his clothes, he filled a wagon with supplies, bought 3,000 Texas longhorns, hired 27 cowboys, gave them the finest Remington breech-loading rifles, and headed north for the gold fields. At Ft. Kearny (see p. 437 for more on this notorious fort), Col. Carrington forbade them from continuing north through Sioux country since they did not have the required 40 armed guards. (Some feel that Carrington actually hoped to requisition the cattle for his men; most of the Army's had already been stolen.) In response, an angry Story thumbed his nose at the government, heading north under cover of darkness. Discovering his departure, Carrington was forced to cave in, sending 15 soldiers along to bring Story's force up the legal minimum. Although one man died, the rest of the men and cattle made it to Virginia City on December 9. Nelson Story had gained himself a place in history.

Millions of cattle headed into or through Wyoming in the 1870s and 1880s. Ranching looked like a can't-lose business; dump a couple thousand head of cows and calves on the range in spring and return a year later to round them up for market. What could be simpler? Investors from Omaha, New York, England, Scotland, and France quickly took note of the potential fortunes to be made.

By 1883, English and Scottish investors had

TOM HORN

The story of the outlaw Tom Horn will always remain something of a mystery. Over the years, Horn worked as a stage driver, Army scout, deputy sheriff, Pinkerton investigator, and a stock detective for the Wyoming Stock Growers Association. When J.M. Carey (later Wyoming governor and senator) discovered that Tom Horn was out to murder, rather than bring in for trial, the accused rustlers, he had Horn fired from the association. Other cattle barons quickly moved to hire him, however, paying $500 for each man murdered. Horn is generally blamed for

BUFFALO BILL HISTORICAL SOCIETY

ambushing and killing two ranchers (and suspected rustlers) in the Laramie Mountains in 1895, along with two others in Brown's Park, Colorado, five years later.

Wherever Horn went, a trail of dead men was left behind, but nobody was able to pin the blame on him until 1901, when a 14-year-old boy was shot in the back and killed in the Laramie Mountains. It was a case of mistaken identity, since the boy had been wearing his father's hat and clothes. The older man was later shot from ambush but survived. Horn was implicated in the boy's slaying by his trademark: a small stone placed under the victim's head.

Horn would probably have escaped even this heinous crime had he not bragged about it. The confession would never hold up in court today, however, since Deputy U.S. Marshal Joe LeFors had plied Horn with liquor and had a court stenographer listen through a crack in the door as he boasted of the slaying. Tom Horn had little money himself, but his supporters spent $100,000 in his defense, hiring the finest legal council, John W. Lacey, who had never lost any of his 50 previous murder trials (and who, not coincidentally, represented the Wyoming Stock Growers Association and the Union Pacific Railroad).

Despite this, Horn was adjudged guilty and sentenced to hang. Horn's supporters tried to free him with a dynamite blast, and he later did briefly escape from jail, but on November 20, 1903, he was hanged before a large crowd at the corner of Pioneer and 19th avenues in Cheyenne. Until the last minute, everyone expected a pardon, and many wealthy cattlemen feared what Horn might reveal about them, but in the end, his last words were to his friend T. Joe Cahill: "Joe, they tell me you are married now. I hope you're doing well. Treat her right."

poured some £6 million into Wyoming cattle and had turned Cheyenne into a country club for the European gentry. Some were more gullible than others; stories are still told of an Englishman who watched as the cattle he was buying were driven by to be counted, not noticing that the same cattle had come around the hill a couple of times before. The use of "book counts" also inflated the value of the herds; frequently nobody bothered to make sure that numbers in the books equalled cattle on the range. The

aristocracy were regarded with a mixture of humor and disdain by the hardened cowboys whose every other utterance came out a swear word. One British lord rode up to a cowboy in his buggy, asking, "My good man could you tell me where your master is?" The cowboy glowered back, spat out his tobacco, and said, "The son-of-a-bitch ain't been born yet!"

During the early years of ranching in Wyoming, cattle were allowed to roam at will and were not sorted out until the annual roundup.

BRANDS

Branding dates back to the Egyptian pharaohs, who branded not only their cattle, camels, and donkeys, but even their slaves. (Slave branding was also practiced in America.) The American tradition of branding comes from the Spanish conquistadors and their vaqueros, but was adapted to the spacious western plains. Because there were no fences, cattle belonging to various ranchers became intermixed, leading to inevitable questions of ownership, which brands helped clear up.

Brands appear almost anywhere on an animal, and a given ranch may have a half-dozen or more for its cattle, sheep, and horses. An individual animal often has several different brands or marks. To make them easier to identify on the hoof, cattle are frequently distinctively marked by cutting a notch in the ear, slicing the skin that hangs under the cow's throat (the dewlap), or hacking a flap of hide (a wattle) so that it hangs loose from the neck.

In Wyoming, having a brand is something of a status symbol, and the Wyoming Brand Book lists more than 27,000 currently in use (one for every 17 residents!). Not everyone who has a brand has stock; some are simply used for mailbox decorations on suburban ranchettes. The more complex ones aren't likely to appear on a cow since they become illegible as the scar heals. Brands that are hard to alter or of historic significance may be worth more than $5000 when sold. Getting a desired brand can be a problem, since the state looks askance on brands that resemble others in the same area, or that might be easily altered by rustlers (they still exist). One 19th-century rancher became so fed up with having his brand suggestions rejected that he wrote the brand department, demanding, "Send me a brand P.D.Q." They complied by giving him the brand PDQ. Reading brands is an art gained by years of experience. They are read from left to right, top to bottom, and outside to inside.

Branding usually takes place in the spring before cattle and calves are driven into the higher pastures or set loose on the plains. A branding iron is heated to a dull red in a fire and then pressed against the calf as it is held down. Freeze branding is also often used. Most male calves are castrated at the same time.

Sounds fine in theory, but in practice a few flaws showed up, notably the problem of mavericks. (The term maverick refers to an unbranded calf or cow of questionable ownership, or, as writer Struthers Burt put it, "A calf whose mamma has died and whose father has run off with another lady cow.") Unbranded calves were generally divvied up among the ranchers on the basis of which herd they were with, but when herds became mixed together, conflicts were inevitable. In addition, multiple roundups meant that the first cowboys on the scene could pretty much decide for themselves which calves were theirs. Some even went so far as to slit the tongues of calves so they could no longer suckle and would not follow their mothers, thus becoming instant mavericks.

Cattle Barons And Rustlers

To curb the temptations for such "sooners," the powerful Wyoming Stock Growers Association—an organization dominated by the wealthiest of the cattlemen—gained the authority to dictate when roundups could be held. The organization dominated the political landscape of Wyoming for many years; by the 1880s, a third of the members of the state legislature were association members. The 1882 Maverick Bill gave the association control over all cattle roundups in the territory, with proceeds from the sales of mavericks going into the association's coffers. It could blacklist cowboys as "rustlers" on the basis of hearsay, and cattle shipped without the association's permission risked being impounded by inspectors in Chicago or Omaha. Even worse, ranchers suspected of rustling (which seemed to include anyone except members) were sometimes ambushed and murdered by enforcers, the most notorious of whom was Tom Horn. Whole regions of Wyoming were terrorized by the practice of dry-gulching, in which suspected rustlers would be shot from behind and left in an out-of-the-way gulch.

Meanwhile, the big cattlemen—commonly called cattle barons—also ran into trouble, especially in the Powder River country. The fierce winter of 1886-87 decimated their herds; some lost all their cattle, while others had just 20 or 30 percent of the numbers from the previous year. Big ranching outfits also found themselves hemmed in by homesteading settlers who fenced the land. (Fences created a hazard, since cattle often moved with the winter winds until they hit the fences and then piled up there to die.)

The big cattlemen accused these "nesters" of not only of fencing the land, but also of taking stray cattle for themselves. Using a "long rope" and a "running iron" they could easily alter the brands and soon have their own herd. The cattle barons decided to put an end to this thievery once and for all with the infamous Johnson County War of 1892, but the invasion proved a complete fiasco (see p. 443). Two men died on each side in pitched battles between the "barons" and the "rustlers." Although the invaders managed to escape prosecution, the small nesters and rustlers had won the day. From that time on, the range would increasingly be fenced in.

SHEEP

History
Cattle arrived in most parts of Wyoming a decade or so before the first sheep munched their way across the grazing lands, but by 1902, the rangeland was crowded with close to six million sheep. Cattlemen considered the public land their own by right of previous use, though legally all this was open range owned by the government. As competition increased, cattlemen declared "dead lines" across which no sheep would be allowed. Conflicts quickly erupted, and the single herder and his dogs proved no match for a gang of cattlemen on horseback. Herders were murdered throughout the state, and the violence escalated into the infamous Ten Sleep Raid of 1909 (see p. 410), in which three sheepmen were brutally murdered. After this, things quieted down as the land became increasingly settled and government policies divided up the areas. Some cattlemen even turned to raising sheep, but animosity still remains between sheepmen and cattlemen in some areas.

Times have not always been easy for herders. Alfred Mokler in *History of Natrona County* describes one horrific night:

During a severe storm the latter part of March, 1895, Noel R. Gascho was with a band of sheep on the open range. The band became unmanageable and drifted with the storm. Gascho went with the sheep, which was the only thing to do. The snow came down in blinding sheets, the cold wind swept over the bleak prairie and hundreds of the sheep were frozen. Gascho said it seemed as though the blood in his veins and the marrow in his bones were frozen. He became numb and sleepy and to keep awake he would stick his legs with a knife blade. About midnight he caught one of the sheep, cut its throat and drank the blood. Then he set fire to the wool on the dead sheep and the greasy wool burned readily. Before daylight, he had burned six sheep after he had cut their throats and drank of their blood. This was all that saved his life.

Sheepherding
Over the years the number of sheep in Wyoming has steadily dropped; today there are around 837,000 at any given time. Sheep are generally moved up into the mountains each spring to graze in the high meadows, and then back down in the fall. A long drive along country roads is a sight straight out of the history books.

Sheep are sheared in spring, generally just before lambing season. By fall the lambs are big enough to send to market, and the ewes are bred.

A good many of the first sheepherders in Wyoming were from the Basque region. Many preferred to take sheep instead of a salary and so gradually gained flocks of their own. The frugal ones eventually became ranch owners in their own right. The herding business has not changed much over the years, however, and herders still spend weeks at a time alone, seeing nobody but the camp mover when he arrives to help move the outfit to new feedgrounds. Today many herders are immigrants from Mexico, although some Basque and American herders are around. The herder's life is a simple and quiet one, with plenty of time for reflection. It takes someone with the right temperament to be a sheepherder.

The sheepherder's wagon—an early-day RV—was invented by James Candlish, a Rawlins blacksmith, and later improved and marketed by Casper's Schulte Hardware Company. The design proved an efficient one, and herders still use the old wagons, though rubber tires have replaced wagon wheels and the roof is now tin instead of canvas. The layout is simple: a Dutch door opens into a small space filled by a bed at the back with drawers underneath and shelves above. A small wood stove near the entrance is used for both heating and cooking. Almost every Wyoming museum seems to have one tucked away in a corner, but many more are still in use on the lonely high plains.

ENERGY BOOM AND BUST

Wyoming's first oil well was drilled in 1884, and by 1908—the year of the first oil boom—production approached 18,000 barrels per year. Production continued to climb over the decades, reaching a peak in 1970 when more than 155 million barrels were pumped. Since then, the figures have dropped as older fields are exhausted and as low prices discourage exploration. By 1991, production had fallen to 95 million barrels. The decline in oil production has been offset somewhat by dramatic increases in two other energy sources: natural gas and coal. During the 1980s, both industries nearly doubled their production levels in Wyoming.

The Arab oil embargo of 1973 and subsequent price rises turned Wyoming upside down. The oil-patch towns—particularly Casper, Rock Springs, Evanston, and Green River—turned into madhouses of pickup trucks, heavily muscled oil workers, honkytonk bars, strip joints, fast-food outlets, and trailer courts. Drugs, crime, prostitution, and gambling ripped across the state. The population of Rock Springs doubled in two years. In the heady rush of new workers and high-paying oil jobs, many towns embarked on ambitious construction projects such as schools and housing developments, while trailer parks sprouted up across the countryside. (Wyoming still holds top honors as the state with the highest percentage of mobile homes.)

This economic bubble collapsed with the sudden halving of oil prices in 1982, and Wyoming's population actually dropped by almost three percent during the 1980s. The bust left many towns struggling to survive as unemployment skyrocketed, the state government was forced into consolidation mode, and local residents were left with a bloated set of facilities. In the late 1980s and early '90s, the economy has rebounded, and recent years have seen efforts to diversify. Still, the inevitable booms and busts associated with the energy and mining industries will affect Wyoming for the foreseeable future.

ECONOMY AND GOVERNMENT

Due to financial restraints, the light at the end of the tunnel will be turned off until further notice.
　　　—sign in Hot Springs County Library

In recent years, Wyoming rode an economic bucking bronco as oil prices shot up and then suddenly dove, throwing this energy-rich state out of the saddle. The decade of the '80s was not kind to Wyoming—the population actually declined and the economy floundered. Things have turned around more recently as communities begin to emphasize tourism and small industries. During the 1990s, folks are once again moving into Wyoming, but this time because they want to live here, rather than just to make money and run.

Wyoming's economy is affected not only by private developments, but also by the government. The federal government owns almost 47% of the land, while the state government holds another 10%—leaving 43% in private hands. The largest public land agency, the Bureau of Land Management (BLM), owns nearly 18 million acres in Wyoming, but most of this exists in a checkerboard of small parcels with limited public access. The BLM manages only a few patches of wilderness scattered around Wyoming. The U.S. Forest Service has 8.7 million acres within nine national forests that cover the state's largest mountain ranges, and the National Park Service has another 2.3 million acres in five national parks, monuments, and recreation areas. Warren Air Force Base—the most important ICBM base in North America—is located in Cheyenne and represents the state's only major military installation. The military also owns land in other parts of Wyoming today; notably the Camp Guernsey training area north of Wheatland and a Naval Petroleum Reserve at Teapot Dome. Partly because of all this federal land, Wyoming residents are on the receiving end of generous federal monies; the state is second only to Alaska in per-capita federal aid.

Working For A Living

Today, Wyoming's economy is based on several industries: oil and gas extraction, coal and trona mining, cattle and sheep ranching, and tourism. Of these, the most important from a financial point is the oil and gas industry, contributing nearly half of the state's tax base. Some 1,000 fields annually produce 95 million barrels of oil (sixth in the nation) and 700 million cubic feet of natural gas (fifth in the nation). A quarter of the nation's coal reserves lie beneath Wyoming, and in recent years it has become the largest coal-producing state, outstripping (pun intended) West Virginia and Kentucky. Nearly all the 185 million tons extracted each year comes from enormous open-pit mines, primarily in the Powder River Basin. With perhaps a *trillion* tons of coal still below the surface, Wyoming is one of the largest energy storehouses anywhere on the planet. Vast deposits of trona (used primarily in glass and chemicals) occur in southwestern Wyoming, where mines produce 90% of the nation's supply. The state is also a major producer of bentonite, helium, and sulfur. Uranium was once an important industry—a third of America's reserves are in Wyoming—but since Three Mile Island, production has dropped to almost nothing.

Tourism has grown rapidly in recent years and now contributes $1.5 billion annually to the state's economy. It is particularly important in northwestern Wyoming (Yellowstone and Grand Teton national parks). More than five million people come to enjoy the state's abundant recreational opportunities each year.

The state's most obvious industry, and the one that encompasses 90% of its land base, is agriculture. Surprisingly, however, grazing and farming employ less than six percent of the population. Wyoming is second in the nation in terms of sheep and lamb production and has 1.3 million cattle and calves. It takes 35-40 acres to support a single cow, which is why the average Wyoming farm is nearly 4,000 acres (versus a national average of 463 acres). Only four percent of

WYOMING LINGO

Absaroka—Alternatively pronounced ab-SOR-ka or ab-SOR-aka, the word means "People of the Large-beaked Bird" (hence the name Crow Indians). The Absaroka Mountains lie east of Yellowstone National Park.

Arapaho—The word is often spelled Arapahoe. An Indian tribe of Algonquin stock originally living on the Canadian plains, the Northern Arapaho now live on the Wind River Reservation. The name comes from a Crow Indian term meaning "Tattooed People." They call themselves simply "Our People."

bentonite—A special kind of clay that originates from volcanic ash, bentonite absorbs large amounts of water, increasing in volume by 30 percent. Bentonite is used in oil drilling, to line ponds, and even in candy bars. Wyoming is the nation's largest producer of this mineral.

booshway—the boss at a mountain men rendezvous

buck and rail fence—Consisting of X-shaped supports and connecting poles, these are the classic fences of Jackson Hole, where the soils proved too rocky for ranchers to dig postholes. The abundant lodgepole pines made fine fences. Today, buck and rail fences are built more for beauty than function.

calcutta—The auctioning off of various rodeo teams or contestants; it's a popular way to wager bets on rodeo events. Rules vary.

cattle baron—a cattle owner with extensive holdings; primarily used during the heyday of the giant cattle spreads in the 1880s

chaps—pronounced "shaps," protective leather leg coverings, useful when riding horses through brush

chislers—Ground squirrels, also called ground cougars. The lemmings of Wyoming; they seem to delight in waiting till the last minute and then dashing toward car wheels. Lots of them get nailed on dirt roads all across the state.

coup—Pronounced "coo"; a Plains Indian word that signified great skill and daring, it involved striking an enemy in the midst of a battle or some other deed of valor. "Counting coups" was similar to gaining today's military medals of honor. Those with many coups wore warbonnets with many feathers.

coyotes—Fans of these ubiquitous critters call them "ki-O-tees," while those who regard them as "varmints" tend to pronounce the word "KI-oats."

creek—Everyone knows what it is, but old-timers in Wyoming pronounce the word "crik."

dead line—A line established by turn-of-the-century cattlemen who feared competition from sheep. Those herders who brought sheep across the imaginary line risked death and the destruction of their flocks.

dogger—A rodeo term used for steer wrestlers; it originated from Will Pickett, an early wrestler who threw steers to the ground by biting their lips in the manner of a bulldog. The name stuck, even though the lip-biting part didn't.

dogie—A motherless calf. A famous old cowboy poem begins:

As I walked out one morning for pleasure,
I spied a cowpuncher all riding alone;
His hat was throwed back and his spurs
was a-jingling,
As he approached me a-singin' this song,

Whoopee ti yi yo, git along, little dogies,
It's your misfortune, and none of my own.
Whoopee ti yi yo, git along, little dogies,
For you know Wyoming will be your new
home. . . .

dog-trot—A type of log cabin common on old Wyoming ranches. Two cabins were connected by a breezeway, making a favorite place for dogs to hang out on hot summer days. This cabin style actually originated in the southern Appalachians.

dude—This is a term that has changed in meaning over the years. Writer Nathaniel

Burt originally called the dude "any fancy-pants young man who wore a boutonniere and parted his hair in the middle." Later, the term came to mean a wealthy easterner vacationing on a western ranch, in contradistinction to "tourists," who were viewed as an inferior species. Today Wyoming's many dude ranches are more proletarian. The wealthy elite generally prefer "guest ranches," which are really luxury resorts with a few horses thrown in.

emigrants—The dictionary defines emigrants as people who leave one place to settle elsewhere, in contrast to immigrants, who come into a new place. Guess it all depends on your perspective, but for some reason folks heading west on the Oregon Trail were almost always called emigrants, not immigrants.

hazer—A rodeo term used in steer wrestling. It refers to a cowboy who rides beside the steer to keep it in position for the dogger.

hog ranch—An establishment of ill repute where booze, gambling, and loose women were the primary attractions. The most famous were located near military forts in Wyoming, notably Fort Fetterman and Fort Laramie. The name is generally attributed to the appearance of the women, but may also refer to the tiny, squalid rooms where they plied their wares. Author David Lavender called them places offering "the poorest whiskey and women in the west."

hooey—A tie used in calf-roping events at rodeos. Three feet are wrapped with a piggin' string and completed with a half-hitch knot.

jackalope—an antlered jackrabbit found most commonly in the vicinity of Douglas, Wyoming, but proliferating throughout the west

maverick—An unbranded cow or calf of questionable ownership. The term originated from Samuel Maverick, owner of a two-million-acre Texas ranch in the 1840s. Because many of his cattle were never branded, cowboys coming across unbranded cattle on the open range would joke that they were Maverick's. Eventually the term was applied to all unbranded cattle.

piggin' string—a short piece of rope used to tie a hooey around the feet of a roped calf or steer at a rodeo

rendezvous—French for "appointed place of meeting." Between 1825 and 1840 the annual rendezvous was the big shindig for Rocky Mountain trappers, Indians, and traders. Modern-day versions try to recreate this trading and partying atmosphere.

runnin' iron—an improvised branding iron used by rustlers

rustler—A cattle thief or someone accused of taking cattle from the cattle barons; during the Johnson County War the term actually became a badge of honor in parts of Wyoming. "Packing a long rope" became the common term applied to folks who rustled.

sage hen—Another name for the sage grouse, a common bird across Wyoming. This was also a cowboy term for women.

scoria—A red rock commonly used on Powder River Basin roads. It was formed when coal beds caught fire and burned underground, baking adjacent shales and sandstones to create a bright red slag. The red comes from iron oxide. Clinker is another word commonly used for scoria.

Shoshone—An Indian tribe on Wyoming's Wind River Reservation. The word is also frequently spelled Shoshoni, and is generally pronounced with a long *e* at the end.

Sioux—The word was derived from a derogatory Chippewa Indian term meaning "enemy" or "snake" and used to describe the Indians who lived just to their west. The Sioux actually called themselves Dakota, meaning an "Alliance of Friends."

trona—a mineral (sodium sesquicarbonate) used in glass, detergents, baking soda, and other products; mined in huge underground mines west of Green River

varmint—any animal you don't like; especially used for prairie dogs, ground squirrels, and coyotes

wapiti—Pronounced WOP-a-tee. The Indian word for elk, it is occasionally used by biologists who consider it a more precise term.

the state is cultivated, with sugar beets, barley, alfalfa hay, wheat, oats, and dry beans the primary crops. These are mainly grown within Bighorn Basin and Wind River Basin, and along Wyoming's eastern plains. The state has no truly large manufacturing plants, though every town has its own specialty, from cheesemaking to computer manufacturing.

POLITICS

During the campaign in those days there were always a great many 'doubtful voters,' and it sometimes required several quarts of liquor and an unlimited number of cigars to convince them.

—Alfred J. Mokler, describing the 1898 election campaign for Frank W. Mondell, running for U.S. Senate (he won)

Unlike in many states, where apathy reigns, Wyomingites take their right to vote seriously, with turnout during presidential election years sometimes topping 80% of registered voters. Wyoming has 64 elected state representatives who serve two-year terms, along with 30 state senators elected for four-year terms of office. The elected statewide officials—governor, secretary of state, auditor, treasurer, and superintendent of public instruction—all stand for office every four years.

Republicans have controlled both houses almost since statehood, although Democrats have retained the statehouse since 1975. Governor Mike Sullivan easily won reelection in 1990, but the congressional delegation has been staunchly Republican for quite a while, and appears set to stay that way. Sierra Clubbers and leftists are advised to lay low in most parts of Wyo-

ming. (I actually met someone in Greybull, Wyoming, in 1992 who considered Dan Quayle America's best hope!) The two U.S. senators are Malcolm Wallop and Alan Simpson, while the state's lone U.S. representative is Craig Thomas.

State Symbols

As Wyoming's official governmental emblem, the Great Seal of the State of Wyoming is filled with symbolism. The two dates commemorate establishment of the territorial government in 1869 and statehood in 1890. Roman numerals (XLIV) represent Wyoming as the 44th state to be admitted to the Union; the male figures represent the livestock and mining industries, while the central female figure stands for political equality. Wyoming was without a state seal for several years since in early versions the woman was unclothed; legislators quickly sensed the problems inherent in nudity on Wyoming's official emblem. A swath of cloth made everything acceptable, and it was finally adopted by the second state Legislature in 1893.

Wyoming's best-known symbol is its bucking horse, a figure that has appeared on state license plates since 1936. The silhouette was created by artist Allen True of Denver and was reputedly inspired by the rodeo cowboy Albert ("Stub") Farlow. The bucking horse insignia had been used earlier by Wyoming soldiers during World War I.

Wyoming has all kinds of other official designations: the state flower (Indian paintbrush), bird (meadowlark), tree (cottonwood), stone (jade), mammal (bison), fossil (knightia, a fish), and fish (cutthroat trout). The state nickname seems to suffer from a split personality, being both "Equality State" and "Cowboy State." The state flag includes both the state symbol and an outline of a bison.

OUTDOOR RECREATION

Fishing And Hunting

Outstanding fishing opportunities abound throughout Wyoming, and a number of places—notably in the Yellowstone area—have attained recognition as some of the finest in America. Cutthroat, brown, rainbow, brook, and lake trout are favorites of many anglers, but the state's waters also contain mountain whitefish, kokanee, grayling, channel catfish, smallmouth bass, largemouth bass, and others. Nonresident fishing permits cost $20 for five days, $30 for 10 days, or $50 for a season. Youths (age 14-19) pay $10 for a season permit. Kids under 14 don't need a license if they are with an adult who has a valid fishing license. Get permits at most sporting-goods stores or at Game and Fish offices.

For detailed hunting and fishing information, contact the Wyoming Game and Fish Department at 5400 Bishop Blvd., Cheyenne, WY 82006, tel. 777-7735. Note that Wyoming game laws are enforced with a vengeance, so out-of-state hunters must be sure they know and obey the regulations thoroughly. Access to private land is often available only for a fee, and trespassers are subject to stringent prosecution.

Skiing

Downhill skiing enthusiasts will be pleased to find developed facilities at 11 different Wyoming locations. The finest are in the Jackson area: Jackson Hole, Grand Targhee, and Snow King. Other ski areas are Snowy Range (west of Laramie), Hogadon (near Casper), Sleeping Giant (west of Cody), and Antelope Butte (east of Greybull). More limited facilities can be found at High Park (east of Worland), Eagle Rock (near Evanston), Pine Creek (east of Cokeville), and Snowshoe Hollow (near Afton). See appropriate chapters for descriptions.

Cross-country skiers will discover an overwhelming choice of places to ski. The only developed Nordic areas are around Jackson Hole, but any of the mountain ranges fill with deep snow, providing an inexhaustible opportunity for discovery. (See p. 291-294 for more on cross-country skiing opportunities and precautions.)

Snowmobiling

Wyoming has some of the most extensive snowmobile trails in America, covering more than 1,100 miles. The most popular snowmobile areas lie within the mountains of northwestern Wyoming, the Medicine Bows, the Wind River Range, the Big Horn Mountains, and the Laramie Range. Snowmobile trail maps are available from the Wyoming Recreation Commission, 122 W. 25th, Cheyenne, WY 82002, tel. 777-7695. For trail conditions around the state, call the snowmobile hotline in Cheyenne at 777-6503. See specific areas for snowmobile rental information.

GETTING INTO THE WILDERNESS

To get a real feel for Wyoming, you need to abandon your car, get away from the towns, and head out into the vast undeveloped public lands. Wyoming's most popular backcountry areas are in the Wind River Mountains, the Medicine Bows, the Big Horn Mountains, and the entire northwest corner of the state, including Yellowstone and Grand Teton national parks. The Yellowstone region contains one of the largest nearly natural ecosystems and some of the most remote country in the lower 48 states.

Many campers prefer to use horses for longer trips, but backpacking is very popular on the shorter trails, especially in the Wind Rivers and the national parks. Backcountry permits are required only within Yellowstone and Grand Teton. It is, however, a good idea to check in at a local Forest Service ranger station to get a copy of the regulations since each place is different in such specifics as how far your tent must be from lakes and trails and whether wood fires are allowed. Be sure to take insect repellent along on any summertime trip, since mosquitoes, deerflies, and horseflies can be quite thick, especially in July and early August.

A number of hiking trails, mostly two- or three-day hikes, are described for each of Wyoming's best-known backcountry areas. For more detailed hiking information on Yellowstone, Grand

STANDING BEAR

We did not think of the great open plains, the beautiful rolling hills, the winding streams with tangled growth as wild. Only to the white man was nature a wilderness, and only to him was the land infested with wild animals and savage people. To us it was tame. Earth was bountiful, and we were surrounded with the blessings of the Great Mystery. Not until the hairy man from the east came, and with his brutal frenzy, heaped injustices upon us and the families we loved, was it wild to us. When the very animals of the forest began fleeing from his approach; then it was that for us, the "wild west" began.

—*Sioux Chief Standing Bear*

Teton, the Big Horns, or the Wind Rivers, see the "Booklist." A fine overall guide is *The Hiker's Guide to Wyoming* by Bill Hunger (Falcon Press, Helena, Montana). The National Park Service and Forest Service can also provide specific trail information.

Horses

For many people, the highlight of a Wyoming vacation is the chance to ride horseback into wild country. Although a few folks bring their own horses, most visitors leave the driving to an expert local outfitter instead. (If you've ever worked around horses in the backcountry, you'll understand why.) Horse packing is an entirely different experience from backpacking. The trade requires years of experience in learning how to properly load horses and mules with panniers, which type of knots to use for different loads, how to keep the packstrings under control, which horses to picket and which ones to hobble, and how to awaken when the horses decide to head down the trail on hobbles at three in the morning. Add to this a knowledge of bear safety, an ability to keep guests entertained with campfire tales and ribald jokes, a complete vocabulary of horse-cussing terms,

and a thorough knowledge of tobacco chewing, and you're still only about 10% of the way to becoming a packer.

Dozens of outfitters are scattered across Wyoming, but especially in the Jackson Hole, Pinedale, Cody, Dubois, Sheridan, and Saratoga areas. For a listing of outfitters in a given region, contact the local chamber of commerce office. The **Wyoming Outfitters Association,** Box 2284, Cody, WY 82414, tel. 527-7453, can provide a statewide listing.

Horse and Wagon Tours

A unique way to discover the old West is the not-for-profit **Outlaw Trail Ride** in mid-August. This six-day, 100-mile trip follows the Outlaw Trail from the Hole-in-the-Wall country of the "Wild Bunch" to Thermopolis. You'll need to bring your own horse, bedroll, and gear, but meals are provided for a fee. There is a limit of 100 riders. Call (800) 443-6235 for information.

Great Divide Tours, tel. (800) 458-1915, has Oregon Trail wagon trips, a cattle drive along the Sweetwater River, treks into Hole-in-the-Wall country, and other great adventures. More Wild West adventures are available from **Historic Trail Expeditions,** tel. 266-4868 (Casper). They lead a wide range of Conestoga wagon and horse trips (from three hours to two days; $25-150 pp) along the Oregon Trail and even a weeklong cattle drive into Hole-in-the-Wall country. On some of the trips the riders dress in 19th-century garb. **Trails West,** tel. 332-7801 or (800) 327-4052, offers three-day wagon-train treks from South Pass along the old Oregon Trail. The cost is $350 including food ($250 for ages 6-12 and $100 for children under six). For covered-wagon trips in the mountains around Jackson Hole, contact **Bar-T-5,** tel. 733-5386, or **Wagons West,** tel. (800) 447-4711.

Backcountry Ethics

Wyoming's wilderness areas represent places to escape the crowds, to enjoy the beauty and peace of the countryside, and to develop an understanding of nature. Unfortunately, as more and more people head into the backcountry, these values are becoming endangered. To keep the wild places wild, you need to practice minimum-impact hiking and camping. This means using existing campsites and fire rings, locating your campsite well away from trails and streams, burning only dead and down wood, extinguishing all fires, digging latrines at least 100 feet from lakes or streams, and hanging all food above the reach of bears. Your tent site should be 100 yards from the food storage and cooking areas to reduce the likelihood of bear problems. Wood fires are not allowed in many areas, so be sure to bring along a portable gas stove. And, of course, haul your garbage out with you. Burning cans and tinfoil in the fire lessens their weight (and the odors that attract bears), but be sure to pick them out of the fire pit before you depart.

Trail Etiquette

Because horses are so commonly used in Wyoming, hikers should follow a few rules of courtesy. Horses and mules are not the brightest critters on this planet, and they can spook at the most inane thing, even a bush blowing in the breeze or a brightly colored hat. Hikers meeting a pack string should move several feet off the trail and not speak loudly or make any sudden moves. If you've ever seen what happens when just one mule in a string decides to act up, you'll appreciate the chaos that can result from sudden noises or movements. Anyone hiking with a dog should keep it well away from the stock and not let it bark. Last of all, never walk closely behind a horse, unless you don't mind spending time in a hospital. Their kick is definitely worse than their bite.

Range Etiquette

Wyoming's land-ownership pattern includes many areas where private and public lands are intermingled in a complex checkerboard pattern. This creates all sorts of problems for management of, and access to, public lands, as well as for private owners. The conflict is most apparent in grazing country, where many ranchers jealously guard their land from trespassers for any reason. There are places—most notably in the Hole-in-the-Wall country of northeastern Wyoming—where access to public lands is blocked by private landowners who have had problems in the past. A gate left open by a careless visitor or sheep sent running by a barking

dog can quickly sour even the most generous rancher. Many of them are living marginal existences already, so every little problem becomes magnified, especially if done by a cityslicker (or even worse, a cityslicker with California license plates).

Private boundaries are not always marked by No Trespassing signs, so it's a good idea to have a detailed map (such as those sold at BLM offices) to be sure you are walking on public land. This is a particularly big issue during the fall hunting season, when many ranchers require a hefty "trespass fee" for access. If you *do* hunt despite warning signs, don't expect any help from the state, since Game and Fish officers are very supportive of private-property rights. And since we're talking ethical issues, here's some more advice: never ask a rancher how many cattle he has; it's like asking someone how much money he earns.

BACKCOUNTRY SAFETY

Beaver Fever

Although Wyoming's lakes and streams may appear clean, you may be risking a debilitating sickness by drinking the water without treatment. The protozoan *Giardia duodenalis* is found throughout the state, spread by both humans and animals (including beaver). Although the disease is curable with drugs, it's always best to carry safe drinking water on any trip or to boil water taken from creeks

Giardia duodenalis

or lakes. Bringing water to a full boil is sufficient to kill Giardia and other harmful organisms. Another option is to use water filters such as First Need, available from backpacking stores. Note, however, that these may not filter out other organisms such as Campylobacter bacteria that are just 0.2 microns in size. Chlorine and iodine are not always reliable, taste foul, and can be unhealthy.

BEAR COUNTRY

Old-timers joke that bears are easy to differentiate: a black bear climbs up the tree after you, while a grizzly snaps the tree off at the base. Black bears are found in forested areas throughout Wyoming, but grizzlies exist only in Yellowstone National Park and surrounding country. Although grizzlies are generally a much greater threat to humans, black bears can also be dangerous, and backcountry travelers need to take similar precautions against both.

Grizzlies once ranged across the entire Northern Hemisphere, from Europe across what is now Russia and through the western half of North America. Unfortunately, as white settlers arrived, they came to view these massive and powerful creatures (average adult males weigh 500 pounds) as a threat to themselves and their stock. The scientific name, *Ursus arctos horribilis,* says much about human attitudes toward grizzlies. They were shot, trapped, and poisoned nearly to the brink of extinction in the lower 48, so that today they now exist in only a few of the most remote parts of Montana, Wyoming, Idaho, and Washington. Wyoming has perhaps 200 grizzlies.

Avoiding Bear Hugs

Bear encounters are rare, but frightening, experiences. Although there is considerable variability among individuals, most bears hear or smell you long before you realize their presence, and they hightail it away. Surprising a bear, especially a sow with her cubs, is the last thing you want to do in the backcountry. Before heading out, check at a local ranger station to see whether there have been recent bear encounters. Larger groups are less likely to have problems. Make noise in areas of dense cover or when coming around blind spots on trails. Some people tie bells to their packs for this purpose, while others regard this as an annoyance to fellow hikers.

Before camping, take a look around the area to see if there are recent bear tracks or scat. If so, you should find another spot. Keep a clean camp, and be sure to hang all food and other items that bears may smell at least 12 feet off the ground and four feet from tree trunks. Bears are attracted to odors of all sorts, including food, horse feed, soap, toothpaste, deodorants, and perhaps menstruation. If you discover an animal carcass, be extremely alert since a bear may be nearby and may attack anything that might threaten its food. Get away from such areas. Other potential problem areas are along streams where fish are spawning and in grassy or brush areas where a resting bear may be hidden from your sight.

If you do happen to encounter a bear and it sees you, try to stay calm and not make any sudden moves. Do not run, since you could not possibly outrun a bear; they can exceed 40 mph for short distances. If a good-sized tree is nearby, climb it as high as you can with safety and stay there until you're certain that the bear has left the area. If no tree is close, your best bet is to remain still or back slowly away. Sometimes dropping an item such as a hat or jacket will distract the bear, and talking also seems to have some value in convincing bears that you're a human. If a grizzly bear does attack, curl up facedown on the ground in a fetal position with your hands wrapped behind your neck and your elbows tucked over your face. Your backpack may help protect you somewhat. Remain still even if you are attacked, since sudden movements may incite further attacks. Many people have survived such attacks, despite being bitten and clawed. Many authorities now recommend against dropping to the ground if you are attacked by a black bear, since they tend to be more aggressive in those situations. You are better off fighting back with whatever weapons are at hand if attacked by a black bear.

Recently, capsicum (pepper) sprays such as Counter Assault (Bushwacker Backpack & Supply Co., Box 4721, Missoula, MT 59806) have proven useful in fending off bear attacks. They are not, however, cure-alls or replacements for being careful in bear country.

BOB RACE

Hypothermia

Anyone who has spent much time in the outdoors will discover the dangers of exposure to cold, wet, and windy conditions. Even at temperatures well above freezing, hypothermia—the reduction of the body's inner core temperature—can prove fatal. In the early stages, hypothermia causes uncontrollable shivering, followed by a loss of coordination, slurred speech, and then a rapid descent into unconsciousness and death. Always travel prepared for sudden changes in the weather. Wear clothing that insulates well and that holds its heat when wet. Wool and polypro are far better than cotton, and clothes should be worn in layers to provide better trapping of heat and a chance to adjust to conditions more easily. Always carry a wool hat, since your head loses more heat than any other part of the body. Bring a waterproof shell to cut the wind.

If someone in your party begins to show signs of hypothermia, don't take any chances, even if the person denies needing help. Get the victim out of the wind, strip off his clothes, and put him in a dry sleeping bag on an insulating pad. Skin-to-skin contact is the best way to warm a hypothermic person, and that means you'll need to also strip and climb in the sleeping bag. If you weren't friends before, this should heat up the relationship! Do not give the victim alcohol or hot drinks, and do not try to warm the person too quickly since it could lead to heart failure. Once the victim has recovered, get medical help as soon as possible. Actually, you're far better off keeping close tabs on everyone in the group and seeking shelter before exhaustion and hypothermia set in.

ACCOMMODATIONS AND FOOD

LODGING CHOICES

Lodging in Wyoming covers the complete spectrum, from the very finest of luxury accommodations where a king would feel pampered all the way down to flophouses so tawdry that even town drunks think twice. In general, visitors will find motel costs considerably less than what they might pay in other parts of America. This is especially true in the smaller towns and in places where the economy is weak from the bust following the oil boom. During the summer, rates at the mom-and-pop motels that line the streets of every Wyoming town start around $25 for one person or $30 for two people. Tack on another $5-10 for slightly fancier places with the AAA sign out front. Come wintertime, rates may drop 25% or more.

The exception to these low rates is the northwest corner of the state, notably Cody, and most egregiously, Jackson. Expect to pay at least $45 s or $55 d during peak summer or winter season in Jackson Hole. Beware that rates for Cheyenne motel and hotel rooms skyrocket during Cheyenne Frontier Days (late July). Also note that motel prices have a way of changing even in a given day. The law of supply and demand holds, and many owners raise prices as the evening progresses and the rooms start to fill up, when a convention comes to town, and on weekends.

Some places (I try to keep them out of this book) seem to operate on the let's-make-a-deal school of pricing and get evasive when asked to quote a rate. Always ask to see the room before deciding to stay at a motel—places that I consider more than adequate may be beneath your standards. In general, however, visitors will be very pleased with Wyoming motels. The low rates reflect a less expensive economy, not shoddy conditions. Don't be scared off by a price that seems too low by New Jersey standards!

The annual *TourBook* for Idaho, Montana, and Wyoming (free to members of the American Automobile Association) is a helpful guide to the better hotels and motels, offering current prices and accurate ratings. For a complete listing of motels, hotels, bed and breakfasts, dude ranches, and camping places in Wyoming, request a copy of the free *Wyoming Accommodations Directory* from the Wyoming Travel Commission, I-25 at College Dr., Cheyenne, WY 82002, tel. 777-7777 or (800) 225-5996. The booklet lists lodging and campgrounds in every part of the state. Throughout this book I have listed only two prices for most lodging places: one person (single, or s) and two people in one bed (double, or d). The accommodations charts are arranged from least to most expensive.

Hotels

Most of the traditional hotels that once offered lodging for weary Wyoming travelers have either fallen to the wrecking ball or have been turned into residence flophouses. Only a few of these historic gems have been restored to their glory; they include Cheyenne's Plains Hotel, Cody's Irma Hotel, Jackson's Wort Hotel, Medicine Bow's Virginian Hotel, and Saratoga's Wolf Hotel. Yellowstone National Park offers some of the finest old-time luxury accommodations anywhere in America: Old Faithful Inn, Lake Hotel, and Mammoth Hot Springs Hotel.

Motels

The various motel chains—Best Western, Days Inn, Holiday Inn, La Quinta, Motel 6, and Super 8—all operate motels across the state, primarily in the larger towns. These cinderblock monuments to the bigger-is-better school of lodging stand on the edges of town, their towering signs acting as glaring eyesores. Each chain publishes its own brochure, listing locations and rates. Pick up a copy at a chain motel near your home or call their toll-free numbers.

Every town in Wyoming has its locally owned small motels, generally run by an elderly woman with a yip-dog slightly larger than a small shrew (and twice as feisty). These motels vary widely in quality and price but tend to offer the best rates and friendliest service.

Bed And Breakfasts

Bed and breakfasts are a relatively recent addition to Wyoming's lodging picture, but more are appearing each year. These range from remote places where the accommodations are not unlike a guest ranch to historic Victorian homes in the center of town. Some of the best are found in Big Horn, Buffalo, Cheyenne, Cody, Douglas, Dubois, Guernsey, Jackson Hole, Lander, Laramie, Lusk, Rawlins, Saratoga, Shell, and Wheatland. Get a brochure from Wyoming Homestay & Outdoor Adventures (WHOA) at the B&Bs listed in these pages.

Dude Ranches

An old and respected Western tradition is the dude ranch, which began as a sideline to the business of raising cattle. Friends from the East would remember old Jake out there in wild Wyoming where the buffalo roam and the antelope play and would decide it was time for a visit. So off they would head, living in the ranchers' outbuildings and joining in the chores. The "dudes," as they became known, soon told their friends, and Jake found his ranch inundated. After a couple of years of this, the next step was obvious: get those eastern rascals to fork over some cash for the privilege of visiting. Pretty soon the

Horseback riding is a popular activity at many Wyoming dude ranches.

CATHY CARLSON

dude ranching business was born. At its peak in the 1920s, dude ranching spread through much of Wyoming and the West. Dude ranching saved many cattle ranches from extinction by providing a second source of income, and it simultaneously brought these magnificent lands to the attention of people who had the money to prevent their development (most notably Grand Teton National Park).

At the older ranches, generations of families have returned year after year to vacation in the Wild West. Many dude ranches now call themselves guest ranches, a term that reflects both the suspicious way some people view the word *dude* and the changing nature of the business. Many city folks today lack the desire or skill to actually saddle up their own horse, much less push cattle between pastures. As a result, guest/dude ranches tend to emphasize grand scenery, horseback riding, campfires, hearty meals, chuckwagon cookouts, sing-alongs, and evenings around the fireplace. Some folks even camp overnight out there in the fearful wilderness where the coyotes howl and the mice chew into your stash of potato chips. There aren't too many places left where you actually work alongside the cowboys. Playing is a lot more fun.

Wyoming has literally dozens of dude ranches and ranch resorts, offering accommodations ranging from Spartan to so sumptuous that they bear absolutely no resemblance to ranch life. Not all dude ranches are created equal—some are slick and modern with tennis courts and hot tubs while others are funky and old-fashioned with delightful rough edges. Dude ranch rates generally start around $700 pp (double occupancy) for a one-week stay, including everything from fine meals to horse rides. The fanciest resorts will set you back over $2000 a week.

Ask plenty of questions ahead of time, such as what activities are available, what to bring in the way of clothing, what sort of meals to expect (vegetarians may have a hard time on many ranches), if there are additional charges, what the living accommodations are like, and how many other guests are likely to be there at the same time. Note that it is considered proper to tip the ranch hands, kitchen help, and others who work so hard to keep the ranch running. For many of them, this is a way to fund their college education (or buy a winter in Belize).

Camping

Wyoming has dozens of public campsites scattered across the state, primarily on Forest Service and Park Service lands. Most of these have running water, garbage pick-up, and outhouses, but no showers. The fee is generally $5-8 per night, and most are open from early June to mid-September. After that, many of the campgrounds remain open (no charge) but do not have garbage pick-up or running water. It's generally legal to camp for free on undeveloped Forest Service or BLM land throughout the state, but check at local offices for specifics.

Every town of any size has at least one private RV park and so-called campground. Most of these are little more than vacant lots with sewer and electrical hookups, showers, and toilet facilities. These private campgrounds generally charge $2-4 for showers if you're not camping there. A better deal in many towns is to use the shower in the local public swimming pool, where you get a free swim thrown in for the entrance charge.

FOOD AND DRINK

Wyoming is not a state known for its haute cuisine. This is cattle country, the land of the free and the home on the range, where juicy steaks and the finest prime rib can be found in every podunk town in the state. (The two best steakhouses may well be in the don't-blink-or-you'll-miss-it town of Hudson.) Or if you don't like that, try chicken-fried steak, the house specialty at every truck stop and greasy spoon in Wyoming. Wash it down with a beer, and then sit back for a big hunk of apple pie. For breakfast, it's pretty much standard all-American fare, accompanied by a dark brew that folks in these parts call coffee. Real cowboy coffee, made only over an open smoky fire and not available within 20 miles of any town, is a potent medicine, not advised for children and the weak-kneed. Check local outfitters for the prescription.

Unfortunately, in Wyoming—like the rest of the nation—the real dining-out kings are McDonald's, Wendy's, Domino's, Dairy Queen, and all the other fast-food outlets that are turning regional differences into a bland mediocrity of frozen burgers and whipped-shortening "milk shakes." For Mexican fare, many locals head to the appropriately named Taco John's, a Wyoming chain that will hopefully never be unleashed on the rest of America.

Actually, Wyoming food is not quite as uniformly bland as might be imagined, and travelers will discover several innovative and surprisingly reasonable restaurants in Laramie, Jackson, and Cody, fine Mexican eateries in Rawlins and Cheyenne, authentic Chinese food in Cheyenne and Casper, and nouvelle-cuisine restaurants scattered around the state. The most creative (and pricey) food can probably be found in the tourist town of Jackson and the college town of Laramie.

> *Astronomical eclipses are of infrequent occurrence, but there is an eclipse taking place on Eddy Street daily and nightly. It is Professor McDaniel's Museum, which eclipses every other place of amusement in Cheyenne. The more money you invest with the Professor the greater equivalent you receive. Call upon him, imbibe one of those Tom and Jerrys, etc., and if not satisfied we pronounce you incorrigible. "Ye Gods!" What nectar the Professor concocts in those little china mugs. Better than the dew on a damsel's lips. Speaking of damsels just step into the museum and you'll see 'em large as life, besides 1,001 other sciences, embracing every known subject. It is an awe-inspiring view.*
>
> *—ad for McDaniel's Theater and Museum in the 1860s, quoted in The Magic City of the Plains: Cheyenne 1867-1967*

On The Town

In many Wyoming towns, drinking and carousing hold as much interest as eating, especially on Friday and Saturday nights. Every burg of any size has its resident country-western band, and saloon dance floors fill up with duded-up cowboys and cowgirls out for a night on the town. Many of these bands also play Eagles-style rock tunes for variety. The larger cities and tourist towns have several nightclubs, some with disc jockeys, others with basic rock-and-roll fare. Don't expect a steep cover charge to get in the door—most places are free.

EVENTS AND ACTIVITIES

During the summer months, every town in Wyoming has its own main event, generally centered on a morning parade, an afternoon rodeo, and an evening of country music and dancing. Rodeos are the definitive Wyoming activity, reflecting an enduring nostalgia for cattle and cowboys. Daily summertime rodeos can be found in Cody and Jackson, and twice-weekly rodeos in Laramie and Casper. Riverton has weekly rodeos in the summer. Informal roping events go on all summer long around the state; ask locally for times. See "Rodeo Today" below for more details.

Wyoming's most famous event is **Cheyenne Frontier Days**, a 10-day bash that fills every hotel for a hundred miles and makes Cheyenne streets look like a miniature Los Angeles. It starts the last full week of July each year. The centerpiece of Frontier Days is, of course, the rodeo, which attracts the nation's finest riders,

but there are also parades, pancake feeds, art exhibits, and much more. Don't miss this one! The **Cody Stampede** (early July) is another very popular rodeo, parade, and all-round chance to party. The **PRCA Rodeo Finals**—Wyoming's largest indoor rodeo—comes to Casper each October.

A Taste Of History

The **Gift of the Waters Pageant** arrives in Thermopolis in early August. It celebrates Chief Washakie's gift of this wonderful hot springs to the federal government to be used by all people. The *Legend of Rawhide,* an outdoor play held each July since 1947, has a cast that seems to include half the town of Lusk. The story is based on the 1849 killing of a Sioux girl by a white gold-seeker and the Indians' retaliatory skinning-alive of the protagonist (hence the name). For a more sanguine view of life in the early days, visit one of the many mountain men rendezvous held around the state. The biggest and best are the **Fort Bridger Rendezvous,** held each Labor Day, and Pinedale's **Green River Rendezvous** in July. Also of note are those in Lander (early June), Riverton (early July), and Jackson (mid-July). A good time is had by all in an authentic and picturesque setting. (See below for more on rendezvous.) To get another taste of the mountain man era, be sure to attend a performance of *Ballad of the West,* a dramatic musical held in Cody each July and August. Wyoming's largest powwows are the **Plains Indian Powwow** in Cody each June, Ft. Washakie's **Eastern Shoshone Powwow and Rodeo** in early July, and the **Labor Day Powwow** in Arapahoe.

Other Events

Thousands of people flood the tiny settlement of Encampment for the **Woodchopper's Jamboree** in late June. Another big attraction is the **Wyoming State Fair,** held in Douglas during mid-August. County fairs are held in each of Wyoming's 22 counties during the summer. Casper's two biggest events are the **Central Wyoming Fair and Rodeo** in early August and the **Casper Classic Bicycle Races.** The latter races (held late June to July 4) attract 500 of the top cyclists in America with a $75,000 purse.

Jackson Hole has a number of popular events through the year, including the highly acclaimed **Grand Teton Music Festival** during July and the **Fall Arts Festival,** which attracts entries from all over the world. Jackson's annual **Elk Antler Auction** in late May attracts aphrodisiac (!) buyers from all over the globe. For something completely different, head to Chugwater in late June for the **Chugwater Chili Cook-Off.** Bring along a bottle of Maalox.

All of these events—plus many more—are described in greater detail in appropriate sections of this book. For a complete calendar of Wyoming events, contact the Wyoming Travel Commission, I-25 at College Dr., Cheyenne, WY 82002, tel. 777-7777 or (800) 225-5996.

MODERN-DAY RENDEZVOUS

In recent years the mountain men rendezvous has become a major summertime attraction in Wyoming. These are rather strange affairs, attracting both tourists and locals to gawk at guys in buckskin pants or breechcloths and women in tanned leather skirts. Unlike the original rendezvous, you won't see many Indians at these get-togethers. The participants are a mixture of Joe Blow Businessman who likes a little diversion, Wendy Waitress who dreams of simpler times, and a lot of folks who look like they're either former/current hippies or bikers and who find this a great way to live the simple life in a semilegitimate way. More long hair, beards, braless women, and barefoot kids than you've seen in two decades.

Participants live in tipis, bake bread over fires, race horses bareback, and mug for the clicking cameras of tourists. Lots of beef jerky, Indian tacos, and fry bread for sale. This isn't a good place for the animal-rights crowd, since many of the trade items at the modern rendezvous (as at the original ones) are from wild animals. Most of the people who attend a rendezvous have something to offer: old beads, leather clothing, tomahawks, knives, moccasins, woven crafts, tanned hides, and lots of fox, coyote, rabbit, ermine, and other furs.

Events at a rendezvous include black-powder shooting contests, storytelling, fiddle music, dancing, hide-tanning demonstrations, tomahawk and knife throwing, and footraces for the kids. In the evening when all the gawkers head back to their air-conditioned motel rooms, the rendezvous really comes to life with big campfires, more storytelling, carousing, drinking, and a raucous good time for all. But woe be the one who shows up after dark in modern-day civilian clothes!

RODEO

Sometimes I think life is just a rodeo. The trick is to ride and make it to the bell . . .
—John Fogerty

It may come as a revelation to many people, but rodeo is one of the most popular sports in America; more people watch professional rodeos than attend NFL football games! In Wyoming—a state where even the license plate is graced with a cowboy astride a bucking bronc—it should come as no surprise that rodeo is king.

Every small town in the state has a rodeo of some sort during the summer, and the larger cities have world-class rodeos attracting hundreds of riders and ropers from the Professional Rodeo Cowboys Association (PRCA). (By the way, in Wyoming, rodeo is always pronounced ROE-dee-oh.)

History

Although rodeo seems to have a few drops of Spanish bullfight in its blood, and many of the words—rodeo, bronco, lariat, arena, and honda—have Spanish origins, its true origins were in the days of cowboys and cattle in the Wild West. Gradually, groups of cowboys got together to show off their riding and roping skills and to compete with neighboring outfits. Everyone argues over the official origins of rodeo, but credit is generally given to a bucking and roping competition between the Mill Iron and Hash Knife outfits who met near Deer Trail, Colorado, in 1869.

As the West began to be fenced in, the cowboy events moved into the nearby towns as organized "buckin' shows." Buffalo Bill Cody probably had more to do with popularizing the sport than any other person. For many years his Wild West Show traveled the world, providing a spectacle that included several of the events in present-day rodeos. Lander lays claim to the oldest rodeo in Wyoming. Begun in 1893, the Lander Pioneer Days rodeo still comes around each July. By far, the most famous Wyoming rodeo is the "Daddy of 'em All," Cheyenne Frontier Days, one of the top four rodeos in the world.

TODD CLARK

Rodeo Today

Over the years, rodeo has become more professional and less connected to the true cowboy. Many participants today come from cities and have never spent time herding cattle or working on a ranch; some of the finest have come from Harlem and the Bronx. Of course, many other cowboys still come from more traditional farming and ranching backgrounds, though they may work part-time at the local grocery store to fund their travels around the rodeo circuit. When they get enough money, they attend a weeklong rodeo school, picking up pointers from past champions.

Those who make it to the top do so the hard way. Grand National winners are decided on the basis of rodeo earnings, meaning that they must compete almost continuously, flying from one rodeo to another, staying in cheap motels, or living out of their RVs. Semipros and amateurs compete in the hundreds of smaller rodeos that dot Wyoming and the West, hoping to make it to the professional level. Most don't even come close, losing their stiff entry fees to more experienced competitors and taking home only bruises or broken bones.

The major rodeo events generally fall into two categories, riding and roping. Riding events include saddle bronc riding, bareback bronc riding, and bull riding, while roping events include steer wrestling, calf roping, and steer roping. Women's barrel racing, clown bullfighting, and chuckwagon races complete the roundup. In most of the events, luck has much to do with who wins. Much of the scoring is based on the difficulty of the ride (the toughest broncs or bulls are favorites because they mean higher scores), and times for ropers are dependent upon the speed and behavior of the calf or steer they are trying to tackle.

Many rodeo riders are young, skinny-as-a-rail types, while ropers tend to be bulkier and older. The two groups don't mix much and generally have disparaging words to say about the "skinny cowboys on their rocking horses" or "those fat bulldoggers with no style and no skill." But behind this bluster lies respect, especially for competitors in a cowboy's own events. Hang around the chutes a while and you'll discover a surprising generosity to fellow riders and ropers as they warn what to expect from a given bronc, help cinch down the straps, and joke over the new shiner from the horseshoe firmly planted in the bareback rider's face. And they party together late into the night, looking for the rodeo queens and the girls who like the smell of horse sweat. Small-time winners often spread the loot back among the losers, buying drinks and renting a motel room where everyone can sneak in for a night's rest. Writer Fred Schnell, in *Rodeo! The Suicide Sport,* described a story that seems to epitomize rodeo life:

Once, when rodeo announcer Mel Lambert explained to the audience that a champion who had just made a good ride neither drank nor smoked and was a college athlete, Jim Shoulders, who has won 16 world titles, turned to a friend behind the chutes and said disgustedly, "Isn't that the worst crap you've ever heard? What the hell is rodeo coming to?"

One thing newcomers soon notice about rodeo cowboys is the clothes they wear—long-sleeve shirts, cowboy hats, Wrangler jeans (never Levi's—the seam is in the wrong place for riding), and cowboy boots. As writer Mary S. Robertson suggested, "In no other sport but rodeo do the players and the spectators dress alike." Interestingly, the PRCA actually has a rule requiring long-sleeve shirts and cowboy hats; apparently at one time too many riders and ropers were wearing baseball caps and T-shirts, so the more traditional attire was made mandatory. And of course, there is one additional piece of attire worn by rodeo cowboys, the plate-sized silver and gold belt buckles. Top winners get these as awards for surviving a season of abuse; others buy them for flash and dash.

The Suicide Sport

A title occasionally used for rodeo is "the suicide sport." It is, unfortunately, all too true. Accidents are very common and rodeos always have an EMT ready to tend to the inevitable smashed legs, kicked-in ribs, and broken collarbones. Many cowboys are crippled for life and at least several die each year in the sport, including two at Cheyenne Frontier Days in the 1980s. Even the nation's top riders and ropers can be killed. Most dangerous of all are the bull rides, but just

watching a "dogger" leaping off his horse onto the horns of a speeding steer can give the crowd pause. Rodeos are criticized by animal-rights activists as unnecessary cruelty to animals—steers occasionally die from broken necks and broncs sometimes injure themselves (and their riders) by trying to jump out of the chutes—but the cowboys really do all they can to prevent injury to the animals they ride or rope.

Steer Wrestling

Steer wrestling, or bulldogging, involves leaping from a quarter horse onto the back of a 700-pound Mexican steer running at 25 miles an hour, grabbing his horns, and wrestling him to the ground. If you think that sounds easy, try it some time! Steer wrestling originated in 1903 when Bill Pickett, a black Texas cowboy (many early cowboys were black), jumped on the back of an ornery steer, grabbed its horns, bent over its head and bit the steer's lower lip like an attacking bulldog. Soon he was repeating the stunt for the 101 Ranch Wild West Show. Others copied this feat, and though the lip-biting part has long since disappeared, the name bulldogging has stuck.

Steer wrestling is a complex endeavor involving two men: a dogger and a hazer. When the steer hurtles into the arena, the two spur their horses in quick pursuit, with the hazer trying to force the steer to run straight ahead while the dogger gets into position to leap onto the steer's horns, wrestling him to the ground with his feet and head facing the same direction. Since they are competing with other doggers on time, every second counts. Good doggers can get a steer down in less than seven seconds.

Calf Roping

Calf roping originated in the Old West when ropers would pull down a calf and quickly tie it up for branding. Today, this is the most competitive of all rodeo events, and there is often big money for the winners. Calf ropers chase a 300-pound calf on their expertly trained horses, roping it and then quickly throwing it on its side. After a quick wrap of the piggin' string around three ankles, followed by a half-hitch knot ("hooey"), the calf is allowed to try to break free. If it can't within six seconds, the time stands and an untie man rides in to free the calf. Time is of the essence in calf roping, and the most valuable asset for a roper is his horse. The best horses are in high demand and are often rented to other riders for a cut of any winnings.

Steer Roping

The most controversial of all rodeo contests is steer roping, an event that has been banned from most rodeos because it is so hard on the animals. Cheyenne Frontier Days is one place it is still done. The procedure is essentially the same as calf roping, but with a much larger animal. When the 700-pound steer is jerked back by the rope and then thrown down with a thud, you can almost feel the impact. Fortunately, injuries to the tough old steers are uncommon.

Saddle Bronc Riding

When you say the word *rodeo,* many people immediately think of saddle bronc riding. The oldest of all rodeo sports, it originated from cowboys' attempts to train wild horses. Rodeo saddle bronc riding is more complex than this, however, requiring a special "association" saddle, dulled spurs, and very precise rules. It is a judged event, with points taken away for not being in the correct position or in control. The bronc is saddled up in the chute (a fenced-in enclosure along the edge of the arena) and the rider climbs on, grabbing a thick hemp rope in one hand and sinking his boots into the stirrups. When the gate opens the bronc goes wild, trying to throw the rider off. The smooth back-and-forth motion of a good saddle bronc rider makes it appear that he is atop a rocking chair. Rides only last eight seconds (leading to lots of ribald cowboy jokes); when the horn sounds, a pick-up man rides alongside the bronc and the rider slides onto the other horse.

Bareback Bronc Riding

Bareback riding is a relatively recent sport, having arrived on the scene in the 1920s. The rules are similar to saddle bronc riding, but the cowboy rides with only a minimum of equipment—no stirrups and no reins. A small leather rigging held on by a leather strap around the horse is topped with a suitcaselike handle. A second wool-lined strap goes around the flank of the horse to act as an irritant so that he bucks more. The cowboy holds on with one hand and

bounces back and forth in a rocking motion, an effort akin to trying to juggle bowling pins while surfing a big wave. Eight seconds later it's over and a pick-up man comes in to rescue the rider (if he hasn't been thrown to the ground).

Bull Riding And Rodeo Clowns

Bull riding is in a class of danger all its own. Unlike broncs, which just want that man off their back, bulls want to get even. When a bull rider is thrown off (and this is most of the time, even with the best riders), the bull immediately goes on the attack, trying to gore or trample him. Many bull riders are seriously injured and some die when hit by this 2,000 pounds of brute force. There are no saddles in bull riding, just a piece of thick rope wrapped around the bull's chest with the free end wrapped tightly around the bull rider's hand. A cowbell hangs at the bottom of this contraption to annoy the bull even more. When the chute opens, all hell breaks loose as the bull does everything it possibly can to throw his rider off—spinning, kicking, jumping, and running against the fence.

If the rider hangs on for the required eight seconds (style isn't very important), the next battle begins—getting out of the way of one very angry bull. Here the **rodeo clowns** come in. Dressed in bright red-and-white shirts and baggy pants, they look like human Raggedy Andy dolls. In reality they are moving targets. Clowns use every trick in the book—climbing into padded barrels that the bulls butt against, weaving across the arena, mocking the bulls with matador capes, and simply running for their lives to reach the fence ahead of the bull. Frequently, two clowns work in tandem to create confusion, one acting as the barrel man and the other as a roving target. The rodeo clown also plays another role, that of entertainer between events. A clown's stock of supplies includes rubber chickens, trick mules, a series of pantomimed jokes with the announcer, and anything else that might keep folks from getting restless.

In a few of the larger rodeos there are clown "bullfights." In them a clown is pitted against a bull in a specially constructed small arena. He taunts the bull in every possible way, running past and around the bull, touching him, and maybe even leaping over him, all the while trying to stay out of the way of those horns and hooves. These last only 45 seconds, but that seems like an eternity of danger. No wonder they call this the suicide sport!

Other Events
One of the funniest of all rodeo events is the **wild horse race,** a zany event that since 1897 has ended each day's events at Cheyenne Frontier Days. Twelve teams of three cowboys try to rope, saddle, and then race a collection of the wildest horses imaginable. If they manage to get on the broncs, their next problem is convincing the horses to run around the half-mile track in the right direction. It seems the definition of bedlam, with horses breaking loose and starting off in opposite directions, crashing into mounted riders and other horses. For sheer chaos, wild horse races would even put a Democratic Convention to shame!

Another crowd favorite at Frontier Days is the **chuck wagon race,** a Canadian invention with mostly Canadian teams. It is a confusing, fast-paced, chaotic, noisy, and dusty sport that involves four wagons, each pulled by four horses. Each team also has two "outriders," boys on horseback. At the sound of the starting gun, an outrider throws a 50-pound "cookstove" into the back of the chuckwagon and climbs back on his horse to chase the wagons. Then everyone takes off on a tight figure-eight course around several barrels and then onto the half-mile circular track. The outriders ride in pursuit; they must cross the finish line near their chuckwagons. Needless to say, with four wagons pulled by 16 horses running at a full gallop, and another eight horses running alongside, the race is both exciting and dangerous. When the wagons come around the last corner, everyone in the stands is on their feet, yelling and cheering.

Barrel racing—one of the only female-dominated events—is found at nearly every rodeo and consists of a triangular course of three barrels arranged a hundred feet apart. The event requires riding a fast horse in a set pattern around these barrels, trying not to knock any over. The fastest time wins.

Some rodeos also have what is called the **calf scramble** (featuring dozens of children from the stands chasing a calf to get the ribbon off its tail) and the **colt race,** in which young colts are let loose in a race toward their mares. Both are real crowd pleasers.

INFORMATION AND SERVICES

Events and specific chamber of commerce information are listed for each town described in this book. There are large **state information centers** in Cheyenne, Evanston, Jackson, Laramie, Pine Bluffs, Sheridan, and Sundance. For a helpful overall guide to Wyoming, along with a listing of events, chamber of commerce offices, plus lodging and camping places, request a copy of the free *Wyoming Vacation Guide* from the Wyoming Travel Commission, I-25 at College Dr., Cheyenne, WY 82002, tel. 777-7777 or (800) 225-5996. They also have free **state maps,** or pick up these maps at any chamber of commerce office in Wyoming. A great way to check the pulse of Wyoming is by reading the letters to the editor in the *Casper Star-Tribune.* They fill several pages every day and are sometimes quite amusing.

For a complete listing of more than 225 **museums and galleries,** contact the Wyoming Arts Council, 2320 Capitol Ave., Cheyenne, WY 82002, tel. 777-7742. The finest large museum—Cody's Buffalo Bill Historical Center—should not be missed, but a visit to the smaller and less-known museums is also well worth your time. Some of the best are found in Buffalo, Casper, Cheyenne, Douglas, Fort Laramie, Grand Teton National Park, Jackson, Lusk, Pinedale, South Pass City, and Thermopolis. See appropriate chapters for specifics.

The telephone **area code** for all of Wyoming is 307. Throughout this book, **summer** is defined as Memorial Day to Labor Day, except when otherwise noted.

BEST OF WYOMING

It isn't just the spectaculars of Wyoming that make it wonderful—Yellowstone, the Tetons, or Devils Tower—but also the lack of such spectacles, the lack of "sights," the lack of people, the lack of civilization. This is a land of rutted dirt roads and a sky that envelops it all. The following places offer a cross section of Wyoming's delights. This highly selective list features just a few of the many places worth exploring; this book is filled with hundreds of other places.

The "Biggies" that everyone should see

Big Horn Mountains
Bighorn Canyon National Recreation Area
Buffalo Bill Historical Center
Devils Tower National Monument
Fort Laramie
Hot Springs State Park
Jackson Hole
Grand Teton National Park
Snowy Range
Wind River Mountains
Yellowstone

Lesser-known places well worth a visit

Ayres Natural Bridge
Casper Mountain
Castle Gardens
Flaming Gorge National Recreation Area
Fort Bridger
Fossil Butte National Monument
Frontier Prison, Rawlins
Guernsey State Park
Hell's Half Acre
Independence Rock
Killpecker Dunes
Medicine Lodge State Park
Medicine Wheel
Oregon Trail Ruts, Guernsey
Sacagawea Cemetery, Ft. Washakie
Sierra Madre Range
Snake River Canyon
South Pass City
St. Stephens Mission
Sunlight Basin
The Black Hills
Trail Town, Cody
Vedauwoo Rocks
Wyoming Territorial Park

Interesting Offbeat Attractions

Accidental Oil Company, Newcastle
Charcoal kilns, Piedmont
Crimson Dawn Museum, Casper Mountain
Elk antler arch, Afton
Elk antler arches, Jackson
Giant wind generator, Medicine Bow
J.C. Penney house, Kemmerer
Jackalope statue, Douglas
Joss House, Evanston
Little America
Midwest-area pumpjacks
Mother Featherlegs monument, Lusk area
Star Valley Cheese factory, Thayne
Torrington Livestock Auction
World's "Oldest" Building, Como Bluff
Wright-area coal mines

Great Country Roads

Little Sandy Road (partly gravel) between Farson and Boulder
Sinks Canyon Road (partly gravel) between Lander and Atlantic City
State 24 between Devils Tower and Aladdin
State 70 between Encampment and Baggs
State 89 between Cokeville and Alpine
State 230 between Laramie and Encampment
State 296 (partly gravel) through Sunlight Basin
State 414 between Mountain View and Manila

State 487 through Shirley Basin
US 14 and 14A over the Big Horn
    Mountains
US 14-16 between Ucross and Gillette
US 14-16-20 between Cody and
    Yellowstone
US 16 between Worland and Buffalo
US 18-85 between Newcastle and Lusk
US 26-287 between Dubois and Moran
    Junction
US 212 between Cooke City and Red
    Lodge

Fascinating Small Towns:

Aladdin	Hartville
Atlantic City	Medicine Bow
Buffalo	Meeteetse
Dayton	Saratoga
Dubois	Sundance
Elk Mountain	Ten Sleep
Encampment	Wilson
Jay Em	

TRANSPORTATION

By Air

Commercial airline service to Wyoming is limited to the towns of Casper, Cheyenne, Cody, Gillette, Jackson, Laramie, Riverton, Rock Springs, Sheridan, and Worland. Four major airlines serve the state—United, Continental, Delta, and American—but most connections are via Denver or Salt Lake, even if you want to fly from one part of Wyoming to another. Deregulation at work!

By Car

Given the expansiveness and small population of Wyoming, it comes as no surprise that the automobile is the primary means of transportation (actually, pickup trucks are the most common vehicles in rural areas). Wyoming has many thousands of miles of paved and gravel roads. See Dan Lewis's *8,000 Miles of Dirt: A Backroad Travel Guide to Wyoming* (Casper: Hawks Book Co.) for descriptions of these interesting back roads. Be forewarned, however, that flying gravel is a constant problem, since drivers seldom slow down when meeting. This is even a problem on paved roads. Make sure your insurance pays for windshield repairs!

Cars can be rented at all the larger towns, and those with airports generally have the national chains (Hertz, Avis, etc.). See individual city descriptions in this book for local rental companies.

Bikes

Because of Wyoming's small population and long distances, cyclists will find uncrowded roads to ride. The long distances between towns, windy conditions, and frequent summer thunderstorms add to the adventure. Many thousands of miles of gravel and dirt roads provide excellent places to explore on mountain bikes; check at local bike shops for nearby routes. Get the excellent BLM area maps (available at most BLM offices) before heading out. Mountain bikes can be rented in most of the larger towns.

Rail Travel

In 1991, **Amtrak** reinstated daily passenger train service across southern Wyoming following an eight-year hiatus. The Pioneer Line now connects Seattle and Chicago, with Wyoming stops in Evanston, Green River, Rock Springs, Rawlins, Laramie, and Cheyenne. Trains run once each day in both directions. Each train has a dining car and a lounge car, plus sleeping cars (available by reservation only). For price and scheduling information, call Amtrak at (800) 872-7245. This is an excellent way to reach Wyoming and is leading to the revitalization of the state's wonderful old train depots. One warning on Amtrak: don't expect on-time service, since the trains often run far behind schedule.

WYOMING TRIVIA

Size: 62,664,960 acres, or 97,914 square miles (9th-largest state)

Lowest Point: 3,125 feet, where Belle Fourche River leaves Wyoming

Highest point: 13,804 feet, Gannett Peak

Number of people in 1990: 453,588

Number of cattle: 1,330,000

Number of antelope: 360,000

Number of people per square mile: 4.6

Percentage of people in Wyoming with four or more years of college: 7

Ethnic makeup (1980):
  white: 446,488 (includes Hispanic)
  Indian: 7,094
  black: 3,364
  Asian: 1,969
  Other: 10,642

One-time Wells Fargo agent in Cheyenne and later restaurant critic who had a cake mix named for him in 1949: Duncan Hines

Former president who once worked as a Yellowstone park ranger: Gerald Ford

Founder of a chain of retail stores who started out calling his Kemmerer store the Golden Rule Store: J.C. Penney

Number of Democratic governors: 10
  Republican: 11

Number of years the Democrats controlled both houses of the Legislature between 1890 and 1990: 4
  Controlled by Republicans: 93

World's largest piece of jade: a 3,366-pound nephrite jade boulder found near Lander in the 1940s

National rank in terms of:
  coal production: 1st
  trona production: 1st
  bentonite production: 1st
  mobile homes: 1st
  average size of farms: 2nd (4,000 acres)
  wool production: 2nd
  per-capita federal aid: 2nd
  sheep and lambs: 2rd
  natural gas production: 6th
  oil production: 4th
  sugar beets: 7th
  dry beans: 9th
  per-capita alcohol consumption: 8th
  cattle: 33rd
  population: 50th
  average value of farmland: 50th ($136/acre)

Estimated Wyoming coal resources: 1 trillion tons

Years Wyoming's coal would last if it supplied all the world's coal: 230

Size of Sweetwater County, Wyoming: 10,495 square miles

Size of Rhode Island, Delaware, and Connecticut combined: 7,859 square miles

Number of Wyoming farms in 1920: 15,800
In 1988: 8,700

Percentage of water behind North Platte River dams in Wyoming used to irrigate Wyoming fields: 20%

Used for Nebraska fields: 80%

Number of acres submerged by the Pathfinder dam: 22,000

Number of acres irrigated in Wyoming by the Pathfinder dam: 4,000

Cost of a trip from Cheyenne to Deadwood by stagecoach in 1880: $20 (first class)

Cost of the same trip by bus in 1990: $60

Number of MX missiles in the Cheyenne area: 50

In the rest of the nation: 0

Nation's first national park: Yellowstone

continued

Nation's first national monument: Devils Tower

Nation's first national forest: (now Shoshone National Forest)

Nation's first polo field: north of Sheridan

"Oldest" building on earth: cabin built from dinosaur bones at Como Bluff

Oldest military building in Wyoming: Fort Laramie's Old Bedlam

First state to grant women full citizenship: Wyoming (in 1868, while still a territory)

First woman governor in America: Nellie Tayloe Ross (1925)

First artificially lit football game: in Midwest, Wyoming (1925)

First female voter: Louisa Gardner Swain ("Grandma Swain") on September 6, 1870, voted in Laramie

World's first female jurors: in Laramie during 1870

World's first female prison chaplain: Mrs. May Slosson at the Laramie Penitentiary in 1899

World's first female fire lookout: Lorraine Lindaley, who was stationed at Medicine Bow Peak Lookout (west of Laramie) in 1921

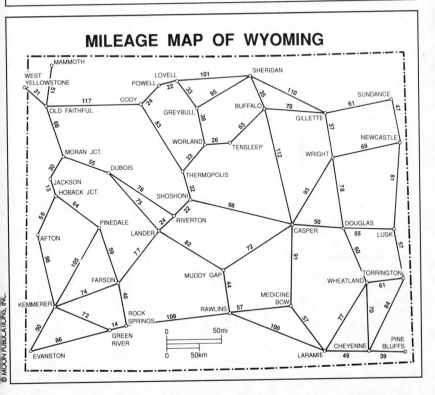

MILEAGE MAP OF WYOMING

Buses

Greyhound covers the southern end of Wyoming along I-80, while **Powder River Transportation,** tel. 266-1904 or (800) 442-3682, focuses on the rest of the state. Powder River has daily service to Cheyenne, Wheatland, Douglas, Casper, Buffalo, Gillette, Sheridan, Thermopolis, Worland, Greybull, and Lovell, as well as Billings, Montana, and Rapid City, South Dakota. Unfortunately, there is no bus service to many western Wyoming towns, including Jackson, Cody, Lander, Pinedale, Dubois, and Riverton. An option is to take a tour bus (summer only) from Jackson or Cody into Yellowstone, where you can connect with **Karst Stage,** tel. (406) 586-8567, and Greyhound out of West Yellowstone, Montana. See the appropriate chapters for specifics. Note: If you're planning to travel by Greyhound and are coming from out of state, get an Ameripass, available only in New York, Miami, Los Angeles, and San Francisco. International travelers can knock approximately $100 off Ameripass rates by showing their passports.

Winter Travel

During the winter months, Wyoming travelers need to take special precautions. Snow tires are a necessity, but you should also keep a number of emergency supplies, including tire chains, a shovel and a bag of sand in case you get stuck, first-aid kit, booster cables, flares, flashlight, dehydrated food, water, ice scraper, and sleeping bag. Call the Wyoming Highway Department at one of the following 800 numbers for road and travel conditions in various parts of Wyoming: 442-7850 (western), 442-2535 (north-central), 442-2555 (northeast), 442-2565 (east-central), and 442-8321 (southeast).

SOUTHEAST WYOMING

Southeast Wyoming is farming and ranching country, part of the vast prairie region that drapes America's heartland. In many ways, it is indistinguishable from western Nebraska or eastern Colorado, one long continuum of grass, grain, and grazing. Folks drive big American cars and Ford pickups. Instead of the saddleries and oil companies elsewhere in Wyoming, you'll find farm-equipment dealers and more feed caps than cowboy hats. They hold down better in the wind that seems to never stop blowing.

Buffalo roamed through southeast Wyoming for thousands of years, hunted by nomadic tribes of Plains Indians. Now sheep and cattle follow the same trails, and farmers grow wheat where Cheyenne Indian villages once stood. Alternating bands of wheat and fallow land give some areas a candy-striped appearance, while in others the expansive prairie extends in all directions. Old windmills, white farmhouses, hip-roofed barns, rusting retired farm machinery, and tall silos mark the old homesteads that became permanent farmsteads. The gravel roads cut straight across this gently rolling land, with sudden right-angled jags around old homestead boundaries. Drive out on these roads and the pace slows to country speed. Folks raise a hand to wave as you pass and stop to chat on the crest of a hill. Tune in the radio and you're likely to hear country music, farm market reports, and Paul Harvey commentaries. This is Wyoming's most important agricultural region.

The capital city of Cheyenne dominates the economy of southeast Wyoming, one of only two real cities in the state (the other being Casper). The other major settlements—Wheatland, Torrington, and Lusk—are small agricultural focal points and governmental centers for their respective counties.

Southeast Wyoming experiences typical high-plains weather. It is hot and windy in the summer, cold and windy in the winter. The wind—averaging over 13 mph—is a given; great country for kites, but not much fun when the gales of winter slice through like a knife. Partly because of this wind, however, Cheyenne has some of the cleanest air in the nation. Explore the back roads and you'll find busy cattle ranches, abandoned mining towns, remnants of many historic trails, archaeological sites, dinosaur bones, and old sod homesteads. Hiking through the gently undulating plains is a delightful experience, for vast expanses of this land remain almost unchanged from the time when bison roamed the great grasslands of the West.

CHEYENNE

As you drive west toward Cheyenne (pop. 50,000), the Colorado Rockies loom on the southwestern horizon like whitecaps in a sea of barely rolling plains, snow fences, stunted grass, and the highway slashing toward the boundary of sight. You catch quick glimpses of the great mountain ranges that ramble across Wyoming—like tantalizing flashes in a burlesque show. Gradually they grow larger, and finally you know that the Great Plains will soon be left behind. It's easy to imagine how this must have looked to the railroad passengers who passed this way in the 1860s, watching the mountains loom on the horizon as they rolled into Wyoming. Suddenly you're shaken into the present by the highway sign, "Cheyenne Next 4 Exits." Suburban homes crowd over the gentle hillsides, and the state capitol gleams in the setting sun. You have arrived at Wyoming's political and transportation fulcrum.

The city of Cheyenne hunkers down in the southeastern corner of Wyoming, just 10 miles from Colorado and 40 miles from Nebraska. Its wide, tree-draped urban streets form a gridwork through downtown, while suburbia spreads its tentacles over the surrounding prairie. Cheyenne is remarkably similar to (albeit smaller than) another state capital—Lincoln, Nebraska. For many visitors, it offers a taste of the West without leaving the Midwest. Folks in Casper or Cody view Cheyenne as the capital of eastern Wyoming, and as a city whose ties are really closer to the markets of Denver or Omaha than to the sagebrush, oil, and coal of Wyoming. People in Cheyenne brush aside these criticisms. They know everyone else is just jealous.

As the state capital, the largest city, home for a strategic military base, a center for various governmental agencies, and a major transportation hub, Cheyenne is a big fish in the small pond called Wyoming. The city has one of the most stable economies in the state. Its largest employer (nearly 5,000 people) is giant Francis E. Warren Air Force Base, with several thousand other folks working for the federal, state, and local government agencies around town. Railroad tracks of the Union Pacific and Burlington Northern railroads head to the four points of the compass, and Cheyenne is right at the junction of two of the primary transportation routes across the Plains and Rockies: I-25 and I-80. Some 800 folks work for Union Pacific, with hundreds more employed in trucking, communications, and shipping firms.

HISTORY

Like so many other Wyoming cities, Cheyenne is a creation of the railroad. It is the oldest of Wyoming's railroad towns, established as the Union Pacific was racing westward in 1867. When Gen. Grenville M. Dodge was planning the new railroad's route, he decided to establish a major rail terminal in the plains just before the long climb over the Laramie Mountains. He named the new settlement Cheyenne, for the Indians who lived in this country. The word is from a Sioux Indian term Shey an nah, meaning "People of a Strange Tongue." (Some have suggested a less complimentary origin for the word, the French term chienne, meaning "bitch.") While Dodge was there, Indians attacked a Mormon grading crew, killing two men. The graveyard was started before the first building was up. By November of that year the new town of Cheyenne had swollen to 4,000 people, earning the nickname "Magic City of the Plains." It was easily the largest town in Wyoming and has remained that way for much of the state's history.

At first, Cheyenne consisted of the usual hell-on-wheels railroad settlement of tents and hastily erected buildings. Railroad workers and Army men from nearby Fort D.A. Russell turned the town into a rip-roaring place—every second building was a saloon, and burlesque shows

SOUTHEAST WYOMING

were the rage. At center stage stood a 36-by-100-foot tent housing Headquarters Saloon. Reporter James Chisholm noted:

The wildest roughs from all parts of the country are congregated here, as one may see by glancing into the numerous dance-houses and gambling halls—men who carry on the trade of robbery openly, and would not scruple to kill a man for ten dollars.

SETTLING DOWN

Within a decade, however, Cheyenne had settled into a more urbane stage. The railroad provided access to the East, not only allowing cattle to be shipped but also keeping the town abreast of the latest fashions and furnishings and bringing news of world events. With the discovery of gold in the Black Hills, Cheyenne became the primary shipping center for supplies to the Black Hills and gold bullion from the smelters.

By the 1880s, Cheyenne had grown to a cosmopolitan small city of 14,000 people and was declared the wealthiest city per capita in the world. It was one of the first cities in the West to have electric lights—a powerplant charged batteries during the day and then delivered them by wagon in time for the evening's use. In 1882, the elaborate Cheyenne Opera House opened with great fanfare. With seating for up to 1,000 people, luxurious furnishings, and a huge 52-light gas chandelier overhead, it was regarded as the equal of any in New York and attracted such performers as Lily Langtry, Sarah Bernhardt, P.T. Barnum, Buffalo Bill Cody, and the Royal Opera Company.

Despite its edge-of-the-state location, Cheyenne was the logical place for Wyoming's territorial capital. The railroad was here, along with Fort D.A. Russell and most of the wealthy cattlemen. In 1869, the first territorial governor, John A. Campbell, made it the temporary capital, with the legislature meeting in rented quarters. Five years later it almost lost that title to Laramie in a rump session of the legislature, but after completion of the capitol building in 1888 it became obvious that the governmental seat would remain in Cheyenne.

Rule Of The Cattle Barons
Destruction of the once-vast herds of bison and the decimation of Indians who had lived in Wyoming suddenly opened up nearly all the territory to cattle grazing. Cheyenne became the focal point for hundreds of cattlemen who rushed in to

FRANCIS E. WARREN

One of Wyoming's best-known politicians was Francis E. Warren (1844-1929). A lifelong Republican, Warren served as both a territorial and state governor before being elected to the U.S. Senate in 1890. One of the millionaire cattle barons, his ranch once had more than 100,000 sheep. This land would later get him in trouble when he was charged with fencing public land for his own gain but his friendship with President Theodore Roosevelt helped keep him out of prison. While territorial governor in the 1880s, Warren was an ardent agitator for statehood. His 37 years in the U.S. Senate made him one of its most powerful members, and newspapers labeled him the "Boss of Wyoming." With Warren's backing, Fort D.A. Russell always got more than its share of the pork barrel, and after his death, it was renamed in his honor. Cheyenne's old **Warren Mansion,** at 222 E. 17th St., was once owned by Francis E. Warren. President Theodore Roosevelt stayed here as a guest of Warren, and its ornate interior features are still intact. The building was built in 1889 from stone rejected for use in the state capitol building. Over the years the stone began to deteriorate and the outside walls had to be covered with stucco.

WYOMING STATE MUSEUM

make a killing on the booming cattle market. (At the time, Laramie County extended all the way to the border with Montana, so it was logical that Cheyenne would be the center of ranching activity in the state.) The most famous of these men was Alexander Swan, founder of a spread so large that it required a special book to keep track of all its cattle brands. Other parttime residents included members of English nobility such as Moreton Frewen (nephew of Sir Winston Churchill) and Sir Oliver H. Wallop, seventh earl of Portsmouth.

One of the most unusual organizations in frontier Wyoming was the **Cheyenne Club,** first established in 1880 as an exclusive English country club. With membership limited to 200, it included only the wealthiest of the cattlemen, men who quickly became known as cattle barons. Many came from aristocratic social backgrounds, graduates of the finest universities on the East Coast and in Europe. Some were millionaires who summered in Cheyenne and

then sailed back to Europe for winters. With the growing prosperity of the cattle business, the Cheyenne Club claimed the finest French-Canadian chef and steward in the country and was said to be the first club in America to have electricity. Dinner dress was always formal. Despite strict rules on behavior (no card cheating, pipe smoking, or profanity), one member did manage to shoot a hole through a painting of a cow and bull—he claimed it to be an abomination against purebred cattle. With the sudden bust that followed the harsh winter of 1886-87, the cattle barons were abruptly brought back to reality. Many went out of business, and the club quickly followed. The historic Cheyenne Club was razed in 1936.

Fort D.A. Russell

In 1862, President Lincoln approved creation of a military fort to guard the then-proposed transcontinental railroad from Indian attacks. When the railroad finally arrived—five years later—the Army established a fort near the new town of Cheyenne. (Both the town and fort were officially named on the same day.) Originally named for a Civil War general—David A. Russell—the new fort grew into America's largest cavalry outpost. Troops from the base were sent out to protect railroad survey and construction parties and later served as guards along the route. An important supply depot, **Camp Carlin,** was established adjacent to the fort, providing equipment for a dozen Army posts scattered throughout the Indian frontier. It was abandoned in 1890.

With the Indians' forced relocation to reservations, the role of Fort D.A. Russell changed into a training center and strategic garrison for the Rockies. New brick barracks and officers' quarters were completed in 1885, and the dusty parade ground was planted with grass and trees. Wyoming's Senator Francis E. Warren had long "brought home the bacon" by gaining political plums for his constituents, one of the biggest being continued support for the fort in Cheyenne. After his death in 1929, the fort was renamed in his honor. The base served as a training center and POW camp in WW II and was transferred to the newly created Air Force in 1947.

The fort's current role began in 1958 when the arrival of Atlas missiles made Warren the nation's first nuclear-missile base. The event was greeted with glee by Cheyenne's then mayor Worth Story, who exclaimed, "Cheyenne is proud to be the nation's number one target for enemy missiles." Today, the city enjoys a similar privilege as the only place in the nation where the 10-warhead MX nuclear missiles are based. Cheyenne even has a Missile Drive. Warren Air Force Base operates 150 Minuteman III missiles, plus all 50 MX missiles in existence, making it one of the most important intercontinental ballistic missile (ICBM) centers in America. (We're talking 40% of the nation's ICBMs here!) The missiles are dispersed over a 150-mile radius in Wyoming, Nebraska, and Colorado, creating an attractive bullseye target centered on Cheyenne. Missile silos are manned by two crew members working some 60 feet underground on 24-hour shifts. Each of these "capsules" controls 10 missiles in surrounding areas.

SIGHTS

An excellent introduction to Cheyenne is to take one of the **trolley tours** that depart from 16th and Capitol daily in the summer. These two-hour tours cost $6 ($3 for children) and include visits to several historic buildings, F.E. Warren Air Force Base, and the Old West Museum. Get tickets at the visitor's bureau on weekdays or the Wrangler Store, 1518 Capitol Ave., tel. 634-3048, on weekends.

State Capitol
Capitol Avenue—one of the primary streets in Cheyenne—seems to symbolize the city's history. State government buildings line the street, and at either end are the two main reasons for Cheyenne's existence: the Union Pacific depot to the south and the State Capitol to the north. The Capitol is open Mon.-Fri. 8-5 and Sat. 9-4 (closed weekends in winter) with free guided tours during the summer. Call 777-7220 for more info.

Wyoming's Capitol building falls in the tradition of ostentatious political structures and is modelled after the Capitol in Washington, D.C. The initial structure was authorized by a $150,000 appropriation from the territorial legislature in 1886. The cornerstone was laid on May 18, 1887, and the central portion was completed the following year, with the two wings added later. When completed in 1917, the building measured its present 300 feet in length. The 146-foot-tall dome has been regilded with gold four times, most recently in 1986. Don't bother trying to climb up to steal any; the entire dome is covered with less than an ounce of gold.

The Capitol's central rotunda has a checkered marble floor with cherrywood staircases leading to the second floor. Directly overhead is a beautiful blue stained-glass window imported from England. Interesting historical photographs line the second floor walls. The senate chambers are in the west wing, with the house meeting in the east wing. You can view the Legislature from the third-floor balconies when it is in session. Inside the legislative chambers are four Western murals painted by Allen T. True (designer of Wyoming's bucking-bronco symbol), along with others by Joseph Henry Sharp and Bill Gollings. Look upward in each chamber to see the large Tiffany stained-glass ceilings with the state seal.

From the outside, the Capitol dome seems strangely tall; rumor has it that architects once voted it the nation's ugliest state capitol. Out front is a bronze statue of **Esther Hobart Morris,** the person incorrectly credited with making Wyoming the first state to grant women the right to vote. Directly behind the Capitol building is the sparkling new **Herschler Building,** named for the only Wyoming governor to serve three terms, Ed Herschler. It has an attractive interior atrium and houses the offices of various state agencies. In between the two buildings is an 18-foot-tall bronze statue by Edward Fraughton, *Spirit of Wyoming,* a bucking horse and rider that seem almost suspended in space. It is perhaps fitting that the two mottos of Wyoming—the Equality State and the Cowboy State—are symbolized by statues on either side of the State Capitol. Wander around the flower-garnished grounds and you'll discover a monument to the Spanish-American War, a statue of a bison, and a copy of Philadelphia's Liberty Bell.

Historic Governors' Mansion

Located at 300 E. 21st St., tel. 777-7878, the old governors' mansion is open year-round Tues.-Sat. 9-5. There is no charge. A 10-minute video provides information about the house and its inhabitants, including the nation's first woman governor, Nellie Tayloe Ross, who lived here from 1925 to 1927. The 2½-story brick building was completed in 1905 at a cost of $33,000; it is in the Georgian style with four Corinthian columns out front. Inside are furnishings from a variety of periods. The current governor's mansion, completed in 1976, is near the intersection of Central Ave. and I-25. It is open summers for group tours only; call 777-7398 for appointments.

Wyoming State Museum

The free Wyoming State Museum in the Barrett State Office Building at 24th and Central,

---

CHEYENNE AND BLACK HILLS STAGE

With the 1874 discovery of gold in the Black Hills, a stampede of miners headed north in search of riches. A fierce competition quickly developed between Cheyenne, Wyoming, and Sidney, Nebraska, to be the jumping-off point for miners. With support for road construction from the Wyoming Territorial Legislature, a 300-mile-long stage route was soon laid out, and the first coach headed north on February 3, 1876. The Cheyenne and Black Hills Stage, Mail and Express Line had begun.

The line operated almost straight north from Cheyenne to the vicinity of present-day Lusk before veering into Dakota Territory and ending at Deadwood. Drivers made the trip in three days and three nights, with station stops every 15 miles that lasted just long enough to change horses, usually less than three minutes. It was a strenuous and tiring journey, passing through Sioux Indian territory, over treacherous river crossings, and past hideouts of notorious road agents. On the long trip south from the mines, special armored coaches carried gold bullion in steel strongboxes, protected by four to six armed guards. Often they held up to $100,000 in gold dust and nuggets and sometimes as much as $350,000! Outlaws—including Frank and Jesse James, and Big Nose George Parrot's gang—targeted these coaches, riding off with both the gold and the horses. One of the most infamous attack sites was near the Robber's Roost Stage Station, along the Cheyenne River north of Lusk. Here the stages were frequently attacked, sometimes every day.

The "Deadwood Coaches" (such as the one used by Buffalo Bill in his Wild West Show) were actually the famed Concord coaches built by Abbott and Downing of Concord, New Hampshire. They could jam nine passengers inside (first and second class) for $15-20 a head, and an equal number on top (third class) at $10 apiece. Riders on top sometimes had to get off and push the stage up hills. (Despite the attention given to stagecoaches, much of the traffic along the goldfields route was in freight wagons, pulled by long strings of oxen.) Upon completion of the Chicago and Northwestern Railroad to Rapid City, traffic on the Cheyenne to Deadwood Stage dropped, and the last coach ran on Feb. 19, 1887. In just 11 years, the stage line had carved out a big piece of history, and its closing marked the end of one of the most romantic chapters in the history of the west.

DOWNTOWN CHEYENNE

tel. 777-7022, is open Mon.-Fri. 8:30-5, and Sat. 9-4 during the summer (reduced Sat. hours in winter). It is not large but does have a number of fine displays on the Plains Indians, sheepherding, cattle ranching, and rustling. Also here are an art gallery with changing displays and a gift shop containing regional books and Wyoming-made crafts, including some impressive belt buckles, bolo ties, and beaded earrings.

Frontier Days Old West Museum

Located right next to the rodeo grounds in Frontier Park, this is one of the nicest museums in Wyoming. It's open Sat.-Sun. 10-5 and Mon.-Fri. 8-6 June-Aug., and Mon.-Fri. 9-5 and Sat.-Sun. 11-4 the rest of the year. During Frontier Days the doors are open daily 8 a.m.-9 p.m. Admission is $3 for adults, $2 for seniors, $6 for families, and kids under 12 free. Call 778-7290 for details. The museum's focus is on horse-drawn transportation of all types, including over 125 vehicles spread through the recently expanded facilities. On display are dozens of carriages (many of which appear in the annual Frontier Days parade), including a Cheyenne-to-Deadwood stage, sleighs, a buckboard (the name came from the lack of springs on the axles), and of course, a surrey with a fringe on top. Be sure to check out the luxurious landau, sort of an early-day convertible. Also on display are exhibits on the Union Pacific Railroad and Tom Horn. One room houses traveling art exhibits, and the gift shop sells various Frontier Days souvenirs.

Botanic Garden

One of Cheyenne's lesser-known attractions is the fine city-run Botanic Garden in Lions Park, tel. 637-6458. Hours are Mon.-Fri. 8-4:30, Sat. and Sun. 11-3:30; no charge. Troubled kids, handicapped people, and seniors grow flowers and vegetables in the botanic gardens. Visitors find it a pleasant place to relax, especially during the winter when the warmth and the showy flowers are delightful surprises. Inside the passively solar-heated greenhouse (look for the black metal drums filled with water) are three sections containing everything from vegetables to cacti. The central portion of the greenhouse has tall banana plants and tropical flowers, plus a pond containing goldfish and turtles. The angel's trumpet with its beautiful orange flowers is the centerpiece. Upstairs is a small library with various gardening magazines and books. Outside are pleasant picnic tables and a gazebo set among the flowerbeds and shade trees.

F.E. Warren Air Force Base

For something different, try a visit to Wyoming's primary military base. The entrance to Warren Air Force Base is flanked by three missiles, but the buildings are actually quaint, with hundreds of two- and three-story brick buildings set back from the tree-lined streets. Expansive green lawns give it a country-club feeling. This is essentially a self-supporting city, with childcare facilities, schools, stores, a veterinary clinic, and of course that old neighborhood standby, nuclear warheads. During Frontier Days, jets take off constantly from the airport, suddenly screaming overhead in sharp climbs that bring gasps from the crowd. A small **Base Museum,** tel. 775-2980, is open to the public Wed., Fri., Sat., and Sun. 1-4 during the summer, and Wed., Fri., and Sat. 1-4 the rest of the year. Two-hour tours of Warren—including visits to missile simulators—are available on Thurs. at 7:45 a.m. during the summer and monthly in winter. Call 775-3381 for details. You'll need to stop at the gate for permission to enter.

First Day Cover Museum

Stamp collectors will enjoy a visit to the free First Day Cover Museum, 702 Randall Blvd., tel. 634-5911. The attractive museum is open Mon.-Fri. 9-5 and houses first day covers worth close to $1 million, including Great Britain's 1840 Penny Black. In addition to U.S. covers, you'll also find covers from such diverse areas as Swaziland and Fiji. (First day covers are released only on the initial day of issue for new stamps and are postmarked at just one location.) Pretty obscure stuff, but interesting if you are into philately.

Historic Buildings

The **Whipple House,** located at 300 E. 17th St., is a wonderful Victorian home built in 1883 by Ithamar C. Whipple, a wealthy merchant, cattleman, mayor, and state legislator. The home was later occupied by attorney and one-time Wyoming Territorial Supreme Court Justice John

W. Lacey, who defended both the notorious outlaw Tom Horn and the equally infamous oilman Harry Sinclair. The building is on the National Register of Historic Places but is not presently open to the public. Cheyenne has several of Wyoming's most ostentatious and interesting churches. **St. Mark's Episcopal Church,** 1908 Central Ave., tel. 634-7709, is the oldest, begun in 1886 but not completed until 1893. It has an exterior of red lava stones with traditional stained-glass windows, including one by Tiffany. This was the home church for many of the transplanted British and Scottish cattle barons, so it is fitting that the funeral for gunman Tom Horn (who worked for some of them) was held here in 1903. Two other impressive churches are **St. Mary's Catholic Cathedral,** 2107 Capitol Ave., tel. 635-9261, built in 1907 of native standstone in the Gothic Revival style, and the **First United Methodist Church,** 18th and Central avenues, tel. 632-1410, also made from sandstone, and completed in 1894. The previous Methodist church on the same site was where marshal, gunman, and gambler Wild Bill Hickok married a circus performer, Agnes Lake Thatcher, in 1876. The officiating clergyman wrote in the registry, "Don't think they meant it." Just five months later Wild Bill was shot in the back in a Deadwood saloon.

Railroad Paraphernalia

The railroad business reached its peak in the 1940s, when Cheyenne had the finest equipment and service anywhere in America. The railroad is still an important part of Cheyenne's economy, with freight trains rumbling through town day and night. Drop by the gorgeous old **Union Pacific Railroad depot** at the south end of Capitol Ave. to see one of the finest remaining depots in the West. Built of red and gray sandstone in 1886, the structure was for a time the largest building in the territory and the most elaborate depot between Omaha and San Francisco. (The depot was a reward to Governor Francis E. Warren for restoring order after the 1885 massacre of Chinese workers at the Union Pacific's vital Rock Springs coal mines.) It occupies an entire block, with the clock tower and Romanesque arched openings adding a touch of class. Despite the recent return of Amtrak service, the depot remains closed, awaiting costly removal of asbestos. Holliday Park along E. 17th St. has a **Big Boy locomotive,** one of only 25 ever made and one of the largest steam locomotives ever built. It was used to haul freight over the mountain tracks between Cheyenne and Ogden, Utah. A couple of blocks east of here is a boxcar from the **French Merci Train,** given as a thank-you for food Americans had given the French after WW II.

Wyoming Hereford Ranch

In 1883, cattle barons Alexander and Thomas Swan, backed by European investors, formed the Wyoming Hereford Association, placing 400 purebred Hereford bulls and cows on a ranch near Cheyenne. This was the first real attempt to bring quality cattle to the state and was at one time the world's largest herd of thoroughbred cattle. Gradually other ranchers followed this lead, as the rangy longhorns of Texas were replaced by the more manageable Herefords (now the dominant breed in Wyoming). The 60,000-acre Wyoming Hereford Ranch has survived for more than a hundred years and has many historic structures in immaculate condition. It is five miles east of Cheyenne off I-80. Call 634-1905 for free tours. The current owner is a local surgeon, Dr. Sloan Hales.

Other Sights

Cheyenne has quite a number of interesting old Victorian buildings. Stop by the chamber of commerce for a brochure that takes you on a **walking tour** of historic downtown. Of particular note are the Victorian homes of "Cattle Baron's Row" on 17th Street. The **Wyoming Department of Game and Fish** at 5400 Bishop Blvd., tel. 777-7735, has a small museum with wildlife dioramas, an aquarium with trout, and wildlife photographs; open daily 8-5 in summer and Mon.-Fri. 8-5 the remainder of the year.

ACCOMMODATIONS

Motels

Choose from more than two dozen different lodging places in Cheyenne. Generally, space is not a problem, but when Frontier Days comes to town, motel rates often double or even triple, with motels and campgrounds booked up six months in advance. Even towns as far away as Torrington are affected, so be sure to plan well ahead for accommodations during this time. Be certain to take a look around before paying for a room at the cheaper motels.

Cheyenne is fortunate in having one of Wyoming's only remaining historic lodging places, the **Plains Hotel.** Built in 1911, the hotel was completely refurbished in 1986. For many years this was the political center of Cheyenne, with politicians retiring to the bar to discuss whatever politicians discuss. Note the tile mosaic of Chief Little Shield in the sidewalk along Central Avenue. Also of interest is the **Terry Bison Ranch,** tel. 634-4171, located eight miles south of Cheyenne. This 27,500-acre dude ranch offers overnight visits as well as extended stays and runs one of the largest bison herds in the state.

Campgrounds
Cheyenne's closest public campgrounds ($4) are in **Curt Gowdy State Park,** 26 miles west on State 210, tel. 632-7946. There are also campsites ($5) within the scenic Pole Mountain area of Medicine Bow National Forest (see p. 116). **Greenway Trailer Park,** 3829 Greenway St., tel. 634-6696, has paved RV lots for $13 and showers for $3; open year-round. **AB Camping,** 1503 W. College Dr., tel. 634-7035, charges $10 for tents and $12 for RVs; open all year.

CHEYENNE ACCOMMODATIONS

NAME	ADDRESS	PHONE	RATES	FEATURES
Pioneer Hotel	209 W. 17th St.	634-3010	$18 s or d	flophouse
Big Horn Motel	2004 E. Lincolnway	632-3122	$20 s, 22 d	kitchenettes available
Round-Up Motel	403 S. Greeley Hwy.	634-7741	$22 s, $25 d	kitchens available
Cheyenne Motel	1601 E. Lincolnway	778-7664	$25 s, $30 d	kitchenettes available
Fleetwood Motel	3800 E. Lincolnway	638-8908 (800) 634-7763	$25 s, $31 d	AAA approved, pool
Sands Motel	1100 W. 16th St.	634-7771	$26 s, $30 d	
Plains Hotel	1600 Central Ave.	638-3311	$26 s, $31 d	airport shuttle, historic place
Atlas Motel	1524 W. Lincolnway	632-9214	$27 s, $31 d	kitchenettes available
Stage Coach Motel	1515 W. Lincolnway	634-4495	$29 s, $30+ d	AAA approved
Motel 6	1735 Westland Rd.	635-6806	$29 s, $35 d	pool
Lariat Motel	600 Central Ave.	635-8439	$30 s, $33 d	see rooms first
Frontier Motel	1400 W. Lincolnway	634-7961	$30 s, $40 d	
American Family Lodge	5401 Walker Rd.	632-8901 (800) 876-8901	$30+ s, $35+ d	pool, airport shuttle
Sapp Brothers Big C Motel	six miles east	778-8878	$27 s, $31 d	AAA approved
Home Ranch Motel	2414 E. Lincolnway	634-3575 (800) 999-7188	$28 s or d	AAA approved
Super 8 Motel	1900 W. Lincolnway	635-8741 (800) 800-8000	$34 s, $39 d	pool

continued

CHEYENNE ACCOMMODATIONS
(CONT.)

NAME	ADDRESS	PHONE	RATES	FEATURES
Comfort Inn	2245 Etchepare Dr.	638-7202 (800) 221-2222	$35+ s, $38+ d	AAA approved, pool
Luxury Inn	1805 Westland Rd.	638-2550	$37 s, $44 d	AAA approved
Rodeway Inn	3839 E. Lincolnway	634-2171	$39 s, $43 d	pool
La Quinta Inn	2410 W. Lincolnway	632-7117	$45+ s, $53+ d	AAA approved, pool
Holiday Inn	204 W. Fox Farm Rd.	638-4466 (800) 465-4329	$50+ s, $54+ d	AAA approved, pool, jacuzzi, sauna, airport shuttle, exercise room
Hitching Post Inn (Best Western)	1700 W. Lincolnway	638-3301 (800) 528-1234	$50+ s, $55+ d	AAA approved, pools, jacuzzi, sauna, airport shuttle, exercise room
Little America	2800 W. Lincolnway	634-2771 (800) 445-6945	$52+ s, $59+ d	AAA approved, pool, airport shuttle
Days Inn	2360 W. Lincolnway	778-8877 (800) 325-2525	$54+ s or d	jacuzzi, sauna, exercise room

BED AND BREAKFASTS

NAME	ADDRESS	PHONE	RATES	FEATURES
Porch Swing B&B	712 E. 20th	778-7182	$40 s, $50 d	antique-furnished historic home
Howdy Partners B&B	six miles N	634-6493	$40 s, $50 d	
Adventurer's Country B&B	15 miles E	632-4087	$60 s or d	ranch house
Raven Cry Ranch B&B	15 miles E	632-4087	$60 s or d	full breakfast,
Rainsford Inn B&B	219 E. 18th	638-2337	$75+ s or d	historic home, whirlpool

The most complete local camping facility is **Restway Travel Park,** 4212 Whitney Rd., tel. 634-3811, (800) 442-2854 (in Wyoming), or (800) 443-2751 (outside), which charges $12 for tents and $14 for RVs. Showers for non-campers are $3; open all year. Restway offers shuttle-bus service ($3 RT) to Frontier Days and also has horseback rides, chuckwagon dinners, and other activities. Friendly folks. RV sites are also available at **Terry Bison Ranch,** tel. 634-4171.

FOOD

The city of Cheyenne offers a surprisingly diverse choice of eateries, from greasy spoons to Chinese restaurants. In addition to all the places listed below, the city is jammed with all the fast-food chains, particularly along E. Lincolnway. The **Cheyenne Farmers Market** is held on summer Saturdays 8-1 in the big parking lot at 16th and Carey. This is the best place to get fresh produce.

Breakfast And Lunch
One of the real treats in Cheyenne is downhome **Lexie's,** 216 E. 17th St., tel. 638-8712. Great breakfasts and the best burgers in town. The place gets crowded with locals most days. **Driftwood Cafe,** 200 E. 18th St., tel. 634-5304, is also popular. The huge **Little America** coffee shop, 2800 W. Lincolnway, tel. 634-2771, is open 24 hours a day, offering better-than-average truck-stop food and a fine Sunday brunch. **Ruthies Sub Shoppe,** 1651 Carey Ave., tel. 635-4896, makes good sandwiches for lunch. For a taste of the East Coast, try a Philly steak sandwich or pierogie from **Little Philly,** 1013 Logan, tel. 632-6824. A downtown lunch and dinner favorite of many locals is **Albany Restaurant,** 1506 Capitol Ave., tel. 638-3507. The cheapest meal deal in Cheyenne is in the state government cafeteria in the **Herschler Building** (directly behind the Capitol), where a filling lunch will set you back less than $4. The indoor atrium is spacious and very pleasant. Open Mon.-Fri. 6-4, with limited service after 1:30 p.m. A different experience can be had at **Phyneas' Pfine Pfood and Sody Saloon** at 1501 Carey Avenue. Good sandwiches (try the bacon cheeseburger), sarsaparillas, and an old-west atmosphere pfor pflunch. Get pastries at **Cookie Jar Bakery,** 3219 Snyder Ave., tel. 632-2488.

International Eats
Several places in town make very good south-of-the-border food. The best and most authentic is **Los Amigos,** 620 Central Ave., tel. 638-8591, but two others offer reasonably good fare: **Emanuel's Mexican Cuisine,** 1607 Carey Ave., tel. 632-1744; and **Estevan's Cafe,** beside the K mart on Yellowstone Rd., tel. 632-6828. Wyoming is not known for its Chinese food, but Cheyenne has two relatively authentic Chinese restaurants that are worth a visit: **Twin Dragon Restaurant,** 1809 Carey Ave., tel. 637-6622, and **Oriental House,** 1602 E. Lincolnway, tel. 635-1411. Twin Dragon's lunchtime buffet is a very good deal.

Stuff yourself at **Avanti Restaurant,** 4620 Grandview Ave., tel. 634-3422, where an all-you-can-eat Italian-American evening buffet costs under $8. **Pete's Pizza,** 1801 Warren Ave., tel. 632-2267, claims to make "the world's best pizza," but most folks in Cheyenne seem to prefer **Pizza Hut,** 2215 E. Lincolnway, tel. 635-4151.

Dinner
A new and immensely popular Cheyenne eatery is **Applebee's,** located at 1401 Dell Range Blvd., tel. 638-3434. Although it's part of a chain, the grilled specialities, crunchy munchies, and decadent desserts mean long waits into evenings. Get there early. Outstanding BBQ ribs at **Hickory House,** 2001 E. 11th, tel. 638-1445. **Owl Inn,** 3919 Central Ave., tel. 638-8578, has been around since 1935 and is still a popular family dining establishment (famous homemade chicken noodle soup). It's also a good place for a quiet drink with friends. **Poor Richard's,** 2233 E. Lincolnway, tel. 635-5114, has Cheyenne's only Saturday brunch. The prime rib and seafood are excellent and reasonably priced, and the salad bar is one of the best around. Enjoy a drink at the fireside lounge. **Carriage Court** at Hitching Post Inn, 1700 W. Lincolnway, tel. 638-3301, is the place to go for fresh fish or oysters. **Little Bear Inn,** three miles north on I-25, tel. 634-3684, is quite an experience. Good steaks, but the rest of the menu sometimes varies in quality. For prime rib, fly up to **Cloud 9 Restaurant** at the airport (300 E. Eighth Ave.), tel. 635-1525.

ENTERTAINMENT AND EVENTS

All summer long, visitors gather at Lincolnway and Carey streets to watch the **Cheyenne Gunslingers** put on a Hollywood-style shoot-'em-up. Hope I don't give anything away, but the good guys invariably win. Pretty tacky, and absolutely no relationship to Cheyenne's history. The "gunfights" take place at 6 p.m. on weekdays and "high noon" on Saturdays (more often during Frontier Days). Also here at "Gunslinger Square" is a replica of the gallows used to hang Tom Horn (no hangings, alas). Each September, the Tom Horn "Kick and Growl" includes reenactments of his trial and visits to sites associated with his reign of mayhem.

During July and August, tourists fill the historic Atlas Theatre at 211 W. 16th St. to watch comic melodramas by the **Little Theatre Players.** Lots of audience participation, plus popcorn, pizza, and beer for sale. Tickets for the nightly shows are $6.50, or $4.50 for kids and seniors. Call 635-0199 for details. For something more sedate, you may want to attend winter performances of the **Cheyenne Symphony Orchestra.** Call 778-8561 for specifics.

Nightlife

Cheyenne is a hopping town when it comes to nightlife, especially during Frontier Days when every C&W band this side of the Mississippi finds a place to play. **Cowboy South,** 312 S. Greeley Hwy., tel. 637-3800, is the biggest and best country-music bar in town. Another favorite, especially with the Air Force crowd, is the similarly spacious **Cheyenne Club,** 1617 Capitol Ave., tel. 635-7777. **Hitching Post Inn Lounge,** 1700 W. Lincolnway, tel. 638-3301, and **Little Bear Inn,** three miles north of Cheyenne, tel. 634-3684, are also popular C&W hangouts, as is **Mayflower Tavern,** 112 W. 17th, tel. 634-2761, where the rodeo cowboys jingle their spurs. (Cowpokes have been known to ride horses through its doors.) **Cristy's** at Holiday Inn, 204 W. Fox Farm Rd., tel. 638-4466, has a lounge with Top-40 DJ music most nights, while **Little America,** 2800 W. Lincolnway, tel. 634-2771, sometimes has easy-listening music. Also check at **Shenanigans Bar,** 222 W. 16th, tel. 637-5043, and **Mingles,** 1318 Stillwater, for rock music. **Les and Carol's Lamp Lounge,** 101 W. Sixth, tel. 635-7557, is a fun pool-shootin' locals' bar. For something more risqué, head 10 miles south of town to the Wyoming-Colorado border where **The Clown's Den,** tel. 635-0765, features topless performers with names like Amber, Candy, Tiffany, Passion, and Priscilla. Cowgirl wet-T-shirt contests every night.

FRONTIER DAYS

Cheyenne Frontier Days—the "daddy of 'em all"—is Wyoming's largest and most famous annual event, with all sorts of entertainment, from professional rodeos to parades. Festivities begin the last full week of July and continue for 10 action-packed days. There is something for everyone at this memorable event, but the rodeo is the main attraction for upwards of 300,000 visitors from all 50 states and many other nations. The largest number commute in from Denver, while others jam the campgrounds and motels for a hundred miles in all directions.

History

There are several versions of the origin of Cheyenne Frontier Days, the most plausible being that it was inspired when a Union Pacific employee, F.W. Angier, watched a group of cowboys from the Swan Land and Cattle Company trying to load an ornery horse into a railroad car. The show he saw sparked his imagination, and when he suggested the idea of a Wild West buckin' and ropin' contest, others quickly jumped on the bandwagon. Just one month later (September, 1897), the first Cheyenne Frontier Days celebration began. It was a rip-roaring success, with 15,000 people in attendance. In addition to various cowboy contests, Frontier Days included several events that you won't see today—a staged battle between Sioux Indians and the U.S. Cavalry, Pony Express demonstrations, and a mock stage holdup and hanging by vigilantes. Obviously, the production had been influenced by Buffalo Bill's Wild West Show, then touring Europe. Most amusing of all was the dog and hare event, where a rabbit was released to be chased by dogs. Unfortunately, the dogs in the race were quickly joined by many more from the stands, so no winner was declared, although the loser was obvious. Cheyenne Frontier Days has grown over the years to a 10-day celebration (two weekends) and is regarded as one of the top-four rodeos in the world (the others being the Salinas California Rodeo, the Calgary Stampede, and the Pendleton Round-Up). Local enthusiasts call it the world's largest outdoor rodeo.

Activities

Frontier Days centers on the daily rodeos, with the nation's top rodeo cowboys showing their stuff. The rodeo has all the standard contests: bareback bronc riding, saddle bronc riding, Brahma bull riding, steer roping, calf roping, and steer wrestling. Other events include exciting and dangerous chuckwagon races, chaotic and amusing wild horse races, and a real crowd pleaser, the colt race (where young colts race toward their mares). With a purse of more than $400,000 (largest regular-season payoff in rodeo), Frontier Days attracts more than 1,000 contestants, so many of the timed events must begin at seven each morning!

Frontier Park is the center for all sorts of other activities during Frontier Days, including daily performances by the **Southern Plains Indian Dancers** and a **tipi village** on the south end of the parking lot. Each evening brings musical performances, including some of the top names in country music. A large and well-run **carnival** provides stomach-churning rides, sugar and grease in all forms (cotton candy, candy apples, ice cream, corn dogs, burgers, etc.), plus thousands of stuffed animal prizes, stretched-out coke bottles, velvet paintings, and other necessities. Other entertainment includes country-music performers, balloon "sculptors," Indian dancers, magicians, and

cloggers. After all this debauchery, try attending the **cowboy church services** held nightly at 7 p.m. on the rodeo grounds. Also in Frontier Park is the Cheyenne Frontier Days Old West Museum (see description above), where the annual **Governor's Invitational Art Show** offers the chance to view or purchase works from more than 50 different Western artists.

Not everything happens in Frontier Park. On Mon., Wed., and Fri. during Frontier Days, a free **pancake feed** stuffs close to 10,000 folks. The feeding frenzy lasts 7-9 a.m. Check out the cement mixer used to stir up 3,600 pounds of pancake batter or the Boy Scouts trying to catch the furiously flying flapjacks. Visitors sit on bales of hay and are treated with performances by Indian dancers and musicians of all stripes. For many children, the four **parades** (held at 9:30 a.m. on both Saturdays, as well as on Tues. and Thurs.) are a special treat, featuring the largest collection of horse-drawn vehicles in the nation. You'll see everything from popcorn wagons to hearses. Other events during Frontier Days include square dances, chili cookoffs, and an **open house** at Warren Air Force Base where you can check out Air Force jets of all types (including the C-130 Hercules, a plane big enough to hold seven buses), demonstrations by military bands, tours of historic homes and the missile-launch control center, plus a hair-raising air show by the USAF Thunderbirds. Ride the shuttle bus to the base from Frontier Mall.

In addition to Frontier Days, Cheyenne plays host each January to the **Mountain States Circuit Finals Rodeo** at Laramie County Community College. Another popular event is the **Laramie County Fair,** held the first full week in August.

Specifics

For information on Frontier Days, including a schedule of events, call 778-7222 or (800) 227-6336. Rodeo tickets cost $8-12 pp, while tickets to night shows are $10-18. A package ticket includes rodeo entrance, a night show, and admission to the Old West Museum for $18.50. Get tickets from the ticket office, south of the main grandstand, or by calling the 800 number. Entrance to the midway is $1 for adults, but persons holding tickets to Frontier Days events are admitted free. Parking costs $4 per vehicle in the huge lot along Carey and Eighth avenues. (Note, however, that overnight camping is not allowed here.) Because of the large number of participants in the calf-roping, steer-roping, and steer-wrestling contests, preliminary events are held each morning 7-10 a.m., with no entrance fee charged. The main rodeo events start promptly at 1:30 p.m. and last three hours. Information wagons are in various locations around the park.

OTHER PRACTICALITIES

Recreation
One-hour horseback rides are available at **Blue Ribbon Horse Center**, 406 N. Fort Rd. (two miles west of Cheyenne), tel. 634-5975. They also offer chuckwagon suppers. Rides are also available at **Terry Bison Ranch**, eight miles south of town, tel. 634-4171. Swim at the **Lions Park** indoor pool for $2.50 ($2 for seniors and kids). Sloans Lake is a popular swimming hole in the summer. The park also has a flower garden, an 18-hole **municipal golf course** (tel. 637-6418), picnic areas, playgrounds, ponds that turn into skating rinks in the winter, and even several bison. The city is also home to three other public golf courses.

Shopping
Cheyenne is an automobile town, so most folks shop at one of the big malls scattered around the edges of the city. **Frontier Mall** at 1400 Dell Range Blvd. is one of the state's largest, with more than 75 stores. WalMart and a mega-K mart add to the shop-'til-you-plop allure. Cheyenne has several good bookstores. **City News**, 18th and Carey streets, tel. 638-8671, has many Wyoming titles, while **Waldenbooks** in Frontier Mall, tel. 634-7099, is another good-sized shop. For used books, head to **Book & Record Exchange**, 318 W. 17th, tel. 635-2665, or **Book Rack**, 3321 E. Pershing, tel. 632-2014. **Abundance**, 1809 Warren Ave., tel. 632-8237, will fill your new-age needs for crystals and metaphysical books.

Downtown Cheyenne has two of the largest western clothing stores in the state: **Wrangler** (owned by Corral West), 1518 Capitol Ave., tel. 634-3048, and **Cheyenne Outfitters**, 210 W.

16th, tel. 775-7550. Both are great places to pick up a cowboy hat or cowboy boots. The latter also publishes a national catalogue for mail orders, tel. (800) 234-0432. Another place for quality western wear and other gear is **Snubbing Post**, 1802 Dell Range Blvd., tel. 638-6421.

Peoples Sporting Goods, 217 W. 16th, tel. 638-8981, and in the Frontier Mall, tel. 638-8985, offers a wide variety of outdoor gear as well as topographic maps and rents skis in winter months. Check out the dragoon pistols at the downtown location. Nearby is **Marv's Pawn Shop** run by a decidedly unique owner. His ads brag of offering the "worst free coffee in town." Give it a taste. For cheap clothes, stop by the large **Salvation Army Thrift Store** at 1401 E. Lincolnway, tel. 637-8073.

Cheyenne has quite a few art galleries, including **Gallery West**, 122 W. 16th, tel. 632-1258; **Manitou Gallery**, 1715 Carey Ave., tel. 635-0019; **Wild Horse Ranch Studio** (ceramics), 3 ½ miles east, tel. 634-3428; and **De-Selms Fine Art**, 215 W. 17th St., tel. 632-0607. **Cheyenne Artists Guild**, 1010 E. 16th St., tel. 632-2263, is the state's oldest art guild (since 1949) and has a nonprofit gallery in Holliday Park.

Information And Services
The **Cheyenne Convention and Visitors Bureau** can be found at 309 W. Lincolnway, tel. 778-3133 or (800) 426-5009. Hours are Mon.-Fri. 8-6 in summer (longer hours during Frontier Days) or Mon.-Fri. 8-5 the rest of the year. A **"Howdy Wagon"** a few doors east is staffed Sat. 11-5 and Sun. 10-3 in the summer. The state also maintains a spacious **Wyoming Information Center** at the College Dr. exit along I-25, tel. 777-7777 or (800) 225-5996. The expansive **Laramie County Public Library**, 2800 Central Ave., tel. 634-3561, is open Mon.-Thurs. 10-9, Fri. and Sat. 10-6. Between mid-Sept. and May it is also open Sun. 1-5. **Laramie County Community College**, 1400 E. College Dr., tel. 778-5222, has both day and night classes for some 3,500 students. Founded in 1968, it focuses primarily on technical fields, although there are two-year degrees in everything from accounting to wildlife conservation. The 271-acre campus has 18 buildings, most of the ugly concrete-box style common in the early 1970s.

Transportation

Amtrak offers daily train service to points east (via Denver) as well as westward. Ironically, Cheyenne—the city that was built around the railroad and that still has the finest depot in Wyoming—has no direct rail service. Because of inadequate tracking and costly repairs needed in the downtown depot, trains now stop at the railroad siding called Borie, 10 miles west of Cheyenne. It is just a brown trailer in the middle of nowhere, but a free shuttle bus provides service from downtown. Call 788-3912 or (800) 872-7245 for schedules and tickets.

The bus depot is right in front of the downtown train station on the south end of Capitol Avenue. **Greyhound,** tel. 634-7744, provides connections east and west along I-80, and south to Denver, while **Powder River Transportation,** tel. 635-1327 or (800) 442-3682, has daily bus service from Cheyenne north to Wheatland and much of northern Wyoming.

Cheyenne Airport is just south of Dell Range Blvd., with the entrance at the east end of Eighth Avenue. **United Express,** tel. (800) 241-6522, and **Continental Express,** tel. (800) 525-0280, have daily flights to Denver. **Denver Express,** tel. (800) 658-3231, has daily van runs to Denver's airport. At the airport you can rent cars from **Avis,** tel. (800) 331-1212, **Budget,** tel. (800) 527-0700, **Dollar,** tel. (800) 800-4000, **Econo-Rate,** tel. (800) 289-1417, **Enterprise,** tel. 632-1907, **Hertz,** tel. (800) 654-3131, and **National,** tel. (800) 227-7368. **Affordable Rent A Car,** 701 E. Lincolnway, tel. 634-5666, **Second Hand Rose,** 1009 E. 7th St., tel. 632-4237, and **American West Rentals,** 120 Greeley Hwy., tel. 634-0665, have used cars for better rates. Five local taxi companies to choose from in town: **A-A Taxi,** tel. 634-6020, **A-1 Veterans Cab,** tel. 634-4444; **Ace Taxi,** tel. 637-4747; **Checker Cab,** tel. 635-5555; and **Yellow Cab,** tel. 633-3333.

CURT GOWDY STATE PARK

The 1,645-acre Curt Gowdy State Park is located 26 miles west of Cheyenne along State 210, the scenic "back way" to Laramie. Here, two small lakes offer recreation for anglers, boaters, snowmobilers, and cross-country skiers. The lakes are a part of Cheyenne's water supply (no swimming) and were constructed between 1904 and 1910. An elaborate Rube Goldberg scheme completed in 1964 now carries 12 million gallons of water from the west, crossing the Continental Divide, the Sierra Madre, the Snowy Range, and the Laramie Range to bring it to thirsty Cheyenne. In 1971, the two lakes at the eastern end were set aside as a state park and named for Wyoming native Curt Gowdy, a Hall of Fame baseball player and well-known TV sportscaster. Camping here costs $4 per day at any one of five sites. There's pleasant hiking in the surrounding pine-covered country-

side, but by late summer the lakes tend to get drawn down rather severely. There are some interesting granitic formations to explore and climb. Also in the park is the historic Hynds Lodge, a stone structure completed in 1923 and available for families and groups to rent. For details, call park headquarters at 632-7946. An outstanding lodging option is **A. Drummond's Ranch Bed and Breakfast,** tel. 634-6042, located just a mile and a half away from the park. Rooms and a full breakfast cost $70+ s or d, including access to an outdoor hot tub. Other meals are available for an additional charge. This is a very nice place to splurge.

Happy Jack Mountain Music Festival comes around the last Saturday in June at Curt Gowdy, offering a fun chance to listen to bluegrass tunes, sample the wares at a crafts fair, or participate in a fishing derby. Tickets are $6 per day.

PINE BLUFFS

Pine Bluffs (pop. 1,100) is a small agricultural and transportation center on Wyoming's eastern border. It is so close to Nebraska that one gas station—Smitty's Stateline Truckstop—straddles the border, with a line painted down the middle of the building. Pine Bluffs feels like western Nebraska, with ponderosa pines crowding the long ridge south of town. The countryside is filled with silos, farm equipment, and rifle-racked pickup trucks, while the airwaves contain market reports and hog futures. Wheat fields and irrigated potato fields surround Pine Bluffs. The spuds head to the potato-chip factory here; look for Rocky Mountain brand (crunchiest chips anywhere) in Wyoming stores. The town itself is middle America, with spreading shade trees and quiet homes along the side streets and deserted buildings lining Main Street.

Sights

The most interesting sight in Pine Bluffs is the ongoing **archaeological excavation** near a major Indian occupation site that dates back 8,000 years. Indians pitched their tipis atop the pine-covered bluffs here and headed down to the fertile valley below to hunt and collect berries. Their tipi rings are still visible. Each summer, University of Wyoming students under the direction of Dr. Charles Reher (who was born in Pine Bluffs) arrive to slowly dig through the soil to find a buried treasure trove of prehistory. The staff will be happy to answer your questions. The site is located right next to the tourist information center at the I-80 rest area. Also here are several painted tipi replicas; pick up the brochure describing the various designs. Get to the top of the bluffs by following the two-mile **hiking trail** that departs from the rest area. The hills are also accessible by car by following Beech St. south under the freeway and turning right on the dirt road at the crest of the hill. This is an excellent place to watch sunrises and sunsets or to enjoy a picnic lunch amid the pines.

The town of Pine Bluffs lays right along the great **Texas Trail**; at its peak in 1871, more than 600,000 cattle were trailed north from Texas past this point. Pine Bluffs became not just a watering place for cattle, but also a vital shipping point. For several years, more cattle were shipped from the railroad station at Pine Bluffs than anywhere else in the world. A monument to the Texas Trail stands in the adjacent park. The free **Texas Trail Museum** at Third and Market streets, tel. 245-3713, houses a Conestoga wagon, old photos, and a small collection of homesteading and ranching items. Be sure to see the hand-crocheted snowflakes in the museum gift shop. It's open daily 9-5 during the summer, or by appointment (stop by town hall) at other times. Next to the museum are a caboose (these are becoming almost as common as sheep wagons in Wyoming museums) and several historic buildings: a one-room schoolhouse, an old church, and a railroad boardinghouse. The **University of Wyoming High Plains Archaeology Field Lab and Visitor Center** (try saying this one fast) is located at Second and Elm and is open daily during the summer. Inside are interesting archaeological displays and artifacts. These will be moved into a new domed facility near the I-80 excavation site in 1994. Tiny **Albin** (pop. 130) is 18 miles north of Pine Bluffs and has an interesting old sod house. The annual event here is Albin Days, held in July each year. Call 246-3444 for details.

Practicalities

Sunset Motel, 315 W. Third, tel. 245-3591, charges $24 s or $26 d, while **Gator's Travelyn Motel,** 515 W. Seventh, tel. 245-3226, has comfortable rooms for $28 s or $34 d. **Pine Bluff Mobile Village** is a half mile east of town, tel. 245-3665, with tent spaces (no shade) for $9 and RV sites for $14. Showers are an exorbitant $5 for noncampers; open mid-April to mid-October. Restaurant options are pretty slim in Pine Bluffs. Best bet is **Pizza Place,** 715 Parsons, tel. 245-3443, where you'll find decent sandwiches, pizza, and fast food. Locals also eat at the restaurant in the Phillips 66 station, 600 Parsons, tel. 245-9365. It's a cigarette smoker's definition of heaven and a nonsmoker's hell. Open 24 hours for your breathing enjoyment. Check **Jim's Bar** and **Pal's Pub** for live music. Get groceries in **Texas Trail Market,** Third and

Elm, tel. 245-3302. This is a cooperatively run store, as is the auto-repair shop at 700 Parsons and the local grain elevator. Socialism in a rock-ribbed Republican state!

The primary hangout in Pine Bluffs is the local bowling alley, **Pine Bowl,** at Third and Pine, tel. 245-3622. No chamber of commerce office in town, but the state-run **Tourist Information Center** at the I-80 rest area has both local and statewide info. It is open late May-September. The **library** at 108 E. Second, tel. 245-3646, is open Tues.-Fri. 8:30-5 and Sat. 8:30-12:30. Pine Bluffs has a free outdoor **swimming pool**

(summers only) at 200 E. Eighth, tel. 245-3783.

Pine Bluffs Trail Days comes around the first weekend in August, with rodeos, barbe-cues, a parade, a melodrama, and dancing. A few mountain men types rendezvous in the bluffs above town. There are also **calf and team roping** events at the rodeo grounds on most Sunday afternoons through the summer, with practice roping on Tues. and Thurs. evenings. **Greyhound,** tel. 634-7744 (in Cheyenne), stops at Redimart (Eighth and Parsons) in Pine Bluffs, with connections in both directions along I-80.

CHUGWATER

Chugwater (pop. 200) was once headquarters for the giant Swan Land and Cattle Company, the greatest of Wyoming's cattle spreads during the 1880s. The town itself was founded in 1913 on land sold by the Swan Company. Today it is best known for Chugwater Chili, (though it is not actually packaged in town). The chili mix is a creation of Dave Cameron, who calls himself a "hunting guide, chili cook, and real estate broker, in that order." Get a free taste at 210 First Street. Chugwater has to have one of the strangest origins of any town name in America, coming from the Indian practice of driving buffalo over cliffs into the creek. The "chug" sound they made as they hit the water led Indians to call it "Water at the Place Where the Buffalo Chug."

Practicalities

Chugwater has a free small **museum** located in a historic bank with an impressive collection of

brands, open Sat.-Sun. 1-5 only. **Buffalo Grill,** tel. 422-3458, makes home-cooked meals served with gusto. The **Diamond Guest Ranch/Chugwater KOA,** tel. 422-3567, is located on a historic 75,000-acre cattle ranch 15 miles west of town and is very popular with families and retirees. The ranch was begun in 1884 and was for many years a breeding center for Clydesdale and Morgan horses. It has been a guest ranch since 1968. All sorts of outdoor recreation here, including hayrides, swimming, and trail rides. Also here are a restaurant and a bar. Campsites cost $12 for tents or $17 for RVs. Cabins are also available. The annual **Chugwater Chili Cook-off** is held at Diamond Ranch each June, attracting several thousand fire-breathing chili-eaters. **Powder River Transportation,** tel. (800) 442-3682, has daily bus service north and south from Chugwater.

WHEATLAND

With a name like Wheatland (pop. 3,300), it should be pretty obvious that you're in farming country. Actually, wheat is not the primary crop grown here; sugar beets, dry beans, and barley are. The 1,650-megawatt coal-fired Laramie River Station powerplant, built in the 1980s, is five miles north of town and supplies electricity to a grid that feeds an eight-state area. It's the biggest local employer. Another substantial employer is a local marble quarry operation that mines dolomite in the Laramie Mountains and crushes it for use in everything from aquarium gravel to cattle feed. Don't let on that I told you, but Wheatland has Minuteman III nuclear missiles out in the country near the power plant. Perhaps for this reason, Wheatland claims to have one of the highest per capita number of churches anywhere; 23 different houses of worship crowd the town.

History

An early settler in this part of Wyoming called it "a desolate looking place, nothing but sagebrush, cactus, rocks, mudhole, rattlesnakes and coyotes." It took water to change all this. Wheatland is a creation of the Wyoming Development Company, founded in 1883 by a number of individuals, including senators Joseph M. Carey and Francis E. Warren. In one of the few successful applications of the famous Carey Act in Wyoming, the company built a dam on Big Laramie River and canals to carry the water to some 50,000 acres where homesteaders formed the Wheatland Colony. (This is still the largest privately owned irrigation system in the nation.) In 1905 the town of Wheatland was incorporated—the name won out over Wheatdale and Wheatridge—becoming the hub of activity for the region, and later the Platte County seat.

SWAN LAND AND CATTLE COMPANY

The most famous of all Wyoming ranches was the Swan Land and Cattle Company, Ltd., founded in 1883 by Alexander and Thomas Swan with enormous financial backing from Scottish investors: £600,000 the first year and an additional £1.6 million spread over the next three years. At its peak in the mid-1880s, the company's holdings reached from its headquarters along Chugwater Creek westward for 120 miles to the North Platte River near Rawlins. More than 110,000 cattle ranged across this vast expanse. The company bought 550,000 acres of Union Pacific Railroad land (and therefore controlled the checkerboard of public land in alternating sections) and purchased government land along major creeks in the area. By doing this, it controlled access to water in this semiarid country, thus keeping others from settling on surrounding public lands. All told, the Swan Land and Cattle Company had its tentacles over nearly a million acres with more than 30 different ranches. The company had dozens of different brands, but locals knew it as the "Two Bar." Cowboys loved the company, for it always provided good working conditions and wages ($20 a

month to start), plus the best grub around.

In the mid-1880s things began to turn sour, and by 1886 the Scottish investors accused Alexander Swan of fraud and misrepresentation; the 110,000 cattle shown on the books did not all exist on the hoof. A lawsuit led to his firing, but another factor caused considerably more devastation: the severe winter of 1886-87 that killed off thousands of the firm's cows and calves, pushing the company to the brink of bankruptcy. Amazingly, the reorganized company managed to survive for more than 50 years, though it began raising sheep instead of cattle after 1903. It was quite prosperous during WW I, when wool prices soared, but its fortunes gradually declined as the economy turned down. By 1950, the vast operation had been entirely liquidated. Some folks claim that a wild bronc from the old Two Bar Ranch—Steamboat—was the inspiration for Wyoming's bucking horse symbol (as appears on license plates). Many of the historic ranch's buildings are still intact, and the complex has been designated a National Historic Landmark.

During the late 1970s and early '80s, Wheatland followed the boom pattern common to other Wyoming towns, with oil and gas exploration nearby and construction of the giant powerplant attracting thousands to town. When things went bust, Wheatland was pulled down; it still has not really recovered. That old standby, agriculture, has gained increasing importance.

Sights

The free **Laramie Peak Museum** on 16th and Elliot streets is open Mon.-Fri. 1-5. It houses a variety of homestead-era flotsam and jetsam ranging from turn-of-the-century tricycles to a stuffed vulture! A saddle and cowboy hat here have burn marks from when lightning struck a local cowboy (he lived). The marble-columned **Platte County Court House** at Ninth and Walnut is easily the most imposing structure in Wheatland. It was built in 1911. Call 322-9601 for tours of the huge **Laramie River Station** powerplant just north of Wheatland.

Approximately 30 miles southwest of Wheatland on State 34 is the Wyoming Game and Fish Department's **Sybille Wildlife Research Center** (pronounced suh-BEEL), which houses elk, moose, deer, antelope, bighorn sheep, and black-footed ferrets. The visitor center here is open daily during the summer and Mon.-Fri. the rest of the year and includes exhibits and videos on the endangered black-footed ferret. TV monitors show activity in the adjacent ferret facility, where more than 140 of these cute little furries live. This is a unique opportunity to glimpse one of the rarest mammals on earth.

Accommodations

Blackbird Inn Bed & Breakfast, 1101 11th St., tel. 322-4540, rates near the top of my list of places to stay in Wyoming. Run by a friendly local schoolteacher, Dan Brecht, this old Victorian home (built in 1912) has been lovingly restored. Excellent full breakfasts are served during the summer, but even the continental breakfast offered the rest of the year will fill you up. Another unique lodging place is **Hubbard's Mountain Cupboards**, tel. 322-4441, located in the pines northwest of Wheatland. Cabins with kitchens cost $20+ s or $25+ d and are open May-October. On weekends co-owner Dan Lilly leads very informative herbal walks ($15) detailing the medicinal properties of wild plants. Also here are a small gallery featuring local artists and a bar with occasional live music. Get here by driving 20 miles north on I-25. Take the El Rancho exit and follow the signs 20 more miles west to the cabins. See the chart for other lodging options in Wheatland. You can camp for free at 40-acre **Lewis Park**, right in town (with showers and RV hookups), or pay $9 for RVs or $5 for tents to stay at **Squaw Mountain R.V. Camp**, 2005 N. 16th, tel. 322-3253. Showers for non-campers here cost $2; open year-round.

Food

For the best local breakfasts (especially the omelettes), head to **Breakfast Inn**, 86 16th St., tel. 322-9302. **Granny's Goodie Shop**, 719 Ninth St., tel. 322-5321, makes good sandwiches for lunch (including cabbage burgers!) and serves hot coffee and donuts for a quick break-

WHEATLAND ACCOMMODATIONS

NAME	ADDRESS	PHONE	RATES	FEATURES
Plains Motel	208 16th St.	322-3416	$21 s, $27 d	
Parkway Motel	1257 South Rd.	322-3080	$22 s, $28 d	
Wyoming Motel	1109 9th St.	322-5383	$25 s, $29 d	
Motel West Winds	1756 South St.	322-2705	$26 s, $31 d	outdoor pool
Blackbird Inn B&B	1101 11th St.	322-4540	$30 s, $35 d	AAA approved
Vimbo's Motel	203 16th St.	322-3842	$32+ s, $36+ d	historic place
Torchlite Inn (Best Western)	1809 N. 16th St.	322-4070 (800) 528-1234	$42+ s, $52+ d	AAA approved

fast. Pseudo-Mexican food comes to you courtesy of the Korean chefs at **El Gringo's,** 705 10th St., tel. 322-4402, and standard family dining at **Vimbo's Restaurant,** 203 16th St., tel. 322-3725. For fast food, be sure to eschew the Burger King and Arby's, heading instead to **Casey's Drive In,** 1556 S St., tel. 322-9616. Very good burgers.

Wheatland's surprise is **J.J.'s Little Brown Derby,** 1707 Ninth St., tel. 322-4257. Located in a 1950s-era trailer house with appropriately tacky decor, it has great food, reasonable prices, and huge portions. The burgers and chicken-fried steak are famous. For something different, stop by on Friday nights for the prime rib specials. Even the Burlington Northern freight train stops so the crew can come over for dinner! **Pizza Hut,** 1801 N. 16th St., tel. 322-4001, is the only place open late most nights. Groceries are available at **Safeway** and **Jack and Jill Market.**

Events

The **Platte County Fair and Rodeo** comes to town the second week of August, offering a street breakfast, barbecue, parade, professional rodeo, and entertainment, plus all the usual fun of a country fair. Most enjoyable of all is the pig wrestling. Two other local events are worth noting: **Community Fest** in mid-July has bake sales, homemade crafts, and a carnival, plus there are amateur rodeo events at **Miles Mitchell Memorial Day Rodeo.**

Information And Services

The **Wheatland Chamber of Commerce** office is in the basement of city hall at 600 Ninth St., tel. 322-2322. Hours are Mon.-Fri. 8-5. **Platte County Library,** 904 Ninth St., tel. 322-2689, is open Mon.-Thurs. 10-8, Fri. 10-5, and Sat. 10-2. There is a fine outdoor **swimming pool** (tel. 322-9254) in Lewis Park, open only during the summer. Entrance costs 75 cents for adults; free for kids under six. Find the nine-hole **Wheatland Golf Course** at 1253 Cole, tel. 322-3675. For something unique, stop by 1556 Cedar, where Lucy Gorman makes woven-wheat wall hangings. **Powder River Transportation,** tel. 322-2725 or (800) 442-3682, has daily bus service to Cheyenne and most of

BLACK-FOOTED FERRETS

On September 25, 1981, near Meeteetse, Wyoming, a dog walked up to its master with a strange creature in his mouth. It was a black-footed ferret, a sleek, black-masked animal last seen in 1972 and feared extinct. Biologists soon discovered that a nearby prairie dog colony housed the only living population of the ferrets, the world's rarest mammals. Ferrets eat prairie dogs and were once found in their colonies from Saskatchewan to Texas. The colonies were huge—one along the Cheyenne River in eastern Wyoming stretched for a hundred miles—but the prairie dogs went the way of many other animals, hunted and poisoned by settlers and their land taken over by plowed fields. Although still present in Wyoming, prairie dog colonies are now much smaller and more isolated. The population of ferrets declined with their shrinking food source.

With the discovery of ferrets living near Meeteetse, national attention focused on saving the population from extinction. A 1985 an outbreak of canine distemper threatened to kill all the remaining wild ferrets, so they were captured and taken to the Wyoming Game and Fish Wildlife Research Unit at Sybille. After inoculations, an ambitious captive breeding program was begun. It proved so successful that in 1989 the population was split up (to reduce the chance that all would be killed in an accident such as a tornado), with some sent to the National Zoo in Virginia and others to Omaha's Henry Doorly Zoo. In 1991, a small number of ferrets were returned to the wild in Shirley Basin (north of the town of Medicine Bow). Others can be seen at the Sybille research center. Eventually, researchers hope to reestablish ferrets in at least 10 separate areas around the West. Because of their relatively short lifespan (two to three years in the wild) and their susceptibility to predators such as owls and coyotes, as well as diseases, ferrets may remain endangered for many years.

northern Wyoming. The buses stop at DJ's Gas Station, 16th and South.

GUERNSEY AND VICINITY

Guernsey (pop. 1,200) is a scenic railroad and ranching town along the once mighty North Platte River. The river is now just a trickle in late summer, thanks to all the upstream dams. Guernsey was named after Charles A. Guernsey, a prominent local rancher and legislator who came here in the late 19th century. The town is right at the heart of the Oregon Trail, with Fort Laramie just 11 miles east and numerous historical markers from the 19th century. The Wyoming Army National Guard maintains Camp Guernsey, a large trooptraining facility just north of town.

Emigrant Trail Sights

The Oregon Trail ran just on the other side of the North Platte River from Guernsey. One mile south of town are some of the deepest **Oregon Trail ruts** anywhere along the historic route. A short trail leads uphill to four-foot-deep gouges cut into the soft sandstone. The paths of bullwhackers are visible alongside. The old wagon trail is easy to follow in both directions, and the surrounding landscape has probably changed but little since the last wagon train rolled past. Perhaps better than any historic photos or written descriptions, these deep ruts serve as permanent reminders of the great westward migration. Not far away is a white obelisk marking the grave of Lucindy Rollins, one of the thousands who died on the hard road west.

The hundred-foot-tall **Register Cliff** is four miles south of Guernsey. Here the soft limestone made a perfect place for passing emigrants to carve their names, and thousands took the time to do so. The oldest—dating to the 1850s—are now behind a chainlink fence to keep folks from defacing them further. Hundreds of swallows nest on the cliff here. North of Guernsey, ruts of the historic Mormon Trail are visible along **Emigrant Hill,** where Mormon pioneers struggled to hoist their wagons up the steep slope. Another important nearby site was **Emigrants' Washtub,** a warm springs where weary travelers stopped to bathe and wash clothes.

Practicalities

No bunkhouse accommodations at the **Bunkhouse Motel,** tel. 836-2356, but nice motel rooms for $26 s or $32 d. Talk to the mayor while you're here. **Sagebrush Motel,** tel. 836-2331, charges $26 s or $32 d. **Annette's White House,** 239 South Dakota, tel. 836-2148, has delightful bed-and-breakfast accommodations for $25 s or $30 d. Owner Annette Dombeck has one of the finest gardens in town. Pleasant riverside campsites are found at the city-run **Larson Park** for $5 tents and $7 RVs including showers. **Crazy Tony's** serves very popular Saturday-night Italian dinners, while **S & S Cafe,** tel. 836-9301, has homemade baked goods and good breakfasts. The best steaks in Guernsey are at **Trail Inn,** tel. 836-2573. **Burrito Brothers** offers up fast food. Get groceries at the **Jack and Jill Food Center.**

Guernsey has a small **visitor center/museum** that is open during the summer months. It's located right in front of the town swimming pool, which is also open during the summer. A nine-hole golf course provides a place to putt around, and there is a small library open Mon.-Saturday. Guernsey's airport is surprisingly large and well equipped, not because of any commercial service but because of nearby National Guard training facilities. Rent canoes from **Quick Canoe Rentals,** tel. 836-2039. They will even drive your car downstream to the takeout point. Each Fourth of July, the **Old Timer's Rodeo** comes to Guernsey, offering all the standard small-town fun: a parade, rodeo, barbecue, street dance, and fireworks. **Labor Day** brings a demolition derby and an arts-and-crafts fair to town.

HARTVILLE AREA

Six miles north of Guernsey on State 270 is the picturesque old mining community of Hartville (pop. 100). Established in 1884, it is the oldest incorporated town in Wyoming. The town is named for Colonel Verling Hart, an officer at nearby Fort Laramie and owner of a copper mine here. The Hartville Uplift region (as it is known by geologists) is one of the most mineral-rich in Wyoming. Indians used its iron as pigment to make war paint. During the 1870s, prospectors found gold, silver, copper, onyx, and iron ore in these scenic pine-and-juniper-dotted hills. Copper brought the first miners, but by 1887 it had been mostly mined out, and they turned to iron ore. Hartville arose as a shopping, gambling, boozing, and whoring center for the miners; many of the historic stone and false-front buildings still stand.

Of note is the **Miners Bar**—the state's oldest drinking establishment—and the old stone jail just up the block. The cherrywood back bar was made in Germany in 1864 and shipped to Fort Laramie, moving to Hartville in 1881. Also in Hartville is **Venice Bar,** where homemade Italian dinners are served on Saturday evenings, but only if you can get 12 people together and reserve ahead! Call 836-2881 for details. This is a fun place to put quarters in the jukebox and listen to the country tunes with locals. **Hartville Merc Co.** has groceries and **Wild Bill's Antiques** is another fun place to explore. The local cemetery is crowded with the bodies of men who died wearing their cowboy boots—this was one town where gunfights really did take place on Main Street—so it is fitting that the local annual festivities are **Boot Hill Days.** Drop in on Labor Day weekend for the melodrama, street games, mock shootouts, and plenty of food. (The last gunfight took place on Labor Day in 1912.)

The mining ghost town of **Sunrise** (closed to the public) is just a mile east of Hartville. An extraordinarily rich body of iron ore was discovered here in 1887, and a dozen years later the Colorado Fuel and Iron Corp. established an open-pit iron mine, a mine that would eventually reach 650 feet in depth, the largest glory hole in the world. It closed in 1980 and reclamation work has restored the gaping glory hole to a more natural contour. When the mine first opened the company hired some 750 predominantly Italian and Greek emigrants to dig the ore, which was shipped to a smelter in Pueblo, Colorado. To house the workers, the clean, well-planned company town of Sunrise sprang up. The mine was closed in 1980 due to a lessened demand for ore, and its brick buildings now stand abandoned. Sunrise claims a miniscule footnote to trivial history: "Ripley's Believe It or Not!" noted that the town had the longest string of car garages in the world. They are still standing.

The Hartville area is part of the so-called **Spanish Diggings,** an extensive archaeological site that covers hundreds of square miles. Early settlers believed this to be the site of a Spanish gold mine (hence the name), but it is now known to have been used instead by Indians gathering flint for arrowheads. They mined quartzite, jasper, moss agate, and chalcedony here for perhaps 10,000 years. Stone flakes and countless old pits (up to 15 feet deep and 50 feet across) abound in this region. Hundreds of tipi rings and rock chips can be found here, and the material mined was carried all the way to the Missouri River. One of the most important aboriginal places in Wyoming is in this area, an 11,000-year-old paleo-Indian site called **Hell Gap.** Excellent three-hour tours of Hell Gap, the Spanish Diggings, the Cheyenne-Deadwood Stage Route, and historic ranches are given by a local rancher and archaeologist, George Ziemens. Call 837-2724 for info and rates.

The road north from Hartville (State 270) leads over pine-carpeted hills and then descends through rolling grassland with a backdrop of rocky buttes and antelope grazing beside old windmills. There are dramatic views of Laramie Peak from the hilltops. At **Manville** (pop. 100) the road meets US 18, which leads to Lusk. Not much in Manville other than a few old buildings (including one of the smallest post offices in Wyoming), a water tower, a school, and a gas station/cafe/bar. The latter (Conners Corner) is noteworthy for its "Porn O' Plenty" vending machine in the men's restroom!

GUERNSEY STATE PARK

Two state parks are found along the North Platte River in eastern Wyoming. Guernsey is the smaller of the two (about seven miles long and covering 6,538 acres), but it is far more interesting than its sister, Glendo State Park. The south entrance to Guernsey State Park is a mile northwest of Guernsey, and the road connects through to the Hartville area. The park surrounds

Guernsey Reservoir, backed up behind a 105-foot-tall, 560-foot-long earthen dam completed in 1927. Originally, the dam stored 74,000 acre-feet of water, but half that capacity has been lost due to siltation. To reduce this problem, the reservoir is now drained down each summer, killing off many of the fish and sometimes creating havoc with boaters (it can take place with almost no warning). Don't bother bringing your fishing pole. Guernsey is surrounded by scenic grass-and-sage-covered hills topped with juniper and pine. The drive from Hartville through the park is a surprise after the open sage-and-grass country north of here. Pink-walled sandstone cliffs suddenly appear as the narrow, winding road (not for RVs) enters the canyon, hugs the cliffs as it passes the lake, and then climbs into the pines. There is a pleasant sandy beach five miles west along the southern shore, and there are seven campgrounds, each costing $4 per night. The water is quite warm, making this a popular swimming hole. Entrance to

Guernsey State Park costs $3, but it may not be collected after mid-September.

Other than the scenery, the main attractions in Guernsey State Park are the wonderful stone structures built by the Civilian Conservation Corps during the 1930s, some of the best examples of CCC craftsmanship in existence. **Guernsey State Park Museum**—built in 1936 —is the finest of all, with an arched stone entrance that faces impressive Laramie Peak, 35 miles to the west. Inside are enormous hand-hewn timbers, wrought-iron light fixtures, and flagstone floors. This place was built to last! The museum (tel. 836-2900) is open daily 10-6 in summer (closed in winter) and houses 14 displays created by the CCC to illustrate the geology and human use of the surrounding country. Take a look at the historical slide show. Other park structures built of native material include roads, overlooks, rock walls, culverts, bridges, picnic shelters, and the famous "million-dollar privy," located on the southwest side of the park.

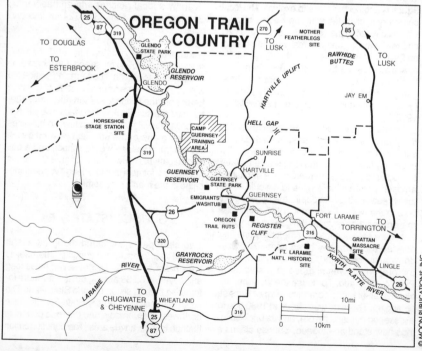

Outstanding vistas from this area at sunset. Also within Guernsey State Park are eight miles of hiking trails and a short nature trail near the museum. Pick up a trail guide inside.

GLENDO STATE PARK

Located 25 miles east of Douglas and 32 miles north of Wheatland, 10,000-acre Glendo State Park surrounds Glendo Reservoir. A 167-foot-high earthen dam backs up water for 14 miles and generates some 24,000 kilowatts of electricity. This is one of the largest reservoirs on the North Platte River, with almost 80 miles of shoreline. (Note, however, that drought years sometimes reduce the reservoir to little more than a puddle.) The surrounding country is treeless and windy, but the towering 10,272-foot summit of Laramie Peak dominates the skyline to the west. The surprisingly warm water at Sandy Beach makes this a favorite play area for families. Other attractions are the Red Cliffs, where cliff divers agonize over the long drop, and Muddy Bay, where anglers look for walleye, perch, or trout (lunker walleyes here). Dozens of small coves can be explored by boat, or you can float down the river below the dam. The wind can really blow, making for good windsurfing conditions but also creating hazards for folks who go out in small boats.

Practicalities
There are seven state park campgrounds ($4) on the eastern end of Glendo Reservoir. Get permits from park headquarters (tel. 735-4433) near the dam. The little town of **Glendo** (pop. 200) is just two miles from Glendo State Park, near the site of the old **Horseshoe Creek Stage Station.** Built by Mormons in the 1850s, the station was later burned by them to keep it out of government hands. A small **Glendo Historical Museum** is open seasonally, with Indian and early settlers' gear. Lodging is available at **Howard's Motel,** 106 A St., tel. 735-4252, for $18 s or $22 d. **Glendo Marina** near the dam, tel. 735-4216, has rustic motel accommodations overlooking the lake for $30 s or $35 d, plus a restaurant, a grocery store, and RV hookups ($10). Rent fishing boats here for $60 a day. The marina is open year-round, but the other facilities are closed in winter. **Glendo Days** comes around each July with a rodeo and street dance.

FORT LARAMIE NATIONAL HISTORIC SITE

One of the most important historic sites in all Wyoming is old Fort Laramie, located three miles south of the town of the same name. The fort played a changing series of roles as the West was developed: Indian trading post, emigrant way station, and military center. Fort Laramie stood at the crossroads of history. The budding territory's first school and post office opened here, and nearly every famous citizen of the frontier era—from Jim Bridger to Mark Twain—stopped in. Today Fort Laramie is one of the most popular stopping points for visitors who want a taste of the rich history of this region.

HISTORY

In 1834, trader William Sublette halted along the banks of the Laramie River near its confluence with the North Platte. With him were 35 mountain men, their pack animals weighted down with trade items for the annual rendezvous along the Green River. Sublette had a bold plan, to build a permanent trading post here, one that would make it easier to bring supplies west and beaver furs and buffalo robes back east, a place where Indians and whites could parlay, with both profiting. He left behind a dozen men to begin work on what would become Fort William (as in William Sublette) and hurried west to the rendezvous. The men threw up a cottonwood stockade, with blockhouses on the corners and a tunnel to the outer gate for trading with the Indians.

Over the next two years the post changed hands a couple of times (and names—to Fort Lucien), becoming an important trade center for Pierre Chouteau's American Fur Company. By 1841, competition from another trading post—built just a mile away—forced the com-

FORT LARAMIE NATIONAL HISTORIC SITE

MARRIED NCO QUARTERS

HOSPITAL

CAVALRY BARRACKS

ARTILLERY DEMONSTRATION AREA

ENTRANCE

PARKING

TRADER'S RESIDENCE

VISITOR CENTER / COMMISSARY STOREHOUSES

SAWMILL

POST TRADER'S STORE

BAKERIES

PIT TOILET

LT. COLONEL'S QUARTERS

SURGEON'S QUARTERS

MAGAZINE

MESS ROOMS AND KITCHENS

OFFICER'S QUARTERS

OLD BEDLAM

FLAG POLE

GUARDHOUSE

PICNIC AREA

PARADE GROUNDS

GENERAL SINK

COMMANDING OFFICER'S RESIDENCE

BARRACKS

CHICKEN HOUSE

GUARDHOUSES

OFFICER'S QUARTERS

ADMINISTRATION BUILDING

CAPTAIN'S QUARTERS

OPEN BUILDINGS ▪

NOT TO SCALE

STANDING OR VISIBLE RUIN □

BUILDING SITE ⋯

© MOON PUBLICATIONS, INC.

pany to start again. This time they spent $10,000 building a whitewashed adobe fort near the old one that was already rotting. Fort John-on-the-Laramie was the official name given to the second fort, but this was quickly shortened to Fort Laramie.

During the next eight years, Fort Laramie emerged as a strategic center for the Indian trade, with more than 10,000 buffalo robes purchased each year. (Traders generally paid the equivalent of $1 per robe in the form of gunpowder, hatchets, tobacco, coffee, sugar, blankets, and of course, liquor; the robes were sold in St. Louis for $4 each.) But trade with the Indians was gradually supplanted by a new role for the fort: aiding the growing migration of people westward. Fort Laramie stood right along the main trail to Oregon and California. It was a

third of the way from Missouri to the Columbia River mouth and provided a much-anticipated break before the long, desolate trek over the Continental Divide. In 1843, nearly a thousand people passed the fort, and the numbers increased each year, reaching a crescendo after gold was discovered in California in 1849. Soon thereafter, more than 50,000 emigrants were trudging into Fort Laramie each summer. They stopped to repair wheels at the carpentry and blacksmith shops, purchase food and whiskey at the store, or trade tired stock for fresh oxen and horses. The latter was the best deal for traders at the fort; all they had to do was put the oxen and horses they had gotten in trade (generally a two-for-one deal) out to pasture for a couple of weeks and then trade them as fresh stock to subsequent emigrants.

The Army Takes Over

The great migration westward had its negative consequences. Indians complained that buffalo were being shot and forced away from their traditional migration routes and that the thousands of stock brought by the emigrants were destroying the grass. The inevitable conflicts began as young warriors halted wagon trains demanding "tolls" in the form of tobacco, coffee, or sugar. Quickly, this escalated into attacks against the emigrants, and a great hue and cry went up for protection from the "savages." Thus it was that Congress gave Fort Laramie a new role: as a military garrison to protect the Oregon Trail.

In 1849, the Army purchased Fort Laramie for $4000, establishing the first military post in what would become Wyoming. Some 180 men —both cavalrymen and infantrymen—were assigned to the post. A rapid expansion program was begun, with the old adobe fort serving as temporary quarters while more elaborate facilities were built. The Army's Fort Laramie did not fit the Hollywood stereotype of a frontier fort, having no log perimeter or blockhouses. The fort was instead laid out around a central parade ground, with clapboard and "lime grout" concrete buildings forming a loose perimeter. In case of attack, the Army was prepared to retreat to a single, heavily fortified building. Despite this general lack of protection, the fort was never attacked by Indians (though the horses were brazenly driven off one time), and most soldiers never engaged in battle with the Indians.

Fort Laramie was essentially a male bastion, though a few officers' wives were present. The only exceptions were laundresses, hired generally on the basis of their physical appearance—the less attractive the better, so as to not appeal to the soldiers' prurient interests. A small group of Indians (termed derisively "Laramie Loafers") soon attached themselves to the fort, camping nearby and providing scouts, interpreters, errand boys, and paramours. Fort Laramie was not a pleasant place. The food was deplorable, discipline so strict that even the smallest infraction could land a man in the brig, and sanitary conditions were so bad that by 1880 it was getting hard to find a place to dig latrines that had not already been contaminated. The infrequent paydays turned into drunken brawls. No wonder so many men deserted their post and slipped off for the promising gold fields of California! The inevitable "hog ranches" also grew up near the fort, offering an escape from the day-to-day monotony of the soldiers' lives. In 1877, Lt. John G. Bourke described the ranches as:

> tenanted by as hardened and depraved a set of witches as could be found on the face of the globe. Each of these establishments was equipped with a rum-mill of the worst kind and each contained from three to half a dozen Cyprians, virgins whose lamps were always burning brightly in expectance of the coming of the bridegroom, and who lured to destruction the soldiers of the garrison. In all my experience I have never seen a lower, more beastly set of people of both sexes.

For the next four decades, Fort Laramie served as the nerve center for this part of the plains, providing troops and cavalry to retaliate against Indian attacks and serving as a meeting place for treaty arrangements when the political wind shifted toward negotiation instead of confrontation. The first of these treaties came in 1851, under the forceful leadership of Indian agent Thomas Fitzpatrick, a former mountain man. More than 10,000 Indians attended, representing the Sioux, Cheyenne, Arapaho, and Shoshone, Crow, Gros Ventre, and Assiniboin tribes. The treaty consisted essentially of annual bribes (annuities) to be given to the Indians to compensate them for their losses to whites. The various tribes would be assigned to distinct territories but could hunt in other areas. After signing the treaty, a mountain of presents awaited, the first of the $50,000 in annuities for each of the next 50 years. Shortly thereafter, the federal government reneged on the promise, increasing the annual amount to $70,000 per year but cutting the time to just 10 years. Peace lasted but a short while.

Grattan Massacre

One of the few Indian-white conflicts to occur in the vicinity of Fort Laramie took place in 1854. It began innocently enough when a Mormon emigrant's lame cow wandered off and was butchered by a hungry Miniconjou Indian waiting for the government to dispense annuities. A hot-headed young lieutenant, John Grattan, was sent out to bring in the Indian. Unfortunately, Grattan's interpreter was drunk and began immediately shouting insults at the Sioux in whose village the man was camped. Grattan himself was anxious for a fight, hoping to gain a piece of fame, so when the Sioux refused to give up the man—offering instead to pay for the cow with two horses—Grattan would have nothing of it. His soldiers opened fire and were themselves immediately attacked by a vastly superior force of Sioux. All 29 soldiers died in the massacre that followed, and Fort Laramie stood in danger of being destroyed. But the Indians instead raided local storehouses for the promised annuities and headed out. The Army used the Grattan Massacre as proof that the Indians could not be trusted. In reality, the entire incident was one of utter stupidity on the part of the Army.

More Trouble

One of the least distinguished post commanders at Fort Laramie was the hard-drinking and ill-tempered Colonel Thomas Moonlight. In 1865, he publicly hanged two Sioux subchiefs who had brought in two white women captives for reward. Their bodies were left dangling in chains for several days, an act that brought condemnation from the Eastern press. In retaliation, the Sioux killed several soldiers and then managed to drive off most of the horses from Colonel Moonlight's cavalry. A sullen Moonlight led his almost horseless cavalry in the 120-mile-long hike back to the fort. Shortly thereafter, he was stripped of his command. (Moonlight later served as a politically appointed territorial governor of Wyoming.)

With the decline in importance of the Oregon Trail, Fort Laramie became a staging area for military expeditions against the Indians. In the Treaty of 1868, signed at Fort Laramie, the Sioux were guaranteed the Powder River country "as long as the grass shall grow and the buffalo shall roam." But the discovery of gold in the Black Hills abruptly changed the picture, for now whites wanted the land itself, not just a road through it. They eventually got it, but not before the massacre of Custer and his men at Little Big Horn in 1876. After this, with the Indians tucked away on reservations, most of the hostilities died down and the fort lost its strategic importance. The railroad had long since supplanted the Oregon Trail as the primary route west, and for the decade of the 1880s, Fort Laramie served as a way station along the Cheyenne-to-Deadwood stage road. During this time the fort grew more genteel, with the planting of trees and completion of numerous substantial homes.

The Army Departs
By 1889, it was clear that Fort Laramie had outlived its usefulness, and it was ordered closed. The following year the 35,000 acres of military land was opened to homesteaders, with the buildings auctioned off. Because of the scarcity of wood in the area, many were stripped and hauled away to become cabins or other structures. Others remained on the site, used as homes, businesses, or barns. For the next half century the historic fort slowly deteriorated, but in 1937, the state of Wyoming purchased the site and donated it to the federal government. The following year it was declared a national monument, to be managed by the National Park Service. A lengthy and difficult restoration process managed to stabilize the ruins and restore a dozen of the historic structures, but it was not until 1964 that the fort was restored to something approaching the conditions in the 1880s.

FORT LARAMIE TODAY

Each year nearly 90,000 visitors come to historic Fort Laramie for a rewarding traipse back in time. The clear, tree-lined Laramie River still flows close by, and the spacious parade ground engenders a feeling of this fort's importance, while the bleak, windswept setting speaks of its hardships.

Visiting The Fort
Buildings and grounds of the 830-acre Fort Laramie National Historic Site are open year-round from sunrise to sunset. Entrance costs $1 pp (kids under 16 free). No camping, but there is a pleasant picnic area. For a good orientation to Fort Laramie, head to the **visitor center/park headquarters** building (tel. 837-2221), which houses excellent displays, including a scale model of the fort, an 1876 Gatling gun, and many photos. The center is open daily 8-7 mid-May through mid-Sept., and daily 8-4:30 the rest of the year. Videos about the fort and the old West are shown during the summer, and the bookstore has a large selection of Wyoming and frontier history books, along with such authentic items as lye soap and hardtack. Ask here about interpretive talks and tours, as well as the dramatic firings of historic weapons such as the mountain howitzer and long arms. (The howitzer was once used to drive away Indian attacks.)

The **living history** program helps bring Fort Laramie to life each summer, with employees dressed in a variety of period costumes. They will be happy to explain their roles at the fort. Buy a root beer or apple cider at the enlisted men's bar and taste fresh bread in the bakery. If you're in the area in early July, be sure to drop by Fort Laramie for an **Old-Fashioned Fourth of July Celebration** with all sorts of festivities, including a traveling medicine show and fiddlers. Many locals join in by dressing up in period clothing and taking part in the activities, which range from cannon salutes to fashion shows. In late August Fort Laramie is host to **Native American Heritage Days**, a unique chance to attend programs about the first inhabitants of this land and to purchase crafts or traditional foods.

Historical Buildings

By the time it was abandoned in 1890, Fort Laramie had approached the size of a small town, with 60 buildings of all types scattered around the grounds. The remains of 21 of these old buildings are still visible, some simply lime-grout concrete ruins, maintained in a state of arrested decay. A dozen have been completely restored and refurbished, with authentic period pieces behind Plexiglas doors. The Park Service has an informative Historic Buildings Guide for 20 cents, available at the visitor center. See it for descriptions of the various buildings. Several of these are particularly noteworthy: the cavalry barracks, Old Bedlam, the bakery, and the guardhouse.

Most of the men who soldiered out of Fort Laramie lived under crowded conditions with little privacy. Sometimes this meant living in tents for long periods. The **cavalry barracks** (on your left as you enter the fort) were not much of an improvement. Walk up to the restored second floor to find row upon row of cots, where an entire company of 60 men slept. Then try to imagine all the snoring and the smelly feet after being out on duty for weeks at a time! Baths were taken (in theory) every Saturday night in a half barrel.

The oldest and most prominent building at Fort Laramie is **Old Bedlam**, an attractive clapboard structure that dominates the west end of the parade grounds. Built in 1849, it was the center of life at the fort. Old Bedlam served a variety of roles when the military was here, initially as post headquarters, but later as a hotel of sorts for bachelor officers and as housing for married officers and their families. The name apparently comes from the bedlam that existed with so many folks jammed together, particularly after payday, when parties raged. Old Bedlam is now refurnished to represent two different periods. Upstairs are displays representing the living quarters of Lt. Colonel William O. Collins, while the bachelor officer's quarters are downstairs.

Behind the attractive **Captain's Quarters** on the south end of the parade ground is a model of adobe-walled Fort John, which stood on this spot in 1841. (The "bat house" near here was recently built in an attempt to keep bats from roosting in the Captain's Quarters.) A footpath leads to the Laramie River where a **fur trader's camp** has been set up. The old stone **guardhouse** on the east side of the fort could house up to 40 prisoners, ranging from soldiers who had violated minor conduct rules to those charged with murder. The basement jail had no furniture, toilet, or light, and no heat even in the dead of winter. Stop by the historic **bakery**—one of four built here at different times—for a taste of bread. One loaf of bread, along with greasy salt pork, beans, rice, and rotgut coffee, were the typical daily allotment for soldiers. Fresh vegetables were often unavailable for months at a time, and scurvy was a constant threat. In the field, the rations were even worse, generally consisting of salt pork, beans, and wormy hardtack.

One of the less-visited sights in the area is **Old Bedlam ruts,** two miles northwest of Fort Laramie. A gravel road leads to the location; get a map from park headquarters. The ruts (marked by posts) climb up into the gentle hills west of the old fort, offering a marvelous panorama of a landscape that has not changed much in the last century. From here, it's easy to imagine emigrants looking back on the fort, their last touch with civilization for hundreds of miles. Laramie Peak is prominent to the west. Nearby is the grave of Mary Homsley, one of the thousands who died along the difficult trek west. The ruts can be traced all the way to Guernsey, where they grow even deeper. A similar series of ruts extends eastward from the fort. If you're heading to Wheatland from the fort, try the "back way" via Grayrocks Reservoir. The road is rough for the first eight miles or so, but it is paved beyond here and offers an enjoyable taste of the rugged countryside around the reservoir. Signs point the way to Wheatland.

Fort Laramie (The Town)

The town of Fort Laramie (pop. 240) is three miles north of the historic fort and across the North Platte River. Wyoming's oldest post office is here, begun in the 1880s when the Army was occupying the nearby fort. A mile south of town is an **iron bridge** built in 1875. It doesn't look like much—and has been superseded for more than 30 years by a concrete span just upriver—but is of historic importance. Funded by a $15,000 congressional appropriation, the bridge ensured the establishment of the Cheyenne-

Deadwood Stage and Express through here. It remained the major route north for many years thereafter. A highway monument east of town along US 26 notes the site of the **Grattan Massacre** (see above).

Margaret's Cafe serves home-style meals, or if you're in a hurry head to **Chuckwagon Drive-In** for fast food. **Rustic Inn**, tel. 837-2960, has motel rooms. Pitch tents for free at the town park, just across the railroad tracks on the south side of town, or stay at the friendly **Bennett Court Campground**, tel. 837-2270, where tent sites cost $8 and RV sites $9. Showers for noncampers are just $1; open year-round. **Chuckwagon Campground**, tel. 837-2828, is open April-Nov. only and charges $9 for RVs or tents. A small log-cabin **visitor center** on the main street is staffed daily during the summer months.

TORRINGTON

Torrington (pop. 5,700) is a quiet farming town located just eight miles from the Nebraska border. It is the county seat for Wyoming's most important agricultural county, Goshen (alias "The Land of Goshen"). Lots of sugar beets, alfalfa, oats, dry beans, corn, and hay are grown here. The tree-lined North Platte River drifts lazily through town. Torrington's economy is relatively stable, with a Holly Sugar factory (the biggest local employer) on the edge of town and many productive farms in the surrounding countryside. Two long waterways—Fort Laramie Canal and the Interstate Canal—provide irrigation water to much of this farmland. Trains filled with coal from Campbell and Weston counties constantly rumble through toward the south and east; a stench from the sugar refinery hangs in the air; and the livestock auction is the big daily event. A walk along Main Street is a trek through the American heartland. But bring your earplugs along; loudspeakers on Torrington's downtown street corners blare muzak!

History
Although several hundred thousand emigrants passed through Goshen County on their way to Oregon, California, or Utah, none bothered to stop. The area was not settled until cattlemen came in the 1880s, followed by homesteaders around the turn of the century, including many from Russia and Germany. Many of the "soddies" and wooden shacks these emigrants built still stand in the fields around the county. Named for Torrington, Connecticut, the town was incorporated in 1907 as a ranching and farming center. Completion of the Interstate Canal in 1915 and the Fort Laramie Canal in 1924 brought North Platte River water, making it possible to grow a wide variety of crops. The Burlington Railroad arrived from the east in 1900, but it was not until 1926 that the Union Pacific built a line connecting Torrington with Pine Bluffs to the south. That year proved a pivotal one, for it brought a new train depot and the Holly Sugar Company plant. The town has grown slowly over the years and, except for a brief flirtation with oil and gas in the 1970s, has remained true to its farming and ranching roots.

Homestead Museum
Located right at the crossroads of the Oregon Trail, the Cheyenne-to-Deadwood stage route, the Mormon Trail, and the Texas Cattle Trail, the Homestead Museum seems to sit atop history. It is housed in the old brick-and-masonry Union Pacific depot just south of town, built in 1926. The last train stopped at the depot in 1964. The museum, tel. 532-5612, is open Sun. 1-4 and Mon.-Sat. 10-5 during the summer, and Mon.-Fri. 10-4 in winter. Although it contains a substantial paleo-Indian collection, the museum focuses on the thousands of turn-of-the-century homesteaders who flocked to eastern Wyoming. The Yoder Ranch collection (artifacts from 1881 on) is particularly noteworthy. Other displays include items from the 4A Ranch and the Bordeau Trading Post near Fort Laramie, a homemade baseball bat from 1920, plus a marvelous collection of old black-and-white photos. Sit down and spend some time looking through these pictures; they will quickly transport you back to a

TODD CLARK

TORRINGTON

(Map labels:)
HOSPITAL
EASTERN WYOMING COLLEGE
GARRETT ST.
WESTERN MOTEL
MAVERICK MOTEL
26
85
ROUSE ST.
WEST VALLEY RD.
GOSHEN COUNTY FAIRGROUNDS
29th AVE.
28th AVE.
27th AVE.
26th AVE.
SHOEMAKER ST.
JIRDON PARK / SWIMMING POOL
GRASS ROOTS TRAIL
E ST. D ST. C ST. B ST. A ST.
MAIN ST.
25th AVE.
24th AVE.
23rd AVE.
22nd AVE.
TO FT. LARAMIE & GUERNSEY
TORRINGTON LIVESTOCK COMMISSION CO.
CHAMBER OF COMMERCE
POST OFFICE
CITY HALL
LIBRARY
21st AVE.
AIRPORT RD.
BRONCO BAR
THE BAKE HAUS
20th AVE.
19th AVE.
18th AVE.
17th AVE.
16th AVE.
15th AVE.
SUPER 8 MOTEL
JACK & JILL FOOD STORE
KING'S INN
ST. JOSEPH CHILDREN'S HOME
OREGON TRAIL LODGE
GOLF COURSE RD.
GOLF COURSE
PIONEER PARK (CAMPING)
14th AVE.
11th AVE.
BLUE LANTERN MOTEL
TRIPLE M BIKE SHOP
KELLY'S SUPER MARKET
TRAVELERS COURT
IDEAL GROCERY
HOLLY SUGAR FACTORY
NORTH PLATTE RIVER
1st AVE.
2nd AVE.
SOUTH MAIN ST.
HOMESTEAD MUSEUM
BURLINGTON NORTHERN RAILROAD
EAST VALLEY RD.
26
TO SCOTTSBLUFF, NEBRASKA
0   0.25 mi
0   0.25 km
UNION PACIFIC RAILROAD
TO CHEYENNE
4th AVE.
5th AVE.
85

© MOON PUBLICATIONS, INC.

simple era when pioneers scratched out a hard-scrabble life on the mixed-grass prairie in wooden or sod shacks. Once you're through these, check out the box of freebees: pieces of old stone knives and scrapers from a nearby archaeological dig. The KKK robe displayed in the museum comes from the 1920s when a vehement anti-Catholic spirit dominated rural America. Outside are an old homestead cabin, a windmill, and a caboose housing historic railroad photos and memorabilia.

Other Sights
Over 120,000 cattle are raised in Goshen County each year—more than in any other Wyoming county—so it is logical that Torrington should also be at the center of the livestock trade. Each year more than a quarter-million cattle are marketed at Torrington's two livestock sales barns. These are fascinating places to visit, offering an authentic taste of ranching life. **Torrington Livestock Market**, on US 26 at W. E St., tel. 532-3333, has auctions beginning at 10 a.m. every Fri., with additional Wednesday load lot auctions in the fall. **Stockman Livestock Auction**, tel. 532-7079, is two miles south of Torrington on US 85, then a half-mile west on State 154. Here you'll find cattle sales every Thurs. at 10 a.m. Two-hour tours of nearby cattle ranches are available through a local women's group,

the **Goshen County CowBelles**. Advance arrangements are necessary; call 837-2510. For a nice walk, saunter along the **Grassroots Trail**, built atop an old irrigation canal that slices along the northern edge of Torrington.

STARVING TO DEATH ON A GOVERNMENT CLAIM

My name is Frank Taylor, a bachelor I am,
I'm keeping old batch on an elegant plan,
You'll find me out West in the county of Lane
A-starving to death on a Government claim.

Hurrah for Lane County, the land of the free,
The home of the bedbug, grasshopper and flea,
I'll sing of its praises and boast of its fame
A-starving to death on a Government claim.

My clothes they are ragged, my language is rough,
My bread is case-hardened and solid and tough,
But I have a good time and live at my ease
On common sop-sorghum and old bacon grease.

How happy am I on my Govenment claim,
I've nothing to lose and I've nothing to gain,
I've nothing to eat and I've nothing to wear,
And nothing from nothing is honest and fair.

Oh, come to Lane County, there's room for you all,
Where the wind never stops and the rains never fall,
Oh, join in the chorus and sing of her fame,
A-starving to death on a Government claim.

Oh, don't be downhearted, you poor hungry men,
We're all just as free as the pigs in the pen,
Just stick to your homestead and fight with your fleas,
And pray to your Maker to send some more breeze.

Now all you poor sinners, I hope you will stay
And chow on your hardtack till you're toothless and grey,
But as for myself I don't aim to remain
And slave like a dog on no Government claim.

Farewell to Lane County, the pride of the West
I'm going back East to the girl I love best
I'll stop in Missouri and get me a wife,
And live on corn doggers the rest of my life.

—Anonymous

Accommodations And Camping

See the chart for local motels. Note that noisy freight trains roll through Torrington at all hours of the night, so you may want to choose a lodging place as far as possible from the tracks. Or bring earplugs. Camp for free in **Pioneer Park** along the North Platte River on the edge of town. Open year-round, but during the winter you'll need to get water elsewhere. **Travelers Court**, 750 S. Main, tel. 532-5517, has shady riverside tent sites for $8 and RV sites for $12. Showers for noncampers cost $1. Open year-round. **Kountry Kids Kampground**, three miles east of Torrington on US 26, tel. 532-2356, charges $8 for tents and $12 for RVs. Also here are all sorts of other recreation opportunities, from go-carts and miniature golf to cookouts and canoe float trips down the North Platte River. Popular with families.

Food

For reasonable breakfasts (try the buttermilk hotcakes) and fresh baked goods, head to **The Bake Haus**, 1915 Main St., tel. 532-2982. Lots of locals hang out here in the morning. The Friday and Saturday night prime rib is another favorite here. Also popular for breakfast is **Daylight Donuts**, 2106 Main St., tel. 532-2888. **Jimar's Chinese Cuisine**, 1932 Main, serves up a good lunch buffet for a little over $5, or try the local **Subway** at 1934 W. A for lunch. **Jose Paizano's**, 1918 Main St., tel. 532-4822, cooks up Mexican or Italian dishes (including pizzas), and **Kings Inn**, 1555 S. Main St., tel. 532-4011, has prime-rib specials on Friday and Saturday nights. For reasonably priced steaks and seafood, head to **Little Moon Lake Supper Club** on the state line, eight miles east on US 26, tel. 532-5750. Two grocers are in Torrington: **Kelly's Super Market** on S. Main, tel. 532-3113, and **Jack & Jill Food Store**, 1542 S. Main, tel. 532-3401.

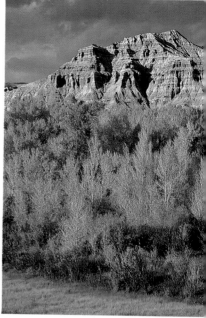

(previous page) Devils Canyon, within Bighorn Canyon National Recreation Area, drops more than a thousand f
(this page top) bales of hay, near Lander; (bottom left) Soda Mountain; (bottom right) badlands, near Dubois
(photos by Don Pitcher)

TORRINGTON ACCOMMODATIONS

NAME	ADDRESS	PHONE	RATES	FEATURES
Blue Lantern Motel	1402 S. Main St.	532-9986	$18 s, $21 d	kitchenettes
Oregon Trail Lodge	US 26 & F St.	532-2101	$22+ s, $24+ d	
Maverick Motel	1.5 miles W on US 26-85	532-4064	$27 s $29 d	
Western Motel	1.5 miles W on US 26-85	532-2104	$32 s $34 d	
Super 8 Motel	1548 S. Main St.	532-7118 (800) 800-8000	$34 s, $45 d	
King's Inn (Best Western)	1555 S. Main St.	532-4011 (800) 528-1234	$40 s, $43 d	pool

Entertainment And Events

Broncho Bar, 1924 Main St., tel. 532-4285, has live country music on weekends. Many locals also head over to the **Stateline Oasis**, tel. 532-4990, next to the Nebraska line, for the chance to dance to rock or C&W tunes. The biggest annual event in Torrington is the Goshen County Fair, held the second full week in August with everything from a parade to pig wrestling. It's a good place to check out all the 4-H hogs and sheep on display.

Information And Services

The **Torrington Chamber of Commerce** office, 350 W. 21st Ave., tel. 532-3879, is open Mon.-Fri. 8-5. The **public library**, 2001 E. A St., tel. 532-3411, is open Mon.-Sat. 10-5 in winter with reduced Sat. hours (10-noon) in summer. **The Christmas Store**, 119 E. 19th Ave., tel. 532-7433, has some used books for sale. **Eastern Wyoming College**, 3200 W. C St., tel. 532-7111, is one of the oldest junior colleges in the state, first established in 1948 as an extension of the University of Wyoming (but now independent). The hilltop campus has 1,800 full- and part-time students studying in nearly 60 vocational and academic fields. Torrington has an outdoor **swimming pool** (tel. 532-7798) in Jirdon Park that is open summers only. Kids will love the 180-foot water slide. Entrance costs $2, or $1.50 for children. There is also an 18-hole municipal **golf course** north of town, tel. 532-2418. **Denver Express**, tel. 532-7151 or (800) 658-3231, has daily van runs to Denver. **Triple M Bike Shop**, 1112 S. Main St., tel. 532-

7833, rents bikes ($5/day), while cars can be rented from **Platte Valley Motor Co.**, 510 W. Valley Rd., tel. 532-2114.

TORRINGTON AREA

The town symbol for Torrington is the ring-necked pheasant, a fitting one in this farming country. **Downar Bird Farm**, 17 miles south on US 85, raises some 7,000 pheasants each year. It is run by the Wyoming Game and Fish Department, which releases the birds each fall for area hunters. This is basically a release-and-shoot operation, since the birds are let go in unfamiliar territory just in time for hunting season. The farm is an interesting place to visit, with 27 different pheasant breeds. (By the way, the ring-necked pheasant so common in the Midwest is a native of China.)

The tiny town of **Veteran** (pop. 20)—basically a post office and general store located 15 miles southwest of Torrington—was established by Iowa veterans of WW I. During WW II, a prisoner-of-war camp was established here. The little farming village of **LaGrange** (pop. 220) is 35 miles south of Torrington. Just to the north is 66 Mountain, so called because it supposedly has the number hidden in its profile. Stop by in August for the **Mini Fair & Rodeo**.

Heading North

Ten miles northwest of Torrington is the farming crossroads called **Lingle** (pop. 500). Here you'll find two fine places to eat. **Lira's**, tel. 837-2826, offers authentic Mexican food that attracts folks from many miles around. Also here is **Stagecoach Inn**, tel. 837-2614, with all-you-can-eat dinner specials on Thursday and Friday evenings and the largest salad bar in the area. Lingle's **Harvest Festival** takes place each August. North of Lingle on US 85, the irrigated pastures and green fields give way to endless prairies. This is a land of sandy hillocks carpeted with short grasses, similar to the sandhill country of western Nebraska that lies just a dozen miles eastward.

Halfway between Lingle and Lusk, the road passes the almost-ghost town of **Jay Em** (pop. 15), named for the cattle brand of rancher Jim Moore. Just to the north lies his old Jay Em Ranch. A few people still live in the old wooden houses of Jay Em, and the post office becomes a meeting place each morning, but the town is otherwise deserted. It's a peaceful spot to stop and walk along narrow Rawhide Creek among the cottonwood trees and tall grass. The rustic old buildings (the town is a National Historic District) are a photographer's treat. Continuing north to Lusk, the country again opens into grassland, windmills, and cattle, with a few tree-topped hills and small rocky buttes.

LUSK

Lusk (pop. 1,500) is the county seat of Wyoming's least-populated county. Just 3,200 people live in rural Niobrara County—an average of almost 524 acres per person! It's remote grassland country here, with long, straight highways heading out in the compass directions. The oil industry that once was so prominent here has faded considerably in recent years, but ranching provides a relatively stable, albeit limited, economic base. The town itself has a quiet, Midwestern feel, with tree-lined streets and attractive older homes.

History

The first settlers in this part of Wyoming were miners in search of copper, silver, and gold. They built a small settlement around the Silver Cliff Mine but moved a mile east when the Fremont, Elkhorn, and Missouri Valley Railroad arrived in 1886. Lusk was named for Frank Lusk, a local rancher who donated land for the new townsite. In 1917, oil was discovered along Lance Creek, 20 miles north of here, and almost overnight Lusk became a boomtown, reaching more than 10,000 residents during the peak years of oil production. Pipelines were built to the 200 producing wells, and a refinery was added in Lusk. By the 1940s, Lance Creek had become Wyoming's largest oil field. More recently, oil production has declined, and the old standby of ranching has regained prominence. In 1984, the town succeeded in getting a women's correctional center built in Lusk. This is now the second-largest employer in the county (after the local school district).

Lusk has seen its share of lust over the years. The Yellow Hotel brothel occupied a place of local importance until the 1970s; rumor has it that the madam, Del Burke, was allowed to keep it open because she owned most of Lusk's water bonds! Ten miles southwest of Lusk is a marker to **Mother Featherlegs** (so named because she often rode horseback with her red pantaloons blowing in the wind). A well-known madam, she was murdered in 1879, apparently for money. Some claim that a fortune in gold she had buried nearby is still waiting to be claimed. A marker 10 miles southwest of Lusk notes the site of her old place of entertainment and is said to be the nation's only historical marker commemorating a prostitute. In 1990, Lusk locals swept into a Deadwood saloon and recovered her famous pantaloons, which had been stolen from the historic site in 1964.

Sights

Lusk has one of the nicer historic collections in the state, the aptly named **Stagecoach Museum,** 342 S. Main. It's open daily 10-5 and 7-9 p.m. in July and Aug., and Mon.-Fri. 1-5 during May, June, Sept., and October. Climb up the steep, narrow stairs to find the reason for its name, an old coach built by Abbott & Downing of Concord, New Hampshire, in the 1860s. Used for many years on the famed Cheyenne and Black Hills Stage and Express Line, the stage-

LUSK ACCOMMODATIONS

NAME	ADDRESS	PHONE	RATES	FEATURES
Hospitality House Motor Hotel	201 S. Main	334-2120	$20 s, $23 d	upstairs rooms
Townhouse Motel	565 S. Main	334-2376	$24+ s or d	AAA approved
Rawhide Motel	805 S. Main	334-2440	$26+ s or d	
Pioneer Court (Best Western)	731 S. Main	334-2640 (800) 528-1234	$30+ s, $40+ d	AAA approved, pool
Covered Wagon Motel	730 S. Main	334-2836 (800) 341-8000	$38 s or $46 d	AAA approved, pool, jacuzzi, sauna, exercise room
Trail Motel	305 W. Eighth	334-2530 (800) 333-5875	$43+ s or d	AAA approved, pool

coach is one of only two in existence; its sister resides in the Smithsonian Institution. The museum also houses a treasure chest broken open during the Canyon Springs Stage robbery of 1879. (It contained gold bullion from the Black Hills destined for Cheyenne.) Other items in the Lusk museum are more standard fare—an old buggy, a sulky, a dray wagon, and covered wagons, along with various Indian artifacts and arrowheads. Notice the collection of photos from Niobrara County's many old one-room schoolhouses, and above the staircase, a 31-star U.S. flag from 1876. Try not to snicker at the kitschy doll collection dressed up as the wives of various presidents. Out back is an old one-room schoolhouse. The city park at 14th and Linn contains a **homestead cabin** that was built in the 1880s and originally located at Running Water Stage Station. Another site of minor historical interest is on the east side of town along the railroad tracks. Here you'll find a **redwood water tank** built in 1886 to supply water for steam engines of the Chicago and Northwestern Railroad. It is one of only six still standing in the nation.

Accommodations And Camping

See the chart for a list of local motels. **Wyoming Whale Ranch** six miles east of Lusk, tel. 334-3598, is a fun lodging option. Noal Larson, a third-generation rancher, also offers three-day wagon camping tours of historic sites along the Cheyenne-Deadwood Stage Route. Recommended. **BJ's Campground,** 902 S. Maple St., tel. 334-2462, has clean (but unshaded) campsites at $10 for tents and $14 for RVs. Showers for noncampers cost $3. Open year-round. **Pink Panther Campground,** two miles west of Lusk on US 18-20, tel. 334-2827, may or may not be open but isn't particularly attractive anyway.

Food

The best breakfasts in town are at **Coffee Cup Cafe,** 206 S. Main, tel. 334-3303. **The Diner,** 234 S. Main, tel. 334-3606, offers basic greasy-spoon fare: pancakes for breakfast and decent Friday-night tacos. **Fireside Inn,** 904 S. Main, tel. 334-3477, is a bit expensive but has very good family-style meals. The Sunday brunch is a bargain, and the soup and salad bar offers an inexpensive way to pig out. **Cindy's Cafe,** on the south end of town, tel. 334-3085, serves meals 24 hours a day. Live C&W music at the downtown **Cowboy Bar,** 904 S. Main, tel. 334-3634. Lusk has a **Safeway** store at 405 S. Main.

Information and Services

The **Lusk Visitor Center,** in the caboose at Main and Griffith Blvd., tel. 334-2950 or (800) 223-5875, is open summers Mon.-Fri. 1-5. Winter hours are hit-or-miss. The chamber of commerce is located in the museum and can also provide local information. The local **library,** at 425 S. Main, tel. 334-3490, is open Mon.-Wed. and Fri. 10-6 and Thurs. 10-8. Swim at the **Lusk Plunge** on the north side of the tracks during the summer. The local country club is one of the best nine-hole golf courses in the state. The **Niobrara County Fair** comes to Lusk in early August, but the major local event is the *Legend of Rawhide.*

LEGEND OF RAWHIDE

In 1946, the people of Lusk were looking for an event to attract visitors; something, say, along the lines of Cheyenne Frontier Days, only different. A local doctor, Walter Reckling, faintly remembered a tale that had been passed down for generations—the legend of Rawhide Buttes. It was one of the enduring yarns of the Old West, an event claimed to have occurred in half a dozen different states, and there were probably a thousand different versions. In the story an emigrant wagon train headed west to the California goldfields, carrying along a young man who boasted that he would shoot the first Indian he saw. He killed an innocent Indian girl (a princess, of course) and her tribe retaliated by attacking the wagon train and forcing the young man to surrender. He was skinned alive in revenge. Nobody has ever been able to substantiate the tale, but then again, nobody has proved it didn't happen, either.

Dr. Reckling managed to stir up considerable interest for the idea in Lusk and then found a local college student, Eva Lou Bonsell, who was studying theater in Colorado. She wrote a play to be pantomimed

as a narrator described the scenes, and the *Legend of Rawhide* was off and running. The first production gained a measure of reality by being staged in the midst of a thunderstorm. The crowd of 10,000 loved it. The *Legend of Rawhide* made the covers of *Life* and *Look* magazines at various times and ran from 1946 to 1966. It was revived again in 1986. Today, the annual production is still a decidedly local affair, with a cast of 200 folks from the surrounding area. The spectacle has evolved over the years with the addition of 13 "soiled doves," Father DeSmet, and Jim Bridger, along with some 15 wagons and several dozen Indians on ponies. The skinning alive of bad guy Clyde Pickett is the gory climax. (It's also quite a trick, but I won't give away the secret.)

The *Legend of Rawhide* is put on the second weekend in July every year and begins at 8 p.m. on Fri. and Sat. nights. General admission is $5, or $3 for kids under 12, with reserved seats in the covered grandstands for $8. Other activities include afternoon parades and an art show. For more information, call 334-2950 or 334-3764. Whether or not the story is true, the **Rawhide Buttes** actually do exist; they are 10 miles south of Lusk. (Some stories give a less interesting version for the origin of the name Rawhide Buttes: that they were the site where raw buffalo hides were prepared for shipment east.) A highway marker notes the Cheyenne and Deadwood Stage station that once stood here. Two miles west of Lusk on US 18-20 is a historical marker along the Cheyenne-Deadwood Trail. The ruts are still visible for a ways here, and George Lathrop, one of the best-known stage drivers, is buried nearby.

HEADING NORTH

US 18-85 heads due north from Lusk toward Newcastle, passing through mile after mile of rolling and windy grassland with scattered rocky buttes, a few wearing top hats of ponderosa pines. For the first dozen miles the road parallels the historic Cheyenne-Deadwood Stage Route. Bottomland creeks curl through, with cottonwoods and willows on both sides. This is gorgeous big-sky country; the land seems almost an afterthought. It's about as remote a place as you'll find, with just a few ranches, windmills, and cattle for company.

Some 13 miles north of Lusk is a sign noting the old **Fort Hat Creek Stage Station,** mistakenly built (in 1876) along Sage Creek, Wyoming instead of Hat Creek, Nebraska! Easy to see how the country could start to blend together in the endless hills here. The old stage station itself is two miles east of here on a paved road and then one mile southwest on a gravel road. It is an impressive two-story log structure built in 1887 to replace the original buildings, which had burned. The small fort garrisoned 40 soldiers who rode out to protect the Cheyenne-Deadwood Stage from attack. Hat Creek was typical of other stage stations along the route. One writer of the time, Leander P. Richardson, noted: "At any of these places a traveler can purchase almost anything, from a glass of whiskey to a four-horse team, but the former article is usually the staple of demand."

Tiny **Lance Creek** (pop. 180) lies in the middle of Niobrara County and is surrounded by the Lance Creek oil fields. An oil boom peaked here during WW II, but more recently, production has declined and the community ekes out a minimal survival. The Lance Creek area is famous as the site for discoveries of horned dinosaurs (Ceratopsians) and other fossils. Beginning in the 1880s, scientists found an incredible number of fossil plants, dinosaurs, and ancient mammals, including at least 75 different species of vertebrates, many of which were previously unknown. There are no signs or facilities to mark the location. Halfway between Lusk and Newcastle is **Mule Creek Junction,** consisting of a state rest area along with a combination gas station/cafe/junk-food shop. A couple of miles north of this, US 85 crosses Cheyenne River, near the site of the aptly named **Robber's Roost Stage Station.** Here outlaws sometimes attacked the Cheyenne-Deadwood Stage when it slowed to cross the river. In an 1878 robbery attempt an outlaw was killed here by the shotgun messengers, but his partners managed to escape with the mail sacks.

MEDICINE BOW COUNTRY

West from Cheyenne, I-80 climbs a long, gentle ramp into the Laramie Mountains, reaching the highest point on its 3,000-mile trek across America, and then abruptly beginning a steep descent onto the spacious Laramie Plains. A distinctly frontier feeling envelops this land: mountains rim the valley, and as you continue west the grass is intermixed with more and more sagebrush. You are entering the real West of mountains, sage, and sky.

Medicine Bow Country consists of Albany County, with Laramie and the Laramie Plains at its center and the Laramie and Medicine Bow mountains on either side, along with Carbon County, where Rawlins is the main town and the Sierra Madre mountains dominate the southern horizon. The name Medicine Bow has a convoluted origin. The mountains in southern Wyoming were considered a sacred place, and each year Indians gathered nearby to celebrate powwows and to build bows from the cedarwood. The Indian term for "medicine" means something spiritually powerful, as symbolized by the mountains, by the cedar that made fine bows, and by the annual powwows. Whites combined the various tribal activities into "Medicine Bow" and applied the name to a river, a mountain range, a national forest, and a town.

The land is remarkably diverse in terms of both topography and vegetation. Laramie Basin contains the highest short-grass prairie in the world, some 7,200 feet above sea level. Three mountain ranges cross through this region: the Laramie Mountains, the Medicine Bow Mountains (also called the Snowy Range), and the Sierra Madre. Mountain slopes are covered with lodgepole pine, Engelmann spruce, and subalpine fir, while alpine meadows, tundra, and rock dominate the highest elevations. To the north and west of these mountain ranges, the country is a dry landscape of sage and desert.

History

For many centuries this land was filled with buffalo, elk, and deer, providing a rich home for wandering tribes of Indians. By the time whites arrived in large numbers, the area was claimed and fought over by many tribes, including Oglala Sioux, Northern Arapaho, Eastern Shoshone, Northern Cheyenne, and White River Utes. Al-

MEDICINE BOW COUNTRY

though this part of Wyoming was long trapped by mountain men, it remained off the beaten path for many years, with emigrants preferring the Oregon Trail through central Wyoming. This began to change in 1862 when the Overland Trail was opened across southern Wyoming. Ben Holladay's stage traversed the route, as did many thousands of emigrants who found it shorter and generally safer from Indian attack. As with the rest of southern Wyoming, the coming of the Union Pacific Railroad transformed this from a place to get through into a place to live. The railroad provided the region's lifeblood for many years. Later, Laramie gained the University of Wyoming and Rawlins the state penitentiary.

Economy

The economy of the Medicine Bow region is much like that of the rest of Wyoming—heavily dependent upon grazing and energy. More than 170,000 cattle and 75,000 sheep graze over this land of sage and grass, while mines near Hanna produce large amounts of low-sulfur coal. Wells in Carbon County pump more than 37 million cubic feet of natural gas each year. Other important pieces of the regional economy are the University of Wyoming in Laramie and tourism, particularly in the Snowy Range and Upper North Platte River Valley. Transportation has long been a vital factor in the region. Ben Holladay's stage traversed the desolate plains on the Overland Trail, followed by the Union Pacific Railroad, and eventually by I-80, the primary artery across America for truckers and travelers. The remote stretch of I-80 between Laramie and Elk Mountain is commonly called the "Snow Chi Minh Trail," a joking reference to the ceaseless blowing snow that sometimes shuts down traffic for days at a time during the winter. Gale-force winds have even been known to blow semis over!

LARAMIE

The countryside around Laramie (pop. 27,000) differs little from much of Wyoming—arid plains abruptly broken by rugged mountain ranges—but the town itself offers a real change of pace. True, Laramie does have rodeos, restaurants with names like the Cavalryman, and great C&W tunes at the ever-popular Cowboy Saloon, but it also seems to violate one's expectations of a Wyoming town. It has to be the only place in the state where the Chuckwagon Restaurant would feature cappuccino! Take a stroll along downtown's Ivinson Ave. and you'll discover The Chocolate Cellar, with fancy chocolates from all over, and Whole Earth Grainery, selling bulk organic foods in a hippie decor. Nearby are vegetarian restaurants and bars that attract reggae or blues bands. With the recent addition of the beautiful new American Heritage Center and the development of Wyoming Territorial Park, Laramie will certainly draw an increasing number of visitors.

Laramie is one of my favorite cities in Wyoming, a place that has a sense of intelligence without being stultified, where culture mixes with fun and games. Tourist brochures call Laramie "Gem City of the Plains." It has the laid-back college town feel of a Chico or Fort Collins. The students add a playful, educated atmosphere—there are bikes on the streets, heady conversations over beers, and lots to do, from rock concerts to theatrical productions. Laramie has both crowded fast-food outlets and sophisticated restaurants offering more substantial fare. It is probably the only place in the state (other than Jackson) where a restaurant would have the temerity to put descriptions of wines on the menu: "An excellent varietal aroma of apples and butter. It has a full rich flavor and a nicely balanced, clean finish. . . ."

The Union Pacific Railroad splits Laramie into two distinct parts. The campus, the more stately older homes, and nearly all the city lie on the east side, while less pretentious quarters lie on "the other side of the tracks." Long freight trains roll through every few minutes at all hours of the day and night, piled high with double-deck containerized freight boxes destined for Chicago, Denver, or Las Vegas.

Located close to the Medicine Bow Mountains (hiking and skiing), Vedauwoo Rocks (rock climbing), Lake Hattie (windsurfing), and the Colorado Rockies (John Denver?), Laramie is a haven for those who love the outdoors. The only problem is the midwinter wind that makes life in this part of the state difficult. Temperatures may be relatively mild—in the low 20s—but add in a 30-mph wind and it feels like 20 below zero. Bitter gale-force winds can howl through for days on end in this open country.

HISTORY

The city of Laramie—along with all sorts of other places in eastern Wyoming—has the name of a French-Canadian trapper who was killed by Arapaho Indians in the mountains now named in his honor. Nearly everything else about the man is open to question. Jacques LaRamee (or was it Joseph De la Ramie?) was killed in 1820 (or 1821) by Arapahos (or another tribe) who stuffed his body under the ice in a beaver pond (or left his body in his cabin). Be that as it may, in death he attained a far more lasting legacy than in anything he did while alive.

Fort Sanders

The first permanent settlement in the Laramie area was Fort Sanders (originally known as Fort John Buford), built in 1866. Located approximately two miles south of present-day Laramie, it served to protect emigrants and stagecoaches along the Overland Trail and later to protect Union Pacific Railroad construction workers. At its peak, Fort Sanders housed nearly 600 soldiers. As with other posts on the frontier, desertions were rampant; 41 men went AWOL in a single month, taking with them whatever supplies they could grab. As the threat from Indian attacks lessened over the years, so did the value of Fort Sanders. It was abandoned in 1882.

The Union Pacific Arrives

Laramie City (as it was first called) was named and established by Gen. Grenville Dodge, the man in charge of planning the Union Pacific's route westward. The location was chosen because of a major spring that still produces millions of gallons of water, and because ties could be cut in the mountains to the west and brought down the Laramie River. The proximity of Fort Sanders also influenced the location. By the time the first train rolled into Laramie City on May 10, 1868, many "sooners" had already set up business in tents. The first passengers were met with 23 saloons, one hotel, and no churches. Within three months, Laramie had 5,000 people.

Many of the earliest to arrive were the usual end-of-the-track types: hoodlums, gamblers, prostitutes, and others out to make a fast buck. When the tracks headed on westward, the riffraff stayed behind, kept busy by the soldiers. Within a short time, a saloon owner named Asa Moore gained the support of various gambling houses, brothels, and other bars to create a rump town government with him as mayor. The man they appointed town marshall had recently left Cheyenne after being acquitted on a murder charge, and his assistant was caught stealing mules. Laramie quickly became one of the wildest towns on the frontier, with murders al-

© MOON PUBLICATIONS, INC.

most daily. Men who were arrested often faced a trial in a back room of Asa Moore's saloon, where his men robbed and then killed them, burying their bodies out on the plains. Stories tell of up to 10 men disappearing in a single night.

Seeing that the law was in the hands of criminals, the more respectable citizens decided to put an end to the mayhem. More than 500 men joined a vigilance committee that swept into the saloons, brothels, dance halls, and casinos on the night of Oct. 18, 1868. Three men died in gun battles (including a musician and a vigilante) and dozens of others were wounded. Another three were hanged by vigilantes, including the mayor, Asa Moore. The next day, outlaw Big Steve Young met the same fate, and more than a hundred crooks were piled into railroad cars and sent west. These actions calmed things down rather quickly, and thereafter Laramie City became something of a model town. It is perhaps fitting that, four years later, Laramie would be awarded the territorial prison.

For many years the main reason for the existence of Laramie was the presence of the railroad and the operations it established, including a roundhouse, iron foundry, tie-treating plant, machine shops, and a mill for reprocessing old rails. Gold discoveries in the Snowy Range to the west helped Laramie's economy grow, but the railroad remained the largest employer in Laramie until the 1950s, when it was supplanted by the university.

Women's Suffrage

Laramie was the site of two of the most notable events in the history of women's rights. On September 6, 1870, Louisa Gardner Swain ("Grandma Swain") became the first woman in the nation to vote in an open and public election. A few months before this, a judge in Laramie established the world's first jury with women members. (Reporters noted that the female jurors hid behind heavy veils and held crying babies on their laps.) The women brought about a change in the jury system: breaks for boozing and gambling were ended, while smoking and chewing tobacco in the jury box were halted. The women also proved more likely to

convict men of murder than their male peers, who regarded killing humans a less serious crime than rustling cattle. A stone monument near First and Garfield streets marks the location where the first all-woman jury met.

The University

In 1886, Laramie received a gift from the state legislature that would eventually transform it from a cow town into a college town. Under the leadership of Col. Stephen W. Downey ("Father of the University"), the Legislature voted to establish the new University of Wyoming. It was part of a deal that carved up Wyoming: Cheyenne became the capital city, while Rawlins landed the prison, and Evanston the state asylum. The bill was signed into law by Gov. Francis E. Warren in 1886, four years before Wyoming achieved statehood. The school opened the following year with a single building—now

women's suffrage, from Frank Leslie's Illustrated Newspaper, 1888

BILL NYE

Laramie lays claim to one of the most popular humorists of the 19th century, Edgar "Bill" Nye (1850-1896). Born in Maine and raised in Wisconsin, Nye arrived in Laramie in 1876 and soon began writing columns for a local newspaper. His sharp wit and wry sense of humor quickly showed through the news. Local Republicans backed him in publishing his own paper, the *Laramie Boomerang*—named for a flea-bitten gray mule that kept returning no matter how hard Nye tried to get rid of him. The paper first rolled off his "lemon-squeezer" press in 1881. When the news wasn't all that interesting, Nye would embellish it: "[I] write up things that never occurred with a masterly and graphic hand. Then, if they occur, I am grateful; if not, I bow to the inevitable and smother my chagrin."

Even Nye's appointment as Laramie City postmaster (a political plum gained because of his connection with the dominant Republican party) became grist for his humor mill. He wrote the postmaster general, noting, "I look upon the appointment, myself, as a great triumph of eternal truth over error and wrong. It is one of the epoches, I may say, in the Nation's onward march toward political purity and perfection. I do not know when I have noticed any stride in the affairs of state, which so thoroughly impressed me with its wisdom. . . ." Nye only kept the position for a year.

In 1883, an attack of spinal meningitis forced him to leave high-elevation Laramie for a lower climate. By the time he departed, Nye's newspaper was in dire financial condition, but it managed to survive under new, more responsible, management. The *Boomerang* is still published today and is one of the state's few daily papers. The old livery stable where it was published is on the corner of Third and Garfield; Nye's office was on the second floor.

Bill Nye's witty *Boomerang* columns gained a national following, and by the 1890s he had become the best-paid humorist in America. Nye would eventually author 14 books of humor; *Bill Nye's History of the United States,* published in 1894, sold an incredible 500,000 copies. Unfortunately, the intense stress of being constantly on the road helped shorten his life. Nye died of a stroke when just 45 years old.

Much of Nye's humor falls flat today, and its racial stereotypes are certainly dated, but some of the short pieces still have a delightful zing, particularly when he tweaks the nose of famous people such as Oscar Wilde (whom Nye called, "Thou bilious pelican from o'er the sea"), or a competing newspaper editor—"We have nothing more to say of the editor of the Sweetwater *Gazette.* Aside from the fact that he is a squint-eyed, consumptive liar, with a breath like a buzzard and a record like a convict, we don't know anything against him . . . ." The only book of Nye's works still in print is *Bill Nye's Western Humor,* a collection of his pieces published by the University of Nebraska Press.

The following commentary on Wyoming agriculture and "reclamation" efforts is typical of Nye's tongue-in-cheek writing:

AMERICAN HERITAGE MUSEUM

I do not wish to discourage those who might wish to come to this place for the purpose of engaging in agriculture, but frankly I will state that it has its drawbacks. In the first place, the soil is quite course, and the agriculturist, before he can even begin with any prospect of success must run his farm through a stamp-mill in order to make it sufficiently mellow. This, as the reader will see, involves a large expense at the very outset. Hauling the farm to a custom mill would delay the farmer two or three hundred years in getting his crops in, thus giving the agriculturist who had a pulverized farm in Nebraska, Colorado, or Utah, a great advantage over his own, which had not yet been to the reduction works . . . .

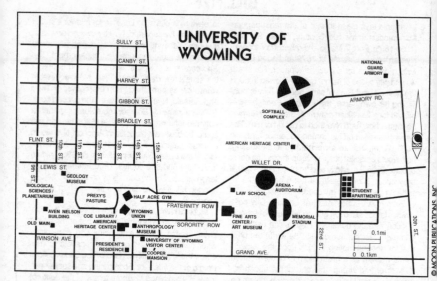

called Old Main—built at a cost of $49,000. The new program had five professors and 42 students (both men and women), who paid $7.50 each to attend. Over the years, the railroad gradually lost in importance while the university added more and more to the local economy, until it became the biggest local employer. It remains so today. Because of the university, Laramie has never really experienced the economic booms and busts common to much of Wyoming.

UNIVERSITY OF WYOMING

Wyoming is unique as the only state to have just one baccalaureate-granting institution. The University of Wyoming campus in Laramie thus gains the state's undivided financial support, much to the chagrin of the two-year colleges. The university lays claim to being the highest university campus in the nation; at 7,200 feet, it makes Denver's mile-high claim to fame look puny. Although not a major research institution, UW has respected research programs in atmospheric sciences (ozone depletion studies), aquatic toxicology, oil recovery technology, water management, agricultural research, and infrared

astronomy. Approximately 12,000 students attend the university.

The university provides a wide spectrum of degree programs, some 110 at the undergraduate level along with 125 graduate programs. It operates on a semester system, with a summer session open to visiting students. A summertime Elderhostel provides classes for folks over 60, and various noncredit classes are also offered throughout the year, covering the spectrum from ballroom dancing to LSAT preparation. For a copy of the school's *General Bulletin,* call the Admissions office at 766-5160 or (800) 342-5996, or write: University of Wyoming Admissions Office, P.O. Box 3435, Laramie, WY 82071.

Seeing The Campus
Begin your campus visit at the **University of Wyoming Visitor Information Center,** 1408 Ivinson Ave., tel. 766-4075. It's open summers Mon.-Fri. 8-4 and Sat. 8-noon; or Mon.-Fri. 9-5 and Sat. 9-1 the rest of the year. No tours of campus, but they can provide maps and complete info on the school. On rainy days this is a good place to watch videos. Right next door is the historic **Cooper Mansion,** built in 1920 in the Mission/Pueblo style and now on the National

Register of Historic Places. There is also an **information center,** tel. 766-3160, in the Wyoming Union building that is open Mon.-Fri. 8-7:30. Check the ride board here if you're looking for or offering transportation. Also stop by for a listing of campus activities. The main campus buildings center around **Prexy's Pasture,** where the school's first president grazed his personal cattle. Today Prexy's is a favorite place to relax on sunny days, and it's still legal to leave your horse here.

American Heritage Center

The newest addition to the UW campus is the $20-million American Heritage Center (open in fall 1993). The center serves dual purposes as a major research facility and as an exhibition space for art and historical pieces. Designed by famed architect Antoine Predock, this multi-leveled conical building contains expansive art galleries and a restaurant, plus thousands of manuscripts, rare books, and artifacts from Wyoming and the west. The building was designed to represent the mountains surrounding Laramie and features stunning interior spaces and a spacious outdoor sculpture court. Take in dramatic window views of the Laramie Mountains and the Snowy Range; the building is oriented so that one small section is lit by the sun during the summer solstice.

Some of the more unusual items on display are a beautifully ornate saddle presented to actor Tim McCoy by the Shoshone Indians in 1918, along with obscure Hollywood memorabilia such as the six-guns worn by Hopalong Cassidy, scripts from *Captain Kangaroo* (he really used a script?), and even Jack Benny's violin. Of far more value are the 19th-century Plains Indian prints by George Catlin, etchings and watercolors by Yellowstone painter Thomas Moran, and oil paintings by W.H. Jackson, Bill Gollings, Henry Farny, and Frederic Remington. Probably the best-known work is Alfred Jacob Miller's oil painting, *The Rendezvous Near Green River—Oregon Territory,* valued at $750,000. Miller was the only artist to ever witness a mountain men rendezvous.

The American Heritage Center, tel. 766-4114, is open Mon.-Fri. 7:30-4:30 and Sat. 11-5 during the summer, and Mon.-Fri. 8-5 the rest of the year. These hours will be expanded once the new building opens. (The AHC's collection will remain on the third and fifth floors of the Coe Library until moving to the new facility in fall 1993.)

Geology Museum

One of the more interesting campus sites is the Geological Museum, tel. 766-4218, open Mon.-Fri. 8-5 and Sat.-Sun. 10-3. Free tours are available. A life-size bronze *Tyrannosaurus rex* greets visitors at the entrance, while dinosaur bones surround the doorway. Inside the museum are fossil and mineral displays from around the state. An enormous mammoth skull found near Rawlins is one of the most impressive fossils, but the museum's centerpiece is a 75-foot-long and 15-foot-tall skeleton of an *Aptosaurus excelsus,* better known as a Brontosaurus. Excavated along Sheep Creek in Albany County, it's one of just five mounted specimens in the world. Right next door is the **Wyoming Geological Survey Building,** with tons of fun maps of all types, along with a number of good guides to the state's geology.

Art Museum

The excellent, free University Art Museum exhibits paintings, sculpture, and other works of art from its collection of 5,000 pieces. Most are by 19th- and 20th-century artists, including paintings and drawings by Thomas Hart Benton, Charles M. Russell, Paul Gauguin, Andy Warhol, Thomas Moran, and Pablo Picasso. The spacious downstairs gallery provides space for a variety of displays, while upstairs is a small gallery with student and faculty works. The museum is located in the Fine Arts Center, tel. 766-2374, and is open Tues.-Fri. 11:30-5 and Sat.-Sun. 1-5. Another place to see artwork on campus is **Gallery 234,** which exhibits student pieces. It is located in the Wyoming Union building (open Mon.-Fri. 8-5).

Other University Sights

The first campus building was **Old Main,** completed in 1887 and now housing the administrative offices. The prominent tower that once adorned the building was removed in 1915. Look for Wyoming's territorial seal over the west entrance. Head to the Anthropology Building to view the university's **Anthropology Museum,** representing a small portion of the department's extensive cultural collection. The museum (tel. 766-5310) is open Mon.-Fri. 8-5 and focuses on the Plains Indians. A mammoth skull is here, along with a display on the Vore Site buffalo jump in northeastern Wyoming, where thousands of buffalo were trapped and killed.

Located in the basement of the Science Complex near the Science Library, the **Planetarium** offers Wed. evening programs during the school year. It specializes in the history of astronomy, with a recorded tape and slide show on the solar system. In the Agriculture Addition Building is the **Entomology Museum,** which houses thousands of insect specimens. Although primarily for research, it is open to the public. Also in the same building is the **Range Herbarium,** considered one of the most complete collections of grasses in the western states. It is open Mon.-Fri. 7:30-4:30. More impressive is the **Rocky Mountain Herbarium,** on the third floor of the Aven Nelson building, tel. 766-2236, where you'll find one of the nation's largest herbarium collections. Open to the general public only by prior arrangement.

WYOMING TERRITORIAL PARK

In 1869, the territorial Legislature voted to construct a penitentiary at Laramie. (Wyoming prisoners had previously been housed in the Detroit House of Correction at a cost of $1.25 a week.) The imposing three-story stone building was dedicated to "evil doers of all classes and kinds"; fittingly enough, a bottle of bourbon was deposited in the cornerstone. It remained a prison until 1902, when the inmates were transferred to a new facility in Rawlins. After the prisoners were moved out, the building was turned over to the university for use as an experimental livestock farm, with the cells becoming cattle stalls and the prison broom factory becoming a sheep barn. In the 1980s, the university farm moved to a more modern facility elsewhere and the historic prison was officially established as Wyoming Territorial Park. Both state and local funds ($5 million worth) were used to transform the badly deteriorated buildings into one of the largest western-heritage parks in existence. Some of the stuff here gets a bit cutesified and corny— children help recapture "Butch Cassidy" on his

DOWNTOWN LARAMIE

© MOON PUBLICATIONS, INC.

daily escapes from prison (the real outlaw never escaped)—but the park does offer a unique and fascinating way to step into Wyoming's frontier past.

Prison

The cornerstone of Territorial Park is the beautifully restored prison. A wooden stockade surrounds the sandstone building and adjacent broom factory where prisoners were forced to work. Other prisoners made candles or furniture, braided leather, and made musical instruments. Pick up a self-guided tour brochure as you enter the prison. The interior has been reconstructed using the original cells and period fixtures; modern additions include excellent short videos describing the prisoners' lives. The convicts who served time here, pictured in giant photos, glare down from the walls, and tour guides take on the roles of such individuals as Butch Cassidy—inmate number 187—and a U.S. marshal. Each cell held two prisoners in a tiny six-by-eight-foot arched brick enclosure sealed with an iron door. They slept on straw mattresses. Walk inside one of the cells to get a feeling for the claustrophobic conditions. No wonder Butch Cassidy promised to "never molest the state of Wyoming again" when he was pardoned after serving 18 months here! Be sure to also stop by the ongoing archaeological dig at the site of the prison bakery, just outside the prison itself.

Horse Barn

The old horse barn has been transformed into a museum and dinner theatre. Downstairs is the **U.S. Marshals' Exhibit,** housing everything from frontier-era artifacts—including a bullet-riddled Wells Fargo cash box—to displays on the crack-cocaine busts of today. The Marshals Service is the oldest civilian law enforcement agency in the world and was responsible for managing the Wyoming Territorial Prison. Visitors will enjoy finding John Wayne, Clint Eastwood, and Ronald Reagan in the film clips that feature Hollywood's version of old-west marshals. (As a trivial aside, the five-pointed star worn by U.S. Marshals was derived from a pentacle worn by 17th-century soldiers. It was supposed to make them bullet-proof.)

Upstairs you'll find a noontime cafe that turns into a **dinner theatre** each evening as a professional cast puts on a musical revue. Pretty foolish, but the production and singing are first-rate, and the meal is well prepared. The Horse Barn Dinner Theatre runs daily (except Mon.), with Sat. and Sun. matinee productions (lower prices). The dinner theatre is also the scene of Monday evening talks by various historical speakers and folk artists.

Frontier Town

Just west of the prison lies an "end-of-the-tracks town," featuring simple wood and canvas buildings that come alive with living history characters such as Calamity Jane (played by her great-great niece) and fur trapper Jacque LaRamee. There are candlemakers, woodcarvers, a seamstress, spinners and weavers, and a blacksmith (who in "real life" is chairman of UW's language department), all turning out authentic period items. Many of these can be purchased in the various shops that make up the town. Other buildings house a printing press that cranks out "wanted" posters, saloon, photo studio, general store, livery stable, and depot (but no whore-house). Stagecoach rides are available, and the amphitheater provides entertainment of all sorts throughout the day. Future additions include a Plains Indian camp, a mountain men rendezvous site, and a cavalry outpost. During the summer, visitors can watch more living history as crews lay railroad track for the narrow-gauge steam train.

Practicalities

Wyoming Territorial Park, located west of town on Snowy Range Rd., is open daily 9-6 from Memorial Day to Labor Day. Entrance costs $9.50 for adults, $8.50 for seniors and children (free under age eight). Combination tickets for park entrance and the evening dinner theatre are $28 for adults, $26 for seniors and kids, and $11 under age eight. Frontier Town shuts down after Labor Day, but the other exhibits remain open till mid-Oct. (self-guided tours) at a reduced entrance fee: $3.50 for adults or $2.50 for seniors or kids. Dinner theatre performances continue through the end of December. A gift shop sells souvenirs and books. The entire park, including the old prison, is handicapped accessible. For more information, call 745-6161 or (800) 845-2287.

MORE LARAMIE SIGHTS

Ivinson Mansion

Although its official name is the Laramie Plains Museum, this historic site is known to most folks as the Ivinson Mansion. Located at 603 Ivinson, the home is a delightful example of the Queen Anne style of Victorian architecture. Now on the National Register of Historic Places, it was built in 1892 for a millionaire merchant turned banker and politician, Edward Ivinson. That same year, Ivinson ran unsuccessfully for governor, intending to make his palatial new home into the governor's mansion. After his death, the mansion became an Episcopalian girls' school. When the school closed, locals managed to raise more than $74,000 to buy the mansion and turn it into a museum.

The Ivinson Mansion spreads over an entire

city block, with a carriage house out back and attractively landscaped grounds. Few of the original furnishings remain, but much of the interior woodwork (including a freestanding stairway built without nails or screws) is still here. The museum has been furnished with antiques, including some elaborate hand-carved furniture built at the Wyoming Penitentiary in 1901, handmade toys (including a 160-year-old doll), a piano that arrived by covered wagon, and a number of Indian artifacts. More unusual are such items as a quilt that took 60 years to complete (listed in "Ripley's Believe It or Not!"), a seven-headed shower that looks like a medieval torture chamber, and a square Steinway grand piano. In the back carriage house, be sure to buy a couple of the amusing postcards from 1907. Also on the grounds is a one-room log schoolhouse built in 1924.

The museum, tel. 742-4448, is open Sun. 1-5 and Mon.-Sat. 9-8 June-Aug., and Mon.-Sat. 10-3 the rest of the year. Guided tours are given throughout the day, with the last one starting an hour before closing. It costs $4 for adults, $3 for seniors, $2 for students and children. During the summer, the museum has free programs (tel. 766-3031) for children every Wednesday morning.

Downtown

Laramie's downtown buildings are on the National Register of Historic Places, with many of them dating from the 19th century. Along Ivinson Ave., a major renovation turned what had been a collection of sleazy flophouses and bars into a lively, attractive, and fun section of town. The chamber of commerce office provides a city map that includes a **walking tour** of town. **St. Matthew's Cathedral,** at the corner of Third and Ivinson, is one of Wyoming's more interesting churches. The limestone church was built in 1868 and funded by banker Edward Ivinson.

Laramie has a number of small art galleries in addition to the those at the university. If you are around on the first Friday of the month, join in the evening **gallery walk** that features artists and authors. **El Cuero Del Toro,** 205 Grand Ave., tel. 721-8893, sells South American baskets, hats, and woven wall hangings, as well as other crafts from around the world. Other noteworthy galleries are **Gallery West,** 121 Ivinson Ave., tel.

742-3245, and **Artisans' Gallery,** 213 S. Second, tel. 745-3983.

Laramie Plains Civic Center

A couple of places are worth visiting at the civic center, 710 Garfield. The **Wyoming Children's Nature Center and Museum,** tel. 745-4732, on the second floor, is open Tues. 8:30 a.m.-12:30 p.m., Wed.-Fri. 1-5, and Sat. 10-4 during the summer (closed Wed. and Fri. the rest of the year), and provides kids a hands-on experience with the natural world, including a visit with Hiss the great horned owl. Admission is $1.50 for adults or $1 for children. Also on the grounds is the **East Side School**. Built in 1878, this is the oldest stone schoolhouse in Wyoming. Inside the civic center theater are six **murals**, painted in the early 1930s by noted muralist Florence E. Ware.

Farther Afield

A granite monument to **Fort Sanders** is two miles south of town on Kiowa Street. Not much remains of the fort other than the ruins of the old stone guardhouse and the powder house. One of Fort Sanders' wooden buildings was moved to LaBonte Park, at Ninth and Canby streets in Laramie, and is now used as a recreation center. **Hutton Lake National Wildlife Refuge** is six miles south of Laramie on State 230, then three miles south on County Road 37. It is a quiet, peaceful place to look for ducks, shorebirds, and migratory birds.

Wyoming/Colorado Scenic Railroad

Begun in 1901, this railroad was intended to serve the mining area of Gold Hill, due west of Centennial. By the time the railroad reached the mountains, however, the gold could be transported in a teaspoon (the train was often beseiged by bandits), so a new plan was hatched, to head south to the lumber mills, cattle ranches, and coal mines of Colorado. The Laramie, Hahn's Peak and Pacific Railway as it was called, operated until 1914 when it was sold to new owners. (The Pacific part of the name came from pretensions of eventually reaching the West Coast, even though the rails never made it beyond northern Colorado.) Because of constant problems with deep snow, equipment failures, and a lack of capital, the railroad was a target of local jokesters who renamed it the "Late, Hard Pressed and Panicky" or the "Lord Help Push and Pull." Over the years, the little railroad went through several incarnations in an attempt to survive, finally becoming the Wyoming/Colorado Railroad in 1987. Its primary customers over the years have been cattlemen and miners in Colorado, but in recent years the excursion trains have become a favorite of visitors.

This unique and very popular train provides day-long excursions between Laramie and Fox Park, 108 miles to the southwest. The train runs mid-April through Nov., with daily service in July and August. Call 742-9162 to make reservations (required). Fares are $26 for adults or $20 for children ages 5-12 (free for younger kids). First-class fare ($38) entitles you to the private parlor car, plus free hors d'oeuvres and champagne. Lunch is included in all fares. Along the way the conductor describes landmarks and the railroad's history. The tracks head west across the Laramie Plains and then climb up three complete circles (the "Albany loops") into the beautiful Snowy Range, cresting at an elevation of 9,055 feet. This is one of the highest standard-gauge railroads in North America. Recommended.

ACCOMMODATIONS

Motels
Space is generally not a problem at Laramie's motels, although you should reserve well ahead during graduation week (mid-May), Cheyenne Frontier Days (mid-July), and on football weekends. The old rule of supply and demand holds here, so rates also rise considerably at these times. One of the homiest places to stay in Laramie is **Annie Moore's Guest House.** The old Victorian house—built in 1912—is now a bed and breakfast, and has an attractive, sunlit, natural wood interior. **Vee Bar Guest Ranch** is 20 miles west on US 130, tel. 745-7036, with weekly accommodations ($840 pp and up) in summer and B&B nightly rates ($75 s or $85 d) in winter. **Two Bars Seven Ranch,** tel. 742-6072, is in the tiny town of Tie Siding, 27 miles south of Laramie on State 287, and provides dude-ranch accommodations at a working cat-

tle ranch. The "city slicker cattle drive" in June and October is a unique chance to assist in moving cattle into or out of the high country.

Camping
The closest public campground ($5) is in the scenic Pole Mountain portion of **Medicine Bow National Forest,** approximately 10 miles east of Laramie. Other public campsites are 30 miles west in the Snowy Range. See below for details on both areas. **Curt Gowdy State Park,** 22 miles east of Laramie on State 210 (Happy Jack Rd.), has campsites for $4. See above for more on this park. The local private "camping" options are pretty miserable, unless you enjoy treeless gravel lots. **Riverside Kampground,** I-80 at Curtis, tel. 721-7405, charges $7 for tents and $9 for RVs and is open year-round. Showers for noncampers run $3. **Laramie KOA,** 1171 Baker, tel. 742-6553, charges $9 for tents and $15 for RVs. Showers cost $3 for non-campers; open mid-March through mid-November. **N-H Trailer Ranch,** 1360 N. Third., tel. 742-3158, charges $11 for RV parking with hookups; open year-round.

FOOD

If you like reasonable prices, creative cooking, and a wide selection (who doesn't?), you're bound to appreciate all that Laramie has to offer in the way of dining out. You'll discover some of the best food in Wyoming here, from thick, juicy steaks to nouvelle cuisine.

American
For earthy breakfasts and hearty dinners, visit **The Overland,** 100 Ivinson Ave., tel. 721-2800, a very popular cafe with a wine list of more than 125 different varieties. **Roundhouse Restaurant,** 1560 N. Third, tel. 745-4948, features standard American fare at reasonable prices. The Sun. brunch and Fri. seafood buffet are favorites. For more traditional steaks and seafood, **The Cavalryman Supper Club,** 4425 S. Third, tel. 745-5551, is considered the best around. Also well-liked is **Cowboy Bar & Grill,** 309 S. Third, tel. 742-3141, where a fun atmosphere makes it popular with families. Good breakfasts, as well as burgers and steaks later in the day. Inexpensive cafeteria food, as well as pizza, ice cream,

LARAMIE ACCOMMODATIONS

MOTEL	ADDRESS	TELEPHONE	RATE	FEATURES
Motel 8	501 Boswell Dr.	745-4856	$22+ s, $30+ d	kitchenettes
Motel 6	621 Plaza Lane	742-2307	$22 s, $28 d	
Thunderbird Lodge	1369 N. Third St.	745-4871	$25 s, $31 d	kitchenettes
Ranger Motel	453 N. Third St.	742-6677	$27 s, $31 d	kitchenettes
Travel Inn	262 N. Third St.	745-4853	$36 s, $40 d	AAA approved, pool
University Inn	1720 Grand Ave.	721-8855 (800) 869-9466	$32 s, $35 d	kitchenettes, nice rooms
Camelot Motel (Budget Host)	523 Adams	721-8860 (800) 876-6788	$30+ s, $36+ d	AAA approved,
Annie Moore's Guest House	819 University Ave.	721-4177	$40+ s, $50+ d	historic home bed & breakfast
Gas Lite Motel (Best Western)	960 N. Third St.	742-6616 (800) 942-6610	$49+ s, $59+ d	AAA approved, pool
Laramie Inn	421 Boswell Dr.	742-3721	$38+ s, $40+ d	AAA approved, pool
Super 8 Motel	1987 Banner Rd.	745-8901 (800) 800-8000	$46 s or d	AAA approved
Sunset Inn	1104 S. Third St.	742-3741	$48+ s, $55+ d	AAA approved, jacuzzi, pool, kitchenettes
Holiday Inn	I-80 & US 287	742-6611 (800) 465-4329	$49+ s, $55+ d	AAA approved, airport shuttle, pool
Inn on Ivinson B&B	719 Ivinson Ave.	745-8939	$50 s or d	full breakfast
Foster's Country Corner Motel (Best Western)	1561 Jackson St.	742-8371 (800) 526-5145	$56+ s, $62+ d	pool, hot tub, overpriced

and deli food, can be found at the **University Cafeteria,** downstairs in the Wyoming Union building on campus. **CowBelle Cookouts** are put on by local ranches four times each summer. Just $6 brings a tour of a ranch, along with a BBQ beef dinner and entertainment. Call 745-5711 or 742-4963 for reservations.

International Eats

Several places offer Mexican food in town; best are **E¹ Conquistador,** 110 Ivinson Ave., tel. 742-2377, and **Las Mariachis,** 615 S. Second, tel. 742-4771. **Chelo's,** 357 University Ave., tel. 745-5139, is a tiny greasy spoon that locals rave over. Judge for yourself. Two places offer decent Chinese food: **Hong Kong West,** 1665 N. Third, tel. 742-8138, and **The Mandarin,** 1254 N. Third, tel. 742-8822. The latter serves up more spicy and authentic fare and has an under-$5, all-you-can-eat lunch buffet. **Grand Avenue Pizza,** 301 Grand Ave., tel. 721-2909, bakes some of the best homemade pizzas in Wyoming.

Eclectic

Jeffrey's Bistro, 123 Ivinson Ave., tel. 742-7046, is a personal favorite. The menu is on the light side and includes creative vegetarian specialities and great homemade bread served in a pleasant brick, oak, and brass atmosphere. Next door is **Jeffrey's Too,** tel. 742-0744, offering salads, sandwiches, and other healthy fast food (is this a culinary oxymoron?) to go. Each Jeffrey's is well worth a visit.

For a fine night on the town, locals head to **Cafe Jacques,** 216 Grand Ave., tel. 742-5522, where the varied menu emphasizes high quality and nouvelle cuisine. Dinner entrees start around $12, with lunches for $6 and up. Highly recommended. Next door (same management and phone) is **Third Street Bar & Grill.** Lighter fare, lower prices, and a friendly bar make this a relaxing place to munch on the best burgers in town, tip a brew (50 to choose from!), and watch a ball game.

Bakers And Grocers
Australian bakers Allison and Kim Campbell crank out delicious homemade breads and pastries at **Home Bakery,** 304 S. Second, tel. 742-2721. This building served as the second office of Bill Nye's *Boomerang* newspaper. A bakery has been on the premises since 1901. More fresh-baked goods plus espresso coffees at **Second Street Cafe,** 160 N. Second, tel. 745-3048. **The Chocolate Cellar,** 115A Ivinson Ave., tel. 742-9278, sells imported chocolates from all over the world. **Ideal Foods,** 1575 N. Fourth, tel. 742-2188, has a good deli counter and salad bar. **Whole Earth Grainery and Truck Store,** 111 Ivinson, tel. 745-4268, is a funky and friendly grocery with all sorts of organic produce, dried foods, teas, spices, and coffees. Not many places like this in Wyoming!

OTHER PRACTICALITIES

Entertainment
Plenty of night action in this vigorous, youthful town. Laramie's oldest saloon—dating to 1890—is the **Buckhorn Bar,** 114 Ivinson Ave., tel. 742-3554. Mounted heads of all types and an antique bear trap adorn the walls, while students adorn the pool table and bar stools. Notice the bullet hole in the mirror behind the bar, the result of a 1971 incident in which a man opened fire on the bartender (he missed). The Buckhorn is a popular place for TV sports, and when school is in session the back room thumps to rock or blues most weekends. Three other places for rock, pop, or blues tunes are **Ranger Lounge,** 463 N. Third Ave., tel. 745-9751, **Shooters,** 303 S. Third, tel. 746-7676, and **Fireside Bar,** 201 Custer, tel. 721-5097. Oldies fans head to **Depot Lounge** (at the Roundhouse Restaurant), 1560 N. Third, tel. 742-7149.

For hot C&W music, duded-up cowboys, and fresh-faced cowgirls, saunter on down to **The Cowboy Saloon,** 108 S. Second, tel. 721-3165. It's a spacious place with a big dance floor, two bars, and several pool tables. More country tunes at **Mulligan's,** 1115 S. Third, tel. 745-9954. **Mingles,** 3206 Grand Ave., tel. 721-2005, is a popular place to shoot pool at any of the 14 tables. **Bud's Bar,** 354 W. University Ave., tel. 745-5236, is the big hangout for sports enthusiasts. Everyone goes there before and after university football or basketball games; sort of like the "Cheers" bar (or so claims *Sports Illustrated*). Students hang out at the **Beergarden** in the basement of the Wyoming Union building, which has live music during the school year.

Events
Each year, the university puts on a **summer theater** with lighthearted productions at the Laramie Plains Civic Center, 710 Garfield. Call 742-6641 for details. During June and July, **band concerts** are held at the Washington Park Bandshell on Wednesday evenings. A **Mountain Man Rendezvous** is held at the Territorial Park on the Fourth of July and features some 50 costumed traders and trappers. **Laramie Jubilee Days** rolls around in mid-July, with rodeos, parades, fireworks, barbecues, a free pancake breakfast, a street dance, melodramas, square dancing, a quarterhorse show, and other activities to celebrate Wyoming's statehood. Call (800) 922-9461 to order rodeo tickets.

During June, July, and August, **Laramie River Rodeo,** tel. 721-4866, provides down-home shows most Thurs. and Fri. evenings at the fairgrounds. Events include most of the standards, plus a kid's calf scramble and lady's ribbon roping in which the audience gets to participate. Get there early for the preshow to learn more about rodeos. The annual **Ranch Tour** includes a visit to four local ranches in mid-July. Contact the chamber of commerce for specifics. Another midsummer event is **Galley on the Green,** a crafts fair featuring more than 100 regional artisans. The ever-popular **Albany County Fair** is held in early August.

Sports

The biggest attraction in Laramie comes each fall with the arrival of football season. Half the state seems to turn out to join in the festivities at War Memorial Stadium, with tailgate parties, rooting sections, and rock-'em-sock-'em helmeted soldiers battling it out against other citadels of higher learning. Up to 30,000 fans crowd the stadium Saturday afternoons to cheer on the Wyoming Cowboys (better known as the "Pokes," as in "Cowpokes"). The football team has a mixed record over the years—a Cody rodeo announcer once joked that Nebraska and Wyoming were uniting so that Nebraska could share Yellowstone, while Wyoming would have a real football team! Needless to say, the crowd did not appreciate the humor. The university also competes in a number of other sports, with men's basketball being a primary draw. The athletic facilities are among the finest in the nation and include a modern 15,000-seat arena-auditorium for basketball games, concerts, and other events. For tickets, call 766-4850 or (800) 442-8322.

Recreation

The public **swimming pool** at 11th and Reynolds, tel. 721-4426, charges $1.25. Square dancers should check out the three-times-a-month dances in Laramie at **Quadra Dangle Square Dance Club,** 3905 Grays Gable Rd., tel. 742-6008. **Jacoby Park Golf Course** on N. 30th, tel. 745-3111, is an 18-hole public course. Rent skis and get details on local conditions from **Cross-Country Connection** in West Laramie, tel. 721-2851. Other ski rental places are **Fine Edge Ski Shop,** 1657 Jackson, tel. 745-449, and **Lou's Sport Shop,** 217 Grand Ave., tel. 745-8484. **West Laramie Fly Store,** 1657 Snowy Range Rd., tel. 745-5425, is the place to go for fishing gear. **Adventure Is,** 209 S. Second, tel. 742-3191, offers beginning windsurfing classes at windy **Lake Hattie,** 20 miles southwest of Laramie on State 230. During the summer, this shallow lake is a good place to swim or

fish for kokanee or rainbow trout. Rent mountain bikes or in-line skates at **Pedal House,** 207 S. First, tel. 742-5533, for $6/day. The folks here are very knowledgeable about local cycling trails and offer mountain-bike tours in the Medicine Bows. They may also be renting bikes out of Centennial.

Shopping

Bradley Mountain Wear, 213 S. First, tel. 742-9490, manufactures (and sells) packs, outdoor clothing, and other high-quality mountaineering gear. They also rent tents, sleeping bags, and packs, and sell climbing gear. Climbers heading to Vedauwoo rocks should stop here to talk with the owners. Other good outdoor shops are **Lou's Sport Shop,** 217 Grand Ave., tel. 745-8484, and **Adventure Is,** 209 S. Second, tel. 742-3191. For a different type of clothing, **The Hourglass,** 210 S. Second St., tel. 745-3288, claims to have the largest selection of lingerie in the Rockies! Some of the nicest stained-glass work anywhere can be found at **The First Tree,** 113 Ivinson Ave., tel. 745-5876.

Information And Services

The **Laramie Chamber of Commerce,** 800 S. Third St., tel. 745-7339 or (800) 445-5303, is open Mon.-Fri. 8-5. Look for the summer-only visitor center in the caboose on the south end of town; open daily 9-5. The University of Wyoming also has its own visitor centers (described above). If you're heading out to the Medicine Bow mountains, be sure to stop by the **Forest Service office** at 2468 Jackson St., tel. 745-8971, for maps, plus up-to-date trail and campground information. The office is open Mon.-Fri. 7:30-5 and Sat.-Sun. 8-4.

Libraries

Albany County Library, 310 S. Eighth, tel. 745-3365, is open Mon.-Thurs. 10-9, and Fri.-Sun. 1-5 (closed Sun. in summer). Much more impressive are the eight university libraries that house nearly a million volumes—including the most complete collection of Wyoming books in existence—plus 150,000 maps and 13,000 periodicals. Most of these publications are in the **William Robertson Coe Library,** tel. 766-5312, which also has a map room, an extensive depository of government publications, and the outstanding Hebard Collection of historical books about Wyoming and the West. Also of note are the **Geology Library** in the Geology Building, tel. 766-3374, the **Science and Technology Library** in the Science Complex, tel. 766-5165, and the **Law Library** in the College of Law, tel. 766-2210.

Bookstores

Laramie is home to several of the finest bookstores in Wyoming. The spacious **University Bookstore,** in the student union, tel. 766-3264, has many regional titles and lots of travel books. **Chickering Bookstore,** 307 S. Second, tel. 742-8609, is a small and friendly bookshop in downtown Laramie. **Personally Recommended Books,** 107 Ivinson, tel. 745-4423, is a relaxing upstairs place to look over local literary favorites while enjoying fresh coffee or a pastry. (Ask for their mocha walnut muffin recipe!) **High Country Books,** 306 S. Second, sells both new and used books, along with rare titles and some of the funniest Wyoming postcards anywhere. This is the place to find those obscure (by Wyoming standards) magazines such as *Yellow Silk* or *Vegetarian Times.* **Books a-Go-Go,** 408 University Ave., tel. 745-5835, carries some 1,800 different magazines—biggest choice in the state—and an enormous selection of paperbacks.

Transportation

Amtrak, tel. (800) 872-7245, operates twice-daily service from the Laramie depot at First St. between Sheridan and Kearney. Built in 1923, the depot was recently restored and features a display of railroad photographs. It is open daily 10-5. Laramie Airport is just west of town on State 130. **United Express,** tel. (800) 241-6522, has daily flights from Laramie to Denver, while **Airport Express,** tel. (800) 321-0404, provides van service to Denver's airport. **Greyhound** buses stop at the Handy Truck Stop at I-80 and Curtis, tel. 721-7405. Buses operate daily in both directions along I-80. Rent cars from **Avis,** tel. (800) 331-1212, or from **Burman Motors,** 3600 Grand Ave., tel. 745-8961. **Laramie Taxi Service,** tel. 745-8294, provides local cab service.

POLE MOUNTAIN AREA

Heading east from Laramie on I-80, the freeway climbs steadily up into second-growth ponderosa and lodgepole pine forests of the Pole Mountain area. It's a scenic land punctuated by unusual and colorful rock formations. For many years much of the land here belonged to the military and was used as a target and maneuver area for the Army's version of off-road vehicles, tanks. Amazingly, the land seems to show little sign of all this abuse today.

Ten miles east of Laramie is the Summit Rest Area, located on the highest point (8,640 feet) along I-80. A 12-foot-tall bronze bust of **Abraham Lincoln** looks over the freeway from atop a granite base. It was created by Robert I. Russin, a former art professor at the university and Wyoming's best-known sculptor. The old road through this pass was known as the Lincoln Highway, and the sculpture was placed here in 1959, the 150th anniversary of Lincoln's birth. (The Lincoln Highway—completed in 1923—was the first transcontinental highway.) The sculpture was moved to the present location in 1968 when the interstate highway came through.

The visitor center here has information on nearby areas and is open daily 9-7 May-October.

Choose from three Forest Service campgrounds ($5, open late May-Oct.) in the Pole Mountain area, or camp for free on land away from the roads. **Headquarters National Recreation Trail** extends five miles from the Summit Rest Area to the Headquarters Road. During the winter, Pole Mountain becomes a popular cross-country ski area (groomed trails). Many others come to play on the tubing and tobogganing hill near Happy Jack Trailhead.

East of the summit, I-80 follows a long open plateau and then drops gradually into the shortgrass prairie of southeast Wyoming via "The Gangplank." The Colorado Rockies form a jagged southern horizon line. This crossing of the Laramie Range was discovered by General Grenville Dodge in 1865. While exploring the railroad's new route, an attack by a party of Indians forced his men to flee eastward. In the process they discovered this gentle ramp to the plains of Cheyenne. Unfortunately, today the route is marked for miles by a dominolike line of billboards advertising everything from McDonald's to Giant Western Fireworks. Too bad the billboards could not all be toppled like dominoes to reveal the expansive grassland beyond!

Vedauwoo

Just five miles east of the summit is the turnoff to strange rock formations known as Vedauwoo (pronounced VEE-dah-voo), a name meaning "earthborn" in Arapaho. The area was considered a sacred place where young Indian men went on vision quests. These oddly jumbled rocks form all sorts of shapes—mushrooms, balancing rocks, feminine curves, rounded knolls, lizards, faces, turtles, and anything you might dream up. Imagine it as a Rorschach test. Indians believed that the rocks were created by animal and human spirits. Today, Vedauwoo is considered one of the best places to practice rock climbing in Wyoming. Climbs go from a difficulty level of 5.0 all the way up to 5.14, with many easy places to practice crack climbs. Nonclimbers come just to view the rocks, to ride mountain bikes along the dirt roads, to hike in the countryside, or to scramble up for marvelous vistas of the surrounding land. Vedauwoo Glen Road connects with Happy Jack Rd. for a nice loop trip. No campgrounds right at Vedauwoo, but you can pull out on the side roads to pitch a tent. Beware, however, that freeway noise may keep you awake. **Tressle Tours,** tel. 742-6049 or 742-7616, offers four-hour tours ($15) of the country around Vedauwoo, including historical railroad sights such as remains of the Dale Creek Bridge, once the longest suspension bridge in existence.

Pyramid Power

Head two miles south from the Vedauwoo exit to one of the strangest monuments in Wyoming: a 60-foot-tall pyramid in the middle of nowhere. The monument commemorates Oakes and Oliver Ames, two of the most influential figures in the building of the transcontinental railroad. As a U.S. congressman, Oakes Ames gained passage of a bill that allowed the railroad to sell bonds equal to the amount loaned by the federal government, some $60 million. The company they established to handle this financing was the infamous Credit Mobilier of America. Later it would be learned that Oakes had bribed fellow congressmen with discount railroad stock and had greatly exaggerated construction costs for his own gain. A congressional investigation labeled Oakes "King of Frauds" and censured him. He died before he could stand trial, and the money was never recovered.

Despite this bit of infamy, the monument to the Ames brothers was built in 1882 at a cost of nearly $65,000. It was originally located at the highest elevation of the transcontinental railroad route near the town of Sherman, a place where trains halted to check their brakes before the long descent on either side. In 1902, the tracks were rerouted a couple of miles to the south, leaving the grandiose pile of rocks by itself. Nothing remains today from the Sherman townsite except a cemetery. The Ames Monument seems to bring out two conflicting emotions, dismay at the obscenity of this monstrosity, and amusement at the irony that so much money was wasted on a self-aggrandizing monument that was soon abandoned even by the railroad that the Ames brothers had helped build.

MEDICINE BOW VICINITY

Two roads head west from Laramie. Most people follow I-80 straight to Rawlins, but US 30-287 (the old Lincoln Hwy.) gets you there in about the same time and provides a strong flavor of the old west. The almost-ghost town of **Rock River** (pop. 200) has a bar, a motel, a general store, a cafe, a pretty red-door church, and not much else. **Longhorn Lodge Motel,** 362 N. Fourth, tel. 378-2226, charges $20 s or $25 d.

West from Rock River, the road sails through desolate treeless country, with sagebrush to the horizon and the impressive summit of Elk Mountain rising to the southwest. The Union Pacific Railroad parallels the highway most of the way, and antelope glance up at the passing trains. Anyone coming through in the winter will appreciate the miles of snow fences along the south side of the highway. Still, the snow streams over the roadway almost constantly.

COMO BLUFF

Halfway between the towns of Rock River and Medicine Bow on US 30-287 is a long, low ridge known as Como Bluff. Not much to distinguish this from countless other buttes in the West, but paleontologists consider it one of the most important sites ever discovered, a place one author likened to Darwin's *Origin of the Species* in terms of its impact on scientific thought. This was the first large discovery of dinosaurs anywhere, and the first place where Diplodocus dinosaurs—the largest ever found—were discovered. The mammals discovered here are prized around the world and include all but three of the 250 known Jurassic mammals found in North America. Combined, the dinosaur and mammal fossils from Como Bluff make up a major part of the collections of Yale's Peabody Museum, the Smithsonian Institution, the New York Museum of Natural History, and the National Museum in Washington, D.C., as well as many others around the world.

History

In July of 1877, Professor Othniel Charles Marsh of Yale College received a letter from two Wyoming men calling themselves Harlow and Ed-
wards. They told of finding "a large number of fossils, supposed to be those of the Megatherium, although there is no one here sufficient of a geologist to state for a certainty." Marsh was in stiff competition with other paleontologists around the country, and his rival, Professor E.D. Cope from the Philadelphia Academy of Sciences, had just scooped him on a major dinosaur discovery in Colorado. The letter from "Harlow and Edwards" piqued Marsh's curiosity. An assistant sent to investigate wrote that the find was indeed substantive and suggested that Marsh immediately hire the two discoverers— they were actually two railroad employees, William Reed and William Carlin—to keep them from revealing the secret. Reed would later work for many years as a collector for the University of Wyoming, and eventually as an instructor in geology and curator of the Geology Museum on the Laramie campus.

Work began almost immediately and continued right through the blizzards of winter, but despite efforts to keep the find a secret, Professor Cope soon had his own men working at Como Bluff. The rivalry almost came to blows, and Marsh's men made it a point to smash any bones left behind after their digging was complete and to backfill the quarries with rocks, even if their rivals were working below. Excavations continued until 1889 when most of the finest specimens had been unearthed.

Today geology and paleontology classes still come to Como Bluff, but the quarries where the bones were found are now abandoned and can't be seen from the road. Como Bluff itself is visible a little over a mile north of US 30, and a sign describes the site. Travelers will want to stop at **"the world's oldest building"** at Como Bluffs ($1, or 50¢ for kids), a small museum/gift shop built from dinosaur bones and run by friendly down-home folks. Inside are more bones and some jewelry for sale. It's open daily 9:30-7 in summer. Worth a stop.

MEDICINE BOW

The little town of Medicine Bow (pop. 400) is the sort of place where headlines in the weekly *Med-*

icine Bow Post complain of dogs getting into garbage or barking at kids. For the most part it's a nondescript town with old boxlike houses and newer boxlike trailers. Medicine Bow differs very little from hundreds of similar places all over the West, but it was here that novelist Owen Wister had his legendary cowboy hero, the Virginian, face off with Trampas. Over a game of cards, Trampas called the Virginian a "son-of-a-bitch," leading to the famous encounter in which the Virginian pulls his pistol and says, "When you call me that, smile!" It remains one of the classic lines in American folklore. *The Virginian* set the prototype for the western adventure; it was made into three movies and a TV series.

History

The town of Medicine Bow began in the 1870s as a Union Pacific pumping station along Medicine Bow River and grew into a local supply point and minor Army garrison. It has always been a center for the ranchers who run thousands of livestock in the surrounding countryside, so it was a logical place to base Wister's cowboy hero. During the 1930s, Medicine Bow prospered because it lay along the Lincoln Hwy. (US 30), but following completion of I-80, it lapsed into decay. The coal mines of Hanna (20 miles west) and uranium and oil explorations in Shirley Basin led to temporary energy booms, but the economy is now back to its ranching base.

Sights

Medicine Bow's main attraction is the boxy, three-story **Virginian Hotel,** built in 1909 (seven years after *The Virginian* came out). At the time, it was the largest hotel between Denver and Salt Lake City. It is still a marvelous building, with the upstairs rooms lovingly restored to Victorian elegance. Take a look around, even if you aren't planning on staying here. Just down the street is the modern **Diplodocus Bar** (alias "the Dip"), containing the largest jade bar in existence, cut from a 4.5-ton jade boulder discovered near Lander. Look down for the only hand-painted dance floor west of the Mississippi. While you're here for a beer, be sure to ask owner Bill Bennett to show his unusually intricate woodcarvings.

Town, as they called it, pleased me the less, the longer I saw it. But until our language stretches itself and takes in a new word or closer fit, town will have to do for the name of such a place as Medicine Bow. I have seen and slept in many like it since. Scattered wide, they littered the frontier from the Columbia to the Rio Grande, from the Missouri to the Sierras. They lay stark, dotted over a planet of treeless dust, like soiled packs of cards. Each was similar to the next, as one old five-spot of cards resembles another. . . . Yet this wretched husk of squalor spent thought upon appearances; many houses in it wore a false front to seem as if they were two stories high. There they stood, rearing their pitiful masquerade amid a fringe of old tin cans, while at their very doors began a world of crystal light, a land without end, a space across which Noah and Adam might come straight from Genesis. Into that space went wandering a road, over a hill and down out of sight, and up again smaller in the distance, and down once more, and up once more, straining the eyes, and so away.

—From Owen Wister's The Virginian

Across from the hotel is the **Medicine Bow Museum,** housed in the old wooden railroad depot (1913). Out front is a cabin built by Owen Wister that stood in Jackson Hole until being moved here in 1976, along with a petrified-wood monument to Wister. The museum contains the typical things found in small-town museums—various homesteading items, a lamb warmer, a coyote scare (made from sawdust and firecrackers), and old fire equipment. Kind of like wandering through an old attic, where you wonder how half the stuff was ever used. There is an old caboose on the side. The museum, tel. 379-2383, is open daily 10-6 summers. The rest of the year it's open Mon.-Thurs. 10-3:30.

Five miles south of Medicine Bow is a giant **wind turbine** built in 1982 for the U.S. Department of the Interior. The largest wind generator in existence, it's located in one of the windiest spots in America. Originally there were two such windmills here, each one producing five million kilowatt hours of electricity a year. Supporters envisioned an enormous wind farm with perhaps another 50, but these 400-foot-tall monsters proved unwieldy embarrassments and were abandoned by the government when it was discovered that repairs would be prohibitively expensive. One of the $6 million turbines was blasted over with dynamite and sold for $13,000 on the scrap market in 1988. The remaining turbine is now privately owned and still produces electricity.

Practicalities

Rooms at the historic **Virginian Hotel,** tel. 379-2377, are remarkably inexpensive, starting at just $22 s or $25 d with a bath down the hall. Sleep in the suite where Owen Wister stayed for $55 d. If you miss your TV and private bath, try a room in the annex next door. The downstairs restaurant provides good homecooking, and most Saturday nights will find country bands in the bar. **Trampas Lodge,** tel. 379-2280, also has rooms for $26 s or $28 d. Open May-Oct. only. Pitch your tent or park RVs at the town park. Groceries are available from **Bow Market,** and pastries at **Pearle's Kitchen.**

Medicine Bow Days is the annual celebration in town, held each July and including rodeos, black-powder shoots, parades, live music, and dancing. The "highlight" is the hanging of Dutch Charlie at high noon. (Dutch Charlie and Big Nose George were both lynched for the murder of two deputies.)

SHIRLEY BASIN

State 487 heads north from Medicine Bow into the vast and remote **Shirley Basin,** some of the finest cattle rangeland in Wyoming. The road is smooth with wide shoulders (perfect for bikes), and the vistas are dramatic—colorful badlands, rolling hills covered with sage and grass, and cottonwood-lined creeks. Lots of wildlife here too—especially antelope and deer, but also some of the largest remaining prairie-dog towns in existence. Because of this, Shirley Basin was the first area where the endangered black-footed ferret was released back into the wild. Forty-nine ferrets were released here in

1991. Despite high mortalities, many are not only surviving but also reproducing. Extensive deposits of uranium have been discovered in Shirley Basin—some of the largest and richest in the world—but low prices and an oversupply have all but halted the uranium-mining business. Ask in Medicine Bow for directions to the petrified forest. Nearly every yard in town has a piece out front.

HANNA

The growing town of Hanna (pop. 1,100) lies at the center of one of the state's major coal fields. Lots of mobile homes and company housing in Hanna, but there is nothing particularly interesting about the town, unless you care to check out the Miners Monument or the enormous Union Pacific snowplow. Near Hanna are two large coal mines: the Medicine Bow strip mine 23 miles west, and the larger Cyprus Shoshone mine five miles north. Mining has been a mainstay of the local economy since coal was discovered here in the late 1800s. Two disastrous mine explosions in 1903 and 1908 killed 228 miners, but the mines remained open until 1954. They were reactivated in the 1970s. The mining ghost town of **Carbon** —established in 1868 as the state's first coal town—once stood a few miles east of here. The coal ran out in 1902, and today only a few ruins and the graveyard remain.

Practicalities

Golden Rule Motel, tel. 325-6525, charges $22 s or $24 d. Very friendly owners. This is the de facto chamber of commerce office. **The Tucker Box,** 624 Madison, tel. 325-6353, serves good breakfasts and lunches on weekdays. **Jade Drive-In,** tel. 325-6355, offers up the best fast food around. Use Hanna's fine **recreation center** with sauna, pool, jacuzzi, and gym for $2.50. Groceries are available at **Hanna Market.**

ELK MOUNTAIN

The tiny settlement of Elk Mountain (pop. 170) stands halfway between Laramie and Rawlins, and just off I-80. *Do* take this exit! Although it is almost within sight of the freeway, the town seems a world apart. Big cottonwoods line the

Rock Creek Stage Station, 1861

quiet streets and the Medicine Bow River flows right through town. Several buildings are noteworthy: the majestic old New England-style community church, the general store (one of the best in Wyoming), and an enormous log barn still in perfect condition after more than 100 years. Directly behind town is the rounded, snow-topped 11,162-foot summit of Elk Mountain, one of the most prominent natural landmarks anywhere along I-80. Unusual clouds frequently hang off its peak, making it a valuable site for the University of Wyoming's atmospheric research program. Ask in town for access information; you'll need to get permission from local ranchers.

Elk Mountain Hotel, tel. 348-7774, built in 1905, is furnished with Victorian-style accoutrements and costs $20 s or $28 d (bath down the hall). The hotel also runs a bar and restaurant that specializes in steaks and seafood, or you can try the attractive **Noon Camp Cafe,** tel. 348-7478, for lighter fare. Still standing in Elk Mountain is Garden Spot Pavilion, a dance hall that in the 1930s and '40s attracted all the big-name orchestras, including Louis Armstrong, Tommy Dorsey, Glenn Miller, and Lawrence Welk. Five miles west of town, a stone monument marks the site of **Fort Halleck,** a short-lived military post built in 1862 to guard the Overland Trail. With the arrival of the transcon-

tinental railroad, it was abandoned in 1866, and its fixtures moved east to Fort Buford (later called Fort Sanders) near present-day Laramie.

ARLINGTON

Approximately 30 miles west of Laramie is a freeway crossroads with lots of history, Arlington. Stay at the **Arlington KOA,** tel. 378-2350, where tents are $13, RVs $16. In Arlington are several buildings from the **Rock Creek Stage Station,** which stood along the Overland Route, including a log cabin built around 1860, one of the oldest buildings in Wyoming. Also here is a combination blacksmith shop/dance hall/gambling palace. (These are located on private land south of the freeway.) In 1865, Indians attacked a wagon train near the Rock Creek Stage Station and captured two girls, Mary and Lizzie Fletcher. Mary was eventually sold to a white trader, but Lizzie remained with the Arapahos for the rest of her life. It wasn't until 35 years later that Mary discovered that her sister was alive and living on the Wind River Reservation. Having grown accustomed to the Arapaho way of life and enjoying a high status in the community, Lizzie chose to stay in her home. She is buried next to her husband, Broken Horn, in the St. Stephen's Mission Cemetery.

MEDICINE BOW MOUNTAINS AND VICINITY

Medicine Bow National Forest is scattered over four disjunctive areas in Wyoming. The northern portion—the Laramie Mountains—is discussed in "Central Wyoming" (pp. 176-178), while the Pole Mountain section is described on p. 107. The other two mountainous areas are west of Laramie: the Medicine Bow Mountains (locally called the Snowy Range) and the Sierra Madre Range. Most of this has been Forest Service land since 1902, although the name and boundaries have changed over the years. Mining was the big attraction in the late 1800s, but the major gold and copper deposits were quickly mined out, and logging became the primary use of this mountainous country. Between 1867 and 1940, millions of railroad ties were brought out of the Laramie and Medicine Bow mountains by tie hacks who logged almost every driveable creek they could get their hands on. The area provided ties for not only Wyoming, but western Nebraska and Colorado as well. Logging for lumber is still important in the Medicine Bow National Forest, but recreational use is increasing each year as more and more people discover this very scenic country. The Supervisor's Office for Medicine Bow National Forest is in Laramie, with district offices in Saratoga and Encampment. Pick up a copy of the Medicine Bow National Forest Map ($3) at any of these offices before heading out.

LARAMIE PLAINS VICINITY

Heading west from Laramie on State 130, you pass through some of the most desolate country in Wyoming, with flat grassland stretching in all directions, interrupted by mountains to the east, south, and west. An enormous windswept bowl here—**Big Hollow**—was created by howling winds during the last ice age. The only other place like this is in Russia. Laramie Basin is also unique in having the highest short-grass prairie in the world, some 7,200 feet above sea level. Eleven miles west of Laramie, State 130 crosses the historic **Overland Trail,** which carried emigrants, mail, and freight west between 1862 and 1868 when the railroad replaced it. The wagon ruts are still visible, with markers tracing the old route. As you approach the Medicine Bow Mountains, the highway dips down to sample the tree-lined beauty of Little Laramie Creek and then begins the long ascent to Snowy Range Pass.

Albany

State 11 heads south along Little Laramie Creek to the foothills town of Albany, passing rolling grass and sagebrush country with pine-topped hills. Old ranches are sprinkled around this gorgeous little valley. Rustic cabins at the **Albany Lodge,** tel. 745-5782, are $25 s or d, and the bar has hundreds of baseball caps tacked to the ceiling. On Saturday nights this is a popular place, with tasty $11 prime-rib dinners. A dirt road continues south from Albany to Woods Landing, but it is often closed by blowing snow in the winter. Albany is a very popular base for snowmobilers.

Centennial

Thirty-five miles west from Laramie, State 130 widens to include the funky old mining town of Centennial (pop. 50). Situated at the foot of the Snowy Range, Centennial was founded in 1875 and gained its name the following year, the centennial of the founding of America. (James Michener claims not to have known of the town when he wrote his book of the same name about an early Rocky Mountain town.) Prospectors came here in search of gold. That first year the Centennial Mine produced more than $90,000 worth, but when the vein ran out, only a few people stayed around. A short boom created by infusions of cash from a Boston financier brought a fish hatchery, hotels, mining explorations, and an exclusive country club to Centennial, but the bubble burst again when the expected gold deposits failed to materialize. Eventually, Centennial became a minor ranching center and train stop. Today, it is a tourist way station with a devil-may-care mix of old log homes and house trailers.

The small **Nici Self Museum** in the old railroad depot building (built in 1907) contains exhibits on the area's mining and logging history and is open weekends 1-4 from July 4 through Labor Day, or by appointment the rest of the year (tel. 742-7158 or 742-8612). Out front is a Union Pacific caboose and various old farm implements. Check out the "police car" as you roll through town. **Pat's Old Corral Motel,** tel. 745-5918 or (800) 678-2024, has rooms in a brand new lodge for $35 s or $43 d; open year-round. The restaurant here serves outstanding "dream steaks" in a comfortably rustic atmosphere and has live music during the summer. **Friendly Motel,** tel. 742-6033, has rooms for $27 s or $32 d. Across the road is **Trading Post Restaurant & Lounge,** tel. 721-5074, where you'll find country, blues, or rock on Saturday nights. They also have two cabins for rent ($30+ s or $40+ d including kitchen facilities); open year-round.

Snowy Range Camp, seven miles west of Centennial, tel. 721-3867, is a unique nonprofit camp offering health and ecology classes in the summer, and skiing (cross-country and tele-marking) classes in the winter. The lodge was built in the 1920s and served as a university science camp for many years. Lodging is also available for those not taking classes, with dorm spaces costing $15 pp and rustic cabins starting at $25 (sleeps four). Make reservations a couple of weeks ahead for the winter months, when the skiing is some of the best to be found. The historic **Mountain Meadow Guest Ranch,** tel. 742-6042, is three miles west of Centennial and sometimes has rustic cabins for rent, plus horse-back rides.

SNOWY RANGE

In between the Laramie Plains and the valley created by the upper North Platte River lie the Medicine Bow Mountains, locally called the Snowy Range. The latter is an appropriate name; it can snow here at any time of the year, and 10-foot drifts are not uncommon in the winter, with snow remaining on high passes until late summer. The Snowy Range contains the **Savage Run Wilderness** (15,260 acres) and the **Platte River Wilderness** (22,749 acres), both lying along the southwestern end of the the range just above the Wyoming-Colorado border. Most visitors simply enjoy the drive over

SNOWY RANGE

TO SAND LAKE

ROCK CREEK KNOLL
(ELEV. 11,125 ft.)

DEEP LAKE

SHEEP LAKE

SHEEP LAKE TRAIL

NORTH TWIN LAKES

QUEALY LAKE

QUEALY LAKE TRAIL

NORTH GAP LAKE TRAIL

RESERVOIR LAKE

GAP LAKES

BROWNS PEAK
(ELEV. 11,722 ft.)

BROOKLYN LAKE

TELEPHONE LAKES

OPEN AIR CHAPEL

BROOKLYN LAKE GUARD STATION

TO CENTENNIAL

MEDICINE BOW PEAK
(ELEV. 12,013 ft.)

LEWIS LAKE

LIBBY LAKE

SUGARLOAF RECREATION AREA

SUGARLOAF MOUNTAIN
(ELEV. 11,398 ft.)

LOOKOUT LAKE

LAKES TRAIL

SNOWY RANGE PASS

LIBBY FLATS

MEDICINE BOW OBSERVATION AREA

SNOWY RANGE CAMP

130

MIRROR LAKE

LAKE MARIE

130

TO SARATOGA AND ENCAMPMENT

0   1 mi

0   1 km

the mountains and the chance to camp beside an alpine lake with a backdrop of 12,000-foot mountains. Numerous short hiking trails make this a favorite spot for locals.

The Forest Service has detailed forest maps and helpful brochures on these mountains at its Laramie office, 2468 Jackson St., tel. 745-8971. There are also Forest Service information centers (open daily 8-5 mid-May through Oct.) on both sides of the Snowy Range along State 130. One of these is located a mile west of Centennial, and the other is 20 miles east of Saratoga.

Over The Top

The 40-mile drive on State 130 over the Snowy Range is one of the most dramatic in Wyoming and is designated a National Scenic Byway. The pass is closed by snow from late October to Memorial Day, but it is open to just beyond the Snowy Range Ski Area on the east side and 20 miles up from the west side year-round. Higher-elevation parts of the road are very popular with snowmobilers and cross-country skiers. West of Centennial, the highway climbs sharply through lodgepole and spruce forests to beautiful Snowy Range Pass at 10,847 feet (second highest in the state).

Be sure to stop at **Sugarloaf Recreation Area,** just east of the pass. Sharp glacially carved spires rise above the small lakes, and islands of stunted Engelmann spruce dot the alpine country. Trails head out to nearby lakes and flower-covered alpine meadows. At the summit, a viewing platform provides panoramic vistas of Libby Flats, massive Medicine Bow Peak, and the valleys on both sides. Pull off at the Medicine Bow Peak Observation Point for a three-quarter-mile hike to the picturesque remains of an old mine. Just west of here, **Mirror Lake** and **Lake Marie** are two of the most photographed spots in Wyoming, with a spectacular backdrop of steep mountain faces reflecting in the dark blue lake waters. Campgrounds and picnic areas are all along here. A wheelchair-accessible path leads along one shore of Lake Marie, and the west parking lot acts as a trailhead for the path up **Medicine Bow Peak** (see below). On the western side of the pass, the highway drops steadily down through the forest, eventually reaching the rolling sage and grass of the Upper North Platte River Valley.

Route 230

Another route west is State 230. While this highway is not as dramatic as the Snowy Pass trek, it is open year-round and is still quite scenic. The road curves around the southern end of the Snowys, passing through Woods Landing en route to the Colorado border. **Woods Landing Resort,** tel. 745-5770, has a gas station/country store/bar with cabins for rent and country music on some weekends. It represents the only real settlement between Laramie and Encampment, a distance of 87 miles. There's excellent fishing for brown trout along the Big Laramie River. The mining ghost town of **Old Jelm** is four miles south of Woods Landing and contains a number of old clapboard buildings. Ask locally for permission to visit. The university's **Jelm Mountain Observatory** is up a five-mile dirt road from here. Call the university in advance (tel. 766-6150) for a tour of the largest infrared telescope in the continental United States.

Beyond Woods Landing, State 230 dips south, passing several mountain lodges, including **WyoColo Lodge,** just north of the state line, tel. 742-4230, where rustic cabins cost $15 s or $25 d (these rates will rise once remodelling is completed in late 1993). Also here is a bar, or you can get light meals; open year-round. The road continues into Colorado for nine miles along Colorado 127, then back north on Colorado 125 for another nine miles before again crossing into Wyoming on State 230. Much of this is open rangeland with hills on either side. Only a few abandoned cabins and fences mark the presence of humans on this vast land. The huge white hip-roofed barn of the Big Creek Ranch is one of the most beautiful in all Wyoming. Turn around for outstanding views of the Colorado Rockies.

Camping

There are 23 different Forest Service campgrounds ($5-7 per site) within the Snowy Range portion of Medicine Bow National Forest. Most of these are open June-Sept., but some remain open longer. A few of the campgrounds—those with no water or trash pickup—are free. Because of heavy use during the summer, you should arrive at the most popular sites early in the day. All of these campgrounds may be reserved by calling (800) 283-2267 ($6 extra). In addition to the official campgrounds, dispersed camping is permitted in most areas (but not near Sugarloaf Recreation Area) as long as you're off the main roads. Check with the Forest Service for specifics.

Trails

The Medicine Bows are ideal for short one- to five-day hikes. The three-mile-long **Medicine Bow Peak Trail** climbs 1,600 feet to the summit of this 12,013-foot mountain, highest in southern Wyoming. Extraordinary vistas from the top. The trail leaves from the Lake Marie picnic area and is in exposed alpine terrain most of the way. A loop hike (approximately six miles) can be made by following this route to the top and then dropping down the east side to the **Lakes Trail** that takes you past rock-rimmed Lookout Lake (keep a lookout for marmots) and on to Mirror Lake. Your starting point is just down the road. Medicine Bow Peak can also be climbed via a shorter trail (four miles RT) that leaves from the Lewis Lake Trailhead.

North Gap Lake Trail departs from the Lewis Lake parking lot in the Sugarloaf Recreation Area and follows a gentle grade past Gap Lakes, continuing on to Sheep Lake. Beyond these, hikers can continue north to Sand Lake, nine miles from your starting point, or loop back to State 130 via the **Sheep Lake Trail**. The latter route ends at Brooklyn Lake, where you can hitch a ride back to your starting point (or leave a vehicle). This entire area is crisscrossed with other alpine trails, some of which are not shown on topographic maps. Check with the Forest Service for details.

Platte River Trail, a five-mile-long path, parallels the river through North Gate Canyon, a long stretch of whitewater in the Platte River Wilderness. The banks are lined with ponderosa pines and Douglas firs. Access is from the south via Sixmile Gap Campground. The trail is on the western bank of the river, but by late summer the river can sometimes be forded, allowing hikers to continue another 1½ miles northward to Pickaroon Campground. **Savage Run Trail** crosses the wilderness area of the same name. It is nine miles long and follows Savage Run Creek, dropping 2,400 feet along the way. Access is too confusing to describe, but not that hard if you have a Medicine Bow National Forest map.

Snowy Range Ski Area
Located in the mountains 32 miles west of Laramie on State 130, the Snowy Range Ski Area has four lifts and 23 different runs. Outside of Jackson Hole, this is the best place to ski in Wyoming, with a good variety of skiing conditions, uncrowded slopes, and soft powder snow. Snowy Range is open mid-Nov. through mid-April and charges $23 for adults ($18/half day) and $11 for kids ages 6-12 and seniors ($9/half day). Children under age six are free. It's open Wed.-Sun. 9-4 (daily in late Dec. and early Jan.), with ski rentals and lessons available. The lodge has cafeteria food, beer, and a fireplace. For more information, call 745-5750 or (800) 462-7669.

Other Winter Sports
The Forest Service maintains dozens of miles of groomed Nordic ski trails in the mountains around Snowy Range Ski Area, with a wide variety of loops and longer treks available for those willing to strike out on their own. An overnight ski hut is available for rent (tel. 745-8971) near the Libby Creek Trail. Snowmobiling is one of the most popular winter activities in the Snowy

Range, and parking lots on all sides of the range fill with vehicles on winter weekends. More than 200 miles of groomed trails follow summertime roads. For details on both cross-country skiing and snowmobiling, stop by the various Forest Service offices. Historic **Medicine Bow Lodge**, just inside the western Forest Service boundary along State 130, tel. 326-5439, offers cross-country ski rentals, along with lodging and meals. Luxury cabins (sleep four) are $75, including a hot tub. The lodge first opened in 1917, and the main building is still in use.

River Recreation
The North Platte River forms a major focal point for visitors staying in Saratoga and Encampment. The trout fishing is excellent, and the scenery grand; no wonder they call this the "Good Times Valley!" Many travelers float downriver either on their own or with a guide. Check with local Forest Service offices for river access information and a list of river guides. In Saratoga, **Great Rocky Mountain Outfitters**, 216 E. Walnut, tel. 326-8750, sells quality fly-fishing gear and can fill you in on the latest fishing and floating conditions. Rent rafts for $65/day or canoes for $35/day. They can also provide shuttle services as well as guided two-day canoe trips ($125 pp) and all-day fishing trips ($235 for two people). Another Saratoga outfit, **Platte Valley Anglers**, First and Bridge, tel. 326-5750, provides all-day scenic float trips ($45 pp) and guided fishing trips ($240 for two people). **Grand & Sierra Outfitters** in Encampment, tel. 327-5200, also offers fishing and float trips down the North Platte.

As the North Platte River enters Wyoming from Colorado it drops into **North Gate Canyon**, a class-III and -IV stretch of whitewater with several hairy sets of rapids. Beyond Sixmile Gap, the river broadens and becomes a gentler float. If you are a whitewater enthusiast, get here early since the water level drops after June. Check with the above places for guided whitewater trips in May and June.

SARATOGA

The friendly, laid-back town of Saratoga (pop. 2,000) is one of two towns in Wyoming that centers around hot springs (the other is Thermopolis). The name was borrowed from another well-known spa: Saratoga, New York. Wyoming's version of Saratoga straddles the North Platte River and putters along on a mixed economy. Louisiana Pacific Company has a large lumber mill in town, and many cattle graze in the beautiful river-bottom country along the North Platte. Saratoga is also something of a bedroom community for coal miners who work in Hanna but prefer the country around Saratoga. Others commute as far as Rawlins to work.

Like many places in Wyoming, Saratoga has long depended upon various extractive industries for a livelihood and is only now discovering how attractive the land itself is. With mountains on both sides, "blue ribbon" trout fishing, river float trips, a free hot springs, a rich history, and lots of wildlife, it is almost certain that tourism will grow increasingly important.

History

Indians called Saratoga Hot Springs "Place of the Magic Water"; it was a place of healing where various tribes could mingle without fear of attack. When whites arrived and first bathed here, the Indians noted that the waters boiled more violently than before, indicating an evil spirit. Thereafter most shunned the hot springs, but an 1874 smallpox epidemic forced some to return. Patients were soaked in the hot water in an attempt to boil out the disease, and then dipped in the cold river water. When all the patients died, the Indians decided that whites had turned the waters from good medicine to bad medicine. The area was littered with the graves of smallpox victims. Thereafter, the Indians moved even farther away from the hot springs.

In 1877, William H. Cadwell homesteaded near the springs and built a wooden bathhouse on the site, offering hot baths, meals, and a place for travelers to stretch out for a night's sleep. People flocked here from all over the region, and some even came from England to soak in the waters that were claimed to cure "rheumatism, eczema, paralysis, stomach trouble, kidney disease, nerves, and all forms of blood and skin disease." The copper-mining boom in the Sierra Madre brought prosperity as miners came to Saratoga to relax, and freighters used it as a way station and supply center. A spur route from the Union Pacific line was built south to Saratoga in 1907 to haul ore from the mines, but they closed shortly thereafter and the town was forced to turn to other pursuits, becoming a ranching and logging center.

Sights

The main attraction in Saratoga is **Hobo Pool**, on the east end of Walnut Ave., where an outdoor concrete pool is fed by the odorless 117-128° F water of Saratoga Hot Springs. It's open 24 hours a day and is handicapped-accessible. No charge. A heated changing room has showers. A larger swimming pool (not mineral water) is adjacent and is open daily 11-4 and 6-9 p.m. during the summer; $2 per swim. The mineral

SARATOGA ACCOMMODATIONS

MOTEL	ADDRESS	TELEPHONE	RATES	FEATURES
Brooksong B&B	24 miles SE of Saratoga	326-8744	$29 s, $39 d	log home, full breakfast
Wolf Hotel	101 E. Bridge St.	326-5525	$29+ s, $35+ d $65 s, $75 d	classic hotel, suites
Riviera Lodge	303 N. First St.	326-5651	$33 s, $38 d	riverside
Silver Moon Motel	412 E. Bridge St.	326-5974	$28 s, $30 d	kitchenettes
Sage and Sand Motel	311 S. First St.	326-8339	$29 s, $34 d	kitchenettes
Saratoga Inn	E. Pic Pike Rd.	326-5261	$40+ s, $46+ d	resort, hot springs
Hacienda Motel	½ mile south	326-5751	$36+ s, $45 d	
Hood House B&B	214 N. Third	326-8901	$40 s, $50 d	historic home, antique furnishings

(previous page) Lower Falls, Yellowstone River;
(this page top) near Encampment; (bottom) PK Ranch cattle drive (photos by Don Pitcher)

baths attract both old and young, with more adventurous types sprinting down to the adjacent North Platte River to cool off. Other hot springs feed directly into the river, keeping some stretches open year-round. Because of this, **Odd Fellows Park** at River and Main streets is a good place to see ducks and geese at all times of the year.

Saratoga's wonderful **Wolf Hotel**, 101 E. Bridge St., was built in 1893 by a German emigrant named Frederick Wolf. Today it is a national historic landmark. The old brick building with steeply gabled windows served for many years as a stage stop along the road to the mines of the Sierra Madre. It was restored with antique furnishings during the 1970s and '80s and now offers an enjoyable taste of the past.

Saratoga Museum, on the south end of town across from the airport, tel. 326-5511, is housed in the old railroad depot. Inside are items from the region's ranching, logging, and sheepherding past, along with a hands-on archaeology exhibit. It's open daily 1-5 during the summer or by appointment the rest of the year. The **North Platte River** from the Wyoming-Colorado border to the mouth of Sage Creek (65 miles north) is the only "blue ribbon" trout fishery in southern Wyoming, with outstanding fishing for rainbow and brown trout. Studies have found over 4,200 catchable wild trout (averaging 13-17 inches) per mile in the river. Indian petroglyphs can be found along the bluff above the river just north of Saratoga. (As a trivial aside, the North Platte is one of the only rivers in the U.S. that flows north for a good portion of its length.) Fish are raised at the **Saratoga National Fish Hatchery,** four miles north of town, tel. 326-5662; open daily 8-5. Constructed in 1915, the hatchery produces fingerling cutthroat, rainbow, and brook trout for Wyoming rivers and lakes.

Accommodations And Camping
See the chart for lodging places in Saratoga. **Saratoga Lake Campground,** 1½ miles north of town, has campsites around this small lake for $5 ($7.50 with RV hookups). Bike campers pay just $1. No trees or showers. It's open May-October. The closest Forest Service campground is 25 miles to the east, with many more campgrounds ($5-7) as you continue up State 130 over Snowy Range Pass. **Saratoga RV Park,** 116 W. Farm Ave., tel. 326-8807, has tent spaces for $8 and RV sites for $12. Showers cost $2 for noncampers. Although right in town, the riverside location has lots of shade. **Saratoga Inn,** E. Pic Pike Rd., tel. 326-5261, has RV sites for $18, including access to a pool, spa, and other facilities.

Food And Entertainment
Mom's Kitchen, 402 S. First, tel. 326-5136, is a good family-style breakfast place with fast, friendly service and monstrous cinnamon rolls. **Family Diner,** on the north side of town, serves Mexican cookery, along with burgers and other standard fare. Get espresso coffees and ice cream at **Lollypops** on E. Bridge Street. For pizzas and lunchtime sandwiches, you won't go wrong at **Stumpy's Eatery,** 218 N. First, tel. 326-8132.

Historic **Wolf Hotel** serves up a complete range of food—from grilled cheese sandwiches to king crab. The bar is the local hangout and offers live C&W music periodically. **Saratoga Inn Restaurant** (closed in winter) also delivers fine steaks and seafood. This is a popular place for Sunday brunches, and its bar (open year-round) has live country or rock music on most nights. The **Rustic Bar,** 124 E. Bridge, tel. 326-5965, is known for its "fighting" mountain lion mounts.

Get groceries at **Valley Super** on the south end of town. The deli here has baked goods, or you can hang out with the locals over coffee and donuts at **Billy's Donuts** on W. Bridge Street. Actually the best place to find locals is the 7-11, where Saturday mornings find the high school's entire junior and senior classes parked out front. It's obviously the place to be seen.

Events
The **Saratoga Arts Festival** is held around July Fourth each year and features a juried art show, street musicians, a parade, and melodrama, along with the obligatory fireworks show. At the end of August, the **Sierra Madre Muzzle Loaders Rendezvous** brings mountain men (and women) to town. The **Ice Fishing Derby** each January is considered one of the top derbies in the Lower 48. The following month brings **cutter races** and **draft-horse pulls.** Lots of excitement as two-horse teams race down the straightaway.

Shopping

Eaton's, 117 E. Bridge, tel. 326-5314, is a delightfully funky and friendly old Western clothing store. The aisles are packed with so much stuff that you have to dig through them to find anything. **Whitney's Saddle Shop,** 107 W. Bridge, tel. 326-5935, also sells quality Western clothing. **Blackhawk Gallery,** 100 N. First., tel. 326-5063, sells Western artwork, and **Medicine Bow Mt. Gallery,** 117 W. Bridge St., tel. 326-5513, has jade jewelry and local gifts. Bill Naylor of **Peg Leg Mountain Furniture,** 413 E. Bridge, tel. 326-5022, makes unique lodgepole items, from walking sticks to bunk beds.

Information And Services

The **Saratoga Chamber of Commerce,** 114 S. First St., tel. 326-8855, is open Mon.-Fri. 9-5. Another source for information is the small kiosk in front of the **Forest Service Brush Creek Ranger Station,** 212 S. First, tel. 326-5258. Ask at the ranger station about guided tours of historic tie hack camps. The **library,** 503 W. Elm St., tel. 326-8209, is open Mon. and Fri. 2-5, and Tues.-Thurs. 11-8. A real surprise in Saratoga is the airport, with its 8,400-foot runway. No commercial service, but during the summer and fall, wealthy businessmen (alias "the conquistadors") flock here for a rendezvous at local dude ranches, jamming the tarmac with corporate jets and turning Shively Field into the third-busiest jetport in Wyoming. There is no bus service to Saratoga.

ENCAMPMENT AND RIVERSIDE

The small logging and tourism town of Encampment (pop. 500) lies in the gorgeous foothills of the Sierra Madre, country that was once home for thousands of copper miners. Today the area abounds with ghost towns from that era. Encampment's twin settlement of Riverside (pop. 90) lies just a mile to the east. This is a very popular area with hunters, who come for deer, antelope, and elk, as well as photographers who enjoy the colorful autumn leaves and anglers who cast about for trout. It's the sort of place where visitors roll into town and silently say to themselves, "I'd love to live here." The community is decidedly conservative: bumper stick-

ers proclaim "Wilderness—Land of No Use," and each fall finds the back roads crowded with gun-racked pickup trucks and silent, orange-capped hunters scanning the horizon for bucks. Back in town, the smoky bars are filled each night with tales of the chase and old men winking at the waitresses over their Budweisers.

History

Encampment takes its name from the Grand Encampment of French-Canadian trappers who rendezvoused along the Encampment River in 1838. Miners had long suspected that the Sierra Madre contained a wealth of minerals, but it was not until 1896 that the first significant gold strike was made. It was another mineral, however, that transformed the region. Encampment itself began in 1897 when British sheepherder Ed Haggerty discovered a rich vein of copper in the Sierra Madre to the west. The mine he developed was named Rudefeha, a word concocted from the letters of the various partners' names—J.M. Rumsey, Robert Deal, George Ferris, and Ed Haggerty. In the first three months of digging, miners recovered $300,000 worth of copper ore. Haggerty took his 10% share and returned to England.

As the wealth of the discovery became known, Chicago promoter and newspaperman Willis George Emerson purchased the mine and built a 16-mile-long aerial tram to haul the ore up over the 10,600-foot Continental Divide and then down to the Boston-Wyoming Smelter at Encampment (elevation 7,200 feet). The tram consisted of 304 wooden towers with buckets supported on thick steel cables. Each bucket held 700 pounds of ore and moved at four miles an hour. The tram could carry almost 1,000 tons of ore a day and was powered by water flowing through a four-foot wooden pipeline. Thousands of men flocked to the mines, creating almost overnight the settlements of Elwood, Battle, Copperton, Dillon, Halfway House, and Rambler. A railroad was completed from the smelter to the main Union Pacific line at Wolcott in 1905, and by 1908 more than 23 million pounds of copper had been produced.

The main regional settlement was Encampment, located at the foot of the mountains and numbering 1,500 rough and hardened souls at its peak. By 1900, the town featured three gen-

ENCAMPMENT AND RIVERSIDE ACCOMMODATIONS

MOTEL	ADDRESS	TELEPHONE	RATES	FEATURES
Lazy Acres Motel	Riverside	327-5968	$20 s, $25 d	
Bear Trap Cafe	Riverside	327-5277	$20s, $25 d $25 s, $30 d	rustic cabins, modular units, open May-Nov.
Elk Horn Motel	508 McCaffrey	327-5110	$21 s, $25 d	open May-Oct.
Riverside Cabins	Riverside	327-5361	$28 s or d	rustic cabins, kitchenettes
Platts Guides & Outfitters	12 miles South of Riverside	327-5539	$35 s, $45 d	working cattle ranch
Grand & Sierra B&B	1016 Lomax	327-5200	$38 s, $48 d	modern log home

eral stores, two lodging houses, two hotels, two restaurants, and three lumber yards, along with nine saloons and two houses of prostitution. Nearby Riverside served as a shipping center for the mines. (Originally known as Dogget, the name was changed to Riverside after folks began calling it "Dog Town.") Another 1,500 people lived in the other mining towns. The mining boom came to an abrupt halt after two disastrous fires destroyed the concentrating mill, smelter, boiler room, and powerhouse. When this combined with falling copper prices, the company was forced into bankruptcy. Soon, all sorts of illegal actions surfaced, including overcapitalization and fraudulent stock sales.

All but a few diehards left the area, and what had once been the town of Grand Encampment was eventually relegated to a lesser status, simply Encampment. Logging, first for ties and mine supports, and later for lumber, became an important part of the economy; today the Hammer Sawmill is the largest local employer. Tourism is becoming increasingly important in the area.

Sights

The excellent **Grand Encampment Museum** includes items from the turn-of-the-century mining camps that filled the Sierra Madre. Displays include historic photographs, 19th-century clothing, Indian artifacts, Forest Service memorabilia, and even a folding bathtub from the 1890s. Teddy the (stuffed) dog greets visitors. Most interesting of all are the 14 authentic historic buildings set up as a frontier town with wooden boardwalks. These include a tie-hack cabin, a bakery, a lookout tower, and a stage station. The transportation barn even houses Noah's Ark (probably not the original one, alas). Oddest of all is a two-story outhouse modelled after one used in the mining ghost town of Dillon. The lower level was used in summer, with the upper floor reserved for wintertime when the snows drifted many feet deep. The Australian term for privies, "long drop," is especially applicable here! Also at the museum are parts of the 16-mile-long aerial tramway that brought ore from the Rudefeha mine.

The museum is open daily 1-5 p.m. during the summer, and Sat.-Sun. 1-5 during Sept. and October. After that, the museum is open by special appointment (tel. 327-5205). There is no charge. Retired locals provide informative tours throughout the day, and you can even buy bars of homemade soap inside the main building. On Memorial Day weekend the museum has turn-of-the-century living history demonstrations. At the museum, pick up a copy of the local **walking tour,** which describes some of the most interesting buildings in town. Be sure to also see the pretty white Presbyterian Church at Ninth and Rankin. Also ask at the museum for directions to the Indian Bathtubs, natural geologic formations that collect water and were once used for bathing.

Lodging And Camping

Although this area is popular with visitors all year, it is doubly so during the fall hunting season. Be sure to book ahead if you're coming through then. See the chart for local cabins, motels, and B&Bs. Platt's is a nice place with friendly folks, great fly-fishing, and horse trips. Recommended.

Pitch your tent for free (no RVs) on the south side of **Grand View Park** next to the museum, where locals have begun a Japanese garden! The nearest Forest Service campsite ($5; open June-Oct.) is **Bottle Creek Campground,** seven miles southwest of town on State 70. Eight more campgrounds lie west of here in the Sierra Madre. Ask locally for directions to three BLM campgrounds: Bennett Peak, Corral Creek, and Encampment River (the closest). Bennett Peak costs $3, while the others are free. **Lazy Acres RV Park** in Riverside, tel. 327-5968, has shady RV and tent sites for $6 and RV sites for $11. Showers for noncampers are $1.50. It's open May-October.

Food
Encampment has three restaurants: **The Oasis,** 706 Rankin, tel. 327-5129, **Encampment Cafe,** 623 Freeman, tel. 327-5207, and **Beverly's House of Steaks,** 518 McCaffrey, tel. 327-5203. The last of these is the best place for steaks in town, though the others are fine for simpler fare. An interesting old two-story brick building at 706 Freeman houses both **Kuntzman's Cash Store** and the **Sugar Bowl,** tel. 327-5271, which has an old-fashioned soda fountain. **Bear Trap Cafe** in Riverside, tel. 327-5277, serves standard American food. A very nice place for picnic lunches amid the cottonwoods is Riverside's town park.

Entertainment And Events
Both **Pine Lodge Saloon,** 518 McCaffrey, tel. 327-5203, and the **Mangy Moose** in Riverside, tel. 327-5117, have live music periodically throughout the summer. One of the most popular events in Wyoming is the **Woodchoppers Jamboree and Rodeo** at Encampment in late June. Begun in 1961, this is the state's largest loggers' show, with all sorts of events, including tree-felling, chainsaw log-bucking, hand-saw-ing, pole-throwing, and axe-throwing contests. Other activities include a fun amateur rodeo, parade, barbecue, and a melodrama featuring "dancehall girls." The town erupts with lots of drunk-and-rowdy behavior at night, befitting such a festival. Each Feb., the **Sierra Madre**

Winter Carnival includes dogsled and snow-mobile races, snow sculptures, broom ball, a casino night, a melodrama, dances, and other activities.

Information And Services
There is a small summer-only information cabin in Riverside, or get local info at the Grand Encampment Museum. Encampment's **city hall** is in the historic Opera House, a wooden building with a bell tower that looks like a lighthouse. The **Encampment Library,** 202 Rankin Ave., tel. 327-5775, is open Tues. and Thurs. 10-2 and Wed. 1-8 p.m. The local place for clothing and other supplies is **Big R,** 614 McCaffery, tel. 327-5444.

SIERRA MADRE

The historic Sierra Madre cover a small section of Wyoming, a finger from the Medicine Bow Range that stretches south into Colorado. This is one of the lesser-known parts of the state. Worth a visit are the many mining ghost towns and historic mine sites, plus quite a few miles of wilderness trails. The highest mountain in the range is 11,004-foot Bridger Peak, named for mountain man Jim Bridger. Before heading out, get maps ($3), camping, and hiking information from the Forest Service's **Hayden Ranger Station** at 204 W. Ninth, tel. 327-5481, in Encampment. Ask for the self-guided auto tour brochure.

Sights
Battle Hwy (State 70) crosses the Sierra Madre from Encampment on the east to Baggs on the west, a distance of 57 miles. Approximately five miles of this is gravel, though this final stretch will be paved by the end of 1994. The rest of the way is smooth with wide shoulders for bikes. It is extraordinarily scenic, especially in the fall when the aspens turn golden. Lodgepole pines are the dominant trees at higher elevations. During the winter, State 70 is closed at the forest boundary, although snowmobilers and skiers may continue up the road. Approximately 10 miles west of Encampment the road reaches the the Continental Divide at 9,916-foot Battle Pass. This is the location of **Battle,** one of many ghost towns that cap the Sierra Madre. Battle is named

for an 1841 fight between Indians and whites that took place near here.

A 4WD road (good for mountain bikes) heads north from the east side of the pass to the summit of Bridger Peak and then down the western side to the Ferris-Haggerty mine site at the ghost town of **Rudefeha,** where remains of the tramway towers are still visible. A mile to the west are the remains of **Dillon,** established after the company town of Rudefeha banned saloons; the owners simply moved a short distance away and started anew, and in no time at all Dillon was the largest town in the Sierra Madre. Many buildings remain here, hidden in the trees.

Two miles west of the Continental Divide on State 70 is a pullout overlooking pretty Battle Lake and a monument to **Thomas A. Edison**. While vacationing here in 1878, Edison was pondering over what substance to use as a filament for incandescent lights. One night he threw a broken bamboo fishing pole in the fire and was intrigued by the way the frayed pieces glowed. Carbonized bamboo would make a fine non-conducting filament for his bulbs. This tale has been passed down as fact through the years, but in reality Edison didn't come up with the idea until a year later. (Maybe he remembered the old fly rod at that time.)

The town of **Rambler** once stood along the lake shore, with the Doane-Rambler copper mine nearby. The mine operated from 1879 to 1902, producing a half-million tons of copper. Another six miles west are a few remains from the settlement of **Copperton**.

Aspen Alley

The western slopes of the Sierra Madre are carpeted with extensive stands of quaking aspen trees that came up after fires swept this region during the mining era. These reach for many miles along State 70. A favorite of photographers is **Aspen Alley,** a half-mile stretch of fabulously flamboyant fall foliage. Get here by turning north onto Deep Creek Rd. (Forest Rd. 801). The colors generally peak in late September, but this varies, so you may want to call ahead (try the Encampment Forest Service office) to get there at the best time. Sandstone Campground (no charge; open June-Oct.) is just up the road, and adventurous souls will enjoy the 50-mile drive north to Rawlins.

Once the gravel road emerges from the national forest, the land broadens into sage and grass before once again climbing over the Continental Divide. Stop here on a fall night and listen to the quiet. A few clouds hang on the western horizon. A few pickups churn clouds of dust up the road—en route to either hunting grounds or a bar. The night lays over the land like a blackened canvas splattered with stars. There aren't many places like this anymore.

Camping

The Forest Service maintains seven campgrounds ($5-6, open mid-June to mid-Sept.) in the Sierra Madre, five of which are located along the main road across the mountains, State 70. These campgrounds are not nearly as crowded as those in the Snowy Range to the east.

Huston Park Wilderness

The 31,300-acre Huston Park Wilderness straddles the Continental Divide just south of Battle Pass. It contains spruce, fir, aspen, and lodgepole forests, as well as open alpine country that reaches to 10,500 feet. **Huston Park Trail** provides an enjoyable high-elevation trek along the Continental Divide. Not a developed trail, this 16-mile-long route is marked with rock cairns and blazed trees. Trailheads are located one mile south of the Battle townsite and 2½ miles west of Hog Park Reservoir.

The nine-mile-long **Baby Lake Trail** is an enjoyable overnight trip through high meadows and along a mountain creek. Take in excellent vistas of the Snake River Valley from the Continental Divide. The trail is accessible from State 70 on both ends, but the easiest hiking is by starting from a trailhead at the end of a two-mile gravel road just south of Battle Pass. From here, the trail drops 2,600 feet in elevation to a second trailhead located off Forest Rd. 811 (near Lost Creek Campground).

North Fork Encampment Trail takes you two miles up North Fork Creek to Green Mountain Falls. Get to the trailhead by driving west from Encampment to Bottle Creek Campground, and then south on Forest Rd. 550 for 1½ miles. This is one of the few waterfalls in the area.

Encampment River Wilderness

At just 10,400 acres, Encampment River Wilderness is one of the smallest and least-visited wilderness areas in Wyoming. The centerpiece is the Encampment River with its narrow canyon, rushing rapids, and quiet pools (fine fishing). Despite the Encampment's current wilderness status, much of this land was logged over at the turn of the century to supply railroad ties and mine timbers for the Union Pacific Railroad. Old cabins and mines offer endless opportunities to explore. The well-maintained **Encampment River Trail** is a 15-mile-long path that follows this wild and scenic river through the heart of the wilderness. Roads provide access from either end, so the trail is easier to hike if you can shuttle a second vehicle to the other end. Start from a trailhead near the BLM's Encampment River Campground, located two miles south of Encampment. The trail follows the river, beginning in low-elevation sage-and-grass country and gradually climbing into dense lodgepole and spruce forests. The first five miles are considerably easier hiking than higher up, where the canyon narrows and becomes more rugged. The trail ends at Hog Park, near the Colorado state line.

Another off-the-beaten-path sight near the Encampment River Wilderness is an old fire tower (no longer in use) at **Blackhall Mountain,** approximately 15 miles south of Riverside on Forest Rd. 409. The last several miles are narrow, but passable. From the top are long vistas into the mountains of Wyoming and Colorado.

Winter Recreation

During the winter months, the Forest Service maintains more than a dozen miles of **cross-country ski trails** around the Bottle Creek Campground, 5½ miles west of Encampment. A parking area at the forest boundary provides access. Many forest roads in the Sierra Madre are used extensively by snowmobilers.

LITTLE SNAKE RIVER VALLEY

The Little Snake River Valley is one of the most isolated parts of Wyoming; it lies right along the Colorado border, with the desolate Red Desert to the west and the Sierra Madre to the east. Three tiny towns spread out along the ir-

rigated farmland that follows Savery Creek: **Baggs** (pop. 270), **Dixon** (pop. 70), and **Savery.** Baggs was named for rancher George Baggs and his notorious wife Maggie; this was a gathering place for outlaws. Butch Cassidy helped build a place in Baggs known as Matthew's House. It is still standing. Another noteworthy building is the historic **Bank Bar Club.** An unusual two-story log blockhouse built by mountain man Jim Baker is in Savery next to the **Little Snake River Museum.** The museum contains Jim Baker's canoe, plus other historical items. Also of note is the **Little Snake River Valley Rodeo** held each July in Dixon and the **Cutting Horse Contest,** where cowboys work specially trained horses to move cattle.

Stay at **Drifters Inn,** tel. 383-2015, in Baggs for $30 s or d. **Savory Creek Thoroughbred Ranch,** near Savery, tel. 383-7840, is a special riding ranch for those who are serious about horses. Beautiful country all around, and gracious lodging in an antique-furnished home.

FORT FRED STEELE

History

Fort Fred Steele—named for Civil War hero Maj. Gen. Frederick Steele—was built in 1868 as one of three Wyoming posts established to protect the transcontinental railroad from Indian attacks. Soldiers from the fort fought against the Utes in northern Colorado during their 1879 uprising against tyrannical Indian agent Nathan C. Meeker. The troops also helped reestablish peace after the 1885 anti-Chinese riots in Rock Springs.

After the fort was abandoned by the Army in 1886, civilians took over the buildings, turning this into a supply base for ranchers and sheepherders. It was headquarters for the Carbon Timber Company, a company that controlled the enormous tie market for the Union Pacific Railroad in the Rockies and owned nearly 25,000 acres of timberland. Lodgepole pine were felled in the Medicine Bow Mountains and floated down the North Platte River during high flows each spring. At Fort Steele, they were caught by a log boom and loaded onto railway cars or used in the sawmill or box factory. The tie industry remained important well into this century, with 300,000 ties being sent down the North Platte River in 1938 alone, but when the Union Pacific stopped using hand-hewn ties in 1940, the town of Fort Steele suffered. With the loss of its main industry and the moving of the Lincoln Hwy. (in 1939), all but a few people moved away.

Fort Steele Today

Fort Steele is now a 137-acre state park located nine miles east of Sinclair on I-80. A small visitor center (open daily 7-7 May-Oct.) in the old bridge tender's house contains many historical photos of the fort and Carbon Timber Company. Historical plaques are scattered over the grounds, but not much remains from what had been a substantial settlement, just a couple of clapboard buildings, some sandstone foundations and chimneys, and the walls of a house once owned by Fenimore Chatterton (who served as governor from 1903 to 1905). Stone walls from the military quartermaster's corral are just west of the parade grounds, but a disastrous arson fire on New Year's Eve, 1976, destroyed two enlisted men's barracks that had stood here for more than a century. Just up the hill from the fort site is a square stone ordnance magazine (1881) with an adjacent cemetery containing the graves of civilians who died in the area. Only a few headstones remain. The slow-moving North Platte River right next to the fort is a great place for picnics (but no camping). Despite the paucity of historical buildings, there is something rather nice about the authenticity of the site. Stop in at dusk on a summer evening, and you'll hear the distant rumble of freight trains, while coyotes howl from nearby hills, and the North Platte River rolls quietly away from this lonely place.

SINCLAIR

Sinclair (pop. 500) is one of the more distinctive small settlements in Wyoming. In 1923, the Pro-ducers Oil and Refining Company (Parco) established a 50,000-barrel-a-day oil refinery here and built a town to house its employees, naming the town Parco. When the Sinclair Oil Company bought the refinery in 1934, the town's name changed. Today, the refinery still lights up the night sky for miles around, and hundreds of giant oil tanks stand behind the facility. Interstate 80 passes right by Sinclair, and most folks don't bother to stop, except to fill up at the Burns Brothers Truckstop a mile east of town or at the Sinclair station in town. Actually, Sinclair is a pleasant little resting place and a nice place for a shady picnic lunch.

When Parco built the company town, everything was constructed in Spanish-mission style (red-tile roofs and stucco walls), including the large Parco Inn at the center. You'd think you were in southern California. An elaborate fountain and a nice small park stand across from the now almost-abandoned building. Only the bar remains open. A pair of Civil War-vintage cannons guard the water fountain from attack by marauding oil executives. They were brought here originally to blow holes in burning oil tanks, allowing the oil to drain into the surrounding dykes before the tanks could explode from the heat.

The **Sinclair/Parco Museum** is located in the old bank building and contains a number of local items, including the high point, a newspaper headlined "Nixon Resigns." Open summer weekdays, or stop at the town hall (next door) for access to the museum if it's closed. While here check out the police car, perhaps the only Chevy Cavalier station wagon patrol vehicle anywhere (I'm assured that it was purchased at a bargain price!). The small branch library is open Mon., Tues., and Thursdays. Of note in Sinclair is **Su Casa Cafe,** tel. 328-1745, which makes genuine Mexican food. No motels in town, but the road north of Sinclair leads to popular Seminoe and Pathfinder reservoirs, where camping is available (see "Central Wyoming," pp. 196-197). Sinclair also has a nine-hole golf course, site of the biggest Fourth of July fireworks display in the area.

RAWLINS

The small city of Rawlins (pop. 9,400) sits right in the middle of southern Wyoming. To the east and south lie mountain ranges and rich grazing land; to the west is the Great Divide Basin and a vast expanse of desert country. During the late 1970s and early '80s, Rawlins was a hub of development as the "Oil Patch" blossomed and energy companies pumped petrodollars into the economy. But like in so many other Wyoming towns, the inevitable bust that followed was traumatic. Layoffs affected everyone in town in one way or another, and Rawlins still shows signs of being down in the dumps, with quite a few empty storefronts. Not everyone packed up and left, however. Most of the people who lived here before the oil boom stayed around when the bust hit, scraping by on business brought in by traffic from the freeway, local ranchers, and the energy companies. Many Rawlins work-

ers now commute 40 miles to work in the Hanna coal mines. With restoration of the old state prison, Rawlins is trying to broaden its limited tourism base.

HISTORY

Rawlins is named for Gen. John A. Rawlins, the secretary of war under President Grant. In 1867, as the railroad route was being surveyed westward, the crew of Gen. Grenville Dodge met up with soldiers under Rawlins' command. When they discovered a clear, alkali-free spring at the base of a hill, Rawlins remarked, "If anything is ever named after me, I hope it will be a spring of water." Dodge immediately decided to name this Rawlins Spring. When a division point on the Union Pacific was established here in 1868, the town was also named Rawlins Spring. Its name was later shortened to Rawlins.

In 1886, the Wyoming Legislature appropriated $100,000 for a state penitentiary in Rawlins. Two years later, construction began, with enormous slabs of sandstone cut and hauled by wagon from a quarry south of town. Because of inadequate funding, the new prison was not completed and occupied until Dec. 1901, some 13 years after it was begun. By that time the town had grown, and what had been a relatively remote location was now in central Rawlins. For the next eight decades, this would be Wyoming's only state prison, housing its most hardened criminals. The prison was finally abandoned in 1981, when the inmates were transferred to a new facility south of Rawlins.

FRONTIER PRISON

Rawlins' main attraction is the Frontier Prison at Fifth and Walnut streets, first opened in 1901 and in use until 1981. (Actually, it was a state prison for all of its existence, but locals prefer to call it a frontier prison since construction began while Wyoming was still a territory.) The imposing turret towers and stonework of the prison's exterior give it the oppressive appearance of a medieval castle. Inside, conditions for the inmates were almost as primitive, bordering on ghastly. There was no plumbing or electricity for the first 15 years, and it was 1978 before hot water was installed in one block of cells. A special dungeon house was built for uncooperative inmates, and beatings were common in the early years. Ten prisoners were hanged (one by fellow inmates), and another five were executed in the gas chamber in Rawlins, the last dying in 1965. The gallows were a uniquely gruesome device in which the victim actually hung himself through an elaborate mechanism by which his weight displaced a water counterbalance, thus releasing a trap door and leaving him hanging by a noose. It was built to hang notorious cattle detective and murderer Tom Horn in 1903 (see p. 27) and moved into the prison later. (Tom Horn was never in this prison.) The instrument did not always work; one man had to be strangled by the "humane" guards when he didn't die fast enough. Death-row in-

mates in Wyoming now face lethal injection instead. Science marches onward!

The old prison was the scene of several escape attempts, including one in which four death-row inmates tunneled out as far as the west wall before being caught. The dirt was secreted away in the ceiling panels; it's still visible there. Two other breakouts were successful—one involved 28 men—although nearly all the escapees were later caught or killed in the surrounding community. In later years the penitentiary housed 500 prisoners and employed 100 guards and other workers.

In 1987, the grade-B movie *Prison* was filmed on location here, with a number of locals as extras. Parts of the movie set are still visible, and some of the prison floors are still red from the fake blood. If you missed it in the theaters, don't despair; this is one of those god-awful flicks that will eventually make it to the 4 a.m. movie dregs slot on some obscure cable-TV station.

The Lone Bandit

The most famous inmate to spend time here was William Carlisle, the "gentleman train robber." In three Union Pacific train robberies in Wyoming, Carlisle netted barely $1,000. He never took money from female passengers and was reported to have bought gifts for children with the money. After the third robbery, he was caught and sentenced to life in prison. Carlisle was sent to Rawlins in 1916 but escaped in a shirt crate three years later. In another train robbery Carlisle was shot and wounded but still managed to remain free for two weeks before a posse caught up with him. The last conviction landed him with another life sentence, but the governor pardoned Carlisle in 1936. He walked out a changed man and eventually became a respected Laramie motel owner and author of a book about his life, *The Lone Bandit*. Carlisle died in 1964.

Practicalities

During the summer months, the prison is open Mon.-Sat. 8:30-4:30 and Sun. 10:30-4:30, with guided tours every hour. These excellent, hour-long tours cost $3.50 for adults, $3 for seniors or kids (children under six free), and $12 for families. During the rest of the year, tours are generally offered between 10:30 and 3:30 daily, but call ahead (tel. 324-4422) for times. Be sure to bring a sweater or coat with you, since the stone prison is a chilly place, even in midsummer. For a scarier visit, ask about the nighttime flashlight tours ($4.50 pp), offered in summer by reservation only.

The Smell Of Sage

Outlaw Mercantile in front of the old prison sells gifts (T-shirts, leather belts, paintings, and other items) made by inmates at the new state penitentiary just south of Rawlins. A portion of the old prison has been turned into a small museum housing photos and descriptions of various inmates, and a souvenir shop selling postcards, books, and other items. One book well worth a look is *The Sweet Smell of Sagebrush.* This is a collection of stories by William Stanley Hudson, a man who served four separate sentences here for such crimes as horse stealing and passing stolen checks. It offers not only a glimpse of turn-of-the-century prison life but also a fascinating account of criminal logic. The title comes from his release from prison after serving his first sentence:

i thought little of those things that august day as i walked out from the damp prison air into the glorious sunshine of this enchanted land. i felt only a desire to get away somewhere out of sight. after walking towards the buisness part of town a short way, i turned and went straight out of town untill i reached the high sagebrush. the smell of the sage was that day sweeter to me than a breath from a bed of rarest flowers. for an hour i was content to sit and breathe the pure mountain air and enjoy the warm sunshine.

Hudson's fate is unknown. After release from his fourth incarceration in 1921, he disappeared. Perhaps he was a reformed man. Perhaps he learned enough to avoid being caught again.

OTHER SIGHTS

Carbon County Museum

Housed in an old Mormon church at Ninth and Walnut streets, tel. 324-9611, the Carbon County Museum is open Mon.-Fri. 1-4 p.m. June-Aug., with reduced winter hours. There is no charge. The museum is a mixed bag, containing a few Indian relics, a 1920 hook-and-ladder truck, along with various stage-station and Civil War artifacts. Easily the strangest object in the Carbon County Museum is a pair of two-tone shoes made from the skin of Big Nose George Parrot, a train robber and murderer. These were crafted by Dr. John E. Osborne, who also decided to saw open George's skull to see if the brains of desperadoes differed from common men. The skullcap became an ashtray. (This is the same Dr. Osborne who would serve as governor of Wyoming from 1893 to 1895!) The bottom of the skull is also on display here, along with Big Nose George's death mask and a photo of the old whiskey barrel that Osborne decided to store the body in. The barrel wasn't discovered until 1950 when a construction crew found it while digging at an old Rawlins drugstore. Looking for more criminals? Try **St. Joseph's Cemetery** where two early-day train robbers are buried. Ask at the museum for the exact grave locations. Still more crooks? Try the state penitentiary, south of town; you'll meet real live ones there.

Larson Hardware

Hardware stores don't generally fit in the category of local attractions, but Larson Hardware at 208 W. Cedar is an exception. The old store houses several thousand arrowheads that have been picked up over the years by J.W. Larson. It is one of the largest arrowhead and artifact collections anywhere in Wyoming, with 44 different display cases surrounding the walls. Drop in and talk to the friendly folks here.

Buildings

Quite a number of interesting old sandstone buildings are scattered around downtown, built from stone quarried around Rawlins. Notable ones include the Shrine Temple at Fifth and Pine (completed in 1909), the Elks Club at Fourth and Buffalo (completed in 1909), and the Presbyterian church at Third and Cedar (built in 1882). The Union Pacific Railroad depot at 400 W. Front was built in 1901 of granite and brick and was in use until 1983. It's still in good condition, but for some reason Amtrak stops at the small shed next door! One of the most attractive buildings in Rawlins is the **Ferris Mansion** at 607 W. Maple, built for the widow of an early mining pioneer, George Ferris, and now open as a B&B. An old **steam locomotive** can be seen in Tully Park on Elm St. next to the hospital.

"Rockology"

The country around Rawlins is a geologist's and rock hound's paradise, with jade, petrified wood, agate, and other minerals to be discovered. Of course, oil, gas, and coal are what geologists are most interested in around here. The **Rawlins Uplift** (a thrust-faulted anticline) rises immediately north of town, providing a textbook example of stratigraphy. Plenty of fish and invertebrate fossils here too. **Alex Semryck**, tel. 324-3566, a retired geologist, provides free half-day tours of the Rawlins Uplift during the summer months, an excellent way to learn geology from a local expert. Recommended. As a side note, the paint known as "Rawlins Red" originated from iron oxide mined just north of the town. The color is still used for barns and buildings in the eastern U.S., and this was the color originally chosen by Gen. Rawlins to paint the Brooklyn Bridge—as Secretary of War, he approved the bridge plans.

BIG NOSE GEORGE PARROT

George Manuse, better known as Big Nose George Parrot, was one of the most notorious outlaws in the West. In 1878 his gang attempted to derail a Union Pacific train by pulling up a piece of track and waiting in ambush. Unfortunately for the outlaws, an alert UP employee discovered the missing rail before the train arrived, and a manhunt ensued. A posse followed the gang's tracks into Rattlesnake Canyon and then stopped in a camp that had been recently deserted. As a deputy sheriff bent over to check the coals, he commented, "They're hot as hell." Immediately, a voice came from behind the bushes, "We'll show you how hot hell is." Two deputies were shot dead.

Two years later, the law finally caught up with Big Nose George in Montana, and he was taken back to Rawlins in shackles. When the train pulled into town, 15 armed men forced the sheriff to release the prisoner to them and hauled him off to be hanged. Big Nose George managed to avoid his fate this time by noting that, "Dead men tell no tales," but he was convicted of the murders the following spring and sentenced to hang. In an escape attempt shortly after the trial, George cracked the skull of a guard with his shackles before finally being subdued. When word of the escape attempt spread through Rawlins, a mob of masked men broke into the jail. Big Nose George was hauled out and lynched in the street, though it took two tries—the rope was too long the first time. The Rawlins jail register notes that Big Nose George Parrot, "Went to join the angels via hempen cord on telegraph pole front of Fred Wolf's saloon."

PRACTICALITIES

Accommodations

Given its relatively small size, Rawlins has a surprising number of places to stay. Partly this is a holdover from the boom era, when housing was tight and many workers lived in motels and mobile homes; partly it is the result of the influx of tired I-80 travelers each night. See the chart for a complete listing. Of particular note is **Ferris Mansion Bed and Breakfast**, a classic Victorian home built in 1903 and on the National Register of Historic Places.

Campgrounds

The nearest public campground (free; open June-Oct.) is at **Teton Reservoir**, 17 miles south of Rawlins. More public facilities ($4; open year-round) are in Seminoe State Park, 28 miles north of Sinclair; see pp. 196-197, for details. A pair of parking lot/campgrounds can be found in Rawlins. Expect to pay $9 for tents or $16 for RVs at **Western Hills Campground**, 2500 Wagon Circle Rd., tel. 324-2592, or **RV World Campground**, 2401 Wagon Circle Rd., tel. 328-1091. Great places to swelter in the simmering heat of summer as you listen to the freeway traffic.

Food

No real standouts on the Rawlins breakfast scene, but **Square Shooter's Eating House**, 311 W. Cedar, tel. 324-4380, has standard American fare served in an enjoyable downtown place with animal heads on the walls. Good for lunches and dinners too. One of Wyoming's dining-out gems is **Rose's Lariat** at 410 E. Cedar, tel. 324-5261. The ads claim, "Best Mexican food in town. Ask anyone!" Some folks claim that this is one of the best and most authentic Mexican restaurants in Wyoming. Not to be missed, but be ready to wait in line at dinner time. If you can't get in the door, try **El Jardin**, 401 W. Cedar, tel. 324-2639, which also offers good south-of-the-border cooking. Another excellent dinner choice is **The Pantry**, 221 W. Cedar St., tel. 324-7860, located in a building built in 1881. This is a fine, family-run place with reasonable prices and all-American food. Lots of grub for the buck.

For pizza, try **Cappy's**, 18th and W. Spruce, tel. 324-4847, or **Pizza Hut**, 506 Higley Blvd., tel. 324-7706. The latter usually has lunchtime specials. Fast service and decent truckstop grub

at **Gay Johnson's Restaurant**, two miles west of Rawlins, tel. 324-3463, and **Rip Griffin's Truckstop**, I-80 at Higley Blvd., tel. 328-2103. **Rocky's**, 1915 E. Murray, tel. 328-0308, is the local sandwich joint, or head to the deli counters at **Ideal Foods** or **City Market**.

Entertainment And Events

The lounge at **Days Inn**, 2222 E. Cedar, tel. 324-6615, has Top-40 DJ tunes most nights and occasional rock bands. For live country music, traipse on down to **Golden Spike Inn**, 1617 W. Spruce, tel. 324-2271. Another place to try is **The Keg**, 307 E. Cedar, tel. 324-9826.

The main local event is the **Carbon County Fair and Rodeo**, held the second full week of August each year. At the same time, Rawlins celebrates **Outlaw Days**, featuring lots more

RAWLINS ACCOMMODATIONS

MOTEL	ADDRESS	TELEPHONE	RATES	FEATURES
Golden West Motel	822 W. Pine	324-4452	$18 s, $20 d	
Ideal Motel	1507 W. Spruce	324-3451	$18 s, $22 d	kitchenettes
Hi Top Motel	713 W. Spruce	324-4561	$20 s, $22 d	
Rifleman Motel	1915 W. Spruce	324-2263	$20 s, $24 d	
La Bella Motel	1819 W. Spruce	324-2583	$22 s, $26 d	
Jade Lodge	499 W. Spruce	324-2791	$22 s, $28 d	
Cliff Motor Lodge	1500 W. Spruce	324-3493	$23 s, $24 d	
Bucking Horse Lodge	1720 W. Spruce	324-3471	$24 s, $26 d	kitchenettes
Holiday Lodge	2011 W. Spruce	324-7878	$25 s, $30 d	
Sunset Motel	1302 W. Spruce	324-3448	$26 s, $30 d	AAA approved
Bridger Inn	1902 E. Cedar	328-1401	$29 s, $32 d	AAA approved
Golden Spike Inn	1617 W. Spruce	328-1600	$30 s, $32 d	
Key Motel	1806 E. Cedar	324-2728	$32 s or d	AAA approved
Rawlins Motel	905 W. Spruce	324-3456	$32+ s or d	AAA approved
Weston Inn	1801 E. Cedar	324-2783	$35 s or d	
Days Inn	2222 E. Cedar	324-6615 (800) 325-2525	$45+ s, $50+ d	
Super 8 Motel	2338 Wagon Cir.	328-0630 (800) 800-8000	$46 s or d	
Ferris Mansion Bed and Breakfast	607 W. Maple	324-3961	$50+ s or d	AAA approved, historic place
Bel Air Inn (Best Western)	23rd and Spruce	324-2737 (800) 528-1234	$59+ s, $65+ d	AAA approved, pool, sauna

local activities. In early July, **Old West Summerfest** includes booths, races, local tours, and country music.

Recreation

The **Rawlins Family Recreation Center**, 1616 Harshman, tel. 324-7529, has racquetball, basketball, and volleyball courts, along with a weight room and other facilities. Swim at the high school pool year-round or during summers at the Washington Park pool. **Galaxy Skate Center**, Third and Cedar, tel. 324-7850, has evening skating for $3, including skates, or you can join the locals for bingo at the Moose Lodge.

Information And Services

The **Rawlins-Carbon County Chamber of Commerce** is right in front of the old prison at Fifth and Walnut, tel. 324-4111 or (800) 228-3547, and is open Mon.-Fri. 8-5. **Carbon County Public Library**, Third and Buffalo, tel. 328-2618, is open Mon. and Wed. 10-6, Tues. and Thurs. 12-8, and Fri. 10-5. **Carbon County Higher Education Center**, 600 Higley Blvd., tel. 328-9204, provides night classes and a variety of two-year degree programs. The **BLM district office** is at 1300 N. Third, tel. 324-7171. **Cedar Chest Gallery**, 416 W. Cedar, tel. 324-7737, is a gift shop and art gallery with a small collection of Wyoming books.

Transportation

Amtrak, tel. (800) 872-7245, has daily train service heading both east and west. Trains stop next to the old downtown depot. **Greyhound**, 301 W. Cedar, tel. 324-5496, has bus service along I-80 in both directions, but no direct connections between Rawlins and Casper or other cities in the northern part of Wyoming; the nearest connection is via Cheyenne or Rock Springs. Rent cars from **McGee Murphy Ford**, Seventh and Spruce, tel. 324-3434. There's no commercial air service to Rawlins.

HEADING NORTH

US 287-State 789 points north from Rawlins into Wyoming's heartland, crossing the Continental Divide twice along the way as it dips into the Great Divide Basin and then back out again. Once inside the basin, the highway throws itself straight across this sandy land from point A to point B, with not much in between to deflect it. No need to touch the steering wheel here. The fences collect both tumbleweeds and bits of miscellaneous junk. To the northeast the tilted face of 10,037-foot Ferris Mountain rises, but your sense of distance falters in the featureless desert land where only fences and a few gullies halt the relentless horizontal geography. Geologists love this place: long, eroded ridges, and scarps in the distance that appear so parched of water their barren slopes could be the bleached rib cages of some prehistoric monster. Some amazing badlands formations are here as well.

Forty miles north of Rawlins, the highway climbs through **Whiskey Gap**, with Green Mountain to the west and the Ferris Mountains to the east. The gap got its name in 1862 when Maj. Jack O'Farrell caught his soldiers drinking from an illegal barrel of whiskey in a trader's wagon. The whiskey was dumped on the ground, but some flowed into a spring that one soldier later called the "sweetest water he had ever tasted." Another five miles north is the junction of US 287-State 789 and State 220 at **Muddy Gap**. Not much here other than a run-down motel, gas station, and store, but travelers will enjoy stopping to talk with Frank Erickson at the store. The road diverges, with one fork leading northeast to Casper, passing the Oregon Trail landmarks of Devil's Gate and Independence Rock along the way, and the other heading northwest to Lander, with Split Rock and Jeffrey City along the way. In either direction you will find stereotypical Wyoming sights—sagebrush, grass, cattle, and sky.

SOUTHWEST WYOMING

Southwest Wyoming is the state's forbidden quarter, a place seen most frequently from Interstate 80. Most folks consider it a stark, barren, and worthless chunk of earth. In 1866, Gen. William T. Sherman wrote, "The Government will have to pay a bounty for people to like it up here." Others said people wouldn't come, no matter how many incentives the government might offer. But despite the lack of trees, the broiling hot summers, and the wind-iced winters, people *have* settled here, primarily to extract the area's immense energy and mineral resources. Southwest Wyoming contains both the state's largest county (Sweetwater) and its smallest (Uinta), along with Lincoln County, seemingly named for its L-shape. The Green River cuts across this part of Wyoming, eventually joining the Colorado River in Utah.

History

When whites first arrived in southwest Wyoming, they found the Shoshone and Ute Indians hunting buffalo and antelope in this desert country. The first mountain men rendezvous took place here, and many of the vital emigrant routes passed through, including the Oregon, Mormon, and Overland trails, along with the Pony Express and the transcontinental telegraph. But it was the Union Pacific Railroad that opened the land to settlement. Completion of the railroad in 1869 brought about the establishment of Rock Springs, Green River, and Evanston, while coal mines were developed in the Rock Springs, Evanston, and Kemmerer areas to fuel these trains. Men of all nationalities came to work the mines, creating a racial diversity still visible.

Just as the coal mines began to close in the 1950s, enormous trona deposits were developed in western Sweetwater County, and many miners simply switched employers. Other mines extract phosphates and coal, while the natural-gas fields of Sweetwater and Uinta counties are the most productive in Wyoming. Southwest Wyoming has the world's biggest coal mine, coke-producing plant, trona mine, and helium plant. Put all this together, and it is obvious that despite the desert setting and small population, southwest Wyoming is in some ways the most industrialized part of the state.

THE RED DESERT

The eastern half of Sweetwater County contains a vast treeless area known as the Red Desert, so named because of the brick-red soil that stretches in all directions. It is a place not to be trifled with. Less than nine inches of precipitation fall each year, and summertime temperatures frequently top 100° F in this forbidding, lonely place—the largest stretch of unfenced land in the lower 48. Some of the biggest remaining herds of wild horses roam here, along with desert elk and one of the last wild herds of bison. Antelope are found throughout this country, along with a few cattle and lots of sheep. The signs of humans are few and far between: dirt roads, oil and gas wells, and a few wind-scoured buildings.

Interstate 80 is most folk's sole acquaintance with the Red Desert, two double-wide rivers of asphalt cracking open the desiccated land. Not many sights to see, unless you pull off the main road and slow down. Despite its harshness, the Red Desert has a desolate beauty that grows on you. Pick what may seem the least interesting place where the ramp ends at a cattle crossing and the road immediately turns to gravel. When you're far enough from the interstate that you can no longer hear the trucks, get out of your car and use all your senses to grasp this place. Feel the intensity of the sun on a blistering summer day. Look at the way the thin-crusted snow lies in the lee side of the sage in the winter, worn out by the constant wind. Listen to the "scree!" cry of the red-tailed hawk. Taste a couple of the the pungent sage leaves; smell the rusty air as the first drops of a sudden shower pummel the road dust. Watch a herd of antelope bound away and then turn warily back to see who might be stopping in such a place. Or simply let the stillness of this vast land sweep over you, broken by the howl of a distant coyote. This is Wyoming.

The Red Desert lies within **Great Divide Basin,** a 90-mile-long region where the little water that falls never makes it to either ocean. Red Lake—a salty playa—fills with water during rare rainy spells, only to have it soak into the sandy soil or evaporate in the summer sun. The Continental Divide splits south of Great Divide Basin and then rejoins on its northern margin, leaving a bowl in the middle. Highway travelers thus cross the Continental Divide twice.

As you head west from Rawlins toward Rock Springs (108 miles away), the only town worth noting—and marginally so—is **Wamsutter** (pop. 240). Natural-gas wells now sprinkle the country to the west and south. Butch Cassidy's Hole-in-the-Wall gang robbed a Union Pacific train nearby in 1900. Two places to rest your head here: **Sagebrush Motel,** tel. 328-1584, and **Wamsutter Motel,** tel. 324-7112. The latter has kitchenettes. At **Point of Rocks,** 25 miles east of Rock Springs, the state has restored an Overland Stage station built in 1862. Ruins of the stables are nearby. The station served as a jumping-off point for a road to South Pass City during the gold-rush years. The historic stone building is well worth the brief side trip from I-80. Coal is pulled out of the ground at two large strip mines not far away. The Jim Bridger Mine feeds directly into the huge Jim Bridger Power Plant, built in the early 1970s to supply power for Utah and Wyoming. North of here are the **Natural Corrals,** an area where caves reach into the volcanic hills and often contain ice even in midsummer. Check with the Rock Springs BLM office for directions and precautions.

KILLPECKER DUNES AREA

North of Rock Springs, White Mountain rises like a cresting wave over the valley through which US 191 passes. Approximately 11 miles up is the turnoff to Tri-Territory Rd., providing access to the Killpecker Sand Dunes, the largest active dunes in North America. The dunes— some topping 150 feet in height—extend eastward for 55 miles in a band that averages two to three miles wide but sometimes reaches 10 miles wide. The constantly shifting dunes are formed from Eden Valley dirt that blows east on the prevailing winds. Signs point the way to most of the sights in the Killpecker Dunes area.

Petroglyphs And Boars Tusk

Follow gravel Tri-Territory Rd. 12 miles east from US 191 and head left at the turnoff to **White Mountain Petroglyphs,** a very rough four-mile track that ends at a low sandstone cliff. (Avoid this road after rains or early in the year.) Some 100 or so petroglyphs were carved into the soft rock by the Indian peoples who lived here in centuries past. Look closely to find elk, bison, horses, feather headdresses, and even a human footprint. Many petroglyphs relate to hunting. Because of the horses pictured here (they did not reach this region until the 16th century), it is likely that many of the petroglyphs are of relatively recent origin. Look up the cliff to find several large raptor nests. Juniper and sage poke up through the remote desert landscape.

Return to the main gravel road and turn left to get to other interesting sights. Six miles to the east the road splits. Turn right to reach the ORV area of the dunes or left to visit **Boars Tusk** and dunes where vehicles are not allowed. Follow the latter road a mile and a half to an unmarked road that leads to the base of Boars Tusk, a prominent rocky spire (actually a volcanic plug) that's a favorite of local rock climbers. The 2½-mile side road to Boars Tusk may be passable in a high-clearance vehicle, but 4WD is recommended.

The Dunes

The dunes begin a mile and a half beyond the turnoff to Boars Tusk (22 miles from US 191). This fascinating area is most beautiful in the early morning or at dusk, when sunlight gleams off the sand. Because it is a wilderness study area, vehicles are not allowed off the roads. Animals are surprisingly common in the Killpecker Dunes, and even a cursory examination will reveal tracks of coyotes, deer, elk, birds, and insects. Small pools of water are on the lee side of some dunes. This is a great place to hike, but be sure to come prepared for a desert climate and to bring food and water, a compass, and a topographic map. The dirt roads are also fine for mountain biking. See the BLM office in Rock Springs for more details on this unusual area.

ROCK SPRINGS

As an energy and transportation center, Rock Springs (pop. 19,000) is western Wyoming's largest city. It's also Wyoming's whipping boy, the place people joke about and consider a local version of hell-on-earth. Despite recent renovation efforts, the city is still not particularly noteworthy except as a place to rest up on the way to somewhere else. Pull off the freeway and you'll find the standard grouping of fast-food eateries, chain motels, gas stations, and convenience stores that could be Anywhere, U.S.A. The rest of Rock Springs consists of a crazy patchwork of dead-end streets, trailer parks, and split-levels sprawling in various directions, with the train tracks cutting through the middle of it all. The convoluted street system is a legacy of the coal-mining era, when paths taken by miners walking to work gradually evolved into a road network. Rock Springs makes the spiderweb streets of Boston look like a model of city planning!

Like most other mining and energy towns, Rock Springs has always experienced booms and busts. Most of the underground coal mines are closed, but they still create a hazard as they settle, dropping the overlying buildings down as they go. The subsiding mines are perhaps a symbol of what happened to Rock Springs in the late 1980s as the energy-dependent economy collapsed and the oil-field workers fled for greener pastures, leaving a plague of abandoned businesses. In the last couple of years the citizens of Rock Springs have started cleaning up their image. Extensive restoration work on the historic city hall (now a museum) and along Front St. are helping transform downtown into a more likeable place.

History

Rock Springs began as a stage station along the Overland Trail but grew because of the Union Pacific's need for coal to run its trains. The Railway Act granted the Union Pacific rights to all coal along the transcontinental route. Although nearly all of Sweetwater County is underlain with coal, in Rock Springs the coal was close to the surface and easily accessible; the mines actually ran underneath the tracks in many places. Eventually the mines would spread over a mile in various directions, creating a honeycomb of tunnels under Rock Springs.

Water And Coal

Despite the fact that Rock Springs is named for flowing water, the lack of water has always been a problem. Rock Spring dried up once coal mining began, and Bitter Creek provided only muddy, bitter water. Killpecker Creek, a sometimes-stream that flows through Rock Springs, was named by soldiers who noted the alkaline water's rather painful biological effects when they visited the outhouse. Honest. In the early years, Rock Springs was so short on drinking water that it had to be brought by train from Green River. Baths were once-a-week events despite the coal dust that blackened everyone in Rock Springs.

Coal mining brought workers from all over the globe; locals call it the 57-variety town. Many arrived from Great Britain or Ireland, but others included Chinese, Italians, Scandinavians, Austrians, Hungarians, Yugoslavians, and Czechs. It was an uneasy melting pot. They lived in company housing, in riverbank dugouts, or in shanties, and used Bitter Creek—already notorious because of its undrinkable alkaline water—as the local cesspool and garbage dump. Rock Springs continued to expand as more mines were opened by the UP, and the Chinese Massacre of 1885 (see below) had only a minimal impact on production. By 1892, some 943,513 tons were being hauled out by 1,500 miners.

Although various companies mined coal, it was the Union Pacific Coal Co. that really owned Rock Springs and its miners. And it was the UP that was to blame for many of the problems: the filth, the poor housing, the lack of water, and the working conditions that spawned racial hatred. After Union Pacific engines switched from coal to diesel in the 1950s, the underground mines were closed and the economy began to fade. During another boom in the '70s, Rock Springs's population doubled, and by 1982, high-paying energy and construction jobs had made it the wealthiest city in the nation on a per-capita basis. With the crash in oil prices,

ROCK SPRINGS

however, many companies fled town and the economy went into a tailspin. More recently, the city has once again rebounded as coal and trona mining bring steady jobs to Rock Springs. An open-pit mine located east of Rock Springs now provides coal for the enormous Jim Bridger Power Plant—largest power plant west of the Mississippi—while the Black Buttes strip mine in the same area feeds power plants elsewhere in the nation. The latter mine may eventually spread its tentacles over 60 square miles of desert land. There are also two underground mines in the vicinity.

Sights

The newly remodelled **Rock Springs Museum** in the old city hall, 201 B St., tel. 362-3138, is open summers Mon.-Sat. 11-7, and Fri.-Sat. 1-5 during the winter. No charge. Built in 1894, this attractive sandstone building looks more like a medieval castle than a city hall. Inside, the local memorabilia—some dating to the 1880s—spreads over two floors. Be sure to pick up a copy of the excellent historical walking tour while here. Another interesting building—once a butcher shop—is at 432 Main. It was while working here and in other local butcher shops that Robert LeRoy Parker (Butch Cassidy) acquired his nickname "Butch." The walking tour details several other Cassidy hangouts, plus the beer garden where Calamity Jane "announced her appearances in town by emptying both of her six shooters and 'shouting verbal oaths well tarnished.'"

The site of **Camp Pilot Butte** (see "The Chinese Massacre") is now occupied by the Saints Cyril and Methodius Catholic Church at 633 Bridger, a major Slavonian center in the community. Only one of the original buildings remains, a soldiers' barracks now used as a parish school. Chinatown was just north of here. The second J.C. Penney store ever opened was housed in the building at 531 N. Front St.. The **Fine Arts Center** is next to the main library at 400 C St., tel. 362-6212, and is open Mon.-Saturday. There is some pretty surprising work here, including paintings by Conrad Schwiering, Hans Kleiber, Grandma Moses, and Norman Rockwell! Also here is a painting of the Chinese Massacre.

The **Reliance tipple,** five miles north of town on US 191 and then two miles in on County Rd. 4-42, was used to load coal into railroad cars in the 1930s. Today the impressive structure is open for self-guided walking tours. A paved path passes several interpretive signs describing the facility. Several miles northwest of Rock Springs is **Pilot Butte,** a prominent spire visible for miles in all directions, and a marker for emigrants along the Overland Trail. Get there via Gookin-White Rd. on the west side of town. You'll need a 4WD or mountain bike, unless you want to hoof it. Another interesting rock formation stands across from Plaza Mall on Dewar Drive. **West-**

THE CHINESE MASSACRE

Rock Springs has the dubious honor as the site of one of the most infamous incidents in Wyoming history, the Chinese Massacre. In 1875, the Union Pacific Railroad tried to step up coal production at its Rock Springs mines, but the miners refused when they found their wages simultaneously being cut. To fill the gap, the company brought in Chinese contract laborers who were willing to work for less money. They immediately became targets of harassment. The railroad hired more and more Chinese at the same time whites were turned away, and within a decade, more than 500 Chinese miners were in Rock Springs.

Things came to a head on Sept. 2, 1885 when the supervisor of one of the mines began assigning Chinese workers to locations where whites had previously been working. Whites attacked the Chinese, first with picks and shovels, then with rifles. The violence spread, and Chinatown—a ramshackle assemblage of shacks along what is now Ahsay Ave.—was burned to the ground. A mob of 60 men swept after the defenseless Chinese workers, robbing and then murdering them. Twenty-eight Chinese died in the melee and many more fled and may have died while trying to cross the desert. The sheriff came down from Green River to protect the whites, but did nothing to stop the murders in Chinatown. No one ever faced trial for the attacks.

The riots spawned similar anti-Chinese violence and strikes all over the West, and led Gov. Francis E. Warren to call for federal troops to protect the remaining Chinese workers. As a result, Camp Pilot Butte was established to serve as a buffer between the Chinese and whites. This was the only place in America where an international treaty post was ever established. Some 250 soldiers remained here until the Spanish-American War forced the fort's abandonment in 1899.

The workers—both white and Chinese—gradually filtered back after the riots, and by December, the mines had 85 whites and 457 Chinese workers. The massacre led the U.S. to pay the Chinese government $149,000 in compensation (used to fund Chinese student scholarships in America). In 1920s and '30s, the Union Pacific Coal Company finally rewarded the few remaining Chinese workers with passage back to their homeland and endowments to pay for their retirement. Only one of the men remained in Rock Springs all his life. The bones of others who died were shipped home to China.

An unusual legacy of the riots is a still-burning coal mine at Potter Street in Rock Springs. During the melee, several miners stole a large amount of Chinese tea and stored it in a mine tunnel, hoping to sell it later. When the authorities came for it, the miners set it on fire, and the burning tea ignited an adjacent coal seam. Smoke still emerges from the ground at what is now called Burning Mountain.

ROCK SPRINGS ACCOMMODATIONS

MOTEL	ADDRESS	TELEPHONE	RATES	FEATURES
Cody Motel	75 Center St.	362-6675	$19 s, $23 d	
Knotty Pine Motel	1234 Ninth St.	382-6600	$19 s, $25 d	kitchenettes
Rocky Mt. Motel	1204 Ninth St.	352-3593	$19 s, $25 d	
El Rancho Motel	1430 Ninth St.	362-3763	$20 s, $25 d	
Saddle Lite Motel	1411 Ninth St.	362-1846	$20 s, $25 d	
Motel 8	108 Gateway Blvd.	362-8200	$22+ s, $32 d	
Motel Thunderbird	1556 Ninth St.	362-3739	$23 s, $28 d	
Elk Street Motel	1100 Elk St.	362-3705	$25 s, $28 d	
Lamplighter Friendship Inn	1004 Dewar Dr.	362-6673	$27 s, $30 d	AAA approved, kitchenettes
Motel 6	2615 Commercial	362-1850	$28 s, $34 d	pool
Springs Motel	1525 Ninth St.	362-6683	$30 s, $35 d	AAA approved
Nomad Inn	1545 Elk St.	362-5646 (800) 341-8000	$33+ s, $37+ d	AAA approved, pool
American Family Inn	1635 N. Elk St.	382-4217	$34 s, $39 d	AAA approved, pool, whirlpool
Comfort Inn	1670 Sunset Dr.	382-9490 (800) 221-2222	$37+ s, $41+ d whirlpool	AAA approved, pool,
La Quinta Motor Inn	2717 Dewar Dr.	362-1770 (800) 531-5900	$42+ d $50+ d	AAA approved, pool
Inn at Rock Springs	2518 Foothill Blvd.	382-9600 (800) 442-9692	$49+ s, $55+ d	AAA approved, pool, exercise room
Holiday Inn	1675 Sunset Dr.	382-9200 (800) 465-4329	$50+ s, $56+ d	AAA approved, pool, jacuzzi
Outlaw Inn (Best Western)	1630 Elk St.	362-6623 (800) 528-1234	$57+ s, $63+ d	AAA approved, pool

ern Wyoming College, 2500 College Dr., tel. 382-1600, is a two-year college in attractive brick buildings with fine views of town. Inside, find a small art gallery, a surprising display of dinosaur bones, plus a museum containing archaeological and natural-history collections. Check out the giant pendulum and the spacious atrium in the student center.

Accommodations

Rock Springs has quite a number of reasonably priced places to stay; see the chart for specifics. The nearest public camping (free; open mid-May to mid-Sept.) is at **Firehole Campground,** 27 miles southwest of Rock Springs in Flaming Gorge National Recreation Area. A **KOA Kampground,** two miles west of town on North Service Rd., tel. 362-3063, provides great scenic vistas of the oil storage tanks, plus you won't need to worry about trees blocking the sun. If you still want to stop, tent sites are $10, RVs $12; open June-September.

Food

Ask someone in Rock Springs where they go for meals, and they're likely to say, "Green River." Interestingly, the same question posed to someone from Green River elicits the response, "Rock Springs." Something strange is going on here. Rock Springs does have one place you should not miss: **Grub's Drive In,** 415 Paulson, tel. 362-6634, where the thick shakes, greasedrenched (but exceptional) fried chicken, and homemade fries are favorites of both locals and visitors. This old-time family operation features Shamrock burgers which come loaded down with all the fixin's. You can almost feel your arteries clogging up. The best place for a down-home breakfast (in a greasy-spoon atmosphere) is **Renegade Cafe,** 1610 Elk St., tel. 362-3052. **Killpeppers,** 1030 Dewar Dr., tel. 382-8012, offers quality family cooking and good lunches at a slightly higher price.

For cheap lunches and a very pleasant atrium setting overlooking Rock Springs, head to the cafeteria at **Western Wyoming College,** 2500 College Drive. Three places in town offer decent Chinese-American fare (in quantity): **Lew's Family Restaurant,** 1506 Ninth St., tel. 382-9894, **Hong Kong House,** 1676 Sunset Dr., tel. 382-5462, and **Sands Cafe and Bar,** 1549 Ninth St., tel. 362-5633. The latter has probably the best all-around meal deal in Rock Springs, but service can be very slow. Try **Santa Fe Trail,** 1635 Elk St., tel. 362-5427, for distinctive Mexican and Native American cooking. Three excellent steak and seafood places are located off I-80 west of town: **Log Inn Supper Club,** tel. 362-7166; **Ted's Supper Club,** tel. 362-7323; and **White Mountain Mining Co.,** tel. 382-5265. You won't go wrong at White Mountain Mining.

Entertainment
In 1903, some 40% of the businesses in Rock Springs were bars, and even during Prohibition, many "soft drink parlors" dispensed Kemmerer moonshine. To produce this booze, 100 train cars of grapes arrived in Rock Springs within a two-month period! Quite a few places still offer nightlife, although many are on the sleazy side, particularly those places along the railroad tracks. The best places for live country-western music are **White Mountain Mining Co.,** west of Rock Springs, tel. 382-5265, and **Saddle Lite Saloon,** 1704 Elk St., tel. 362-8704. **Killpeppers,** 1030 Dewar Dr., tel. 382-8012, is very popular with the rock and pop crowd most nights. For something a bit more risqué (exotic dancers), try **Diamond Lil's,** 1549 Elk, tel. 382-6400, or **Fantasia,** 1549 Mountain View Dr., tel. 362-7760. Fantasia offers rock bands on weekends.

Events
Two rodeos attract contestants to Rock Springs: the **All Girl Rodeo** in early May is the biggest rodeo of its type in the West, while **Red Desert Round Up** in early Aug. is the second-largest professional rodeo in Wyoming, and the main summertime event. The latter also features a Saturday-morning pancake breakfast followed by a parade. **Sweetwater County Fair** is held here in early August, right after the Round Up. **Sweetwater Downs** at the fairgrounds has weekend quarter-horse and thoroughbred races from late May through mid-June. Auto-racing enthusiasts will find stock-car racing and other events all summer long at **Sweetwater Speedway.** If you're in the area in early July, be sure to ask about the **Desert Balloon Extravaganza** that includes some 30 different hot air balloons. In late August, the **Rocky Mountain Polka Festival** attracts polka dotties from all over the nation.

Recreation
The outstanding **Rock Springs Recreation Center,** 3900 Sweetwater Dr., tel. 382-3265, has an indoor pool and gym, ice arena, racquetball and tennis courts, weightroom, sauna, and jacuzzi. Entrance is $3.75 adults, $1.25 seniors, or $2 children. Out front are unique carved-brick sculptures. Similar facilities and prices are at the **civic center,** 410 N St., tel. 362-6181. There is also a third pool at Western Wyoming College. **White Mountain Golf Course,** tel. 382-5030, has an 18-hole course three miles north of town.

Information And Services
The **Rock Springs Chamber of Commerce,** 1897 Dewar Dr., tel. 362-3771, is open Mon.-Fri. 8-6 and Sat 9-1 summers, and Mon.-Fri. 8-5 the rest of the year. The **library** at 400 C St., tel. 362-6212, is open Mon.-Thurs. 10-9 and Fri.-Sat. 10-5. Inside, you'll find a good collection of Wyoming books. **White Mountain Library** at 2935 Sweetwater Dr., tel. 362-2665, has the same hours and is a wonderful place to enjoy the view of White Mountain or stroll through a pleasant rock garden. There is a paperback book swap just inside the front door. The biggest bookstore in town is **B. Dalton** in White Mt. Mall, tel. 382-4900. You can also buy books at **Special Place,** 400 Second, tel. 362-8249, or the **Cam-**

pus Bookstore, tel. 382-1600, at the college.

Wild Horses

There are still more than 1,500 horses in south-west Wyoming. Although wild horses are often seen east of Rock Springs along I-80, the best place to view them is along the west side of US 191, approximately 28 miles north of Rock Springs. Other Wyoming places to see them are near Lander, Worland, Cody, and Lovell. The **Bureau of Land Management (BLM)** has two offices in Rock Springs: 1993 Dewar Dr., tel. 362-6422, and north of town on US 191, tel. 382-5350, either of which can supply info on the Killpecker Dunes area. Contact the latter

for information on adopting a wild horse ($125 for horses and $75 for burros) from one of their Red Desert roundups, or write the BLM at P.O. Box 1869, Rock Springs, WY 82901, for a brochure. Visiting hours at the wild-horse facility are 3-4:30 p.m. Mon.-Friday.

Transportation

Rock Springs airport is eight miles east of town and has daily service to Denver on **Continental Airlines,** tel. (800) 525-0280. Rent cars at the airport from **Hertz,** tel. (800) 654-3131, or **Avis,** tel. (800) 331-1212. **Greyhound Bus,** 1655 Sunset Blvd. (behind Burger King), tel. 362-2931, has I-80 service in both directions.

GREEN RIVER

Green River (pop. 13,000), which straddles the river of the same name, is a prosperous trona-mining and transportation town. It is the seat for Sweetwater County. Interstate 80 cuts a swath just north of town, plunging through tunnels beneath memorable badlands topography. The huge Union Pacific Railroad yard slices the town in half. Run-down buildings crowd the railroad tracks, but elsewhere Green River appears vibrant. Wander through the older parts of town to find small but tidy wooden frame homes, while ranch-style suburbs spread to the south. During the 1970s and '80s, Green River saw an enormous growth surge as the trona mines expanded their operations, and as oil and gas explorations attracted thousands of roustabouts. The population jumped from less than 5,000 in 1970 to almost 13,000 in 1980 and has been holding steady since then.

History

Green River was established in 1868 as the Union Pacific Railroad was being constructed across southern Wyoming. Three years later, Frederick Dellenbaugh described the town he found in less than flattering terms:

This place, when the railway was building, had been for a considerable time the terminus and a town of respectable proportions had grown up, but with the completion of the road through this region, the terminus moved on,

and now all that was to be seen of those golden days was a group of adobe walls, roofless and forlorn. The present 'City' consisted of about thirteen houses, and some of these were of such complex construction that one hesitates whether to describe them as houses with canvas roofs, or tents with board sides.

In May of 1869, Major John Wesley Powell brought fame when his expedition of 10 men climbed off the train at Green River City and began a long float down the Green and Colorado rivers. (While in Green River awaiting orders, the men "tried to drink all the whiskey there was in town. The result was a failure, as Jake Field persisted in making it faster than we could drink it.") They made it all the way through the Grand Canyon in stout wooden boats. Seven men survived; three who decided to hike out rather than face the treacherous rapids were never seen again. Powell returned in 1871 for a second voyage that included a large contingent of scientists who helped map this region. Powell would later direct the U.S. Geological Survey.

Green River claims title to a minor legal footnote. In 1931, Green River passed an antipeddling ordinance that achieved national notoriety and has been copied by many other towns and cities. The "Green River Ordinance" declared uninvited peddlers or hawkers to be a nuisance, punishable by a fine of $25 and up.

GREEN RIVER ACCOMMODATIONS

MOTEL	ADDRESS	TELEPHONE	RATES	FEATURES
Flaming Gorge Motel	316 E. Flaming Gorge	875-4190	$20 s, $25 d	
Mustang Motel	550 E. Flaming Gorge	875-2468	$24 s, $27 d	
Desmond Motel	140 N. Seventh	875-3701	$24+ s, $28+ d	AAA approved
Coachman Inn Motel	470 E. Flaming Gorge	875-3681	$25+ s, $28+ d	AAA approved
Western Motel	890 W. Flaming Gorge	875-2840	$30+ s, $35+ d	AAA approved
Super 8 Motel	280 W. Flaming Gorge	875-9330 (800) 800-8000	$33 s, $38 d	AAA approved

The Fuller Brush Company unsuccessfully fought the ordinance all the way to the U.S. Supreme Court.

Trona Mining

Wyoming leads the world in the mining of an obscure but important mineral known as trona. With processing, trona—sodium sesquicarbonate—becomes soda ash and is used in glass, detergents, pulp and paper, metal refining, and baking soda. Trona is found in a few widely scattered places around the globe, but mined commercially only in a thousand-square-mile area located 25 miles west of Green River. Most trona occurs in a 10-foot-thick bed some 1,500 feet underground. No chance of running out soon; there's enough here to supply the world for several thousand years. The mineral was deposited 50 million years ago when a saline lake developed, reaching 100 by 60 miles and up to 2,000 feet deep. As the climate fluctuated, the lake periodically dried out, precipitating sodium salts. The trona deposits were first discovered in the 1930s, when an unsuccessful natural-gas well brought up core samples containing trona.

Today, the six major trona mines are the region's largest employers. The world's largest trona mine is run by FMC Corporation and has 2,000 miles of tunnels, more than all the streets of San Francisco! Its tunnels are 14 feet wide and eight feet tall, big enough to use as two-lane roads. Miners get around by driving diesel-powered jeeps or electric golf carts through the maze. Mining methods include a continuous mining machine that grinds out six tons of trona a minute, a longwall process by which hydraulic rams hold the roof up as it is being mined and then allow the walls to collapse behind after the ore has been removed, and solution mining, by which the trona is dissolved underground and pumped to the surface. Once at the surface, trona is processed and sent out on railroad tank cars or in 100-pound bags of soda ash. The production is staggering: at FMC's plant alone the mine extracts more than 900 tons an hour.

Sights

Sweetwater County Historical Museum, in the county courthouse at 80 W. Flaming Gorge Way, tel. 875-2611, is open Mon.-Fri. 9-5 and Sat. 1-5 July and Aug., and Mon.-Fri. 9-5 the rest of the year. Inside, find dioramas showing prehistoric Indian life, an interactive display on trona mining, photographs from the Powell expedition, plus an impressive *Tyrannosaurus rex* footprint found in a nearby coal mine. There is even a very rare dugout canoe discovered along the Green River. Also of interest are the brass gongs, ceremonial drum, and other items that were once part of the Chinese Joss House in Evanston.

The most distinctive feature of the country around Green River is **Castle Rock,** the stunning rocky butte that rises above the freeway north of town. Other unusual buttes are **Tollgate Rock** on the northwest end of town and **Mansface Rock** behind the post office. **Expedition Island**—a National Historic Site—is where John Wesley Powell began expeditions down the Green River. A small plaque memorializes these voyages of discovery.

Accommodations And Camping

See the chart for a listing of local motels. The

GREEN RIVER

closest public camping is at **Buckboard Crossing** in Flaming Gorge ($5; open mid-May to mid-Sept.), 25 miles south of Green River on State 530. **Tex's Travel Camp,** four miles west on State 374, tel. 875-2630, is right along the river and has some shade trees. Tenters camp for $11, RVs for $16. Showers cost $5 for non-campers. Open May-September. If you are on a bike, ask about pitching a tent next to the chamber of commerce office.

Food

Some of the most popular local restaurants lie on the way east; see "Rock Springs" above for details. **Ember's Family Restaurant,** 95 E. Railroad Ave., tel. 875-9983, has good breakfasts (including a $1.49 special), home-style cooking, and delicious prime rib. Have a cup of coffee at **Cowboy Cafe,** 580 E. Flaming Gorge, tel. 875-4770, the local greasy-spoon hangout, and the only place open after the bars close. Good sandwiches and lunch deals at **Down-**

town Deli, 176 E. Flaming Gorge, tel. 875-8743, or try **Roosters,** 375 Uinta Dr., tel. 875-9052, for chicken and ribs. The best local pizza is at **Pizza Hut,** 615 E. Flaming Gorge Way, tel. 875-4562. Try **Rita's Mexican Food,** 520 Wilkes Dr., tel. 875-5503, for authentic and cheap south-of-the-border fare. **China Gardens,** 190 N. Fifth, tel. 875-3259, has a good lunch buffet on weekdays. More distinctive is **Cajun Dock,** on the corner of Center and Railroad, where the menu includes catfish, jambalaya, and even alligator!

The real surprise in Green River is **Trudel's Restaurant'e,** 3 E. Flaming Gorge Way, tel. 875-8040. The cook (Trudel Lopez) is German, but her husband (Armando Lopez) is Mexican, and the menu shares a similar eclecticism. Most of the time you'll find Mexican and American cookery, but two Saturday nights a month Trudel's has hearty German fare. Decidedly different and decidedly recommended. Get groceries and baked goods at **City Market,** 400 Uinta Dr., tel. 875-2577, or **Smith's Food Store,** 905 Bridger Dr., tel. 875-6900. Both are open 24 hours.

Entertainment And Events

Given its blue-collar base, it's no surprise that Green River has lots of bars. You'll find half a dozen along Railroad Ave., including **The Brewery,** 50 W. Railroad Ave., tel. 875-9974, housed in an amusing castle built in 1900. **Cowboy Bar,** 580 E. Flaming Gorge, tel. 875-4770, has C&W music on Fri. and Sat. nights, as does **Finer Edge,** 950 W. Flaming Gorge Way, tel. 875-6455. **Mast Lounge,** 24 E. Flaming Gorge Way, tel. 875-9990, is a biker hangout with rock music, go-go dancers, and striptease artisans. **Flaming Gorge Days,** in early July, features a parade, country music, horseshoe contests, a flea market, and other activities. The **Antique Car Show** follows in late July, attracting participants from throughout the Rockies.

Recreation

The excellent **Green River Recreation Center,** 1775 Hitching Post Dr., tel. 875-4772, has an Olympic-size pool, a gym, a weight room, and even nursery services. Entrance costs $3 ($1 seniors or $2 for kids). During the winter, rent cross-country skis here for $10 a day to use in the nearby Uinta Mountains. **Fergy's River Rats,** tel. 875-2754, offers Green River float trips and raft rentals. This is a rather gentle float.

Information And Services

The **Green River Chamber of Commerce** office at 1450 Uinta Dr., tel. 875-5711, is open Mon.-Sat. 8-5 and Sun. 8-4:30 in summer, and Mon.-Fri. 9-5 the rest of the year. Be sure to stop here to see the large relief map of Flaming Gorge and to purchase Forest Service maps or local books. **Greyhound** no longer stops in Green River except by special request, and there are no local taxis. **Wyoming Treasures,** 142 E. Flaming Gorge, tel. 875-7702, sells unique Wyoming items, from salsa to old license plates. Right next door is **Dona's Doll Den,** selling handmade porcelain dolls. Another interesting shop is **Back in Time Antiques,** on First near Flaming Gorge Way. There is a small bookstore in the Green River campus of **Western Wyoming College** on College Way, tel. 875-2278. The school sits atop a hill just south of town and offers a fine view of the surrounding badlands. **Sweetwater County Library,** 300 N. First East, tel. 875-3615, is open Mon.-Thurs. 10-9 and Fri.-Sat. 10-5. It was built over an old cemetery and seems to be filled with ghosts; librarians have seen the ghosts, heard voices from empty rooms, and watched gates open on their own.

GREEN RIVER VICINITY

LITTLE AMERICA

Find Little America approximately 20 miles west of Green River. From either direction along I-80, billboards announce, "Little America, only 350 (250, 150, 100 . . .) miles ahead!" And then, out in the desolate, windblown landscape, drivers suddenly come to this oasis of consumption where you can cozy up to cable TV or enjoy fresh produce trucked in from California. The repair bays can hold half a dozen semis at once and often do. Ten bright red fuel tanks have "Little America" emblazoned on their sides, flanked by two emperor penguins.

Little America had its origins in the mind of S. M. Covey, a sheepherder who spent a fearful winter near here in the 1890s. Covey resolved to build a way station for travelers, a place to escape from the blizzards and wind. Many years later, he saw a photo of Admiral Byrd's "Little America" in Antarctica and was inspired in 1932 to create his own Little America, adding over the years a restaurant, motel, and dozens of gas pumps. He died in the 1960s, and the operation was bought by Earl Holding. Other Little America stations are flung across the West—Cheyenne, Sun Valley, Flagstaff, Salt Lake City, and even San Diego—but this is the real thing, and the only one that rates a name on the map.

Practicalities

Little America Motel, tel. 875-2400 or (800) 634-2401, has immaculate rooms starting for $42 s or $48 d. The coffee shop is always open and good; reasonably priced meals can be had here or in the restaurant. The pastries and pies are divine. Get a 25 cent ice cream cone to go. But the real reason for Little America's existence is fuel to propel you on down the road. It seems fitting that a place with such an all-American name should be built to worship the internal-combustion engine. There are 65 gas pumps out front. (OK, one of them is a propane tank.)

West of Little America, I-80 lies across colorful badlands country, passing a temple of a different kind—**Church Buttes**. Brigham Young and his Mormon pioneers held religious services under these churchlike spires in 1847. Access today is via a gravel road north of the interstate.

SEEDSKADEE NATIONAL WILDLIFE REFUGE

The 13,812-acre Seedskadee National Wildlife Refuge is 37 miles northwest of Green River town on State 372. The word comes from the Shoshone Seeds-kee-dee, meaning "River of the Prairie Chicken." The refuge stretches 35 miles along the Green River, containing marshes and riparian areas that provide outstanding waterfowl and wildlife habitat. It is one of the finest birding areas in the state; over 200 species have been sighted. Canada geese are common, along with sandhill cranes, coots, shorebirds, great blue herons, and a variety of ducks. Good fishing here, and canoeists and rafters will see quite a few moose, deer, and antelope along the banks. This is a relatively gentle float trip, though you will need to watch for boulders placed in the channel to improve fish habitat. Camping is not allowed within the refuge, but you can camp upstream from the refuge at the BLM-run Weeping Rock and Slate Creek campgrounds. Refuge headquarters (tel. 875-2187) is just northwest of the intersection of State highways 372 and 28.

FLAMING GORGE NATIONAL RECREATION AREA

Flaming Gorge National Recreation Area covers 94,308 acres of wild country, reaching 91 miles from the town of Green River into northeastern Utah. The region is named for the impressive canyon that Major John Wesley Powell described in his famous 1869 expedition down the river:

> *At a distance of from 1 to 20 miles a brilliant red gorge is seen, the red being surrounded by broad bands of mottled buff and gray at the summit of the cliffs, and curving down to the water's edge on the nearer slope of the mountain. This is where the river enters the mountain range—the head of the first canyon we are to explore, or rather, an introductory canyon to a series made by the river through the range. We name it Flaming Gorge.*

Flaming Gorge Reservoir backs up behind a 502-foot-high concrete arch dam, which was completed in 1964 and is located 15 miles south of the Wyoming border. The dam has three enormous generators, each producing 50,000 kilowatts of power. The reservoir also provides irrigation water for Utah farmers and recreation for boaters, waterskiers, and anglers. Many osprey nest on the rocky pinnacles and cliffs around the edges, while below the dam is a river runner's funhouse. The area attracts over two million visitors annually.

ACCESS AND SIGHTS

The landscape surrounding the Wyoming portion of Flaming Gorge is typical high desert country, but once you cross into Utah, the road climbs into mountains covered with forests of pinyon pine, juniper, lodgepole, and ponderosa pine. This area was a favorite hideout of Butch Cassidy and other outlaws, who operated out of nearby Brown's Hole. Flaming Gorge Reservoir is encircled by roads—total loop distance 160 miles—providing a pleasant overnight break from the grinding I-80 routine. The main roads don't come particularly close to the dramatic gorge itself (except at the dam), but side roads do provide access.

One of the most interesting ways to reach Flaming Gorge is via State 414 heading southeast from the town of Mountain View. The road climbs past colorful, eroded badlands topography—as though an enormous skeletal landscape were showing through—before emerging into wide-open spaces carpeted with grass and sage. Then the road dips down along the Henry's Fork, where cottonwoods and willows form a border to lush green pastures. Huge piles of hay crowd the pastures. Keep your eyes open for the many historic log structures. A sign notes the location of the first mountain men rendezvous in 1825 when 120 trappers traded furs for supplies from the East. Butch Cassidy and other outlaws later frequented Uncle Jack's Cabin Saloon, which stood nearby. Today, there is a small store and post office in **McKinnon**, but that's about it till you reach Manila, Utah. This is the real West!

Flaming Gorge National Recreation Area is administered by the U.S. Forest Service. Get information and topo maps at the Ashley National Forest offices in Manila, Utah, tel. (801) 784-3228, or Green River, Wyoming, tel. 875-2871. The Manila office is open daily 8-4:30 in the summer. The Bureau of Reclamation maintains a year-round **visitor center** atop the dam, with self-guided dam tours available daily April-October. A second visitor center at **Red Canyon Overlook** is open daily 9:30-5 in summer and offers breathtaking canyon views. Campfire programs are given on Fri. and Sat. evenings in the summer. Check at the visitor centers for a current schedule of activities.

US 191 heads south from the Rock Springs area over the dry sage-and-juniper landscape. Take the paved turnoff to **Firehole Canyon**, where there is a campground ($8 including showers; open May-Sept.) and some interesting geological treats, including the two fingerlike projections known as North and South Chimney Rocks. Look for sheepherders tending huge flocks nearby. A dirt road continues south along the canyon to the Wyoming border, or you can return to US 191 to eventually reach the dam. Utah Hwy. 44 meets US 191 near the dam and climbs through the scenic mountain country to the west before dropping down to the town of Manila, where it joins State 530 heading north.

Sheep Creek Geological Area is a side loop from the southwestern end of the NRA and has all sorts of craggy rock formations. It's a good place to witness a billion years of geologic history and to watch for bighorn sheep. A road leads west from here to **Ute Mountain Fire Tower**, an old wooden lookout with grand vistas. Built in 1935 by the CCC, it is still in use today and is open Fri.-Mon. 9-5 in summer. **Swett Ranch**, located just south of Flaming Gorge Lodge, is another historic site open to the public in the summer. Just northeast of Manila and barely in Wyoming are a number of unusual Indian petroglyphs; ask at the Forest Service office for directions. As you continue north along the western side of Flaming Gorge (State 530), the road passes **Haystack Buttes**, a series of bee-hive-shaped rocky mounds, followed by the barren, eroded badlands of **Devils Playground**, where sagebrush, sand, and cactus extend as far as you can see.

PRACTICALITIES

Accommodations And Food

Because of the popularity of this area, it's a good idea to reserve a week or two ahead during the summer to be ensured of a motel room, or in July if you need a place on Labor Day weekend. **Flaming Gorge Lodge** is four miles south of the dam, tel. (801) 889-3773, and has motel rooms for $39 s or $45 d. The town of Manila, Utah, is just three miles south of the Wyoming border on the west side of the reservoir and has several lodging places. Cheapest is **Steinaker's Motel**, tel. (801) 784-3363, where rooms are $22 s or $25 d. (Stop by the Chevron station to check in here.) **Grubb's Motel**, tel. (801) 784-3131, charges $28 s or $36 d for rooms and also has a very friendly cafe. **Vacation Inn**, tel. (801) 784-3259, has condos with kitchens for $40 s or d. Very clean and nice, but open only April-October. **Niki's Motel**, tel. (801) 784-3117, is a modern and comfortable place to stay for $36 s or $44 d. Niki's Inn also serves meals. One of the nicest places in the area is **Red Canyon Lodge**, on Hwy. 44, tel. (801) 889-3759. Rustic cabins start at $24 s or $34 d, and luxury units with kitchenettes (sleep four) are $85. Also here is a fine restaurant. Get groceries and sandwiches at the small **Crossroads Market**, tel. (801) 784-3392, and Mexican food at **The Hub**, located on State 530 just across the Wyoming-Utah border. The Hub also has a Sunday buffet breakfast and live music most weekends. **Spring Creek Ranch**, tel. (801) 880-8772, is 12 miles north of Dutch John of US 191. Here visitors can take part in all sorts of Western adventures—from guided horseback rides to cattle drives. Room and board costs $100 pp per day.

Camping

The Forest Service maintains 18 different roadside campgrounds in the Flaming Gorge NRA ($7-10; open mid-May to mid-September). Most are on the Utah side, particularly around the dam. Reservations (extra charge) can be made for several of the campgrounds by calling (800) 283-2267. It is also possible to camp for free in undeveloped parts of the Flaming Gorge. There is a **KOA Kampground,** open May-September, in Manila, Utah, tel. (801) 784-3239, with tent sites for $15, RV sites for $19. Showers for noncampers cost $4.

Hiking

Three trails are noteworthy in Flaming Gorge. **Little Hole Trail** follows the north bank of Green River from just below the dam to Little Hole, seven miles away. You may want to set up a car shuttle to save having to hike back the same way. **Canyon Rim Trail** is a scenic five-mile path connecting Greendale Overlook with the Red Canyon Visitor Center. It is also accessible from the Skull Creek, Greens Lake, and Canyon Rim campgrounds. The steep **Hideout Canyon Trail** drops 3½ miles from Dowd Mountain Overlook to Hideout Boat Campground. If you want to explore further, head 30 miles west of Manila, Utah to the wonderful **High Uinta Wilderness**. This area is very popular with hikers and cross-country skiers from the Evanston and Green River areas and includes Kings Peak, highest mountain in Utah. Several access roads come in from the north; see the Forest Service office in Evanston for details.

Fishing

Flaming Gorge Reservoir is famous for its monster fish, including a record 51-pound Mackinaw and a 33-pound brown trout. In addition to these two species, anglers catch lake and rainbow trout, kokanee, smallmouth bass, and largemouth bass. **Flaming Gorge Fishing Derby** in mid-May is one of the biggest such events in Wyoming. The reservoir has three places where you can rent boats (approximately $60/day) and fishing gear or hire a fishing guide: **Buckboard Marina,** tel. (307) 875-6927; **Cedar Springs Marina,** tel. (801) 889-3795; and **Lucerne Valley Marina,** tel. (801) 784-3483. Below the dam, the Green River is considered the finest fishing in Utah, with up to 20,000 trout per mile. Because the reservoir lies in both Utah and Wyoming, be sure you have the appropriate fishing license.

Float Trips

One of the most popular summertime activities is floating down the Green River below Flaming Gorge Dam. An entry station below the dam has safety information. The first several miles of the river are relatively gentle (although there are a half-dozen small rapids) and can be run without a guide, but life jackets are mandatory. Most folks put in just below the spillway and take out at Little Hole, seven miles downriver. Plan on three hours for the run. Overnight camping is not allowed along this stretch, but campsites are available below Little Hole. It is also possible to continue on down the river to Gates of Lodore, 31 miles beyond Brown's Park. Check at the various visitor centers for details and precautions for these longer float trips.

Rafts can be rented ($35 for a six-person raft) from **Flaming Gorge Recreation Services** in Dutch John, (801) 885-3191, **Flaming Gorge Lodge,** four miles south of the dam, (801) 889-3773, and **Flaming Gorge Flying Service** in Dutch John, tel. (801) 885-3338. All these companies offer guided fishing trips ($125 pp and up) or shuttle services ($30 for up to eight people from Little Hole). Flaming Gorge Flying Service also has hot showers for $3. Note that river levels may fluctuate due to varying releases from the dam, pushing the river up or down by three to four feet in a matter of 15-30 minutes.

BRIDGER VALLEY

Beautiful Bridger Valley is a large splotch of green in the midst of desert country, nourished by numerous irrigation ditches off the Blacks Fork River. This was the first place in Wyoming to be farmed, having been settled by Mormons in 1853. (By the way, the various branches of the Green River—Smiths Fork, Blacks Fork, Henrys Fork, La Barge, and Hams Fork—are all named for trappers in Jedediah Smith's party of mountain men, who first spread over this country in 1824. These were considered the richest beaver-trapping waters ever discovered.)

LYMAN AND MOUNTAIN VIEW

Lyman (pop. 1,900) consists of a wide main street and not much else. The town was named for a Mormon leader, and many of those who settled here were members of that religion. Lyman's pretentious new town complex is the only building of note, although more because of its size than any architectural merit. A small **Trona Mining Museum** is on the top floor. Stay at **Valley West Motel,** tel. 787-3700, where comfortable rooms (including some kitchenettes) are $30 s or $32 d. For meals, try **Golden Eagle Cafe,** tel. 787-3822, or buy groceries at **Foodtown,** tel. 787-3344. There is a **KOA Kampground,** tel. 786-2762, just north of town. The charge is $12 for tents or $14 for RVs; it's open mid-May to mid-October. **Greyhound,** tel. 787-6192, stops at Paramount Dry Goods, 110 N. Main in Lyman. Since this is a Mormon town, July 24 has a special meaning; it was on this date in 1847 that pioneers first reached Salt Lake City. Lyman's **Days of '47 Celebration** on this date includes a rodeo, a parade, and a dance.

. The town of Mountain View (pop. 1,200) is appropriately named; to the south, the Uintas form a rough-edged horizon line. Mountain View is in the heart of farming and ranching country. Not much to see in the town itself. The best food can be found at the local **Pizza Hut** or the **Thriftway** grocery store. For entertainment,

well, there's always the bowling alley. **Hoedown on the Smiths Fork** comes to Mountain View on Labor Day weekend, featuring polka, bluegrass, and cowboy poetry. The closest public campground is 22 miles away along the Wyoming-Utah line. For details, stop by the Wasatch National Forest district office in Mountain View, tel. 782-6555. Both Lyman (tel. 787-6333) and Mountain View (tel. 782-3525) have public swimming pools.

PIEDMONT

The ghost town of Piedmont is a rarely visited part of Wyoming but worth the seven-mile drive south from I-80. Take the LeRoy Rd. exit (mile 24) and head west on County Rd. 128, following an old railroad grade south. Continue straight at the intersection, and keep your eyes open for the herd of wild buffalo that roam this country. Established as a water and wood refueling station for the Union Pacific, Piedmont was also the scene of an incident in 1869 when 300 railroad workers blocked a train carrying UP vice-president Dr. Thomas Durrant en route to ceremonies at Promontory Point. The workers demanded $200,000 in back pay before they finally let Durrant proceed.

Around 1869, Moses Byrne built five **charcoal kilns** near Piedmont, each 30 feet high and 30 feet across and made of stone and mortar. Wood was sealed in the ovens and slowly burned until it turned into charcoal for Utah's Pioneer smelter. Three of these massive kilns still stand, like three oversized breasts emerging from the plains. A half-mile south are a dozen buildings from the ghost town of Piedmont, abandoned when the railroad tracks were moved farther north in 1901. The last store closed in 1940. A local legend claims that Butch Cassidy buried loot from one of his bank holdups near here. Treasure hunters still search for it. The father of Calamity Jane, who was gunned down in a saloon, is buried in an unmarked grave in the small Piedmont cemetery.

FORT BRIDGER

The most interesting historic site in Southwest Wyoming is Fort Bridger, located in the town of the same name. The Uinta Mountains form a majestic backdrop to the south, and the Blacks Fork River winds through. The old fort is just three miles off I-80, providing an easy diversion from the interstate-highway blahs.

History

Fort Bridger was built in 1843 by the famed mountain man Jim Bridger and his Mexican partner, Louis Vásquez. The location—right on the Oregon and Mormon trails—quickly made this a vital stopping point for emigrants heading west to California, Oregon, or Salt Lake. In a letter dictated by Bridger, Vásquez remarked,

> I have established a small store with a black-smith shop, and a supply of iron in the road of the emigrants, on Black Fork of Green River, which promises fairly. They, in coming out are generally well supplied with money, but by the time they get there, are in want of all kinds of supplies, horses, provisions, smithwork, etc. They bring ready cash from the states, and should I receive the goods ordered, will have considerable business in that way with them, and establish trade with the Indians in the neighborhood, who have a good number of beaver among them.

The new "fort" consisted of a few crude log huts and a corral surrounded by a log stockade, while the lush riverside country provided pasturage for stock. Conflicts quickly developed between Bridger and the Mormon emigrants, who eyed his prosperous trade with envy and his good relations with the Indians as competition for their own efforts to turn them against the U.S. government. Under the pretext that Bridger was supplying weapons to Ute Indians, Brigham Young ordered Bridger arrested, sending 150 men to do the job. Bridger managed to escape, hiding in a nearby eagle nest while the men searched in vain. He finally fled with his Indian wife to Fort Laramie but lost all his merchandise, livestock, and buildings to the invaders.

The Mormons then built their own base, **Fort Supply,** 12 miles south of Bridger's trading post and established the first agricultural settlement in Wyoming. Soon Fort Supply had more than 100 log buildings surrounded by a palisade. In 1855, they purchased Fort Bridger from Vásquez (without Bridger's knowledge or consent) and added a variety of structures. When the so-called Mormon War began two years later, the Saints decided to leave nothing for the U.S. Army. They burned both the forts and fled to Salt Lake City.

Jim Bridger leased his land to the Army in 1858 for $600 a year. The Army rebuilt the fort with room for the 350 troops who called this place home. A Pony Express station was established in 1860, followed later by an Overland Stage station. The fort was the site of the first newspaper published in Wyoming (1863) and also served as a base for Chief Washakie's band of Shoshone Indians until a treaty signed here in 1868 set aside the Wind River Reservation. Fort Bridger was abandoned by the military in 1890, with many of its buildings sold at auction. Thirty years later, the state of Wyoming bought the site and has since restored or reconstructed many of the structures.

Sights

Fort Bridger, tel. 782-3842, is open daily 9-5:30 June-Oct. 15 and Sat.-Sun. 9-4:30 the rest of the year. Entrance costs $1. A number of buildings are open to the public during the summer, although only the museum is open the rest of the year. The grounds themselves are open year-round from 8 a.m. to sunset. Between June and Aug., the staff dresses in 1880s costumes and provides living-history demonstrations and historical information. Various activities take place throughout the year, including a mountain men rendezvous (see below), a frontier soldiers association encampment in mid-June, and special moonlight tours ($3) in July when you meet various characters from the past. Call several months ahead to book for this popular tour.

The attractive grounds are sprinkled with aspen and cottonwood trees and beautifully restored buildings. First stop is the **museum/visitor center,** housed in the enlisted-men's barracks. Inside, find a model of the old fort, displays of Army uniforms and weapons, Indian artifacts (including a bowl made from a buffalo hump), a chuckwagon, and even a working telegraph on which to practice your Morse code. Be sure to look for Jim Bridger's old powderhorn. Behind the front desk is a "young" Jim Bridger created by computerized reverse aging! Visitors can watch a slide show on the fort's history. The **Bridger-Vasquez Trading Co.** stands in one corner of the fort. This replica of Bridger's original trading post is open May-Sept. and is run by Dick and Sandy Gregory, who will be happy to talk about the trapper's life or to sell trade beads, furs, Indian sweetgrass, clothing, and even bull scrotum bags! Be sure to ask how to use the fire steels. Other noteworthy sights at the fort include the ongoing archaeological dig (summers), Wyoming's oldest schoolhouse, and the fenced-in grave of Thornburgh the dog.

Practicalities

The town of Fort Bridger contains **Wagon Wheel Motel,** tel. 782-6361, where rooms start for $25 s or $28 d. There is a restaurant on the premises, or you can get groceries at **Fort Bridger Cash Store,** tel. 782-6744. Wagon coach rides are offered during the summer by **Black's Fork Stageline,** tel. 782-3945.

Fort Bridger Rendezvous—held on Labor Day weekend—is the largest modern-day mountain men rendezvous in Wyoming. Tents and tipis sprawl across the fort grounds. Events include cannon shoots, muzzle-loading shoots, Indian dancing, Dutch-oven cooking contests, tomahawk throwing, live music, and clothing contests, plus all sorts of trading and food. Be sure to attend *A Ballad of the West,* written by a great-grand nephew of Jim Bridger. The rendezvous attracts 400 buckskinners, squaws, hunters, and pilgrims, along with over 10,000 spectators.

EVANSTON

The attractive, friendly town of Evanston (pop. 11,000) lies just six miles from the Utah border and only 80 miles from Salt Lake City. It is a typical small town, with a mixture of prosperity and difficulty. On the outskirts of Evanston, fireworks stands crowd the freeway off-ramps, waiting to lure Utahans who create weekend traffic jams in the pursuit of booze, bars, and betting. Evanston's economy depends upon gas and oil wells, tourists, ranching, and a state hospital. (In 1886, the territorial Legislature offered Uinta County representatives the choice of either the university or the insane asylum. They chose the asylum.)

History

As the transcontinental railroad's construction crews raced across Wyoming in 1868, the settlement of Evanston was established as the last division point before the Wasatch Range. The town received its name from the railroad's surveyor, James A. Evans. By 1887, it had 1,500 people, many of whom worked at the Union Pacific car and machine shops, at an ice plant, or on the tracks. Others logged railroad ties in the mountains or raised sheep and cattle. Rich deposits of coal were discovered four miles north of Evanston, and several mines soon opened, creating the town of **Almy.** In 1869, hundreds of Chinese miners were hired as strikebreakers at the mines, creating tensions that would later erupt into race riots and force the temporary abandonment of Evanston's Chinatown. The Almy mines became notorious for deadly methane-gas explosions. At least 60 whites and uncounted Chinese miners were killed in blasts in 1881, 1886, and 1895. The mines closed in 1906, leaving many of the fires unextinguished; evidence of the smouldering fires is still visible. Many of the old mine buildings can be seen at the townsite, but the town itself is long since abandoned.

The Overthrust Belt

Evanston lies at the center of the energy-rich Overthrust Belt that extends from Canada to Mexico. This 40-mile-wide uplift was formed when two land masses smashed together, thrusting the western portion atop the eastern half and creating folds that trapped oil and gas. It was long believed to contain rich energy deposits, but hundreds of dry holes were drilled

JIM BRIDGER

Legendary figures fill the history of the West, but only one man—Jim Bridger—ranks as the uncrowned king of the mountain men. Like many other frontiersmen from the 19th century, Bridger never learned to read or write, but his deep knowledge of the mountains and Indians gained him the name "Old Gabe." His skills were said to rival those of the angel Gabriel. Jim Bridger has 21 different Wyoming places named for him, more than any other individual.

Bridger was born in 1804 in Virginia, moving with his family to Missouri. When both his parents died, he was sent off to apprentice with a blacksmith, but the wild country beckoned, and when William Ashley advertised for "Enterprising Young Men" to go into the Rockies to trap beaver, Bridger quickly joined up. He was on the first keelboat that headed out in 1822, and wintered that year on the Bear River of southern Idaho. When men began speculating on where the Bear River led, Bridger volunteered to find out, thus becoming the first white man to discover Great Salt Lake. Bridger took any challenge in stride. When Ashley needed a volunteer to test the possibility of running furs down the Bighorn River, Bridger stepped forward. He nearly died taking his log raft through the wild waters of Bighorn Canyon, but the adventure added to his growing reputation.

Bridger entered the fur trading business in 1830 when he and four others bought the Rocky Mountain Fur Company from Ashley. They in turn sold the business to William Sublette five years later. Bridger continued to lead trapping parties until the last rendezvous in 1840, then turned his attention to the growing tide of emigrants heading west to California and Oregon. Together with partner Louis Vásquez, Bridger built a trading post (Fort Bridger) along the Blacks Fork of the Green River. He later served as a scout for the U.S. Army in the Powder River, although his sage advice was often ignored.

Like many other mountain men, Jim Bridger had several wives. His first was a white Mormon woman, but when Jim refused to join her religion, they separated. He later married three different Indian women, none of whom spoke English. The first two died early, but the last one—daughter of the great Shoshone Chief Washakie—returned to Missouri with him.

Bridger's knowledge of sign language was legendary; he once kept an audience of Sioux and Cheyenne Indians in rapt attention for over an hour as he signed a lengthy adventure. In one of his yarns told to a naive British army captain, Bridger described how the Indians had him trapped in a canyon with his only escape up a 200-foot waterfall. When the captain insisted upon discovering how he escaped this predicament, Bridger wryly went on, "Oh bless your soul, Captain, we never did get out. The Indians killed us right there!" Partly because of such stories, few believed Bridger's true accounts of the geysers and hot springs he had found in Yellowstone or of the stream that split along the Continental Divide, with waters flowing in both directions. Bridger died on his Missouri farm in 1881 at the age of 77.

Jim Bridger

BUFFALO BILL HISTORICAL SOCIETY

before one finally hit home. In 1976, the Yellow Creek Oil Field was discovered, producing both oil and natural gas and unleashing a boomtown atmosphere. Many more oil and gas fields have been discovered since then. Although Uinta County is Wyoming's smallest, it is easily the largest in terms of natural-gas production. In 1990, more than a third of the state's production came from here, some 173 million cubic feet of gas.

Sights

Uinta County Museum, 36 10th St., tel. 789-2757, is open Mon.-Fri. 8-5 year-round, plus Sat.-Sun. 10-4 during the summer. Outside are various old wagons. Inside, look for the Coletti Still, said to have made the nation's finest Prohibition-era moonshine. Also of interest here are various Chinese items—including opium pipes, an impressive turn-of-the-century dragon, a Buddha figure, and lanterns—along with hundreds of historic photos. While here, pick up a walking tour of Evanston that details many of the older buildings in town. The historic **Evanston Depot** is next door. Built in 1900, it was one of the finest along the line and had separate waiting rooms for men and women. A 1944 Union Pacific dining car and caboose stand outside the depot. Amtrak trains now stop here twice daily. The **Beeman-Cashin Implement**

EVANSTON ACCOMMODATIONS

MOTEL	ADDRESS	TELEPHONE	RATES	FEATURES
Hillcrest DX Motel	1725 Harrison Dr.	789-1111	$16 s, $24 d	
Alexander Motel	248 Bear River Dr.	789-2346	$17 s, $22 d	
Sunset Motel	196 Bear River Dr.	789-3763	$18+ s, $28 d	kitchenettes
Vagabond Motel	230 Bear River Dr.	789-2902	$19+ s, $24+ d	
Whirl Inn Motel	1724 Harrison Dr.	789-9610	$20 s, $25 d	
Weston Super Budget Inn	1936 Harrison Dr.	789-2810 (800) 255-9840	$20+ s, $25+ d	pool
Evanston Inn	247 Bear River Dr.	789-6212 (800) 443-1982	$24 s, $34 d	kitchenettes
Bear River Inn	261 Bear River Dr.	789-0791	$25 s, $32 d	
Big Horn Motel	202 Bear River Dr.	789-6830	$25+ s, $30+ d	AAA approved
Super 8 Motel	70 Bear River Dr.	789-7510 (800) 800-8000	$27 s, $31 d	
Prairie Inn	264 Bear River Dr.	789-2920	$27s, 34+ d	AAA approved, continental breakfast
Pine Gables Inn	1049 Center St.	789-2069	$32 s, $38 d	AAA approved, historic B&B
Weston Plaza	1983 Harrison Dr.	789-0783 (800) 255-9840	$45 s, $50 d	AAA approved, pool, hot tub
Dunmar Inn (Best Western)	1019 Lombard	789-3770 (800) 528-1234	$68 s, $74 d	AAA approved, pool

Depot across the road is used for dances and community activities. Built around 1886 and restored in 1986, this unique wooden structure has no supporting posts.

Early in this century, Evanston had a prominent Chinatown located along the north side of the tracks. Life centered around the **Joss House,** a Taoist temple built in 1894 and one of just three in the nation (the others were in San Francisco and New York). Pilgrims came from hundreds of miles away to worship here. After the Chinese workers returned to their homeland, the building was destroyed in a suspicious 1922 fire that leveled much of Chinatown. A replica of the Joss House was completed in 1990 and furnished with a new dragon and various Chinatown artifacts. It is open daily 11-8 in the summer; ask at the museum the rest of the year. Inside are historic photos and various cultural items. Be sure to see the video on Mormon Charlie and China Mary, the only Chinese who remained after 1922. (The few Chinese-Americans in Evanston today moved here more recently.)

Accommodations

There are quite a few inexpensive places to stay in Evanston; see the chart for specifics. Reserve ahead on summer weekends to be sure of having a place, and on Labor Day you'll need to reserve a month ahead. The homiest lodging in Evanston is at **Pine Gables Inn B&B,** tel. 789-2069, built in 1883 and used as a European-style bed and breakfast during the 1920s and '30s. The house was restored in 1981, furnished with antiques, and reopened as a delightful bed and breakfast. The nearest public campgrounds are in the Uinta Mountains, 30 miles to the south. **Sunset RV Park,** 196 Bear River Dr., tel. 789-3763, charges $10 for tents or $13 for RVs. Noncampers can shower for $3. **Phillips RV Trailer Park,** 225 Bear River Dr., tel. 789-3805, charges $11 for tents or $13 for RVs. Both places are open year-round and offer shaded sites.

Food

Meet the Evanston cops over coffee and donuts at **Main Street Deli,** 1025 Main St., tel. 789-

1599. A great breakfast bargain is the tortilla, eggs, and home fries. **Legal Tender Dining Room** in the Dunmar Inn, 1019 Lombard, tel. 789-3770, is an attractive and popular local establishment offering standard steakhouse fare and all-you-can-eat weekday specials. It's a bit pricier than some of the other local eateries. **Last Outpost,** 205 Bear River Dr., tel. 789-3322, grills buffalo burgers and great steaks in a rustic atmosphere, but the salads leave something to be desired.

New Garden Cafe, 933 Front, tel. 789-2882, offers very reasonably priced Chinese and American cooking. The American fare is quite good, but heavy on the grease. **Chico's,** Ninth and Front streets, is the place to find good Mexican fare. Try more international eats at **Sorella's,** 123 10th, tel. 789-8720. The menu features delicious seafood and pasta, with ice-cream cocktails for dessert. Best pizza around is at **Pizza Hut,** 134 Yellow Creek Rd., tel. 789-1372, although **Shakey's,** 350 Front St., tel. 789-8281, offers a reasonable lunchtime special. Be assured that Evanston also has most of the fast-food chains, including Subway, Little Caesar's, and McD's. **Hamblin Park,** next to the fairgrounds on Bear River Drive, is a very pleasant place to enjoy a picnic lunch beneath tall cottonwood trees.

Entertainment

Evanston is jam-packed with liquor stores and lounges, here to quench the parched thirst of Utahans who cross the border in droves. **Legal Tender Lounge** at Dunmar Inn, 1019 Lombard, tel. 789-3770, has two bars: an upstairs disco and a downstairs saloon where you can dance to rock bands most nights. This is mainly a young crowd. For more rock tunes, try **Pete's Rock-N-Rye Club,** east of town on US 30, tel. 789-2135. You'll find country and oldies music most weekends at **Last Outpost,** 205 Bear River Dr., tel. 789-3322. A popular pool-shootin' spot is **Pink Elephant Bar** on Front Street. Looking for a cozier place? Try **Cinnamon's** at the Weston Super Budget, 1936 Harrison Dr., tel. 789-2810.

Events

One of the most unusual Evanston events is **Chinese New Year,** featuring a parade, fire-

works, and of course, the dragon. (There are very few Chinese-Americans in Evanston today, so many of the performers are from other backgrounds.) On summer weekends, **Wyoming Downs Racetrack,** 12 miles north of Evanston on State 89, tel. 789-0511 or (800) 842-8722, has horse racing with pari-mutuel betting. These are particularly popular with folks from Salt Lake, since horse racing is illegal in Utah. Race enthusiasts can also watch and wager off-track bets on races as far away as California from the Weston Super Budget Inn.

In mid-June, stop in Evanston for both the 80-mile-long **High Uinta Bike Race** and the very popular **Chili Cookoff.** July brings miniature-train rides, steam engines, railroad movies, model-train displays, and more during **Railroad Days.** The **Uinta County Fair** in early August includes a greased-pig contest, animal judging, carnival rides, music, and dancing. **Bear River Rendezvous** is held in late August and includes all the standard mountain-men trading and other activities.

The big event in Evanston is, predictably, the annual rodeo, here known as **Cowboy Days.** Labor Day weekend festivities pack all the motels in town as folks come from Wyoming, Idaho, and Utah to watch professional cowboys show their stuff at "the biggest little rodeo in the world." The three-day event also includes musical entertainment, dances, an arts-and-crafts fair, a parade, a pancake breakfast, a spaghetti dinner, and clowns.

Recreation

The excellent **Evanston Recreation Center,** 275 Saddle Ridge Rd., tel. 789-1770, features a swimming pool, gyms, racquetball courts, a weight room, and a hot tub. Entrance costs $2.50 for adults or $1.25 for seniors or youths. Cross-country skiers head to the **Lily Lake Touring Area,** 30 miles south of Evanston in the Uintas. Call 789-7588 for details. More trails can be found in Bear River State Park (next to the I-80 information center). There is also a small wintertime ice rink (free) on Sixth Street. **Purple Sage Golf Course** is a nine-hole public course on Country Club Lane, tel. 789-2383.

Information And Services

Evanston has two places to go for information. If

you're entering the state from the west, be sure to stop at **Bear River Information Center** at Exit 6, just off I-80, tel. 789-6540. The center has a wealth of statewide information, along with a pleasant picnic area and short trails. It's open summers daily 7-7 and winters daily 8-5. The Bear River—just a creek here—flows northward, eventually draining into Great Salt Lake. At 400 miles in length, it's the largest river in the Western Hemisphere that doesn't reach the ocean. The **Evanston Chamber of Commerce**, 36 10th St., tel. 789-2757 or (800) 328-9708, is housed with the county museum and has more local info. Hours are Mon.-Fri. 8-5, plus Sat.-Sun. 10-4 in the summer.

Uinta County Library, 701 Main, tel. 789-2770, is open Mon. and Tues. 10-9, Wed.-Thurs. 10-8, and Fri.-Sat. 10-5. **Curiosity Book Shoppe**, 927 Main St., tel. 789-7855, is a friendly little place located in the restored **Blyth-Fargo Building**, site of the first hardware/grocery store chain in the West. **Mountain View Ranger Station**, 1565 S. State 150, tel. 789-3194, has maps of Wasatch National Forest, but not much else. A tiny corner of the forest comes into Wyoming.

Transportation

Amtrak trains arrive at the Evanston depot twice a day, once from each direction. Call (800) 872-7245 for schedule information. **Greyhound** runs buses both east and west on I-80 and stops next to the Burger King at 1945 Harrison Drive. **Big Horn Taxi**, tel. 789-1060, has 24-hour service. Rent cars from **Evanston Motor Co.**, 2000 US 30 W, tel. 789-3145, or from **Affordable Used Car Rental**, 101 US 30, tel. 789-3096. No commercial service at the airport.

North To Kemmerer

North of Evanston, US 189 follows a long valley most of the way to Kemmerer. A hogback ridge hems you in to the east. Stop to take a look behind to the ragged snow-topped Uintas that form a southern horizon line. Near the junction with State 412 (36 miles up) is the small **Cumberland** cemetery, enclosed within a white picket fence. Turn down State 412 to see what's left of the ghost town of Cumberland. This was a booming coal-mining town between 1920 and 1935, with four underground mines going at once. Today all that remains are the sandstone Ziller ranch buildings—they were a whorehouse and saloon—and the cemetery. The buildings are not open to the public.

KEMMERER

The twin towns of Kemmerer (pop. 3,000) and Diamondville (pop. 900) are at the center of the coal industry in southwest Wyoming. Kemmerer is the Lincoln County seat and is located on the Hams Fork River; Diamondville lies just a few yards away. The surrounding country is dotted with mining and energy plants of various types. The world's largest strip mine is a few miles south, and a nearby Exxon plant is the world's largest manufacturer of helium (and the state's largest consumer of electricity). Another major employer is the FMC coke plant providing coke for a phosphorous plant in Pocatello, Idaho. It too is the largest such operation in the world. Natural gas, oil, and sulfur are also very important locally. Given this blue-collar setting it should come as no surprise that this is a pickup-truck town, or failing that, you better drive a Mustang with growling mufflers.

HISTORY

Coal Mining

Explorer John C. Frémont first chanced upon coal here in 1843, but it wasn't until 1881 that the Union Pacific opened the first underground mine. Things really began to boom when Patrick J. Quealy and his partner Mahlon S. Kemmerer established the Kemmerer Coal Company. Hundreds of men died in mine accidents; worst was a 1923 explosion that killed 99 miners, mostly emigrants. The operation moved above ground in 1950, and the Kemmerer mine became the Pittsburg & Midway Coal Company, now a subsidiary of Chevron. Located six miles south of Kemmerer along US 189, it is the world's largest open-pit coal mine, an 800-foot-deep monstrosity. Two-thirds of the coal is used at the adjacent Utah Power & Light Naughton Plant, which produces 710 megawatts of power. The mine (the longest continuously operating mine in Wyoming) and power plant are the largest employers in the region. Call 877-9081 for tours.

Moonshine And Shady Ladies

During the 1920s, Kemmerer became a national center for bootlegging and a major supplier for Chicago. Kemmerer "moon" was a favorite of speakeasies, with winemakers ordering grapes by the trainload. A 1931 bust near Kemmerer found 24,000 gallons of liquor! All this ended when Prohibition was repealed in 1933.

With all the coal miners, the ratio of men to women in Kemmerer was nearly 50 to one, prime pickings for the world's oldest profession. Into these conditions stepped Madam Isabelle Burns, fresh off the train from Salt Lake City, with considerable experience in the "sporting" trade. She arrived in 1896, looking for somewhere to invest the $28,500 inheritance from her husband's suicide. With $5000 in cash she bought a dance hall with convenient side rooms, enough to house 50 prostitutes. In a short while, the Green House was a roaring success, allowing Madam Isabelle to build what was then the most elegant house in town (still standing at 301 Ruby Street). Because of the demand for "evening wear," it is claimed that Kemmerer's shoe store sold more high-heeled satin slippers than any store west of the Mississippi! A nude painting of one of the Green House ladies with her brother (and lover) is now in the Golden Nugget Bar in Las Vegas. Madam Isabelle quit the business in 1926, left town, and married a New Orleans physician. Her business went on in fresh hands.

Several deaths took place at the Green House, leading to a grand conflagration when a man whose sons had been murdered there burned one of the women to death, igniting the building in the process and leaving it a pile of ashes. After the 1926 fire, it was replaced by the Southern Hotel. A newly elected sheriff finally shut things down in 1967, despite pleas from locals that the loss of all the Utah and Idaho clients would hurt business in town. For more on this tantalizing bit of history, see Ray Essman's *Only Count the Sunny Hours* (Winona, Minn.: Apollo Books).

SIGHTS

The most unusual sights in Kemmerer relate to **James Cash Penney,** founder of the J.C. Penney chain. Penney moved to Kemmerer in 1902 from Evanston to open a dry goods store for the booming mining town, and his Golden Rule Store quickly achieved a reputation for quality and honesty. By 1912 there were 34 Golden Rule stores, and the following year their name was changed to J.C. Penney.

The **J.C. Penney Home** is a six-room cottage where Penney lived between 1903 and 1909. The house is right behind the chamber of commerce office downtown and is open summers Sun. 1-6 and Mon.-Sat. 9-6. During the rest of the year, ask at the chamber for a tour. No charge. Guides are ready to show you around or to put on a video about the company's history. The J.C. Penney "mother store" is also in Kemmerer, just a few doors up the street.

Fossil Country Frontier Museum, 400 Pine Ave., tel. 877-6551, is open Mon.-Fri. 9-5, no charge. It contains a variety of art, mining, and archaeological exhibits, along with dozens of kinds of barbed wire dating from the 19th century. The small gift shop sells inexpensive fossil fish. The nicely restored **Lincoln County Courthouse** at Sage and Topaz streets was built in 1925 and contains a fine collection of fossils. Stop by the post office at Cedar and Sapphire streets to view the attractive fossil murals painted by WPA artists in 1938.

PRACTICALITIES

Accommodations

See the chart for local motels. The closest public campground ($5) is **Fontenelle Creek Campground,** 25 miles northeast of Kemmerer on US 189 beside Fontenelle Reservoir. Three free campgrounds are located along the river below the dam. **Riverside Trailer Park,** 216 Spinel St., tel. 877-3416, has RV spaces for $12 (no tent sites and no shade). It's open mid-May to mid-October.

Food

For a reasonably priced Chinese-American

KEMMERER ACCOMMODATIONS

MOTEL	ADDRESS	TELEPHONE	RATES	FEATURES
Chateau Motel	601 Pine Ave.	877-3701	$18 s, $21 d	see rooms first
Burnett's Motel	1326 Central Ave.	877-4471	$20 s, $24 d	
Antler Motel	419 Coral St.	877-4461	$20+ s, $28+ d	
Fossil Butte Motel	1424 Central Ave.	877-3996	$26 s, $29 d	
Energy Inn	Diamondville	877-6901	$30 s, $34 d	kitchenettes
Fairview Motel	501 N. US 30	877-3938	$30+ s, $44+ d	AAA approved

lunch, visit **Nishi's Corner Cafe,** 801 S. Main, tel. 877-4007. **Kirkwood Kitchen,** 1433 Central Ave., tel. 877-6633, serves all-American fare for a reasonable price. **Polar King Drive In,** US 189, tel. 877-9448, is the place for burgers, as well as surprisingly good breakfasts. **Luigi's Supper Club,** 819 Susie Ave. in Diamondville, tel. 877-6221, has excellent Italian-American cooking, or try **Pizza Hut,** in Diamondville, tel. 877-6969. **Bon Rico's,** 12 miles south of town, tel. 877-4503, is another favorite place to stuff yourself with Italian food, steak, or fish. Some locals also like **Lake Viva-Naughton Marina,** 15 miles north of Kemmerer on the reservoir, tel. 877-9669, for seafood and steaks, but the atmosphere leaves something to be desired. Instead, I'd try the historic **Frontier Saloon & Restaurant,** north of town on State 233, tel. 877-9922, in business since 1898. Try their great Saturday-night prime-rib specials too.

Entertainment And Events
The **Stock Exchange Bar** downtown has a pool table and fills with locals most nights. **Luigi's Supper Club,** 819 Susie Ave. in Diamondville, tel. 877-6221, sometimes has live music, as does **Bon Rico's,** 12 miles south of town, tel. 877-4503. On weekends, try **Lake Viva-Naughton Marina,** 15 miles north of Kemmerer, tel. 877-9669, for country music.

Turn of the Century Days comes around the last weekend in July and includes a chili cook-off, carnival, Little Buckaroo Rodeo, parade, bed races, and other activities.

Recreation
Kemmerer Recreation Center, 1776 Dell Rio Dr., tel. 877-9641, has a pool, racquetball courts,

weight room, jacuzzi, and sauna. Entrance costs $2 for adults, $1 for seniors and youths. There is also an outdoor pool (tel. 877-9641) in **Archie Neil Park** open during the summer. The town's nine-hole golf course is north of town on US 189, tel. 877-6954.

Information And Services
The **Kemmerer Chamber of Commerce** is housed in a log cabin in Triangle Park at the center of town, tel. 877-9761. (Locals joke that Kemmerer is too small to have a town square, so it has a town triangle instead.) It's open summers Mon.-Sat. 9-6 and the rest of the year Mon.-Fri. 10-2 (plus additional weekend hours in Sept. and October). Inside are displays of fossils and historical pictures, and you can buy local books and old Wyoming license plates. They can also provide helpful information on nearby fossil-fish quarries. The **Rock & Wash**—a combination car wash and rock shop at 502 Coral, tel. 877-3220, is a fun place to get petrified wood and other interesting rocks. See "Fossil Collecting" below for a list of places to get fish fossils. The **Forest Service district office** is in Diamondville at US 189 and 30, tel. 877-4415, and the **BLM office** is on US 189 N, tel. 877-3933. **Lincoln County Library,** 519 Emerald St., tel. 877-6961, is open Mon.-Wed. 10-8, Thurs.-Fri. 10-6, and Sat. 10-2.

FOSSIL BUTTE NATIONAL MONUMENT

Established in 1972, Fossil Butte is an 8,198-acre natural area managed by the National Park Service and located 15 miles west of Kemmerer. The dominant feature is a 1,000-foot-tall escarpment rising above the arid plains. Within this butte are millions of fossil fish, insects, snails, turtles, and plants. This is also one of the few places in the world where fossilized birds and bats have been found. The Green River Formation fossils were first collected by geologist Dr. John Evans in 1865, but the site now known as Fossil Butte was not discovered until a railroad grade cut exposed the fossils.

Origins

Fossil Butte is not unlike countless other buttes throughout Wyoming: an exposed rocky cliff lit with the red, yellow, and buff colors representing millions of years of deposition and erosion. Despite the arid conditions today, this land once supported a subtropical climate similar to that along the Gulf Coast. During the Eocene Epoch (50 million years ago), palm trees grew along the shore of a lake now called Fossil Lake, and the waters teamed with fish, crocodiles, turtles, stingrays, and other animals. Over a period of two million years, changing salinity levels and variations in runoff from calcium-rich streams caused calcium carbonate to precipitate out. Dead animals or plants on the deep lake bottom were covered with a blanket of fine sediment. Eventually they were fossilized, and when the lake dried up, the sedimentary deposits were gradually thrust upward by geological forces.

Visitor Center

The sparkling new **Fossil Butte Visitor Center,** tel. 877-4455, is open daily 8-7 in summer and 8-4:30 in winter. There is no charge. The visitor center is 3½ miles off US 30 (follow the signs) and houses a variety of displays on the area's geology, paleontology, and natural history. Two videos—one an orientation to the area and the second on fossil preparation—are available for viewing, and the shop sells a variety of natural-history books. Rangers lead informative walks originating at the visitor center, along with evening campfire programs at the picnic area. Check at the visitor center for specific times. Camping is not allowed at Fossil Butte, and the nearest lodging is in Kemmerer.

Hiking

The 2½ mile (RT) **Historic Quarry Trail** on the south side of the monument provides access to an old fossil quarry site (600 feet up) and has various interpretive signs along the way. It is illegal to take fossils or other items.

Fossil Lake Trail begins from a pleasant picnic area located three miles north of the visitor center. It provides an enjoyable one-mile loop hike through open sage country and a grove of aspen trees. Many varieties of flowers are blooming in midsummer. Keep your eyes open for mule deer, coyotes, sage grouse, prairie dogs, and other animals on these paths. The visitor center has a brochure on these trails. Other than these two, you're on your own, although the open country makes hiking relatively easy.

Fossil Collecting

Although it is illegal to collect fossils within the national monument, several nearby areas are open for a fee. These are only open in the summer months. The best known—its fossils are exhibited in the Smithsonian—is **Ulrich's Fossil Gallery,** tel. 877-6466, located just outside the national monument. Out front are enormous dinosaur tracks found in a nearby coal mine. They have a nearby quarry on state land where

Diplomystus *are the most common specimens found at Fossil Butte National Monument.*

you can dig your own fish fossils for $45 (advance reservations required). You're allowed to keep a wooden pallet full of the most common species, although the state gets any rare specimens that might turn up. They also sell prepared fossils at the gallery. **Tynsky's Fossil Fish Shop,** next to the J.C. Penney store in Kemmerer, tel. 877-6885, has fossil fish for sale.

Ask about quarrying your own ($25 for two hours). **Warfield Fossil Quarry,** tel. 883-244, 15 miles south of Kemmerer on US 189, charges diggers $25 per day. Both Tynsky's and Warfield are located on private land. **Severns Studio,** located five miles west of Kemmerer, tel. 877-9402, also sells fish fossils.

KEMMERER VICINITY

OREGON TRAIL SIGHTS

Ten miles north of Kemmerer on State 233 are the still-noticeable ruts of the Oregon Trail's Sublette Cutoff. A few miles to the west is the grave of a young emigrant, Nancy Hill. An 1852 letter written by her uncle describes how suddenly life could end on this treacherous journey west:

July the 6th. Since left off writing we have made slow progress in traveling on account of sickness and lame cattle. On last Friday & Saturday we layby on account of abe. He was very bad but is now in a fair way to get well. This day was called on to consign to the tomb one other of our company N.J. Hill. She was in good health on Sunday evening, taken unwell that knight worse in the morning & a corps at nine o'clock at knight. We had two doctors with her. They pronounced her complaining cholera but I believe it was nothing more than cholera with conjestion connecter.

Names Hill

There are three well-known places in Wyoming where Oregon Trail travelers paused to carve their names into the rocks: Register Cliff, Independence Rock, and—westernmost of the three—Names Hill. The last of these is six miles south of the tiny oil and gas town of **La Barge** (pop. 500) near the Lander Cutoff of the Oregon Trail. Hundreds of old names are carved in the sandstone cliff, along with far too many recent additions. A fence surrounds one carving that says, "James Bridger 1844 Trapper." It's authenticity is dubious since Bridger always signed

his name with an X; he could neither read nor write. (Give it the benefit of the doubt—maybe a companion carved it for Bridger while he watched.) **Fontenelle Reservoir** lies just west of Names Hill and backs up behind a 137-foot earthen dam on the Green River. As you head north from here, the red-and-yellow badlands rise along the east side of the Green River, while oil pumpjacks punctuate the land in all directions.

COKEVILLE

Cokeville (pop. 500) is situated in a long, fertile valley along the Idaho border and south of Star Valley. Directly behind the town is an impressive triangular mountain, **Rocky Point.** The ranching and farming country is punctuated with small white farmhouses, but many locals commute to work at the coal mine and power plant near Kemmerer. Nearly everyone is Mormon here. The town of Cokeville was founded in 1874 with the arrival of the Oregon Shortline Railroad and is named for the coal that was used to produce coke. By the turn of the century, it had become the "sheep capital of the world" and claimed more millionaires per capita than anywhere else on earth. Cokeville's proximity to the state line also made it a haven for outlaws; with Utah and Idaho just six miles away, they found it easy to leave the posse behind as they fled to a different jurisdiction.

Practicalities

Valley Hi Motel, tel. 279-3251, has rooms for $30 s or $32 d and up, while **Hideout Motel,** tel. 279-3281, charges $24 s or $28 d and up. Get meals at **Texico Cafe** (open 24 hours), or fast food at the summer-only **Hideout Drive-In**. A small **Cokeville Visitor Center**, tel. 279-3223, is open for summer. **Pine Creek Ski Area**, six miles east of Cokeville, tel. 279-3201, consists of a chairlift and rope tow with a 1,200-foot vertical rise. Ski rentals and instruction are available. It's open Tues., Sat., and Sun., Jan.-March. The mountains east of Cokeville also contain many miles of groomed snowmobile trails during the winter.

Lake Alice

Take an enjoyable side trip to Lake Alice, a pristine mountain lake at the end of a 1½ mile trail in Bridger-Teton National Forest. Three-mile-long Lake Alice was created many centuries ago when a mountain slid across the valley, damming the creek. Get here by heading northeast from Cokeville on State 232 and bearing right at the Y where the pavement ends (12 miles up). The gravel road continues another 13 miles to the trailhead, where you'll find the very nice **Hobble Creek Campground**. Good fishing both in the creek and at Lake Alice. The country around here is some of the only unroaded land left in the Wyoming Range.

STAR VALLEY

West of the Wyoming Range, the mountains seem exhausted as they dip into a broad, fertile farming valley that stretches across the Idaho border. This is Star Valley, a place with closer ties to Idaho—in terms of geography, farming, sheep ranching, transportation, and even religion—than to Wyoming. Locals call it the "home of 5,000 people and 20,000 cattle." The valley reaches 10 miles across and 40 miles from north to south; an early settler labeled it "The Star of all Valleys." Star Valley is a very pretty place, with the Salt River (so named because of salt deposits and saline springs along its banks; the water is not salty) creating an oasis of greenery and the mountains establishing a grand backdrop. Irrigation ditches flow alongside the roads, barbed wire stretches between old lodgepole posts, and dairy cows graze in the velvet green farm fields. Spacious old ranches—built to house large Mormon families—alternate with more modern ranch-style homes. A single main road, US 89, heads north across the full length of Star Valley, with a network of side roads and scattered pinprick settlements.

History

The **Lander Cutoff** of the Oregon Trail angles through the southern half of Star Valley, following the Salt River as far as the Auburn area and then cutting northwest along Stump Creek. The trail—constructed in 1858 under the direction of Frederick W. Lander—was the first federal road built west of the Missouri River. (The route had been used by fur trappers for 45 years before Lander's men upgraded it for wagon travel.) The Lander Cutoff saved Oregon-bound travelers over 100 miles but also entailed climbing over a rugged 9,000-foot pass. Parts of the route are readily visible along the south end of Greys River Rd., where it is marked by concrete posts and emigrant graves.

The first white settlers came to Star Valley from Idaho in the 1880s, fleeing laws restricting the number of wives a man could have. Polygamy, while outlawed by the federal government in 1882, was winked at by Wyoming authorities for many years; they needed all the settlers they could get, especially the conservative, hardworking Mormons. When Frank W. Mondell was running for Congress in 1894, he came to Star Valley and found the Afton mayor a polygamist. Mondell noted:

We assured our friend we were not disposed to question the propriety of his family affairs and would be glad to accept his hospitality. Thereupon our party partook of a fine supper in the modest home of very pleasant and comely wife No. Three, and thereafter, leaving Miss Reel with her, the remainder of our party was comfortably housed in the larger homes of Wives One and Two.

Polygamy has long since been outlawed, but a large brick LDS church still stands in every podunk town in Star Valley.

AFTON

Afton (pop. 1,400) is the primary settlement in Star Valley. It is a typical small American town, the sort of place where parents complain of kids partying with kegs and making out on the back roads. Meanwhile the high schoolers complain of nothing to do. The local economy has suffered in recent years as farmers struggle on fertile land in a marginal climate. The Tricon Timber sawmill belches smoke from its plant, which processes much of the 4.5 million board-feet of timber cut annually on adjacent Forest Service lands. Aviat, Inc., also in Afton, manufactures a variety of aircraft, including the Pitts Specials, considered the finest aerobatic planes in existence (alas, no tours of the plant). Quite a few workers also commute to Jackson Hole—69 winding miles each way—where service jobs are plentiful.

Sights

Afton's best-known attraction is the world's largest **elk antler arch,** an 18-foot-high arch that extends over the main street. Built in 1958, it contains 3,011 antlers. At today's antler prices (they are prized as aphrodisiacs in Asia), the antlers would be worth over $300,000! The small **Pioneer Museum** at 46 Fifth Ave. is open Mon.-Sat. 1-5 June-August. No charge. Inside are various items collected by the Daughters of the Utah Pioneers, including a loom, a spinning wheel, and other miscellaneous memorabilia. The enormous **Afton Tabernacle**—LDS of course—sits at the corner of Jefferson and Third and serves as a community focal point. This impressive sandstone building (architects call this a Middle

English design) was begun in 1904, with further additions in the 1940s.

The town of **Auburn,** eight miles north and west of Afton, contains a small area of travertine terraces and hot springs on private land. The nearby countryside is filled with old log homes, cabins, and barns. A historic stone church sits across from the tiny Auburn post office, and nearby is the Davis Ranch, where Butch Cassidy and his gang holed up one winter. West of

Pitts Specials, made in Afton, are world-famous stunt planes.

Auburn on County Rd. 134 is **Auburn Fish Hatchery,** where some 50,000 trout are raised annually. It's open daily 8-5. The road to the hatchery parallels the Lander Cutoff of the Oregon Trail for several miles.

Periodic Spring

Afton's most unusual sight is **Periodic Spring,** located in Swift Creek Canyon, six miles east of town (take Second Avenue). The largest of only three intermittent springs known to exist, it is reached via a three-quarter-mile trail. Periodic Spring feeds Swift Creek, the water source for Afton, and is so pure that no chlorination is needed. When the spring is operating, it seems as though there were a timer and an on-off switch buried in the mountain. Icy water gushes from a gaping opening in the cliff for approximately 18 minutes, then stops for an equal period of time. The Shoshones regarded this as a sacred place of healing and said that a powerful medicine man was able to turn the waters on and off by command. Today, hydrologists believe that a large underground chamber periodically fills and then empties of water through a natural siphon in the porous limestone rock. The spring loses its intermittence in spring, when it flows constantly. Best time to see it in action is in late summer or early fall.

Accommodations And Camping

See the chart for a complete list of Star Valley motels. The Forest Service's attractive **Swift Creek Campground** ($5; open mid-May to mid-Sept.) is only a mile and a half east of Afton (take Second Avenue). Periodic Spring is farther up the same road. RVers may want to pull into the summer-only **Camp Fire RV Park** ($10) on the north side of town or **Wagon Wheel RV Park** ($12) closer to the center of town. Showers for noncampers cost $2 at Camp Fire. Neither RV lot is recommended.

Food

Get standard American breakfasts at **Golden Spur Cafe,** 486 Washington, tel. 886-9890, or the somewhat nicer **Elkhorn Restaurant,** 465 Washington, tel. 886-3080. The latter also has good lunch specials and a big salad bar. **Red Baron Drive-In,** 838 Washington, tel. 886-3745, is the hangout for folks who want burgers and fries. Pizza and sandwiches are available at **The Dough Box,** 458 Washington, tel. 886-5529, or try the lunchtime buffet at **Pizza Hut,** 228 Washington, tel. 886-9794. **Silver Stream Lodge,** seven miles north of Afton, tel. 883-2400, has a popular steak and seafood restaurant and cocktail lounge. **Colter's Bar,** 355 Washington, tel. 886-9597, grills fine steaks and chicken in a rustic old-west atmosphere. Eat outside on the patio during the summer. **Homestead Restaurant,** just south of town, tel. 886-3878, offers the area's finest prime rib. Try the double-fudge desserts. Get groceries at **Thriftway,** just north of Afton, tel. 886-5550.

Entertainment And Events

For live C&W or rock music, head to **Colter's Bar,** 355 Washington, tel. 886-9597, where the young crowd hangs out, or **Valley Vineyard,** 967 Washington, tel. 886-9215. The **Lincoln County Fair** is held in Afton during early August.

STAR VALLEY AND ALPINE ACCOMMODATIONS

MOTEL	ADDRESS	TELEPHONE	RATES	FEATURES
Star Valley Sunset Motel	Thayne	883-2462	$25 s, $29 d	
Horse Shoe Motel	Etna	883-2281	$27 s, $33 d	
Corral Motel	161 Washington Afton	886-5424	$30 s, $34 d	AAA approved, pool, whirlpool, open April-Oct.
Lazy B Motel	219 Washington Afton	886-3187	$30 s, $34 d	AAA approved
Flat Creek Cabins	Thayne	883-2231	$30 s or d	cabins with kitchenettes
Silver Stream Lodge	Grover	883-2440	$35 s or d	cabins
Swiss Mountain Motel	Thayne	883-2227	$38 s or d	
Hi Country Inn (Best Western)	3/4 mile south of Afton	886-3856 (800) 528-1234	$40 s, $45 d	AAA approved, pool, whirlpool
Mountain Inn	one mile south of Afton	886-3156	$42 s, $47 d	AAA approved, pool, sauna, whirlpool
Alpine Alpen Haus	Alpine	654-7545	$30+ s, $40+ d	AAA approved, whirlpools
Palisport Motel	Alpine	654-7540	$34 s, $38 d	open mid-May to mid-Oct.
Three Rivers Motel	Alpine	654-7551	$40 s, $45+ d	
Lakeside Motel	Alpine	654-7506	$41 s, $45 d	open May-Oct.
Greys River Lodge	Greys River Rd.	654-7777	$45 s, $55 d	bed & breakfast, log home
Flying Saddle Lodge	Alpine	654-7561	$48+ s or d	AAA approved, pool, whirlpools, open late May to mid-Oct.
Nordic Inn	Alpine	654-7556	$48 s, $52+ d $125+ chalet	classy place, spa, open late May to mid-Oct.

Recreation

Country Gardens Pool, just north of town, tel. 886-5507, is open May-Sept. and costs $3.50 for adults or $2.50 for kids, including hot tub. Golfers will find a pair of nine-hole courses (one of these—Valli-Vu Golf Course—is free if you're staying at a local motel), plus two 18-hole courses at Star Valley Ranch Resort in Thayne. During the winter, the town operates Snowshoe Hollow, tel. 886-9831, a small ski area just east of Afton. The hill has a rope tow and snack bar.

Stop by the Forest Service office for information on the half-dozen groomed cross-country ski trails in Star Valley. The mountains to the east offer unlimited opportunities for further exploration by skiers. A variety of groomed snowmobile trails is also available.

Information And Shopping

Afton has a summer-only visitor center at Second and Washington, tel. 886-3156 or (800) 426-8833, that is open Tues.-Sat. 10-6. Directly across the road is the **Forest Service Greys River District Office,** tel. 886-3166. Stop here for local maps, natural history books, and info on nearby recreation opportunities. **Star Valley Branch Library,** 261 Washington St., tel. 886-3158, is open only Wed. 10-6, Thurs. 10-8, and Sat. 10-2. Lots of genealogy titles. If you are looking for local crafts, visit **Star Valley Treasures,** next to the arch on Washington Street. Although some of the stuff is unadulterated kitsch, you'll also discover beautiful handmade quilts for sale. For a real dose of Star Valley culture, drop by the **Hastings Store,** 422 Washington, tel. 886-3503. Inside is a large selection of LDS books along with a world history map showing where local kids have gone as Mormon missionaries (15% discount for outgoing missionaries!).

GREYS RIVER LOOP ROAD

Star Valley is bordered on the east by two parallel mountain ranges: Salt River Range and Wyoming Range. The Greys River flows between them, and alongside it is an 80-mile-long gravel road that is popular with vacationers, hikers, anglers, and hunters. The road begins south of Afton and goes all the way to Alpine. Excellent fishing for cutthroat, rainbow, brown, and brook trout in the river, and good opportunities to see deer and moose along the way. All this country lies within Bridger-Teton National Forest. Considerable logging and oil exploration take place in the mountains, and many thousands of sheep and cattle graze the open areas, but much of the land remains wild and beautiful. It is an almost unknown part of Wyoming.

Another fascinating drive (great for mountain bikes) is to continue east through Snider Basin to the town of Big Piney on Forest Rd. 10128. The road parallels the still-visible Lander Cutoff of the Oregon Trail for a long distance, and a number of emigrant graves are noted along the way. Keep your eyes open for elk and deer on the slopes and beaver dams in Piney Creek. The high country is lodgepole-pine forests, passing into open sage land as you descend toward Big Piney. Note that this route can be confusing (signs are often missing) and sometimes muddy, so be sure to get a Forest Service map and current conditions before heading out from Afton.

Camping And Hiking

Camping ($5; open mid-June to mid-Sept.) is available at seven places along the Greys River Rd.; nicest are ones at Murphy Creek and Forest Park. (At other times of the year the campgrounds are open at no charge, but you'll need to bring in water and haul out your own garbage.) You can also camp off the road for free in most parts of the national forest. More than 450 miles of trails cut across this country, including the 70-mile-long **Wyoming Range National Recreation Trail** that climbs through beautiful alpine meadows and over narrow, rocky ridges. A side road off the Greys River Rd. leads to a two-mile trail that climbs 11,363-foot **Wyoming Peak,** tallest in the range. During the winter, cross-country skiers will find four groomed ski trails, while snowmobilers can cruise on 100 miles of groomed routes. See the Forest Service office in Afton for maps and recreation information. The chamber of commerce has a listing of local guides and outfitters. **Star Valley Llama,** in Bedford, tel. 883-2174 or (800) 554-2174, provides llama trips of various lengths in the Salt River Range as well as into the Yellowstone backcountry. Overnight trips start at $175 pp.

OTHER TOWNS

Thayne

Thayne's (pop. 270) claim to fame is the **cutter races,** a sport invented here in the 1920s. It's said that racing began with dairymen who used sleighs to haul milk to the local creamery. To avoid having to wait in line, there was often a race to get to the creamery ahead of other farmers, and this sparring eventually grew into a competition that now encompasses seven western states. (The "world finals" are held in Pocatello, Idaho.) In a cutter race, horses pull chariots over a frozen field at breakneck speeds; the world record stands at 21.8 seconds for the quarter-mile run! Races are held in Thayne on most Saturdays between Dec. and February.

Star Valley Cheese, tel. 883-2510, is one of the most unusual eating places in Wyoming. The restaurant—an old-fashioned place straight out of the 1950s—serves reasonably priced burgers, homemade pies, ice cream, and other fare, or you can buy fresh cheeses from the coolers. It's open daily May-October. Some 60,000 pounds of mozzarella, provolone, and ricotta cheese are made in the plant right behind the shop. Everything here gets the Star Valley label, although the plant is now a part of Western Dairymen Cooperative. Well worth a stop. Across the highway is a rock shop selling fossils and crystals. Also in Thayne is **Caribou Saddle Shop,** tel. 886-3061, where you'll find some of the finest handcrafted saddles in the area. **JH Ranch Cafe,** tel. 883-2357, has homemade breads and pastries, along with "The Thing." **Dad's Bar,** tel. 883-2300, offers live music on weekends and the best steaks in the area. This is also home to a small cutter-racing museum; the sport was established by "Dad" Walton.

Flat Creek RV Park south of Thayne, tel. 883-2231, charges $12 for RVs, or $5 for tents. Showers cost $2. It's open year-round. Just north of Thayne is **Star Valley Ranch Resort,** tel. 883-2457, an obscenely elaborate place with several hundred summer homes, a restaurant, RV park, two pools, two golf courses, and tennis courts. Ugly billboards announce its presence for miles in both directions. This is the sort of development that is ruining the west.

Bedford
The tiny farming and sheep-ranching settlement of Bedford lies near the center of Star Valley. On fall days you're likely to meet huge herds of sheep being driven down the main roads as they return from a summer in the mountains. Drop by the Bedford store, where the talkative owner will welcome you to "Hooterville without the train." Across the street is the occasionally-open **Bedford Mercantile,** tel. 883-2136, which sells handmade quilts.

Freedom And Etna
Freedom (pop. 100), Star Valley's oldest settlement, straddles the Idaho-Wyoming border. The town was established by Mormons in 1879 and offered an escape from Idaho Territory's efforts to ban polygamy. Arthur Clark named the town for his freedom to have multiple wives. Today, Freedom has a small country store just a few feet from the border where you are free to buy Idaho lottery tickets. **Horse Shoe Cafe** in Etna is a classic small-town cafe, filling with lo-

cals every day and deer hunters on cool fall mornings. Freedom is famous in gun circles for a small factory, **Freedom Arms,** tel. 883-2468, that makes handguns, including the monstrous .454 Casull, the world's most powerful revolver (and one of the most expensive at $1100 apiece). No surprise that Clint Eastwood owns one. Don't ever get on the wrong end of this deadly instrument. Visitors can watch a short video and view a gun display here.

Etna lies near the northern end of Star Valley and has a small country store and an outsized brick LDS church that looks big enough to house the entire population of 200. In late summer, the sweet scent of new-mown hay hangs in the air.

ALPINE

The crossroads settlement called Alpine (pop. 180) consists of several motels, restaurants, and bars strung out in all directions along the intersection of US 26 and 89. Almost everything here is aimed at tourists en route to Jackson Hole. The area is called Lower Valley and borders on Palisades Reservoir. Approximately 1,000 elk gather each winter at the **Elk Feedground,** located a mile south of Alpine on US 89. The elk can be viewed from the parking area here, and they often approach parked cars rather closely. Best time to visit is in the mornings, when they are fed.

Practicalities
See the chart for a list of local motels. Reservations are advisable during July and August. **Palisport Campground,** tel. 654-7540, has tent sites for $10 and RV sites for $15; it's open mid-May to mid-October. Showers for noncampers cost $3. Lots of public camping nearby; see "Snake River Canyon" (below) or "Greys River Loop Road" (above). Contact **Alpine Riding & Rafts,** tel. 654-9900, for horseback rides in the area and raft trips down the Snake River Canyon. Float trips can also be booked at **Nordic Inn,** tel. 654-7556. Many similar operations are run in nearby Jackson.

Restaurants And Entertainment
Lakeside Restaurant, tel. 654-7507, features homemade food. **Bette's Coffee Shop,** tel. 654-

7536, serves delicious, reasonably priced breakfasts and lunches on weekdays, plus dinners Fri.-Sun. nights. Recommended. The real surprise in Alpine is **Brentoven's Restaurant,** where the chef—Brent Johnston—is not only talented in the kitchen but is also an international concert pianist. You'll find everything from fresh fruit crepes for breakfast to steak and venison for dinner. The bar here has a fine wine selection, and owner Mike Clinger will be happy to discuss opera or tell you about his distinctive Colonial home located behind the Nordic Inn. **Jeep's Bar,** tel. 654-7585, has live music (mostly C&W) on weekends and is one of the most popular weekend hangouts in the Star Valley/Upper Valley vicinity.

SNAKE RIVER CANYON

Above Alpine, the country abruptly changes as US 89-26 enters Snake River Canyon, paralleling it all the way to Hoback Junction, 23 miles away. In places, the highway hangs high over the river, with only a guardrail blocking the way (and sometimes not even that). This is a delicious way to enter Jackson Hole, offering numerous pullouts where you can view the roiling rambunctious rapids of the sinuous Snake River as it slithers through millions of years of rocky cliffs. At sunset, the river glows a silver ribbon of light. A big, powerful river, the Snake eventually feeds into the Columbia River in Washington state. Riverbanks are lined with ancient cottonwoods, while the higher slopes exude lodgepole pines.

The whitewater of Snake River Canyon is a favorite of recreationists, and during the summer you're bound to meet cars with kayaks on their roofs and vans filled with happy rafters heading back to Jackson. See "Jackson Hole," pp. 281-282 for details on the many river-running options. River access is generally via the West Table Creek and Sheep Gulch boat ramps. A half-dozen Forest Service **campgrounds** ($5; open late May to mid-Sept.) are scattered all along the way. Many fill up early in the day during midsummer. Undeveloped camping spots along the way are also used by many travelers.

Boar's Tusk

CENTRAL WYOMING

The counties of Natrona and Converse enclose definitive Wyoming country: sage-and-grass-carpeted plains, desolate badlands, impressive tree-draped mountainsides, and the big, lazy North Platte River. This is grazing country; each year nearly a quarter of the sheep raised in Wyoming, along with 120,000 cattle, come from these two counties. The dominant industry, however—and the one that dictates the region's economy—is oil. It means jobs for roughnecks in dozens of oil fields, but it also greases the wheels of city life, offering refinery and transportation work, government positions, and a wave of other impacts in the local community as the wages pass on to construction workers, shop owners, and schoolteachers. Without oil, Casper—Wyoming's second-largest metropolitan area—would be little more than a cattle-town crossroad on the way to Yellowstone.

The Land

Geographically, central Wyoming is quite diverse. The north portion is an open, expansive place. Driving across the long, straight highways that divide this land is like sailing a boat over an ocean of gentle rollers—the mountains are so far in the distance that they could well be islands. Golden eagles spin giant loops in the sky, and the coal black clouds of distant summertime thunderheads are pierced by brilliant slashes of lightning. The wind blows on, bending the grass as it passes in waves of motion, whirling the old windmills that pump water to sheep, cattle, and deer. This is rolling mixed-grass prairie and sagebrush country, with sharp ridges appearing suddenly, topped by narrow bands of ponderosa pine and juniper.

South of this rangeland lies the North Platte River, carving a slow curve first to the north, then east, and finally southeast toward Nebraska. Giant dams hold back the water for irrigation and electricity. A green stripe of riparian forests and irrigated fields borders the river. South of the Platte, the land changes again, with the Laramie Mountains rising in a rough-edged jumble of rugged canyons and pine-covered peaks. Elk stand along mountain meadows, bugling in the cool air of late fall. Pickup trucks slow as wild turkeys speed-walk across the gravel roads. Clear mountain brooks cascade down mountain slopes. West of here, central Wyoming becomes drier and more desolate, wrinkled by the badlands of Hells Half Acre and the barren crests of desert mountain ranges.

Casper dominates the central Wyoming economy with oil refineries, the only statewide newspaper, the state's largest junior college, and its biggest shopping mall. The towns of Douglas and Glenrock go their own ways, with a mix-ture of ranching, oil, coal, and tourism. Farther north, the tiny settlements of Midwest and Edgerton cap the vast Salt Creek oil field. Between these few outposts of civilization lie hundreds of square miles of sagebrush and grass, jackrabbits, and rattlers. Only the scattered roads, oil pumpjacks, windmills, and old ranch houses mark the presence of humans.

DOUGLAS

Douglas (pop. 5,100) epitomizes life in small-town America. It's the sort of place where the big summertime events are the state fair and weekly drag races, where a night on the town means joining a bowling league or doing the two-step at the LaBonte Inn, and where men hang out in the Corner Barber Shop to talk politics, retiring next door to the historic College Inn Bar for a beer. On both ends of Douglas are more modern slices of Americana—suburban ranch-style homes cover the hills. It's a friendly, conservative town with pickup trucks, dense American food, and an unusual history.

HISTORY

Douglas came into existence with the arrival of the Fremont, Elkhorn, and Missouri Valley Railroad. Platted in 1886, the town was named for Stephen A. Douglas, the senator from Illinois best known for his debates with Abraham Lincoln. It quickly boomed to 1,600 people that first year, boasting three newspapers, several restaurants and hotels, two dance halls, 12 stores, and 21 saloons (easy to see where priorities lay). Once the railroad construction had moved

DOUGLAS

on down the line to Casper, the population dwindled, and it became a sleepy little ranching center for the next 70 years. Only the late-summer state fair brought Douglas to life each year.

World War II

One of the strangest pieces of Douglas history is its prisoner-of-war camp, built in 1943 along the North Platte River. The camp contained 180 barrack-style buildings and housed up to 3,000 prisoners of war. The camp was surrounded by an electrified fence, watchtowers, German shepherds, and Army guards. One prisoner was shot by a guard, and a few others escaped, but they

didn't get far in this remote country, 2,000 miles from the sea. Though some of the prisoners at Douglas were German Nazi and SS officers, the majority were Italians, many of whom were happy to be away from the war.

The prisoners worked in local agricultural fields, harvesting potatoes and sugar beets for $4 a day or at a variety of art projects in the camp. Most impressive was the work of several Italian artists who painted the interior of the U.S. officers' club with 15 murals of old-west scenes. After the war, the prisoners returned home, though some have returned to visit in later years. The land was sold to Converse County for $1, and the barracks were dismantled or bought by locals who moved them to other parts of town. Today the POW campsite is an open meadow on the west bank of the North Platte south of Richards Street.

Boom And Bust

Like much of Wyoming, Douglas has watched its fortunes wax and wane over the years. In the 1950s, with the Cold War at fever pitch, prospectors combed Wyoming with Geiger counters, discovering major uranium deposits just north of Douglas. Others found oil, gas, and coal. A giant coal-fired power plant opened in nearby Glenrock, and by the late '70s the region was one of

the most prosperous in the state. At the peak of the oil-and-uranium orgy in the early 1980s, the town of Douglas had doubled in size to over 10,000 people.

The tourist brochures claim "growth has leveled off," but in reality it fell off a cliff, dropping perhaps 50% in a couple of years. Longtime locals had mixed feelings when the balloon suddenly burst in the mid '80s—they were happy to see the rabble leave town, but suddenly burdened with paying for all the new schools, roads, and other facilities ordered up in the heady heyday. Today, the economy of Douglas is back to its old mixture of ranching and energy, with some people commuting 60 miles each way to

JACKALOPES

Definition: Jackalope—a mammal that moves by bounding, found originally in Converse County, Wyoming, but now distributed throughout the western states. It has the horns of an antelope, the body of a jackrabbit, and the stealth of both. First observed by trapper Roy Ball in 1829, and later noted by cowboys and others after too little sleep, too many days in the saddle, and too much cheap whiskey. Nocturnal animals, jackalopes are never seen during the day. These powerful and vicious animals are reputed to attain speeds approaching 90 mph and often sing and mate during thunderstorms. The hornless does are commonly seen by tourists, while the bucks remain elusive. Westerners feel that the federal government is hushing the true story of these dangerous critters to make cowboys look like liars.

Okay, I admit to liking plastic pink flamingos and tacky postcards, but jackalopes are another story. The first time you see a mounted jackalope specimen, it is mildly amusing, but with each tourist junk shop west of the Mississippi offering more jackalopes, the originality quickly fades. The town of Douglas takes credit for this harebrained idea, though its claim is a bit suspect. In the 1920s, a Douglas resident saw a jackalope mounted in a store in Buffalo, Wyoming. He described the creature to his grandson, Douglas Herrick, who was intrigued by the animal. In 1941, he attached the antlers of a deer to the head of a large jackrabbit he had shot and sold the specimen to the LaBonte Hotel. The rest is history. Douglas Herrick's son, Jim Herrick, follows in his father's footsteps, offering

BOB RACE

everything from fighting jackalopes to jackalope "love mounts" at Big Horn Taxidermy on Smylie Road.

In 1960, the State of Wyoming gave the Douglas Chamber of Commerce "jackalope" as a registered trademark. Today jackalopes are everywhere in Douglas: the town symbol contains one, an eight-foot-tall jackalope statue greets visitors at Jackalope Square, another statue has hopped atop the LaBonte Hotel, a roadside sign warns "Watch Out For Jackalope," cans of jackalope milk are sold in the stores, you can drink "Rabbit Punch" at a local bar, jackalope hunting licenses are available around town, and of course, the critters multiply like rabbits on the shelves of local shops.

coal mines near Wright. Most folks are happy to live a simpler life. Of course, the next energy boom could be just around the corner.

SIGHTS

Pioneer Museum

The people of Douglas point with pride to their local museum, easily one of the finest in Wyoming. Located just inside the fairgrounds, the spacious museum, tel. 358-9288, is open Mon.-Fri. 8-5 in winter, and daily in summer (extended hours). Free. The main room is filled with old rifles and saddles (including one that belonged to outlaw Tom Horn). Check out the special "running irons" used by rustlers to alter cattle brands. Fittingly enough, the rifle of Nate Champion—a rustler murdered in the Johnson County Wars—is also here. Look around the other rooms and you'll discover the bison-fur mittens worn by Portugee Phillips on his ride to get help for Fort Kearny, and an Army trumpet and bullets from the Custer battlefield.

On a kinder and gentler note, take a look at the large doll collection and many unusual women's fans, along with a description of "fan language." A back room contains Indian artifacts, including beautiful pottery, Sioux and Crow war clubs, a bow from the Custer Battlefield, and a tipi used in the movie *Dances with Wolves*. Downstairs are several wonderful old quilts and a collection of homestead items. The stairwell features the 64-inch-waist overalls that belonged to flamboyant C.B. Irwin. He weighed 500 pounds. Outside are seven old train cars in various stages of disrepair, along with a schoolhouse built in 1886.

More Sights

The old **officers' club** from the Douglas POW camp is now an Odd Fellows Hall at 115 S. Riverbend Dr., tel. 358-2421. Ask to take a look inside at the wall-to-wall murals painted by Italian artists/prisoners during WW II. One of Wyoming's oldest churches is the **Christ Episcopal Church,** built in 1896 and now on the National Register of Historic Places. The attractive white structure is located at 411 Center, tel. 358-5609. The **Plains Complex,** 628 E. Richards, tel. 358-4489, has several historic structures, hauled in from all over this part of

Wyoming. Included are the old officers' quarters from Fort Fetterman and a POW-camp building. The ice-cream parlor served at various times as a barn, a boardinghouse, and a maternity center. Check out the doors on the ceiling of the ice-cream shop. The **Douglas Park Cemetery,** on the east end of Pine St., has a number of interesting old graves, including that of horse thief "Doc" Middleton. Also here is the grave of George W. Pike.

PRACTICALITIES

Accommodations

There are 10 lodging places to choose from in Douglas; see the chart on the next page for specifics. In July and August you should book motel reservations up to two months ahead. This is especially true when the state fair arrives each August. Many locals rent out rooms in their homes to visitors while the fair is going on; get a list from the chamber of commerce. Dormitories are also available for temporary lodging on the fairgrounds; call 358-2398 for details.

In addition to the places listed, visitors may want to spend time at **Deer Folks Ranch,** 24 miles south of Douglas, tel. 358-2033. This is a good chance to join in on cattle drives and other activities on a working cattle ranch.

Camping

Pitch tents or park RVs for free at **Riverside Park** along the North Platte River. The free showers have an amusing Western-decor bathroom covered with "branded" wood. Camping is limited to two nights, and the sprinklers come on at 8 a.m., so get up early! Two nearby camping places—Ayres Natural Bridge Park and the Laramie Mountains—are described on pp. 176-178. The RV crowd heads to **Jackalope KOA,** tel. 358-2164, west of Douglas on State 91. Rates are $12 for tents or $17 for RVs. It's open year-round.

Food

Restaurant food in Douglas is pretty standard Wyoming fare. Breakfast time means bacon and eggs at **LaBonte Inn,** 206 Walnut St., tel. 358-9856, or big portions at the **Broken Wheel Truckstop,** just east of town, tel. 358-4446

DOUGLAS ACCOMMODATIONS

MOTEL	ADDRESS	TELEPHONE	RATES	FEATURES
Four Winds Motel	615 Richards	358-2322	$20 s, $22 d	
Plains Motel	628 E. Richards	358-4484	$22 s, $24 d	kitchenettes
Vagabond Motel	430 Richards	358-9414	$22 s, $26 d	
LaBonte Hotel	206 Walnut	358-9856	$25 s or d	
Chieftain Motel	815 Richards	358-2673	$25 s, $29 d	AAA approved
1st Interstate	2349 E. Richards	358-2833	$25 s, $32 d	AAA approved
Super 8 Motel	314 Russell Ave.	358-6800 (800) 800-8000	$30 s, $34 d	AAA approved
Alpine Inn	2310 E. Richards	358-4780	$31 s, $36 d	friendly staff
Akers Ranch B&B	81 Inez Rd.	358-3741	$40 s, $50 d	AAA approved, full breakfast, ranch living
Holiday Inn	1450 Riverbend Dr.	358-9790 (800) 465-4329	$49+ s, $61+ d	AAA approved, pool, whirlpool, sauna, exercise room

(open 24 hours). LaBonte is also the place to head for prime-rib dinners. Both **Pizza Hut,** 1830 Richards, tel. 358-3657, and **Clementine's,** 1199 Mesa Dr., tel. 358-5554, have all-you-can-eat lunch specials. The **Plains Complex,** 628 E. Richards, tel. 358-4489, has a so-so coffee shop (open 24 hours) and an old-fashioned ice-cream parlor. For the best and biggest burgers anywhere around (they cook them *your* way, and use locally raised stock), head to **Grumpy's,** 1213 Teton Way, tel. 358-5702. Surprisingly good ice-cream sundaes, too.

Come dinner time, there are several choices. Clementine's has steak and prime rib, pizza, and Mexican food in a pleasant atmosphere. **El Quico's,** in the American Legion at Sixth and Oak, tel. 358-2317, serves reasonable Mexican food; or try **Chute's Eatery** in the Holiday Inn, 1450 Riverbend Dr., tel. 358-9790. Their soup and salad buffet is a good deal. Also popular is the elegant **Country Inn,** 2341 E. Richards, tel. 358-3575. It has a reasonable salad bar, plus good burgers, sandwiches, and chicken-fried steak.

Douglas has three grocery stores: **Peyton Bolln Grocery,** 100 S. Third, **Decker Food Center,** 1100 Richards, and a **Safeway,** 130 S. Fourth. For fresh-baked pastries, head to **Home Bakery,** 119 N. Third, tel. 358-9251.

Recreation

The free **Douglas Recreation Center** at the high school, 1701 Hamilton, tel. 358-4231, houses a pool, gyms, racquetball courts, and a weight room. Seven miles south of Douglas on Esterbrook Rd. (State 94) is **Jackalope Plunge Swimming Pool,** tel. 358-2820, fed by the 86° F water of Douglas Warm Spring. No chlorine. This is a fun place to play volleyball, enjoy a picnic, or practice your diving. Entrance is $3 adults, $2 under age 11. It's open summers only, Tues.-Thurs. 11-5:30, and Fri.-Sun. 11-7. A couple of miles south of Jackalope Plunge, you can see ruts of the old Oregon Trail; ask at the chamber of commerce for directions.

An 18-hole **golf course,** tel. 358-5099, is southeast of Douglas. (There are no sand traps because the fierce winter winds kept blowing them away.) **Riverside Park,** along the western bank of the North Platte River, contains a two-mile-long paved bike path that makes for a pleasant evening stroll. Take along your fishing pole to try for trout, walleye, or channel catfish. If you have your own raft or canoe, the river provides pleasant, leisurely float trips.

Entertainment

Chutes Lounge in the Holiday Inn, 1450 Riverbend Dr., tel. 358-9790, has lounge-lizard tunes six nights a week, a big-screen TV, and free hors d'oeuvres on weeknights. **LaBonte Lounge,** 206 Walnut, tel. 358-5210, is the place for weekend bands. More country two-stepping at the **Plains Complex,** 628 E. Richards, tel. 358-4489. Farther afield, you can dance on summer weekends at **Esterbrook Lodge,** 32 miles south of Douglas. The historic **College Inn Bar,** 103 N. Second, tel. 358-9976, is a favorite place for major-league drinking with the locals.

Wyoming State Fair

In 1905, the Wyoming Legislature appropriated $10,000 for a Wyoming State Fair in Douglas. With land donated by the Chicago and Northwestern Railroad, the "Show Window of Wyoming" opened that summer, offering a variety of agricultural exhibits, plus horseback wrestling, Roman races, and concerts. To top it off, two cavalry soldiers added their own drama by putting on an impromptu gunfight. Later, auto polo and motorcycle-riding events were added, but the big hit was Professor Carver's High Diving Girl, who leapt with her horse off a 40-foot platform into a pool of water.

The Wyoming State Fair is held the third week of August each year, drawing thousands of visitors from all over the nation. The 113-acre fairgrounds is right next to town and includes a 4,300-seat grandstand, an arts-and-crafts building, a cafeteria, an arena, an open-air pavilion, livestock barns and stalls, and of course, plenty of carnival rides, cotton candy, and stuffed-animal prizes in the midway. Keep yourself entertained at the market swine evaluation, the 4-H vegetable judging, the demolition derby, or the sheep-to-shawl contest. A free "people shuttle" (tractor-pulled wagon) takes folks around the fairgrounds and into town. Other attractions include evening C&W concerts, the Miss Rodeo Wyoming contest, and a Saturday morning parade. Since this is Wyoming, the biggest events at the fair are the **PRCA rodeos** held the final three days.

Other Events

Both locals and visitors enjoy the **High Plains Oldtime Country Music Show & Contest** held in mid-April. Plenty of hot fiddle, guitar, and banjo players offer entertainment. **Fort Fetterman Days,** held the third weekend in June at the old fort, attracts a troop of soldiers and other folks dressed in costumes from the 1870s. There are black-powder contests, old-time music, and games.

In late June, **Jackalope Days** offers a western art show, a street dance, a carnival, and a pancake breakfast, along with live music and poetry. All summer long, the grandiosely named Douglas International Raceway on the southeast edge of town hosts **drag races** of all types. It's considered one of the top quarter-mile strips in the nation. The biggest races come in mid-July.

Information And Services

The **Douglas Area Chamber of Commerce** office, 318 First St., tel. 358-2950, is open Mon.-Fri. 9 a.m.-noon and 1-4 p.m.. **Converse County Library,** 300 Walnut St., tel. 358-3644, is open only Mon., Tues., and Fri. 10-6, and Thurs. noon-8 p.m. **R-D Pharmacy,** 206 Center, tel. 358-3266, sells Wyoming books. Visit the **Meadowlark Gallery** at 300 S. Fourth St., tel. 358-3808, for local arts and crafts. The Forest Service's **Laramie Peak District Office,** 809 S. Ninth St., tel. 358-4690, has maps and info on both Medicine Bow National Forest and Thunder Basin National Grassland. **Powder River Transportation** buses, tel. (800) 442-3682, stop at Broken Wheel Truckstop, just east of Douglas, providing connections to most of Wyoming.

DOUGLAS VICINITY

FORT FETTERMAN

Seven miles northwest of Douglas on State 93 is Fort Fetterman State Historic Site. The fort was named for Lt. Col. William J. Fetterman, who was killed by Indians in the Fetterman Massacre of 1866 (see "Powder River Country," pp. 438-439). Begun in 1867, this was the last fort built in the Rockies. With the signing of the Fort Laramie Treaty of 1868, forts Casper, Reno, Phil Kearny, and C.F. Smith were all closed, leaving Fort Fetterman as the only Army base in northern Wyoming. The hilltop location afforded commanding views along the infamous Bozeman Trail in both directions, but the location proved inhospitable. A report to headquarters the first winter noted "officers and men were found under canvas exposed on a bleak plain to violent and almost constant gales and very uncomfortable." Even after the buildings were completed, the fort remained a dreaded, windswept, lonely place, and many soldiers deserted as soon as they could get to the nearest railroad. The regimen was strict, with daily parade drills and the prospect of long rides to fight Indians in the surrounding country. Soldiers called the place "Hell Hole," while the Sioux derisively labelled it "Fort Fetterman Reservation." Not far away stood the "Hog Ranch"—sin city on the plains—where gambling, drinking, and women offered a choice of ways to spend the $13 a month cavalrymen received.

Fort Fetterman served as a supply base for the Army during the mid-1870s, and both Gen. Crook and Col. MacKenzie led expeditions from here to attack the Sioux, but the fort itself was never the scene of any conflicts. After the battles had finally died down, the fort was abandoned in 1882. Instead of immediately disappearing, however, "Fetterman City" became the center of ranching and trade in the area. For a while, at least, it was a wide-open town with enough gunfights, hangings, whoring, gambling, and drunkenness to give "Miami Vice" a run for the money. In his novel *The Virginian,* Owen Wister used Fetterman as the basis for his rough-and-tumble town of "Drybone."

Alferd Packer

One of the characters attracted to Fetterman was a prospector who called himself John Swartz. When a waiter was slow in bringing water to his table at a local restaurant, he pulled a gun, saying, "Damn you, ain't you going to bring me that water?" Service quickly improved. The man turned out to be Alferd Packer, wanted for robbing, killing, and then eating his five mining partners in Colorado during the winter of 1875. (Packer called human breast meat the sweetest he'd ever eaten.) After escaping from a Colorado jail, he remained free for the next decade, before finally being recognized in Fetterman City. The sheriff captured him at a nearby ranch and spent several nervous nights on the long stage ride to Rock Creek before finally turning Packer over to Colorado authorities. Although convicted of murder, Packer managed to escape from prison again, his body was found in the Rockies in 1903.

The Fort Today

After the railroad arrived in 1886, Douglas became the new center for trade, and Fetterman quickly faded from the scene. Most of the buildings were torn down or moved to Douglas, and only two of the original buildings remain: an adobe ordnance warehouse and a log officers' quarters. Inside the officers' quarters is a small state-run **museum** (free) that includes historic displays on the fort, Indians battles, and Fetterman City. The buildings are open daily 9-5 in summer, or by appointment (tel. 358-2864) the rest of the year. You can visit the grounds at any time. The surrounding country still exudes a sense of barren loneliness, and it's easy to see how much the soldiers must have hated this windswept post. Ask the museum staff to point out the faint tracks of the "Bloody Bozeman" Trail to the south.

THUNDER BASIN NATIONAL GRASSLAND

Thunder Basin National Grassland is an expansive blend of high rolling plateaus, steep rocky escarpments, and gentle plains. It's one of the few places in Wyoming where mountain ranges are not visible, giving the countryside a North Dakota feel. Most of the grassland is covered with a mixture of western wheatgrass, blue grama grass, and big sagebrush, but some of the ridges have stands of ponderosa pine and juniper, while creek bottoms contain cottonwood trees or greasewood. There are 170 known golden-eagle nests on Thunder Basin—one of the biggest concentrations in Wyoming—along with abundant populations of sandhill cranes, turkeys, antelope, mule deer, elk, and coyotes. Many bald eagles winter here. Look out for the jackalopes, too; lots of the antlerless variety get hit by cars.

Thunder Basin National Grassland covers 1.8 million acres within Powder River Basin. The land is a checkerboard of private ranches and property belonging to the Forest Service, the BLM, and the state. The federal government owns 572,000 acres of the total, managed from the Forest Service office in Douglas, at 809 S. Ninth St., tel. 358-4690. Get a copy of the detailed Thunder Basin map here for $3.

History

Thunder Basin came about during the glory days of the New Deal and remains today an enclave of pseudosocialism within the rock-ribbed Republican state of Wyoming. Although ranchers had grazed sheep and cattle in the area since the mid-19th century, the arrival of homesteaders caused the land to be divided into smaller parcels. In the arid mixed-grass prairies of eastern Wyoming, it was nearly impossible for a family to survive—the rains fell too infrequently for farming, and profitable cattle or sheep operations required more than 640 acres of grazing land.

PRAIRIE DOGS

Prairie dogs are cat-sized rodents that live in underground communities and feed on roots and plants. Prairie-dog towns sometimes cover thousands of acres, with burrow holes spaced every 50 feet or so. Two species dwell in Wyoming: white-tailed and black-tailed prairie dogs. The latter are found in at least 180 towns covering more than 28,000 acres within Thunder Basin National Grassland. Local ranchers complain of lost grazing range due to digging by the dogs and injuries from horses and cattle stepping into their holes. Because of this, the Forest Service for many years systematically poisoned prairie-dog colonies for "range improvement" (translation: cattle grazing).

Sightings of the endangered black-footed ferret on the national grassland helped end most of this poisoning in the 1970s, and prairie-dog populations have rebounded dramatically. Unfortunately, the Forest Service continues its poisoning program in places. In addition, because prairie dogs are still considered varmints, "sport" hunters aren't limited on how many they can shoot. Hunters from South Dakota—having already decimated prairie-dog populations in their own state—are coming to the prairie-dog colonies of Wyoming, shooting as many as they can. Meanwhile, the Department of Game and Fish is raising a covey of once-wild ferrets at its Sybille Canyon facility, hoping to someday return them to such places as the national grassland (see p. 75 for more on the black-footed ferret). By trying to contain the prairie-dog population to small areas, the hunters, Forest Service, and private ranchers may well be endangering the long-term survival of the world's rarest mammal, the black-footed ferret. If you're interested in seeing prairie dogs, ask at the Douglas Forest Service office for a copy of their prairie-dog town map. The largest area—covering at least eight square miles—is along Horse Creek in the Rochelle Hills. Smaller prairie-dog colonies lie along North Antelope Road.

BOB RACE

Overgrazing, soil erosion, and five consecutive drought years in the 1930s combined to force many families off the land. Counties risked bankruptcy because of lost tax revenue. The Agricultural Adjustment Administration finally began purchasing homesteads in 1934, giving money to the counties in lieu of taxes. Programs were begun to reestablish grasses to protect the soil and to develop water sources for livestock, while private land ownership was consolidated into larger, more economically manageable units.

Management

Today, local ranchers use the grassland in a cooperative grazing scheme that allows 21,000 cattle and an equal number of sheep on the federal land. Improvements such as dams, wells, and fences are cooperatively developed. In addition to livestock grazing, practically every acre of Thunder Basin has been leased for petroleum exploration. Currently, over 375 oil and gas wells pump from 58 oil fields. Vast deposits of sub-bituminous coal underlie almost the entire area, and there are five gigantic strip mines, including Black Thunder Coal Mine, the largest coal producer in the nation. Revenues from oil and coal developments on the grassland bring in nearly $20 million a year to the federal treasury, a figure unmatched anywhere else in the Forest Service system. Bentonite—a lubricant and absorptive clay used in everything from oil-drilling muds to candy bars—is also mined on the grassland, and major uranium deposits wait for the public to forget about Three Mile Island and Chernobyl.

Recreation

A network of over 775 miles of gravel and dirt roads crisscrosses Thunder Basin National Grassland, but there are no developed trails, campgrounds, or other facilities. You can, however, camp for free anywhere on the public lands. A couple of areas are popular with hunters, birdwatchers, photographers, and others looking for a chance to get out and about.

The **Rochelle Hills** area, a forested volcanic escarpment near the corner of Converse, Campbell, and Weston counties, is one of the prettiest parts of the national grassland, though a recent fire has blackened some of the trees. A scenic gravel road takes you in a long loop north of the tiny settlement of **Bill** (the name came from four early homesteaders, all of whom had the same first name—Bill), and then for 50 miles through the Rochelle Hills before dropping back to State 59 eight miles south of Wright. The Forest Service office in Douglas has an informative brochure describing the Rochelle Hills route. The Upton-Osage area also contains miles of ponderosa-pine-topped hills and many small ponds that attract birds.

Because of the patchwork quilt of land ownership on the grassland, many federal parcels are accessible only across private property, and you may need to get permission from the landowners first. Ask at the Forest Service office for access information. As with much of Wyoming's rangelands, you should be on guard for prairie rattlesnakes, especially around rockpiles and prairie-dog towns. Also, beware of thunderstorms and the lightning that can strike in this open country—they don't call this Thunder Basin for nothing. Because of the lack of drinking-water sources, carry plenty with you in your travels.

LARAMIE MOUNTAINS

The Laramie Peak portion of Medicine Bow National Forest lies approximately 30 miles south of Douglas, cutting from northwest to southeast along the Laramie Mountains. The mountains are draped with stands of ponderosa, lodgepole, and limber pine, along with Engelmann spruce and subalpine fir at higher elevations. Lower elevations are dominated by grass and sagebrush. It is pretty, but rugged, country, with deep valleys dividing the high granitic ridges and peaks. Several exceed 9,000 feet. Deer, elk, antelope, and wild turkeys are commonly seen in the Laramie Mountains, while rainbow, brook, and brown trout are found in the creeks. Public and private lands are intermingled here, with only a few large tracts of Forest Service property, the biggest being around Laramie Peak, an impressive mountain clearly visible from Douglas and a landmark for travelers along the old Oregon Trail. (They called this country the Black Hills.) There is some logging around Esterbrook and Albany Peak, especially in insect-killed forests, but Laramie Peak is de facto wilderness.

LARAMIE MOUNTAINS

91
TO DOUGLAS
94
TO DOUGLAS

LARAMIE

LABONTE CREEK

TO GLENDO
653

BUFFALO PEAK

SQUAW MOUNTAIN

CAMPBELL CREEK CAMPGROUND

CURTIS GULCH CAMPGROUND

LABONTE CANYON

ESTERBROOK

614

ESTERBROOK CAMPGROUND

WARBONNET PEAK

658

BIG BEAR CANYON

611
TO SHIRLEY BASIN

MEDICINE BOW

NATIONAL FOREST

FRIEND PARK CAMPGROUND

BLACK MOUNTAIN FIRE LOOKOUT

HUBBARDS MT. CUPBOARDS

LARAMIE PEAK

618

EAGLE PEAK

TRAIL

620

ARAPAHOE

MOUNTAINS

653

TO WHEATLAND

0   5mi
0   5km

671

TO MEDICINE BOW

TO ROCK RIVER & LARAMIE

633

MOON

The **Esterbrook** area, 32 miles south of Douglas on State 94, began as a copper-mining town in 1886 but never really had much to show for its effort. Esterbrook is famed for an old log church whose rear window frames snowcapped Laramie Peak. It's a very popular place for weddings. A fine campground (free; open June-Oct.) is close by, along with **Esterbrook Lodge,** offering small cabins, a restaurant, and bar with summertime live music on weekends. There's free camping at three other small Forest Service campgrounds (also open June-Oct.) in the Laramie Mountains; see the map for access.

Hiking

Some of the finest hiking in central Wyoming is found along the **Laramie Peak Trail,** a five-mile path (OW) that climbs to the top of 10,272-foot Laramie Peak. The trail begins right behind Friend Park Campground, 48 miles south of Douglas (via a rough gravel road). The first mile is relatively easy as the trail parallels Friend Creek, but after this it's a long, arduous climb. Two miles from the start is a pretty cascade; fill your water bottles here if you're hiking in late summer, since water can be hard to find above this point. Periodic forest openings offer dramatic vistas as you continue up the mountain, gaining 2,800 feet along the way. On top find expansive vistas in all directions—including into Nebraska, Colorado, and South Dakota on a clear day. Communication buildings and towers are also here.

Another route, the **Friend Park Trail,** also begins at the Friend Park Campground. This three-mile trail gains 400 feet as it climbs over a saddle and passes through open parklike forests to the **Arapahoe 4WD Road.** Hikers can follow this road back down to create a seven-mile loop trip. Check with the Forest Service office in Douglas for the exact routing of this new trail.

The two-mile-long **LaBonte Creek Trail** offers both pleasant hiking and good fishing for brook trout. The trailhead is at Curtis Gulch Campground, 38 miles south of Douglas. The path drops down a gorgeous steep-walled canyon (keep your eyes open for bighorn sheep and elk) and ends at a big-game refuge. Along the way are meadows, forests of poplar and Douglas fir, and flowers galore. Also near the Curtis Gulch Campground is a 4WD road/hiking trail that climbs for three miles up Big Bear Canyon to scenic Devils Pass.

Another good climb is up the 4WD road to **Black Mountain Lookout,** one of the last operating fire towers in Wyoming, open June-September. Great views down pristine Ashenfelder Creek. Get there by following Forest Rd. 633 south of Esterbrook Campground for six miles to the Laramie Peak Scout Camp. The 4WD road is just beyond this on the right.

Winter Recreation
Come winter, the Laramie Mountains offer excellent cross-country skiing opportunities, with many miles of scenic country and untracked snow. Over 20 miles of groomed trails surround the Esterbrook area, used primarily by snowmobilers, but also by skiers. A warming hut is also here. Pick up a map of snowmobile trails from the Douglas ranger station.

AYRES NATURAL BRIDGE PARK

One of the most unusual geologic formations in Wyoming lies 14 miles west of Douglas on I-25. Take Exit 151 and continue five miles south to tiny 22-acre Ayres Natural Bridge Park, where the main attraction is a 100-foot-long and 50-foot-high rock arch over LaPrele Creek. This natural arch was formed when a meander bend in LaPrele Creek gradually eroded the base of the rock face, leaving the upper part of the cliff unscathed. Eventually the weakened rock gave way, and the creek flowed through the hole that had been created at the bend. The ancient creek bed is now 300 feet away from the present creek and 50 feet higher.

History
For the Indians who first lived in this country, the natural bridge was a deadly place. A young brave had been struck by lightning and killed while hunting in the canyon, and thus began a legend that an evil spirit lived below the bridge, ready to grab anyone who ventured into his lair. When white settlers realized this, they used the natural bridge as a place to escape from Indian attacks, knowing they would not be pursued across the arch. Early-day mountain men lived in caves here, and Mormon settlers built cabins nearby in the 1850s. It took an expedition by Dr. Ferdinand V. Hayden, director of the U.S. Geological Survey in 1869, to bring the rock arch to national attention. He found it odd "that so great a natural curiosity should have failed to attract the attention it deserves." In 1881, Alva Ayres bought the land and used the lush LaPrele Creek country as headquarters for a freighting business. The natural bridge and surrounding land were donated to Converse County in 1920 by Ayres' heirs.

Seeing The Bridge
Today, Ayres Natural Bridge offers a surprisingly beautiful side trip. Box elders and cottonwoods line LaPrele Creek, fluorescent green patches against the brilliant red sandstone and the rich blue sky. Along one face of the red-walled amphitheater that circles the park are carved the names of many visitors, some dating from the 1880s. This is a popular weekend picnic and swimming spot and a great place to watch birds or to spend a quiet night at the small free campground. Ayres Natural Bridge Park is open daily 8-8 April-October. A gate blocks the road during the winter, but you can walk in the last half-mile. Call caretaker Ray Morton at 358-3532 for more information.

GLENROCK

The podunk cattle-and-coal town of Glenrock (pop. 2,200) lies halfway between Casper and Douglas at the confluence of Deer Creek and the North Platte River. The town's name comes from Rock in the Glen, a large rocky outcrop just to the west. Deer Creek was a favorite camping spot along the Oregon Trail, a place to rest up, do a little fishing, and let the stock graze on the lush creekside grass. Starting in 1847, Mormon emigrants mined the coal visible along the north bank of the river; this proved to be the first coal mined in Wyoming. The first bridge to span the North Platte River was built here in 1851 but was washed out in a flood the following year. Deer Creek Station was established in the 1850s, operating first as a trading post and later as a relay terminal for the Overland Stage and as a home station for the short-lived Pony Express. Later, when telegraph wires replaced the Pony Express, Deer Creek became a telegraph relay station. Indians burned the station to the ground in 1866 and it was never rebuilt.

Boom And Bust

Around the turn of the century, several underground coal mines opened, transforming the quiet settlement of Glenrock into a raucous mining town. They closed in 1916, just as oil was discovered west of Glenrock. Some 5,000 oil workers flooded the town, along with a raft of less-honorable professionals. Two oil refineries were built, fed by 200 Big Muddy oil wells. One refinery closed in the 1920s, the other in the '50s. More oil was found in 1949 and again in 1973, leading to temporary booms. The massive coal-fired Dave Johnston Powerplant became one of the largest local employers when it opened in 1958, and the discovery of uranium 25 miles northeast of Glenrock attracted hundreds of people to the area when several large uranium mines opened. In the late 1980s they began to shut down, and Glenrock has experienced hard times. Downtown shows this decline in a number of boarded-up old storefronts.

Sights

Rock in the Glen, a half-mile west of Glenrock, has the carved names of a few of the 19th-century emigrants who passed by on the way to Oregon, California, or Utah. Several **graves** from this era are scattered around Glenrock, sad reminders of the thousands who never made it. One is that of A.H. Unthank, just east of the Dave Johnston Powerplant on Tank Farm Rd., who died of cholera just a week after carving his name in Register Cliffs near present-day Guernsey. Four miles west of town is the grave of Ada Magill, a young girl who died of dysentery in 1864 as her parents headed west in a wagon train. Stones were piled on top of the grave to keep wolves from digging up her body.

In Glenrock City Park is a granite monument to **Dr. Ferdinand V. Hayden,** a physician who devoted his life to explorations of the West. Hayden helped found the U.S. Geological Survey and led the famed Hayden Yellowstone Expedition of 1870. The Indians considered Hayden a bit wacky, calling him "Man-who-picks-up-stones-running." Hayden used the Deer Creek Station at present-day Glenrock as a base of operations for several of his expeditions around Wyoming, hence the monument—placed here in 1931 by his photographic partner on these trips, William H. Jackson.

The country around Glenrock is laced with energy projects of all types. Immediately west of town is the Big Muddy oil field, where more than 2.6 million barrels have been pumped out over the last 40 years. The giant **Dave Johnston Powerplant** is six miles east of Glenrock along the North Platte River. It's one of the largest coal-fired power plants in the Rockies, generating 810,000 kilowatts of electricity for the Pacific Northwest. A private railroad feeds the plant with coal from the Glenrock Coal strip mine, 16 miles to the north.

Accommodations

Glenrock has two motels and a wonderful old hotel. **All American Inn,** 500 W. Aspen, tel. 436-2772, has rooms starting for $19 s or $22 d; $5 extra for kitchenettes. **Glenrock Motel,** 108 S. Third, tel. 436-2281, charges $18 s or $20 d and up. Kitchenettes are $28 and up. **Higgins Hotel,** 416 W. Birch, tel. 436-9212 or (800) 458-0144, is plain vanilla on the outside—red asbestos shingles on a building built in 1916—but the inside is a real surprise. The entire hotel has been lovingly furnished with antique brass beds, wardrobes, lamps, and a ticking old grandfather clock. Rooms cost $30 s or $37 d, ($38 s or $55 d including breakfast). For a taste of Western hospitality, stay just out of town at **Opal's Bed & Breakfast,** 24 miles south of Douglas, tel. 358-2033.

Camping
Free camping at **South Recreation Complex,** three miles south of Glenrock along the river. **Deer Creek RV Park,** on the east end of town, tel. 436-8121, is open mid-April through October. Tent sites cost $8, and RVs $12. Showers for noncampers are $3.

Food And Entertainment
The owners of the Higgins Hotel also run a fine gourmet restaurant here, **The Paisley Shawl,** named after the delicate old Scottish shawl—a family heirloom—in the dining room. The restaurant (Tues.-Sat. only) has a statewide reputation for its lunches, as well as its prime-rib, steak, and veal dinners. Get pizzas at **Classic Cafe & Pizza,** 201 S. Fourth, tel. 436-2244. Another

Glenrock eating establishment is **Four Aces Dining Room,** 316 W. Birch, tel. 436-9010. Get groceries at **Williams' Town & Country Food Center,** 218 W. Cedar, tel. 436-2344. At least one of the local bars (**Four Aces, El Diablo,** or **Deer Creek Lounge**) will have a country-western band on most weekends.

Information And Services
Stop by the **First Insurance Agency,** 217 W. Birch, tel. 436-2564, for local information. There is a free indoor **swimming pool** at the monumental middle school (a heritage of early 1980s boomtimes), 225 Oregon Trail, tel. 436-9201. **Glenrock Library** is at 518 S. Fourth, tel. 436-2573. **Real Wyoming Gifts,** 302 W. Birch, tel. 436-8604, sells all sorts of locally made items.

The big annual event is **Deer Creek Days,** a mid-July carnival with parades, games, a mountain men rendezvous, dancing, and lots of drinking. For something tamer, visit the **Glenrock Livestock Exchange,** just east of town, tel. 436-5327, where cattle, sheep, pigs, and even a few goats are auctioned off on Mon. and Sat. during the summer months. This is an enjoyable way to learn about ranching and to rub shoulders with local cowboys.

CASPER

Wyoming's second-largest city, Casper (pop. 47,000) is in transition from an oil-dependent economy to a more diversified base. The city sprawls across both sides of the North Platte River and is surrounded by the outlying settlements of **Evansville** (pop. 1,400), **Mills** (pop. 1,600), and **Bar Nunn** (pop. 800), with more suburbs filling the intervening land. As "Oil Capital of the Rockies," the city has long been chained to the fortunes of oil. Casper sits at the center of several large oil fields and is home to two refineries and a giant tank farm. Oil-related manufacturing and service industries crowd the city; the Casper yellow pages contain 32 different types of oil-related listings—from oil and gas exploration companies to directional drilling outfits.

With its central location, substantial population, spacious convention facilities, and ties to the state's energy and ranching industries, Casper considers itself the true heart and soul of Wyoming. The only statewide newspaper, the *Casper Star-Tribune,* is based here, along with one of the state's premier medical centers. To Casperites, arch-rival Cheyenne is just a Nebraska city that happened to sneak into Wyoming. (The rest of Wyoming, however, views Casper with equal suspicion; in 1904 Casper aspired to become the state capital but failed miserably, coming in third behind Cheyenne and Lander in a statewide vote.) A working-class town, Casper will never become a major tourist destination. Despite this, there are outstanding recreational opportunities on nearby Casper Mountain, at local reservoirs, and along the North Platte River, plus a surprising variety of cultural activities centered around Nicolaysen Art Center, Casper College, and the spacious Casper Events Center.

HISTORY

The Astorians

Although Casper is identified today with oil, the city began as a way station along the Oregon Trail. Seven of John Jacob Astor's fur traders led by Robert Stuart first traveled through this area in 1812 on their return from Oregon, arriving in late October. Knowing they could not make it back to St. Louis in their emaciated condition, the explorers constructed a rock-walled cabin (the first Anglo building in Wyoming) and covered it with buffalo hides. Game proved amazingly plentiful. They returned from a hunting trip with 47 bison, 28 deer and bighorn sheep, and a bear! But five weeks later, a band of 23 Arapaho warriors appeared, on their way to raid the Crow Indians farther north. Intimidated, the Astorians invited them in for a meal. They stayed for a day and a half, promising to return in two weeks. The Astorians quickly decided discretion was the better part of valor and moved to a new camp just across what is now the Nebraska border. They finally reached Missouri the following spring.

Ferries And Bridges

The route pioneered by the Astorians eventually became a virtual highway to the West. The North Platte River was one of the main barriers to this migration, with many emigrants choosing to ford near what is now Casper. In early summer. when the river ran dangerously high, people often died trying to cross. Others lost their wagon or watched as their oxen and horses were swept downriver. When Brigham Young's party of Mormon emigrants arrived here in 1847, they built a 23-foot-long raft and floated their wagons across. The Mormon ferry became Casper's first business venture, with gentiles charged $1.50 per wagon. Business boomed. By 1849, several different ferries were competing with the Mormon ferry, but there were still delays of up to a week as wagons waited in line to cross. (This has to rate as one of Wyoming's only recorded traffic jams!)

In 1852, a French-Canadian trader named John Reshaw built a long wooden toll bridge at present-day Evansville, charging $5 in gold per wagon (less when the river was low and folks would risk fording). To stifle competition, he

bought the Mormon ferry for $300 and shut it down. Edwin R. Bird, an 1854 Oregon Trail pioneer, wrote of the toll bridge in his diary:

Here we found a good bridge far better than some I have seen at home. There is a store & other buildings connected with it. In the store saw two Frenchmen gambling. The owner of the bridge says he took in seventeen thousand dollars last season. He charges five dollars for a team & five cents a head for loose stock.

In 1859, another bridge was built six miles upriver by Louis Guinard to compete for the lucrative Oregon Trail traffic. Guinard's bridge must have been one of the most impressive structures along the entire 2,000-mile route. Built at a cost of $40,000, the bridge was 17 feet wide, 1,000 feet long, and supported by 28 log and rock cribs. It soon became the preferred crossing point along the North Platte, and the old Reshaw bridge was torn down, with the lumber used to build a fort (Platte Bridge Station) to protect the new bridge. Guinard made so much money at the toll station that he reportedly threw handfuls of gold into the river, exclaiming, "You have given me all my wealth; I now give back to you a tithe!"

Red Cloud's War

Platte Bridge Station served as a trading post for travelers, a Pony Express mail stop, and later a telegraph office. A volunteer force of up to 50 soldiers was posted to protect the telegraph and those traveling along the Oregon Trail from Indian and Mormon attacks. In retaliation for a massacre of Indians at Colorado's Sand Creek in 1865 (see p. 16), a full-scale war broke out between Indians and whites. One of these battlegrounds that July was at the Platte Bridge Station. Expecting a wagon train with vital supplies and ammunition, 20 men under the command of Lt. Caspar Collins left the fort to escort the expected convoy. Once across the bridge, the soldiers found themselves surrounded by Red Cloud and 3,000 of his Sioux warriors. In their flight back across the bridge, five soldiers died. Collins was killed when he stooped to rescue a

wagon trains crossing the Platte River

fellow soldier and his horse bolted, carrying him into the onrushing warriors. Other soldiers said that when last seen, he had his reins in his teeth and was firing pistols from both hands. Caspar's body was found two days later with 24 arrows in it.

A second battle followed that afternoon—Custard's Wagon Train Fight. When the supply wagons of Sergeant Amos Custard came within sight of the fort, the soldiers tried to warn them with cannon fire. Three men from an advance guard made it to safety within the fort, and the others quickly corralled the three wagons together. Although they put up a fierce fight, within hours Red Cloud's men had killed and mutilated the 23 defenders and burned their wagons. In honor of Caspar Collins, Platte Bridge Station was renamed Fort Caspar. (Fort Collins, Colorado, is named for his father, William Collins.) Due to a never-corrected error by an Army telegraph operator—he typed a dot instead of a dot-dash—the town that eventually grew up nearby was misspelled Casper. Two years later, when most traffic on the Oregon Trail had been rerouted south to avoid conflicts with the Indians, Fort Caspar was abandoned. Shortly thereafter, the bridge and fort were burned by the Sioux.

Lawless Days And Nights
In 1888, the Fremont, Elkhorn, and Missouri Valley Railway extended its line up the North Platte River to the site of old Fort Caspar. A tent city quickly sprang up, followed by more permanent buildings. For the next 17 years the town of Casper lay at the end of the tracks. It was an exceptionally violent place; employees of the first grocery store surrounded their beds with sacks of flour for protection from stray bullets, and Casper's first public building was a jail. Even the mayor got in the act, murdering his business partner in an 1890 gun duel on main street. The jury let him go free. When the ruffians became too much to tolerate, a street trial was held, and those who refused to leave town faced the prospect of being strung up in a "necktie party." Pinned to the shirt of one murderer lynched by a vigilance committee was the following note: "Process of law is a little slow, so this is the road you'll have to go. Murderers and sinners, Beware! People's Verdict."

Oil Changes Everything
In 1851 Jim Bridger, Cy Iba, Kit Carson, and Basil Cimineau Lajeunesse discovered an oil spring just west of Casper at Poison Spider Creek. The oil was mixed with flour and sold as axle grease for wagon trains. By 1889, when the first oil well was drilled near Casper, it was clear that much more oil lay beneath the ground. Land speculators and claim jumpers flocked to Wyoming, and battles quickly broke out over who had staked the first claim; the winner generally had more burly men, guns, and lawyers. Soon the massive Salt Creek oil field (40 miles north of Casper) was producing, with wagons towed by teams of up to 20 horses hauling the oil back to Casper. A small refinery was built in 1895, the first in Wyoming. It was later replaced by more modern facilities, including the now-closed Standard Oil plant, at one time the largest refinery on earth, handling 25,000 barrels of oil per day. Over time, Casper became a center for oil and refining in the Rockies.

Boom And Bust
Casper grew into a major industrial town with development of Salt Creek and other oil fields. So many roustabouts flooded Casper that they had to sleep in shifts at the tents, motels, garages, basements, or shacks. Dozens of illegal gambling houses and speakeasies helped make a trip to town memorable, while more than 2,000 prostitutes pursued their own boomtimes in the Sandbar district. (Prostitution was blatant until the 1950s.) Oil production peaked in the 1920s, but the crash of 1929 ruined this economic bubble, cutting the city's population in half within five years. World War II sent oil prices and Casper's economy soaring. An Army air base—home to 4,000 men—opened nearby; it's now the site of Casper's airport. In the late '50s, new technology—injecting water to force the remaining oil to wellheads—helped boost recovery dramatically at Salt Creek, and there followed another boom for Casper. The discovery of massive uranium deposits in the Pumpkin Buttes, Gas Hills, and Shirley Basin also fueled this growth.

The roller coaster ride has continued in recent decades: down in the late '60s, back up in the '70s. When oil prices soared following the OPEC oil embargo in 1973, Casper experienced such

DOWNTOWN CASPER

an orgy of growth that planners predicted a population rivaling Denver's by the year 2000. After oil prices plummeted in the 1980s, however, these optimistic—or apocalyptic, depending upon your point of view—predictions failed to materialize. Sales tax receipts dropped by half, and many of downtown Casper's storefronts were covered with plywood. The economy has improved in recent years as Casper diversified its industrial base to include everything from a copper foundry to mace manufacturing. New stores—including a Wal-Mart—have invigorated the commercial sector. Downtown is thriving, the suburbs are once again creeping over the countryside, and Eastridge Mall (Wyoming's largest shopping mall) is packed with chain stores.

SIGHTS

Fort Caspar

Although the original fort had long since disappeared, in 1936 the WPA reconstructed a half-dozen of Fort Caspar's log buildings. Included are a blacksmith shop, an overland stage station, a commissary storehouse, a barracks building, and a sutler's store (where you can buy various western items). Many supports from Guinard's long bridge across the North Platte are still visible as mounds of rock, and a small section of the bridge has been reconstructed, along with a replica of the Mormon ferry. During summer months, guides dressed as 1860s cavalrymen answer your questions.

A newer brick building at the fort houses an excellent small museum (free) where you'll find a variety of items including a reconstructed Mormon handcart and a W.H. Jackson painting of Platte Bridge Station. Summer hours for the museum, tel. 235-8462, are Sun. 12-5, Mon.-Fri. 9-6, and Sat. 9-5. The rest of the year, it's open Sun. 1-4 and Mon.-Fri. 9-5. Ask about the free Wednesday night lectures on Wyoming history held during the summer. The fort buildings are open only in summer, but you can wander around the grounds at any time of year. Over in Evansville, the **Town Hall** contains a collection of other items found along the Oregon Trail.

Nicolaysen Art Museum

One surprising aspect of Casper is an emphasis on art and culture as exemplified by the Nicolaysen, Wyoming's finest contemporary art exhibition space. Originally a power plant, this beautifully refurbished brick building houses seven different gallery spaces. Exhibits change throughout the year, but you're unlikely to see the standard moose-in-the-meadow pieces here. The permanent collection includes some 1,900 drawings by German-American illustrator Carl Link, and a variety of Native American paintings, pottery, and rugs. Children of all ages love the fine **Discovery Center** here, the only children's museum in Wyoming. A gift shop sells books and work by local artisans. The "Nic" is located at 400 E. Collins, tel. 235-5247, and is open Mon.-Sat. 10-5, and till 8 p.m. on Thursday. Entrance costs $2 for adults, $1 for kids, or $5 for families (free on the first and third Thurs. evening of the month).

More Art

One legacy from Casper's oil boom-times is an abundance of outdoor sculptures, including three pieces by Laramie sculptor Robert Russin. His energetic bronze **Prometheus** livens the library entrance at 307 E. Second St., while **Man and Energy** at the chamber of commerce, 500 N. Center, symbolizes Casper's ties to oil and coal. Neither is as controversial as **The Fountainhead,** a $230,000 red-and-blue-metal sculpture placed in front of the new city hall in 1981. A statue of Caspar Collins on horseback guards the Casper Events Center, while a monument to sheepherders stands in front of the Wyoming Wool Growers Building at 117 Glenn Road. Other places to see distinctive artwork are **West Wind Gallery,** 1040 W. 15th, tel. 265-2655, **Artist's Choice,** 1910 E. 21st St., tel. 234-1315, and the student art gallery at Casper College.

Casper College

Casper College first opened its doors in 1945 and has grown into the state's largest junior college, with over 6,000 full- and part-time students. The college's brick buildings sprawl up a long hillside. Although many students live in dorms, most commute from around town, making for traffic jams in the parking lots and along adjacent city streets.

Casperites fought for many years to turn their college into a four-year school, but the university at Laramie successfully fended those moves until recently. In something of a joint venture, the University of Wyoming now operates a limited number of bachelor's degree programs at the Casper College campus. A fine 78,000-volume **library** on campus includes a rare-book room with unusual Wyoming titles. An **Elderhostel** program runs at Casper College during the summer, and the excellent **Fitness Center** is open to the public. In the College Center building you'll find a cafeteria, a small bookstore, and other facilities.

Visitors will enjoy stops at two Casper College museums. **Tate Mineralogical Museum,** tel. 268-2110, is open Mon.-Fri. 10-5 during the summer and Mon.-Fri. 2-5 p.m. during the school year. Entrance is free. Inside, you'll find one of the largest mineralogical collections in the Rockies, including several meteorites, various types of petrified wood, Indian artifacts, and fossils. Purchase polished stones at the entrance. **Werner Wildlife Museum,** 405 E. 15th, tel. 235-2108, is open Mon.-Fri. 10-5 during the summer and Mon.-Fri. 2-5 p.m. in winter; no charge. The museum houses the usual stuffed critters from Wyoming—dozens of antelope heads, deer mounts, bears, bison, and many birds—along with several African trophies.

More Sights And Sounds

One of Casper's minor claims to fame is having Wyoming's largest convention and performance center. Here you might run across a mining trade show, a cat-judging event, or even a monster-truck pull. Located on a hill overlooking the city, the **Casper Events Center** is a spacious, modern building with room for over 10,000 people. Call (800) 442-2256 for upcoming events. **Casper Planetarium,** 904 N. Poplar, tel. 577-0310, is open nightly during the summer, with programs starting at 7:30. Admission costs $2, or $5 for a family. **Stage III Community Theatre,** 4080 S. Poplar, tel. 234-0946, puts on plays Sept.-July. The **Casper Symphony Orchestra,** tel. 266-1478, is Wyoming's only professional orchestra, with winter performances.

ACCOMMODATIONS

Casper motels cover the complete quality spectrum, from dumpy little hole-in-the-walls to an elaborate Hilton Inn. In general, you'll find prices in Casper to be among the cheapest in Wyoming. More than two dozen of the city's lodging establishments are listed in the chart on p. 188. At the cheapest places, you'd better take a look at the rooms before plunking down any money.

Camping

The nearest public camping ($4) is in the pines on Casper Mountain, 10 miles south of Casper and 3,000 feet higher in elevation. Well worth the drive. See "Casper Mountain," below, for details. Casper's three private campgrounds all have swimming pools. The **Fort Caspar Campground,** tel. 234-3260, is on the river and just beyond the old fort site. Sites are $10 for tents or $15 for RVs. It is open year-round. **Casper KOA,** 2800 E. Yellowstone, tel. 237-5155, charges $11 for tents and $16 for RVs, and it's also open year-round. **Antelope Run Campground,** 1101 W. Prairie Lane, tel. 577-1664, in Bar Nunn has tent sites for $11 and RV sites for $13. Showers for noncampers cost $3; open May-September.

FOOD

Casper has a wide range of dining-out options that will suit almost any taste. For a homestyle, reasonably priced breakfast, visit **Paradise Valley Cafe,** 5755 CY Ave., tel. 266-9914. On the other end of town is the **Red and White Cafe,** 1620 E. Yellowstone, tel. 234-6962, a popular

CASPER ACCOMMODATIONS

MOTEL	ADDRESS	TELEPHONE	RATES	FEATURES
Parkway Motel	5102 W. Yellowstone	234-2162	$14 s, $18 d	kitchenettes
Bel Air Motel	5400 W. Yellowstone	472-1930	$14 s, $16 d	kitchenettes
Travelier Motel	500 E. First St.	237-9343	$17 s, $20 d	AAA-approved
Virginian Motel	830 E. A St.	266-9731	$18 s, $22 d	
Topper Motel	728 E. A St.	237-8407	$19 s, $23 d	
Galley Motel	310 N. Center	234-4330	$19 s, $24 d	
Commercial Inn	5755 CY Ave.	235-6688	$20 s, $24 d	kitchenettes
Royal Inn	440 E. A St.	234-3503 (800) 967-6925	$23 s, $28 d	AAA-approved, pool kitchenettes
Motel 6	1150 Wilkins Circle	234-3903	$21 s, $27 d	
Yellowstone Motel	1610 E. Yellowstone	234-9174 (800) 352-6551	$22 s, $26 d	
Sand & Sage Motel	901 W. Yellowstone	237-2088	$22 s, $26 d	
Showboat Motel	100 W. F St.	235-2711 (800) 341-8000	$24 s, $31 d	AAA-approved
I-25 Inn	Wyoming Blvd. at I-25	234-9125	$25 s, $30 d	AAA-approved
Super 8 Motel	3838 CY Ave.	266-3480 (800) 800-8000	$27 s, $31 d	
Westridge Motel	955 CY Ave.	234-8911 (800) 356-6268	$28+ s or d	AAA-approved
Casper Inn	I-25 at Center	235-1777	$30 s, $34 d	
Bessemer Bend B&B	11 miles south	265-6819	$30 s, $40 d	riverside location
Kelly Inn	821 N. Poplar	266-2400 (800) 635-3559	$31 s, $35 d	AAA-approved, whirlpool, sauna
La Quinta Motor Inn	301 E. E St.	234-1159 (800) 531-5900	$37+ s, $45+ d	AAA-approved, pool
Durbin St. Inn B&B	843 S. Durbin	577-5774	$40 s, $50 d	friendly, full breakfast
Best Western East	2325 E. Yellowstone	234-3541 (800) 528-1234	$43+ s or d	AAA-approved, pool
Shilo Inn Evansville	739 Luker Lane	237-1335 (800) 222-2244	$41 s, $47 d	AAA-approved, whirlpool, sauna, pool
Days Inn	400 W. F St.	235-6668 (800) 325-2525	$48+ s or d	AAA-approved, sauna, pool, airport shuttle
Holiday Inn	300 W. F St.	235-2531 (800) 465-4329	$48+ s, $60+ d	AAA-approved, whirlpool, sauna, pool, airport shuttle
Hilton Inn	I-25 and Poplar	266-6000 (800) 445-8667	$54+ s, $64+ d	AAA-approved, whirlpool, pool, airport shuttle

greasy-spoon hangout. A fine Sunday brunch place is **Circle T Restaurant,** 7800 W. Hwy. 220, tel. 237-0012, where the extensive all-you-can-eat buffet costs just $8. **Herbo's,** 4755 W. Yellowstone, tel. 266-2293, is one of the local restaurants where big servings win out over quality. Packed with Casperites. More stuff-yourself eating at **King's Table Buffet,** 111 Star Lane, tel. 577-6013. During the school year, visitors will find Casper's cheapest eats at the **Casper College cafeteria**. The best place for lunchtime sandwiches and soups is **Cheese Barrel,** 544 S. Center, tel. 235-5202.

Steak And Seafood

Casper's old-time steakhouse is **Benham's,** 739 N. Center, tel. 234-4531. A bit pricey, but the varied menu of steak, seafood, and ribs is a palate pleaser. The popular Pump Room, in the same building, has Mexican food, "gourmet hamburgers," and mixed drinks. **Dorn's Fireside,** 1745 CY Ave., tel. 235-6831, is another popular beef-and-seafood house. In the same vein is **Goose Egg Inn,** nine miles southwest of Casper on State 220, tel. 473-8838, where prime rib, seafood, and pan-fried chicken are house specialities. Well worth the drive! **Crazy Crab,** 144 S. Center, tel. 266-3474, specializes in fresh fish, crab, and clam chowder.

Italian

Casper has two decent Italian restaurants: **Anthony's,** 241 S. Center, tel. 234-3071, is more centrally located and a bit fancier, but the down-home **Bosco's,** 847 E. A St., tel. 265-9658, really packs them in, particularly over the lunch hour. If you're looking for good pizza in Casper, give up. The best of a bad lot is probably at **Little Big Men Pizza,** 3350 CY Ave., tel. 235-0786. You could also try the various chains, such as Godfather's and Pizza Hut.

Mexican

For Mexican food, everyone in Casper goes to **El Jarro's,** 500 W. F St., tel. 577-0538. Be ready for a long wait most any evening. (Their second restaurant, at 2807 CY Ave., tel. 234-4818, has the same food but doesn't attract the crowds.) The El Jarro's phenomenon exists for a number of reasons: inexpensive prices, big margaritas, crispy chips, tangy salsa, and mass

quantities of food. Besides, the bleached-blond hostesses and the beefy waiters (who gather around tables to sing happy birthday at least a dozen times each hour) make for lots of ogling. Be forewarned, however, that this is Americanized Mexican food; we're talking something that looks like mushroom soup over the chile rellenos! For far more authentic Mexican fare, try **La Casacita,** 633 W. Collins, tel. 234-7633. Recommended.

Chinese

A real surprise in Casper is the large number of Asian restaurants that dot the town—eight places at last count. The food has suffered a bit from Americanization, but two of these places are quite good. **South Sea Chinese Restaurant** has two locations: 2025 E. Second, tel. 237-4777, and 116 W. Second, tel. 265-9711, and offers the more authentic fare. Also good is **Peking Chinese Restaurant,** 333 E. A, tel. 266-2207. The **Mekong,** 144 S. Center, tel. 237-6728, has a good reputation for its Vietnamese cuisine.

Coffee, Bakeries, And Groceries

Get espresso and pastries at **Uncle Bruno's** (upstairs at Taubert's), 125 E. Second, tel. 234-2500. For fresh-baked goods, head to **Casper Cake and Donut,** 604 E. Second, tel. 234-1180. They have another bakery outlet in Eastridge Mall. All the big grocery chains also have in-store bakeries and delis. Casper has a number of giant grocery stores scattered across the city—Albertson's, Buttrey, Safeway, and Smith's—and even a small Asian food store, **Wilson's Oriental Mart,** 382 W. Collins Dr., tel. 237-3715. If you're looking for fresh produce, be sure to check out the **Farmers Market** at the fairgrounds each Saturday morning during the summer.

ENTERTAINMENT

Casper's downtown movie theaters usually have some of the cheapest flick-viewing to be found: $1.50 for all shows. See the *Casper Star-Tribune* for the latest on the movie scene, as well as local nightlife. The biggest and best-known place for live music every night of the week is the

Beacon Club, 4100 W. Yellowstone Hwy., tel. 577-1503, with country tunes and a fun, trendy crowd. Both **Bronco's Lounge,** 1200 W. Collins Dr., tel. 266-5111, and the **Avalon Club,** 260 E. Yellowstone Hwy., tel. 473-7544, offer Western dance bands most nights. Free dance lessons on Wednesday nights at Bronco's. **Drake's Lounge** in the Holiday Inn, 300 W. F St., tel. 235-2531, has live top-40 music most evenings and free hors d'oeuvres on weeknights. More rock at **Moonlight Lounge,** 2305 E. 12th, tel. 234-7787, and **The Wonder Bar,** 256 S. Center, tel. 266-2330. Other places to check for musical entertainment and dancing are **Shilo Inn Motel,** 739 Luker Lane, tel. 237-1335; **Colonial Lounge,** 4370 S. Poplar, tel. 265-9988; **Goose Egg Inn,** 10580 Goose Egg Rd., tel. 473-8838; **Caspar Inn,** I-25 at Center, tel. 235-1777; **Little Big Men Pizza,** 3350 CY Ave., tel. 234-0786; and **Viking Restaurant and Lounge,** 2740 E. Third, tel. 234-5386.

EVENTS

Casper features a multitude of fun events throughout the summer months; there's bound to be something going on when you visit. Each Thursday evening from mid-June to mid-August the **Casper Municipal Band** performs free concerts at Washington Park (McKinley and Eighth). Join locals who sprawl out on the lawn and picnic to the big sounds. In early June, the **Mountain Man Rendezvous** draws dozens of costumed mountain men and Indians to old Fort Caspar. Another June activity in Casper is the **Cowboy State Games,** an Olympic-style multisport festival with teams from all over Wyoming competing in everything from archery to wrestling. See "Crimson Dawn," below, for the year's most unusual event, held atop Casper Mountain during the summer solstice (June 21).

The annual **Wyoming Governor's Cup Regatta** at nearby Lake Alcova in late July is the biggest sailing event in the state. For a glimpse of the city's past, come to Fort Caspar for the **Platte Bridge Encampment** in late July. This taste of history includes period fashion shows, living history demonstrations, and military drills. The **Casper Troopers Drum and Bugle Corps** —one of the finest in the nation—often performs

for the encampment. They have been performing together since 1957. Don't miss them!

Casper's biggest annual event is the **Central Wyoming Fair and Rodeo** in early August. The various arts-and-crafts displays, farm animals, rodeos, and the midway attract both locals and visitors. Rodeo events include exciting chuckwagon races and clown "bullfighting."

For more laid-back action, try the twice-weekly rodeos at North 40, located 10 miles north of Casper on I-25. Call 265-9619 for specifics. Each October, the **PRCA Rodeo Finals** are held at the events center. This is Wyoming's largest indoor rodeo. **Pari-mutuel horse racing** comes to the fairgrounds later in August, lasting through Labor Day.

Cycling Events

The **Casper Classic Bicycle Races** attract over 500 of the top cyclists in America with a $75,000 purse. Beginning on June 28 and continuing up to the Fourth of July, the races encompass eight different events, including a grueling 15-mile-long climb up Casper Mountain. At the same time, **Classicfest** goes on at the Events Center, featuring carnival rides, food booths, live music, and a crafts fair. A smaller, but still exciting bike race is the **Platte River Station Stage Race** held on Memorial Day weekend. Cyclists race in four different stages, including to Glenrock and back and along steep Garden Creek Rd. (speeds to 65 mph). **BMX Races** take place on many summer weekends at Mike Sedar Park, and **Mountain Bike Races** are held each August.

RECREATION

The fine **Casper Recreation Center,** 1801 E. Fourth St., tel. 235-8383, provides racquetball and volleyball courts, a weight room, a gym, and a game room. Entrance costs $2. Same price to skate next door at **Casper Ice Arena** (open Aug.-April), tel. 235-8484. Rent skates here for $1.50. Wyoming's largest roller-skating palace, **Wagon Wheel Roller Rink,** is in Mills at 305 Vanhorn Ave., tel. 265-4214. Mountain bikers will find many miles of roads and trails on Casper and Muddy mountains, south of town. For maps and info, contact **Casper**

Wheelmen, 548 E. A St., tel. 577-9117, or **The Bike Stop,** 515 W. Collins, tel. 577-0115. Ask at Bike Stop about the Wednesday-night bike rides.

If you're looking for a little water activity, check out one of Casper's half-dozen **swimming pools.** Five outdoor pools (tel. 235-8403) are scattered throughout the city and are open summers for $2 (free for kids). The Paradise Valley pool also has a very popular corkscrew water slide. The indoor pool ($1) at Kelly Walsh High School is open on Wednesday evenings, and another indoor pool is at the YMCA, 315 E. 15th, tel. 234-9187. Swim for $2 or use the complete facilities for $6 per day. (Trivia buffs will be interested to know that the Casper High School was the first in the nation to have an indoor swimming pool, built in 1929.)

Three 18-hole golf courses to choose from in town: **Casper Municipal Golf Course,** tel. 234-1037, **Paradise Valley Golf Course,** tel. 234-9146, and **Casper Country Club,** tel. 235-5777. Casper is one of the nation's windiest cities; winds averaging 13 mph make this a great place for kite flying, hang-gliding, and **windsurfing.** Pathfinder and Alcova Reservoirs are both popular windsurfing spots. **Mountain Sports,** 543 S. Center, tel. 266-1136 or (800) 426-1136, sells quality outdoor gear and rents Windsurfers, Alpine and Nordic skis, and snowshoes. While there, take a look at the various rock-climbing maps and books.

Oregon Trail Rides

Looking for a taste of the Old West? **Historic Trail Expeditions,** tel. 266-4868, leads a wide range of Conestoga wagon and horse trips (from three hours to two days) along the Oregon Trail and even a week-long cattle drive into the Hole-in-the-Wall country of Butch Cassidy and the Sundance Kid. On some of the trips the riders dress in 19th-century garb. **Off the Deep End Travels,** tel. (800) 223-6833, offers six-day mountain-bike trips along the old Oregon Trail.

River Recreation

The **North Platte River** flows right through the city of Casper, providing both the city's drinking water and a variety of recreational opportunities. The Platte's slow current and shallow depth (two to four feet in most places) make for a gentle and scenic float trip, with plenty of

wildlife along the way: beaver, muskrats, ducks, geese, hawks, eagles, mule deer, and antelope. For a map and brochure describing public landings, camping, and parking areas along the 45-mile stretch of the Platte between Alcova Reservoir and Casper, contact the Bureau of Land Management at 1701 E. E St., tel. 261-7600.

Wyoming's Choice, 513 N. Lennox, tel. 234-3870, rents canoes ($30/day) and rafts ($40/day) and provides shuttle boat service ($15). In addition, they offer scenic half-day float trips for $25 ($15 for kids), and guided drift fishing ($185 for two). Fishing is excellent for both German brown and rainbow trout; locals call the North Platte one of the west's largest and finest trout fisheries. See the chamber of commerce for a listing of other local fishing guides.

Edness Kimball Wilkins State Park, six miles east of Casper on State 256, is a 1,420-acre riverside park that is perfect for quiet picnics among the cottonwoods, birdwatching, and fishing from the banks. No camping, but several trails provide pleasant day hikes or bike rides, and the pond is a popular swimming hole.

GETTING MALLED

Casper is Wyoming's version of shop-till-your-car-dies. Sprawling suburbia, frantically feckless fast food, and a half-dozen park-anywhere malls combine to make Casper indistinguishable from Modesto, California or Columbus, Ohio. This is the sort of place where even the Highland Park Community Church is housed in what looks like an old K mart store! **Eastridge Mall** is Wyoming's largest shopping mall, with 90 (count 'em) stores, including most of the big chains. If Norman Rockwell were alive today, he would be painting the high school girls eyeing the hunks on parade and the over-60, post-heart attack crowd doing their fast walks around the mall.

Okay, so not all of Casper's stores are in shopping malls. Downtown at 125 E. Second St., tel. 234-2500, is the impressive **Lou Taubert Ranch Outfitters,** a four-level department store with everything from cowboy boots (10,000 pairs in stock!) to gourmet coffee. It's a great place to try on a new cowboy hat. **Mountain Sports,**

543 S. Center, tel. 266-1136 or (800) 426-1136, has a good collection of outdoor supplies of all sorts, from windsurfing equipment to sleeping bags. Get topo maps and local hiking and climbing books here too.

Bookstores

Four places sell new books in Casper: **B. Dalton,** tel. 247-0793, and **Waldenbooks,** tel. 235-2046, in Eastridge Mall; **Ralph's Books** at Hilltop Shopping Center, tel. 234-0308; and **The Book Peddler** at Sunrise Shopping Center, tel. 266-2021. **Westerner News,** 245 S. Center, tel. 235-1022, sells history books, paperbacks, out-of-state newspapers, and all sorts of magazines. **Book Palace,** 225 W. First, tel. 577-1325, offers a fine selection of used books and is a great place to browse. The **Book Nook,** 918 E. Second, tel. 237-2211, also sells used books.

INFORMATION

The friendly **Casper Area Chamber of Commerce,** 500 N. Center, tel. 234-5311 or (800) 852-1889, is the place to go for tourist paraphernalia. Summer hours are Mon.-Fri. 8-7, Sat.-Sun. 10-7. The rest of the year, it's open Mon.-Fri. 8-5. Due to budget cuts, the **Natrona County Library,** 307 E. Second, tel. 237-4935, is only open Mon.-Thurs. 11-7, and Fri.-Sat. 1-5.

TRANSPORTATION

Natrona County Airport is eight miles northwest of Casper on US 20-26. Two airlines provide commuter service (prop planes) to Denver: **Continental Express,** tel. (800) 525-0280, and **United Express/Mesa Airlines,** tel. (800) 241-6522. **Delta/Sky West,** tel. (800) 221-1212, has daily commuter service to Salt Lake City. The airport is an official Foreign Trade Zone.

Powder River Transportation, 596 N. Poplar (across from Dairy Queen), tel. 266-1094 or (800) 442-3682, has daily bus service to Douglas, Gillette, Buffalo, Thermopolis, Worland, and other towns in northern and central Wyoming. Call **RC Cab,** tel. 235-5203, for taxi service.

Rent cars from **Affordable Used Car Rentals,** tel. 237-1733; **Avis,** tel. (800) 331-1212; **Budget,** tel. (800) 527-0700; **Dollar,** tel. (800) 421-6878; **Hertz,** tel. (800) 654-3131; or **National,** tel. (800) 227-7368. The cheapest rates (used cars for $20/day including airport pickup and unlimited miles) can be found at **Aries Car Rentals,** 440 E. A St., tel. 234-3503 or (800) 967-6925.

CASPER VICINITY

CASPER MOUNTAIN

Scenic mountain country is just a hop, skip, and a jump away from Casper. When the thermometer tops 100° F in summertime, Casper folks escape to the cool mountains, just a 15-minute drive from town. Snow often lingers until July. Rotary Park, seven miles south of Casper on S. Poplar St. (State 252), has a number of official and unofficial trails that climb the steep canyon cut by Garden Creek. The creek drops 50 feet over **Garden Creek Falls,** one of the few waterfalls in this part of Wyoming. A viewpoint is just a short distance up the trail, or you can cross the bridge and follow a second path (actually a maze of routes) to the top of the falls, one mile up. Other trails head out to a ridge offering views of the surrounding country.

The steep, winding drive up Casper Mountain has turnouts offering panoramas that stretch all the way to the Big Horn Mountains, 125 miles to the north. Casper Mountain's flattened 8,100-foot-summit is carpeted by ponderosa pine trees and pleasant grassy meadows. Several county parks (Casper Mountain, Crimson Dawn, Beartrap Meadow, and Ponderosa) are very popular getaways where deer and elk are found. The five **campgrounds** on Casper Mountain cost $5 per night; all are open year-round. Water is available only at Beartrap (the nicest) and Casper Mountain campgrounds. Red Valley separates Casper Mountain from its neighbor five miles to the south, **Muddy Mountain.** The gravel road climbs up Muddy Mountain, where the BLM maintains a campground ($3), a self-guided nature trail, and other scenic paths. For more information on the various Casper Mountain parks, call 234-6821. The short **Lee McCune Braille Trail** on Casper Mountain has 39 stations with plaques describing the natural world in braille and English. Even sighted people find the trail eye-opening. Nearby is a summer camp for the blind.

Hogadon Ski Area

First opened in 1959, the small city-run Hogadon Ski Area is nine miles south of Casper near the top of the mountain. A family area, it includes hills ranging from the easiest bunny slope to black diamonds. Eleven different runs are fed by two chair lifts and a poma lift, with a vertical rise

of 600 feet. Ski rentals and lessons are available, and there's a cafeteria. The slopes are open to telemarkers. Lift tickets are $15 on weekends ($10 half-day) or $11 on weekdays ($8 half-day). Hogadon is open Wed.-Sun. 9-4 from Thanksgiving to Easter. Call 235-8499 or (800) 852-1889 for information, or 235-8369 for snow conditions.

Cross-country Skiing

Casper Mountain often has surprisingly good powder conditions. The county (tel. 234-6821) maintains 28 km of groomed cross-country ski trails, along with a warming hut. Daily passes are $4. Cross-country lessons are available through

Mountain Sports. In addition, there are extensive undeveloped areas where more adventurous backcountry skiers practice telemarking. Rent cross-country skis on Casper Mountain or from **Mountain Sports**, 543 S. Center, tel. 266-1136; **Dean's Sporting Goods**, 260 S. Center, tel. 234-2788; or **Bundy's Ski & Cycle**, 3201 CY Ave., tel. 237-2509. Casper Mountain also has more than 52 miles of groomed snowmobile trails.

CRIMSON DAWN MUSEUM

This is a place best experienced early in the morning, when the crimson light of dawn brushes across the ochre-colored earth and streams into the dark green forests. Come here alone to really feel the magic that captivated Neal Forsling almost 70 years ago. After growing up in Independence, Missouri—and nearly marrying Harry Truman—she headed west to Casper. There Neal married a lawyer, but a bitter divorce sent her fleeing to then-remote Casper Mountain with her two children, looking to start anew as a homesteader. She quickly fell in love with the country and later fell in love with a local rancher, Jim Forsling. They were married and settled into a fiercely independent life without electricity or running water, and with but a few neighbors. The idyl was broken one bitterly cold winter day when Jim was skiing back from town with a backpack filled with supplies. Caught in a blizzard, he froze to death just a few miles from the cabin. He was 38 years old.

Neal adjusted to the loss by turning inward to grasp the spirit of the land, by painting out her emotions, and by opening outward to her own and neighboring children with stories. Over the years these grew into a complex series of fairy tales that detailed the good and evil witches, the leprechauns and trolls who inhabit these woods and fields. Midsummers' Eve was a special time when children and adults could enter this magical spirit world through her storytelling. In 1973, Neal Forsling gave her land and cabin to Natrona County for use as a park. She died a few years later and is buried nearby, but her extraordinary love for the earth is revealed in her small cabin, her mystical paintings, her fairy tales, and in the trails that lead through the woods to shrines celebrating the good witches,

magical creatures, and witty forest spirits who haunt this land. Neal's philosophy is summed up by a sign in her cabin:

> *What I had, I lost*
> *What I saved, I spent*
> *What I gave, I have.*

Today, her old log home is a small museum (tel. 472-0452) that is open Sat.-Thurs. 11-7 from mid-June to "the first big snow" (generally late September).

Eleanor Carrigen grew up on the mountain and spent countless childhood days with Neal Forsling, to whom she is related "by osmosis." She now leads tours of the turn-of-the-century cabin and tells delightful stories. Be sure to ask about the "chocolate war" between two of Forsling's suitors! Inside the cabin are several of Forsling's paintings—seemingly inspired by both Vincent van Gogh and Grandma Moses—that reveal her mystical sensibilities. A framed letter from a Missouri friend (Bess Truman) hangs on one wall. You may want to purchase a copy of *Crimson Dawn*, a collection of Forsling's tales that may soon be a Stephen Spielberg movie. And be sure to wander along the nearby woodland trails to enjoy the 20 shrines created by Neal Forsling. (My personal favorite is Sean the leprechaun.) Get to the park by heading 12 miles south of Casper along State 251 and following the signs to Crimson Dawn.

On **Midsummer's Eve** (June 21), be sure to be in Crimson Dawn for a wonderfully mystical celebration of Casper Mountain's witches and spirits. Visitors get to meet the local denizens in person and to throw handfuls of the dark red earth into the bonfire; if it burns, your wish will come true. Hundreds of Casperites will also be there to celebrate, along with a handful of pompous Bible-thumping protestors from Sunlight Ministries.

BESSEMER BEND

The bucolic Bessemer Bend area—10 miles southwest of Casper along State 220—abounds in history, both real and imagined. A lazy curve in the North Platte River, Bessemer Bend was an important 19th-century crossing point for

WYOMING STATE MUSEUM

Joseph M. Carey

wagon trains. Rock walls from a shelter built in 1812 by the Astorians are still visible on a knoll overlooking the river. Between 1860 and 1861, the Red Butte Pony Express station stood at the river bend, site of the longest of all Pony Express rides, a 320-mile gallop by Buffalo Bill Cody that lasted a grueling 21 hours and 40 minutes. The nearby Red Buttes were also where Custard's Wagon Train Fight took place (see p. 184). Bessemer City sprang up along the bend in 1888, calling itself "Queen City of the Plains." It lasted only a couple of years, and when Casper was voted the Natrona County seat, Bessemer City quietly faded away. Many of its buildings were moved to Casper, and today Bessemer City is just a field of alfalfa.

Along the east side of the North Platte River at Bessemer Bend is the site of the famed **Goose Egg Ranch**, once one of Wyoming's largest cattle spreads. In *The Virginian,* Owen Wister used Goose Egg Ranch for a memorable scene where two drunken cowboys switch blankets on a dozen babies while their parents are dancing, creating havoc when the ranch families drive home with the wrong children. Owned for many years by the Carey family—both father Joseph M. Carey and son Robert Carey served as governor and U.S. senator—it was later renamed the CY Ranch. The southern half of Casper is built on what was once CY land—hence CY Ave., one of the city's main thoroughfares. Ironically, the old Goose Egg ranch house died partly because of the fame brought to it in *The Virginian.* The abandoned stone buildings gradually deteriorated as tourists chipped away for momentos. Fearing that the buildings might collapse, the owners finally tore down the ranch in 1951. John Wayne's oil-field fire movie, *Hellfighters,* was filmed not far away in 1968.

Today folks come to Bessemer Bend to enjoy a steak at Goose Egg Inn or to watch wintering golden and bald eagles in nearby Jackson Canyon (named for famed Yellowstone photographer William H. Jackson). Another five miles down State 220 is **Dan Speas Fish Hatchery,** tel. 473-8890, Wyoming's largest trout-rearing facility. It's open daily 8-5.

THE "LAKE DISTRICT"

The 655-mile-long North Platte River rises in Colorado, heads north into Wyoming, and then curves a long lazy loop to the east, cutting across western Nebraska, and finally joining with the South Platte River near the city of North Platte. The entire basin covers 32,000 square miles and in Wyoming is fed by the Sweetwater, Medicine Bow, and Laramie rivers. The name "Platte" is French for "Broad"; Indians called the river "Nebraska," meaning "Flat." Both are appropriate titles along much of its path. Cottonwood trees line the banks, and the river offers an essential watering hole for wildlife. (Early settlers in Wyoming called the Platte "a mile wide and an inch deep," and "too thick to drink and too thin to plow.")

Once one of the most impressive rivers in the Plains states—at flood stage it ran 150 yards wide and 10-15 feet deep—the North Platte has

THE
"LAKE DISTRICT"

turn 12 to 15 million acres of the state into productive farmland. The Carey Act—named for Wyoming's Senator Joseph M. Carey—tested these claims by having the federal government donate land to the states to be reclaimed by settlers. Wyoming became the first state to try out the new law, but only 10% of the two million acres in the program were finally patented. The costs were simply too high and the return too low; funding for the massive dams and irrigation canals could only come from the federal government. The Reclamation Act of 1902 was designed to do just that.

When the Reclamation Act's money started flowing, the North Platte was one of the first to be dammed (or damned, depending upon one's perspective). It seemed a potential godsend for farmers who had long used waterwheels to lift water from the river into adjacent irrigation ditches. Today, eight giant dams hold back the river and its tributaries in Wyoming: Seminoe, Kortes, Pathfinder, Alcova, and Gray Reef all above the city of Casper, along with Glendo, Guernsey, and Grayrocks farther downstream. Two long irrigation canals—the Interstate Canal and the Fort Laramie Canal—supply water to farms east of Wheatland. Ironically, nearly 80% of the water behind Wyoming dams on the North Platte goes to fields in neighboring Nebraska. This is also true at most of the other large reclamation projects in Wyoming: Bighorn Canyon water goes to Montana, Keyhole Reservoir water to South Dakota, Jackson Lake water to Idaho, and Flaming Gorge water to Utah. Meanwhile, more than 100,000 acres of once-valuable farming and grazing land in Wyoming lie under these massive reservoirs. Wyoming, one of the driest states in the nation, has become an exporter of huge quantities of water to surrounding states.

been reduced to little more than a creek through much of Wyoming. Near Fort Laramie, where wagon trains in the 1850s found a treacherous crossing, the river today sometimes ceases to flow at all, lying in shallow puddles in the late summer sun. A look at the map makes it obvious what has happened to the water; agriculture has siphoned it all away.

Reclamation
Without irrigation, farming was difficult or impossible in much of the arid west, and the thousands of homesteaders who tried to survive on 640 acres soon saw their hopes and dreams fade in the withering summer heat. Irrigation seemed natural for these desert lands. John Wesley Powell's idea of arid lands reclamation through dams and irrigation canals gradually gained favor, and by the 1890s, Wyoming's politicians were claiming that irrigation could

Seminoe Reservoir
Completed in 1939, Seminoe Dam is a 295-foot-high concrete arch dam. It is the farthest upstream of the North Platte dams and holds back more than a million acre-feet of water. A power plant produces 45 megawatts of electricity. The reservoir is bounded by 3,821-acre **Seminoe State Park**, named for the nearby Seminoe Mountains, which in turn were named after the French trapper Basil Cimineau Lajeunesse. (Folks apparently had a hard time spelling

his middle name.) The reservoir stretches almost 20 miles south of the dam, through desolate, rocky mountains and gigantic dunes of white sand. Sandy beaches along the shoreline attract swimmers in late summer. Juniper and ponderosa pine trees dot the hills, while sagebrush, greasewood, yucca, and salt sage grow on the lower slopes. The steep 500-foot knife edge of Horseshoe Ridge is visible on the eastern shore.

BRIAN BARDWELL

Golden eagles nest along the southern arm of Seminoe Reservoir, and bighorn sheep and elk have been reintroduced. The area also abounds with sage grouse.

Seminoe has two state park **campgrounds** ($4, open year-round) along its northwest shore. Water and toilets are available. You can also camp for free on Bureau of Reclamation sand dunes along the lake's southern arm. The reservoir is popular for fishing (rainbow, brown, and cutthroat trout, along with walleye) and water-skiing. Gas and limited provisions are available at Seminoe Boat Club. Access from Rawlins and Sinclair to the western shore of Seminoe is relatively easy via a 34-mile-long paved road, but the 70 miles of mixed pavement and gravel from Casper are a bit harder to take. The eastern shore is even less accessible.

An overlook at the dam site provides views into the steep rocky canyon and the dam that spans the chasm. North of this, the road drops steeply into the canyon and then climbs up through Morgan Creek Canyon, where big ponderosa pines, willows, and cottonwoods line the creek. A few miles beyond this, the road descends over a pass and then down through Hamilton Creek Canyon, finally emerging into open sagebrush country near the **Miracle Mile** of the North Platte River. There is free camping here among the cottonwoods that line the riverbank, and there's excellent trout fishing. More free camping at Sage Creek Rd., a half-mile north of the river crossing. The name Miracle Mile—actually three miles of free-flowing river—

refers to this popular "blue ribbon" fishery, maintained by regulated flows from the 244-foot-high **Kortes Dam** power plant, just upstream. In reality, the miracle is that any stretch of the North Platte still has anything resembling natural flows.

Pathfinder Reservoir

Pathfinder Reservoir is 30 miles southwest of Casper on State 220 and then another 10 miles in along County Road 409. In 1905, the federal government provided funds for this, the first dam in eastern Wyoming, to be built near the junction of the Sweetwater and North Platte rivers. Proponents claimed that the reservoir would irrigate more than 700,000 acres, primarily in Wyoming, but instead, just 130,000 acres were irrigated, nearly all of this in Nebraska.

Completed in 1909, Pathfinder Dam is considered an engineering marvel for its time and is listed on the National Register of Historic Places. The 214-foot-high arched structure is made up of large granite blocks quarried from adjacent hills and held together with cement and steel hauled by wagon teams from Casper, 45 miles away. (The trip sometimes took three weeks.)

Pathfinder is named for explorer John C. Frémont, "Pathfinder of the West." In 1842 he ventured down the river and—against the advice of his guides—decided to run the canyon below the present dam site (now Fremont Canyon). They narrowly escaped alive, as Frémont described:

To go back was impossible; the torrent before us was a sheet of foam; and, shut up in the chasm by the rocks, which in some places seemed to almost meet overhead, the roar of the waters was deafening. . . the boat struck a concealed rock immediately at the foot of the fall, which whirled her over in an instant. . . . For a hundred yards below, the current was covered with floating books and boxes, bales of blankets, and scattered articles of clothing. . . . For a mo-

ment, I felt somewhat disheartened. All our books—almost every record of the journey—our journals and registers of astronomical and barometrical observations—had been lost in a moment.

Pathfinder Reservoir splits into two arms, following the upstream path of the Sweetwater and North Platte rivers. **Pathfinder National Wildlife Refuge** covers 16,807 acres of land around scattered parts of the reservoir and is home to many mammals and birds. Canada geese nest along the shore, and white pelicans nest on an island here. **Camping** is available at Pathfinder Mountain and Bishops Point ($4; April to mid-Sept.), or you can camp for free along much of the lake's hundred-mile shore (except within the refuge). The deep-blue lake is a popular place for anglers in search of cutthroat, brown, and rainbow trout, or walleye. Windsurfers find some of Wyoming's finest sailing conditions. **Pathfinder Marina** has rental boats, fishing gear, gas, and a snack bar.

Not far from the dam is an old stone building that once housed the dam tender but is today used as an **interpretive center**. Summer hours are Sat. 11-5 and Sun. 10-4; ask at the adjacent frame house for a peek inside at other times. A pleasant 1½ mile loop trail crosses the dam, follows Fremont Canyon (lined with hundreds of cliff-swallow nests), and then recrosses the river over an impressive swinging footbridge before returning to the interpretive center. The interpretive center has a brochure describing sights along the path.

The Lynching Of Cattle Kate

Deep beneath the waters of Pathfinder Reservoir lies the site of one of the most infamous Wyoming lynchings. In 1889, James Averell and Ella Watson ("Cattle Kate") operated a ranch here. Local cattle barons accused Averell of housing rustlers and operating a saloon and gambling house for them, with Cattle Kate running a sideline business in which cattle were exchanged for "personal favors." The charges were apparently a smokescreen put up by A.J. Bothwell and other large landowners who were angry that Averell and Watson had filed homestead claims on land being grazed by Bothwell's cattle. When Averell had the temerity to call the

cattle barons "land sharks" in a letter to the Casper newspaper, they responded by sending a party out to eliminate the two. Averell and Watson were found hanging from a tree along the Sweetwater River. Later, the six men who perpetrated the hanging escaped prosecution when the chief witness suddenly disappeared—apparently murdered by one of the lynching party. Bothwell went on to gain title to Averell's and Watson's land, despite national newspaper complaints over "the barbaric lynching of a woman in Wyoming Territory."

Alcova Reservoir

Although much smaller than Pathfinder or Seminoe reservoirs, Alcova is a favorite recreation spot for the people of Casper. Windsurfing sailing, water-skiing, and ice fishing are all popular sports on this windy lake, located 30 miles southwest of Casper. The upper portion of the reservoir reaches into famed **Fremont Canyon**, a mini-Grand Canyon whose red vertical cliffs reach 500 feet above the river. Access is via dirt roads from both sides. The water makes for exciting river-running if you have a kayak and the skills. Golden eagles nest here. It is also very popular with rock climbers. There are dozens of climbs up to a rating of 5.12. For details, stop by Mountain Sports in Casper for a copy of Steve Petro's *Climber's Guide to Fremont Canyon*. Anglers try their luck with the rainbow and cutthroat trout and walleye.

The name Alcova comes from **Alcova Hot Springs** (129° F water), so named because of its location within a series of coves. At the turn of the century, developers tried to turn the hot springs into a spa, but the propensity of Wyomingites to take baths but once a week made the venture a failure. The springs were covered by the reservoir, but an artesian well below the dam pours forth the naturally heated water. Bring your swimsuit!

The 265-foot-high Alcova Dam, part of the depression-era Kendrick Project, was completed in 1938, with a 36-megawatt power plant added in the 1980s. Facilities here include picnic areas, swimming beaches, four campgrounds ($4 for tents; $10 for RVs), and the **Alcova Lakeside Marina**, tel. 472-6666, where you can rent boats and buy gas or supplies. Water leaves Alcova Dam and flows into small **Gray Reef**

Reservoir used to control the fluctuating discharges from Alcova and to generate more power. From here some of the water is diverted into the 62-mile Casper Canal, irrigating 24,000 acres of alfalfa, barley, oats, and corn west of Casper.

OREGON TRAIL LANDMARKS

Three of the most famous landmarks along the entire Oregon Trail lie within Natrona County: Independence Rock, Devil's Gate, and Split Rock. Travelers anticipated these landmarks, for they marked the start of a long, gentle approach to the Continental Divide, 80 miles to the west. The route past these landmarks paralleled the Sweetwater River, a ribbon of lush grass in a rugged, desolate landscape. The names applied to adjacent mountains and creeks offer clues to the land's harshness: Rattlesnake Mountains, Poison Spider Creek, Greasewood Creek, Sulfur Creek, and Stinking Creek. Steamboat Lake, just a few miles north of Independence Rock, was a source of bicarbonate of soda used to bake bread. Cattle that drank the lake's putrid water died, while bread made with this baking soda took on a greenish cast. But along the Sweetwater, horses and oxen could find forage, firewood was available, and the clean mountain water offered a relief from the alkaline springs to the east. (The name Sweetwater arose when a mule team carrying sugar lost its load in the river.) Today, State 220 crosses the old Oregon Trail several miles east of its junction with US 287 at Muddy Gap. The highway parallels the trail for the next 45 miles west.

Independence Rock
Head southwest from Casper along State 220 for 55 miles till the granitic dome of Independence Rock rises above the flat surrounding plain. Though not as spectacular or colorful, the setting seems reminiscent of Australia's Ayers Rock. Independence Rock is 1,950 feet long by 850 feet wide; its smoothly rounded top reaches to 193 feet. Travelers could not resist the chance to note their passing on this gigantic billboard; an estimated 50,000 names were carved, chipped, or painted on Independence Rock during the mid-19th century. Father Jean Pierre DeSmet, a famed Jesuit missionary, labeled it "the Great Register of the Desert." His initials, along with the names of Captain Bonneville, John C. Frémont, and many other explorers, were etched into the rock face.

Independence Rock apparently received its name from explorer and mountain man William Sublette, who arrived here on July 4, 1830, leading the first wagon train across the overland route. Oregon Trail emigrants tried to reach the rock around July 4 to be on schedule for Oregon. When the rock came into view, it was a source of rejoicing, for it offered a welcome place to rest alongside the Sweetwater River. During the heyday of migration along the Oregon Trail, dozens of wagon trains would find themselves at the rock on Independence Day, and the celebrations included patriotic flag-waving, the firing of guns, big dinners, and other festivities. Many people did not make it beyond Independence Rock; dozens of unmarked graves surround the rock.

August 16

Moved on up the creek saw the notable rock Independence with the names of its numerious visitors most of which are nearly obliterated by the weather & ravages of time amongst which I observed the names of two of my old friends the notable mountaneers Thos. Fitzpatrick & W. L. Sublette as likewise one of our noblest politicians Henry Clay coupled in division with that of Martin Van Buren a few miles further up the creek pases through the south point of ruged & solid looking granite rock by a verry narrow pass after passing which we entered a valy Surounded by low ruged mountains except to the West whare a defiel Shews itself the lower vally of this creek is well clothed with short grass the upper with sand & sage the mountains with short scattering pines but in many places nothing but the bear rock in large steep Surfaces made 8 miles & encamped for the night on a good plat of grass

—Mountain man James Clyman describing Independence Rock in 1844

Today, hundreds of the original names carved into Independence Rock are still visible, though weathering and lichen have obliterated many more. Unfortunately, more recent travelers have added their names, sometimes covering up names over a hundred years old. Independence Rock can be climbed from a number of points along the perimeter, providing fine views of the surrounding countryside. Some of the oldest and best-preserved names are on top. An old road circles the rock, making for an interesting mile-long hike. Names can be found on all sides, and you're bound to see deer and other wildlife along the Sweetwater River. A small footbridge crosses the still-visible Oregon Trail route here.

Devil's Gate

Visible from Independence Rock and just seven miles to the southwest is another famed Oregon Trail landmark, Devil's Gate. Over the centuries, the Sweetwater River has gradually sliced a giant cleft through the Rattlesnake Mountains, leaving 370-foot cliffs on both sides of a 1,500-foot-long canyon. (An Indian legend offers an alternative origin for Devil's Gate: a gigantic tusked beast had roamed Sweetwater Valley, and when the Indians finally managed to mortally wound the animal, it gouged out the nearby mountains in its death agony.) Devil's Gate was another favorite emigrant campsite. The cut is hard to miss, especially from the east, the direction of most Oregon Trail travelers. Today, the BLM maintains a historic site along State 220, with a short loop trail and signboards. At least 20 emigrant graves are nearby. The **Tom Sun Ranch**, visible from here, was established in 1872 by a French-Canadian trapper, Thomas De Beau Soleil (Thomas Sun). His original cabin is a National Historic Landmark, and the ranch is still owned by the Sun family. A museum ($3) at the Sun Ranch is open by reservation only, tel. 324-6925. The ranch also provides a number of historical tours of the area.

Martin's Cove, just two miles northwest of Devil's Gate, is the site of the most disastrous experience along the Oregon and Mormon trails. In 1856, a group of 1,620 British converts to the Mormon religion sailed from Liverpool for America, intent upon reaching Salt Lake City before winter. (Total cost of the trip to Utah, including ship passage from England, was just $45 pp.) The converts left Missouri in several groups; last to leave were 576 people under the direction of Edward Martin. They headed out in late August, crossing the North Platte at present-day Casper on October 19. Instead of the usual wagons, many of these poor emigrants pushed or pulled small handcarts that held their few possessions. Soon the weather turned bitterly cold, a blizzard dumped 18 inches of snow on them, and temperatures dropped to -14° F. The elderly and children died first; eventually even the strongest began to die. A rescue wagon from Salt Lake City finally arrived in late October, with rescuer Daniel W. Jones writing:

There were old men pulling and tugging their carts, sometimes loaded with a sick wife or children, women pulling along sick husbands; little children six to eight years old struggling through the mud and snow. . . . The provisions we took amounted to almost nothing among so many people, many of them now on very short rations, some almost starving.

The survivors were escorted 65 miles to Martin's Cove, a protected area near Devil's Gate. The company of foolhardy emigrants finally reached Salt Lake City in late November, but 145 members had died along the way. Another Mormon handcart company, led by James G. Willie, suffered a similar fate that same year, losing 67 people to the elements (see p. 252).

Split Rock

The final of the three geologic landmarks that lined the Oregon Trail through present-day Natrona County is Split Rock, a bite taken out of a solid granite mountain. The cleft was visible for two days as emigrants trudged along; it seemed to be a gunsight aimed toward the west. In the early 1860s, a Pony Express station, an overland stage station, a telegraph station, and a garrison of troops were located nearby. Today, Split Rock is noted at a turnout 10 miles west of Muddy Gap Junction along US 287. Tourists sail past in minutes what took the emigrants many long and treacherous days.

NORTH OF CASPER

Salt Creek Oil Field

Forty miles north of Casper is the Salt Creek Oil Field, considered the largest light oil field in the world. The 10-mile-long field covers a land of sage, sand, and rock that has produced over 600 million barrels of oil and 700 million cubic feet of gas. Much more oil has been found nearby. A drive up State 259 is a trip through a bizarre alien world of desert land carpeted with giant grasshopperlike electric pumpjacks spaced every couple hundred feet to the horizon. (Actually, they look more like the little plastic ostriches sold in tourist shops—the ones that keep tipping down to a bowl of water to "drink.") The pumpjacks don't run all the time, allowing the oil to accumulate in the well before pumping resumes. West of the company town of Midwest, things get even stranger, with an incredible grid of pumpjacks, dirt roads, powerlines, and storage tanks crisscrossing the harsh land.

This famed oil field occupies a classic anticlinal structure that traps oil; hundred-foot cliffs surround the field. Wyoming's territorial geologist, Samuel Aughey, discovered these unusual structures and brought the first speculators here to file placer claims in 1884. The first well in the area was drilled in 1889 by a Pennsylvania oilman, M.P. Shannon. The oil was hauled by horse-drawn wagon to Casper, 50 miles away. In 1904, Shannon sold his small Casper refinery and 105,000 acres of Salt Creek leases to European speculators for $350,000.

Four years later the real boom came when a Dutch-financed company struck black gold at 1,050 feet in the Salt Creek Field, spouting oil in a massive gusher. When the news hit, battles over land claims quickly escalated to the shouting and shooting stage. The Midwest Oil Company was formed, building the first pipeline to Casper in 1911, feeding the new Midwest refinery there. The Fransco Company added another refinery the following year, and Standard Oil of Indiana built a cracking plant to retrieve more gasoline from the crude.

As WW I steamed over the horizon, the field suddenly gained a vital national importance; oil shipped to the allies from Salt Creek was considered an important factor in the defeat of Kaiser Wilhelm. After the war, Standard Oil (now Amoco) bought out all of Midwest's Salt Creek properties, but the 14 remaining companies competed with each other for the crude, with oil derricks within spitting distance of each other.

Production declined as the companies attempted to pump the oil too fast, trying to get it before it flowed into neighboring wells. Finally, in 1939, Salt Creek became the first oil field in America to run as a unitized operation, with joint management of the various wells for greater efficiency and conservation. Production in Salt Creek reached a peak in 1923 (when it produced 5% of the nation's oil), but the introduction of gas injection in the 1920s and water flooding in the 1950s helped push more oil to the wellheads. Although just a third of the oil at Salt Creek has been recovered even today—more than 100 years after its discovery—retrieving the remaining oil will require more sophisticated techniques, such as flooding with carbon dioxide. Salt Creek, yielding 12 thousand barrels per day, still accounts for two-thirds of Natrona County's oil production. It's Wyoming's third-largest producing field.

Midwest And Edgerton

The twin oil towns of Midwest (pop. 500) and Edgerton (pop. 250) lie near the center of the Salt Creek Field. A paved road north of Midwest leads to the Shannon Pool oil field, where oil was first discovered. Thousands of drill holes surround the towns, laced together by a grid of dirt roads, power lines, and pipes.

The company town of Midwest is named for Midwest Oil Company, now a part of Amoco. Its four straight streets contain rows of identical wooden houses built in the '20s, which now show their age. The stench of sulfur from a gas-recovery plant south of town permeates the air. Midwest's golf course is dotted with oil pumps, and folks attending Mass at the Catholic church can hear the quiet, rhythmic "ker-thunk" from a couple of pumpjacks just a hundred feet away. Midwest was especially hard hit by the slide in oil prices in the '80s; assessed valuation plummeted from $9.2 million in 1987 to $1.5 million in 1989! The impact is obvious in a walk around town: peeling paint on the small wooden box houses, boarded-up buildings, aging cars, and a sense of defeat. A small **museum** can be found in the town hall.

The dumpy little town of Edgerton isn't much better. For meals, try **Edgerton Cafe** or Midwest's **Derrick Cafe**. The only lodging place is **Tea Pot Motor Lodge** in Edgerton, tel. 437-6541. Edgerton claims a bit of baseball trivia: it was the first place in America to have a baseball game played under lights. The big local event—including dancing, food, a golf tournament, and more—comes in August, when both towns celebrate **Salt Creek Days**.

Tempest In A Teapot

Twenty-five miles north of Casper along US 87 is a distinctively shaped butte, Teapot Rock. Until a 1962 windstorm knocked down the "spout" that bent away from one side, the rock resembled a teapot. In the first decades of this century, rapid growth in the oil industry sent prospectors and speculators all over the west in search of black gold. To ensure adequate fuel supplies for the Navy's ships after WW I, the government set aside three large oil reserves—Elk Hills and Buena Vista in California, and Wyoming's Teapot Dome Oil Field (named for Teapot Rock).

In 1921 and 1922, Secretary of the Interior Albert B. Fall secretly leased Teapot Dome to Edward Doheny and Harry Sinclair, owners of Mammoth Oil Company. (Could anyone have ever come up with a more fitting name for a corrupt corporation?) Although the action was technically legal, the $100,000 bribe paid by Doheny to President Harding's interior secretary was

decidedly not legal, and Fall was forced to resign. The action brought a plethora of charges against the giant oil companies, and political cartoonists had a heyday with Teapot Dome. Interior Secretary Fall was convicted of accepting bribes and spent a year in prison. Harry Sinclair (for whom both the oil company and the Wyoming town are named) hired detectives to spy on a jury investigating Teapot Dome and was sent to jail in 1929 for contempt of court. He also spent three months in jail for refusing to testify before a Senate committee investigating the scandal. Today, the U.S. Navy still owns thousands of acres at Teapot Dome, and there are hundreds of oil wells a few miles east of the highway. A sign points out Naval Petroleum Reserve Number 3, but you won't find any historical signs mentioning this rather sordid piece of Wyoming history. The mailboxes and nearby white buildings of Teapot Dome Ranch mark the site of Teapot Rock.

HEADING WEST

Powder River

The tiny settlement of Powder River (pop. 50) lies along US 20-26 where it crosses this famous river, 35 lonely miles west of Casper. Not much here today; writer James Conaway called the town "little more than a Texaco station and a bunch of pronghorn antelope looking at it." On the third weekend in July, however, several hundred people flock (pun intended) to town for the annual **Sheepherder's Fair**. It features dog trials, sheep roping, a free BBQ, a "lamb cookoff," and sheepherding demonstrations of all sorts. A band plays C&W favorites late into the evening for a happy throng of dancers.

Hell's Half Acre

Head west from Casper on US 20-26 for 45 miles to one of the freaks of nature, Hell's Half Acre. Actually covering 320 acres, the area includes a strange collection of deeply eroded and colorful badlands surrounded by featureless sage-covered plains. Ancient coal deposits within the badlands caught on fire and burned for many years, and when explorer Captain Bonneville passed by in 1833, he labeled it Devils Kitchen because of these sulfurous fumes. The name Hell's Half Acre was a later title. Indians used these badlands as a buffalo trap, driving herds of them to their deaths over the canyon walls. In the late 19th century, after whites had slaughtered the bison to the brink of extinction, bone pickers gleaned thousands of these bones from Hell's Half Acre for eastern fertilizer plants. Archaeologists later discovered more bones here, along with arrowheads and other artifacts. Hell's Half Acre is well worth a stop, but be forewarned that a kitschy souvenir shop, cafe, motel (tel. 472-0018), and RV park detract from the view. It's a great place to meet busloads of tottering tourists from hell.

Lysite And Lost Cabin
This area is decidedly off the beaten track, located eight miles north of another nowheresville town, Moneta (pop. 10). At one time the main route into the Bighorn Basin and Yellowstone lay along the Lysite road, but with completion of a highway through Wind River Canyon in 1927, traffic bypassed this area. Slow-paced Lysite has an old-time country store and is the sort of place where horses are still a means of transportation. Lysite library is housed in a building slightly larger than a shoe box.

Three miles to the east is Lost Cabin, named for a gold mine in the Big Horn Mountains. Miner Allen Hulburt and two partners discovered a stream filled with gold, but Indians killed his partners and partially burned their cabin. The dazed miner scooped up as much gold as he could carry and fled to Casper, where his tale pricked more than a few ears. Despite repeated efforts by Hulburt and others, the Lost Cabin mine was never again found. (This is only one of many such tales about the fabled mine.)

The flyspeck of a town called Lost Cabin is cen-

BOB RACE

tered around an elaborate mansion by John B. Okie. He came to Wyoming as a cowboy with only the clothes on his back, decided sheep were a better bet, and gradually became a millionaire. Okie once ran 30,000 sheep through the surrounding country, gaining the title "The Sheep King." His mansion—called "The Big Tipi" by local Indians—was built in 1900 for $30,000 and filled with carved fireplaces, Asian chandeliers, imported furniture, stained-glass, and Persian prayer rugs. Surrounding it were a greenhouse filled with flowers tended by Japanese gardeners, a roller rink, a dance hall, and even an aviary housing 140 exotic birds. A power plant was built to supply electricity for Okie's town. In 1930, Okie drowned in a nearby reservoir while hunting ducks. The old mansion is not open to the public but is visible from the gate.

Castle Gardens
A remote and little-known archaeological site is Castle Gardens, located 21 miles south of Moneta on a gravel road and then another six miles east on a rough dirt road. Not recommended for RVs or after rains, when the road turns into a quagmire. Signs at Moneta and at the turnoff keep you from getting lost. Castle Gardens is a desolate area with all sorts of odd sandstone formations: toadstools, spires, and various creatures seem to appear. It's easy to see how this would be a sacred spot for the Indians who came here centuries ago. Small juniper and limber pines grow amid the grey rocks and sand, creating a garden in the castles of Castle Gardens. No camping at the site, but there are picnic tables and an outhouse.

Dozens of Indian pictographs (presumably Shoshonean in origin) have been sharply incised into the soft rock walls. They include many in the shield motif, believed to represent the round shields of Indian warriors. While they may be up to 900 years old, these figures are probably more recent than the pecked style of pictographs present in the Dinwoody Creek and Legend Rock areas. Castle Gardens' figures that show horses or tipis are clearly from the period after A.D. 1700. The most elaborate shield found here—the figure of a turtle painted green, yellow, and red—is now in the State Museum in Cheyenne. The remaining pictographs are protected by chain-link fences, but vandals have marred many of these priceless artifacts with graffiti. The site leaves you with mixed emotions: a multitude of questions about what the images represent, a feeling of closeness to the natural world in this remote and fascinating place, and an utter disgust for those who would destroy this cultural heritage.

West To Shoshoni

The 85 miles of highway (US 20-26) that connect Casper with Shoshoni cross an almost featureless plain, a place that seems to define the word "bleak." No trees in sight, the clouds throw moving shadows across a landscape of sage and grass. This is antelope country. Even the ranches are few and far between out here, and cattle take slow, desultory steps in the summer heat or brace against the bitter winds of winter. For many travelers this is pedal-to-the-metal country, a place to crank up the country tunes and sail on west.

BOB KACE

WIND RIVER MOUNTAINS COUNTRY

The Wind River Mountains—Wyoming's highest and longest range—form a dramatic divide between two of the state's most important rivers. The east side drains into the Wind River, eventually reaching the Atlantic Ocean, while the western slopes drop into the Green River and eventually down to the Pacific. The name Wind River Mountains originated as a Crow Indian reference to the warm chinook winds that blow down the Wind River Valley. (Writer Joe Kelsey noted that the name Wind River Mountains contains three of the ancient Greek's four elements: earth, air, and water.)

The Land
This chapter covers Sublette and Fremont counties, named for two of the state's most famous explorers. Fremont County is a land of sharp contrasts. The eastern end consists of a spacious, arid landscape of sage, grass, and antelope, while to the west are the fluorescent green irrigated fields along the Wind River and the pastel badlands near Dubois. Along the southern and western borders rise the snow-crested Wind River and Absaroka mountains. At almost six million acres, this is Wyoming's second-largest county (after Sweetwater).

The centerpiece of Fremont County is the Wind River Reservation, home to both the Eastern Shoshone and the Northern Arapaho peoples. Within the reservation itself are the tiny towns of Fort Washakie, Ethete, and Arapahoe. The much larger non-Indian settlements of Riverton and Lander border it on the east, while on the south are the historic mining towns of South Pass and Atlantic City. West of the reservation, the town of Dubois provides an entry point into the Absarokas, the Tetons, and Yellowstone.

The Wind River Valley is farming and ranching country, with nearly half of Fremont County's people employed in agriculture. Some 150,000 acres of alfalfa hay, feed and malt barley, sugar beets, and oats are under irrigation each year. This is Wyoming's second-biggest dairy county,

WIND RIVER
MOUNTAINS
COUNTRY

© MOON PUBLICATIONS, INC.

eclipsed only by Park County, and it has the largest number of horses in the state. There is also a substantial amount of oil and natural-gas production on the Wind River Reservation, where energy royalties bring in millions of dollars each year. Uranium was discovered in the Gas Hills area east of Riverton during the 1950s and spawned a major industry in the 1960s and '70s, before plummeting when the Three-Mile Island accident of 1981 brought the dangers of nuclear power to the forefront. Today the main work in the uranium mines is an effort to clean up the abandoned sites.

Sublette County has fewer people than any other county in Wyoming, just 4,500 individuals spread over 10,495 square miles. Cattle exceed people by a 16:1 margin, and there is only one town of any size: Pinedale. A few folks live in the little burgs of Big Piney, Marbleton, Boulder, and Daniel. Not surprisingly, the big industry here is ranching, although tourists are increasingly attracted to the area for its scenic beauty. There are magnificent vistas of the Winds all along the western front—far more dramatic than from the eastern side.

RIVERTON

Located near the confluence of the Big Wind River and Little Wind River, aptly named Riverton (pop. 9,200) is the largest settlement in Fremont County and the eighth-largest city in the state. The Wind River Reservation surrounds Riverton on all sides. It's a mid-America suburbia sort of place where K marts and McDonald's dominate the outskirts. Cheap gas and low-priced hotels make visiting easier. The modern Central Wyoming College attracts students from throughout the area.

History
The Riverton area was the site of two trapping and trading rendezvous, in 1830 and 1838. The land became part of the Wind River Reservation in 1868, but a portion was ceded by the Shoshone and Arapaho tribes in 1904. Almost overnight, the town of Riverton sprang up, as would-be farmers drew lots for prime farmland. It still has the state's largest dairy. Canals were dug and fields planted to crops; more than 100,000 acres of irrigated farmland surround Riverton today.

During the 1960s and '70s enormous uranium deposits were developed in the nearby Gas Hills area. Hundreds of millions of dollars poured into the local economy, creating rapid growth, but when nuclear power suddenly lost its luster, so did Riverton. After the bust that followed, the town began to diversify and has been slowly rebounding. Today the largest private employer is DH Print, a manufacturer of computer equipment. Other major employers are a soda ash

hauling company (Bonneville Transloaders), the Brunton Co. (America's only compass manufacturer), and various government agencies.

Sights
The **Riverton Museum,** 700 E. Park Ave., tel. 856-2665, is open Tues.-Sat. 10-5 May-Sept., and Tues.-Sat. 11-4 the rest of the year. No charge. Local historical exhibits include a tipi that contains a buffalo robe and powwow drum, an Indian cradle board with saddle, a model of the Carissa Mine at South Pass, various old farm and mining equipment, and an interesting exhibit on oil drilling. Take a gander at Desert Demon, a stuffed wild mustang that proved untamable (hence his current more sedate condition; a bullet helped in the "taming" process). While here, also check out the photos of Leslie King, the father of former president Gerald R. Ford and a prominent Riverton-area rancher. (President Ford's parents were divorced, and his mother later married a man whose last name was Ford.) Gerald Ford worked as a Yellowstone National Park ranger after graduating from college in Michigan but is not known to have fallen into any geysers.

Riverton Livestock Auction, located on Fairgrounds Rd., tel. 856-2209, is Wyoming's second-largest livestock auction barn (after Torrington). The monthly horse sales are the most enjoyable.

Accommodations
Riverton has some 15 different places to bed

down for the night, all priced quite reasonably. See the chart for specifics. The nearest public camping ($4; open year-round) is 20 miles north in **Boysen State Park**. **Rudy's Camper Court,** 622 E. Lincoln Ave., tel. 856-9764, charges $14 for RVs and $9 for tents. Showers for noncampers are $3. Open year-round. **Owl Creek Kampground,** six miles northeast of Riverton on US 26, tel. 856-2869, has tent sites for $10, RVs for $14, and showers for noncampers for $3. Open mid-May to mid-September.

Food
One of the best local eateries is, surprisingly, **Airport Cafe** at the airport, tel. 856-2838, where the homemade cinnamon rolls and pies are specialties. Head here for breakfast. The Thursday-night Navajo tacos at **Trailhead Restaurant,** 831 N. Federal Blvd., tel 856-7990, are

worth a taste. **Claimsteak Restaurant,** 1616 N. Federal, tel. 856-6503, has a Mexican buffet on Wednesday night, or try **Dog Patch,** 489 S. Federal, tel. 856-4590. The latter has as much atmosphere as a Taco Bell and closes early each evening. Higher-quality—and pricier—Mexican food, along with prime rib, steak, seafood, and roast duck, is available at **Broker Restaurant,** 203 E. Main, tel. 856-0555.

Valley View Supper Club, 4911 Valley View Rd., tel. 856-2447, is a favorite for steaks and prime rib, but see nearby Hudson for the very best steaks in this part of Wyoming. The biggest salad bar in Riverton is at **Golden Corral,** 400 N. Federal Blvd., tel. 856-1152. **Trade Winds,** 302 N. Federal, tel. 856-7666, serves Americanized Chinese dishes that locals rave over. **New China Restaurant,** 302 N. Federal Blvd., tel. 856-7666, is also popular. All the fast-food chains can be

RIVERTON

© MOON PUBLICATIONS, INC.

RIVERTON ACCOMMODATIONS

MOTEL	ADDRESS	TELEPHONE	RATES	FEATURES
Wyoming Motel	319 N. Federal	856-6549	$21 s, $25 d	
Mountain View Motel	720 W. Main	856-2418	$22+ s, $24+ d	
Driftwood Inn	611 W. Main	856-5811	$23 s, $27 d	
Jackpine Motel	120 S. Federal	856-9251	$24 s, $26 d	
El Rancho Motel	221 S. Federal	856-7455	$24+ s, $36+ d	
Thunderbird Motel	302 E. Fremont	856-9201	$25 s, $30 d	AAA approved
Hi-Lo Motel	414 N. Federal	856-9223	$28 s, $31 d	AAA-approved very clean
Paintbrush Motel	1550 N. Federal	856-9238	$30 s, $33 d	AAA approved, clean and friendly
Circle-B Motel	909 W. Main St.	856-9677	$30 s, $35 d	AAA-approved
Tomahawk Motor Lodge	208 E. Main	856-9205 (800) 341-8000	$30+ s, $35+ d	AAA-approved,
Super 8 Motel	1040 N. Federal	857-2400 (800) 800-8000	$36 s, $40 d	
Sundowner Station Motel	1616 N. Federal	856-6503 (800) 874-1116	$39+ s, $41+ d	pool, jacuzzi, sauna, very nice
Holiday Inn	789 N. Federal	856-8100 (800) 465-4329	$45+ s, $47+ d	AAA-approved, pool, whirlpool, exercise room
Cottonwood Ranch B&B	13 miles northwest	856-3064	$40 s, $45 d	working ranch
Hillcrest Manor B&B	10 miles west	856-6309	$48+ s or d	spacious home

found on N. Federal Blvd., or on the west end of Main Street. The cheapest meal deal in town is at Little Caesers in the K mart store on N. Federal, where you can get pizza by the slice. When everything else is closed, head to the always-open **Silver Spoon Cafe**, 1104 N. Federal Blvd., tel. 856-4085. Get groceries at **Woodward's IGA**, 619 N. Federal and 906 W. Main, or **Smith's**, 1200 W. Main.

Entertainment

The local bowling alley—**Star-Lite Lanes**, 837 N. Federal, tel. 856-5944—has country music nightly. **Good Time Charlie's Lounge**, 502 E. Main St., tel. 856-4285, generally has rock bands on weekends. **Club El Toro**, tel. 332-4627, in nearby Hudson also has live tunes.

Events

Summer kicks off with the **Mountain Man Rendezvous and Music Festival** the first weekend in July near the site of a similar gathering in 1838. The next two weekends are reserved for the **Riverton Rendezvous,** which includes an arts-and-crafts festival, stock-car races, rodeos, outdoor dancing, a melodrama, and all sorts of other activities. The festival ends with a **Hot Air Balloon Rally** on the third weekend in July, where you're likely to see more than two dozen colorful balloons lifting off at sunrise. The event attracts celebrities from the world of ballooning.

Fremont County Fair and Rodeo comes to the Riverton Fairground in mid-August, with stock-dog trials, a demolition derby, a parade, PRCA rodeos, and even a llama show. Other rodeos are held every Tuesday night mid-June to August. In mid-August, the Riverton Museum sponsors a **Folk Festival** with demonstrations of pioneer skills and arts such as storytelling, old-fashioned cooking, and folk music. Meet all sorts of people in turn-of-the-century costumes and on horse-drawn carriages. You can have more fun at the **Cowboy Poetry Roundup** in October, where the cowpokes spin tales. This is the largest cowboy poetry event in Wyoming.

Shopping
Books and Briar, 313 E. Main, tel. 856-1797, is a surprisingly nice bookshop in downtown Riverton, with quite a few Wyoming and Indian titles. Also check out the bookstore on the CWC campus. **Beaver Creek Stitchery,** 415 E. Main, tel. 856-5303, sells authentic western dusters, scarves, and other locally sewn items. **Wind River Trading Post,** 924 S. Federal Blvd., tel. 856-6141, has locally made beadwork and jewelry, along with turquoise jewelry from Arizona. Royce Brown, a local Arapaho craftsman, makes miniature Indian warbonnets. Call **Lone Bear Crafts,** tel. 856-1521, for details.

Recreation
Riverton has an outdoor summer-only pool in City Park at Main and Federal and an excellent indoor **Aquatic Center** at the high school on W. Sunset Dr., tel. 856-4230, with a sauna and whirlpool. Both are free. The 18-hole **Riverton Country Club** is at 4275 Country Club Dr., tel. 856-4779. **Central Wyoming College** offers nature walks to the surrounding mountain country through the summer months. Call 856-9291 or (800) 735-8418 for details.

Information And Services
Riverton Chamber of Commerce is in the old railroad depot at First and Main, tel. 856-4801 or (800) 735-8418, and is open Mon.-Fri. 8-5. The attractive 109-acre campus of **Central Wyoming College,** tel. 856-9291 or (800) 442-1228, is on the west edge of town along US 26. Founded in 1966, it offers two-year programs in more than 50 fields for nearly 1,000 full-time students. Students run Wyoming's only public television station and an excellent National Public Radio station (FM 88.1). The impressive **Arts Center** houses a small gallery with changing exhibits. Riverton's brand new **public library,** 1330 W. Park Ave., tel. 856-3556, is open Mon., Tues., and Thurs. 12-9, Wed. 9-9, Fri. 9-4, and Sat. 9-1. The college also has a good-sized library.

Transportation
Riverton Airport, two miles northwest of town, has daily connections to Denver on **Continental Express,** tel. (800) 525-0280, or **United Express,** tel. (800) 241-6522. No taxis in town, but you can rent cars at the airport from **Avis,** tel. 856-5052 or (800) 331-1212, or **Hertz,** tel. 856-2344 or (800) 654-3131.

RIVERTON VICINITY

SHOSHONI

Shoshoni (pop. 500) is one of the saddest hunks of desolation in Wyoming; only Jeffrey City beats it for top honors in this rather dubious category. During the late 1970s and early '80s this was a booming oil-and-uranium town, but today three-quarters of Shoshoni seems abandoned, with tall grass, peeling paint, and plywood windows. Tumbleweeds tumble down Main St., and locals joke that no one wants to be the last to "turn out the lights" because they're afraid of getting stuck with the electric bill! Fittingly enough, Shoshoni is bordered on the north by Badwater Creek and on the south by Poison Creek. East of Shoshoni is an arid landscape of badlands topography.

Practicalities
The main attraction in town is **Yellowstone Drug Store,** tel. 876-2539. During the summer months, scads of tourists stop here for delicious malts and ice-cream floats at the old-time soda fountain. Peek in the windows of Gamble's store across the street, a crowded, funky old store that was closed by the fire marshal several years ago. Also in Shoshoni is the interesting little **CU Rock Shop.** Tipi rings northwest of town are still visible.

Aside from Yellowstone Drug and the Rock Shop, Shoshoni's only redeeming value is its reasonably priced accommodations. **Desert Inn Motel,** 605 W. Second St., tel. 876-2273, has rooms for $23 s or $28 d; and **Shoshoni Motel,** 503 W. Second, tel. 876-2216, charges $20 s or $ 23 d. **Boysen State Park** is just a few miles north of here, with camping facilities for $4 a night. **Powder River Transportation,** tel. (800) 442-3682, has daily buses to Casper and Thermopolis from Shoshoni.

BOYSEN STATE PARK

Established in 1956, Boysen State Park, tel. 876-2796, surrounds a reservoir named for Asmus Boysen, a Danish emigrant who built the first dam here in 1907-08. When the water from his dam covered tracks of the Burlington Railroad, the railroad sued and had his dam blown up. The dam that now backs up the Wind River is a 230-foot-high earthen structure completed in 1961 and located at the entrance to Wind River Canyon. Boysen Reservoir is a motorboat playground popular with water-skiers and anglers (biggest walleye in Wyoming—to 17 pounds). Its relatively warm waters attract swimmers to the beach near park headquarters.

Boysen Reservoir lies primarily within the Wind River Indian Reservation and is surrounded by open desert country. A nearly straight highway (US 20) rolls north from Shoshoni over the arid hills and rocky buttes, providing a few good vistas across the lake. Southwest of Shoshoni, US 26 crosses an arm of the reservoir. **Boysen Lake Marina,** on the north end near the entrance to Wind River Canyon, tel. 876-2772, has a restaurant, a grocery store, and RV spaces ($13). The reservoir is surrounded by 10 different state park campsites ($4; open year-round). **Wyoming Winter Carnival** comes to Boysen in mid-Feb., featuring souped-up snowmobile races, ice golf, ice bowling, ice sculpture, dog-sled races, and even a "snodeo." The main event is the high-altitude speed run in which funny sleds (more like rockets with runners) reach speeds topping 160 mph.

GAS HILLS

The paved, but almost-untraveled, Gas Hills Rd. (State 136) leads east from the Riverton area to several now-closed open-pit uranium mines, including the Lucky McMine, discovered in 1953 by Neil and Maxine McNeice and mined for many years. Perhaps a third of the nation's uranium reserves remain in these arid hills. Today signs warn trespassers of the nuclear hazard in the abandoned mines. Dirt roads from the end of the pavement (approximately 45 miles east of Riverton) lead south to Jeffrey City, northwest to tiny Waltman, and east to Casper along Poison Spider Road. This is some of the most remote and desolate country you will ever find, with nary a tree in sight. The antelope love this sage-and-grass landscape. Castle Gardens (see pp. 203-204) can also be accessed from Gas Hills Road. A sign on the road (easy to miss) points out the turnoff.

HUDSON

It would be easy to drive through Hudson (pop. 400) without paying any attention to this rather run-down little place. That would be a mistake. Attractions include Big Red's Cafe, Bob's Gun and Ammo, Drive In Liquors, Riviera of Hudson Beauty Salon, and an aging Sinclair sign painted on the side of a brick building. Hudson has a distinct sense of decay, with boarded-up shops along the main drag, but off the main drag are quiet, cottonwood-lined streets, simple frame homes, and gardens filled with tall yellow sunflowers. This place is full of character and characters.

Hudson was established in 1905 and became a major coal-mining center in the early part of this century before the mines closed. Most of those who settled were European emigrants, and the town still maintains a strong ethnic flavor; the old fire truck says "Dago Red" on the front. Nowhere is this ethnic heritage as evident as in the two Yugoslavian-run steakhouses that attract folks from all over the state. **Svilar's,** tel. 332-4516, is the oldest, and its owners are staunchly Republican. Mama Bessie Svilar founded the restaurant in the 1920s to serve the hungry local miners, but soon travelers began going out of their way to visit tiny Hudson. Restaurant critic Red Fenwick noted that Svilar's "put Hudson on the map in big red letters that dripped with gravy and honey and meat juices." Mama Svilar died in 1981, but the food is still great, and the bar remains a popular place for drinks.

Just across the road is **Club El Toro,** tel. 332-4627, owned by the Vinich family and offering similarly fine steaks and other hearty fare.

The homemade ravioli hors d'oeuvres are a speciality. John Vinich is a gadfly Democratic state senator who ran for the U.S. Senate in 1988, losing to Malcolm Wallop by only 1,165 votes out of nearly 180,000 cast. The Vinich family also owns **Union Bar,** just across the street, another very popular local hangout. El Toro has live C&W music on weekends. After stuffing yourself at Svilar's or Club El Toro, ask about the badlands country east of Hudson. Some fascinating eroded formations are just a few miles out.

LANDER

Friendly Lander (pop. 7,000) lies along the banks of the Popo Agie River, with the majestic Wind River Mountains rising just to the west. The town has a state training school for the mentally ill that employs more than 600 people. Also important are government, ranching, and construction-related jobs. Lander is smaller and more homey than nearby Riverton and has become something of a center for those who love the outdoors. The relatively mild winters here make it an attractive place to retire, and Lander's proximity to the Popo Agie Wilderness (see pp. 245-246) makes it a jumping-off place for mountain treks into the high country.

History

Lander began in 1869 when the Army established a small military post, Camp Augur (later Camp Brown), to protect Shoshones from attacks by the Sioux and Arapaho. The rich valley along the Popo Agie River proved easy to irrigate and grew ample crops to feed hungry miners in nearby South Pass. Settlers moved here from the dying gold mines of South Pass in the late 1870s, creating the crossroads settlement of Pushroot (later renamed Lander after Colonel Frederick W. Lander, who had surveyed the Oregon Trail's Lander Cutoff). The town grew more rapidly once the railroad arrived in 1906, but it took local farmers a while to adjust. When the first train rolled into town, people crowded around, and the engineer jokingly yelled from his cab, "Stand back, I'm gonna turn around." The crowd scattered in fear. During the 1960s and '70s, Lander became a mining boomtown as

hundreds of workers commuted to the Columbia-Geneva iron mine and mill near Atlantic City. The mine closed in 1983.

Sights

The **Pioneer Museum,** 630 Lincoln St., tel. 332-4137, is open Mon.-Fri. 10-6 and Sat.-Sun. 1-4 from June to mid-September. The rest of the year its doors are open Mon.-Fri. 1-5 and Sat. 1-4. No charge. Pioneer Museum first opened in 1915, and the original log cabin still comprises its core. The museum houses an outstanding collection of Indian artifacts, including buffalo robes, a sun-dance pole, beaded gloves, painted buffalo hides, and a squaw saddle. The skull of Harvey Morgan—a local farmer killed in an 1870 Indian raid in Deadman Gulch (east of Lander)—is also in the museum, with the 10-inch wagon bolt still gruesomely driven through it. A skilled marksman, he had fired off more than 200 rounds from his rifle before his death. For something completely different, peek in the tiny wedding chapel, popular for spring nuptials. Another room, the One-Shot Antelope Hunt Memorial Room, is devoted to this bizarre sport with its own celebrities.

Accommodations

See the chart for Lander's motels and bed and breakfasts. Camping is free at **Lander City Park,** 405 Fremont St., right along the banks of the Popo Agie River. Pitch tents on the shady grass here or park vehicles in the lot. Local high schoolers often park here for a bit of extracurricular activity, so don't expect a quiet night. **Sinks Canyon State Park,** 10 miles southwest of Lander on State 131, has two campgrounds ($4); see p. 218 for details. There are three private campgrounds in the Lander area. **Rocky Acres Campground,** five miles northwest on US 287, tel. 332-6953, charges $9 for tents and $12 for RVs. **Ray Lake Campground,** nine miles northwest on US 287, tel. 332-9333, charges $7 for tents or $13 for RVs; open May-September. Showers for noncampers are $2. **K-Bar Ranch Campground,** 10 miles southeast on US 287, tel. 332-3836, has tent sites for $8 and RV hookups for $12. Noncampers can use the showers for $2; open year-round.

Food

Highwayman Cafe on the south end of town, tel. 332-4628, has great sourdough pancakes for breakfast. Another favorite breakfast place is **The Maverick,** 808 Main St., tel. 332-4868, where you'll also find excellent prime rib at dinner. On weekends, head to **The Showboat** at First and Main for breakfast or lunch; their all-you-can-eat buffet is the best deal going. **Tony's Pizza Shack,** 637 Main, tel. 332-3900, makes good pizzas using homemade dough; their breadsticks are a local favorite. Get deli sandwiches at **The Breadboard,** 125 E. Main, tel.

Main St., Lander, circa 1883

332-6090, and decent Thai food at **The Loft,** 351 Main St., tel. 332-3102.

Judd's Grub Drive-In, 634 Main, tel. 332-9680, has the best fast food in town (including an enormous one-pound burger and fresh strawberry shakes), as the high school kids will attest. Carhop service too! **The Hitching Rack,** half a mile south on US 287, tel. 332-4322, has a big salad bar and homemade soups. This is the place locals go out for steak and seafood dinners (not open for other meals). Actually, two of the most popular night-out places are 10 miles northeast in Hudson: Svilar's and Club El Toro.

Recreation
When most folks think of recreation in Lander, they think of the wonderful mountain country just a few miles away. See pp. 245-246 for more on the Popo Agie part of the Wind River Mountains. Lander's Olympic-size **swimming pool,** 450 S. Ninth, tel. 332-2272, is open year-round and costs $1.75 for adults, kids 75 cents-$1.25, and seniors free. A weight room and hydrotherapy pool are also here. **Freewheel Sports,** 149 Main, tel. 332-6616, rents mountain bikes ($15/day) as well as cross-country skis. The nine-hole **Lander Golf and Country Club** is on Capitol Hill, tel. 332-4653. During the winter, skate for free at City Park, where you'll also find a warming hut and skate rentals.

Great Divide Tours, 336 Focht Rd., tel. 332-3123 or (800) 458-1915, provides a wide range of enjoyable horseback and wagon trips, including cattle drives, Oregon Trail rides, and trips into Hole-in-the-Wall country—Butch Cassidy's lair. These excellent five-to-seven-day treks cost $750-950 pp.

NOLS
Because of its proximity to the glorious Wind River Mountains, Lander has become a center for the environmental movement in Wyoming. The best-known organization is the National Outdoors Leadership School (NOLS), located in a brick building at 288 Main St., tel. 332-6973. Open Tues., Wed., and Fri. in the summer. NOLS was founded in 1964 by Paul Petzoldt, who participated in the 1938 attempt on K2, setting an American altitude record.

NOLS was established to offer classes in wilderness living skills that would lead people to respect their environment and that would go beyond the Outward Bound emphasis upon survival. Over the years, NOLS folks have achieved a reputation as the purists in the field, emphasizing low-impact camping and respect for the land. Today the school offers classes all over the world, lasting from two weeks to three months, and covering everything from wilderness horsepacking to East African mountaineering. Equipment can be rented from NOLS for the classes. College credit is available, as is a limited amount

LANDER ACCOMMODATIONS

MOTEL	ADDRESS	TELEPHONE	RATE	FEATURES
Downtown Motel	569 Main St.	332-5220	$22 s, $24 d	pool, open June-Sept.
Maverick Motel	808 Main	332-2821	$26 s, $28 d	
Horseshoe Motel	685 Main	332-4915	$27 s, $32 d	
Pioneer Court Motel	Sixth and Lincoln	332-2821	$28 s, $36 d	kitchenettes $8 extra
Edna's Bed & Breakfast	five miles north	332-3175	$28 s, $40 d	working ranch
Western Motel	151 N. Ninth	332-4270	$30+ s or d	kitchenettes
Silver Spur Motel	340 N. 10th	332-5189	$30 s, $32 d	AAA-approved, pool, kitchenettes
Teton Motel	586 Main St.	332-3582	$30 s, $39 d	kitchenettes $45
Empty Nest B&B	1355 S. First.	332-7516	$55 s, $65 d	full breakfast
Holiday Lodge	210 McFarlane Dr.	332-2511	$35 s, $39 d	AAA-approved, whirlpool, kitchenettes $5 extra
Pronghorn Lodge (Budget Host)	150 E. Main St.	332-3940 (800) 999-5233	$37 s, $40 d	AAA-approved, whirlpool
Country Fare B&B	904 Main	332-9604	$40 s, $50 d	historic, full breakfast, open May-Oct.

of financial aid. For more info and a catalog of classes, write NOLS at P.O. Box AA, Lander, WY 82520.

Other Environmental Groups

Also in Lander is the **Wyoming Outdoor Council,** an organization founded in 1967 that emphasizes conservation education and environmental lobbying, especially on such issues as wilderness, wildlife, growth impacts, and waste management. Tax-deductible memberships start at $15 a year. Their address is 201 Main (or P.O. Box 1449), tel. 332-7031. **The Nature Conservancy** has its Wyoming state office at 258 Main, tel. 332-2971. Most of its 17,000 acres are conservation easements or cooperative projects rather than preserves.

Entertainment

Barney's, 432 US 287, tel. 332-7742, often has country tunes or DJ music on weekends, while **One Shot Lounge,** 695 Main, tel. 332-2692, occasionally offers rock and roll. Also check **The Hitching Rack,** half a mile south on US 287, tel. 332-4322, and Hudson's **Club El Toro** for live bands. As a side note, the present **Stock-grower's Bar** at 202 Main (not the original name), was a hangout for the outlaw Butch Cassidy. It was built in 1886 and has C&W music some nights. Befitting its history, the clientele is sometimes on the tough side.

Events

Lander hosts the **Wyoming State Winter Fair** the last weekend in January, with livestock exhibits, dog weight-pulling contests, horse shows, entertainment, and dancing. In early June the **Popo Agie Rendezvous** commemorates the 1829 rendezvous held near here. **Pioneer Days,** a three-day party in early July, is Lander's big event. There is a big parade with dozens of floats, marching bands, vintage autos, and performers, along with Indian dancing, street dances, and evening fireworks. The primary event is the **rodeo,** the oldest paid rodeo anywhere on earth, first established in 1893. Other roping events are held every Wednesday night between late June and August.

The **One-Shot Antelope Hunt** attracts hunters each September, as teams of three head out to see how quickly they can bring down an antelope with just one shot. The governors of

Wyoming and Colorado are "team captains," and celebrities sometimes participate. All sorts of convoluted rules and ridiculous ceremonies make this akin to fraternity initiation rites. Old men find strange ways to amuse themselves.

Getting Jaded

The Jeffrey City area (60 miles east of Lander) is world-famous for its nephrite jade, a mineral found only in Asia, British Columbia, and Wyoming. The jade comes from Crooks Mountain, and much of it was discovered in the 1930s and '40s by Bert Rhoads, who established **Rhoads' Jewelry,** 423 Main, tel. 332-4439. His wife Verla discovered the largest piece of jade ever found—a 3,366-pound boulder that required heavy mining equipment to haul out. Wyoming jade varies greatly in value depending upon the color and the rarity. Some of it sells for around $7.50 a pound, while Wyoming emerald jade can sell for several thousand dollars per karat. Warning: Much of the jewelry sold as "Wyoming jade" actually comes from British Columbia. Buy only from reputable dealers.

Shopping

You'll find unusual homemade lodgepole beds, chairs, tables, and other furniture at **Mountain Breeze,** 875 Lincoln, tel. 332-2160 or (800) 371-2738. **The Booke Shoppe,** 160 N. Second, tel. 332-6221, has a selection of books on Wyoming, and **Cabin Fever Books,** 163 S. Fifth,

tel. 332-9580, offers both new and used titles. **Kottage Krafts,** 343 Main, tel. 332-9722, sells handmade gifts, including Shoshone and Arapaho beadwork. Stop by **Wild Iris Mountain Sports,** 325 Main St., tel. 332-4541, for quality outdoor gear and climbing books. The owner, Todd Skinner, is a world-renowned rock-climber, and the shop is managed by another well-known climber, Amy Whisler (find them on the North Face posters). There is also a climbers' bulletin board in the shop. **Camera Corral,** 329 Main St., tel. 332-2432, is one of the most complete photo stores in Wyoming.

Information And Services

The **Lander Chamber of Commerce** office is in the old railroad depot at 160 N. First St., tel. 332-3892 or (800) 433-0662 (outside Wyoming), and is open Mon.-Fri. 9-6, Sat. 9-noon in summer, and Mon.-Fri. 9-5 the rest of the year. Ask here for directions to the nearby prairie-dog town. **Fremont County Library,** Second and Amoretti, tel. 332-5194, is open Mon., Tues., and Thurs. 12-9, Wed. 9-9, Fri. 9-4 throughout the year, plus Sat. 9-1 in winter. The **BLM District Office** is at 125 Sunflower St., tel. 332-7822, and the Forest Service's **Lander District Office** is at 600 N. US 287, tel. 332-5460. Stop here for Shoshone National Forest maps and hiking information. The closest airport is in Riverton. Rent cars from **Fremont Motors,** 161 State 789, tel. 332-4355.

LANDER VICINITY

EAST ON US 287

A few miles east of Lander on US 287, the highway passes an impressive vermillion sandstone butte. Near here is a beautiful century-old red-rock barn that once stabled horses used on the stage route through here. In 1884, Wyoming's **first oil well** was drilled not far away. The site—now called the Dallas oil field—was known to Indians and had been described in Washington Irving's *Adventures of Captain Bonneville* as the "Great Tar Springs." Nineteenth-century emigrants used the oil to grease wagon axles, for lamps, or as a balm for their aches. Mountain

man Osborne Russell described coming across the spring in 1837:

This spring produces about one gallon per hour of pure oil of Coal or rather Coal Tar the scent of which is often carried on the wind 5 or 6 mls. The Oil issues from the ground within 30 feet of the stream and runs off slowly into the water Camp stopped here eight days We set fire to the spring when there was 2 or 3 Bbls. of oil on the ground about it, it burnt very quick and clear but produced a dense column of thick black smoke the oil above ground being consumed the fire soon went out. This is a beauti-

*ful country thickly clothed with grass inter-
mingled with flowers of every hue. On the west
rises the Wind River range of Mountains
abruptly from the smooth rolling hills until
crowned with Snow above the Clouds On the
East stretches away the Great Wind River plain
and terminates at a low range of Mountains
rising betwen Wind and Powder Rivers.*

As you continue eastward, the Wind River
Mountains gradually diminish in magnitude. Stop
to look up at them for a while. It is easy to see
how the pioneers from the east—where a mountain is anything over 1,000 feet—would watch
these mountains grow closer with each day's
travel and wonder at their rugged crowns. It's
also easy to see why they would choose to
cross around the southern end of this range
(South Pass) instead of over it.

Ice Slough

Forty miles east of Lander, the highway passes
a marker describing Ice Slough, one of many
landmarks along this portion of the Oregon Trail.
Dense grasses in a small marsh kept ice all
through the summer, a real treat for emigrants
on a hot summer day. In *Roughing It,* Mark
Twain described Ice Slough as follows:

*In the night we sailed by a most notable cu-
riosity, and one we had been hearing a good
deal about for a day or two, and were suffering
to see. This was what might be called a natural
ice-house. It was August, now, and sweltering
weather in the daytime, yet at one of the stations the men could scrape the soil on the hillside under the lee of a range of boulders, and at
a depth of six inches cut out pure blocks of ice
—hard, compactly frozen, and clear as crystal.*

Jeffrey City

The bleak, almost-ghost town of Jeffrey City is a
casualty of the bust that followed the uranium-
mining boom of the 1970s. First called Home
on the Range, the town was renamed for a
Rawlins philanthropist, Dr. Charles W. Jeffrey.
The town was built on the nuclear industry, and
as a company town its survival was tied to the
fortunes of Western Nuclear Company. By 1980,

the population had swollen to 3,000. Today,
weeds grow through the concrete sidewalks
around the empty bunkhouses, and Home on
the Range Restaurant, Coats Motel, Drillers'
Delite Lounge, and Jeffrey City Grocery are
all closed. Only a gas station and a bar remain
on this remote stretch of highway. The modern
grade school looks rather forlorn in all this desolation. Ranching, oil, and gas keep Jeffrey
City from drying up and blowing away. Rock-
hounds should ask for directions to the famed
jade deposits around Jeffrey City, but make
sure you're on public land or have permission
from landowners.

East of Jeffrey City lies definitive Wyoming
country with rolling sage and grassland, a few
weathered old homesteads, and distant mountains on all sides. **Cottonwood Campground**
($4; open June-Oct.), a BLM facility, is six miles
east of Jeffrey City and then eight miles south on
Green Mountain Loop Road. You aren't likely to
meet many folks here. See "Central Wyoming,"
pp. 202-204, for more on the country east of
Jeffrey City (including Castle Gardens).

SINKS CANYON AND
THE LOOP ROAD

State 131 climbs south from Lander through
fascinating Sinks Canyon and then over the
mountains to Atlantic City. A popular loop trip is
to follow this road to Atlantic City, returning to
Lander via State 28, a total distance of 56 miles.
(See map on p. 247.) Plan to spend at least a full
day if you want to savor the many sights along
the way. Locally this is known as the Loop Road,
and it is very popular with both visitors and residents. Bighorn sheep were transplanted into
Sinks Canyon in 1987 and are common sights
along the road. Rock-climbers practice their
skills on the steep cliffs of the canyon. Several
campgrounds are here, along with lots of lakes,
trails, and big mountain country. Get to State
131 by heading south on Lander's Fifth Street.
Sinks Canyon begins seven miles away.

The Sinks

The Popo Agie River (usually pronounced po-
PO-zha, but you'll hear lots of other versions) begins in the snowfields of the Wind River Moun-

tains, dropping northeast to its junction with the Wind River near Riverton. **Sinks Canyon State Park** contains one of Wyoming's geological wonders. Here the Middle Fork of the Popo Agie plunges into a cave (the "Sinks"), only to emerge again a half-mile down in a gigantic spring (the "Rise"). The river's name—Popo Agie—is a Crow Indian word meaning "Beginning of the Waters." The stream originally flowed above ground, and still does during high spring runoff, but over time a cave formed in the water-soluble Madison Limestone that underlies this region, allowing the water to disappear into underground caverns. The path connecting the two must be a convoluted one, however. In 1983, researchers put dye in the Sinks. The dye did reappear at the rise, but not until two hours later! Lots of fat rainbow and brown trout congregate in the pool at the Rise, waiting for visitors to toss them bits of food. A vending machine sells fish food (fish do not live by bread alone). No fishing allowed. Also keep your eyes open for the muskrat that lives in the spring here.

Sinks Visitor Center, tel. 332-3077, houses displays of fish and animals, along with geological exhibits. Open daily 8-7 during the summer only. The windows face down this steep-walled canyon, offering dramatic vistas. The cave into which the stream disappears is directly behind the visitor center. This area is a fine place to watch birds. Look for dippers—the odd birds that walk underwater—on the rocks above the Sinks.

Three campgrounds are nearby: state-run **Sawmill Campground** and **Popo Agie Campground** ($4; open May-Oct.), and just up the road, the Forest Service's **Sinks Canyon Campground** ($5; open June-October). Get brochures at the visitor center for the mile-long **nature trail** near Popo Agie Campground. More interesting is the **Popo Agie Falls Trail,** which takes off from Bruce Picnic Ground, a mile above Popo Agie Campground. This 1 1/2-mile trail climbs 600 feet in elevation to a series of attractive waterfalls, the largest being 60 feet. Horses and mountain bikes are allowed on the trail. During the winter, skiers enjoy groomed cross-country trails in the canyon.

Into The Mountains

Beyond the state park, the road turns to gravel and switchbacks steeply up the canyon's south face. The Owl Creek Mountains—50 miles to the north—are visible from the overlook. The road is washboarded in sections, so be ready for a buckin'-bronc ride—and lots of traffic on summer weekends. The rough ride is made worthwhile by excellent vistas and several attractive lakes (enlarged by dams). This is primarily lodgepole and limber pine country, but around Louis Lake you'll discover some huge old Engelmann spruce and subalpine fir trees.

TIE HACKS

Many of the trees cut in Wyoming's forests between 1870 and 1940 went to supply railroad ties for an ever-expanding network of rails throughout the Rockies. The men who cut these ties—tie hacks—spent long, hard months in the mountains, working through the winter. Many of the woodsmen were emigrants from Sweden, Norway, Finland, Austria, and Italy. Tie hacks first felled a suitable lodgepole pine using a bucksaw, and then limbed the tree and used a broadax to hew the tie into shape, finally peeling the remaining bark from the sides and cutting it to length. Hundreds of thousands of ties—each eight feet long and at least five inches on both sides—were produced each year by tie hacks. Horses were used to drag the ties down to a creek bank or flume to await high spring flows when thousands of ties could be sent downriver at once. (The enormous log jams that resulted sometimes required dynamite to loosen.) Downstream booms caught the logs where they could be hauled up and loaded onto railway cars.

Tie hacks found work in many parts of Wyoming, but especially in the Medicine Bow Mountains, Laramie Mountains, Sierra Madre, Big Horn Mountains, and Wind River Mountains, where major streams provided a way for the ties to reach the railheads. In the upper Wind River country, the industry spanned three decades, from 1914 to 1946, and more than 10 million ties were cut and floated downstream to Riverton, where they were used by the Chicago and Northwestern Railroad. A stone monument to the tie hacks stands along US 26-287, approximately 18 miles west of Dubois.

The Forest Service maintains four fine campgrounds ($5) at **Fiddler's Lake, Worthen Meadows, Little Popo Agie Creek,** and **Louis Lake.** Fiddler's Lake has handicapped-accessible facilities and is the highest (9,400 feet). Louis Lake is easily the most popular, made more scenic by a sharp granite cliff that rises directly behind the lake. Good fishing for brown and Mackinaw trout, and moose are commonly seen around the lake's margins. During the summer, **Louis Lake Lodge,** tel. 332-4324, rents very rustic four-person cabins (oil lanterns and handmade furnishings), as well as horses, canoes, and boats. Other folks car camp around Frye Lake or off the road. A number of hiking trails head west from Loop Rd. to the lake-dotted Popo Agie Wilderness (see pp. 245-246).

South from Louis Lake the road opens into a high plateau with limber pine trees and wide vistas south to the Oregon Buttes. Antelope are common in the sagebrush country, while moose are seen in the aspen stands along the road and in the marshes around Fiddler's Lake. The Loop Road meets State 28 beside the now-abandoned U.S. Steel iron-ore mine. From here you can continue back to Lander on the highway or visit the historic South Pass area (see pp. 246-252).

WIND RIVER RESERVATION

At 2.2 million acres, the Wind River Reservation is one of America's largest Indian reservations. It is home to both the Northern Arapaho and the Eastern Shoshone tribes and reaches some 70 miles from north to south, 55 miles from east to west. You'll find some of the most unforgettable vistas in Wyoming here: fabulous badlands on the western edge; the beautiful Wind River, where the cottonwoods glow a brilliant yellow in the cool fall air; deep green irrigated pastures where horses, sheep, and cattle graze; and desolate, wide-open spaces where only cactus, sagebrush, jackrabbits, and rattlesnakes grow. Bright yellow sunflowers add color to the roadsides in late summer, and horses seem to be everywhere. All this is backdropped by the enormous, snowcapped Wind River Mountains. It is said that the eminent guide Jim Bridger attempted to convince Brigham Young that this basin would be a far better home for the Mormons than the deserts around Salt Lake. Young refused to listen. It is just as well, for this was—and still is—Indian country.

The Wind River Reservation was the scene for the classic Zane Grey Western, *War Paint,* a film that featured both Tim McCoy and hun-

dreds of Arapaho and Shoshone Indians. Today, hundreds of people, both Indian and nonnative, come to watch a different form of entertainment: the many powwows that occur throughout the summer months on the Wind River Reservation. The annual sun-dance ceremonies are more intense, spiritual events where outsiders are only tolerated. The Shoshone and Arapaho peoples maintain separate sun dances and powwows; absolutely no cameras or tape recorders are allowed during the sun dances.

One of the most heated legal battles in recent Wyoming history focused on water from the Wind River. In 1989, the U.S. Supreme Court awarded the Shoshone and Arapaho tribes rights to nearly half the river's flow, based upon an 1868 treaty. The tribes then dedicated a substantial portion of the water to instream flows to develop a world-class fishery. Farmers dependent upon this water are angry that they may be left high and dry in some years, but the tribes counter that for years that is exactly what the farmers were doing to the local fish. Don't bring the topic up in a Riverton bar.

Despite the close proximity of the reservation to Lander and Riverton, very little interaction

CHIEF WASHAKIE

The history of Wyoming during the 19th century is one of constant battles between Indians and the invading white settlers. Only one tribe—the Shoshone—provided an exception to this rule. The reason for this stems from Chief Washakie (pronounced WASH-a-key), a man whose life spanned the entire tumultuous century. Washakie was born around 1798 of Shoshone and Flathead parents. His birth name was Pina Quanah, but later in life he gained the name Washakie—literally, "The Rattler"—a reference to a rawhide buffalo rattle he used to scare Sioux ponies during his daring raids. Because his father was killed by the Blackfeet tribe, Washakie lived something of an orphan's existence, growing up among both the Lemhi and Bannock tribes. He eventually joined the Eastern Shoshones and quickly proved himself as a fearless and extraordinary warrior.

In the 1830s, Washakie—fluent in sign language—met and became a close friend of famed mountain man Jim Bridger, and one of his daughters became Bridger's third wife. From Bridger, Washakie learned a few words of English and a realization that a union with whites against his enemies was wiser than trying to fight the countless hordes coming across the plains from the east. Around 1843, after the death of the previous chief, Washakie gained control over a band of Shoshones based in the Upper Green River. As their lifelong chief, he was recognized as an extraordinarily intelligent, kindhearted, and forceful leader. Because of his consistent support, Washakie was sought out by white settlers whenever trouble appeared with other tribes.

Washakie's people had been devastated over the years by smallpox, cholera, and other diseases, and they were no match against the Sioux, Cheyenne, and Arapaho. Because of this, he viewed an allegiance with whites as a way to drive back other tribes. When some of his young warriors began to complain that the old man was losing his warrior abilities and becoming a lackey, Washakie disappeared for a few weeks and returned with seven enemy scalps. The grumbling ended. Those who joined in with others who attacked whites became instant outcasts.

In 1876, Washakie's Shoshones joined with General Crook against the Sioux and Cheyenne in the Battle of the Rosebud. The battle was a standoff, but Washakie's sage advice almost certainly prevented Crook's troops from facing what befell General Custer one week later. When President Chester A. Arthur visited Wyoming in 1883, he asked Chief Washakie to meet him at a reception in Fort Washakie. The proud chief demurred, instead insisting that the president come to him. They met in Washakie's tipi.

Chief Washakie died on the Wind River Reservation on Feb. 22, 1900, and was buried with full U.S. military honors, the only Indian chief ever to be so honored. He was 102 years old and had led his people for over 60 years. With Washakie's death died the tradition of having one man as chief of the Shoshones. Although his name is not nearly as well-known today as that of Red Cloud or Crazy Horse, Washakie deserves a place as one of the great warriors and peacemakers of history. A dozen different Wyoming places are named in his honor, including the Washakie Wilderness and Mount Washakie.

Chief Washakie

goes on between Indians and nonnatives except in business situations. After more than 120 years, the various cultures—Arapaho, Shoshone, and Anglo—are still like oil and water. Whites regard the Indians as disorganized, drunken, and lazy. Indians view whites as pushy, materialistic, selfish, and disrespectful. Relations are not a whole lot better between the Shoshones and Arapaho, who still view each other with an animosity born of constant warfare during the 19th century.

SHOSHONE HISTORY

Originally peoples of the Great Basin, the Shoshones first entered southwestern Wyoming in the 16th century, gradually pushing northward until they controlled most of the land now known as Wyoming, along with territory all the way into Canada. As they moved onto the Plains, and with the acquisition of the horse, Shoshone life changed drastically, from a simple Stone-Age culture of grubbing for roots and eating whatever they could catch by hand to a sophisticated buffalo-centered livelihood. Because Shoshone culture extended far to the south, they came into contact with Spanish traders and were some of the first Indians to have horses. The Shoshone introduced horses to the northern plains region around 1700, forever transforming Plains Indian culture. To the trappers and traders who first encountered the Shoshone, they were known as the Snakes, because of their serpentinelike hand signals used to signify their tribal name. The word *Shoshone* refers to the simple willow-and-sagebrush lodges in which they lived before the great flowering of their culture in the 18th and 19th centuries. The Eastern Shoshone occupied western Wyoming, while their cousins the Western Shoshone lived in Idaho.

In the late 18th century, the expanding Shoshone culture was halted when their enemies—the Sioux, Crow, and Arapaho—forced the Shoshone west of the Laramie Mountains. The Wind River and Fort Bridger vicinities became wintering areas. After a spring sun dance and buffalo hunt, the various tribal members would move into the mountains of northern Utah to hunt, fish, and gather berries and roots. Each fall the entire tribe would gather in the Great Divide Basin and head across the Continental Divide for the fall buffalo hunt in the Wind River and Bighorn basins. Led by Chief Washakie, the Eastern Shoshone—unlike most other Plains Indians—maintained an unbroken friendship with the invading whites.

Onto The Reservation

The Shoshones were not recognized in the great Fort Laramie Treaty of 1851, and the Wind River Basin and Bighorn Basin where they had long lived were assigned to the Crows. The Fort Bridger Treaty of 1863 gave the Shoshones and Bannocks a reservation covering parts of Colorado, Utah, Wyoming, and Idaho. In 1868, this enormous 45-million-acre spread was whittled down to just the Wind River region (with the Bannocks given a separate Idaho reservation).

Several years later, the government lopped off 600,000 acres around the rich gold region of South Pass City, giving Chief Washakie $500 a year and $5000 worth of cattle for five years (around four cents an acre). More land was ceded to the government in 1897 (Thermopolis Hot Springs) for $60,000, and in 1905, 1.4 million acres were opened to homesteaders north of the Wind River. In exchange for the latter, the Shoshones and Arapaho received per-capita payments, schools, payment for water rights, and an irrigation system on what remained of their reservation. This area is now one of the state's most important agricultural regions.

In 1878, Wyoming's territorial governor asked Chief Washakie if the destitute Arapaho—archenemies of the Shoshone—could be allowed to stay temporarily on the Wind River Reservation. Washakie's sympathetic heart finally gave in:

It is plain they can go no further now. Take them down to where Popo Agie walks into Wind River and let them stay until the grass comes again. But when the grass comes again take them off my reservation. I want my words written down on paper with the white man's ink. I want all you to sign as witnesses to what I have said. And I want a copy of that paper. I have spoken.

Despite this agreement, the "temporary" arrangement became permanent, and urgent pleas by Washakie went unheeded. Once again the government had abused its most loyal friend.

Many years after Chief Washakie's death, the Shoshones sued over this gross injustice. In 1937, the tribe was awarded $6.4 million for the land given to the Arapaho, minus the expenses for every building ever built by the government on the fort and any services rendered. The cheapskate federal government even deducted $125 for a silver saddle given by President Grant to Chief Washakie as a token of appreciation! What was left amounted to a grand total of $2350 per capita, distributed almost entirely in various BIA-run programs.

ARAPAHO HISTORY

The Arapaho—a Blackfeet Indian term meaning "Tattooed People"—always called themselves simply "Our People." They originally lived a farming life in what is now central Minnesota, but the arrival of whites on the East Coast created a domino effect among eastern Indians, pushing tribes westward on top of each other. Because of this pressure, the Arapaho, along with the Sioux and Crow, migrated onto the Great Plains in the late 18th century. They quickly adopted the nomadic life associated with Plains Indian culture, a life centered on the buffalo and made possible by the horse. Pressure from the Sioux (who numbered perhaps 25,000 individuals, versus 3,000 Arapaho) forced the Arapaho to join with the Cheyenne and move south to the Arkansas and Platte river regions.

Around 1830, the Arapaho split into northern and southern divisions, due in part to the establishment of Fort Laramie on the Laramie River (Wyoming) and Bent's Fort on the Arkansas River (Colorado). For many years, the Northern Arapaho wintered in northern Colorado, scattering along the North Platte River

with the coming of spring and then gathering again in late summer to hunt buffalo and prepare for winter. In the 1851 Fort Laramie Treaty, the Arapaho and Cheyenne tribes were assigned the area east of the Rockies between the Arkansas and North Platte rivers, but as gold was discovered in the Rockies, whites began to push the Arapaho off this land.

After Cheyenne and Arapaho warriors began raiding white ranches in Colorado during the early 1860s, the governor demanded action. In the Sand Creek Massacre of 1864, a peaceful Cheyenne and Arapaho village was viciously attacked by U.S. cavalry soldiers under Colonel John M. Chivington. The action sparked a massive retaliation as Arapaho, Sioux, and Cheyenne warriors sacked Julesburg, Colorado, tore down miles of telegraph wire, stampeded cattle herds, and burned ranch and stage stations throughout the Rockies.

After this, the Arapaho shifted their living patterns, spending winters along Wyoming's Powder River and summers in the Medicine Bow country to the south. They continued to attack Shoshones on the Wind River Reservation, emigrant trains along the Overland Trail, and miners around South Pass until the early 1870s, but gradually lessened their raids as the futility of their condition became more apparent.

The end came in the Bates Battle of 1874, when the Shoshones and the U.S. Army attacked the Arapaho, leaving them demoralized and without horses or supplies. In the late 1870s, many Arapaho served as Army scouts, and some even joined an Arapaho unit of the Army during the 1880s. Best-known of the Arapaho scouts was Friday, an orphan Arapaho boy adopted by mountain man and Indian agent Thomas Fitzpatrick and taught in eastern schools. He returned to his tribe, becoming their most important translator and a force for peace. It was probably Friday's friendship with Chief Washakie that led Washakie to finally tolerate Arapaho on his reservation.

Onto The Reservation

With the buffalo gone and their way of life under constant pressure from white settlers and the deadly diseases they brought, the Arapaho were in desperate straits, shuttling from one temporary home to another. The government refused to set aside a separate reservation, insisting that they live with the Cheyenne in Oklahoma or with the Sioux in South Dakota, far from their Wyoming home.

In 1878, the Northern Arapaho were shoehorned onto the Wind River Reservation with their hated enemies in what was to be a "temporary" stay. Only 913 Arapaho remained—mostly women and children—from the tribe that had once been so powerful. (Interestingly, the Arapaho now outnumber the Shoshones on the reservation.) The two bands of Arapaho that settled on the Wind River Reservation were led by Chief Black Coal (whose people settled in present-day Arapahoe) and Chief Sharp Nose (whose people settled around present-day Ethete).

The two tribes continue to jointly occupy the Wind River Reservation, with the Arapaho holding the eastern half (the towns of Ethete and Arapahoe) and the Shoshones in the west (the towns of Fort Washakie, Burris, and Crowheart). In 1891, the Arapaho were given equal rights on the reservation, despite Shoshone Chief Washakie's continued attempts to have them removed. Although Chief Washakie's son married an Arapaho woman, there is still very little intermarriage between the tribes and almost no blending of the two cultures, even after more than a century.

POWWOWS

CATHY CARLSON

The Indian "powwow" (an Algonquian term meaning "medicine man") is a colorful celebration of Native American culture that cuts across tribal boundaries. Nobody knows the exact origin of powwows, but they may have developed from the Grass Dance of the Omaha and Pawnee tribes, who passed the dance on to various Plains tribes. The dance was used as a way of communicating with the Great Spirit, and the rhythmic beat of the drum helped send prayers skyward. Buffalo Bill Cody first introduced Indian dancers to audiences all over America and Europe, and in 1887 the Ponca Tribe began the first Indian fair and powwow. Other tribes joined in, and powwows became increasingly popular with the coming of the 20th century. The creation of "fancy dancing" allowed more personalized costumes and dances. Women were allowed to dance, and by the 1940s, Indians began traveling long distances to join other tribal powwows.

Dancers perform to a beat set up by different groups of drummers, who sing a repetitious song as they beat out the rhythm. The chant evokes images of somber ceremonies far out on the plains, and of a lost culture. The dances originated from different tribes but have been adapted using the more colorful synthetic fabrics and beads of today. Professional dancers travel a circuit throughout the western states, and even non-Indians take part in powwows. Contestants wear numbers similar to those at track meets or rodeos and compete for cash awards.

RESERVATION LIFE

In the early reservation years every effort was made to break the spirit of the "savages" and to make them into red-skinned Europeans (today's derogatory term is "Apples"—red on the outside, white on the inside). Even that most basic attribute, one's name, was taken away in the 1890s by the Commissioner of Indian Affairs. Thus, Yellow Calf became George Caldwell and Night Horse became Henry Lee Tyler. Even William Shakespeare and Cornelius Vanderbilt suddenly became tribal members! (The effort was not entirely successful since William Shakespeare was credited with bringing Peyotism—an important Native American religion today—to the Wind River Reservation.) Other measures helped weaken the culture, including the repression of Native religious practices, indoctrination by Christian missionaries, banning of face painting, and the forced cutting of young boys' long black hair. Today, the nation is paying the price for these all-too-successful attempts to destroy Native American culture.

Most of the 4,500 Arapaho and 2,500 Shoshones live in housing built by the tribal council or in the hundreds of mobile homes that dot the reservation. From a non-Indian point of view, they are decidedly untidy, with junk of all sorts piled outside; but then, the folks who live here really don't care what outsiders think. Older log cabins can be found all over the back roads, their sod roofs collapsing and their log walls slowly returning to the earth. A number of missions are scattered throughout this area, marked

Traditional And Fancy Dancing

Two main styles of powwow dance exist. In **traditional dancing**, the movements are slow and graceful, with an adherence to more authentic costumes and traditional dance steps. Male dancers wear bustles of eagle feathers, representing the birds of prey that once gathered over battlefields to feed on dead warriors. They also wear a head roach made from porcupine guard hairs. **Fancy dancing** is more casual, sort of an anything-goes dance in which the steps are decided by the individual dancers. It generally involves lots of spins, bows, and head movements. Men's costumes are equally free-form, with all sorts of gaudy additions, particularly colorful bustles added to the shoulders and arms. Women's costumes for both traditional and fancy dancing are not as showy as the men's, although they do include bells, elk teeth (or plastic copies), and shell decorations on the dresses, along with shawls, and necklaces of hairpipe.

Powwow Activities

The Wind River Reservation has a half-dozen powwows throughout the year, all but one of which are held outdoors. Tipis are set up and the event becomes a joyful celebration of life and culture. These are three-day-weekend events that involve not just singing and dancing, but traditional games, parades, and a "giveaway ceremony." Activities last all day and late into the evening. Things generally begin with a festive parade that includes a military color guard and a powwow queen seated atop a car hood.

CATHY CARLSON

Visitors are welcome at powwows and photos are not usually a problem, although this is less true at Arapaho powwows. For general information on powwows and other events on the reservation, call 332-3040.

by attractive log or stucco churches.

Oil and gas revenues from a number of major fields on the reservation provide millions of dollars each year in the form of monthly dividend payments. These royalties, along with various Bureau of Indian Affairs (BIA) assistance programs, ranching, farming, and tribal-owned businesses, are the main source of income. A Business Council acts as the manager of tribal income. The Arapaho tend to emphasize communal sharing and a purity of race much more than the Shoshones, who are more likely to marry whites and to own private land.

Most people on the reservation are poor, and many are unemployed, having lost their jobs when the uranium mines closed down and oil companies left. Pawnshops in Lander and Riverton often acquire valuable cultural items from desperate individuals when the money runs out before the month does. For many on the reservation, sports are the way out. Every kid, it seems, plays basketball, and there are hoops outside all the trailer homes and government-built houses. For older folks, bingo is a major source of entertainment, with games almost every night of the year.

Despair And Hope

The Wind River Reservation has severe problems with drugs and alcohol; a third of the children are born with fetal alcohol syndrome. Many young people (and older folks too) die in alcohol-related car accidents or fights, while suicide rates and infant mortality are distressingly high. Despite all the problems, there is a genuine sense of pride in the cultural history of the Arapaho and Shoshone peoples. To attack the problems of alcoholism and the loss of self-identity, young people learn their native tongue in special classes and take part in powwows, sun dances, and personal vision quests. The warrior tradition is expressed in a high enlistment in the nation's armed forces.

The reservation is a center for fine beaded clothing and moccasins that are prized by collectors. Arapaho patterns are geometric in nature, with rectangles and trian-

gles appearing frequently. Arapaho women generally use red, black, blue, yellow, orange, and white as the main colors, with mountains, tipis, and butterflies as common motifs. Eastern Shoshone patterns tend to be more circular, with the rose as a popular theme.

ARAPAHOE AND ST. STEPHENS

The town of Arapahoe (known locally as Lower Arapahoe) is a small village on the southeastern edge of the reservation. It came into existence because of animosity between the tribes, as a subagency through which annuities could be distributed to the Arapaho without their having to face the taunts of "beggar" or "dog eater" from the Shoshones at Fort Washakie. A prominent white water tower is visible for many miles. The **Northern Arapaho Powwow** (oldest on the reservation) is held here in early August, followed by the **Labor Day Powwow**.

St. Stephens Mission

In 1884, the St. Stephens Mission was established by Father John Jutz, a Jesuit missionary. Chief Black Coal consented to allow a mission to be built and later proved an ardent supporter of the school for Arapaho children. Until 1939, the Catholic Church operated a boarding school here. It was replaced by a day school that ran until the 1970s, when it became increasingly difficult to find priests and nuns to run the mission.

Visitors entering St. Stephens Mission pass a modern grade school built in 1983 and run by a private nonreligious corporation with an entirely Indian leadership. The most interesting sight at the mission is **St. Stephens Church,** built in 1928. The white stucco exterior is covered with colorful Arapaho geometric symbols. Note the right panel in which a black-robed figure appears to be preaching to a crowd. This is taken from an Indian pictograph at Castle Gardens (see pp. 203-204) and is believed to have been etched into the rock by an Indian who had watched

Father Pierre DeSmet baptize 305 Arapaho during the great council of 1851 at Fort Laramie.

The excellent quarterly magazine *Wind River Rendezvous* is published by the mission and is available for just $10 a year; write them at Box 278, St. Stephens, WY 82524. Although this is a religious organization, the magazine deals with all sorts of historical and social issues. A cemetery near the mission contains the graves of Chief Lone Bear, Francis Setting Eagle, and John Broken Horn, along with that of his wife, Sarah Broken Horn—a white woman (born as Lizzie Fletcher) who had been captured as a child and raised as an Indian. See "Arlington," p. 112, for more on this story. The outlaw Butch Cassidy was a frequent visitor in Chief Lone Bear's camp.

The **North American Indian Heritage Center,** tel. 856-4330, is open Mon.-Fri. 9-5 April-November. Inside is the Singing Horse Gallery with historic photos, plus a fine gift shop containing Arapaho paintings, belts, moccasins, hair ornaments, earrings, necklaces, and other works. Some of the most interesting items for sale are collector dolls dressed in Arapaho costume. The center also runs **Singing Horse Tours,** tel. 856-6688. For $15, visitors are given a tour of the St. Stephens Mission, collector-quality booklets, and a cassette tape and map describing other reservation sites. Indian-escorted tours are also available.

ETHETE

Ethete (pronounced EEE-thuh-tee) is the primary Arapaho settlement on the reservation. People live in trailer homes scattered on small plots around town or in ticky-tacky box houses built by the BIA. (The prefabricated houses are known as the "Easter Egg Village" because of the bright colors.) Tipi poles lean against the barns, and the bright tribal colors and geometric patterns dominate the laundromat/video store. "Downtown" Ethete consists of a stoplight—the only one on the reservation—surrounded by a grocery store (with a few handicraft items), a gas station, a community hall, a high school, and the above-mentioned laundromat. All this is entirely forgettable, except for nearby St. Michael's Mission. The **Ethete Community**

Powwow is held in mid-June, and the annual **Ethete Celebration** is held in late July. In mid-July the Ethete powwow grounds come alive with the **Northern Arapaho Sun Dance** ceremony (no cameras allowed).

St. Michael's Mission

Established in 1887 by Rev. John Roberts of the Episcopal Church, this mission is the town's reason for existence. When Chief Sharp Nose was asked for his approval to build here, the response was "*Ethete,*" meaning "Good." The buildings here were constructed between 1910 and 1917 and are arranged in a circle around a grassy lawn. Most are built from cobblestones, with Arapaho designs on the doors, but the **Church of Our Father's House** is of log. Inside this fascinating building (built in the shape of a cross) are rustic handmade wooden benches and a central Arapaho drum. Altar seats are made of elk antlers, and the back window faces the great Wind River Mountains.

Across the circle is the **Arapaho Cultural Museum,** housing a small but remarkable collection of artifacts that includes beaded garments, medicine pouches, peace pipes, warbonnets, and more. It is open Mon.-Fri. 8-5, Sat. 10-3, and Sun. by request in the summer. If nobody is here, knock on the house next to the church to have someone let you in.

FORT WASHAKIE

Fort Washakie is the center of activity on the Wind River Reservation. The BIA compound is here—locals insist the initials stand for Boss Indians Around—along with headquarters for the tribal council. Fort Washakie was the home of Chief Washakie, the longtime leader of the Shoshones. Behind Chief Washakie's town are a series of dramatic escarpments and canyons, and through a gap in the hills you can peer into the mighty Wind River Mountains.

In 1869, the U.S. Army established a fort, Camp Augur (later Camp Brown), along the Popo Agie River to protect the Shoshones from attacks by Arapaho and Sioux warriors. The fort was later moved a dozen miles west and renamed Fort Washakie, making this one of the only forts ever named for an Indian chief. It re-

SACAGAWEA

Fictional books about Sacagawea (pronounced sah-cah-gah-WEE-ah), describe her as a beautiful Indian maiden, guide, peacemaker, heroine, and mother—sort of the original Superwoman. Historian James Truslow Adams declared her one of the six most important women in American history. The reality is a bit less romantic, but still fascinating. Sacagawea—her name meant "Bird Woman" in Shoshone—was born around 1788 in what is now eastern Idaho. As a child, she was captured by the Minnetaree tribe and later sold to a French-Canadian trapper and interpreter named Toussaint Charbonneau. He eventually made her one of his many wives.

The Lewis And Clark Expedition

In 1803, President Thomas Jefferson negotiated the Louisiana Purchase from the French. For the fire-sale price of $16 million he suddenly doubled the size of the young nation called America. Captains Meriwether Lewis and William Clark were selected to lead a secret exploration of this vast land. They left St. Louis in late 1804, camping that first winter in North Dakota, where they met Sacagawea and her husband Charbonneau. Lewis and Clark didn't think much of the ill-tempered and untrustworthy Charbonneau, but realized the value in having a Shoshone woman who was fluent in English and French. Charbonneau was hired, with the stipulation that his wife come along.

Over the winter, Sacagawea gave birth to a baby boy (Baptiste), and when the troupe headed out two months later, the child was on her back in a cradle board. Contrary to the romanticized novels, her role was not so much as "the guide," but as an interpreter, as one who knew the edible plants along the way, and as a symbol of the expedition's friendly intentions. When the expedition reached the Continental Divide, they met up with

Sacagawea's sister and brother, whom she had not seen since being kidnapped six years before. The Shoshones agreed to provide guides and horses to cross the Rockies.

They reached the Pacific Ocean that fall and built a fort near the mouth of the Columbia River for winter quarters. They recrossed the mountains the following summer, and Sacagawea, Charbonneau, and their son returned to their old existence in Mandan country. The rest of the expedition party reached St. Louis on September 23, 1806, long after everyone but President Jefferson had given them up for dead. The trip proved a vital step in bringing the Northwest under the U.S. flag.

Later Years

From here, the story of Sacagawea becomes murkier. Some researchers claim she died in 1812 of "putrid fever" at Fort Mandan in North Dakota. This version is generally told by Dakota folks. Wyoming partisans prefer another story: that the woman who died so young was one of Charbonneau's other wives, and that Sacagawea continued to live for many more years. After leaving her abusive husband, she wandered all over the West—gaining the name Wad-ze-Wipe ("Lost Woman")—before finally ending up on the Wind River Reservation with her fellow Shoshones. She served a crucial role as translator for Chief Washakie in negotiations to establish the reservation, and was often seen wearing one of the peace medals given out by Lewis and Clark. Sacagawea (or at least the Wyoming version) died on April 9, 1884, and was buried near Fort Washakie in a cemetery overlooking the Wind River. It wasn't until 25 years later that historians began to realize who the "Lost Woman" really was. The 13,569-foot Mt. Sacagawea in the Wind River Mountains is named for the remarkable woman who remained unrecognized much of her life.

BOB RACE

mained open until 1909, when the threat of conflict between the Shoshones and Arapaho had diminished. A few buildings still stand, including a **stone guardhouse**. They are now used by the BIA.

Sights

Despite its minuscule size, Fort Washakie has an array of interesting sights. The **Shoshone Cultural and Resource Center**, tel. 332-9106, is in the "White House" on the BIA compound. Built in 1913, it now serves as an information and heritage center. Upstairs are some historical photos along with a video about powwows (get a powwow calendar here). Young people take cultural and Shoshone language classes here. It's open Mon.-Fri. 8-4:45.

South Fork Rd. west from Fort Washakie passes the **Washakie Graveyard**. A substantial granite memorial notes that Washakie was "Always loyal to the government and his white brothers. A wise ruler." Directly across the road is the **R.V. Greeves Art Gallery**, tel. 332-3557, open by appointment only. Greeves is one of America's best-known sculptors; his *The Unknown* is in the Buffalo Bill Historical Center.

Continue another mile along this road (stay left at the "Y" and turn left again at the Full Gospel Revival Center's log church) to the **Sacagawea Cemetery**, perhaps the most beautiful cemetery in Wyoming. The remote setting offers views of the Wind River Mountains. When I last visited, the sun was playing behind darkly rumbling thunderheads atop the Winds while horses whinnied in the fields below. Sacagawea's gravesite (or at least the Wyoming version) is marked by an impressive granite headstone, and one of her sons, John Baptiste, is buried alongside. A granddaughter and other descendants are up the hill. The graveyard also contains an old log church and a number of old bed frames over graves, a burial practice that was common for many years on the reservation.

The historic **Shoshone Episcopal Mission** is on Trout Creek Rd., 1 1/2 miles southwest of Fort Washakie (turn east just beyond the Hines General Store), and was founded in 1883 by Rev. John Roberts, a Welsh missionary known as "White Robe." A boarding school for Indian girls was built in 1891. The two-story brick-and-stone building still stands, though the school closed in 1945. A simple log mission church is nearby.

Three miles east of Fort Washakie on the way to Ethete is **Chief Washakie Hot Springs**, tel. 332-4530, where 110° F sulfur-rich water flows into a public swimming pool ($4 adults, $2.50 kids, seniors free). This was a favorite place of Chief Washakie. Maybe these mineral waters helped him live to age 102! The facility is a bit run-down and seems to open and close on a whim.

Arts And Crafts

Warm Valley Arts and Crafts, tel. 332-7330, sells handmade Indian beadwork, jewelry, garments, and other items from the reservation. Also on display are Chief Washakie's headdress, leather shirt, and suitcase. It is owned and operated by the Eastern Shoshone tribe and is open Mon.-Fri. 8-5. **Wind River Trading Co.**, next to Hines General Store, has more beadwork, moccasins, and baskets. The setting is more elaborate than Warm Valley, but much of this work is not from the Wind River Reservation. A good place to find quality craftwork is the nursing home, **Morning Star Manor**. Other locals worth contacting for beadwork and art are Nathaniel Barney, Orlean Ute, and Birdie Aaron.

Practicalities

El Ranchito, next to Hines General Store, sells delicious Indian tacos and Mexican food. **Ray Lake Campground**, at the intersection of US 287 and State 132, tel. 332-9333, charges $9 for tents or $13 for RVs. Tipis are also available for rent, and meals are available at the cafe. Open May-September. Very friendly folks here, and the remote country setting offers classic Wyoming scenery. There is no other lodging available on the reservation, although many places are available in nearby Lander, Riverton, and Dubois. **Little Wind River Outfitter**, tel. 332-2409, provides guided horse-packing trips in the Little Wind River drainage on the reservation.

Fishing on the Wind River Reservation requires a special permit ($7/one day or $35/one week), available from the Tribal Fish and Game Office in Fort Washakie, tel. 332-7207. This permit also allows hiking, camping, and boating access. Restrictions apply, and a number of areas (including the entire northern end of the reservation) are closed to the non-Indian public. The map that comes with the permit also lists public camping areas on the reservation. Hunting by outsiders on the reservation is strictly verboten.

Events

In late June, Fort Washakie is home to the **Treaty Day Celebration,** which includes Indian games, dancing, and a feast. It is immediately followed by the **Eastern Shoshone Powwow and Rodeo,** which attracts Indians from all over the west. The all-Indian rodeo features **Indian relay horse racing** in which bareback riders rocket around the track in a chaos of flying dirt and colliding horses. Another Shoshone powwow is held in Crowheart in early June, and an Eastern Shoshone sun dance takes place near Hamilton Dome in late July. In late December, another Shoshone powwow is held at Fort Washakie, but this time inside the local gymnasium.

WEST TO DUBOIS

As you head northwest along US 26-287, the Wind River Mountains and Absarokas grow ever closer, and the Wind River Valley begins to narrow. Crowheart Butte dominates the skyline to the north for many miles, and then you drop over a rise to discover a stunning landscape of red-rock badlands accented by the green of cottonwoods along the Wind River. For the next 20 miles, travelers are treated to a constantly changing panorama of gloriously colorful badlands topography, with 11,635-foot Ramshorn Peak rising in the distance. It's a geologist's dreamworld. Several reservoirs provide irrigation water plus recreation on the Wind River Reservation. Largest is **Bull Lake,** along the western margin. The Shoshones say that it is haunted by a supernatural water buffalo. The aquamarine waters of **Ocean Lake** are well-known for bass and crappie fishing. Other people come to swim or water-ski.

Crowheart Butte

The tiny settlement of **Crowheart** consists of an old-fashioned country store and gas station surrounded by irrigated fields and grazing cattle.

A couple miles northeast of the store—and visible for many miles in either direction—is a regal summit, Crowheart Butte, looking like a pyramid whose top got caught in a giant lawn mower.

The name comes from an 1866 battle over hunting rights in the Wind River Valley between the Shoshones and Bannocks against their enemy, the Crows. The Crows had been "given" the valley in the Fort Laramie Treaty of 1851, while the Shoshones and Bannocks were "given" the same land in the 1863 Fort Bridger Treaty. Four days of intense fighting led to a standoff, and to prevent further bloodshed, the chiefs declared a winner-takes-all fight atop this butte. Charging each other on horseback with lances drawn, both were thrown in the collision, and the fight turned to a hand-to-hand struggle. In the battle, Shoshone Chief Washakie killed Crow Chief Big Robber and then reputedly ate the vanquished leader's heart (or at least carried it around on a spear). Thus the name, Crowheart Butte. When Chief Washakie was later asked about the story, he replied, "When a man is in battle and his blood runs hot, he sometimes does things that he is sorry for afterwards. I cannot remember everything that happened so long ago."

Crowheart Butte is regarded as something of a sacred place by local Indians and is used as a place of spiritual renewal for young men on a vision quest. A small rock shelter stands on the top, used for this purpose. It is illegal for non-Indians to climb Crowheart Butte, and legends claim that those who do so may disappear.

Broken Wheel Ranch

The Broken Wheel Ranch, located near Dinwoody Creek (10 miles west of Crowheart), offers an amusing taste of the Hollywood frontier. During the 1980s, Lee Kozell—a onetime Wyoming cowboy and retired Pittsburgh bartender—built this miniature Wild West town, including a saloon, jail, church, general store, bank, and brothel. Get here by turning south on the dirt road just beyond Dinwoody Creek and following the road 1½ miles to the buildings.

Whiskey Basin

The highway continues its slow, scenic climb to Dubois, crossing the cottonwood-lined Wind River three times en route. Approximately 25 miles west of Crowheart (five miles east of Dubois), a gravel road leads to a state fish hatchery and a big-horn sheep wintering range in Whiskey Basin. A sign points the way. The road is easy at first but approaches 4WD status within a couple of miles as it follows Torrey Creek up past a string of four small lakes. (The lakes were created by retreating glaciers centuries ago, though small dams have enlarged them.) State Game and Fish **campsites** (free) are located along Ring and Trail lakes. A trailhead at the end of the road (12 miles) provides access to the primary route up to Dinwoody Glacier and 13,804-foot Gannett Peak. (See p. 244 for more on the Glacier Trail.) Keep your eyes open for the osprey nest at mile 5. The Audubon Society has a field camp at mile 8.

A number of large Indian **pictographs** are on large boulders in the Trail Lake vicinity. The figures—some four feet tall—are elaborate otherworldly creations with horns and headdresses. Evidence points to their use in shamanistic ceremonies produced under altered states of consciousness. While their age is unknown, they are probably at least 2,000 years old, and from Athapaskan (a Canadian tribe) rather than Shoshonean origins. This is some of the oldest rock art in Wyoming.

During the winter months, Whiskey Basin Habitat Area contains the largest population of Rocky Mountain **bighorn sheep** anywhere on earth. At times more than 1,200 sheep congregate here because of the mild winters and the lack of deep snow. Best time to find them here is Dec.-Feb., but some stick around till April. Bighorn sheep are also sometimes seen in the meadows along the highway or in the hills just above Dubois.

DUBOIS AND VICINITY

Approaching Dubois (pop. 900) from either direction, you drive through the extraordinary red, yellow, and gray badlands that set this country apart. The luxuriant Wind River winds its way down a narrow valley where horses graze in the irrigated pastures, and old barns and newer log homes stand against the hills, while the tree-covered Absaroka Mountains ring distant views. The town of Dubois consists of a long main street that makes a sharp elbow turn and then points due west toward the mountains. It has an authentic frontier feel, with many log buildings and even a few snatches of wooden sidewalks. Locals live in cabins, trailer homes, and simple frame houses. Dubois weather is famously mild (warm chinook winds often melt any snow that falls) and grand scenery reigns in all directions. Snowmobilers, hunters, and anglers have begun to discover that Dubois provides a good place to relax in Wyoming's "banana belt," while at the same time remaining close to the more temperamental mountains. By the way, Dubois is pronounced DEW-boys; other pronunciations will reveal your tenderfoot status. (Actually, locals sometimes jokingly call it "Dubious.")

History

Dubois began in the 1880s when pioneer ranchers and homesteaders settled in the area, followed by Scandinavian hand-loggers who cut lodgepole for railroad ties. The town that grew up along the juncture of Horse Creek and the Wind River was first known as Never Sweat, but when citizens applied for a post office, the Postal Service refused to allow the name. The agency suggested Dubois instead, the name of an Idaho senator who just happened to be on the Senate committee that provided funding for the post office.

Dubois is a town in transition. For most of its existence, Dubois served as a logging and ranching center. In 1987, the Louisiana Pacific sawmill shut down, throwing many loggers and millworkers onto the unemployment rolls. Loggers blamed environmentalists and the Forest Service for sharply reducing the timber available, but environmentalists countered that the company was simply using the reductions as an excuse to close an aging mill. After everyone ran out of mud to sling, they decided to look at what Dubois had to offer and discovered that, lo and behold, they just happened to be sitting in

DUBOIS AREA

TOGWATER PASS (ELEV. 9,644 ft.)

BROOKS LAKE

BROOKS LAKE CAMPGROUND

BROOKS LAKE LODGE

PINNACLE BUTTES

SHOSHONE NATIONAL FOREST

TO DOUBLE CABIN CAMPGROUND

TO YELLOWSTONE AND JACKSON HOLE

FALLS CAMPGROUND

RAMSHORN PEAK (ELEV. 11,635 ft.)

HORSE CREEK CAMPGROUND

DU NOIR CREEK RD.

TIE HACK MEMORIAL

WIND RIVER

HORSE CREEK RD.

WARM SPRINGS RD.

CONTINENTAL DIVIDE

BRIDGER - TETON

NATIONAL

FOREST

LINE SHACK

SHOSHONE

NATIONAL

FOREST

TO LANDER AND RIVERTON

DUBOIS

HATCHERY

287

26

WHISKEY BASIN HABITAT AREA

TORREY LAKES

UNION PASS (ELEV. 9,210 ft.)

TO GREEN RIVER LAKES AND PINEDALE

0   5 mi
0   5 km

an almost-undiscovered recreational and re-tirement gold mine. In the last few years the town has leapt full-force into the tourism business. The transformation of Dubois to a visitor-oriented economy certainly has its downside—elaborate log summer homes are beginning to overrun the lush pastures on both ends of town, and the first condominiums have already appeared. Will the factory outlets and fast-food chains be the next to arrive, or can "industrial tourism" be kept away from this pretty little place? Stay tuned.

Sights

The **Dubois Museum,** 909 W. Ramshorn, tel. 455-2284, is open Mon.-Sat. 10-5 and Sun. noon-5, May-Sept., no charge. It houses exhibits on the Sheepeater Indians and various cultural artifacts, plus petrified wood, and dis-

plays on ranch life, natural history, and the tie hacks. Be sure to check out the hilarious photo of 1930s movie star Tim McCoy teaching golf to a skeptical group of Shoshone Indians!

Just west of Dubois is a signed turnoff to a **scenic overlook.** The gravel road climbs sharply (no RVs) for approximately a mile to this point, where signs note the surrounding peaks. Marvelous views of 11,635-foot Ramshorn Peak from here. **Rocky Mountain bighorn sheep** crowd the Dubois area in the winter. Many are visible on the hills just south of town, with hundreds more gathered in the Whiskey Basin Habitat Area, five miles east (see pp. 230-231).

The historic **Welty's General Store,** 113 W. Ramshorn, tel. 455-2377, was built in 1889. The real surprise inside is a Colt .44 with "Butch Cassidy" carved in the handle. The gun was found by Dubois rancher Leon Warnock in 1936 while hunting in the Wind River Mountains. (Cassidy and his partner Al Hainer had established a ranch up Horse Creek in 1889, using it to hide rustled horses. Cassidy gained the admiration of neighbors that winter after a nonstop 120-mile horseback ride to Fort Washakie to get medicine for a neighbor's child.) Rock hounds will find all sorts of petrified wood, agates, and other colorful rocks up the Wiggins Fork and Horse Creek drainages; ask at the chamber of commerce for directions.

The brand new **National Bighorn Sheep Center,** located next to the museum, is open daily in the summer months. Inside are exhibits on bighorn sheep, where they live, and how coordinated management has brought the population back from the brink of extinction. A theater shows videos and slide programs.

Accommodations

Dubois makes an excellent stopping point on the way to Yellowstone and Grand Teton national parks, with lodging prices well below those in Jackson Hole. See the chart for Dubois-area motels and lodges. Of note is **Twin Pines Lodge,** built in 1939 and nominated for the National Historic Register of Historic Places. Another very enjoyable place is **Jakey's Fork B&B,** located in a century-old homestead east of town. Fine views of both the Wind River Mountains and nearby badlands. Be sure to ask about Butch Cassidy's battle with Indians here! Ten different dude ranches are also found in the Dubois area.

Camping

The closest public camping is at **Horse Creek Campground** ($6; open June-Oct.), located 12

DUBOIS ACCOMMODATIONS

MOTEL	ADDRESS	TELEPHONE	RATE	FEATURES
Red Rock Motel	three miles east	455-2337	$22 s, $28 d	quiet locations
Wind River Motel	519 W. Ramshorn	455-2611	$24+ , $28+ d	open April-Dec.
Trail's End Motel	511 Ramshorn	455-2540	$25+ s, $28+ d	AAA approved, pool, cabins, open May-Oct.
Twin Pines Lodge & Cabins	218 Ramshorn	455-2600	$25+ s, $30+ d	cabins, historic lodge
Branding Iron Motel	401 Ramshorn	455-2893 (800) 341-8000	$27 s, $32 d	AAA-approved, cabins, kitchenettes
Stagecoach Motor Inn	103 Ramshorn	455-2303	$28+ s, $34+ d	AAA approved, pool, kitchenettes, very nice
Red Rock Lodge	13 miles east	455-2944	$28 s, $38 d	riverside location
Black Bear Country Inn	505 W. Ramshorn	455-2344 (800) 873-2327	$34 s or d	AAA-approved, kitchenettes, whirlpool
Chinook Winds Motel	half-mile east	455-2987	$34 s, $36 d	kitchenettes
Rendezvous Motel	one mile west	455-2844 (800) 682-9323	$40 s, $42 d	kitchenettes
Jakey's Fork B&B	four miles west	455-2769	$60 s or d	sauna, jacuzzi, full breakfast, historic
Line Shack	Union Pass Rd. 13 miles west	455-3232	$50 s or d	elaborate
Union Pass B&B	Union Pass Rd. 13 miles west	455-3238	$55 s, $60 d	jacuzzi, pet goat!
Geyser Creek B&B	four miles west	455-2702	$55 s, $65 d	very nice

miles north of Dubois on Horse Creek Road. **Cir-cle-Up Camper Court,** 225 W. Welty, tel. 455-2238, charges $11 for tents (some shade) and $16 for RVs. Kids love the tipis for $15 (bring your own sleeping bag). Noncampers may use the showers here for $3. Open mid-April to mid-Nov., this is one of Wyoming's nicer private camp-grounds. **Red Rock Lodge,** 13 miles east of Dubois, tel. 455-2944, has RV spaces for $8, and showers for noncampers for $3.

Food
Ziggy's Whisker Pete's Cafe, 318 W. Ramshorn, tel. 455-2656, is the place to go for breakfasts; be sure to get the country hash browns. **Cowboy Cafe,** 115 E. Ramshorn, tel. 455-2595, also has good home-style breakfasts with big helpings of biscuits and gravy. For a real artery-clogger, try the steak and eggs. For excellent lunchtime sandwiches, homemade soups, and salads, head to **Wild West Deli,** 128 E. Ramshorn, tel. 455-3354. The **Pizza Pub,** 308 S. First, tel. 455-3480, has tolerable Mexican food (everything seems to be deep fried), and much better pizzas. Open summers only.

    Village Cafe/Daylight Donut, 515 W. Ramshorn, tel. 455-2122, is an interesting fam-ily place, offering donuts and coffee in the morn-ings and steak dinners each evening. **Ramshorn Inn,** 202 E. Ramshorn, tel. 455-2400, serves good charbroiled steaks and seafood. **Rustic Pine Steakhouse,** 119 E. Ramshorn, tel. 455-2772, is a carnivore's de-light, with prime rib on Fri. and Sat. nights and Mexican dishes for lunch. **The Line Shack,** eight miles west and then five miles up Union Pass Rd., tel. 455-3232, is a popular place for Fri. or Sat. night prime-rib dinners. **Red Rock Lodge,** 13 miles east of Dubois, tel. 455-2944, has prime-rib dinner specials on weekends. Get groceries at **Ramshorn Food Farm,** 610 W. Ramshorn. For outstanding fresh-baked pas-tries, breads, and tasty hardtack (made from a special Swedish recipe), be sure to stop by **Cir-cle-Up Camper Court,** 225 W. Welty, tel. 455-2238.

Entertainment
Dubois is a hopping place during the summer, especially on weekends. **Outlaw Saloon,** 204 W. Ramshorn, tel. 455-2387, often has rock tunes, while both **Ramshorn Inn,** 202 E. Ramshorn, tel. 455-2400, and **Rustic Pine,** 119 E. Ramshorn, tel. 455-2430, offer C&W bands. The Rustic Pine also has square dancing on Tuesday nights in July and August. This classic western bar has elk and moose heads, plenty of old wood, and a pool table. Check out the ash-trays that note, "God spends his vacation here." Dudes from local ranches often invade Dubois one night of the week; ask around to avoid this night if you don't want to be overwhelmed with fellow visitors. Two other places that often have live music on weekends are **The Line Shack,** eight miles west and then five miles up wind-ing Union Pass Rd., tel. 455-3232, and **Red Rock Lodge,** 13 miles east of Dubois, tel. 455-2944.

Events
On Memorial Day weekend Dubois hosts a se-ries of enjoyable cowboy **Pack Horse Races.** On the Fourth of July, Dubois comes alive with a street dance, an ice-cream social, a parade, a western BBQ, and rubber-ducky races down the river. Two mountain men rendezvous take place during the summer. In early June the **Lit-tle Fawn Rendezvous** is for kids only and in-cludes tipi living and frontier-skills training. **Whiskey Mountain Buckskinners Wind River Rendezvous** in mid-August is for the oldsters and includes some impressive black-powder marksmanship contests. Don't miss the Dubois firemen's buffalo BBQ during rendezvous week-end.

Recreation
There is a nine-hole **golf course** on the western end of Dubois. The Absarokas and Wind River Mountains around Dubois are extremely pop-ular with snowmobilers during the winter months, and several places rent 'biles in town. Don't ex-pect peace and quiet with all these machines roaring through the backcountry! Most of the activity centers around **The Line Shack,** eight miles west and then five miles up Union Pass Rd., tel. 455-3232. You can rent snowmobiles here ($100/day), stay in the lodge, and get meals at the restaurant. More than 300 miles of trails head out in all directions. **Cross-coun-try skiers** find trails near Falls Campground

and Brooks Lake (both 23 miles west of town), and Togwotee Mountain Lodge (40 miles west), along with an enormity of backcountry areas off-limits to snowmobiles.

Shopping

Trapline Gallery, 120 E. Ramshorn, tel. 455-2800, sells Indian-crafted beadwork, jewelry, and artwork, as well as furs. **Green River Traders,** 104 E. Ramshorn, tel. 455-3345, has an impressive collection of antique trade beads for sale. A few doors down is a nice bookshop, **Two Ocean Books,** tel. 455-3554. **Water Wheel Gift Shop,** 113 E. Ramshorn, tel. 455-2112, also carries a selection of Wyoming titles. Purchase topographic maps at **Welty's General Store,** 113 W. Ramshorn, tel. 455-2377, and fishing supplies from **Wind River Fly Shop,** on W. Ramshorn, tel. 455-2140. Justin Bridges makes and sells high-quality handmade folding knives, sport knives, and other cutlery at **Wind River Knives,** four miles south of town on Fish Hatchery Rd., tel. 455-2769. Many of the handles are made from the horns of bighorn sheep.

Information And Services

The **Dubois Chamber of Commerce,** 616 W. Ramshorn, tel. 455-2556, is open daily 8-7 May-Aug., and Mon.-Fri. 9-12 and 1-4 the rest of the year. Check here for a listing of local horse-packing outfitters, and ask about the **pony express** mail service run by a local boy. Also ask for a map showing old logging flumes, tie-hack cabins, and other historic structures. Stop by the **Forest Service Ranger Station** at 209 E. Ramshorn, tel. 455-2466, for maps of Shoshone and Bridger-Teton national forests ($2) and info on local trails. See "Bighorn Basin," pp. 377-378, for more on the Washakie Wilderness. See p. 244 for details on access to the Fitzpatrick Wilderness.

DUBOIS VICINITY

Anyone who loves the outdoors will discover an abundance of pleasures around Dubois. There is good fishing in the Wind River (rainbow, cutthroat, brown, and brook trout) and in the many alpine lakes (generally rainbow, brook,

and Mackinaw trout), plus lots of deer, elk, and bighorn sheep. Hikers and horse-packers will find hundreds of miles of Forest Service trails in the area. Photographers love the brilliantly colored badlands that frame Dubois on both the east and west sides. And each winter, hundreds of 'bilers climb on their sleds and cross-country skiers strap on their boards to enter the world of deep powder in the Absarokas. The map on p. 206 shows attractions in the Dubois area.

Horse Creek Area

Horse Creek Rd. heads north from Dubois, providing scenic views of the Absarokas. **Horse Creek Campground** ($6; open June-Oct.) is 12 miles north. Forest Rd. 504 continues another five miles, providing access to the Washakie Wilderness via Horse Creek Trail. Forest Rd. 508 splits off near Horse Creek Campground and leads another 17 miles to **Double Cabin Campground** ($6; open June-October). Several trails head into the wilderness from here; most popular are Frontier Creek Trail and the Wiggins Fork Trail. You'll find remnants of a petrified forest six miles up the Frontier Creek Trail, but they have been rather picked over by collectors. (It's illegal to remove petrified wood from a wilderness area.) For other Washakie Wilderness trails info, ask at the Dubois Ranger Station.

Union Pass

The first road across the Absarokas headed through Union Pass, southwest of Dubois. The pass forms a divide between the waters of the Columbia, Colorado, and Mississippi rivers and marks the boundary of the Absaroka, Wind River, and Gros Ventre mountain ranges. Nearby is an interpretive sign and a nature trail through a flower-filled meadow. Union Pass Rd. (gravel) leaves US 26-287 approximately nine miles northwest of Dubois and climbs across to connect with State 352 north of Pinedale. On the west side of the pass the road becomes rougher and should only be attempted in dry weather. A major reconstruction project is in the works for this road.

Union Pass B&B, tel. 455-3238, is five miles up Union Pass Rd. from US 26-287 and features a jacuzzi, plus Casper the friendly goat (bring Froot Loops for him). Ask owner Judith

Bendel about goat day-treks. The country near here is popular with mountain bikers, cross-country skiers, and far too many wintertime snowmobiles from the new and grotesquely huge Line Shack just up the road.

A beautiful 20-mile-long side road takes off from a couple of miles up Union Pass Rd. and heads along Warm Springs Creek, eventually reconnecting with US 26-287. Fantastic views of the Absaroka and Wind River ranges along this route. The remains of an old tie-hack logging flume are visible and a warm spring (85° F) flows into the creek.

OVER TOGWOTEE PASS

The enjoyable drive west from Dubois first cuts through the colorful badlands, playing tag with the Wind River as it begins a long ascent to 9,644-foot Togwotee Pass (pronounced TOE-go-tee). The pass is named for a subchief under Chief Washakie. Togwotee was one of the last independent Sheepeater Indians (a branch of the Shoshones) and the man who led a U.S. government exploratory expedition over this pass in 1873. He even guided President Chester Arthur on his monthlong visit to Yellowstone in 1883.

Togwotee Pass is one of the most scenic drives imaginable, with Ramshorn Peak peeking down from the north for several miles until the road plunges into dense lodgepole forests (Shoshone National Forest) with lingering glimpses of the Pinnacles. At the crest it emerges into grass, willow, and flower-bedecked meadows with Blackrock Creek winding through. Whitebark pine and Engelmann spruce trees cover the nearby slopes. As the highway drops down the western side (Bridger-Teton National Forest), another marvelous mountain range—the Tetons—dominates the horizon in dramatic fashion. There is snow along the roadsides until early July; notice the high posts along the road used by wintertime snowplows. Togwotee Pass is a complete shock after all the miles of sagebrush and grassland that control the heartland of Wyoming. It's like entering another world, a world of cool, forested mountains and lofty peaks instead of the arid land with horizon-wide vistas.

Pinnacle Buttes And Brooks Lake

Dominating the view along US 26-287 for perhaps 15 miles are the castlelike Pinnacle Buttes. Twenty-three miles west of Dubois, you come to the turnoff to Brooks Lake, elevation 9,100 feet. Take it, even if you don't plan on camping here. A five-mile gravel road leads to the cliff-rimmed lake, and a clear creek flows east and south from here. The Forest Service maintains two excellent **campgrounds** ($6, open mid-June through Sept.) along the lakeshore. Facing the lake is historic Brooks Lake Lodge (see below). Back on the main highway, you'll want to stop at **Falls Campground** ($6; open mid-June to early Sept.), where Brooks Creek tumbles into a deep canyon. Very impressive views of **Brooks Creek Falls** from the short trail that begins from the parking lot here. Reservations ($6 extra) may be made for campsites by calling (800) 283-2267. In wintertime, cross-country skiers will find an easy ski trail (signed but not groomed) that heads out two miles from here. Wind River Lake is another five miles up the hill, just below the pass. It's a gorgeous place for picnics, with deep blue water and the sharp cliffs of Pinnacle Buttes behind.

Mountain Lodges

Pinnacle Motor Lodge, 20 miles west of Dubois on US 26-287, has rooms starting from $29 s or $35 d. There are RV campgrounds at **Rawhide Ranch,** 14 miles west of Dubois, tel. 455-2407, and **Triangle C Ranch** (established as the first tie-hack camp in the region), 18 miles west of Dubois, tel. 455-2225. **Double Bar J Ranch,** 20 miles west of Dubois, tel. 455-2681, has guest-ranch accommodations, horseback rides, and a sauna. The gourmet restaurant here features fabulous desserts.

Brooks Lake Lodge, tel. 455-2121, provides some of the most incredible scenery in Wyoming, with a dual backdrop of Brooks Lake and the Pinnacles. The main hall (on the National Register of Historic Places) is filled with big-game trophies from all over the world. Built in 1922, this classic western lodge has long served travelers en route to Yellowstone. It was completely restored in the late 1980s. The lodge is 23 miles west of Dubois and then five miles in from US 26-287 along Brooks Lake Road. It's open July to mid-Sept. and then mid-Dec. to mid-April. During the summer, lodging costs $150/day pp, including meals, horseback rides, canoes, and fishing. Cabin suites are $170 pp/day. There is a three-night minimum. Be sure to reserve far ahead to be sure of a space. Come winter, Brooks Lake Lodge is a popular ski-in or snowmobile-in destination for lunch or evening cocktails (Thurs.-Mon. only). Overnight winter accommodations (Thurs.-Sun. nights only) are available for $115 pp in the lodge or $140 pp in cabins, including breakfast and dinner, as well as skis and ice-fishing gear. **Geyser Creek Dogsled Adventures,** tel. (800) 531-6874, has all-day dogsled tours of the Brooks Lake area for $150 pp ($75 for kids under 10). See p. 309 for info on Togwotee Mountain Lodge, a few miles west of Brooks Lake.

WIND RIVER MOUNTAINS

The Wind River Mountains begin near South Pass and continue 100 miles northwest to Union Pass, forming part of America's Continental Divide backbone. The range is visible for more than a hundred miles across the sagebrush country of central and southwestern Wyoming, its rugged snowcapped peaks gleaming in the light. The Shoshones traversed this range each spring and fall, and Sheepeater Indians hunted in the high country, but to most of the white pioneers whose wagon trains rolled across South Pass, the peaks represented a forbidding, mysterious place. In 1868, writer James Chisholm offered a description of the range that still rings true today:

I think the best inspired painter that ever drew would fail in attempting to describe these mighty mountains. He may convey correctly enough an impression of their shape, their vast extent and sublime beauty. But there is a something always left out which escapes all his colors and all his skill. Their aspects shift and vary continually. Their very shapes seem to undergo a perpetual transformation like the clouds above them. There is a mystery like the mystery of the sea—a silence not of death but of eternity.

Today, the Wind River Mountains are considered Wyoming's premier backpacking area, offering perhaps 800 miles of trails. Much of the country is well above timberline, with glacially carved mountains and countless small lakes. Mountain climbers enjoy practicing moves on thousands of granitic precipices representing all degrees of difficulty. The Winds contain Gannett Peak—at 13,804 feet the tallest in Wyoming—along with all but one of the state's 15 other highest peaks. There are over 150 glaciers in the Winds, including seven of the 10 largest glaciers in the lower 48. All of these formed during the Little Ice Age between A.D. 1400 and 1850. The glaciers that actually carved these mountains were far larger, so massive in fact that they covered the mountaintops to great depths and spilled over to create the hanging valleys, cirques, alpine lakes, U-shaped valleys, and steep cliffs of today.

Three different Forest Service wilderness areas cap these mountains; largest is Bridger Wilderness on the western side of the Continental Divide (in Bridger-Teton National Forest), with Popo Agie and Fitzpatrick Wilderness areas east of the crest (in Shoshone National Forest). Add in the BLM's Scab Creek Wilderness for a total of more than 735,000 roadless acres. The lower elevations of the Wind Rivers are also national-forest lands, but they are managed for other purposes, primarily timberharvesting and grazing. On the northeast border is the Wind River Reservation, which includes some of the high mountain country, but access is restricted. Contact the Tribal Fish and Game Office in Fort Washakie, tel. 332-7207, to purchase a limited hiking, fishing, and camping permit.

Wildlife

Most of the streams and larger lakes in the Winds have been planted with rainbow, cutthroat, California golden, brook, German brown, or Mackinaw trout, along with grayling and mountain whitefish. Although grizzlies no longer roam these mountains, black bears are still here (mainly below treeline), and food should always be hung out of their reach. Actually other creatures—mosquitoes—are more likely to be a problem. Be sure to bring insect repellant during July and August when they are at their worst. Other critters you're likely to see include bighorn sheep, moose, elk, mule deer, and coyotes. Pikas and yellow-bellied marmots are common in the high-country boulder fields.

Access

Three highways circle the Wind River Range: US 26-287 on the northeast, US 191 on the southwest, and State 28 on the southeast. (See p. 206.) The mountains are traversed by only one road, gravel Union Pass Road. Most people cross the relatively gentle southern slopes at South Pass or over Togwotee Pass to the northeast. Access to the three wilderness areas can be gained from either side, but the high passes and long distances keep many hikers on one side or the other. See descriptions of the three different wilderness areas (below) for specific access points.

Most trails in the Winds are relatively free of snow by late June and remain so until mid-October, but the high passes may not open until mid-July. Be prepared for afternoon thunderstorms and the possibility of snow at any time in this mountain country; night temperatures can drop below freezing even in midsummer. Be aware that there is not a lot of wood in many parts of the Winds, so be sure to bring a gas stove to cook on. In addition, wood fires are prohibited at many of the most heavily used sites.

Unlike the mountain country farther north, most of the people who head into the Winds do so on foot rather than atop a horse. Horses are used by a quarter of the people, and "spot-packing" (in which horses bring in supplies for base camps but everyone hikes in on foot) is a popular way to get into the backcountry without carrying everything on your back. Many outfitters offer these services; check with nearby chambers of commerce. Permits are not required within the Winds except for commercial groups or those using stock. **Lander Llama Co.**, 327 Washington St. in Lander, tel. 332-5624 or (800) 582-5262, provides guided llama trips into the Popo Agie Wilderness, as well as the Absarokas near Dubois. One of the unique ways into the backcountry is with a goat from **Wind River Pack Goats** in Atlantic City, tel. 455-2661. They lead wilderness trips and offer goat rentals once you go through a daylong training course.

More Info

Forest Service ranger stations in Lander (Popo Agie Wilderness), Dubois (Fitzpatrick Wilderness), and Pinedale (Bridger Wilderness) can provide information for their respective areas. An area map ($3) of Southern Shoshone National Forest covers the Fitzpatrick and Popo Agie wilderness areas, while a Pinedale area map ($3) covers the Bridger Wilderness. These maps are available at most Forest Service offices in Wyoming.

Briefly described below are a number of the most popular hikes. There are literally hundreds of possible treks one can take in the Winds, so don't think these are your only options. In fact, if you want to avoid the crowds, you should probably pick up a few topo maps and discover your own trails. Finis Mitchell's *Wind River Trails* (Salt Lake City: Wasatch Publications) is a folksy, inexpensive guide by a man who has hiked this country since 1909. Mitchell personally planted trout in dozens of high-country lakes during the 1930s, and even has a mountain named for him. Pick up this guide if you plan to do any fishing. *Climbing and Hiking in the Wind River Mountains* by Joe Kelsey (San Francisco: Sierra Club Books) has accurate information on most of the hiking trails and describes hundreds of technical climbs. Topographic maps are available from sporting-goods stores in the surrounding towns. The most up-to-date Wind River Mountains maps are from Earthwalk Press, 2239 Union St., Eureka, CA 95501, and can be found in most area bookstores and sporting-goods shops.

GREEN RIVER LAKES AREA

The long drive to Green River Lakes is one of the most popular getaways in the Wind River Mountains. The road parallels the Green River as it first drifts northward then makes a U-turn to meander across southwestern Wyoming, even-

PINEDALE AREA TRAILS

TO UNION PASS

ROARING FORK TRAIL

TO TRAIL LAKE

GREEN RIVER LAKE CG.

CLEAR CREEK TRAIL

CLEAR LAKE

BILLY WELLS DUDE RANCH SITE

KENDALL WARM SPRINGS

WHISKEY GROVE CG.

GREEN RIVER LAKES

FLAT TOP LAKE TRAIL

FLAT TOP MOUNTAIN (ELEV. 11,550 ft.)

SLIDE LAKE

SHOSHONE NATIONAL FOREST

PORCUPINE TRAIL

GREEN RIVER

SQUARE TOP MOUNTAIN (ELEV. 11,679 ft.)

THREE FORKS PARK

DOWNS GLACIER

CONTINENTAL DIVIDE

GANNETT GLACIER

FITZPATRICK WILDERNESS

GANNETT PEAK (ELEV. 13,804 ft.)

DINWOODY GLACIER

MT. WARREN (ELEV. 13,720 ft.)

MT. HELEN (ELEV. 13,600 ft.)

MT. SACAGAWEA (ELEV. 13,569 ft.)

FREMONT GLACIERS

FREMONT PEAK (ELEV. 13,745 ft.)

TITCOMB LAKES

TITCOMB BASIN TRAIL

JACKSON PEAK (ELEV. 13,517 ft.)

BULL LAKE GLACIER

NEW FORK TRAIL

DOUBLETOP MT. (ELEV. 10,867 ft.)

SUMMIT LAKE

HIGHLINE TRAIL

NARROWS CG.

NEW FORK CG.

NEW FORK LAKES

DOUBLE TOP MT. TRAIL

PALMER LAKE TRAIL

PINE CREEK CANYON TRAIL

WILLOW CREEK GUARD STATION

BRIDGER WILDERNESS

ISLAND LAKE

INDIAN PASS TRAIL

SENECA LAKE TRAIL

SENECA LAKE

COOK LAKES

FREMONT TRAIL

FREMONT LAKE CG.

TRAILS END CG.

ELKHART PARK

POLE CREEK TRAIL

0   3mi

0   3km

CORA

352

FREMONT LAKE

HALF MOON CG.

HALF MOON LAKE

HIGHLINE TRAIL

191

TO JACKSON

PINEDALE

TO FARSON

191

BURNT LAKE

NORTH FORK TRAIL

BOULDER LAKE CG.

BOULDER CANYON TRAIL

BOULDER LAKE

TO BOULDER

GLACIER TRAIL

INK WELLS TRAIL

© MOON PUBLICATIONS, INC.

tually joining the Colorado River in Utah. Willows line the riverbanks in this open valley, while sagebrush and aspen cover the hills. Cattle and horses graze on the lush grasses. Get to Green River Lakes by heading to **Cora** (six miles west of Pinedale), and then north on State 352. Little Cora has a delightful old log general store. The first 26 miles of the road to Green River Lakes are paved and kept plowed all winter. Approximately 15 miles up, a sign points the way to **New Fork Lake,** located four miles away on a cobblestone (!) road. **New Fork Trail** takes off from the **Narrows Campground** ($5; open June to mid-Sept.), providing one of many routes into the Winds.

At the Forest Service border, state maintenance ends and the road becomes gravel, getting rougher as you go the remaining 18 miles. Watch the weather, since this upper portion can become a quagmire after heavy rains. Fantastic scenery makes the trip worthwhile, despite the washboard conditions. Look for some enormous "erratic" boulders a couple of miles up the road from here, evidence of the glaciers that once scoured this valley, carrying the boulders along with them.

Just inside the Forest Service border, a signboard describes the tie drives that sent several hundred thousand railroad ties down the Green River between 1869 and 1871. They made it all the way to Green River City (130 miles away), where a boom caught them and they were loaded on railcars. The crew boss, Charles Deloney, later became first superintendent of the Yellowstone Preserve and opened the first store in Jackson. The Green River Lumber and Tie Company came here in the 1890s, employing at least 50 men who lived in the town of Kendall. It lasted until 1904, but the tall stumps can still be found in the second-growth forests nearby.

Approximately three miles beyond the Bridger-Teton National Forest border, a rough gravel road splits off and heads over Union Pass to Dubois. Although this route was used by Indians and mountain men, today it probably sees more use by snowmobiles in the winter than summertime cars. A major reconstruction project is in the works. The Forest Service's **Whiskey Grove Campground** ($5; open mid-June to mid-Sept.) is just across the bridge at the site of the old logging town of Kendall.

Kendall Warm Springs

Back on Green River Lakes Rd., you pass Kendall Warm Springs 1¹/₂ miles above the turnoff to the campground, its 85° F waters issuing from a few hundred feet up the hill. This is the only place in the world where the **Kendall dace** can be found. Fully grown, they are just two inches long, or, as the Forest Service notes, shorter than their scientific name, *Rhinichthys osculus thermalis.* The water drops over a 12-foot-high travertine terrace into Green River. The terrace was built up over thousands of years, at the same time the river was cutting into its banks, thus separating these fish and allowing them to survive away from larger predators. To protect them, wading is not allowed in the waters of Kendall Warm Springs.

More Sights

Another two miles up the road are the log-and-red sandstone remains of **Gros Ventre Lodge,** one of Wyoming's first dude ranches. Billy Wells built a hunting lodge here in 1897 and operated it until 1906 when stricter enforcement of game laws made it more difficult to attract clients. The lodge attracted wealthy big-game hunters from England and the East Coast who enjoyed the chance to slaughter wildlife. (Bannock Indians who hunted out of season in nearby Jackson Hole were shot at, while rich white "sportsmen" could take whatever they wanted for trophies.)

The road ends at the popular **Green River Lake Campground** ($6; open mid-June to mid-September). Weekends and the July Fourth holiday may fill the campground to overflowing. A number of unofficial campsites are just off the road below the lake. **Square Top Mountain** stares back across the lake, one of the most photographed spots in Wyoming. It is especially beautiful at sunrise, when the water is calm and the first light catches its cliff faces. By the way, when winter comes, ice drapes the front of Square Top, creating the longest single-pitch ice route in the nation. It has never been climbed. See below for trails in the Green River Lakes area. **Elk Ridge Lodge,** tel. 367-2553, has modern guest-ranch accommodations and also offers pack trips, float trips, and horseback rides.

BRIDGER WILDERNESS

The 428,169-acre Bridger Wilderness reaches 90 miles along the western side of the Wind River Mountains, encompassing 27 active glaciers, 1,300 alpine lakes, and 600 miles of trails. It is named for famed mountain man and guide Jim Bridger and was first designated a primitive area in 1931, gaining wilderness status with the original Wilderness Act of 1964. Despite this status, a considerable amount of sheep grazing still takes place in the southern end of the Bridger Wilderness; it was "grandfathered" in with the wilderness legislation. We're talking close to 20,000 sheep in the wilderness. These "hoofed locusts" or "range maggots" (pick your term) pollute the waters, trample the meadows, and leave behind a barren, overgrazed moonscape. The Forest Service office in Pinedale has been notoriously lax in enforcing controls on high-country grazing by sheep and shows little signs of changing its ways.

Unlike sheep, humans must camp at least 200 feet from lakes or trails in the wilderness. Bridger Wilderness has special regulations that prohibit campfires in seven of the most heavily used areas between July 1 and Labor Day, including those around Green River Lakes, Island Lake, Big Sandy Lake, and Cirque of the Towers. Pick up a map showing the sites and listing other regulations from the Forest Service office in Pinedale. Access to the Bridger Wilderness comes from nine different entrances along the western side of the range. The three most popular points of entry are described below, along with a number of the favorite trails. If you're looking for solitude, you may want to avoid these popular paths.

Green River Lakes Trails

Easily the most scenic entry into the Winds is from Green River Lakes, located on the end of a paved-then-dirt road that leads north from Cora. (See above for sights along the Green River Lakes Road.) The road ends at a campground ($6) facing onto Lower Green River Lake, where the unforgettable 11,679-foot summit of Square Top Mountain dominates the view.

For an easy five-mile day-hike, follow the trails that circle Lower Green River Lake (High-

line Trail on the east and Lakeside Trail on the west). Excellent views of Flat Top Mountain (not to be confused with Square Top Mountain) from the Lakeside Trail, and of the Clear Creek Falls along the Highline Trail. Keep your eyes open for moose and osprey. An interesting side trip is the short hike to Upper Green River Lake, where Square Top proves even more startling. Another side trip heads up **Clear Creek Trail**—it takes off from the southeastern end of Lower Green River Lake, climbs two miles to a natural bridge, and then continues an equal distance to Clear Lake. Some of this country was burned in a 1988 fire. Flat Top is relatively easy to climb; see Finis Mitchell's *Wind River Trails* for the route.

Those interested in longer hikes will find several trails in the Green River Lakes area. **Roaring Fork Trail** climbs up to Faler Lake, 14 miles away and 2,200 feet higher. The **Highline Trail** follows the northeast shore of Lower Green River Lake and then continues south to the uppermost headwaters of the Green River. From there, the trail stays in the alpine much of the way to its destination at the Big Sandy Trailhead on the southern end of the Bridger Wilderness. The total distance is 72 miles, but few people actually follow this path that far, preferring to branch off to other sights. Another popular trek is up **Porcupine Trail** to Porcupine Pass and then down **New Fork Trail** to New Fork Lake (a total of approximately 17 miles). Porcupine Trail begins at the upper end of Lower Green River Lake, splitting off from Lakeside Trail.

Elkhart Park Trails

Elkhart Park Trailhead lies at the end of a 15-mile-long paved road that heads northeast from Pinedale along the east shore of Fremont Lake. During the summer, the Forest Service generally has someone here to answer questions. There is a campground here, too ($5). An overlook provides excellent vistas over Fremont Lake and Bridger Wilderness, with a big parking area that fills with cars in July and August.

Trails head out from Elkhart in two directions. **Pine Creek Canyon Trail** heads north, providing a relatively direct connection with Summit Lake (13 miles) and then down into Green River Lakes (30 miles total). The main drawback with this trail is that it loses 2,000 feet by dropping into Pine Creek Canyon, elevation that must be regained to reach Summit Lake. Also note that Summit Lake has outfitters' camps that distinctly lessen the area's remote aura. A nice loop can be made by heading east from Summit Lake along the Highline Trail to Elbow Lake and Seneca Lake, where you follow the Seneca Lake and Pole Creek trails back to Elkhart Park. This loop takes you through some of the more scenic areas in the wilderness and covers approximately 31 miles.

The most popular destination from Elkhart is **Titcomb Basin.** Access from Elkhart Park is via a series of connected trails: the Pole Creek, Seneca Lake, Indian Pass, and Titcomb Basin trails. Many hikers and climbers overnight at Island Lake, making for very crowded conditions much of the summer. It is 15 miles from Elkhart Park to Upper Titcomb Lake, a mountain cirque with abundant wildflowers. The lakes have been planted with golden trout. A side hike goes up through gorgeous Indian Basin to Indian Pass (three miles). Mountaineers can then descend to the Knife Point and Bull Lake glaciers within the Popo Agie Wilderness.

The valley above Titcomb Basin is open, giving climbers access to the west side of a whole row of peaks, including Mt. Helen (13,620), Mt. Sacagawea (13,569 feet), Jackson Peak (13,517 feet), and **Fremont Peak** (13,745 feet). The last two can be climbed without technical expertise, although Fremont does require some rough scrambling in places. It is most easily climbed from the southwest side; see a topographic map to find the route. There are many outstanding opportunities for those with greater expertise to try their skills on the cliff faces here.

Fremont Peak is named for **John C. Frémont,** the son-in-law of Senator Thomas Hart Benton, the biggest promoter of the Manifest Destiny that would lead Americans all the way to the Pacific. Because of this familial association, Frémont was given the task of exploring and mapping the western territories, work that brought him the nickname the "Great Pathfinder." Some of his ventures—such as floating through the wild waters of Fremont Canyon on the North Platte River, or crossing the Rockies in the dead of winter—were downright stupid, and his guides tried to stop him. Frémont's best asset was his wife, who painted his adventures in such a heroic light that his presidential ambitions were nearly realized.

In 1842, Frémont and his men climbed what appeared to be the highest mountain in the Wind River range, a summit they called Snow Peak, now Fremont Peak. From the west, it is obviously why Frémont and his men would mistake this for the highest: Gannett Peak (59 feet taller) is barely visible from a distance, hidden behind other summits. It was not until years later that the mistake was discovered. Frémont was led on his wilderness treks by men with far more experience—including Kit Carson and Tom Fitzpatrick—and his real role was to transfer their innate knowledge of the land onto maps. (Although most people believe Frémont did climb the peak with his name, there is still some doubt; some say he climbed another peak instead, or none at all. One of his scouts, Basil Lajeunesse, stated bluntly, "Frémont never ascended the peak." Perhaps that would account for the discrepancies between what Frémont described and what is actually there.)

Big Sandy Trails

One of the most popular entry points into the Bridger Wilderness is from Big Sandy Trailhead. Access is from a number of different directions, but all require long stretches of gravel road. Easiest access is from the north. From the town of Boulder, take State 353 where it turns west off US 191 and follow it till it turns to gravel (16 miles). Bear left at the intersection a half-mile up and go another nine miles to another junction (signed), where you again turn left and go seven more miles to the turnoff (left) to the Forest Service's Dutch Joe Guard Station and then on to Big Sandy Opening. The road ends at **Big Sandy Campground** (free; open mid-June to mid-Sept.), where the trails begin. The Forest Service generally has someone stationed here.

Big Sandy Lodge is just to the left near the end of the road, and provides guided trail rides and rustic cabins. The historic lodge (built in 1929) contains a trophy-filled lounge and two stone fireplaces. Spot pack trips and guided pack trips are also available. Write the lodge at Box 223, Boulder, WY 82923, for more info and reservations.

BIG SANDY AREA TRAILS

TO FORT WASHAKIE

MT. BONNEVILLE
(ELEV. 12,570 ft.)

FREMONT TRAIL

RAID LAKE

GRAVE LAKE

PYRAMID LAKE

BEARS EARS TRAIL

PYRAMID PEAK
(ELEV. 12,030 ft.)

SCAB CREEK TRAIL

WASHAKIE PASS

WASHAKIE TRAIL

WASHAKIE LAKE

LIZARD HEAD TRAIL

DICKINSON CREEK CAMPGROUND

MT. WASHAKIE
(ELEV. 12,524 ft.)

SMITH LAKE

SMITH LAKE TRAIL

SHADOW LAKE TRAIL

SILVER LAKE

EAST FORK TRAIL

MARMS LAKE

GROVE OF THE TOWERS

TEXAS PASS

LONESOME LAKE

NORTH FORK TRAIL

BIG SANDY PASS

POPO AGIE WILDERNESS

CHILCOOT TRAIL

TO LANDER

BRUCE PICNIC GROUND

HIGHLINE TRAIL

BIG SANDY LAKE

BLACK JOE LAKE

ICE LAKES TRAIL

PHOTO PARK TRAIL

MIDDLE FORK TRAIL

SHEEP BRIDGE

BRIDGER-TETON NATIONAL FOREST

BIG SANDY TRAIL

BRIDGER WILDERNESS

WIND RIVER PEAK
(ELEV. 13,192 ft.)

WORTHEN MEADOWS RESERVOIR

LITTLE SANDY TRAIL

CONTINENTAL DIVIDE

TO SOUTH PASS CITY

LOOP RD.

BIG SANDY CAMPGROUND

0 — 2mi
0 — 2km

MOON

DUTCH JOE GUARD STATION

TO PINEDALE

TO FARSON

LITTLE SANDY LAKE

ATLANTIC PEAK
(ELEV. 12,490 ft.)

A maze of trails depart from Big Sandy Opening. The **Highline Trail** heads north, extending across the Bridger Wilderness to Green River Lakes, and continuing from there to Union Pass, a hundred miles away. The trail connects with numerous other paths, including **Shadow Lake Trail,** a 2½-mile route to this alpine lake. More adventurous types can continue up through Texas Pass and down to Lonesome Lake in the Cirque of the Towers, a distance of 15 miles. Another side route off the Highline Trail is the **Washakie Trail,** a path used by this famous Shoshone chief during his people's biannual migration between the Wind River Valley and the Green River country. This trail goes into the Washakie Lakes area of the Popo Agie Wilderness, where you can connect with the Bears Ears Trail (see below).

The most popular trail out of Big Sandy Opening is **Big Sandy Trail,** a 5½-mile trek to crowded Big Sandy Lake, where it meets a spider web of trails and cairn-marked paths to other high-country lakes. Beyond the lake, **Big Sandy Pass Trail** climbs up North Creek and over Big Sandy Pass (shown as Jackass Pass on some maps) before dropping into Lonesome Lake and Cirque of the Towers (total distance 8½ miles). Big Sandy Pass Trail is a long slog. A strenuous loop trip consists of the Big Sandy Trail–Big Sandy Pass Trail route combined with the Texas Pass–Shadow Lake Trail–Highline Trail route described above. Total distance is 24 miles.

FITZPATRICK WILDERNESS

The 198,838-acre Fitzpatrick Wilderness occupies the northeast side of the Wind River Mountains, sandwiched between the Bridger Wilderness just over the Continental Divide and the Wind River Indian Reservation to the east. The wilderness is a rugged landscape of rock and ice, with dozens of mountain lakes and cascading mountain brooks. Wyoming's highest mountain, Gannett Peak, forms part of the western border, and 44 active glaciers crowd against the summits; the largest covers 1,220 acres. The Fitzpatrick is a favorite of folks with considerable backpacking or mountaineering experience.

Although long maintained as a primitive area, the Fitzpatrick Wilderness was officially established by Congress in 1976 and is named for Tom Fitzpatrick, a respected mountain man, guide, head of the Rocky Mountain Fur Company, Army scout, and Indian agent. To the Indians, he was "Broken Hand," a name received after he lost three fingers in a rifle accident while being pursued by Blackfeet Indians; despite this he still managed to kill two of his attackers. As an Indian agent, Tom Fitzpatrick pushed for a number of important treaties, including the 1851 Fort Laramie Treaty. His untimely death from pneumonia in 1854 was a blow to the peace process, and few of the agents who followed could match Fitzpatrick's diplomatic skills or knowledge of the West. Fitzpatrick's adopted Arapaho son, Friday (named for the day of the week that Fitzpatrick found him), later became a respected chief and translator for his people.

Access

The primary entrance point into the Fitzpatrick Wilderness is from **Trail Lake.** Head four miles southeast from Dubois on US 26-287 and turn right (south) onto a gravel road. The road leads into Whiskey Basin, with a rutted dirt road continuing to the left past a string of small lakes, the last being Trail Lake. The trails begin here, 12 miles off the highway. (Note that the Cold Springs/Burris and St. Lawrence Basin trailheads mentioned in the Wind River Mountain guidebooks are now closed to the general public.) Forest Service regulations in the Fitzpatrick prohibit camping within 50 feet of trails or lakes.

In addition, no campfires or horses are allowed at the confluence of Dinwoody and Knoll Lake creeks or the base of Dinwoody Glacier.

Trails

Three major trails lead from Trail Lake into the high country. The **Whiskey Mountain Trail** climbs over the peak of the same name and then on to heavily used Simpson Lake, a dozen miles away. From here it's possible for experienced hikers to continue over a pass above Sandra Lake (another 3$1/2$ miles) and then down into the Roaring Fork drainage of the Bridger Wilderness. The **Bomber Basin Trail** leads from Trail Lake Trailhead to Bomber Lake, eight miles away and 2,600 feet higher, crossing the deep canyon created by Torrey Creek on a high bridge. The basin is named for a B-17 bomber that crashed here during WW II when its crew was practicing a strafing run on either a bear or a bighorn sheep. The plane wreckage is still here. The upper portion of this trail (above Bomber Falls) is not maintained, but is passable.

A very popular moderately long hike is up **Glacier Trail** all the way to Dinwoody Glacier. It is a sweaty and difficult 23 miles but passes lots of lakes and ruggedly beautiful alpine country. Bighorn sheep are often seen along the way. The first several miles are without water, so be sure to bring plenty with you. The trail ends at the glacier, providing access for mountaineers who want to scale 13,804-foot **Gannett Peak,** highest in Wyoming. (The peak is named for Henry Gannett, chief topographer for the Hayden Survey of the 1870s, and was first climbed in 1922 by Arthur Tate and Floyd Stahlnaker.) Because it is nearly surrounded by glaciers, most routes require roping up, particularly the popular one across the Gooseneck Glacier. (From the west side, there is also a class 3 gully scramble.) Many mountaineers come up this trail to climb Gannett and the cluster of peaks over 13,000 feet just to the south, including Mt. Woodrow Wilson, the Sphinx, Mt. Warren, Doublet Peak, and Turret Peak. See Joe Kelsey's *Climbing and Hiking in the Wind River Mountains* for details.

POPO AGIE WILDERNESS

The Popo Agie Wilderness is a 101,991-acre parcel of magnificent mountain real estate with jagged peaks, deep valleys, and more than 240 lakes. At least 20 peaks rise above 13,000 feet; Wind River Peak is the tallest at 13,225 feet. Popo Agie was first established as a primitive area in 1932 and enlarged and reclassified as wilderness in 1984. The Popo Agie is bounded to the west by the Bridger Wilderness and to the north by the Wind River Indian Reservation. Access to the Popo Agie Wilderness is generally from the east side in the Lander vicinity, although it is possible to cross the Continental Divide from the Bridger Wilderness. Camping is not allowed within 200 feet of trails, lakes, or streams.

Dickinson Park Access

The primary jumping-off point into the Popo Agie Wilderness is the Dickinson Park area, northwest of Lander at an elevation of 9,300 feet. Get here by turning west on Moccasin Lake Rd. (paved) just south of Fort Washakie at the Hines Store. Stay right where the road turns to dirt and continue to Moccasin Lake/Dickinson Park junction, a total of 19 miles. Turn left here, and head another four miles to **Dickinson Creek Campground** ($5; open mid-June to mid-September). **Allen's Diamond Four Ranch,** tel. 332-2995, is here, offering a variety of trips, ranging from guided horse-packing trips to wagon rides. Many people opt for spot-pack trips. This is popular with those who want to hike while still enjoying the pleasures of a horse-packed base camp. The ranch also offers rustic cabin accommodations.

The Dickinson Park area has trailheads at the Dickinson Park Work Center and the Dickinson Creek Campground, a mile farther up the road. The **Bears Ears Trail** takes off from the work center and climbs quickly into the alpine before going over Adams Pass. It passes Bears Ears Mountain (look for the "ears") and follows through the alpine before dropping into the lake-filled headwaters of the South Fork of the Little Wind River, 14 miles away. Along the way are all sorts of connections to other trails, including a variety of loops. From the Dickinson Campground trailhead, the popular **Smith Lake Trail** heads south and then west to Smith and then Cathedral Lakes (eight miles). The **North Fork Trail** splits off the Smith Lake Trail approximately a quarter-mile up.

This trail will eventually (15 miles) take you straight to Lonesome Lake at the base of the soaring Cirque of the Towers. Unfortunately, the hike requires four different fordings of the North Fork of the Popo Agie River, a dangerous feat when the water is high. It's best to wait till late summer.

Loop Road Access

The Loop Rd. (State 131) cuts south from Lander through Sinks Canyon and then over the mountains to South Pass, providing a number of entry points into the Popo Agie Wilderness. (See "Lander," pp. 217-219, for other sights along this interesting road.) **Middle Fork Trail** begins at **Bruce Picnic Ground,** 13 miles south of Lander on the Loop Rd., and follows the Middle Fork of the Popo Agie River upstream to Sweetwater Gap (16 miles), where you enter the Bridger Wilderness. Many people use this trail to reach the Cirque of the Towers area via the Pinto Park and North Fork trails (total one-way distance approximately 23 miles). The heavily used **Tayo Creek Trail** splits off from the Middle Fork Trail approximately 13 miles up and continues another four miles to Tayo Lakes. **Sheep Bridge Trail** begins at **Worthen Reservoir,** 20 miles south of Lander on Loop Rd., and heads west for three miles to its junction with the Middle Fork Trail. Many people use this to cut distance and elevation off their trek into the Tayo Lake or Cirque of the Towers areas. (It starts 1,200 feet higher than the Middle Fork Trail.)

Cirque Of The Towers

This is one of the best-known and most-visited places in the Wind River Mountains, an incredible semicircle of pinnacles at the headwaters of the North Fork of the Popo Agie River. **Lonesome Lake** is in the center, backdropped by peaks with such names as Warbonnet, Pingora, Sharks Nose, Camels Hump, Lizard Head, and Watch Tower. All of these are well-known in the climbing community and attract folks from around the globe. Lonesome Lake is not so lonesome these days, and there is talk of restricting the number of hikers and climbers. On a typical day in early August you're likely to find a minitown of tents. The water quality suffers from all these people. To lessen the visual impact, some hikers bivouac behind the larger boulders rather than pitching a tent. The most popular way to reach Cirque of the Towers is from the Big Sandy Opening Trailhead (see "Bridger Wilderness" above), but the longer North Fork Trail (described above) is also commonly used and does not require traversing any passes. The other popularly used route is the Sheep Bridge Trail (described above).

SOUTH PASS AREA

At the southern end of the Wind River Mountains, a broad, relatively gentle pass provides a corridor across the Continental Divide. This part of Wyoming is packed with history. Today, State 28 traverses South Pass, climbing south and then west from Lander, past scenic Red Canyon, and close to the almost-ghost towns of Atlantic City and South Pass, before starting the long descent into the Green River Basin and the junction town of Farson. Winters on the pass are long, cold, and windy; the snow fences stretch for miles along the highway.

Gold was first mined here during the middle 1860s, and a long series of booms and busts followed. For a brief time in 1867-68, the **Sweetwater Mines** attracted national attention, and thousands of men (and a few women) flocked to the area. The land was officially part of the Wind River Reservation at the time, but legalities didn't matter much when gold could be found. South Pass was ceded by the Shoshones in 1878. Prospectors still head out each spring in search of the elusive mother lode, and various schemes to reopen the old mines surface periodically. Today the area is enjoyed by thousands of tourists and others attracted by the rich historical and recreational opportunities.

Over The Pass

South Pass was first discovered by the game animals who traversed this country and the Indian hunters who followed them. The first whites to traipse through were the Astorians, fur traders led by Robert Stuart in 1812. The first wagon wheels rolled over South Pass in 1824, and between 1841 and 1866 more than 350,000 emigrants followed what had become the primary route west. Of all the sights along the Oregon Trail, South Pass must have been one of the most anticipated. West of here the waters flow to the Pacific Ocean, and the entire country became known as the Oregon Territory (hence the **Oregon Buttes** south of South Pass). Travelers took great pleasure in stopping at Pacific Springs, happy in the knowledge that its waters eventually reached the Pacific. An important stage and Pony Express station stood here; some of the buildings from a later ranch are still standing.

Today, State 28 drapes a similar route across South Pass. Signboards denote various historic sites along the way. At the signboard that describes the Oregon Trail, a rough dirt road leads a mile back to the clear waters of Pacific Creek, where posts mark the historic route. Don't believe everything you read on the signs, however: the **Parting of the Ways** monument actually marks the South Pass City–Green River stage road where it intersects the Oregon Trail rather than the famous point where the Sublette Cutoff took Oregon- and California-bound travelers west while Mormon voyagers (and others in need of supplies) diverged southwest to Fort Bridger. The true Parting of the Ways lies 10 miles southwest from this marker. The highway west to Farson rolls up and down the sage-carpeted hills, cutting straight as a carpenter's plumb line. The Wind River Mountains dominate the northern horizon, while to the south, the distant Killpecker Sand Dunes slide into view.

SOUTH PASS CITY

Located at 7,800 feet above sea level, South Pass City is one of Wyoming's highest settlements. Although commonly called a ghost town, the town never really died out. South Pass City is now a State Historic Site, providing one of the most interesting and authentic historical settings in the state.

(previous page) Square Top Mountain; (this page top) Big Springs, Thermopolis;
(bottom left) petroglyphs, Dinwoody Lake area; (bottom right) around the roaring campfire, Teton Wilderne
(photos by Don Pitcher)

Gold In The Hills

During the days of '49, many thousands of would-be miners streamed through South Pass on their way to California, little knowing that gold lay beneath their feet. Gold was first found in 1842, but its discoverer was killed by Indians; other miners faced similar fates. First to file a claim was Henry Reedal, who discovered what became known as the Carissa Lode in 1867. Shortly thereafter, the Miner's Delight

SINKS CANYON & SOUTH PASS AREA

Lode was discovered. The finds attracted an onslaught of miners, and by that fall the town of South Pass City had mushroomed to Wyoming's largest settlement, with nearly 3,000 residents.

The discovery of gold at South Pass helped propel the effort to make Wyoming a territory separate from Dakota, a move that took place the following year. At its rip-roaring peak, there was even an effort to make South Pass the Wyoming territorial capital. The town included six general stores, three butcher shops, several restaurants, two breweries, seven blacksmith shops, five hotels, and dozens of saloons and "sporting houses." In 1868, writer James Chisholm described his return to the town after an absence: "Late at night we arrived at Miner's Delight where everything was just as we had left it. The card table in the corner was in full blast. The parties whom we had left on a drunk were now sobering off and those we had left sober were getting on a drunk."

The Carissa Mine's shafts would eventually reach 400 feet down, and the mill would produce gold worth more than six million dollars. But this was primarily hard-rock mining, requiring large capital investments and long hours. The lack of water in this arid country meant that placer mining was possible only in the spring, with summers spent toiling in the hard-rock mines for $5 a day. The Sweetwater mines were a short-lived bubble that burst almost as quickly as it grew. Instead of the hoped-for mother lode, miners found only small pockets of gold. Within five years most of the miners gave up and moved away. By 1875, fewer than a hundred people remained. But South Pass City refused to die. There were more booms (followed by busts) in the 1880s, 1890s, 1930s, and 1960s. Miners still come to these hills in search of gold.

Women's Suffrage

Given the rough mining crowd that jammed the streets of South Pass City, it seems odd to find the town at the center of the effort to gain equal rights for women. In late 1869, the first territorial representative from South Pass City, William Bright, introduced a women's-suffrage bill before the first territorial legislature. It was a measure supported by his wife and a number of other South Pass women, but probably opposed by many of the local men. The measure surprised almost everyone by being passed and signed into law by Governor John Campbell. In anger, the local judge resigned his post as justice of the peace for South Pass City, only to be replaced by a woman, Esther Hobart Morris. She was the first woman judge in America. In her 8$\frac{1}{2}$ months of service, Morris tried 26 cases, gaining recognition for her fairness, along with considerable national exposure.

A greater claim to fame for Morris as the "Mother of Women's Suffrage" is suspect. In 1869, she is supposed to have held a tea party in which the South Pass City women extracted a promise from then-candidate William Bright to introduce legislation granting women the right to vote. The tea party tale was concocted by her son (a newspaper editor) after her death, but gained entry into the history books as fact. A statue of Morris in front of the state capitol credits her with the bill. Morris herself never claimed any such thing, and in fact was not an active suffragist. According to Bright, the reason he introduced the legislation was not because of lobbying by local women but because "if Negroes had the right to vote, women like his wife and mother should also."

South Pass State Historic Site

In 1965, South Pass City's buildings risked being carted off to southern California's Knott's Berry Farm theme park. With the help of "Flaming Mame" Alice Messick, a committee of Wyoming folks outbid the Californians for the buildings and managed to keep them. The following year, the state purchased the site and began the process of restoration. South Pass State Historic Site contains some 25 old buildings and 13,000 authentic artifacts, 90% of which actually came from the area. The buildings are open daily 9-6, May 15-Sept., no charge. Call 332-3684 for details. The rest of the year, visitors can wander the streets and look in the windows, but many items are in storage.

On summertime weekends the old town comes alive with gold-panning and blacksmithing demonstrations by costumed old-timers. Be sure to drop by the Morris cabin for fresh-baked cookies. The old-fashioned **Fourth of July** celebration at South Pass is great fun, with wagon rides, country dancing, a barbecue, exhibits, and lots of folks in old-time costumes. **Trails West,** tel. 332-7801 or (800) 327-4052, offers three-day wagon-train treks from South Pass along the old Oregon Trail. The cost is $350 including food ($250 for ages 6-12 and $100 for children under 6).

Head first to the **visitors center** in what was once a South Pass store for interpretive displays, old photos, and a 28-minute video on the area's history. Pick up the brochure here that describes the buildings. Just to the west is the **Smith-Sherlock Store,** where you can check

---

In 1861, Mark Twain rumbled west through Wyoming on a stagecoach, a trip later made famous in his book, *Roughing It.* At South Pass, Twain found that the pre-mining days settlement was not exactly a hubbub of activity:

Toward dawn we got under way again, and presently as we sat with raised curtains enjoying our early-morning smoke and contemplating the first splendor of the rising sun as it swept down the long array of mountain peaks, flushing and gilding crag after crag and summit after summit, as if the invisible Creator reviewed his gray veterans and they saluted with a smile, we hove in sight of South Pass City. The hotelkeeper, the postmaster, the blacksmith, the mayor, the constable, the city marshal and the principal citizen and property holder, all came out and greeted us cheerily, and we gave him good day. . . . South Pass City consisted of four log cabins, one of which was unfinished, and the gentleman with all those offices and titles was the chiefest of the ten citizens of the place. Think of hotelkeeper, postmaster, blacksmith, mayor, constable, city marshal and principal citizen all condensed into one person and crammed into one skin. Bemis said he was "a perfect Allen's revolver of dignities." And he said that if he were to die as postmaster, or as blacksmith, or as postmaster and blacksmith both, the people might stand it; but if he were to die all over, it would be a frightful loss to the community.

out the old items or buy licorice candy, sarsparilla, and historical books. Other interesting buildings that have been restored and furnished with original items include a blacksmith shop, a butcher shop, a hotel, a miner's cabin, a saloon, a school, and a dugout cave used to keep perishables cool. **Sweetwater County Jail,** built in 1870, is the oldest nonmilitary government building in Wyoming. Melodramas or films are presented at the **Variety Theatre** on summer weekends.

The reconstructed **Esther Morris cabin** stands at the eastern end of the row of buildings. Out front is a granite marker from 1939 that credits her with originating women's suffrage. Next to it is a more recent disclaimer. Adding more insult to injury is the fact that the reconstructed cabin is in the wrong place; summer visitors can watch archaeological work at the actual Morris cabin site not far away.

Just east from the Morris cabin is a half-mile-long **nature trail** along Willow Creek, with the chance to explore the Carie Shields Mine (it produced $35,000 worth of gold) and other mines, cabins, and mill sights. Be careful where you walk around these old structures. Along the creek you're likely to see all sorts of animals, from beavers to bighorn sheep, mule deer, and moose. Pick up a trail map at the Smith-Sherlock Store. The state also has a 10-km **volksmarch trail** that is popular with the RV crowd.

ATLANTIC CITY

The funky, friendly little town of Atlantic City has dirt streets, old log and stone buildings, and a delightfully infectious country atmosphere. It's the sort of town where old-timers plunk themselves atop the Merc's bar stools to talk cattle, football, and the old days, where many homes (and the church too) still have outhouses, and where the big event is the volunteer fire department picnic (late August). Residents pile up huge stacks of firewood to make it through the long, cold winters. The snow can get deep here near the top of the Continental Divide (elevation 7,660 feet). One winter, the drifts topped 27 feet and the snowplows didn't get in for several weeks! Most residents like the quiet beauty that winter brings to Atlantic City, depending upon snowmobiles and skis to get around.

History
Atlantic City was formed in 1868 when gold mines had attracted thousands of miners to the Sweetwater Mining District. As miners arrived in South Pass, they spread out over the nearby country in search of other gold deposits, founding the settlements of Atlantic City, Miner's Delight, and Lewiston at promising locations. As with most frontier towns, saloons vastly outnumbered churches in early Atlantic City. The first county sheriff owned a local brothel! **Fort Stambaugh** was established a few miles to the east in 1870 to protect miners from Sioux and Arapaho raids. It lasted only to 1878, and the buildings were auctioned off four years later.

In the 1880s, another miniboom hit as French capitalist Emile Granier built a 25-mile-long ditch from the Wind River Mountains to Atlantic City for hydraulic mining. The effort failed when the money ran out before the gold could be found. Another boom hit in the late 1920s and '30s when a dredge worked its way down Rock Creek, leaving behind enormous piles of gravel. By the early 1960s, Atlantic City's population had been reduced to a handful of folks. Development of a U.S. Steel iron-ore (taconite) strip mine nearby brought prosperity after 1962, but it closed in 1983, leaving behind a gaping pit now filled with water. Atlantic City now depends upon tourism and summer homes. But as a local brochure notes, "The wind of this old gold town always whispers of another boom on its way."

The Merc
Atlantic City's main attractions are its mining-era buildings, many dating from the turn of the century. The centerpiece is **Atlantic City Mercantile,** built in 1893 from adobe brick. Its false front is covered with old metal siding, while the interior is stuffed with stuffed heads, historic photos, mining artifacts, and a sense of the past. Pick up a brochure inside describing the town's many other historic buildings. The "Merc," tel. 332-5143, rents A-frame cabins for $45 d during the summer. The bar often has live music on Friday and Saturday nights and a piano where you can display your own musical talents at other times. Owners Ron and Michelle Hobill can be found behind the historic bar (it's 125 years old!) most nights; the mirror behind them

CALAMITY JANE

Calamity Jane—born Martha Jane Canary in 1852—is surely one of the most unusual characters to come out of the 19th-century West. It was an era when the few women who found their way west almost invariably fell into one of three categories: housewife, washerwoman, or prostitute. Calamity Jane was all three, plus a lot more. At age 12, Martha Canary's family trekked west from Missouri to Montana. The trip took five months, and by the time they reached Virginia City she noted: "I was considered a remarkable good shot and a fearless rider for a girl of my age." Her mother died shortly after they arrived, and the family had a hard time surviving the harsh winter; Martha and her sisters were forced to beg on the streets. Her father died the following spring, and from that time on, Martha Canary was on her own. She landed in Miner's Delight (near South Pass City) in 1870-71; here she reportedly "entertained" men at Hyde's Hall Saloon. (Whether this is true or not, she certainly was employed occasionally in "the sporting profession.")

A Man's World

It was around this time that Calamity Jane gained her nickname. She claimed in a brief autobiography to have signed on as a scout for Gen. Custer in Fort Russell, Wyoming (Cheyenne), and to have soon thereafter "donned the uniform of a soldier. It was a bit awkward at first but I soon got to be perfectly at home in men's clothes." At other times she even masqueraded as a man, and could certainly work, shoot, drink, and cuss as hard as the rough-edged men around her. While employed as a scout for Gen. Crook's campaign near Sheridan she supposedly rescued the post commander, Capt. Egan, from an Indian raid, helping him to safety. Egan then named her "Calamity Jane, the heroine of the plains." The name stuck for life.

Whether the story is true or not, Calamity Jane *did* live up to the sobriquet many times in later years. She was often found nursing men down with smallpox (she was immune to the disease), buying meals for the destitute, or assisting ill "soiled doves" (even if it meant rolling a man for his money to pay the bills). She certainly saved many lives at a time when life was short and cheap. This is not to suggest that Calamity Jane was Mother Teresa of the Plains; the same woman who could care so much for others could also be loud and obnoxious when drunk—and that was often. Her binges were legendary and

would land her behind bars on numerous occasions, including a monthlong stint in the Rawlins jail for a drunken brawl with one of her many husbands, and an eight-day trip to the Laramie jail for drunkenness. Beer would never do, always "Give me a shot of booze and slop her over the brim" was the bartender's order. As a friend (Dora DuFran) noted:

Her many friends—she had no enemies—would buy her drinks until she reached the howling stage. Then someone would steer her to the next saloon. Her time was limited in each one when that howling began. She would finally wind up by howling up and down Main street. Even the law was paralyzed. Nothing could quell the howling completely, so some friend would escort her home with a quart of whiskey hugged to her breast to act as a night cap and put her to sleep. In the morning she would awaken with a hangover and start all over again. The only way to sober her up was to tell her someone was sick and needed her services. Not another drink would she take. Next day she would be ready for business.

In her autobiography, Calamity Jane said she married Clinton Burk in El Paso and went on to give birth to a girl "the very image of its father . . . but who has the temper of its mother." Nobody knows what became of the girl in later life, but Calamity went on to marry several other men. One author who knew Calamity very well—a Deadwood madam named Dora DuFran—noted that "Jane had a very affectionate nature. There were very few preachers around to bother her, so whenever she got tired of one man she soon selected a new one." Calamity also alludes in her autobiography to an affair with famed gambler and gunfighter Wild Bill Hickock, and after her death a woman professed to be their illegitimate child raised by a wealthy East Coast family. Most folks put less stock in Calamity's relationship with Wild Bill, though the two did end up in Deadwood in 1876. A desperado shot Wild Bill in the back while he was seated at a gambling table;

continued

Calamity claimed to have helped capture the murderer.

Workin' And Boozin'

In later years, Calamity Jane seemed to spin her way across the west, stopping long enough to make money as a prospector, stagecoach driver, laundress, or

YELLOWSTONE NATIONAL PARK

Calamity Jane

some less seemly trade, before getting the urge (or being told) to move on. Given the regimented code of behavior that women lived under in her era, it's easy to see how her appearance brought such a stir. Newspapers trumpeted her arrival in town, and saloons attracted crowds as her exploits grew with each telling. Someone was always willing to buy a round of drinks for the chance to hear Calamity's tales. As a young woman she was certainly attractive, but the years of hard drinking and rough living were not especially kind. As author Ellen Mueller put it, however, "perhaps the men standing in a saloon dead broke and hankering for a drink would have found the woman beautiful who would get drinks 'on the house' for everybody."

Though she spent a brief period with Buffalo Bill's Wild West Show, Calamity Jane's biggest moment of glory came in an 1895 return to Deadwood after a 17-year absence. A masquerade ball was held in her honor, and the local newspaper noted that "she was in great demand by the Dancers, many who were anxious to spend 25¢ to dance with her, just to have it to say they had danced with 'Calamity Jane.' She had a fair sized jag on board, and this, together with a vile cigar which she smoked, made her look anything but the beautiful woman which novelists and story writer have said so much about."

Calamity died in 1904 at just 52 years old. Her deathbed plea was to be buried next to Wild Bill Hickock, who she said was the only man she had ever loved. Her funeral was one of the largest ever for Deadwood. Today, they lie next to each other at the Mt. Moriah Cemetery overlooking town. The testimony of a fellow tough-living woman (Dora DuFran again) sums up her life best:

It is easy for a woman to be good who has been brought up with every protection from the evils of the world and with good associates. Calamity was a product of the wild and woolly west. She was not immoral; but unmoral. She took more on her shoulders than most women could. She performed many hundreds of deeds of kindness and received very little pay for her work. With her upbringing, how could she be anything but unmoral.

suffers from a gunshot wound. The Merc's dinners are renowned throughout this part of Wyoming. In the front, munch on inexpensive but very good burgers and homemade fries, while back-room guests are treated to an old-timey setting of oil lanterns and great aspen-grilled meats and seafood (Thurs.-Sat. nights only). A bit on the pricey side—entrées around $25—but worth it.

More Buildings
The stone structure a block to the east of the Merc housed the **McAuley Store,** later Hyde's Hall. Calamity Jane once provided the entertainment in the saloon here. Up the hill is **St. Andrews Episcopal Church,** a rustic old log church built in 1913. The **Gratrix Cabin,** a block east of the church, was built in the late 1860s and was home to Judge Buck Gratrix, a man who noted that he lived in three different counties, two territories, and one state while living in one place!

One of the most attractive structures in Atlantic City is the mint-condition **Miner's Delight Inn.** Originally known as the Carpenter Hotel, the building was constructed in 1904 and run as a boardinghouse for miners and others until 1961. Today the historic inn (tel. 332-3513) offers comfortable B&B lodging in antique-furnished log-cabin rooms. Open summers only.

Nearby Sights
Rock Creek flows through Atlantic City, and on the west end of town the banks are lined with huge piles of boulders left behind by the gold-dredging operations of the '30s. Fort Stambaugh Rd. heads east from Atlantic City, following a 12-mile loop past the site of Fort Stambaugh (not marked) and the ghost town of Miner's Delight. A side road leads to **Lewiston,** another abandoned gold-mining town. The loop road is a very scenic drive with open grassland and scattered patches of young aspen and lodgepole. (Miners wiped out previous stands.) Antelope are sure to be seen along the way.

Miner's Delight consists of a dozen log buildings in various states of decay. A small beaver pond and graveyard are also in Miner's Delight, with other old mining buildings visible just west of here.

The road west from Atlantic City to South Pass City passes more old gold mines, notably the **Duncan Mine** (two miles out) and the famous **Carissa Mine,** just before the road drops down to South Pass City. Most of the mines and buildings are on private land, and many contain hazardous structures and shafts without covers. Watch your step!

A little over seven miles south of Atlantic City is a monument to the **Willie Handcart Company.** In 1856, a large group of Mormon emigrants led by James G. Willie was caught in a series of early winter storms and camped here awaiting help and provisions from Salt Lake City. Sixty-seven of them died before they could reach the promised land. This and other Mormon handcart monuments at Rocky Ridge and Rock Creek are described in a pamphlet available from South Pass State Historic Site.

Practicalities
See above for descriptions of Atlantic City Mercantile and Miner's Delight Inn. Note that groceries are not available in either Atlantic City or South Pass, so stock up elsewhere. Also in town is **Red Cloud Saloon,** which sometimes has live music. The big attraction here is the pool table. Next door is the mediocre **TNT Cafe,** where you get a dose of local gossip and dense cigarette smoke with your breakfast or lunch. The **Old Rock Shop** (Willow Creek Inn), tel. 332-7396, on State 28 just north of South Pass City, has a cafe and bar, RV lot ($13), and showers ($2), but no rocks. The BLM maintains two attractive campgrounds ($4) in young aspen stands—very pretty in the fall—along the Fort Stambaugh Loop Rd.: **Atlantic City Campground** and **Big Atlantic Gulch Campground.** Big Atlantic Gulch doesn't have water.

FARSON AREA

Farson (pop. 300) stands at the busy highway junction where State 28 and US 191 greet each other. Locals live in trailer homes—the modern versions of log cabins—and work at a couple of local businesses. All around are long, straight roads, flat sagebrush desert, a few irrigated pastures, and antelope. It's a long way from here to anywhere else, so almost everyone stops for a road break. In the simmering summer sun, **Farson Mercantile,** tel. 273-9511, is crowded with people buying ice-cream cones to eat in the shade of the olive trees out front. The old brick two-story store is a classic country market. **Oregon Trail Cafe,** tel. 273-9631, is named for this historic trail that passed right through the center of Farson. It offers standard road grub, along with **Mitch's Cafe,** tel. 273-9606, where you're more likely to find locals amid the burlwood seats. **Sitzman's Motel,** tel. 273-9246, charges just $22 s or $30 d, but is often full in midsummer and during the fall hunting season. RVs can park for free next to Farson Mercantile.

Heading South

Four miles south of Farson is tiny **Eden,** where irrigated green fields bring the arid landscape alive. Of note here is the old **Oregon Trail Baptist Church,** with its brown log walls, quaint bell tower, and back window facing the Wind River Mountains. The view probably makes it hard to concentrate on the service. Kitty-corner across the road is the Eden Saloon, where the view may not be as great, but after a few beers it really doesn't matter. Bicentennial Park makes a shady place to enjoy a picnic. South of Eden, US 191 cruises into the bleak Bad Lands Hills country on its way to Rock Springs. Killpecker Dunes (see p. 134) rise on the eastern horizon.

Heading North

Immediately north of Farson, the highway crosses Big Sandy River, little more than a creek much of the year, with Big Sandy Reservoir (free camping here) holding back much of its water for irrigation. Flat, irrigated fields of hay surround Farson. As you continue northward to Pinedale (58 miles), the jagged snow-topped crowns of the Wind River Mountains loom ever larger and the sagebrush grows more abundant on the arid landscape rolling away to the mountains. The highway crosses both the **Sublette Cutoff**—one of the original routes to Oregon Country—and the 1858 **Lander Cutoff,** the first federal road west of the Mississippi. Tune in to KQSW (96.5 FM) for country tunes to speed you on your way.

A gravel road that begins two miles east of Farson and heads north along Little Sandy Creek and then northwest to Boulder is even more dramatic, passing along the foothills of the Winds. It's used to access the Big Sandy Trailhead for the Bridger Wilderness. This is one of my favorite drives in Wyoming. Clouds often drape the distant mountains, but when they part—like curtains at a Broadway premier—they reveal the 13,000-foot crest of the Wind River Mountains in all their majesty. This is truly one of the classic western vistas, with the interplay of land, light, and sky creating an unforgettable scene.

The land knocks you out: mountains struggling up through the distant plain, bursting aside the sandy sod, crowning the eastern horizon with slanting patches of monstrous rock faces and snow-mantled slopes, reflecting back the light from a westering sun. Antelope glance up as you drive past; a rough-legged hawk hunches down on a fence post; several horses paw the ground. Periodically a narrow set of pickup-truck tracks angles over the horizon to some remote ranch. In places like this, it is hard not to love the wildly beautiful state of Wyoming.

PINEDALE AND VICINITY

PINEDALE

Pinedale (pop. 1,200) is similar in many ways to its neighbor across the mountains, Dubois. Both towns were long dependent upon ranching and logging but are now starting to appreciate the visitors who come to simply enjoy the country. Rich people from all over the nation (and the world) have bought up the old ranches and turned them into summer homes, and small jets crowd the tarmac (if it could be called that) at Pinedale's airport. Most of these folks are corporate bigwigs such as the head of PepsiCo, but others include John Barlow (lyricist for the Grateful Dead) and James Baker (former secretary of state). Residents brag that Pinedale has all the beauty of Jackson Hole with none of the hassles. All around Pinedale are hay-filled meadows, grazing horses, and modern ranchettes. The Wind River Mountains are close and dramatic. In addition to ranching and tourism, Pinedale is also a minor governmental center, with BLM, Forest Service, Game and Fish, and Sublette County offices here. (Warning: Pinedale is cop heaven with eight—count 'em—police and highway patrol officers waiting to nail anyone topping 55 mph.)

History

The first inhabitants of the Upper Green River Valley were the Shoshone, Gros Ventre, Sheepeater, and Crow Indians who hunted buffalo, elk, and antelope in this rich country. Whites first came as explorers and fur trappers in the early 1800s, and by the 1830s this was the "capital" of the fur trade in the Rockies. Six different rendezvous were held along the Upper Green River. The first white settler arrived with his cattle in 1878, and within a few years a small trading center sprang up alongside Pine Creek. The town prospered with development of the tie-hack industry in the late 19th century. Pinedale was platted in 1899, later becoming the Sublette County seat.

The Drift

The Upper Green River is still very important cattle country; in fact, it's the largest range allotment in the national-forest system. Get here in June to watch cowboys ("riders" is a term more commonly used) pushing the cattle into the mountains. Some are driven as far as 90 miles from the winter range in the desert. Cattle graze in the mountains all summer, watched over by a handful of riders who stay in cabins or trailers. Each fall, the cattle drift back down from their summer home in the mountains when cool October weather hits the high country. At Cora (10 miles northwest of Pinedale), cowboys from 20 different ranches sort out the 7,500 cattle that pile up against fences in the "Green River Drift."

Museum Of The Mountain Men

Pinedale's excellent Museum of the Mountain Men, 700 E. Hennick St., tel. 367-4101, is open daily 9-5 mid-May to Labor Day, Tues.-Fri. 9-5 till mid-Oct., and closed the rest of the year. Entrance costs $2.50 adults, $1.50 seniors, and $1 kids (under age 5 free). Located on a hill overlooking town, this modern, spacious museum contains displays, artifacts, and memorabilia from the fur-trapping era. Jim Bridger's rifle is here, along with a covered wagon and a fascinating video about the fur trade. You'll learn about the daily lives of the different types of trappers (free versus company men), how the men trapped beaver and processed furs, and how the market for hats helped open the American west. Downstairs are displays and photos from ranchers and tie-hack loggers. A gift shop sells historical books.

Accommodations

See the chart for a listing of motels and lodges in the Pinedale area. It's a good idea to book a month ahead during July and August to be sure of space. **Campground of Wyoming** (COW!), 204 S. Jackson Ave, tel. 367-4555, charges $10 for tents and $16 for RVs; open mid-April through October. Showers for noncampers are $3. This is ye olde parking lot masquerading as a "campground." **Lakeside Lodge** at Fremont Lake, three miles northeast of town, tel. 367-2221, charges $8 for tents and $12 for RVs. Open mid-May to early September.

PINEDALE ACCOMMODATIONS

MOTEL	ADDRESS	TELEPHONE	RATE	FEATURES
Lakeside Lodge Motel	four miles north	367-2221	$28 s, $30 d	open May-early Sept. rustic cabins $20
Boulder Lake Lodge	24 miles southeast	367-2961	$30 s, $35 d	AAA-approved, pack trips
Teton Court Motel	123 E. Magnolia	367-4317	$31 s, $34+ d	nice place, open May-Oct.
Sun Dance Motel	148 E. Pine	367-4336	$32+ s, $36+ d	AAA approved
Wagon Wheel Motel	407 S. US 191	367-2871	$34+ s, $36+ d	AAA-approved, nice rooms
Bear Country Cottages	129 S. Franklin	367-2722	$35 s, $45 d	kitchens
Rivera Lodge	442 W. Marilyn	367-2424	$36+ s or d	kitchenettes, cabins, open May to mid-Oct.
Pine Creek Inn	650 W. Pine	367-2191	$40 s, $45 d	continental breakfast
Camp O' The Pines	38 N. Fremont	367-4536	$40 s, $45 d	kitchenettes $5 extra, open June-Oct.
Log Cabin Motel	49 E. Magnolia	367-4579	$40+ s, $45+ d	kitchenettes, cabins, historic
ZZZZ Inn	327 S. US 191	367-2121	$40+ s, $48+ d	open mid-April through Oct.
Fort Williams B&B	eight miles east	367-4670	$50 s or d	open May-Oct., horses continental breakfast
Half Moon Lodge	46 N. Sublette	367-2851	$44 s, $54 d	
Window on the Winds B&B	one mile west on US 191	367-2600	$55 s, $65 d	full breakfast, very nice
Elk Ridge Lodge	30 miles north	367-2553	$100 pp	includes meals, horses, and float trips

The closest public camping is at **Fremont Lake Campground** ($6; open June-late Sept.), seven miles northeast of Pinedale along the lake. Even if you aren't staying here or planning any wilderness hikes from the trailheads, *do* take the 15-mile (paved) drive from Pinedale to road's end. The rugged crest of the Wind River Mountains forms a dramatic vista along the way. **Half Moon Campground** ($3; open June to mid-Sept.) is on the northwest shore of Half Moon Lake, 10 miles northeast of Pinedale. A dozen other Forest Service and BLM campgrounds are dotted all along the western side of the Wind River Mountains.

Food

Patio Grill, 35 W. Pine, tel. 367-4611, is a favorite breakfast place with locals. Nice atmosphere and good food. **Wrangler Cafe,** 310 E. Pine St., tel. 367-4233, is another reasonable place for breakfasts, but the service can be slow. **Sue's Bread Box,** 423 W. Pine (behind the post office), tel. 367-2150, serves earthy breakfasts and lunches with homemade soups and sourdough bread. Be sure to get one of the monstrous cinnamon rolls. **Calamity Jane's / Corral Bar,** 30 W. Pine, tel. 367-2469, is the place to go for delicious burgers and fries or for Mexican food and pizzas. **King Cone Drive In,** 513 S. US 191, tel. 367-6404, (open summers only) is famous (infamous?) as "Home of the Road Kill Burger." Best sundaes in town.

McGregor's Pub, 25 N. Franklin Ave., tel. 367-4443, specializes in prime rib, steak, and seafood, but also has good lunches served on an outside deck. I haven't had the desire to try it, but the waitress insists that the "Chilly & Cheeseburger" is tasty; it includes a burger with ice cream, hot fudge, strawberries, and a pickle. **Stockman's Steak Pub,** 117 W. Pine, tel. 367-4563, has the best steaks in Pinedale. **Fremont Peak Restaurant** serves up dense and authentic German food (the owner is from Germany). Eight miles east of town on Fall Creek Rd. is **Fort Williams Recreation Area,** tel. 367-4670, which has thick steaks, beans, and other hearty fare served Thurs.-Mon., May-October. **Sweet Tooth Saloon,** 128 W. Pine St., tel. 367-4724, is an old-fashioned ice-cream parlor. Get groceries at **Faler's Thriftway,** 341 E. Pine, tel. 367-2131. Inside is a deli, plus one of the largest collections of critter heads anywhere. The city park is a pleasant place for picnic lunches.

Entertainment

Both **Cowboy Bar,** 104 W. Pine, tel. 367-4520, and **Stockman's Bar,** 16 N. Maybell Ave., tel. 367-4562, have live C&W tunes most weekends. The latter attracts a younger crowd. **Fort Williams Recreation Area,** eight miles east of Pinedale, tel. 367-4670, is a popular place to unwind in a cozy atmosphere; open May-Oct. only. **The Place Bar,** tel. 367-2585, in Cora (10 miles northwest of Pinedale) has a pool table along with lots of mounted animal heads.

Events

The big summertime event in Pinedale is the **Green River Rendezvous,** held the second Sunday in July. Established in 1936, this is one of the oldest celebrations of the mountain men rendezvous era and commemorates the raucous activities of the 1830s on nearby Horse Creek. A pageant attracts up to 15,000 visitors, and there are all sorts of other activities, including black-powder shoots, historical demonstrations, a parade, square dancing, cowboy poetry, a crafts fair, and rodeos. All summer long visitors can watch roping events on Tuesday nights at the fairgrounds. In early August comes the annual **Fremont Lake Sailing Regatta,** while mid-

August brings the **Fat Tire Challenge** mountain-bike race. The **Championship Rodeo** in early September is the last big event of the year.

Recreation

Golfers will enjoy Pinedale's 18-hole **Rendezvous Meadows Golf Course.** The **Forest Service District Office** at 210 W. Pine St., tel. 367-4326, has maps ($3) and hiking info on trails in the nearby Bridger Wilderness. **Great Outdoor Shop,** 332 W. Pine, tel. 367-2440, sells quality outdoor gear of all sorts. Get topo maps and fishing gear at **Wind River Sporting Goods,** 234 Pine St., tel. 367-2419. **Horseback rides** ($25 for two hours, or $50/day) are available from several local lodges: Ft. William, tel. 367-4670; Elk Ridge, tel. 367-2553; DC Bar, tel. 367-2268; and Boulder Lake, tel. 367-2961. Elk Ridge also offers wilderness pack trips.

On The Water

The east slope of the Wind River Mountains contains several large lakes, created when glaciers retreated after the last major ice age some 10,000 years ago. The terminal moraines they left behind acted as dams, although some have been enlarged with human-created dams in recent years. The lakes are very popular with anglers. **Fremont Lake** is Wyoming's second-largest natural lake, reaching 12 miles in length, a half-mile across, and up to 600 feet deep. It's just three miles northeast of Pinedale and is famous for the Mackinaw that approach 40 pounds. Other lakes of note are **Half Moon Lake, Willow Lake,** and **Boulder Lake.** See "Green River Lakes Trails" (p. 241) for info on the Green River Lakes and New Fork Lakes. All of these lakes have Forest Service campgrounds for $5-7 a night (some are free) and trails that lead into the Bridger Wilderness.

The lakes and streams near Pinedale offer outstanding fishing for cutthroat, rainbow, brook, Mackinaw, golden, and brown trout, plus grayling and whitefish. A number of local outfitters offer float-fishing trips down the Green River (approximately $75 pp/day); see the chamber of commerce for a listing. Canoeists or kayakers will also enjoy floating stretches of the Green. Ask at the Forest Service office for details. There is an indoor **swimming pool** in the high school, tel. 367-2832; $1.50 ($1 for kids). Seniors get in free.

MOUNTAIN MEN

The era of the fur trapper is one of the most colorful slices of American history, a time when a rough and hardy breed of men took to the Rockies in search of furs and adventure. Romanticized in such films as *Jeremiah Johnson,* the trappers actually played but a brief role in history and numbered fewer than 1,000 individuals. Their real importance lay in acting as the opening wedge for the West—as a vanguard for the settlers and gold miners who would follow their paths, often led by these same mountain men.

The Fur Business

Fashion is what sent men into the Rockies in the first place, since the waterproof underfur of a beaver could be used to create the beaver hat, all the rage in the early part of the 19th century. Beavers in the eastern U.S. were soon trapped out, forcing trappers to head farther and farther west. Several companies competed for the lucrative fur market, but John Jacob Astor's American Fur Company proved the most successful. In 1811, Astor sent a party of men across the Rockies to the mouth of the Columbia to build a trading post and then set up a chain of posts across the West. The men—known as the Astorians—were probably the first whites to follow the route that would later become the Oregon Trail.

John Jacob Astor's trappers went head to head against the Rocky Mountain Fur Company—owned at various times by some of the most famous mountain men: Jedediah Smith, David Jackson, William and Milton Sublette, Jim Bridger, Tom Fitzpatrick, and others. Competition for furs became so intense that Astor's men began following Jim Bridger and Tom Fitzpatrick to discover their trapping grounds. After trying unsuccessfully to shake the men tailing them, Bridger and Fitzpatrick deliberately headed into the heart of Blackfeet country, where Indians killed the leader of Astor's party and managed to leave Bridger with an arrowhead in his shoulder that was not removed until three years later.

A large number of Indians (particularly from the Flathead and Nez Percé tribes) were also involved in the fur trade, and a standard Indian trade value was 240 beaver pelts for a riding horse. In the mountains, anything from the world back east had considerable value. Guns sold for $100 each, blankets $40 apiece, tobacco for $3 a pound, and alcohol (often diluted) for up to $64 a gallon. After just two years of such trading, William Ashley retired with an $80,000 profit. Control of the fur market continued to change hands as the Rocky Mountain Fur Company and the American Fur Company competed

with each other and with a mysterious company headed by Capt. Benjamin Bonneville (which some believe was a front for the U.S. Army to explore the West).

Most of the men who trapped in the Rockies were hired and outfitted by the fur companies, while others worked under contract, trading furs for overpriced supplies. Many men found themselves in debt to the company at the end of a season. At the top of the heap were the free trappers, men who worked either alone or with others, but who sold their furs to whomever offered the highest prices. Some men—primarily those who brought trade goods to the rendezvous—became rich in the process. Others, such as John Colter, Jim Bridger, James Beckwourth, Jedediah Smith, Thomas Fitzpatrick, and Kit Carson, would achieve fame for their rich knowledge of the land and their ability to survive insurmountable odds. Many trappers married Indian women, learned sign language and various Indian tongues, and lived in tipis.

Trappers worked through the fall and spring when the pelts were their finest, while most winters were spent in the lower valleys with fellow trappers or friendly Indians. In his *Journal of a Trapper 1834-1843,* Osborne Russell described a campfire scene among fellow mountain men:

A large fire was soon blazing encircled with sides of Elk ribs and meat cut in slices supported on sticks down which the grease ran in torrents The repast being over the jovial tale goes round the circle the peals of loud laughter break upon the stillness of the night which after being mimicked in the echo from rock to rock it dies away in the solitary. Every tale puts an auditor in mind of something similar to it but under different circumstances which being told the "laughing part" gives rise to increasing merriment and furnishes more subjects for good jokes and witty sayings such as Swift never dreamed of Thus the evening passed with eating drinking and stories enlivened with witty humor until near Midnight all being wrapped in their blankets lying around the fire gradually falling to sleep one by one until the last tale is "encored" by the snoring of the drowsy audience The Speaker takes the hint breaks

continued

off the subject and wrapping his blanket more closely about him soon joins the snoring party—The light of the fire being supersed by that of the Moon just rising from behind the Eastern Mountains a sullen gloom is cast over the remaining fragments of the feast and all is silent except the occasional howling of the solitary wolf on the neighboring mountain whose senses are attracted by the flavors of roasted meat but fearing to approach nearer he sits upon a rock and bewails his calamities in piteous moans which are re-echoed among the Mountains.

A good trapper could take in upwards of 150 beaver in a year, worth $4-6 apiece. It was an arduous job, and the constant threat of attacks by the Blackfeet Indians made it even more difficult. The great letting-go came with the summer rendezvous, an event anticipated for months ahead of time.

The Rendezvous

William H. Ashley, founder of the Rocky Mountain Fur Company—the main competition for Astor's American Fur Company—was one of the most important figures in the fur trade. In 1822, he ran an ad in a St. Louis paper that read:

To Enterprising Young Men. The subscriber wishes to engage ONE HUNDRED MEN, to ascend the river Missouri to its source, there to be employed for one, two or three years.—For particulars enquire of Major Andrew Henry, near the Lead Mines, in the County of Washington, (who will ascend with, and command the party) or to the subscriber at St. Louis. —Wm. H. Ashley.

Ashley's company of men—along with $10,000 in supplies—made it up into the Yellowstone River country, where he left them the following year, promising to resupply them in 1825 on the Henry's Fork near its confluence with the Green River, along the present-day Wyoming-Utah border. Thus began the first rendezvous. They would take place every summer until 1840. Ashley failed to bring booze that first summer, and the rendezvous only lasted two days. In future years, however, the whiskey flowed freely and the festivities lasted for weeks.

The rendezvous—a French word meaning "appointed place of meeting"—was a time when the trappers—both white and Indian—could sell their furs, trade for needed supplies and Indian squaws (the women had little say in the matter, but most took considerable pleasure in the arrangement), meet with old friends, get rip-roaring drunk, and engage in storytelling, gambling, gun duels, and contests of all sorts. Horse racing, wrestling bouts, and shooting contests were favorites. (Kit Carson killed Shunar, a big French bully, in a duel during one of the Green River rendezvous.) Debauchery reigned supreme in these three-week-long affairs, and by the time they were over, many of the trappers had lost their entire year's earnings.

During the heyday of the fur trade, a common saying was "all trails lead to the Seedskeedee [Green River]." Six rendezvous were held here in the 1830s, with the others in the Wind River/Popo Agie River area, on Ham's Fork of the Green River, or in Idaho and Utah. Sites were chosen where there was space for up to 500 mountain men and 3,000 Indians, plenty of game, ample grazing for the thousands of horses, and good water. It was no coincidence that all were held in Shoshone country rather than farther east or north where the hostile Sioux, Blackfeet, and Crow held sway. Despite such precautions, over half of Ashley's men were scalped by Indians.

Changing Times

The end of the rendezvous system—and most of the Rocky Mountain fur trapping—came about for a variety of reasons: overtrapping, the financial panic of 1837, and because other materials—particularly the South American nutria and silk from China—were being used more often in hats. In addition, permanent trading posts such as Fort Laramie drew Indians away from the mountains to trade for buffalo robes instead of beaver furs. By 1840, when the last rendezvous was held on the banks of the Green River near present-day Pinedale, it was obvious there would be no more. One of the longtime trappers, Robert Newell, said to his partner, Joseph Meek:

We are done with this life in the mountains—done with wading in beaver dams, and freezing or starving alternately—done with Indian trading and Indian fighting. The fur trade is dead in the Rocky Mountains, and it is no place for us now, if ever it was. We are young yet, and have life before us. We cannot waste it here; we cannot or will not return to the States. Let us go down to the Wallamet and take farms.

Winter Recreation

Cross-country skiers should pick up a copy of the **Skyline Drive Nordic Touring Trails** map from the Forest Service or chamber of commerce offices in Pinedale. The trails are groomed and marked. More adventurous skiers will find all sorts of places to explore in the Bridger Wilderness just a few miles east of Pinedale. The lower elevations of the Wind River Mountains are also extremely popular with snowmobilers, and trails head out right from town. The **Continental Divide Snowmobile Trail** passes right by Pinedale and will eventually stretch to Yellowstone.

Information And Services

The **Pinedale Chamber of Commerce,** 35 S. Tyler, tel. 367-2242, is open Mon.-Fri. 9-1. A summer-only information kiosk on Pine St. near Fremont Ave. is open daily 9-5. The **Forest Service District Office** is located at 210 W. Pine St., tel. 367-4326, and the **BLM Office** is at 431 W. Pine St., tel. 367-4358. **Paperclips to Manuscripts,** 219 E. Pine St., tel. 367-2428, sells books on Wyoming. The **library** is at 40 S. Fremont Ave., tel. 367-4114. **Sublette Stage,** tel. 537-5403, the local taxi company, can provide shuttle service to trailheads. Drivers en route to Jackson Hole should fill up in Pinedale since gas prices will only get higher.

NEARBY TOWNS

Boulder

A dozen miles south of Pinedale is Boulder (pop. 70), consisting of a gas station/grocery store. **Ox-Yoke Acres Campground,** tel. 537-5453, charges $10 for tents (no trees), $12 for RVs. Showers for noncampers are $3; open May-October. **Meadow Lake Outfitting,** five miles east of Boulder, tel. 537-5278, has bed-and-breakfast accommodations for $50 d, including a warm-springs pool. Halfway between Pinedale and Boulder is a roadside telephone pole topped by an active osprey nest.

Daniel

Head 11 miles west of Pinedale and then another mile south on US 189 to tiny Daniel, where the country bar makes some of the best Bloody Marys in Wyoming. A roadside marker north of Daniel notes the site of **Fort Bonneville,** built in 1832 to serve as a fur-trade center run by Captain Benjamin Bonneville. It lasted only a year but gained the nickname "Fort Nonsense" because of the severely cold and snowy winters that made life difficult for Bonneville's men. The fort consisted of two blockhouses guarding a perimeter of tall log posts.

Two miles south and then 2 1/2 miles east of Daniel on a dirt road is a monument to **Father Pierre Jean DeSmet,** who performed mass

THE SUMMER RENDEZVOUS.

the Summer Rendezvous

during the 1840 rendezvous at this site. A small shrine marks the site and is used during a commemorative mass each July. Pinckney Sublette, one of four brothers from this famous family of trappers, is also buried nearby. The access road cuts through barren sage and grass country, but the vista changes abruptly as you reach the Green River. Below you the Green River twists its way through a lush landscape of grass, cattle, and cottonwoods. Pretty easy to see why the rendezvous was held in this area! Get here for a summer sunrise when it is easy to imagine the multitude of Indians and mountain men spread below for the annual festivities. A short distance beyond the monument are the red log barn and white log home of the historic Quarter Circle 5 Ranch, a definitive Wyoming spread.

Big Piney

An oil boomtown in the late 1970s, Big Piney (pop. 450) has faced hard times more recently. The town is not entirely as it may first appear, however. Along Main St. many of the buildings are either run-down or boarded up, but attractive homes line the suburban neighborhoods and a modern brick high school lies on the west end. Stay at **Big Piney Motel**, tel. 276-3352, for $30 s or $38 d. The historic **Frontier Hotel**, tel. 276-3329, charges just $18 s or $20 d, but take a look at the rooms first. No TV or phones. **Lain's Sports Center & Motel**, tel. 276-3303, has dirt-cheap rates of $18 s or d in dumpy old trailers. **Sage Cafe**, tel. 276-3068, serves good all American fare, and has a nice salad bar. **Ye Olde Pizza Parlor**, tel. 276-3546, makes fine pizzas. **Erickson's Cafe** is the local greasy spoon where you'll meet most everyone in town sometime during the day.

The main annual event is the **Big Piney Chuck Wagon Days** on the Fourth of July. Festivities include a rodeo, a parade, fireworks, and a free barbecue. The local library is open Mon.-Fri. 10-5 and Sat. 11-2. The Forest Service also has a **district office** (tel. 276-3375) in Big Piney where you can find out about the route west into the Wyoming Range. There is a fine-arts center in the high school on the west side of town. Also inside is a swimming pool ($1).

Marbleton

Marbleton (pop. 630), just a couple hundred yards up US 189 from Big Piney, consists of a few old log buildings. **Marbleton Inn**, tel. 276-5231, offers excellent dinners and the finest lodging accommodations in the area ($34 s or $40 d). **Country Chalet Inn**, tel. 276-3391, has pleasant rooms for $28 s or $32 d. Campers will be happy to know that the **Laundry Basket Laundromat** in Marbleton has hot showers for $1. The **Waterhole**, tel. 276-3796, is the center of nightlife in the area, offering all sorts of bizarre contests, including gopher races and "cowboy open golf." Ask about the Little Buckaroo Rodeo for children, complete with those ever-wild Shetland ponies. Other rodeos can be found throughout the summer at the fairgrounds. North of Marbleton, the enormous Wind River Mountains become more visible and the highway crosses the **Lander Cutoff**, its ruts now barely visible across the sagebrush. Built in 1858 by Col. Frederick W. Lander and his soldiers, it served two purposes: as a shorter route to California and Oregon, and as a way to bypass the Mormon communities in Utah. The route offered good grazing and water as well as abundant game, and it quickly became the preferred route to California and Oregon.

TO JACKSON HOLE

US 189-191 provides a scenic route to Hoback Junction and Jackson Hole, crossing the Green River and then slowly climbing into the hills. Aspens begin to appear on the hilltops and willows line the creeks. The 11,000-foot-tall Gros Ventre Mountains are visible to the northwest. Gradually, lodgepole pine and aspen begin to replace the sagebrush. At **the Rim,** the road enters Bridger-Teton National Forest. West of here, the land drains into the Hoback River, which joins the Snake River at Hoback Junction, 40 miles away. The road curves gradually down through this mountainous country, crossing the Hoback River again and again.

Bondurant

The spread-out town of Bondurant (pop. 100) straggles along the road through a gorgeous mountain valley, its pastures dotted with enormous piles of hay, creekside willows, and grazing horses. The Gros Ventre Mountains form a dramatic backdrop. Bondurant is named for Sarah Ellen and Benjamin Franklin Bondurant, the first settlers here. Between 1907 and 1927 they ran a popular dude ranch and had as pets all sorts of wild animals: antelope, elk, and even young bears. **Triangle F Lodge,** tel. 733-2836 (built in 1928), has rustic log cabins with wood stoves starting at $15. A cafe here serves standard American fare. **Smiling S Motel,** tel. 733-3457, charges $25 s or d; campground rates are $7 for tents or $12 for RVs. Showers for noncampers are $2. Open late May-September. **Hoback Village,** tel. 733-3631, has modern cabins (but no TV) starting at $40 s or $45 d; open May-October. On the west end of "town," **Elkhorn Bar and Trading Post,** tel. 733-8358, has a general store and country watering hole.

Hoback Canyon

A few miles west of Bondurant, the road clings to the walls of Hoback Canyon as it passes the high face of Battle Mountain, site of one of the few conflicts between Indians and whites in this part of Wyoming. It was here in 1895 that whites from Jackson Hole attacked Bannock Indians who had been hunting "out of season" along the Hoback River. (See p. 266 for more on this sad story.) Just before you reach Hoback Junction, a sign describes John Hoback, the trapper and guide who led the Astorian trappers of Wilson Price Hunt through here in 1811.

Granite Hot Springs

Just west of Battle Mountain on US 189-191 is the turnoff to Granite Hot Springs. *Do* take this very scenic side trip! A washboarded gravel road follows Granite Creek for 10 miles, with impressive views of the Gros Ventre Range and a 50-foot waterfall. The road ends at a parking lot just a short walk from the hot springs. The pool (93-112° F) was built in 1933 by the CCC and is open 10-8 during the summer, or 10-5 in winter. It's closed in fall and spring. The cost is $4.50 for adults, $3.50 for kids. Suits and towels can also be rented. Granite Canyon Rd. is not plowed in winter but is groomed for use by both snowmobilers and cross-country skiers. A nearby campground ($7) is open late June-early Sept., or you can camp along the road in to the hot springs.

JACKSON HOLE AND THE TETONS

Jackson Hole is one of the most-visited slices of wild country in North America. Each year more than two million travelers pass through, stopping to enjoy the energetic town of Jackson, to camp under the stars in Grand Teton National Park, to hike flower-bedecked trails into the mountains, to ride sleighs among thousands of elk, to raft down the Snake River, to ski at one of the local resorts, or simply to stand in wonderment at the view from Snake River overlook. Many continue on north to Yellowstone National Park, another place on everyone's must-see list. Drive north from Jackson toward Yellowstone and you'll quickly discover why so many people are attracted to this place. The Tetons seem to act as a magnet, drawing your eyes away from the road and forcing you to stop and absorb some of their majesty. Welcome to one of the world's great wonderlands.

In the lingo of the mountain men, a "hole" was a large valley ringed by mountain ranges. Jackson Hole, on Wyoming's far western border,

is justifiably the most famous of all these intermountain valleys. Although Jackson Hole reaches an impressive 40 miles north to south and up to 10 miles across, it is the magnificent range of mountains to the west that defines this valley. Shoshone Indians who wandered through this country called the peaks Teewinot ("Many Pinnacles"); later explorers would use such labels as Shark's Teeth or Pilot Knobs, but the name that stuck came from lonely French-Canadian trappers who arrived in the early 1800s: les Trois Tetons, (literally, "Three Tits").

The valley, originally called Jackson's Hole, was named for a likeable trapper, David E. Jackson, one of the men who helped establish the Rocky Mountain Fur Company. When Jackson and his partners sold out in 1830, they realized a profit of over $50,000. Jackson's presence remains in the names for both Jackson Hole and Jackson Lake. Eventually, more polite folks began calling the valley Jackson Hole, in an attempt to end the ribald stories associated with

NORTHWEST WYOMING

the name Jackson's Hole. (It's easy to imagine the jokes with both Jackson's Hole and the Tetons in the same place.) By the way, in 1991, a group calling itself the "Committee to Restore Decency to Our National Parks" created quite a stir by suggesting that Grand Teton National Park be renamed. A letter sent to the Park Service and various members of Congress noted: "Though a great many Americans may be oblivious to this vulgarity, hundreds of millions of French people around the world are not! How embarrassing that these spectacular, majestic mountains are reduced to a dirty joke overseas." After a flurry of letters in response, the hoax was revealed; it was a prank by staff members of *Spy* magazine.

HISTORY

The first people to cross the mountain passes into Jackson Hole probably arrived while the last massive glaciers were still retreating. Clovis stone arrowheads—a style used 11,000 years ago—have been found along the edges of the valley. These early peoples were replaced in the 16th and 17th centuries by the Shoshone, Bannock, Blackfeet, Crow, and Gros Ventre tribes, who hunted bison from horses. When the first fur trappers tramped up the river valleys into Jackson Hole, they found Indian paths throughout the valley.

John Colter

Transport yourself back to the early 19th century, a time when people from the new nation called America saw the world west of the Mississippi River as just a blank spot on the map. In 1803, Thomas Jefferson purchased the Louisiana Territory from France, and to learn more about this gigantic piece of real estate he sent Meriwether Lewis and William Clark on a military expedition to the Pacific coast, a trip that took nearly two and a half years. Although the expedition skirted around Wyoming—heading across Montana instead—it proved the opening wedge for the settlement of the west and, indirectly, for the discovery of Jackson Hole. On the return trip, the party met two fur trappers en route to the upper Missouri River. One of Lewis and Clark's respected scouts, John Colter, was allowed to join the trappers, "provided no one of the party would ask or expect a Similar permission."

After a winter of trapping with his partners, Colter headed alone down the Platte River, but before he could get back to civilization he met up with a company of trappers led by Manuel Lisa. They were on their way to the Rockies, determined to cash in on the huge demand for beaver furs by trapping the rich beaver streams that Lewis and Clark had described. Wealth beckoned, and John Colter gladly turned his tracks around again, guiding Lisa's men up to the mouth of the Big Horn River, where they built a small fort. From there Colter was sent on a mission: contact Indians throughout the region, trading beads and other items for beaver furs.

His wanderings in the winter of 1807-08 were the first white exploration of this region. A map produced by William Clark in 1814 and based upon Colter's recollections shows an incredible midwinter journey around Yellowstone and

The "Colter Stone," with Colter's name inscribed on the face, and the date 1808 on the other.

G. BRYAN HARRY/COURTESY OF GRAND TETON N.P.

THE WHITE SHOSHONE

The quiet little Jackson Hole settlement of Wilson is named after one of the West's most fascinating characters, "Uncle Nick" Wilson. Born in 1842, Nick grew up in Utah, where he made friends with a fellow sheepherder, an Indian boy, and learned to speak his language. Then, suddenly, Nick's life took a strange twist. The mother of Chief Washakie (from Wyoming's Wind River Reservation) had recently lost a son, and in a dream she had been told that a white boy would come to take his place.

Unable to convince her otherwise, Washakie sent his men out to find the new son. They came across Nick and offered him a pinto pony and the chance to fish, hunt, and ride horses all he wanted. It didn't take much persuading, and for the next two years he lived as a Shoshone, learning to hunt buffalo, to use a bow and arrow, and to answer to his new name, Yagaiki. He became a favorite of Chief Washakie, but when word came (falsely) that Nick's father was threatening to attack the Shoshones with an army of men to retrieve his son, the chief reluctantly helped Nick return home.

At age 18, Nick Wilson became one of the first Pony Express riders, a job that nearly killed him when he was struck in the head during a Piute Indian attack. A doctor managed to remove the arrow point, but Wilson remained in a coma for nearly two weeks. Thereafter, Wilson always wore a hat to cover the scar, even inside buildings. He went on to become an Army scout and a driver for the Overland Stage before returning to a more sedate life of farming. Many years later, in 1889, Nick Wilson led a party of five Mormon families over steep Teton Pass and down to the rich grazing lands in Jackson Hole. The town that grew up around them became Wilson. In later years, "Uncle Nick" recounted his adventures in *The White Indian Boy*.

Jackson lakes, crossing the Tetons twice, and up through Jackson Hole. He did not get back to the fort until the following spring, telling tales of huge mountain ranges and a spectacular geothermal area that others quickly laughed off as "Colter's Hell." (In 1931, an Idaho farmer claimed to have plowed up a stone carved into the shape of a human face, with "John Colter 1808" etched into the sides. There is evidence that it was a hoax, carved by a man anxious to obtain a horse concession with Grand Teton National Park. He got the concession after donating the rock to the park museum.)

Colter went on to become one of the most famous of all mountain men, and his later harrowing escape from the Blackfeet in Montana has become the stuff of legends: After being captured and stripped naked, he was forced to literally run for his life, somehow managing to outdistance his pursuers for six miles before hiding in a pile of logs until dark. He walked barefoot the 300 miles back to Manuel Lisa's fort, surviving on roots and tree bark. Shortly thereafter, Colter was reported to have thrown his hat on the ground, declaring, "I'll be damned if I ever come into [this country] again." He returned to St. Louis, married, and established a farm near that of fellow explorer Daniel Boone. Colter lived long enough to give William Clark a description of the country he had visited but died from jaundice just three years later in 1813.

Because of the abundance of beavers along tributaries of the Snake River, Jackson Hole became an important crossroads for the Rocky Mountain fur trade. No rendezvous was ever held in the valley, but many of the most famous mountain men spent time here. They first trapped beavers in Jackson Hole in 1811, but it was not until the 1820s that fur trapping really came into its own as mountain men fanned through the wilderness in search of the "soft gold." This search continued for the next two decades, finally dying out when overtrapping made beavers harder to find and silk hats replaced fur hats. After the last rendezvous in 1840, most of the old trappers headed on to new adventures, the best becoming guides for those en route to Oregon and California. Because Jackson Hole was not close to the Oregon Trail or other routes west, the area remained virtually deserted until the late 19th century.

Settlers

The first Jackson Hole homesteaders arrived in 1884, followed quickly by those coming to escape the law. The settlers survived by grazing cattle, harvesting hay, and acting as guides for rich hunters from Europe and eastern states. Gradually they filled the richest parts of the valley with homesteads. Conflicts soon arose between the Bannock Indians, who had been hunt-

ing in Jackson Hole for more than a hundred years, and the new settlers who made money guiding wealthy sportsmen.

By 1895, Wyoming had enacted game laws prohibiting hunting during 10 months of the year. Claiming that the Indians were taking elk out of season, Constable William Manning and 26 settlers arrested a group of 28 Indians (mostly women and children) who had been hunting in Hoback Canyon. When the Bannocks attempted to flee, an elderly Indian was shot four times in the back and died. Most of the others escaped. Settlers in Jackson Hole feared revenge and called in the cavalry, but the Indians who had been hunting in the area all returned peaceably to their Idaho reservation. Astoundingly, the *New York Times* headlined the incident with "Settlers Massacred—Indians Kill Every One at Jackson's Hole—Courier Brings the News— Red Men Apply the Torch to All the Houses in the Valley." Although none of this was true, the attack by whites succeeded in forcing the Indians off their traditional hunting grounds, an action eventually upheld in a landmark U.S. Supreme Court case.

DOWNTOWN JACKSON

© MOON PUBLICATIONS, INC.

Jackson Hole Comes Of Age

By the turn of the century, the settlements of Jackson, Wilson, Kelly, and Moran had all been established. The towns grew slowly as people survived by ranching and guiding, along with a strange new business, tending to wealthy "dudes" from back east. Eventually, tourism would vastly eclipse raising cattle in importance, but even today Teton County has nearly as many cattle as people. Jackson, the largest town in Jackson Hole, was established in 1897 when Grace Miller (wife of a local banker known derisively as "Old Twelve Percent") bought a large plot of land and planned a town site. In an event that should come as no surprise in "The Equality State," Jackson became the first town in America to be entirely governed by women. The year was 1920, and not only was the mayor a woman (Grace Miller), but so were all four councilmembers, the city clerk, the treasurer, and even the town marshal. They remained in office until 1923.

Over the years Jackson has grown, spurred on by the creation of Grand Teton National Park and the development of Jackson Hole Ski Resort. During the 1980s Jackson Hole began to really boom as tourists flooded the region and wealthy families built elaborate second homes and golf courses. Although much of the area is public land and will remain undeveloped, rapid growth on private land threatens to turn Jackson Hole into another Aspen or Vail.

JACKSON

The town of Jackson (pop. 4,500) lies near the southern end of Jackson Hole, hemmed in on three sides by Snow King Mountain, the Gros Ventre Range, and East Gros Ventre Butte. At 6,200 feet in elevation, Jackson experiences cold snowy winters, wet springs, warm sunny summers, and gorgeous falls. Jackson is quite unlike any other place in Wyoming. Sit on a bench in town square on a summer day and you're likely to see cars from every state in the Union. Tourists dart in and out of the many gift shops, art galleries, fine restaurants, Western-style saloons, and trendy boutiques. The cowboy hats all look as if the price tags just came off. This sure isn't Rock Springs! In fact, about the only thing the two towns seem to share are rumors that the Mafia owns a number of major businesses.

In other parts of Wyoming, Jackson is viewed with a mixture of awe and disdain: awe over its booming economy, but disdain that Jackson is not a "real" town, just a false front put up to sell things to outsiders. Yes, Jackson is almost wholly dependent upon the almighty tourist dollar, but as a result it has a cultural richness that is lacking in other parts of the state. Besides, if you don't like all the commercial foolishness, it's easy to escape to a campsite or remote trail in the wonderful countryside of nearby Grand Teton National Park or Bridger-Teton National Forest.

Keep your eyes open around Jackson and you're likely to see famous (or infamous, depending upon your perspective) residents such as actor Harrison Ford, former Secretary of the Interior James Watt (who resigned in disgrace in 1983), attorney Gerald Spence (of Karen Silkwood and Imelda Marcos fame or infamy), former Wyoming governor Clifford Hansen, Yvon Chouinard (mountaineer and founder of Patagonia), along with members of the Rockefeller family.

SIGHTS

Town Square

One of Jackson's most distinctive and attractive features is its central town square. The Rotary Club planted trees here in 1932 and added four picturesque arches made from hundreds of elk antlers. Today these trees offer summertime shade, and at any time of day or night you'll find visitors admiring or getting their photo taken in front of the arches. During the winter, the town square's snow-covered arches and trees are draped with lights, giving them a festive atmosphere. Surrounded by dozens of boardwalk-fronted galleries, bars, restaurants, factory outlets, and gift shops, the square is the focal point of tourist activity in Jackson. Depending upon the season, horse-drawn carriages, stagecoaches, or sleighs ($3.50 adults or $2.50 kids) wait to transport you on a leisurely ride around town. During the summer, "cowboys" put on a free **shoot-out** for throngs of camera-happy tourists. The shoot-out starts every night except Sunday at 6:30 p.m. With stereotypical players and questionable acting, the "mountain law" system seems in dire need of reform. Most folks love the sham; Kodak loves it even more.

Museums

The small **Jackson Hole Museum,** 105 N. Glenwood, tel. 733-2414, has a surprising homespun charm. Inside are interesting displays and collections from the days of Indians, trappers, cattlemen, and dude ranchers who made this magnificent valley their home. Check out the Paul Bunyan-sized bear trap and the old postcards. Admission costs $2.50 for adults, $1.50 for students and seniors, and $6 for families. Summer hours are Sun. 10-5 and Mon.-Sat. 9:30-6. It is closed mid-Oct. to mid-May. Ask here about the historical **walking tours**

SAVING JACKSON HOLE

In recent years the town of Jackson has boomed as expensive homes spread across old ranchlands, huge retailers such as K mart moved in, and oil companies salivated over oil and gas wells on nearby Forest Service land. Today, despite the fact that 97% of the land in Teton County is in the public domain, the 70,000 acres of private land that remain are rapidly being developed, and Jackson Hole is in grave danger of losing the wild beauty that has attracted visitors for more than a century. There is even talk of a four-lane highway through Spring Gulch, an area now traversed by a gravel road!

The **Jackson Hole Alliance for Responsible Planning,** 260 E. Broadway, tel. 733-9417, is a thousand-member environmental group that works to preserve the natural areas of Jackson Hole and to prevent the town from becoming just another trashy tourist mill. Membership is only $10/year and includes a bimonthly newsletter and a chance to help control the many developments that threaten the valley. Another influential local group is the **Jackson Hole Land Trust,** Box 2897, tel. 733-4707, a nonprofit organization that purchases land and obtains conservation easements to maintain ranches and other land threatened by development. They now protect more than 6,000 acres in the valley, including the 1,740-acre Walton Ranch, visible along the highway between Jackson and Wilson.

($2.50 adults, $1.50 seniors or students) of Jackson's downtown, given Mon.-Sat. at 11 a.m.

Teton County Historical Center, 105 Mercell Ave., tel. 733-9605, is a research facility housing photo archives and many old books from the area, along with a fine exhibit on the fur trade and an impressive collection of Indian trade beads and mountain men paraphernalia. A replica of the "Colter stone" is also on display, along with rotating exhibits through the year. Hours are Mon.-Fri. 9-5 during the summer; free admission.

The excellent **Wildlife of the American West Art Museum,** 110 N. Center St., tel. 733-5771, houses more than 250 paintings and sculptures of western wildlife. It's the largest such collection in the world. Featured artists include Ernest Thompson Seton, George Catlin, Conrad Schwiering, Charles M. Russell, Albert Bierstadt, Karl Bodmer, John Clymer, and many others. The upstairs gallery has oil paintings and bronzes by Carl Rungius. Admission costs $3 for adults, $2 for seniors and students, or $5 for families (kids free); summer hours are Sun. 1-6 and Mon.-Sat. 10-6. Winter hours are Sun. 1-5 and Tues.-Sat. 10-5. Closed during Nov. and April.

For a slice of Americana, visit the **wildlife museum** at 862 W. Broadway, tel. 733-4909. Pay $2 ($1 for kids) for the standard collection of stuffed big bears posed threateningly in front of background murals. **Wyoming Heritage Museum,** 455 W. Broadway, tel. 739-1743, is worse—sort of an Indiana-Jones-kills-every-big-critter-on-the-planet theme. Don't waste your money.

Art In Jackson Hole

Artists have long been attracted by the beauty of Jackson Hole and the Tetons. Mount Moran, the 12,805-foot summit behind Jackson Lake, is named for Thomas Moran, whose watercolors helped persuade Congress to set aside Yellowstone as the first national park. The late Conrad Schwiering's paintings of the Tetons have attained international fame, and one was even used on the Postal Service's Wyoming Centennial stamp in 1990. Ansel Adams's photograph of the Tetons remains etched in the American consciousness as one of the archetypical wilderness images. A copy of the image was included in the payload of the *Voyager II* spacecraft currently en route out of our solar system. Today many artists live or work in Jackson Hole, making this Wyoming's premier center for the arts.

More than 30 galleries crowd the center of Jackson, covering the spectrum from Indian art collections of questionable authenticity to impressive photographic exhibits and shows by nationally acclaimed painters. Unfortunately, many of these galleries offer recycled ideas that are now manufactured in mass quantity with every cliché thrown in. Particularly egregious examples are the southwestern-style pastel pottery, the elk-antler lamps, and the paintings of noble-looking mountain men and Indians set against a Grand Teton backdrop. Local newspapers provide a complete rundown of current exhibitions and displays, along with maps showing gallery locations. Stop by the visitor center for info on upcoming **gallery walks,** held one evening each month and featuring many of the local galleries.

Several galleries are worth a visit, including the excellent Wildlife of the American West Art Museum (described above). One of the largest is **Wilcox Gallery,** a mile north of town on US 89, tel. 733-6450, featuring works from prominent Western painters and sculptors. Ask about the painting workshops here. The spacious **Trailside Galleries,** 105 Center St., tel. 733-3186, has fine paintings, drawings, jewelry, glassware, and sculpture by contemporary artists. **Wapiti Gallery,** 90 N. Center St., tel. 733-1732, emphasizes western paintings and sculpture, both contemporary and traditional. **The Robert Dean Collection,** 172 Center St., tel. 733-9290, specializes in authentic, high-quality Indian art and jewelry. **Rawson Galleries,** 50 King St., tel. 733-7306, features both traditional and avant-garde watercolors, etchings, and other artwork. **River Rock Gallery,** 170 E. Deloney, tel. 733-9181, features fine pottery and invitational exhibitions. Jack Dennis's **Wyoming Galleries,** 50 E. Broadway, tel. 733-7548, specializes in wildlife and traditional landscape paintings. For a different kind of art, **Dancer's Workshop** in Pink Garter Plaza, tel. 733-6398, offers dance classes and performances by the Three Rivers Dance Company.

Many nationally known photographers live or work in Jackson Hole, exhibiting their prints in Jackson galleries. Two photographers have noteworthy galleries. Tom Mangelsen's **Images of Nature Gallery** at 125 N. Cache (upstairs), tel. 733-6179, displays a selection of his outstanding wildlife photos. **Light Reflections,** 35 E. Deloney, tel. 733-4016, includes many of Fred Joy's large-format visions of the American West.

Snake River Institute

Each summer, the Snake River Institute (run by Gov. Sullivan's daughter) offers innovative workshops and seminars on the arts and their connection to the natural world. The programs last one to five days and include everything from "A Life in Hand: The Illustrated Journal" to "Angling Literature of the West." Classes are taught by respected poets, writers, photographers, and scientists, and tuition starts around $200 for a three-day workshop. Also available are special children's classes. In early October, the institute offers "Nature, Culture, and Human Values," a weekend symposium of readings, workshops, and other activities. Snake River Institute is headquartered in the historic Hardeman Homestead in Wilson. Contact them at Box 7724, Jackson, WY 83001, tel. 733-2214, for more information and a class brochure.

NATIONAL ELK REFUGE

Just a couple miles north of Jackson is the National Elk Refuge, winter home for thousands of these majestic animals. During the summer, these elk can be found up to 65 miles away, feeding on grasses, shrubs, and forbs in alpine meadows. But as the snows descend each fall, the elk move downslope, wintering in Jackson Hole and the surrounding country. The chance to view elk up close from a horse-drawn sleigh makes a trip to the National Elk Refuge one of the most popular wintertime activities for Jackson Hole visitors.

History

When the first ranchers arrived in Jackson Hole in the late 19th century, they moved onto land that had long been an elk migration route and wintering ground. The ranchers soon found elk raiding their haystacks and competing with cattle for forage, particularly during severe winters. The conflicts reached a peak early in this century when three consecutive severe winters killed thousands of elk, leading one settler to claim that he had "walked for a mile on dead elk lying from one to four deep."

Fortunately, a local rancher and hunting guide, Stephen N. Leek, had been given a camera by one of the sportsmen he had guided, George Eastman, founder of Kodak. Leek's disturbing photos of starving and dead elk found a national audience and helped pressure the state of Wyoming to appropriate $5000 to buy hay in 1909. Two years later the federal government began purchasing land for a permanent winter elk refuge, a refuge that would eventually cover nearly 25,000 acres. Today it is administered by the U.S. Fish and Wildlife Service. Famed biologist, illustrator, and conservationist Olaus Murie came to Jackson Hole in 1927 to begin his studies of the elk, remaining here until his death in 1963. With his wife Margaret (Mardie) Murie, they chronicled their adventures in *Wapiti Wilderness* (Boulder: Colorado Associated University Press). Conservationist Mardie Murie still lives in Moose, holding near-sainthood status among Wyoming conservationists.

Today more than 9,000 elk—half the local population—spend Nov.-May on the refuge. Because the elk habitat in the valley has been reduced to a quarter of its original size by development, refuge managers try to improve the remaining land by seeding, irrigation, and prescribed burning. In addition, during the most difficult foraging period, the elk are fed pelleted alfalfa, paid for in part by sales of elk antlers collected on the refuge (see p. 280). During this time, each elk eats more than seven pounds of supplemental alfalfa a day, or 30 tons per day for the entire herd. Elk head back into the mountains with the melting of snow each April and May. During the summer months only a few can be found on the refuge.

Visiting The Refuge

The refuge is primarily a winter attraction, although it is also an excellent place to watch birds and other wildlife in summer. Trumpeter swans nest and winter here. Get to the refuge by heading east on Broadway through town till it dead-ends. The signed dirt road curves left here and goes four miles to the refuge.

The **Elk Refuge Visitor Center,** tel. 733-9212, has displays, books, and pamphlets about elk, plus a slide show on elk and the refuge. Wait here for the **horse-drawn sleighs,** the refuge's real attraction. These sleighs offer a unique opportunity to ride among the thousands of elk without disturbing them. (People on foot would scare them.) Sleighs run daily 10-4 between late Dec. and late March, heading out as soon as enough folks show up for a ride (generally just long enough to watch the slide show). The cost is $7.50 for adults or $3.50 for children, and the rides last for 30-45 minutes. Highly recommended.

All Star Transportation, tel. 733-2888, offers shuttle service to the Elk Refuge from Teton Village ($11 RT) and downtown Jackson ($9 RT). **Jackson Hole Transportation,** tel. 733-3135, charges $9 RT from several downtown locations. Four miles north of town and next to the elk refuge is the **Jackson National Fish Hatchery,** tel. 733-2510, which rears a half-million cutthroat and lake trout annually. Open daily 8-4.

ACCOMMODATIONS

As one of the premier centers for tourism in Wyoming, Jackson Hole is jam-packed with hotels, motels, B&Bs, guest ranches, condominiums, and campgrounds. In Jackson alone there are more than 30 lodging places, plus many more in nearby Teton Village, Wilson, and Hoback Junction. See the charts for a complete listing. Other lodging can be found in Grand Teton National Park, see p. 310. Unfortunately, prices at these motels are considerably higher than rates in other parts of Wyoming. Expect to pay a minimum of $45 s or $55 d during the peak visitor seasons: July and Aug., and late Dec. to early January. Rates will be up to 40% lower in the off-seasons. Because of Jackson Hole's popularity, reservations are highly recommended, and during the Christmas/New Year's period you should probably reserve in summer to ensure getting a place. For up-to-date lodging rates in and around Jackson Hole, request the **accommodations brochure** from the Jackson Hole Visitors Council, tel. (800) 782-0011.

Jackson's least expensive lodging place, the **Bunkhouse,** tel. 733-3668, is located in the basement of the Anvil Motel at 215 N. Cache. This "hostel" costs just $15 pp, including kitchen facilities and a TV room. It is right in town and almost always has space. Facilities are similar to a youth hostel's: bunk beds in dorm-type cubicles. No curfew. The kitchen has a refrigerator and microwave but no stove. Folks who aren't staying here can use the showers for $5. Another place to get showers ($3.50) is Jackson Hole Campground, on the south end of town, tel. 733-2927.

It should come as no surprise that jet-set Jackson Hole has a number of elaborate, pricey, and sumptuous places to stay. The oldest and

continued on p. 274

JACKSON HOLE ACCOMMODATIONS

NAME	ADDRESS	PHONE	RATES	FEATURES
Bunkhouse	215 N. Cache	733-3668 (800) 234-4507	$15 pp	hostel with kitchen
The Hostel	Teton Village	733-3415	$34 s or d	very plain
Hillside Lodge	945 W. Broadway	733-3391	$35 s or d	kitchenettes $40+
Motel 6	1370 W. Broadway	733-1620	$36 s, $42 d	pool
Camp Creek Inn	Hoback	733-3099 (800) 228-8460	$40+	cabins
Snow King Lodge Motel	470 King St.	733-3480	$44 s or d	kitchenettes $54
Super 8 Motel	South US 89	733-6833 (800) 800-8000	$45 s, $57 d	
Alpine Motel	70 S. Jean St.	733-2082	$46 s, $54 d	pool, kitchenettes
Elk Refuge Inn	North US 89	733-3582	$48+ s, $52+ d	AAA-approved, kitchenettes
Teton Motel	165 W. Gill St.	733-3883	$49+ s or d	AAA-approved, open May-Oct.
Rawhide Motel	75 S. Millward	733-1216 (800) 835-2999	$49+ s, $55+ d	AAA-approved
Wood's Motel	120 N. Glenwood	733-2953	$50 s or d	AAA-approved, open mid-May through Sept.
Teton Gables Motel	1140 W. Broadway	733-3723	$52 s or d	
Split Creek Ranch	eight miles north	733-7522	$52 s or d	AAA-approved, open June-Sept., kitchenettes $12 extra
Anvil Motel (Budget Host)	215 N. Cache	733-3668 (800) 234-4507	$53+ s or d	jacuzzi, airport shuttle
Wagon Wheel Village	435 N. Cache	733-2357 (800) 323-9279	$53+ s, $58+ d	AAA approved, whirlpool, kitchenettes, cabins, open May to mid-Oct.
Hitching Post Lodge	460 E. Broadway	733-2606 (800) 821-8351	$54 s or d	AAA approved, pool
Prospector Motel	155 N. Jackson	733-4858	$54+ s or d	AAA-approved
Hoback River Resort	Hoback Jct.	733-5129	$55 s or d	
Lazy X Motel	325 N. Cache	733-3673	$55 s, $60 d	AAA-approved
Days Inn	1280 W. Broadway	739-9010 (800) 833-5343	$55+ s, $60+ d	AAA approved, whirlpool, sauna
Sagebrush Motel	550 W. Broadway	733-0336	$58+ s or d	kitchenettes $68
Pony Express Motel	50 S. Millward St.	733-3835 (800) 526-2658	$58+ s or d	AAA-approved, pool
Golden Eagle Motor Inn	325 E. Broadway	733-2042	$60 s or d	AAA-approved, pool, open June-Sept.

JACKSON HOLE ACCOMMODATIONS
(CONTINUED)

NAME	ADDRESS	PHONE	RATES	FEATURES
Buckrail Lodge	110 E. Karns Ave.	733-2079	$60+ s or d	AAA-approved, jacuzzi closed mid-Oct. to Feb.
Virginian Lodge	750 W. Broadway	733-2792 (800) 262-4999	$62 s, $70 d	AAA-approved, pool
Jackson Hole Lodge	420 W. Broadway	733-2992	$64+ s or d	AAA-approved, pool, whirlpools, sauna, exercise room
Ranch Inn Motel	45 E. Pearl St.	733-6363 (800) 348-5599	$68 s or d $100+	whirlpool, kitchenette suites
Trapper Motel	235 N. Cache	733-2648 (800) 341-8000	$68+ s or d	AAA-approved, whirlpools
Western Motel	225 S. Glenwood	733-3291	$68 s, $78 d	pool
Four Winds Motel	150 N. Millward St.	733-2474 (800) 228-6461	$68+ s or d	AAA approved
Horseshoe Motel	285 N. Cache	733-2287	$68+ s, $72+ d	
Stagecoach Motel	291 N. Glenwood	733-3451	$70+ s or d	
Outlaw Motel	265 N. Millward St.	733-3682	$76 s or d	kitchenettes
Antler Motel (Friendship Inn)	50 W. Pearl Ave.	733-2535 (800) 453-4511	$76 s, $80 d	whirlpool
49'er Inn (Friendship Inn)	330 W. Pearl	733-7550 (800) 451-2980	$78 s, $82 d	AAA-approved, whirlpool, sauna, exercise room
Cache Creek Motel	390 N. Glenwood	733-7781 (800) 843-4788	$78 s or d	AAA-approved, kitchenettes
Flat Creek Motel	1935 N. US 89	733-5276	$75 s or d $110	whirlpool, sauna, kitchenettes
Parkway Inn (Best Western)	125 N. Jackson St.	733-3143 (800) 247-8390	$78+ s, $80+ d	AAA approved, pool, whirlpools, sauna, exercise room
Elk Country Inn	480 W. Pearl	733-2364	$78+ s, $82+ d	kitchenettes $4 extra
Crystal Springs Inn	Teton Village	733-4423	$84 s or d	AAA approved
Wilson Motel	292 E. Pearl	733-2956	$86 s or d	pool, kitchenettes
Village Center Inn	Teton Village	733-3155 (800) 735-8342	$86+ s or d	AAA-approved, kitchens
Cowboy Village Resort	120 Flat Creek Dr.	733-3121 (800) 962-4988	$89 s or d	AAA-approved, whirlpools, kitchenettes
Executive Inn (Best Western)	325 W. Pearl Ave.	733-4340 (800) 528-1234	$89+ s or d	pool
Sojurner Inn	Teton Village	733-3657 (800) 445-4655	$105+ s or d	AAA-approved, pool, whirlpool, sauna
Mad Dog Ranch	Teton Village Rd.	733-3729	$110	cabins

JACKSON HOLE ACCOMMODATIONS
(CONTINUED)

NAME	ADDRESS	PHONE	RATES	FEATURES
Alpenhof Lodge	Teton Village	733-3242 (800) 732-3244	$110+ s or d	AAA-approved, pool, whirlpool, sauna
Snow King Resort	400 E. Snow King	733-5200 (800) 522-5464	$110+ s, $120+ d	AAA-approved, pool, whirlpool, sauna, airport shuttle
Wort Hotel	50 N. Glenwood St.	733-2190 (800) 322-2727	$116+ s or d	AAA approved, historic, airport shuttle
The Inn at Jackson Hole (Best Western)	Teton Village	733-2311 (800) 842-7666	$135+ s or d	AAA-approved, pool, kitchenettes, whir'pool
Spring Creek Resort	Gros Ventre Butte	733-8833 (800) 443-6139	$180+ s or d	AAA-approved, pool, whirlpool, airport shuttle

BED AND BREAKFASTS

NAME	ADDRESS	PHONE	RATES	FEATURES
Twin Mountain River Ranch	Hoback Jct.	733-1168	$55+ s or d	full breakfast, sauna
H.C. Richards B&B	160 W. Deloney	733-6704	$65+	motel rooms
Sundance Inn B&B	135 W. Broadway	733-3444	$69 s or d	continental breakfast, motel rooms
Teton View B&B	Wilson	733-7954	$70+ s or d	full breakfast
Fish Creek B&B	Wilson	733-2586	$85+ s or d	full breakfast, jacuzzi, log home
Teton Treehouse B&B	Wilson	733-3233	$90+ s, $95+ d	full breakfast, jacuzzi mountainside home
Twin Trees B&B	575 S. Willow	739-9737	$95 s or d	full breakfast
Moose Meadows B&B	Wilson	733-9510	$110 s or d	full breakfast
Wildflower Inn	Teton Village Rd.	733-4710	$110+ s or d	full breakfast, whirlpool, log house
Rusty Parrot Lodge	175 N. Jackson	733-2000 (800) 458-2004	$145+ s or d	full breakfast, jacuzzi free airport shuttle

best known is the **Wort Hotel,** but several other places offer equally high standards (and prices). Some of the most dramatic vistas are from **Spring Creek Resort,** high atop Gros Ventre Butte (west of town). For a homier visit to Jackson Hole, make reservations at one of the delightful B&Bs. One of the nicest is **Teton Treehouse B&B,** a gorgeous four-story hillside home.

Condominium Rentals

Condominiums provide one of the most popular lodging options for families and groups visiting Jackson Hole. These privately owned places are maintained by a number of local real-estate management companies and range from small studio apartments to spacious five-bedroom houses. All are completely furnished (including dishes), and have fireplaces, cable TV, phones, and midstay maid service. The nicest also in-

JACKSON HOLE CONDOMINIUMS

CONDOMINIUM COMPANIES	# OF UNITS	TELEPHONE	TOLL-FREE
BBC Property Management	20	733-6170	(800) 325-8605
Ely & Associates	30	733-8604	(800) 333-0914
The Inn at Jackson Hole	6	733-2311	(800) 842-7666
Jackson Hole Lodge	24	733-2992	(800) 642-4567
Jackson Hole Property Management	85	733-7945	(800) 443-8613
Jackson Hole Racquet Club Resort	120	733-3990	(800) 443-8616
Jackson Home Management	10	739-3000	
MTA Resorts	24	733-0613	(800) 272-8824
Mountain Property Management	15	733-1684	(800) 992-9948
Real Estate of Jackson Hole	5	733-0205	(800) 443-6130
Spring Creek Resort	70	733-8833	(800) 443-6139
Snow King Resort	16	733-5220	(800) 522-5464
Teton Village Property Management	115	733-4610	(800) 443-6840

clude access to pools and jacuzzis and have balconies overlooking the spectacular Tetons. Many of the condominiums are in Teton Village, right next to the ski area, with others scattered around Jackson Hole.

During the winter holiday season, expect to pay $130-165/night for studios (one or two people). Two-bedroom units (up to four people) cost $185-400/night, while full four-bedroom and loft condos (these sleep eight) start at a lofty $500/night and climb as high as $1200/night. Summer and off-peak rates are approximately 30% lower, with spring and fall rates 50-75% less than these peak winter holiday prices. In fall or spring, condos offer a real bargain for traveling families. Minimum stays of between two and seven nights are required throughout the year.

If you have the luxury of time, do a little comparison shopping before renting a condo. Things to ask about are whether you have access to a pool and jacuzzi, how close you are to the ski slopes, how frequent the maid service is, and whether the units include such amenities as free washing machines. Also be sure to find out what beds are in the rooms, since couples won't enjoy sleeping in twin bunk beds.

Camping

Both the National Park Service and the U.S. Forest Service maintain campgrounds around Jackson Hole. The chart (see p. 276) shows 20 public campgrounds and a dozen private RV parks within 50 miles of Jackson. For more specifics on public sites, contact Bridger-Teton National Forest in Jackson at 340 N. Cache, tel. 739-5500, or Grand Teton National Park in Moose, tel. 733-2880. In addition to these sites, many people camp informally on Forest Service lands at no charge.

Of the private RV parks in Jackson, the only decent place (real trees!) is Jackson Hole Campground, on the south end of town along Flat Creek. The RV park at **Astoria Mineral Hot Springs,** tel. 733-2659, is noteworthy because of a naturally heated mineral pool with 95° F water ($5; or $4 for campers).

FOOD

Jackson stands out from the rest of Wyoming on the culinary scene: chicken-fried steak may be available, but it certainly isn't the house speciality! You won't need to look far to find good food; in fact, the town seems to overflow with impressive (and even more impressively priced) eateries. There are at least 70 local restaurants—in a town that the Census Bureau says

JACKSON HOLE CAMPGROUNDS
YELLOWSTONE NATIONAL PARK

Most Forest Service campgrounds can be reserved ($5 extra) by calling (800) 342-2267. Park Service campsites are available on a first-come, first-served basis only. The campgrounds below are listed by direction and distance from Jackson.

CAMPGROUND	MILES AND DIRECTION FROM JACKSON	APPROXIMATE SEASON	FEE	FEATURES
Jenny Lake	20 N	May 25-Sept. 25	$7	Park Service; tents only; fills by 8 a.m.
Signal Mountain	32 N	May 10-Oct. 15	$7	Park Service; on Jackson Lake; fills by 10 a.m.
Colter Bay	40 N	May 25-Sept. 25	$7	Park Service; on Jackson Lake; fills by noon
Lizard Creek	48 N	June 15-Sept. 10	$7	Park Service; on Jackson Lake; fills by 2 p.m.
Snake River	55 N	June 15-Sept. 10	$7	Park Service; near Flagg Ranch; fills by 2 p.m.
Curtis Canyon	7 NE	June 5-Sept. 10	$6	Forest Service; 6 miles of gravel road
Gros Ventre	10 NE	May 1-Oct. 20	$7	Park Service; along Gros Ventre River; often fills by evening
Atherton Creek	18 NE	June 5-Oct. 30	$6	Forest Service; along Gros Ventre River; 5 miles of dirt road
Red Hills	22 NE	June 5-Oct. 30	$4	Forest Service; along Gros Ventre River; 4 miles of dirt road
Crystal Creek	23 NE	June 5-Oct. 30	$4	Forest Service; along Gros Ventre River; 5 miles of dirt road
Hatchet	40 NE	June 25-Sept. 10	$5	Forest Service; in Buffalo Valley
Turpin Meadow	50 NE	June 25-Sept. 10	$4	Forest Service; in Buffalo Valley
Cabin Creek	19 S	May 25-Sept. 10	$6	Forest Service; along Snake River
Elbow	22 S	June 10-Sept. 10	$6	Forest Service; along Snake River
East Table Creek	24 S	June 5-Sept. 10	$6	Forest Service; along Snake River
Station Creek	25 S	June 10-Sept. 10	$6	Forest Service; along Snake River
Wolf Creek	28 S	June 10-Sept. 10	$5	Forest Service; along Snake River
Hoback	22 SE	June 5-Sept. 10	$6	Forest Service; along Hoback River
Kozy	30 SE	June 5-Sept. 10	$5	Forest Service; along Hoback River
Granite Creek	35 SE	June 25-Sept. 10	$7	Forest Service; hot springs; nine miles of gravel road
Trail Creek	20 W	June 15-Sept. 10	$5	Forest Service; west of Teton Pass
Mike Harris	21 W	June 15-Sept. 10	$5	Forest Service; west of Teton Pass

has just 4,500 people! To get an idea of what to expect at local restaurants, pick up a copy of the free **Jackson Hole Dining Guide** at the visitor center or local restaurants. It includes sample menus and brief descriptions of most local establishments. If you don't find a place to your liking among those listed below, be assured that all the major fast-food outlets line Jackson's streets, ready to grease your digestive tract.

JACKSON HOLE CAMPGROUNDS

PRIVATE RV PARKS

NAME	LOCATION	TELEPHONE	TENTS	RVS	SEASON/FEATURES
Lazy J Corral	Hoback Jct.	733-1554	No	$14	May 15-Sept. 15
Flagg Ranch	Rockefeller Parkway	733-8761 (800) 443-2311	$14	$19	May 20-Oct. 20
Astoria Mineral Hot Springs	Hoback Jct.	733-2659	$14	$17	May 15-Sept. 15 natural mineral pool
Colter Bay RV Park	Moran	543-2855	No	$20	May 15-Sept.
Wagon Wheel Campground	525 N. Cache	733-4588	$15	$20	May-Sept.
Jackson Hole Campground	Hwy. 89 S	733-2927	$15	$22	year-round
S.R. KOA Campground	Moran	543-2483	$16	$21	May-Nov. 15
A-1 Campground	125 S. Virginian	733-2697	$16	$22	June-Sept. 15
Snake River Park KOA	Hoback Jct.	733-7078	$17	$24	April 15-Sept. 30
Holiday Trav-L-Park	Hoback Jct.	733-5240 (800) 323-8899	$19	$19	May 15-Sept. 15
Teton Village KOA	Teton Village	733-5354	$20	$26	May-Oct. 15
Virginian RV Park	750 W. Broadway	733-7189	No	$30	May 15-Sept.

Breakfast

The best breakfast place in Jackson isn't in Jackson. **Nora's Fish Creek Inn** in Wilson, tel. 733-8288, attracts a full house each morning with great, reasonably priced food, friendly waitresses, and an authentically rustic atmosphere. Nora's also serves tried-and-true dinners at a very good price. Highly recommended. In Jackson, locals get their buns into **The Bunnery**, 130 N. Cache, tel. 733-5474, each morning. Tasty pastries, homemade breakfasts, along with great sandwiches and Mexican dishes for lunch. Also very popular for breakfast is **Jedediah's House of Sourdough**, 135 E. Broadway, tel. 733-5671. The old-time crowd heads to Jackson's greasy spoon for breakfast and other meals: **LeJay's Sportsman's Cafe**, 72 S. Glenwood St., tel. 733-3110. Open 24 hours a day, this is the place to go when no other restaurant is open and your stomach is demanding all-American grub.

Lunch

One of the most popular noontime spots in Jackson is **Sweetwater Restaurant,** 85 King St., tel. 733-3553, where the lunch menu includes salads, homemade soups, and a variety of earthy sandwiches. For dinner, try mesquite-grilled lamb or the spinach-and-feta vegetarian casserole. **Pearl Street Bagels,** 145 Pearl St., tel. 739-1218, serves home-baked bagels and good coffee. Try a bagel with cream cheese, walnuts, and honey for $1.50. Pearl Street closes at 6 p.m. Get delicious sub sandwiches on tangy homemade bread at **New York City Sub Shop,** 25 S. Glenwood St., tel. 733-4414— Fastest sandwich-makers in the business. If you're looking for a substantial organic lunch, try the cafe at **Dynamic Health Natural Foods,** 130 W. Broadway, tel. 733-5418. **Jackson Drug,** established in 1912 and in the same place since 1937, has a very popular soda fountain that serves homemade ice cream. It's located right on town square at 15 E. Deloney Ave., tel. 733-2442. (Unfortunately, the quality has dropped since new owners took over in 1992.)

Cafes

New on the Jackson scene—and highly recommended—is **Sugarfoot Cafe,** 145 N. Glenwood, tel. 733-9148. This attractive little cafe is housed within one of Jackson's oldest buildings; it was originally a saddle shop. On the menu are unique specialties, including panini sandwiches stuffed with marinated artichoke hearts, mozzarella, and tomato. Great espresso coffees, or try their lemon granitas—sort of like a Slurpee, but far better—on a hot day. Be sure to ask about the various readings and other productions that take place here throughout the year. Open for lunch and dinner only.

Climbers and ski bums wear their Vuarnets to the oft-crowded **Shades Cafe,** 82 S. King St., tel. 733-2015. The tiny log cabin has a summer-only patio on the side, and delicious salads and burritos, as well as espresso coffees. It's a great place to hang out (though it does close early in the fall, winter, and spring). Teton Village has a second (winter-only) Shades Cafe, tel. 733-7091.

American

The most popular locals' eatery is **Bubba's Bar-B-Que Restaurant,** 515 W. Broadway, tel. 733-2288. Each evening the parking lot out front is jammed with folks waiting patiently for a chance to chew the marvelous BBQ spare ribs, savor the spicy chicken wings, or fill up at the impressive salad bar. Lunch is a real bargain at this four-stars place.

Head three miles south of town on US 89 to find the finest steaks in Jackson Hole at the **Steak Pub,** tel. 733-6977. Dinners are served in a rustic log-cabin setting. A very popular place with both locals and ski bums is the **Mangy Moose** in Teton Village, tel. 733-4913, where you'll find a good salad bar along with decent prices on steak and seafood. More good burgers at the '50s-style **Billy's Burgers,** 55 N. Cache (on the square), tel. 733-3279. Wilson's **Stagecoach Bar,** tel. 733-4407, makes delicious nachos, burgers, and other pub grub. Get chicken fricassee, seafood gumbo, shrimp étouffée, and other Cajun specialties at **The Acadian House** at the intersection of US 89 and State 22, tel. 739-1269.

Pasta and Pizza

Nani's Genuine Pasta House, 240 N. Glenwood, tel. 733-3888, serves regional Italian dishes from a menu that changes nightly. It has delicious handmade pastas, but it's expensive and the portions tend to be small. One of the tried-and-true local restaurants is **Anthony's Italian Restaurant,** 62 S. Glenwood St., tel. 733-3717. Prices are very reasonable, and vegetarians will find several good menu items. Guaranteed to fill you up.

Two pizza places stand out in Jackson. You'll find **Calico Pizza Parlor,** tel. 733-2460, in a garish red-and-white building three-quarters of a mile north on Teton Village Road. During the summer, be sure to get a side salad, fresh from their big garden. The bar at Calico is a very popular locals' watering hole. **Mt. High Pizza Pie,** 120 W. Broadway, tel. 733-3646, is a favorite downtown place with free delivery in Jackson. From mid-Sept. through April, Mt. High's stuff-yourself pizza buffet (Mon.-Fri. 11:30-1:30 and Tues. 5:30-9 p.m.) is the best meal deal in Jackson.

Continental/Nouvelle Cuisine

If you want fine continental dining and aren't scared off by entrees costing $15-25, Jackson has much to offer. In a plethora of fine European restaurants, one stands out: **Stiegler's,** tel. 733-1071, in the Aspens on Teton Village Road. The menu has names big enough to eat—pfeffer steak hasumannsart, or osttiroler schlipfkrapfen—but the dense Austrian cuisine is simply outstanding. If you enjoy German cooking, particularly game and veal, head to the **Alpenhof,** tel. 733-3462, in Teton Village.

Gouloff's, across from the Aspens on Teton Village Rd., tel. 733-1886, features "Teton cuisine" such as pistachio-nut chicken and wild-game meats. Very nice. In Teton Village, be sure to visit **The Range,** tel. 733-5481, where excellent fixed-price nouvelle-cuisine dinners make this a favorite of out-on-the-town locals. For views so spectacular that they make it difficult to concentrate on your meal, don't miss (top) Devils Tower; (bottom) Mormon Row, Grand Teton National Park (photos by Don Pitcher) (top left) Victoria Napoleon from the Pakima Tribe, Fort Washakie; (top right) hikers in the Tetons; (bottom) packers in North Fork Meadows (photos by Don Pitcher)

The Granary, tel. 733-8833, located atop East Gros Ventre Butte, west of Jackson. This is also a very popular place for evening cocktails.

An excellent continental restaurant in town is **The Blue Lion,** 160 N. Millward St., tel. 733-3912. The front patio makes for delightful summertime dining. Try the tempeh crepes. **Bistro 170,** 170 N. Millward, tel. 733-2628, features fine European country cooking, with paella, wild game, and risottos of the day. Nice place. Jackson's most popular nouvelle-cuisine restaurant is **Cadillac Grille,** 55 N. Cache (on the square), tel. 733-3279. The food is artfully prepared and includes a constantly changing menu of seafood and unusual game meats. The art-deco decor of the Cadillac helps make it one of the most crowded tourist hangouts in town. Portions tend toward the small side.

South Of The Border
Get very good Mexican fast-food at **The Merry Piglets,** Cache Dr. at Gill Ave., tel. 733-2966. Try the cheese crisp. **La Chispa,** tel. 733-4790, downstairs from the Cowboy Bar on the square, serves a variety of distinctive Mexican dinner specials at reasonable prices. **Mama Inez,** 380 W. Pearl, tel. 739-9166, has fill-you-up servings of authentic Mexican cooking. **Tortilla Flats** at 145 E. Snow King Ave. (across from the Snow King chair lift), tel. 739-9800, serves delicious southwestern specialities such as blue-corn flautas, fresh sopaipillas, and vegetarian quesadillas. The largest and most popular Mexican restaurant is **Vista Grande,** tel. 733-6964, on the Teton Village Road. The biggest drawing cards here are the pitchers of margaritas.

Chinese Food
Chinatown Restaurant, 850 W. Broadway, tel. 733-8856, makes good Chinese dishes, particularly the mu shu vegetables, lemon chicken, and their spicy pot stickers. They offer a number of under-$5 lunch specials. **Lame Duck Chinese Restaurant,** 600 E. Broadway, tel. 733-4311, serves both Chinese and Japanese specialties.

Groceries
The largest Jackson grocer is **Albertson's,** 520 W. Broadway, tel. 733-9222, but many folks prefer the more friendly **Fred's Super Market,** 185 W. Broadway, tel. 733-2656, or **Food Town**

next to the Pamida store at 970 W. Broadway, tel. 733-0450. For health foods, head to **Dynamic Health Natural Foods,** 130 W. Broadway, tel. 733-5418, or **Here & Now Natural Foods,** 1925 Moose-Wilson Rd., tel. 733-2742.

ENTERTAINMENT

Nightlife
Barflies will keep buzzing in Jackson, especially during midsummer and midwinter, when visitors pack local saloons every night of the week. At least one nightclub always seems to have live tunes; check Jackson's free newspapers to see where. Cover charges are generally only a couple of bucks on the weekends, and many times you'll get in free.

The famous **Million Dollar Cowboy Bar,** on the west side of town square, tel. 733-2207, is a favorite of cowboys and wannabe cowboys. The four pool tables at the front are almost always in use. Inside the Cowboy you'll discover burled lodgepole pine beams, display cases with stuffed dead bears and other cuddly critters, bars inlaid with old silver dollars, and saddles for barstools. Until the 1950s, the Cowboy was Jackson's center for illegal gambling. Bartenders kept a close eye on Teton Pass, where messengers used mirrors to deliver warnings of coming federal revenuers, giving folks at the bar time to hide the gaming tables in a back room. Today the dance floor fills with honky-tonking couples as the bands croon lonesome cowboy tunes six nights a week. Looking to learn swing dancing? Every Thursday you can join a free beginners' class at 7:30 p.m.; then dance up a storm when the band comes on at 9.

Just across the square is the **Rancher Bar,** where the atmosphere is a bit more relaxed and the music closer to countrified rock. There are still a few genuine cowboys here. Upstairs is a big room filled with pool aficionados. **J.J.'s Silver Dollar Bar and Grill,** in the Wort Hotel at 50 N. Glenwood St., tel. 733-2190, offers a setting that might seem more fitting in Las Vegas; gaudy pink neon lights curve around a bar inlaid with 2,032 (count 'em!) silver dollars. It tends to attract an older crowd. You'll have to sing your own tunes at the Silver Dollar since bands don't play here. Four blocks away, at 385 W. Broadway, tel. 733-3853, is **Spirits of the West,** which attracts the young "skids" (ski kids) crowd. No cowboy hats in sight. Spirits has comedy some nights, along with karaoke and open-mike nights. **Shady Lady Saloon,** in the Snow King Resort at 400 E. Snow King Ave., tel. 733-5200, has jazz and acoustic music most nights.

Three other popular bars are in Teton Village. Right next to the tram, the **Mangy Moose Saloon,** tel. 733-4913, attracts a hip skier/outdoorsy crowd with reggae, blues, or rock bands most nights of the week during the summer and winter. It's Jackson Hole's jumpingest pick-up spot. At **The Sojourner,** tel. 733-3657, you can sip a beer and munch on the free hors d'oeuvres while watching basketball games on the big TV. **Dietrich's,** in the Alpenhof, tel. 733-3242, has mellow music along with free tortillas and salsa during the winter.

Out in Wilson, **The Stagecoach,** tel. 733-4407, is the place to be on Sunday nights 5:30-10 p.m. (Wyoming bars close their doors at 10 p.m. on Sunday.) In the early '70s when hippies risked getting their heads shaved by rednecks at Jackson's Cowboy Bar, they found the 'Coach a more tolerant place. Today tobacco-chewing cowpokes show their partners slick moves on the tiny dance floor as the Stagecoach Band runs through the country tunes one more time—the band has performed here every Sunday since Feb. 16, 1969! For more entertainment, try a game of pool on one of the three tables, or a tasty buffalo burger.

Otto Brothers Brewery
Prior to Prohibition in 1920, nearly every town in Wyoming had its own brewery, making such

local favorites as Hillcrest Beer, Schoenhofen Beer, and Sweetwater Beer. After repeal of "the noble experiment," breweries again popped up, but competition from industrial giants such as Anheuser-Busch and Coors forced the last Wyoming operation—Sheridan Brewing—out of business in 1954. It was another 34 years before commercial beer making returned. In 1988, Charlie Otto started Wyoming's only existing brewery, a tiny backyard operation in Wilson that cranks out Teton Ale, Old Faithful Ale (available only in Yellowstone), Moose Juice Stout, and seasonal brews. You'll find Teton Ale on tap at many Jackson-area bars and restaurants. Teton Ale is sold in 22 ounce bottles; a bit pricey, but this is a truly handmade and hand-bottled beer. Or take some home in a "growler," a half-gallon refillable bottle available at local liquor stores. (Note: The so-called Jackson Hole Beer is a watery lager made in Montana and sold to gullible folks who think they're buying a local brew.) A brewpub—Wyoming's first—is in the works for downtown Jackson.

Theaters And Chuckwagon Shows
In addition to the bar scene, summers bring a number of lighthearted acting ventures to Jackson. For musical melodramas with an Old West theme, head to **Dirty Jack's Wild West Theatre,** 140 N. Cache, tel. 733-4775; **Jackson Hole Playhouse,** 145 W. Deloney, tel. 733-6994; or **Pink Garter Theatre,** 49 W. Broadway, tel. 733-3670. These are family favorites. Families also flock to the all-you-can-eat cookouts and western musical performances at three nearby ranches: **Bar J,** Teton Village Rd. near Teton Pines, tel. 733-3370, and **Bar T-5,** 790 Cache Cr. Rd., tel. 733-5386; and **OK Corral,** 9550 S. Henry's Rd., tel. 733-6556. None of these is particularly authentic. **Box K Ranch,** tel. 543-2407 or (800) 729-1410, has horse-drawn wagon rides and cookouts in beautiful Buffalo Valley, 40 miles northwest of Jackson.

EVENTS

Winter And Spring
Kick the year off by watching (or participating in) the annual **torchlight ski parades** on Christmas Eve and New Year's Eve at all three local

ski areas. Each January and February local Shriners hold horse-drawn **cutter races**—essentially a wild chariot race on a quarter-mile of sheer ice—at Melody Ranch six miles south of Jackson. **Ski races** take place all winter long, ranging from elegant "Powder Eight" Championships to blazingly fast freestyle cross-country races. (Volunteer to work one of the gates at a downhill race and you get to ski free the rest of the day.) The ski season ends in early April with the **Pole-Pedal-Paddle Race,** combining alpine skiing, cross-country skiing, cycling, and canoeing in a wild, tough competition. It is the largest such event in the West.

In late May, the world's only public **elk antler auction** takes place on town square, attracting hundreds of buyers from all over the globe. Local Boy Scouts collect three tons of antlers from the nearby National Elk Refuge each spring, with the proceeds helping to fund feeding the elk. This may sound like an odd event, but the high demand for antlers in the insatiable (pun intended) South Korean and Chinese aphrodisiac markets have made antlers worth more than $14 per pound, so the bidding is highly competitive. There is more than a touch of irony in the Boy Scouts making money from the sale of sexual stimulants!

Summer
Memorial Day weekend brings **Old West Days,** complete with parades, Indian dancing, rodeos, a **mountain man rendezvous,** and other festivities. The **Fourth of July** is another big event with a parade and an impressive fireworks show from Snow King Mountain. On Wednesday and Saturday nights during the summer you can watch bucking broncs, rodeo clowns, and hard-riding cowboys at the **Jackson Rodeo** on the Teton County Fair Grounds. Kids get to join in the calf scramble. The rodeo starts at 8 p.m.; call 733-2805 for details. Each August, the **Old Timer's Rodeo** features a special performance of past champions at the fairgrounds.

Don't miss the 30-year-old **Grand Teton Music Festival** at Teton Village, held June-August. Performances of classical and modern works by world-renowned musicians are the highlight of this extravaganza. Call 733-3050 for specific events and prices. Also in late July is the always-fun **Teton County Fair.** The demo-

lition derby gives a bang-up finale to the festivities. In mid-September, the **Jackson Hole One-Fly Contest** attracts anglers from all over, including a number of celebrity competitors.

Fall
Jackson Hole is at its most glorious in the fall, as aspens and cottonwoods turn a fire of yellow against the Tetons. Many of the tourists have fled back home, leaving locals and hardier visitors to savor the cool autumn nights. The major autumn event is the **Jackson Hole Fall Arts Festival,** featuring exhibits by local galleries, concerts, art demonstrations, dance performances, theater productions, and other events. The annual Arts for the Parks award ($50,000!) during the festival attracts thousands of paintings representing scenes from America's national parks. Immediately after the Arts Festival comes **Quilting in the Tetons,** a week of exhibits, classes, and quilting demonstrations.

RIVER RAFTING

Jackson Hole's most popular summertime recreational activity is running Wyoming's largest river, the Snake. Each year more than 125,000 people climb aboard rafts, canoes, or kayaks to float down placid reaches of the Snake or to blast through the boiling rapids of Snake River Canyon. (As an aside, the name Snake comes from the Shoshone Indians, who used serpentine hand movements as sign language for their tribal name—a motion that trappers misinterpreted as a snake and applied to the river flowing through Shoshone land.)

Many different rafting companies offer dozens of different raft trips each day of the summer, so it generally isn't necessary to make reservations until the day you plan to go. Prepare to get wet. You may want to ask around to determine the advantages of each company—some are cheaper but require you to drive a good distance from town; others offer more experienced crews; while others provide various perks such as fancy meals, overnight camps along the river, or boats with fewer people. Also be sure to ask if you get to do any of the paddling or not. Note that this is pretty far from being a wilderness experience, especially in mid-July when stretches of the river looks like a Los Angeles freeway with traffic jams of rafts, kayaks, inner tubes, and other flotsam and jetsam. The rafting companies generally operate from mid-May to late September.

Float Trips

The gentlest way to see the Snake is by taking one of the many commercial float trips. Along the way, you'll be treated to stunning views of the Tetons, plus glimpses of eagles, ospreys, beavers, and perhaps moose or other wildlife along the riverbanks. Many local rafting companies offer five- or 10-mile scenic float trips along the quiet stretch within Grand Teton National Park, generally putting in at Deadman's Bar or Schwabacher Landing and taking out in Moose. Prices run $17-30 for adults and $12-20 for children. Roundtrip transportation from Jackson is included by most companies. A wide variety of special voyages are also available, including overnight camping trips, fishing/floating trips, and even bike and float trips.

Call one of the following raft companies for details, or pick up one of their slick brochures at the visitor center or their tiny offices scattered around Jackson: **Barker-Ewing,** tel. 733-1800 or (800) 365-1800; **Flagg Ranch,** tel. 733-8761 or (800) 443-2311; **Fort Jackson Float Trips,** tel. 733-2583 or (800) 735-8430; **Grand Teton Lodge Company,** tel. 733-2811; **Heart Six Ranch,** tel. 543-2477; **Lewis & Clark Expeditions,** tel. 733-4022 or (800) 442-8640; **Lone Eagle Expeditions,** tel. 733-0759; **Parkland Expeditions,** tel. (800) 328-0290; **Signal Mountain Lodge,** tel. 733-5470; **Solitude Float Trips,** tel. 733-2871; and **Triangle X** (a.k.a. National Park Float Trips), tel. 733-5500.

Whitewater Trips

Below Jackson, the Snake enters the wild Snake River Canyon, a stretch early explorers labeled "the accursed mad river." The usual put-in point for whitewater trips is West Table Creek Campground, 26 miles south of Jackson. The take-out point is Sheep Gulch, eight miles downstream. In between the two, the river rocks and rolls through the narrow canyon, pumping past waterfalls and eagle nests, and then over a series of big rapids with names like Rope and Champagne, before reaching the two biggest, Kahuna

and Lunch Counter. (For a look at the action from the highway, stop at the paved pullout at milepost 124, where a trail leads down to Lunch Counter.) Whitewater trips last around 3½ hours (including transportation from Jackson) and cost $25-30 for adults, or $20-25 for children. Longer voyages including overnight trips cost approximately $90 for adults and $75 for children. Prices drop early or late in the summer. Most companies include roundtrip transportation from Jackson. Don't take your own camera along unless it's waterproof; bankside float-tographers will be happy to sell you pictures for a permanent record of your run.

For details on whitewater raft trips, contact one of the following companies: **Barker-Ewing Whitewater,** tel. 733-1000; **Dave Hansen Whitewater,** tel. 733-6295; **Jackson Hole Whitewater,** tel. 733-1007 or (800) 648-2602; **Lewis & Clark Expeditions,** tel. 733-4022 or (800) 442-8640; **Mad River Boat Trips,** tel. 733-6203 or (800) 458-6008; **Sands' Wildwater,** tel. 733-4410 or (800) 223-4059; and **Snake River Park Whitewater,** tel. 733-7078.

Float It Yourself

Grand Teton National Park in Moose, tel. 733-2880, has useful information on running the park portions of the river; ask for a copy of *Floating the Snake River.* Note that life jackets, boat permits ($5), and registration are required to run the river through the park, and that inner tubes and air mattresses are prohibited. Floating the gentler parts (between Jackson Lake Dam and Pacific Creek) is easy for even novice boaters and canoeists, but below that point, things get more dicey. The water averages two or three feet deep, but it sometimes exceeds 10 feet and flow rates are often more than 8,000 cubic feet per second, creating logjams, braided channels, strong currents, and dangerous sweepers. Peak flows are between mid-June and early July. Inexperienced rafters or anglers die every year in the river. Flow-rate signs are posted at most river landings, the Moose Visitor Center, and the Buffalo Ranger Station in Moran. If you're planning to raft or kayak on the whitewater parts of the Snake River, be sure to contact the Bridger-Teton National Forest office in Jackson, tel. 739-5500, for more information.

Lessons And Boat Rentals

Rent canoes at **Hungry Jack's** in Wilson, tel. 733-3561, for $25/day including roof rack, paddles, and life jackets. Very friendly folks here. **Snake River Kayak & Canoe School,** 145 W. Gill St., tel. 733-3127, offers kayaking classes of all lengths for $70/day including transportation, equipment, and lunch. All-inclusive canoe clinics are $165 for 2¹/₂ days. The school rents canoes ($25/day), kayaks ($40/day), inflatable kayaks ($40/day), and rafts ($50/day), all with roof racks included. Their free brochure describes conditions on various stretches of the Snake River. **Leisure Sports,** 1075 South US 89, tel. 733-3040, also rents rafts ($40/day), canoes ($25/day), kayaks ($30/ day), and inflatable kayaks ($25), along with all sorts of other outdoor equipment. They can also provide a shuttle service. **Riding and Rafts** in Alpine, tel. 654-9900, has six-person rafts for $30.

OTHER SUMMER RECREATION

Horsin' Around

Think of the Wild West and one animal always comes to mind—the horse. A ride on Old Paint gives city slickers a chance to saunter back in time to a simpler era and to simultaneously learn how ornery and opinionated horses can be. In Jackson Hole you can choose from brief half-day trail rides in Grand Teton National Park all the way up to weeklong wilderness pack trips into the rugged Teton Wilderness. The visitor center has a brochure listing more than a dozen local outfitters and stables offering trail rides.

For short rides ($10-15/hour or $45-55/day), try **Jackson Hole Trail Rides** in Teton Village, tel. 733-6992; **Snow King Stables,** behind Snow King Resort, tel. 733-5781; **Spring Creek Resort,** Spring Gulch Rd., tel. 733-8833; **Teton Trail Rides,** tel. 733-2108; or **Bar T-5,** 790 Cache Creek Rd., tel. 733-5386. Rides of all sorts are also available in the park at Jackson Lake Lodge and Colter Bay; call 733-2811 for specifics. **Riding & Rafts,** in Alpine, tel. 654-9900, offers unguided horse rentals for $40 /day. For a different sort of trip, try llama packing with **Jackson Hole Llamas,** tel. 733-1617, or **Black Diamond Llamas,** tel. 733-2877. Half-day llama treks are just $30 per person.

For two- to six-day covered-wagon trips in the mountains around Jackson Hole, contact **Bar T-5,** tel. 733-5386, or **Wagons West,** tel. (800) 447-4711.

On The Water

Jackson Hole has some of the finest angling in Wyoming, with native Snake River cutthroat (a distinct subspecies) and brook trout in the river, along with Mackinaw, cutthroat, and brown trout in the lakes. The Snake is a particular favorite of beginning fly-fishing enthusiasts. Many local companies offer guided fly-fishing float trips down the Snake River (and other area waterways), or you can fish from the riverbanks with lures or flies. Two people should expect to pay $200-250/day ($130-190/half-day) with guide, lunch, and boat. Rental equipment is also available from local shops.

Jackson has half-a-dozen fly-fishing shops. Stop by **Jack Dennis' Outdoor Shop,** 50 E. Broadway, tel. 733-3270 or (800) 522-5755, and pick up a copy of the free *Western Fishing Newsletter* for descriptions of local fishing areas and what lures to try. **Westbank Anglers,** 3670 Teton Village Rd., tel. 733-6483 or (800) 922-3474, is another nationally known fly-fishing dealer with a slick mail-order catalog, excellent fishing clinics, and float trips. **High Country Flies,** 75 E. Broadway, tel. 733-7210, sells fly-fishing equipment and offers guided trips. The visitor center has an up-to-date listing of fishing guides. Note that Wyoming fishing licenses are valid within Grand Teton National Park, but not in Yellowstone.

Jackson Lake is a popular windsurfing place, with moderate winds (perfect for beginners) and an impressive Teton backdrop. **Alpine Windsurfing,** 365 N. Glenwood, tel. 733-4460, rents windsurfing equipment, wetsuits, and roof racks, and offers lessons on the lake. Advanced windsurfers looking for stronger wind conditions head to Slide Lake east of Kelly, or to blow-me-down Yellowstone Lake.

Biking

Jackson Hole offers all sorts of adventures for cyclists, particularly those with mountain bikes. **Teton Cyclery,** 175 N. Glenwood St., tel. 733-4386; **Hoback Sports,** 40 S. Millward St., tel. 733-5335; **Leisure Sports,** tel. 733-3040, 1075

South US 89; and **Mountain Bike Outfitters** in Moose, tel. 733-3314, all rent mountain bikes for $15-25/day. The last of these has a helpful free map of local mountain-bike routes. Local mountain-bike tours (one includes a chair-lift ride to the top of Snow King) are available from **Fat Tire Tours,** tel. 733-5335, for $35-55/day. **Teton Mt. Bike Tours,** tel. 733-0712, offers scenic half- or all-day bike tours of Grand Teton and Yellowstone national parks as well as Bridger-Teton National Forest. Rates are $30-90 pp.

Alpine Slide And Scenic Rides

During the summer, kids love to race down the 2,500-foot-long **Alpine Slide** at Snow King Mountain, right on the edge of Jackson. Rides cost $4 ($3 for kids under 12). Snow King's main chair lift is also in operation during the summer, taking folks to the top of the 7,751-foot mountain for $5 ($3 for kids under 12, or $4 for seniors). On top is a short nature trail and panoramic views of the Tetons. Call 733-5200 for details on both of these rides.

Out in Teton Village, you can ride the **aerial tram** to the top of Rendezvous Mountain (10,450 feet) for $14 ($12 seniors, $7 teens, $2 ages 6-12, and free under age 6). The ride takes 12 minutes and rises over 4,000 feet in elevation. Open daily late May-Sept., this is a spectacular way to reach the alpine. On top are a small gift/snack shop and naturalists who lead free summertime hikes into nearby Rock Springs Bowl. Call 733-2292 for details. Over in Alta, you can ride the Grand Targhee **chair lift** to the 10,200-foot summit of Fred's Mountain for $6.

Other Activities

There are no public swimming pools in Jackson, but you can soak in a wonderful hot mineral pool (105° F) at **Granite Hot Springs,** tel. 733-6318. Head south to Hoback Junction and then up Hoback Canyon to the turnoff for Granite. The pool is another 10 miles along a dirt road (total of 35 miles), and costs $4 for adults, $1-3 for kids. **Jackson Hole Golf & Tennis Club,** a mile north of town, tel. 733-3111, has an 18-hole golf course (rated one of the 25 best in America), a swimming pool ($5), and tennis courts. The Arnold Palmer-designed 18-hole **Teton Pines Country Club,** on Teton Village Rd., tel. 733-1005, is Jackson Hole's second

golf spot. **Jackson Hole Athletic Club,** 875 W. Broadway, tel. 733-8830, has a gymnasium ($7.50/day) with Nautilus and other equipment, along with a variety of exercise classes. Guides from **The Hole Hiking Experience,** tel. 733-7155, lead daylong treks into the mountains around Jackson Hole for $45 ($20 for children). See "Mountain Climbing," pp. 308-309, for other athletic options.

The **Teton County Parks and Recreation Department,** tel. 733-5056, leads summertime hikes for adults every Tuesday for $2 pp. They also provide outings for kids—swimming, hiking, and more—for $3 pp and can rent out volleyballs, horseshoes, croquet sets, and other toys. If you are feeling flush with cash, both **Rainbow Balloon Flights,** tel. 733-0470, and **Wyoming Balloon Co.,** tel. 739-0900, offer hot-air balloon flights (one hour in the air) for around $165 pp.

WINTER RECREATION

For details on the many opportunities for skiing in and around Jackson Hole, see the sections "Downhill Skiing" and "Crosscountry Skiing," below.

Ice Skating

Each winter, the town of Wilson floods a hockey-rink-sized part of the town park for skating. A warming hut stands next to the rink and the floodlights are on most nights. Jackson maintains a smaller ice rink on Glenwood and a broomball rink in Snow King Ballpark. Snow King Resort has a new indoor ice-skating rink open year-round.

Snowshoeing

Grand Teton National Park has excellent free naturalist-led snowshoe hikes several times each week during the winter months. Snowshoes are provided, and no experience is necessary. These generally depart at 2 p.m. from the visitor center in Moose, but for specifics, call 733-2880. Reservations are required.

Slip-slidin' Away

Jackson Hole Resort Service, tel. 733-6657, offers visitors a quaint step back in time. From mid-Dec. through March, horse-drawn **sleighs** pick up Teton Village guests for a romantic 30-

minute ride to a rustic log cabin where they are served a complete prime-rib dinner before heading back to civilization. Make reservations well in advance for this popular trip down memory lane. Prices are $40 for adults or $20 for children under 10. If you don't have that kind of cash, try one of the sleigh rides offered at the Elk Refuge (see pp. 270-271). **Geyser Creek Dogsled Adventures,** tel. 455-2702 or (800) 531-6874, offers two-hour dogsled tours at Togwotee Mountain Lodge (48 miles north of Jackson) for $95 pp ($60 for children under 10).

Snowmobiling

One of the fastest-growing—and most controversial—wintertime activities in Jackson Hole is snowmobiling. Hundreds of miles of packed and groomed snowmobile trails head into Bridger-Teton National Forest as well as Yellowstone and Grand Teton national parks. Some of the most popular places include the Togwotee Pass area (48 miles north of Jackson), Cache Creek Rd. (east of town), and Granite Hot Springs Rd. (25 miles southeast). At least a half-dozen different Jackson companies offer guided snowmobile trips into Yellowstone, with prices starting around $140/day (including breakfast and lunch). The visitor center has a listing of local snowmobile-rental companies and maps of snowmobile trails.

In recent years, one of the most contentious issues in Jackson Hole has been a proposal to construct the **Continental Divide Snowmobile Trail** through Grand Teton National Park, thus connecting the Yellowstone road network with snowmobile trails that reach all the way to Atlantic City at the southern end of the Wind River Mountains. The process is moving slowly, but if Congress appropriates the money, thousands of machines will be roaring through Grand Teton in the near future. If this does happen, it will not only mean far more machines entering the already overcrowded Yellowstone area, but also an unfortunate emphasis upon mechanized travel in previously undeveloped areas. Hopefully, the snowmobiles will be kept out.

INFORMATION AND SERVICES

Anyone new to Jackson Hole should be sure to visit the impressive **Wyoming State Information Center** at 532 N. Cache, tel. 733-3316.

Hours are daily 8 a.m.-8 p.m. between June 15 and Labor Day, and Mon.-Fri. 8-5 and Sat.-Sun. 10-2 the rest of the year. The information center is a two-level, sod-roofed wooden building with displays on local history and sights, a blizzard of free leaflets extolling the merits of local businesses, and an upstairs rear deck that overlooks the National Elk Refuge. Ducks and trumpeter swans are visible on the marsh. There are direct phones to several dozen local motels and hotels, plus a signboard that lights up when the hotels are full. Check out posters over the entrance from some of the 15 movies filmed in Jackson Hole, including *Shane, Any Which Way You Can, Big Trail, Bad Bascomb, Big Sky, The Far Horizons, Spencer's Mountain, Jubal, Mountain Man,* and *Rocky IV.*

If you want general information before coming to Jackson Hole, the **Jackson Hole Visitors Council,** tel. (800) 782-0011, will be happy to provide a detailed vacation-planner brochure. The **Jackson Hole Chamber of Commerce,** also in the State Information Center, has more specific info on local businesses.

Bridger-Teton National Forest has a new **visitor center** (tel. 739-5500) in the log cabin next to their office at 340 N. Cache. Summer hours are Mon.-Fri. 8-5:30 and Sat. 8-4:30. The rest of the year it is open Mon.-Fri. 8-4:30. This is the place to get detailed forest maps ($2, or $4 for waterproof versions) and info on the Teton and Gros Ventre wilderness areas.

Books

The **Teton County Library** at 320 S. King St., tel. 733-2164, is a great place to spend a rainy or snowy day. Built in 1940, this cozy old log structure houses a substantial collection of books about Wyoming and the West. Hours are Sun. 1-5, Mon., Wed., and Fri. 10-5:30, Tues. and Thurs. 10-9, and Sat. 10-5. Unlike many Wyoming towns where the book selection consists of a few romance novels in the local drugstore, Jackson is blessed with two fine bookstores: **Teton Bookshop,** 25 S. Glenwood, tel. 733-9220; and the largest, **Valley Bookstore,** 125 N. Cache, tel. 733-4533. The latter sometimes has author signings and readings.

Living In Jackson Hole

Jackson Hole is becoming an increasingly popular place to live and work. The surrounding country is grand, there are many things to do and places to explore, and you're likely to meet others with similar interests. Jobs such as waiting tables, operating ski lifts, driving tour buses, cleaning hotels and condos, and construction work are generally plentiful, but the wages are not high. Check local classified ads or stop by the Wyoming Job Service Center, 545 N. Cache, tel. 733-4091, to get an idea of available jobs. The best jobs are those that offer either such perks as a free ski pass or give you lots of free time to explore the area.

Unfortunately, because of Jackson Hole's popularity, finding a place to live is quite difficult, especially during the peak summer and winter tourist seasons. Workers are even being bused in from Afton, 70 miles away! Land prices (and hence housing costs) have been rising at an astronomical rate—Teton Village land values shot up 100% in 1989 alone! A few Jackson-area restaurants include inexpensive housing as a way to lure workers, but this is the exception; many employees are forced to live under less-than-ideal conditions such as sleeping in a tent during the summer or jamming into a too-small apartment. The best times to look for a place to live are in April and November. Check the papers as well as local laundromat and grocery-store bulletin boards for apartments or cabins. The "Trash and Treasure" morning program on radio station KMTN (97 FM) is another place to try.

SHOPPING

If you have the money, Jackson is a great place to buy everything from artwork to mountain bikes. Even if you just hitched in and have no cash to spare, it's always fun to wander through the shops and galleries surrounding town square. Factory-outlet stores offer slightly discounted prices on such brand names as Pendleton, Ralph Lauren Polo, London Fog, J. Crew, Benetton, and Fila. Buy used clothing and other items at **Browse 'N Buy Thrift Shop,** 139 N. Cache, tel. 733-7524, and **Orville's,** 285 W. Pearl, tel. 733-3165. Orville's has old Wyoming license plates for just a buck—a big hit with European tourists.

Outdoor Gear
Outdoor enthusiasts will discover several excellent shops in Jackson. Climbers, backpackers, and cross-country skiers head to **Teton Mountaineering,** 120 E. Broadway, tel. 733-3595, for quality equipment, maps, and travel guides. This is America's oldest climbing shop. They also rent tents, sleeping bags, packs, climbing shoes, cross-country skis and other gear. Check their bulletin board for used items. A block away at 50 E. Broadway, tel. 733-3270 or (800) 522-5755, is **Jack Dennis Sports,** a large upscale store that sells fly-fishing and camping gear in the summer and skis and warm clothes during the winter. They also rent almost anything: tents, stoves, cookware, sleeping bags, fly rods, waders, backpacks, skis, and more. **Skinny Skis,** 65 W. Deloney Ave., tel. 733-6094, has more in the way of high-quality clothing and supplies, especially cross-country ski gear. Another place to rent outdoor gear of all types is **Leisure Sports,** 1075 South US 89, tel. 733-3040. The least expensive place to buy rugged outdoor wear, cowboy boots, and cowboy hats is **Corral West Ranchwear,** 840 W. Broadway, tel. 733-0247.

Wyoming Woolens, a local manufacturer of quality warm clothing (the plant is in Afton), has two stores in Jackson: a retail shop near the square at 20 W. Broadway, tel. 733-2991, and a factory outlet with great bargains at 870 South US 89, tel. 733-2889. For high-quality, handmade Lycra and Polarplus clothing, as well as tent or backpack repairs, visit **Columbine,** tel. 733-7179, a small shop in Pink Garter Plaza at 49 W. Broadway.

TRANSPORTATION

Access to Jackson Hole has become easier in recent years with several airlines and summer-only daily bus service. Most summer visitors arrive by car, though a few more adventurous souls pedal in on bikes. If you're looking for or offering a ride, the local radio station, KMTN (97 FM), tel. 733-5686, has a daily ride-finder announcement at 11:20 p.m. Other folks call in with rides on the station's 9:30 a.m. "Trash and Treasure" show.

By Air

At one time, Jackson was considered impossible to get to, but today daily jet service brings visitors from all over the world. Jackson Hole Airport is eight miles north of Jackson in Grand Teton National Park. The only commercial airport within any national park, it is a source of considerable tension, as plans to expand the runway conflict directly with the park's management for natural-resource values. The airport is served by **Delta,** tel. (800) 221-1212; **American,** tel. (800) 433-7300; **United Express,** tel. (800) 241-6522; **Continental Express,** tel. (800) 525-0280; and **Skywest,** tel. (800) 453-9417. Delta and Skywest route all their flights through Salt Lake City, while United Express and Continental Express go via Denver. American Airlines flights go through Salt Lake City, but during the winter they also offer direct service to Chicago.

All Star Taxi, tel. 733-2888, provides airport taxi service to and from motels in Jackson ($5 pp) and Teton Village ($13 pp). These prices are higher if you have fewer than three people. **Jackson Hole Transportation,** tel. 733-3135, has shuttle bus service from the airport to Jackson ($6) and Teton Village ($13 OW or $19 RT). Both companies meet all commercial airline flights, but after 7 p.m. you should make advance reservations to be sure of an airport pickup. Make outgoing reservations a day in advance. For taxi service ($15 to town or $25 to Teton Village), call **A-I Taxi,** tel. 733-5089; **Airport Taxi,** tel. 733-1700; **Buckboard Cab,** tel. 733-1112, or **Tumbleweed Taxi,** tel. 733-0808.

Car Rentals

Most of the national chains (Avis, Budget, Dollar, Eagle, Hertz, National, Payless, and Rent-A-Wreck) have rental cars in town or at the airport, but the best deals (used cars) are at **Rent-A-Wreck,** 1250 S. Carol Lane, tel. 733-5014, which has a few cars for $22/day. Most of these companies also offer 4WD cars. The least expensive new-car rental company (starting at $40/day for "economy" cars!) is **Resort Rent-A-Car,** 345 W. Broadway, tel. 733-1656. Reserve cars at least a month ahead during the summer, two months in peak season.

START Buses

Local buses are operated by Southern Teton Area Rapid Transit (START) and serve Jackson and Teton Village most of the year. This is Wyoming's only true public bus system! START fares are $1 within town and $2 to Teton Village (seniors and children under eight free). Discount coupons are available for multiple rides (winter only). During the summer, buses run seven days a week, approximately every two hours. Winter schedules offer more frequent service to Teton Village. There is only minimal bus service between mid-April and mid-June, and between early Sept. and early December. Pick up bus schedules and route maps in the visitor center. Hours of operation are generally 7 a.m.-11 p.m. Buses stop near most Jackson hotels and motels and are equipped to carry skis (in winter) and bikes (in summer) on outside racks. START buses do not run to the airport or to Wilson. Call 733-4521 for more information.

Buses And Tours

Given that two million tourists cram through Jackson each year, it's hard to believe how limited long-distance bus service is. The only bus connection out of Jackson is a summer-only service to Yellowstone, where you can connect to Greyhound and other bus companies. **Grand Teton Lodge Company,** tel. 733-2811 or (800) 628-9988, offers twice-daily summer shuttle buses between Jackson Hole Airport and Jackson Lake Lodge for $10 OW/$15 RT. Buses depart from 72 S. Glenwood St., with stops at the airport and Jenny Lake upon request.

Daily summertime bus tours of Grand Teton and Yellowstone national parks are available from **Gray Line,** 332 N. Glenwood, tel. 733-4325 or (800) 443-6133. These all-day loop tours cost $36. Gray Line also has one-way service between Yellowstone and Jackson for $25 in either direction (but reserve ahead). In Yellowstone, travelers can connect with other buses to West Yellowstone, Gardiner, or Cody. During the winter, Gray Line has daily bus runs to Flagg Ranch for $25 OW, arriving in time to meet the snowcoach departures for Yellowstone.

DOWNHILL SKIING

Until recently, Jackson Hole was primarily a summertime resort, filled with carloads of screaming kids, French tourists snickering at the name "Grand Teton," and adventurous young people streaming into the mountains. As access has become easier and the facilities more developed, many people have discovered the wonders of a Jackson Hole winter, especially one centered around a week on the ski slopes. Three very different ski resorts attract the crowds: Grand Targhee for down-home, powder-to-the-butt conditions; Snow King for steep, inexpensive, edge-of-town slopes; and Jackson Hole for flashy, world-class skiing. All three places have rental equipment and ski schools and allow snowboards and telemarkers on the slopes. This mixture, along with an incredible abundance of developed and wild places to ski cross-country, combine to make Jackson Hole one of the premier ski destinations in America.

See your travel agent for package trips to any of the Jackson area resorts. For daily ski reports—including downhill and Nordic areas, as well as backcountry reports—listen to KMTN (FM 97) at 7:15 a.m., 8:15 a.m., 8:25 a.m., and 9:15 a.m. Hot tip: If you plan to spend more than a couple of days in the area, it may well be worth your while to join the **Jackson Hole Ski Club.** In return for a $30 annual membership, you receive an impressive number of premiums, including half-price lift tickets and lessons, various freebies, and discounts at more than 90 local stores. Join up at any local ski shop.

Ski Rentals
Rent or buy downhill skis from: **Hoback Sports,** 40 S. Millward St. (also at Snow King Resort), tel. 733-5335; **Ski and Sports,** 485 W. Broadway, tel. 733-4449; **Jack Dennis Outdoor Shop,** 50 E. Broadway, tel. 733-3270; **Wildernest Sports,** Teton Village, tel. 733-4297; or **Teton Village Sports,** tel. 733-2181. Rentals are also available at all three ski areas. For cross-country ski rental, see below.

GRAND TARGHEE SKI RESORT

Grand Targhee was long considered something of a hick ski area, the sort of place where folks skied in overalls and headed back to their farms to feed the cows. The food was dreadful, the lodging facilities were funky at best, and the lift operators wore cowboy hats with plastic covers. But, skiers also discovered that Targhee had some of the most incredible snow in the universe. With an annual snowfall of 504 inches (42 feet!)—most of which is champagne powder—Targhee became the secret spot where powder hounds got all they could ever want. In 1987, Mory and Carol Bergmeyer took over and began transforming Targhee into a first-class ski area—remodelling the facilities, adding new restaurants and services, and inaugurating snowcat skiing. But some things haven't changed: lift operators still wear cowboy hats, the slopes are still beautifully groomed, and customer service still gets high marks. Despite having just four lifts, Grand Targhee has achieved national rankings in ski magazines for its outstanding snow and friendly service. On the drawing boards are all sorts of new developments that have brought major controversy and even litigation by locals anxious to keep their peaceful way of life.

The biggest drawback to Grand Targhee is the same thing that makes it so great—the weather. Lots of snow means lots of clouds, and because it snows so much, there are many days when the name cynics apply—Grand Foghee—seems more appropriate. Many folks who have returned to Targhee year after year have still never seen the magnificent Grand Teton backdrop behind the ski area! Be sure to bring your goggles.

Nuts and Bolts
Targhee has three double chair lifts and one surface lift on the prosaically named Fred's Mountain. The top elevation is 10,200 feet, with

the longest run dropping 2,200 feet and almost three miles. Although only 300 acres are groomed, the remaining 1,200 acres of ungroomed powder mean that you'll always find track-free skiing. And if that isn't enough, try snowcat skiing ($155/day including lunch and guide; $135 if you overnight at Targhee) on adjacent Peaked Peak. You'll get six to ten runs each day and miles of untracked powder (bring your snorkel) with three-mile-long runs. Lift tickets at Grand Targhee cost $28/day ($18/half day) for adults and $14/day for children and seniors (free under age five and over age 70).

Fully seventy percent of Targhee's groomed runs are intermediate, and advanced skiers will find an extraordinary number of deep-powder faces to explore. Snowboarders are also welcome. The ski school offers lessons for all abilities, and children's programs make it possible for parents to leave their kids behind. Cross-country skiers enjoy the Everything Nordic Center (see "Cross-Country Skiing," below). Rental skis and snowboards are available at the base of the mountain. The ski area usually opens in mid-Nov. and closes in mid-April. Lifts operate 9:30 to 4 daily. Call (800) 827-4433 for more on Grand Targhee.

Food And Lodging

Targhee has several places to stay: motel-style rooms in Targhee and Teewinot lodges as well as condominium accommodations in Sioux Lodge. Nightly rates are $70-95 d during the holiday season, but a wide variety of ski/lodging package deals are also available, such as five nights lodging and four days skiing for $625 and up during the holiday season. A heated outdoor pool and hot tub are available for lodge residents. Call Targhee at 353-2304 or (800) 827-4433 to get brochures detailing all these options.

At the base of Grand Targhee you'll find a cafeteria and several restaurants. Especially noteworthy is **Skadi's**, where the gourmet meals led *Snow Country Magazine* to rate it second in the nation among on-mountain restaurants! You can also ride in a horse-drawn sleigh to a Mongolian-style yurt for a home-cooked dinner of steak, chicken, or fish. The price is $27 pp ($13 for kids).

Grand Targhee's social center is the **Trap Bar**, with live music most nights. Other shops here sell groceries, ski equipment, and clothing. For another diversion, try **dog sledding**, at $35 ($20 for kids) for an hour-long ride. On Christmas and New Year's, be sure to stay around for the impressive **torchlit ski parade** down the mountain.

Getting There

Grand Targhee is located 42 miles northwest of Jackson on the western side of the Tetons in Alta, Wyoming. Get there by driving over Teton Pass (occasionally closed by winter storms), north through Victor and Driggs, Idaho, and then east back into Wyoming. A **shuttle bus** provides transport from the Jackson and Idaho Falls airports to Targhee for $20 OW (minimum two people). Make reservations three days ahead by calling the ski area. The **Targhee Express** bus makes daily wintertime trips (90 minutes each way) to Grand Targhee from Jackson and Teton Village. Buses leave Jackson at 7:30 a.m. and return by 6:30 p.m. For $38 (less than a lift ticket at Jackson Hole Resort) you get roundtrip bus transportation to Targhee and a lift ticket. Reserve tickets by calling 733-3101 in Jackson or (800) 827-4433.

Summer Activities

Not far from Grand Targhee are several popular summertime hiking trails. (See "Jedediah Smith Wilderness," pp. 314-315 for details.) The resort itself is a popular place to relax in the summer and offers many activities. You can rent mountain bikes, ride horses, practice moves on the climbing wall, enjoy the spa and pool, or ride the chairlift. Evening brings movies, lectures, hayrides, and campfire sing-alongs. Each Memorial Day, balloon enthusiasts come to Targhee for the **Teton Valley Hot Air Balloon Festival.** Lots of music during the summer, including the **Fourth of July Music on the Mountain,** the **Bluegrass Festival** in early Aug., and **Rockin' the Tetons** (rock, blues, and reggae) in mid-August.

JACKSON HOLE SKI RESORT

Just 12 miles northwest of Jackson is Jackson Hole Ski Resort, the largest and best-known Wyoming ski area. A true skier's mountain, Jackson Hole is considered the most varied and challenging of any American ski area. The powder is usually deep (average snowfall is 38 feet!), lift lines are short, the slopes are uncrowded, and the vistas are unbelievable. First opened in 1965, Jackson Hole Ski Resort has become one of the nation's favorite ski areas.

Superlatives

A recent magazine article referred to Jackson Hole Resort as a place "where the skiing gets tough and the tough go skiing." The slopes are *steep* here; half the runs are in the advanced category, including several of the notorious double-diamonds. Nearly everyone it seems is on K2 Extreme skis. And yes, those death-defying cliff-jumping shots are real; on the tram ride up, check out the infamous Corbett's Coulair, a rocky gully that requires a leap of faith and suicidal urges. With an unsurpassed 4,139-foot vertical drop (tops in the U.S.), 2,400 acres of terrain spread over two adjacent mountains, runs that may exceed four miles in length, and 24 miles of groomed trails, Jackson Hole is truly a resort of superlatives.

Actually, the mountain is so large that even rank beginners will find plenty of bunny slopes on which to practice. Rendezvous Mountain (10,450 feet) is where experts strut their stuff, while adjacent Après Vous Mountain (8,481 feet) is primarily for those who like friendlier slopes. Intermediate skiers could spend all day exploring the various runs here. The most enjoyable way to the top of Rendezvous Mountain is aboard one of the new 63-passenger aerial tram cars. Powered by 500-horsepower engines, they climb nearly 2½ miles in 12 minutes, offering jaw-dropping views across Jackson Hole. There are also five double chairs, a triple chair, a quad chair, and two Poma lifts spread over the rest of the terrain, and you can ski down 60 different named trails.

There is a negative side to Jackson Hole Ski Resort (in addition to the sky-high prices). Recent years saw an ownership battle that reached the courts. Because of this, management of the resort took a back seat, and there were many complaints about deteriorating facilities and poor service. With new owners in 1992, big improvements are expected.

Services And Rates

Get to Teton Village from the town of Jackson by hopping on the START bus ($2 each way). This is the only inexpensive part of a visit to Jackson Hole Resort, with prices for lift tickets approaching the stratosphere. Single-day tickets are $39 for adults ($30/half-day) and $19 ($15/half-day) for kids under 14 and seniors. Multiday tickets—the most common kind bought —are $33/day for adults or $17/day for kids. Tram tickets are an additional $2 each. Lifts are open 9-4 daily from early Dec. till early April.

Skis and snowboards can be rented in Jackson or Teton Village. The ski school is headed by Pepi Stiegler—a 1964 Olympic gold medalist from Austria—and offers a special Kinderschule program for children. You can ski with Pepi Mon.-Fri. at 1:30 p.m.; meet him at the top of Casper lift. Ski hosts are scattered around the mountain, ready to provide information and tours of the slopes. Racers and spectators will enjoy NASTAR events each Sun., Tues., and Thurs., along with various other events throughout the winter.

Teton Village, a Swiss-style resort at the base of the mountain, has lodges, condominiums, restaurants, bars, shops, a small grocery, ski rentals, lockers, a liquor store, car rentals, and even a travel agency for escapes to Hawaii. On-the-mountain facilities include a restaurant and a ski shop in Casper Bowl and a snack bar at the top of the tram. For more information on Jackson Hole Ski Resort, write Box 290, Teton Village, WY 83025, or call 733-2292. For snow conditions (24 hours), call 733-2291. The messages are changed each morning before 5 a.m.

SNOW KING RESORT

Rising directly behind the town of Jackson, Snow King Resort's ski runs make up in difficulty what they lack in size. From below, the mountain (7,871 feet tall) looks impossibly steep and narrow. High atop the big chair lift, the vista provides a panoramic tour of Jackson Hole. Jackson's "town hill," Snow King was the first ski area in Wyoming (opened in 1939), and one of the first in North America. The original chapter of the National Ski Patrol was established here in 1941.

There are more than 500 acres of skiable terrain at Snow King, with the longest run being nearly a mile in length. Two double chairs and a Poma lift climb up the mountainside. Prices for lift tickets at Snow King are well below those at other Jackson Hole resorts: $25/day ($18/half-day) for adults and $16/day ($10/half day) for kids under 15 and seniors. Discount coupons worth $2 off are often available inside Snow King Resort. Hours of operation are 9:30-4:30, with **night skiing** (Tues.-Sat., 5:30-9:30 p.m.) available on the lower sections of Snow King for an additional $12/adults and $8/kids and se-

niors. The ski season is generally early Dec. to early April.

Hoback Sports rents skis at the foot of the mountain. There's a ski school, and guided Nordic tours down the back side of the mountain are available. At the base of Snow King you'll discover an elaborate lodge, two restaurants, the Shady Lady Saloon, and a variety of other facilities. Jackson's town square is only seven blocks away and START buses ($1) offer frequent service. For more info on Snow King Resort, call 733-5200 or (800) 522-5464 (outside Wyoming).

CROSS-COUNTRY SKIING

For many Jackson Hole residents the word "skiing" means heading across frozen Jenny Lake or telemarking down the bowls of Teton Pass rather than sliding down the slopes of the local resorts. Jackson Hole is becoming a national center for cross-country enthusiasts and offers an impressive range of conditions, from flat-tracking along summertime golf courses where a gourmet restaurant awaits you, to remote wilderness settings where a complete knowledge of snow crystal structure, avalanche hazards, and winter survival are essential. Beginners will probably want to start out at one of the five nearby Nordic centers, progressing to local paths and the more gentle lift-serviced ski runs with experience. More advanced skiers will quickly discover the incredible snow in the surrounding mountains.

Ski Rentals
Rent or buy cross-country skis at **Skinny Skis,** 65 W. Deloney Ave., tel. 733-6094, or **Teton Mountaineering,** 86 E. Broadway, tel. 733-3595. All the local Nordic centers also rent equipment.

NORDIC CENTERS

Jackson Hole Nordic Center
Nordic skiing enthusiasts will find three different developed facilities near Jackson, along with ones at Grand Targhee and up on Togwotee Pass. Largest is Jackson Hole Nordic Center,

tel. 733-2292, with 25 km of groomed trails—both set track and skating lanes—covering a wide range of conditions. Call 733-2291 for the snow report. Located in Teton Village, this is the best place to try out cross-country skiing. Rates are $8/day for adults or $5/day for children and seniors. Cross-country, skating, and telemarking equipment are available for rent, and a combination rental package and trail pass is $30 for adults or $18 for kids. Hours are daily 8:30-5. After 12:30 p.m., your Alpine lift ticket at Jackson Hole Ski Resort is good at the Nordic center too (but hey, it better be, since it costs you $39!). The center offers a wide spectrum of lessons, along with naturalist-led tours of Grand Teton National Park or trips to Teton Pass ($40-65 pp) for the more adventurous.

Teton Pines Cross-country Ski Center
Located three miles north on Teton Village Rd., tel. 733-1005, Teton Pines includes 13 km of

BOB RACE

machine-groomed track (both diagonal stride skiing and skating) on a summertime golf course. Rates are $5/day for adults, $4/day for children, and $15/day for a family. Ski rentals and guided tours within Grand Teton National Park are available. Hours are daily 9 a.m. to dusk. The clubhouse here has a pricey restaurant for gourmet après-ski lunches and dinners.

Spring Creek Resort Nordic Center

Located three miles north of US 22 on Spring Gulch Rd., Spring Creek, tel. 733-1004, is open 9:30-5 daily. If you're staying in town, you can catch the free shuttle bus at the Wort Hotel; call the Nordic center for specifics. Guests of the Wort Hotel or Spring Creek Resort ski free. The center has 14 km of gentle groomed trails with skating lanes, perfect for beginners. Rates are $5/day for adults and $2.50/day for children. Ski rentals and lessons are available.

Togwotee Mountain Lodge

Farther afield is Togwotee Mountain Lodge, 48 miles northeast of Jackson, tel. 543-2847 or (800) 543-2847; open daily 8:30-5. Just a couple of miles above the lodge US 26-287 heads over the Continental Divide at 9,658 feet, so expect to find luxuriously deep powder. Teton Wilderness lies just north of here, and when you face west the Teton Range offers up a jagged horizon line. Togwotee Lodge maintains 12 km of groomed single-track trails covering a variety of terrain. Rates are $6/day for adults and $4/day for children and seniors; open 8:30-5 on weekends only. Ski rentals are also available. The lodge itself is a pleasant, rustic place to stay for the night or to enjoy a dinner before returning to Jackson. Extremely popular with the snowmobile crowd.

Brooks Lake Lodge

Drive another 10 miles over Togwotee Pass to Brooks Lake Lodge, tel. 455-2121, for some of the most incredible scenery (and cross-country skiing) in the west. (See "Wind River Mountains," pp. 236-237 for lodging information.) Brooks Lake Lodge is five miles in on a machine-packed road, making a perfect destination for day trips. Once there, you'll find another five km of groomed trails (no charge) plus access to the nearby Teton Wilderness, where skiers can escape the snow-mobiles. At the lodge (closed Tues. and Wed.) you can relax and enjoy lunch or spend the night (advance reservations required).

Grand Targhee

The Grand Targhee Everything Nordic Center, tel. 353-2304, has 12 km of groomed cross-country ski trails covering rolling terrain. Trail passes are $5/day, and lessons and a variety of tours are also available. Rent skis, boots, and poles for $12.50/day or $8.50/day for children. Hours are daily 9-4:30. Guests with Targhee lodging packages can ski free on the cross-country tracks.

ON YOUR OWN

Nordic skiers who would rather explore Jackson Hole and the mountains that surround it will discover an extraordinary range, from beginner-level treks along old roads to places where only the most advanced skiers dare venture. Because Jackson has so many cross-country fanatics (and visiting enthusiasts), trails are quickly broken along the more popular routes, making it easier for those who follow. For complete coverage of all these options, pick up a copy of the free *Cross Country Ski Guide to Jackson Hole* at Skinny Skis, 65 W. Deloney Ave., tel. 733-6094. If you're heading out on your own, be prepared for deep snow (four feet in the valley) and temperatures that often plummet far below zero at night.

The **Teton County Parks and Recreation Department,** tel. 733-5056, leads a variety of all-day cross-country ski outings every Tues. (early Dec. to late March) for $2 pp. Bring your own skis.

Jackson Hole Mountain Guides, tel. 733-4979, runs wintertime ski tours, avalanche courses, ski mountaineering, rock- and ice-climbing classes, along with overnight trips to the Mt. Glory ski hut on Teton Pass ($200 pp guided; $100/night for the hut if unguided). Longer trips, such as a six-day Teton Crest tour, run around $550 pp.

Jackson Area

Even rank beginners will enjoy exploring several local spots. Get to **Moose-Wilson Rd.** by heading a mile north of Teton Village to where the plowing ends. The nearly level road continues for two scenic miles across a creek and through groves of aspen. For more adventure, turn off at the Granite Canyon trailhead and follow the trail up toward the canyon. Conditions get more difficult as you progress, and avalanches are a potential hazard farther up.

The closest place to Jackson for on-your-own cross-country skiing is **Cache Creek Canyon** at the east end of Cache Creek Dr., where the plowing ends at a parking lot. Snowmobiles and other skiers have packed the route.

For a longer trip, take the Rafferty ski lift at Snow King and then ski west through the trees and down to Cache Creek, returning via the road. Ask at Snow King for specifics. Another popular local place is along the **Snake River dikes,** where US 22 crosses the river (a mile east of Wilson). The dikes extend along both sides of the river for several miles, making for easy skiing. It's also a good place to watch ducks, moose, and other critters, or just to listen to the river rolling over the rocks. More flat, easy skiing is on Moose-Wilson Rd. just north of Jackson Hole Ski Resort.

SAFETY IN AVALANCHE COUNTRY

Backcountry skiing is becoming increasingly popular in the mountains surrounding Jackson Hole. Unfortunately, many skiers fail to take the necessary precautions. Given the enormous snowfalls that occur, the steep slopes the snow piles up on, and the high winds that accompany many storms, it should come as no surprise that avalanches are a real danger. If you really want to avoid avalanches, ski only on groomed ski trails or "bombproof" slopes that, because of aspect, shape, and slope angle, never seem to slide. Unfortunately, this isn't always possible, so an understanding of the conditions that lead to avalanches is imperative for backcountry skiers. The best way to learn this is from an avalanche class such as the backcountry and avalanche programs taught by the **American Avalanche Institute,** Box 308, Wilson, WY 83014, tel. 733-3315, **Jackson Community Education,** tel. 733-7425, or **Jackson Hole Mountain Guides,** tel. 733-4979. Failing that, you can help protect yourself by following these precautions when you head into the backcountry:

• Before leaving, get up-to-date avalanche information by calling the 24-hour **Forest Service Avalanche Forecast** at 733-2664. If they say the avalanche danger is high, try skiing on the flats instead.

• Be sure to carry extra warm clothes, water, high-energy snacks, a dual-frequency avalanche transceiver (and know how to use it!), a lightweight snow shovel (for digging snow pits, emergency snow shelters, or excavating avalanche victims), first-aid supplies, a Swiss Army knife, a topo-

graphic map, an extra plastic ski tip, a flashlight, matches, and a compass. Many skiers also carry that cure-all, duct tape, wrapped around a ski pole. Let someone know exactly where you are going and when you expect to return.

• Check the angle of an area before you ski through it; slopes of 30-40 degrees are the most dangerous, while lesser slopes do not slide as frequently.

• Watch the weather; winds over 15 mph can pile snow much more deeply on lee slopes, causing dangerous loading on the snowpack. Especially avoid skiing on or below cornices.

• Avoid the leeward side of ridges, where snow loading can be greatest.

• Be aware of gullies and bowls; they're more likely to slip than flat open slopes or ridgetops. Stay out of gullies at the bottom of wide bowls; these are natural avalanche chutes.

• Look at the trees. Smaller trees may indicate that avalanches rip through an area frequently, knocking over the larger trees. (Avalanches can, however, also run through forested areas.)

• Know how much new snow has fallen recently. Heavy new snow over older weak snow layers is a sure sign of extreme danger on potential avalanche slopes. Most avalanches slip during or immediately after a storm.

• Learn how to dig a snow pit and how to read the various snow layers. Particularly important are the very weak layers of depth hoar or surface hoar that have been buried under heavy new snow.

Grand Teton National Park Area

A bit farther afield, but well worth the detour, are several trails in Grand Teton National Park. Orange markers denote the paths. Park at the Cottonwood Creek bridge (the road isn't plowed beyond this), and head out for **Jenny Lake** (nine miles RT) or **Taggart Lake** (three miles RT). Just three miles south of Moose on Moose-Wilson Rd., you may also want to try the trail to **Phelps Lake** (five miles RT). Or, if you have more ambition and skill, longer routes could take you far up into the canyons of the Tetons. Be sure to stop at the Moose Visitor Center for current conditions and a copy of their trail map. Ski mountaineers and overnight ski tourers must also register here.

For unsurpassed vistas of the Tetons, try skiing to the top of 8,252-foot **Shadow Mountain**, 14 miles northeast of Jackson. (The name comes from the shadows of the Tetons that fall across the mountain's face each evening.) From the town of Kelly, drive another five miles north to a parking area (the road isn't plowed beyond this) and then ski up the nearby Forest Service road that snakes up Shadow Mountain. It's fairly steep in places and 10 miles RT. Snowmobilers also use this road.

Granite Hot Springs

One of the most popular ski- and snowmobile-in sites is **Granite Hot Springs,** tel. 733-6318, a delightful 105° F hot-spring-fed pool on Forest Service land. Get there by driving 25 miles southeast of Jackson into Hoback Canyon and then skiing 10 miles in from the signed parking area. The route is not difficult, but due to the distance it isn't recommended for beginners unless they are prepared for a 20-mile RT trek. The pool ($4) is open 10 a.m. to an hour before dark. Bring your swimsuit. Ask the attendant about places to snow camp nearby.

Teton Pass

Locals head to 8,429-foot Teton Pass when they really want to test their ability. The summit parking area fills with cars on fresh-snow mornings, as everyone from advanced-beginners to beyond-advanced mountaineering skiers heads out for a day in the powder or a week of wilderness trekking in the Tetons. Snow depths of eight feet or more are not uncommon in midwinter. (The snow once became so deep on the pass that it took plows two weeks to clear the road!) The slopes around Teton Pass cover the full spectrum, but be sure you know your own ability and how to avoid avalanches. There are avalanche chutes all over here.

Before heading out, check the above-mentioned Skinny Skis *Cross Country Ski Guide* for specifics on Teton Pass, or talk to folks at Skinny Skis or Teton Mountaineering. This is the backcountry, so there are no signs at the various bowls; ask other skiers if you aren't sure which is which. Avalanches do occur in some of these bowls, and it's possible to get lost up here during a storm; so be prepared. Skiers frequently ski the five miles down old Teton Pass road.

GRAND TETON NATIONAL PARK

Grand Teton National Park remains one of the preeminent symbols of American wilderness. The Tetons rise abruptly from the valley floor, their bare triangular ridges looking like broken shards of glass from some cosmic accident of creation. With six different summits topping 12,000 feet, plus some of the finest climbing and hiking in Wyoming, the Tetons are a paradise for lovers of the outdoors. They have long been a favorite of photographers and sightseers and once even appeared in an ad promoting Colorado tourism! The Tetons change character with the seasons. In summer the sagebrush flats are a garden of flowers set against the mountain backdrop. When autumn falls on the land, the cottonwoods and aspens become swaths of yellow and orange. Winter turns everything a glorious, sparkling white, set against the fluorescent blue sky.

GEOLOGY

Building A Mountain Range
The precipitous Teton range contains perhaps the most complex geologic history in North America. Although the Tetons are ancient by any human scale, they are the youngest mountains in the Rockies, less than 10 million years old (versus 60 million years for the nearby Wind River Mountains). The Tetons are a fault-block

range, formed when the earth's crust cracked along an angled fault. Forces within the earth have pushed the western side (the Tetons) up, while the eastern portion (Jackson Hole) dropped down like a trapdoor. Geologists believe the fault could slip up to 10 feet at a time, producing a violent earthquake. All this shifting has created one of the most dramatic and asymmetric mountain faces on earth.

Unlike typical mountain ranges, the highest parts are not at the center of the range, but along the eastern edge where uplifting continues. The western slope that drops gently into Idaho is much less dramatic, though the views are still very impressive. This tilting-and-subsidence process is still going on today. The town of Wilson in Jackson Hole now lies 10 feet below the level of the nearby Snake River; only riverside dikes protect the town from flooding.

As the mountains rose along this fault, millennia of overlying deposits were stripped away by erosion, leaving three-million-year-old Precambrian rock jutting into the air above the more recent sedimentary deposits in the valley. Because of this shifting and erosion, sandstone deposits atop Mt. Moran match those 24,000 feet below Jackson Hole.

Rivers Of Ice
In counterpoint to the uplifting actions that created the general outline of the Tetons, erosion-

GEOLOGIC CROSS-SECTION OF THE TETON RANGE

REDRAWN FROM U.S.G.S. MAP OF THE GRAND TETON NATIONAL PARK

CUTAWAY VIEW OF A TYPICAL VALLEY GLACIER

SNOW
SNOW LINE
CREVASSES
LATERAL MORAINE
LATERAL MORAINE
ICE
DEBRIS ON ICE
DEBRIS IN ICE
BEDROCK
TERMINAL MORAINE
ICE DEPOSITED DEBRIS
KETTLES (DEPRESSIONS)
OLD TERMINAL MORAINE
OUTWASH PLAIN
MELTWATER STREAMS
OUTWASH

REDRAWN FROM *CREATION OF THE TETON LANDSCAPE* BY J.D. LOVE AND JOHN C. REED, JR.

al processes have been wearing them down again. Glaciers—created when more snow falls than melts off—have proven one of the most important of these erosional processes. After a period of several years and under the weight of additional snow, the accumulated snow crystals change into ice. Gravity pulls this ice slowly downhill, creating what is essentially a frozen river that grinds against whatever lies in the way, plucking loose rocks and soil and polishing hard bedrock. This debris moves slowly down the glacier as if on a conveyer belt, eventually reaching its terminus.

When a glacier remains the same size for a long period of time, large piles of glacial debris accumulate at its end, creating what glaciologists call a terminal moraine. One of these, Jackson Lake, was created when a huge glacier dumped tons of rock at its snout. After the glacier melted back, this terminal moraine became a natural dam for the waters of the Snake River. Similar mounds of glacial debris dammed the creeks that formed Jenny, Leigh, Bradley, Taggart, and Phelps lakes within Grand Teton National Park.

Streams flowed from the ends of the glaciers, carrying along gravel, sand, silt, and clay. The cobbles and sands from these glacial streams were dropped on the flat valley below, while the finer silts and clays continued downstream, leaving behind soils too rocky and nu-

trient-poor to support trees. Only sagebrush grows on this flat plain today, while the surrounding hills and mountain slopes (which were spared this rocky deposition) are covered with lodgepole and subalpine fir forests. Trees can also be found covering the silty terminal moraines that ring the lakes.

Other reminders of the glacial past are the "potholes" (more accurately termed "kettles") that dot the plain south of Signal Mountain. These depressions were created when large blocks of ice were buried under glacial outwash. Only a dozen or so small glaciers remain in the Tetons; largest is the 3,500-foot-long Teton Glacier, visible on the northeastern face of Grand Teton. For a more detailed picture of Teton geology, read *Creation of the Teton Landscape* by J. D. Love and John C. Reed, Jr. (Moose: Grand Teton Natural History Association).

WILDLIFE

Grand Teton National Park is an excellent place to look for wildlife. Moose are often seen in the willow meadows along Jackson Lake, south of the settlement of Moose, or along the Snake River. Herds of pronghorn antelope are common on the sagebrush flats near Kelly. Elk (park biologists prefer the term wapiti) are frequent sights in fall as they migrate down from the high

country to the elk refuge near Jackson, but they can also be seen in the park during the summer. (Grand Teton is the only national park outside Alaska that allows hunting. The rules are pretty strange, however, requiring elk hunters to become temporarily deputized park rangers before they head out!) Grizzlies are currently found only on the park's northern margins, but black bears are present in wooded canyons and river-bottoms.

Bison (buffalo) are commonly seen in the Moran Junction area. They were present historically (hence the name Buffalo River), but had been extinct for perhaps a century when eight bison were released into Grand Teton National Park in 1969. The population grew slowly for the first decade until they discovered the free alfalfa handout at the elk refuge north of Jackson. With this winter feed, the population has grown to 100 animals, much to the chagrin of the elk-refuge managers. A public hunt has been instituted to control bison numbers. Other animals to look for are bald eagles and ospreys along the Snake River and trumpeter swans and Canada geese in ponds and lakes. The best times to see animals are in the early morning or at dusk.

HISTORY

Once the wonders of Yellowstone came to widespread public attention, it took only a few months for Congress to declare the area a national park, but the magnificent mountain range to the south proved an entirely different story. Early on, there were suggestions that Yellowstone be expanded to include the Tetons, but it would take decades of wrangling before Jackson Hole would finally be preserved.

"Damning" Jackson Lake

Jackson Lake represents one of the sadder chapters in the history of northwestern Wyoming. Jackson Lake Dam was built in the winter of 1910-11 to supply water for Idaho potato and beet farmers. The town of Moran was built to house construction workers for Jackson Lake Dam, and at one time included more than a hundred ramshackle structures. Nothing remains of the town. The 70-foot-tall dam increased the size of the natural lake, flooding out more than 7,200 acres of trees and creating a tangle of floating and submerged trunks and stumps. To some, the dam seemed like the serpent in the Garden of Eden, a symbol of the developments that would destroy the valley if not stopped. The trees remained in Jackson Lake for many years, creating an eyesore until the Park Service and the CCC finally launched a massive cleanup project in the 1930s. The dam was completely rebuilt in 1988-89, and while the lake now looks quite attractive, it remains yet another example how Wyoming provides water for farmers in surrounding states. Late in the fall—especially in recent dry years—the lake can be reduced to a large puddle with long stretches of exposed bottom at the upper end. Fortunately, Idaho irrigators did not succeed in their planned dams on Jenny, Leigh, and Taggart lakes.

Dudes And Development

Because of the rocky soils and long winters, Jackson Hole has always been a marginal place for cattle ranching, and only in the southern end of the valley are the soils rich enough to support a decent crop of hay. It was this poor soil and harsh climate that saved Jackson Hole from early development and forced the ranchers to bring in dudes to supplement their income. (One old-timer noted, "Dudes winter better than cattle.")

The first Jackson Hole dude ranch, the JY, was established along Phelps Lake by Louis Joy. It was quickly followed by the Bar BC Ranch of Struthers Burt, an acclaimed East Coast author who had come west as a dude but learned enough to go into the business for himself. The dude ranchers were some of the first to realize the value of Jackson Hole and to support its preservation. Burt proposed that the valley and mountains be saved not as a traditional park, but as a "museum on the hoof" where ranching and tourism would join hands to stave off commercial developments. The roads would remain unpaved, all homes would be log, and Jackson would stay a frontier town.

The movement to save Jackson Hole coalesced in a 1923 meeting at the cabin of Maude Noble. Horace Albright, superintendent of Yellowstone National Park, was there, along with local dude ranchers, businessmen, and cattlemen anxious to save the remote valley from exploitation. To accomplish this goal, they proposed finding a wealthy philanthropist who might be willing to invest the two million dollars that would be needed to buy the land. Fortunately, one of Struthers Burt's friends happened to be Kenneth Chorley, an assistant to John D. Rockefeller, Jr. Burt used this contact to get Rockefeller interested in the project.

Rocky To The Rescue

In 1926, Rockefeller traveled west for a 12-day trip to Yellowstone. Horace Albright used the chance to take him on a side trip into Jackson Hole and to proselytize for protection of the valley. What they saw portended badly for the future: the Jenny Lake dance hall, roadside tourist camps and hot dog stands, rusting abandoned cars, and a place that billboards proclaimed "Home of the Hollywood Cowboy." Rockefeller was angered by the prospect of crass commercial developments blanketing Jackson Hole and quickly signed on to the idea of purchasing the land and giving it to the Park Service.

To cover his tracks as he bought the land, Rockefeller formed the Snake River Land Company. (If ranchers had known that the Rockefeller clan was behind the scheme, they would have either refused to sell or jacked up the price.) Only a few residents—mostly supporters—knew of the plan. The local banker, Robert Miller, served as land-purchasing agent, although even he opposed letting the Park Service gain control of the valley. Miller used his position to buy out ranches with delinquent mortgages to his Jackson State Bank and then resigned, claiming the whole thing was part of a sinister plot to run the ranchers out and to halt "progress." In 1929, Congress voted to establish a small Grand Teton National Park that would encompass the mountains themselves—which stood little chance of development—but not much else. Conservationists knew that without preservation of the valley below, the wonderful vistas would be lost.

A National Battleground

Rockefeller and Albright finally went public with their land-purchasing scheme in 1930, releasing a tidal wave of outrage. Antipark forces led by

Sen. Milward Simpson (father of current Sen. Alan Simpson) spent the next decade fighting the park tooth and nail, charging that it would destroy the economy of Jackson Hole and that ranchers would lose their livelihood. Rockefeller's agents were falsely accused of trying to intimidate holdouts with strong-arm tactics. Congress refused to accept Rockefeller's gift, and local opposition blocked the bill for more than a decade.

Finally, in 1943, President Roosevelt made an end run around the antipark forces by accepting the 32,000 acres purchased by Rockefeller, adding 130,000 acres of Forest Service land, and declaring it the Jackson Hole National Monument. The move outraged those in the valley, prompting more hearings and bills to abolish the new national monument. Wyoming's politicians attacked Roosevelt's actions. A bill overturning the decision was pocket-vetoed by the president, but for the next several years, the Wyoming delegation kept reintroducing the measure.

Things came to a head when Wallace Beery—a Reaganesque Hollywood actor—threatened to "shoot to kill" park officials. Beery organized a cattle drive across the monument (he had to use a stepladder to climb on his horse), but unable to find anyone to fire on in the new monument, his cadres sat on a creek bank and drank a case of beer, cussing out the damn bureaucrats. So much for the Wild West.

By 1947, the tide had turned as increasing postwar tourism revitalized the local economy. Finally, in 1950, a compromise was reached granting ranchers lifetime grazing rights and the right to trail their cattle across the park en route to summer grazing lands. The new-and-improved Grand Teton National Park had finally come to fruition.

Postmortem

Some of the early fears that Rockefeller would use the new park for his own gain seem at least partly justified. His descendants still own the old JY Ranch and use Phelps Lake as something of a semiprivate playground, while most of the other dude ranches have long since been taken over by the Park Service. Rockefeller also built the enormous Grand Teton Lodge along Jackson Lake, plus facilities at Colter Bay and Jenny Lake, leading some to accuse the family of attempting to monopolize services within the park. The company, Rockresorts, was finally sold in 1986 to CSX Corporation.

Looking back on the controversial creation of Grand Teton National Park, it's easy to see how wrong park opponents were. Teton county has Wyoming's most vibrant economy, and millions of people arrive each year to enjoy the beauty of the undeveloped Tetons. As writer Nathaniel Burt noted, "The old enemies of the park are riding the profitable bandwagon of unlimited tourism with high hearts and open palms." Park opponents' claims that the Park Service would "lock up" the land ring as hollow as similar antiwilderness claims today by descendants of the same politicians who opposed Grand Teton half a century ago. Without inclusion of the land purchased by Rockefeller, it is easy to imagine the valley covered with all sorts of summer home developments, RV campgrounds, souvenir shops, motels, billboards, and neon signs. Take a look at the town of Jackson to see what might have been.

TOURING THE PARK

Grand Teton National Park has fewer "attractions" than Yellowstone—its big sister to the north—and an easy day's drive takes you past the road-accessible portions of Grand Teton. The real attractions are the mountains and the incomparable views one gets of them from Jackson Hole. This is one backdrop you will never tire of seeing.

Roads

Grand Teton is bisected by the main north-south highway (US 26-89-191) and by the road heading east over Togwotee Pass (US 26-287). Both of these routes are kept open year-round, although wintertime plowing ends at Flagg Ranch, just south of the Yellowstone boundary. In

---

BEAVER DICK LEIGH

Around 1863, Richard "Beaver Dick" Leigh became the first white man to attempt a permanent life in Jackson Hole. An Englishman by birth, Beaver Dick lived in a log cabin with his Shoshone wife, Jenny, and their four children, scraping out the barest existence by hunting, trapping, and guiding. As guide for the 1872 Hayden Survey of the Jackson Hole area, Beaver Dick gained the respect of the surveyors who named Leigh Lake for him and Jenny Lake for his wife. Today a local bar denigrates this remarkable man by calling itself "Beaver Dick's" while using a cartoonish image of him in its ads. The real man was nothing like this, and reading his diaries and letters is a lesson in how difficult life was for early Wyoming settlers. On one terrible Christmas in 1876, Beaver Dick watched his entire family—Jenny, his newborn baby, and the four other children—all slowly die from smallpox. Their deaths left him badly shaken, as he related in a letter to a friend:

i got Dick in the house and to bed and Tom went over to get Mr. Anes. Wile Tom and Anes was sounding the ice to see if a horse could cross my wife was struck with Death. she rased up and looked me streaght in the face and then she got excited . . . and she sade she was going to die and all our childron wold die and maby i wold die . . . she was laying very quiet now for about 2 hours when she asked for a drink of water. i was laying downe with one of my daughters on eatch arme keeping them quiet because of the fevor. i told Anes what she wanted and he gave hur a drink and 10 minuts more she was ded . . . i can not wright one hundreth part that pased thrue my mind at this time as i thaught deth was on me. i sade Jinny i will sone be with you and fell asleep. Tom sade i ad beene a sleep a half hour when i woke up everything was wet with presperation i was very weak. i lade for 10 or 15 minuts and saw William and Anne Jane had to be taken up to ease themselves every 5 minuts and Dick Juner very restlas . . . Anne Jane died about 8 o clock about the time every year i used to give them a candy puling and thay menchond about the candy puling many times wile sick . . . William died on the 25 addition, a paved park road cuts south from Jackson Lake Dam to Jenny Lake and Moose. Only the southern end of this is plowed in winter, with the remainder becoming a snowmobile and cross-country ski route. South of Moose, a narrow, winding road connects the park to Teton Village, nine miles away. It is rough dirt in places (no trailers or RVs) and is closed in winter. The following tour takes you past the points of interest along the main roads. The route follows a general clockwise direction beginning and ending at the **Moose Visitor Center**. Before heading out, step inside the center for an introduction to the park and a look at the natural-history videos, books, and oil paintings.

Menor's Ferry Area

Just inside the South Entrance to Grand Teton National Park, a side road leads to **Chapel of the Transfiguration** and **Menor's Ferry**. The rustic log church (built in 1925) is most notable for its dramatic setting. The back window faces directly toward the Tetons, providing ample distractions for worshippers. The bell out front was cast in 1842. Nearby Menor's Ferry is named for William D. Menor, who first homesteaded here in 1894 and later built a cable ferry to make it easier to cross the river. His old whitewashed house still stands. A 1990 ferry reconstruction floats in the river; check out the ingenious propulsion mechanism that uses the current to pull it across. For many years, Menor's ferry served as the primary means of crossing the river in the central part of Jackson Hole. Wagons were charged 50 cents, while those on horseback paid 25 cents. (William Menor's brother, Holiday Menor, lived on the opposite side of the river, but the two often feuded, yelling insults across the water at each other and refusing to acknowledge one another for years at a time.)

Menor sold out to Maude Noble in 1918, and she ran the ferry until 1927 when a bridge was built near the present one in Moose. Her cabin now houses an excellent collection of historical

about 9 or 10 o clock in the evening . . . on the 26th Dick Juner died . . . Elizabeth was over all danger but this, and she caught cold and sweled up agane and died on the 28 of Dec about 2 o clock in the morning. this was the hardist blow of all . . . i shall improve the place and live and die near my famley but i shall not be able to do enything for a few months for my mind is disturbed at the

sights that i see around me and [the] work that my famley as done wile thay were liveing.

But the human spirit is remarkably resilient. Beaver Dick later married a Bannock girl, raised another family, and guided for others, even meeting Theodore Roosevelt on one of his hunting trips. Beaver Dick Leigh died in 1899 and was buried on a ridge overlooking Idaho's Teton Basin.

YELLOWSTONE NATIONAL PARK

Beaver Dick and Jenny Leigh with their children

photos from Jackson Hole. Maude Noble gained a measure of fame in 1923 when she hosted a gathering of residents to save Jackson Hole from development, a movement that would eventually lead to the creation of Grand Teton National Park.

Heading northwest beyond the Menor's Ferry area, the main road climbs up an old river bench (created by flooding from the rapid melting of the glaciers) and passes the trailhead to the turquoise waters of **Taggart Lake**. The land around here was burned in the 1,028-acre Beaver Creek lightning fire of 1985, and summers find a riot of wildflowers. A very popular day-hike leads from the parking area here to Taggart Lake and then back via the Beaver Creek Trail, a distance of four miles roundtrip. A side loop to **Bradley Lake** adds another two miles to this. These trails provide a fine way to see up close the glacial moraines that created the dams that formed these lakes.

Jenny Lake Area

The most loved of all the Grand Teton lakes is Jenny Lake, nestled at the foot of Cascade Canyon and surrounded by a luxuriant forest of Engelmann spruce, subalpine fir, and lodgepole pine. Jenny Lake is named for Jenny Leigh, the Shoshone wife of Beaver Dick Leigh (as in nearby Leigh Lake). A one-way loop road leads south past Jenny and String lakes, providing excellent views of the **Cathedral Group:** Teewinot, Grand Teton, and Mt. Owen. This is the most popular part of the park, and day-hikers will find a plethora of trails to sample, along with crowds to contend with. Paths lead around both Jenny and String lakes, while another nearly level trail follows the east shore of Leigh Lake to several pleasant sandy beaches. String Lake is narrow but very pretty and makes a fine place for canoeing or swimming.

One of the most popular attractions in the area is **Inspiration Point**, located on the west side of Jenny Lake. It's two miles by trail from the Jenny Lake Ranger Station, or you can ride one of the summertime shuttle boats that cross the lake every 20 minutes or so for $3.50 RT or $1.75 for kids (this fee may increase). Scenic boat cruises are also available. From the boat dock, the trail climbs a half-mile to **Hidden Falls**, and then another quarter-mile to Inspiration

Point, which overlooks Jackson Hole. It is 400 feet above Jenny Lake. Many day-hikers continue up Cascade Canyon (see "Backcountry Hiking," below).

Signal Mountain Area

As the road approaches Jackson Lake, a paved but narrow side road (no RVs or trailers) turns east and leads to the summit of Signal Mountain, 800 feet above Jackson Hole. Fine panoramic views of the Tetons, Jackson Lake, the Snake River, and the long valley below. To the south are **The Potholes**, a hummocky area created when huge blocks of ice were left behind by retreating glaciers. The melting ice created depressions, some of which are still filled with water. Signal Mountain was burned by a massive 1879 fire and offers a good opportunity to see how Yellowstone may look in a century.

Signal Mountain Lodge hugs the southeast shore of Jackson Lake and includes a full range of facilities, from campsites to a bar. Just east of the lodge is **Chapel of the Sacred Heart**, a small Roman Catholic church. The road then crosses **Jackson Lake Dam,** which raises the water level by 39 feet, alters the river's natural flow, and inundates a large area upstream. Many conservationists fought to have Jackson Lake excluded from the park, concerned that it would establish a bad precedent for allowing reservoirs in other parks. Nevertheless, once you get away from the dam, the lake seems relatively natural today.

Along Jackson Lake

A pullout near Jackson Lake Junction provides views over the **Willow Flats,** where moose are frequently seen, especially in the morning. Impressive **Jackson Lake Lodge** was built in the 1950s· with the $5 million financial backing of John D. Rockefeller, Jr. The building tops a bluff overlooking the willow flats. Architects are not thrilled about the design (one author termed it "the ugliest building in Western Wyoming"), but the 60-foot-tall back windows frame an unbelievable view of the Tetons and Jackson Lake. A historic U.S.-Soviet diplomatic meeting was held here in 1989 between Soviet Foreign Minister Eduard Shevardnadze and Secretary of State James Baker. Immediately across from the lodge is a trail leading to **Emma Matilda** and

Two Ocean lakes. It is 14 miles RT around both lakes, with lots of wildlife along the way, including moose, trumpeter swans, pelicans, and ducks. You may have to contend with large groups on horseback.

Colter Bay Village is one of the most developed parts of the park, with a full marina, stores, restaurants, and acres of parking. The main attraction here is the visitor center, which houses the **Colter Bay Indian Arts Museum**, tel. 543-2467. Open daily 8-5 from mid-May through Sept. and till 7 p.m. in midsummer; no charge. Inside is the extraordinary David T. Vernon collection of Indian pieces, said to be the finest of its kind in any national park. The collection spreads through several rooms on two floors and includes beaded buckskin dresses, moccasins, kachina dolls, masks, ceremonial pipes, warbonnets, shields, bows, and other decorated items. Indian craft-making demonstrations are sometimes offered.

An almost-level trail leads from the marina out to **Hermitage Point** and then back again, a distance of nine miles roundtrip. Along the way you pass beaver ponds and willow patches where trumpeter swans, moose, and ducks are commonly seen. Get a map of this trail from the visitor center. The **Colter Bay Nature Trail** (one mile) provides another nearby loop hike.

North To Yellowstone

North of Colter Bay, the highway cruises along the shore of Jackson Lake for the next nine miles, providing a number of fine vantage points across to the Tetons. The burned area on the opposite shore was ignited by lightning in the 1974 Waterfalls Canyon Fire that consumed 3,700 acres. By late fall each year, Idaho spud farmers have drawn down water in the lake, leaving a long, barren shoreline at the upper end.

Shortly after the road leaves the upper end of Yellowstone Lake, a signboard announces your entrance into **John D. Rockefeller, Jr. Memorial Parkway**. This 24,000-acre parcel of land was transferred to the National Park Service in 1972, in commemoration of Rockefeller's unstinting work in establishing Grand Teton National Park. The land forms a connection between Grand Teton and Yellowstone and is managed by Grand Teton National Park. Much

of this area was severely burned by the 1988 Huck Fire that began when strong winds blew a tree into power lines. Despite immediate efforts to control the blaze, it consumed 4,000 acres in the first two hours and later grew to cover nearly 200,000 acres, primarily within the Forest Service's Teton Wilderness.

On the northern end of Rockefeller Parkway is **Flagg Ranch**, where facilities include a store, a gas station, a motel, a restaurant, and a campground. **Grassy Lake Road** takes off just north of Flagg Ranch and continues 52 miles to Ashton, Idaho. It's a scenic drive, but don't attempt this narrow and rough dirt road with a trailer or RV. This route provides a shortcut to the Bechler River area of Yellowstone and is a popular wintertime snowmobile route.

Jackson Lake To Moran Junction

Heading east and south from Jackson Lake, the road immediately passes **Oxbow Bend**, where the pullout is almost always filled with folks looking for geese, ducks, moose, and other animals. The oxbow was formed when the meandering river cut off an old loop. The calm water here is a delightful place for canoes, though the mosquitoes can be a major annoyance in midsummer. Come fall, photographers line the shoulder of the road for classic shots of flaming aspen trees with Grand Teton and **Mt. Moran** in the background. Mt. Moran is the massive peak with a flattened summit, a skillet-shaped glacier across its front, and a distinctive black vertical diabase dike that looks like a scar from some ancient battle. It rises 12,605 feet above sea level. The peak is named for Thomas Moran, whose beautiful paintings of Yellowstone helped persuade Congress to set aside that area as the world's first national park.

At **Moran Junction** you pass the Buffalo Entrance Station and meet the road to Togwotee Pass and Dubois. A post office and school are the only developments here. The epic Western *The Big Trail* was filmed nearby in 1930, starring an actor named John Wayne in his first speaking role. (John Wayne had never ridden a horse before this.) An interesting side trip is to head east from Moran on US 26-287 for three miles to **Buffalo Valley Road**. This narrow, scenic road leads to Turpin Meadow, a major entryway into the Teton Wilderness (see pp. 311-313). Very pretty —especially in early summer when the fields are carpeted with flowers. Buck and rail fences line the road and the pastures are filled with horses and cattle. Purty country. Beyond Turpin Meadow, it turns to gravel and climbs sharply uphill, rejoining the main highway a couple of miles below Togwotee Lodge.

Moran Junction To Moose

Heading south from Moran, US 26-89-191 immediately crosses the Buffalo River (a.k.a. Buffalo Fork of the Snake River), where bison were once abundant. With a little help from humans, bison have been reestablished and are now often seen just south of here along the road. The turnoff to the **Cunningham Cabin** is six miles south of Moran Junction. The structure actually consists of two sod-roofed log cabins connected by a covered walkway (a "dogtrot"). Built around 1890, it served first as living quarters and later as a barn and smithy. A park brochure describes the locations of other structures on the property.

Pierce Cunningham came here as a homesteader and with his wife Margaret settled to raise cattle. Although this was some of the better land in this part of the valley, the soil was still so rocky that they had a hard time digging fencepost holes. Instead, they opted to build the buck-and-rail fences that have become a hallmark of Jackson Hole ranches. Cunningham Ranch gained notoriety in 1893 when a posse surrounded two suspected horse thieves who were wintering at Cunningham's place while he was away. Vigilantes shot and killed George Spencer and Mike Burnett in an example of "mountain justice." Later, however, there was some suspicion that hired killers working for wealthy cattle barons had led the posse, and that the murdered men may have been innocent. **Spread Creek** is just north of the Cunningham cabin, gaining its name by having two mouths, separated by a distance of three miles.

The highway next rolls past **Triangle X Ranch**, one of the most famous dude ranches in Jackson Hole. Although it's on park land, the Turner family has managed Triangle X for over 60 years. (One of the owners, John Turner, was President Bush's director of the Fish and Wildlife Service.) Stop by just after sunup to watch wranglers driving 120 head of horses up from the lower pastures. It's a scene straight out of a Marlboro ad. Southwest from Triangle X, the road climbs along an ancient river terrace and passes hidden **Hedrick Pond** where the 1963 movie *Spencer's Mountain* was filmed. Starring Henry Fonda, it was supposedly set in Virginia! Trumpeter swans are sometimes seen on the pond. Several turnouts provide very popular photo-opportunity spots, the most famous being **Snake River Overlook**. Ansel Adams's famous shot of the Tetons was taken here, and has been repeated with less success by generations of photographers. Throughout the summer, a progression of different flowers blooms in the open sagebrush flats along the road, adding brilliant slashes of color. They are prettiest in late June. (In the high country, the peak comes a month or more later.)

Just north of Snake River Overlook is the turnoff to **Deadman's Bar**. An extremely steep dirt road (4WD recommended) drops down to one of the primary river-access points used by river rafters. The river bar received its name from an incident in 1886. Four German prospectors entered the area, but only one—John Tonnar—emerged. Bodies of the other three were found along the Snake River, and Tonnar was charged with murder. The jury in Evanston believed his claim of self-defense, and he was set free, an act that so angered locals that they vowed to take care of future Jackson Hole criminals with a shotgun. A skull from one of the victims is on display in the Jackson Hole Museum. Another popular put-in for river runners is **Schwabacher Landing**, located at the end of a one-mile gravel road that splits off just north of the Glacier View Turnout. This is a pleasant place for riverside picnics.

A mile north of the turnoff to Moose, the Antelope Flats Rd. heads east along Ditch Creek. **Blacktail Butte** lies just south of here, a timbered knoll rising over the surrounding sagebrush plains. It's a favorite of rock-climbers. Keep your eyes peeled for the much-photographed old farm buildings known as **Mormon Row**. The farmland here was homesteaded by Mormon (and non-Mormon) settlers in the early 1900s but was later purchased by Rockefeller's Snake River Land Company and transferred to the Park Service. A few of the buildings are still occupied, but most are abandoned and gradually collapsing under the heavy winter snows.

Teton Science School

Hidden away in a valley along upper Ditch Creek is Teton Science School, a fine hands-on school for both young and old. Founded in 1967 as a summer field-biology program for high-school kids, it has grown into a year-round program with classes that run the gamut from elementary-school level all the way up to intensive college courses and adult seminars. Summertime visitors will enjoy their one- to five-day seminars on such diverse subjects as environmental ethics, alpine butterflies, river channels, and wolves. Their excellent month-long wilderness EMT course ($1225) is one of the few programs of its kind in the nation. During the winter, TSS offers a **winter speaker series** ($3) at Snow King Resort in Jackson, covering a spectrum of scientific, environmental, and social issues. In the spring and fall, they have **fireside chats** at the TSS library, where speakers talk about environmental issues. The cost is $12, including dinner (reservations required).

The school is based at the old Elbo dude ranch (started in 1932), which includes two small dormitories plus a central kitchen, dining area, and other structures. At the main building, visitors will find the large **Murie Collection** of birds, mammal skulls, and other natural-history specimens, including casts of animal tracks used by famed wildlife biologist Olaus Murie in producing his *Peterson's Guide to Animal Tracks*. (Open to the public, but call ahead to be sure it is not being used by a class.) Check out the grizzly scat! Get a copy of the course catalog by contacting TSS at Box 68, Kelly, WY 83011, tel. 733-4765.

Kelly Vicinity

The small settlement of **Kelly** borders on the southeastern end of Grand Teton National Park and has some log homes plus a cluster of Mongolian-style yurts—certainly the most unusual dwellings in Wyoming. The Park Service's **Gros Ventre Campground** is three miles west of here. Gros Ventre Rd. leads east from the Kelly area, passing **Kelly Warm Spring** on the right. Its warm, clear waters are a favorite place for

local kayakers to practice their rolls. A short distance up the road and off to the north are the collapsing remains of the **Shane cabin**, where a scene from this classic 1951 Western was filmed. Beyond this, the road enters Bridger-Teton National Forest and the Slide Lake area, where there is a Forest Service campground.

Gros Ventre Slide

One of the most impressive geologic events in recent Wyoming history took place in the Gros Ventre (pronounced GROW-vont; "Big Belly" in French trapper lingo) Canyon, named for the Gros Ventre Indians of this area. Sheep Mountain, on the south side of the canyon, consists of sandstone underlain by a layer of shale that becomes slippery when wet. Melting snow and heavy rains in the spring of 1925 lubricated this layer of shale, and on June 23, the entire north end of the mountain—a section 2,000 feet wide and a mile long—suddenly slid a mile and a half downslope, instantly damming the river below and creating Slide Lake. A rancher in the valley, Guil Huff, watched in amazement as the mountain began to move, galloping his horse out of the way as the slide roared within 30 feet of him. Huff's ranch floated away on the new lake several days later.

For two years folks kept a wary eye on the makeshift dam of rock and mud. Then, on May 18, 1927, the dam suddenly gave way, pushing an enormous wall of water through the downstream town of Kelly. Six people perished in the flood, and when the water reached Snake River Canyon nine hours later, it filled the canyon to the rim with boiling water, trees, houses, and debris. Today a smaller Slide Lake still exists, and the massive landslide that created it more than 65 years ago remains as an exposed gouge visible for miles around. Geologists say that, under the right conditions, more of Sheep Mountain could slide. Dead trees still stand in the upper end of Slide Lake.

Gros Ventre River

Above Slide Lake, the road turns to gravel (unplowed in winter), becoming quite rutted in spots. Surprising scenery makes the bone-jarring easier to take. The landscape here is far different from the Tetons, with the road passing colorful badlands hills rising sharply above the Gros Ventre River. Two more campgrounds (Red Hills and Crystal Creek) are four miles above Slide Lake. The road continues another 15 beautiful miles along the river, getting rougher at the upper end. The Gros Ventre Wilderness lies immediately south of the road and there are quite a few trailheads along the way. On the way back down the Gros Ventre River valley you will discover some fine views across to the Tetons.

BACKCOUNTRY HIKING

The precipitous Tetons that look so dramatic from the roads are even more impressive up close and personal. Grand Teton National Park is laced with 200 miles of trails, and hikers can choose from everything from simple day-treks to weeklong trips along the crest of the range. Unlike nearby Yellowstone, where most of the country is forested, the Tetons contain extensive

TETON HIKING TRAILS

Alpine scenery. This means, however, that many of the high passes won't be free of snow until late July and may require ice axes before then. Check at the visitor centers or Jenny Lake Ranger Station for current conditions.

The most popular hiking area centers on the crest of the Tetons and the lakes that lie at its feet, most notably Jenny Lake. **Teton Crest Trail** stretches from Teton Pass north all the way to Cascade Canyon, with numerous connecting paths from both sides of the range. Three relatively short (two to three days) loop hikes are described below. For more complete descriptions of park trails, see *Teton Trails* by Bryan Harry (Moose: Grand Teton Natural History Association) or *Hiking the Teton Backcountry* by Paul Lawrence (San Francisco: Sierra Club Books). Get topographic maps at the Moose Visitor Center or Teton Mountaineering in Jackson. Earthwalk Press, 2239 Union St., Eureka, CA 95501, produces an excellent topographic map of park trails (also available locally).

Regulations

The hiking trails of Grand Teton National Park are some of the most heavily used paths in Wyoming, and strict regulations are enforced. Backcountry-use permits (free) are required of all overnight hikers, and you'll need to specify a particular camping zone or site for each night of your trip. Get permits at the visitor centers in Moose or Colter Bay, or at the Jenny Lake Ranger Station. Get there early in the morning during the summer for popular trails. A limited number of backcountry permits may be reserved in advance (Jan. 1-June 1 only) by writing to: Permits Office, Grand Teton National Park, P.O. Drawer 170, Moose, WY 83012. Any off-trail hiking requires special permission; see "Mountain Climbing" below for specifics. Grizzlies are only found in the northern end of Grand Teton, but you still need to hang all food, since black bears roam throughout the park, particularly in the forested areas. Campfires are not allowed at higher elevations, so be sure to bring a cooking stove.

Cascade Canyon To Paintbrush Canyon

One of the most popular hikes in Grand Teton is this 19-mile loop trip up Cascade Canyon, over

Paintbrush Divide, and down Paintbrush Canyon (or vice versa). The trip offers a little of everything: hiking through dense forests, magnificent views of Grand Teton, alpine lakes, and flower-covered meadows. This trip is best done in late summer, since a cornice of snow typically blocks Paintbrush Divide until late July.

Begin at the String Lake trailhead and head south around Jenny Lake, stopping to enjoy the views (and crowds) at Inspiration Point before heading up along Cascade Creek. The trail splits at the upper end of this canyon; turning left takes you to Hurricane Pass and the Teton Crest Trail where you'll discover fine views of the back side of Grand Teton. Instead, turn right (north) and head up to beautiful Lake Solitude. Behind you, Teewinot, Mt. Owen, and Grand Teton are framed by the glacially carved valley walls. Above Lake Solitude, the trail climbs sharply to Paintbrush Divide and then switchbacks even more quickly down into Paintbrush Canyon. The trail eventually leads back to String Lake. Be sure to stop at beautiful Holly Lake on the way down.

Amphitheater Lake

A relatively short but very steep hike begins at the Lupine Meadows trailhead just south of Jenny Lake. It is only five miles to the cirque of Amphitheater Lake, but 3,000 feet higher, making this the quickest climb to the Teton treeline. Many folks day-hike this trail to savor the wonderful vistas across Jackson Hole along the way. Camping is available at Surprise Lake, a half-mile below Amphitheater. More adventurous folks may want to climb **Disappointment Peak**, the 11,618-foot summit directly in front of Grand Teton. (It was named by climbers who mistakenly thought they were on the east face of Grand Teton.) If you plan to do so, be sure to register at the Jenny Lake Ranger Station, and only attempt it if you're able to handle a few areas of class 3 moves.

Rendezvous Mountain To Death Canyon

This 23-mile-long loop hike is different in that much of the way is downhill. Begin at the Jackson Hole tram in Teton Village, where an $11 ticket takes you to the top of 10,450-foot Rendezvous Mountain. From the summit, the trail leads down to a saddle, across the South Fork of

Granite Creek, and up to Teton Crest Trail. Head north on this trail to Marion Lake—a popular camping site—and then over Fox Creek Pass. The trail splits, with the right fork dropping sharply down into scenic Death Canyon, named when a member of a survey party disappeared here in 1903. At the lower end of Death Canyon, cliffs rise nearly 3,000 feet on both sides. The trail forks at Phelps Lake, and from here you can either hike back to Teton Village via the Valley Trail or head to the trailhead at White Grass Ranger Station, 1 1/2 miles northeast of Phelps Lake. Note: If you reverse the direction of this hike you can save your money, since there is no charge for riding the tram down to Teton Village.

MOUNTAIN CLIMBING

The Tetons are considered some of the premier mountaineering country in the nation, with solid rock, good access, and a wide range of climbing conditions. Hundreds of climbing routes have been described for the main peaks, but the goal of many climbers is Grand Teton, better known as "the Grand." At 13,770 feet, this is Wyoming's second-highest summit, exceeded only by 13,804-foot Gannett Peak in the Wind River Mountains.

First To The Top
In the climbing trade, first ascents always rate highly, but the identity of the first to have scaled Grand Teton has long been a matter of debate. The official record belongs to the party of William Owen (as in nearby Mt. Owen), Bishop Spalding (as in nearby Spalding Peak), John Shive, and Frank Petersen, who reached the summit in 1898. Today, however, it appears that they were preceded by two members of the 1872 Hayden Expedition: Nathaniel P. Langford (first superintendent of Yellowstone National Park) and John Stevenson. In addition, another party made it to the top in 1893. Owen made a big deal out of his climb and spent 30 years trying to work himself into the record books by claiming the Langford party never reached the top. The whole thing got quite nasty, with Owen even accusing Langford of bribing the author of a history book to gain top honors. In 1929, Owen con-

vinced the Wyoming Legislature to declare his party the first on top. Few people believe it today, and the whole thing looks pretty foolish since even seven-year-old kids have made it to the top. Several thousand people climb the Grand each summer, many with no previous climbing experience (but excellent guides and a couple days of training). And just to prove that it could be done, in 1971 one fanatic actually skied the Grand (he's the ski-school director at Snow King Resort), followed in 1989 by a snowboarder. Both lived to tell the tale.

Getting There
Most climbing takes place between mid-July and late Sept. when the snow has melted back. Mountain climbing or off-trail hiking requires a special permit available from the Jenny Lake Ranger Station (or the Moose Visitor Center during the winter). You'll also need to check in upon your return. The climbing rangers—one of the most prestigious and dangerous jobs in the park—are all highly experienced mountaineers and can provide specific route information for the various summits.

Many climbers who scale Grand Teton follow the Amphitheater Lake Trail from Lupine Meadows to its junction with the Garnet Canyon Trail. This leads to a saddle separating Grand Teton and Middle Teton where both Exum and the Park Service have base camps. Other folks pitch tents behind boulders in this extraordinarily windy mountain gap. The final assault on the summit requires technical equipment and expertise. Mountaineers can stay at **Climbers' Ranch**, near Taggart Lake, for $5/night including bunk accommodations with showers and covered cooking areas. The ranch is open June 15 to Sept. 10 only. Call 733-7271 for reservations.

Climbing Schools
Jackson Hole is blessed with two of the finest climbing schools in North America, **Exum Mountain Guides**, Box 56, Moose, WY 83012, tel. 733-2297, and **Jackson Hole Mountain Guides**, 165 N. Glenwood, Jackson, WY 83001, tel. 733-4979. Both are authorized concessions of the National Park Service and the U.S. Forest Service and offer a wide range of classes, snow training, and climbs in the Tetons and elsewhere. Exum has been around since 1931,

when Glenn Exum pioneered the first solo climb of what has become the most popular route to the top of the Grand, the Exum Route.

During midsummer, expect to pay $400-500 (including food, gear, and shelter) for an ascent of Grand Teton that encompasses two days of basic and intermediate training followed by a two-day climb up the Grand and back. Rates are lower before mid-July and in September. Basic and intermediate climbing schools cost around $50-70/day. Also available are more advanced classes, plus climbs in the Tetons, the Wind River Mountains, Devils Tower, and other precipices. In addition, Jackson Hole Mountain Guides offers many winter classes, including avalanche safety, ice climbing, guided backcountry skiing, and winter ascents of Grand Teton. If you're planning to climb the Grand during the peak summer season, be sure to make reservations several months in advance to be assured of a spot.

On Your Own

If you already have the experience and want to do your own climbing, the most accessible local spot is **Blacktail Butte**, just north of Moose near Ditch Creek. The parking lot here fills on warm summer afternoons as hang-dogging enthusiasts try their moves on the rock face. Get climbing gear at **Moosely Seconds Mountaineering** in Moose, tel. 733-7176 or (800) 669-7176, or in Jackson at **Teton Mountaineering**, 86 E. Broadway, tel. 733-3595. Both stores rent climbing boots ($5/day). **Teton Rock Gym**, 1116 Maple Way, tel. 733-0707, has an indoor climbing wall where you can practice your moves. For more detailed info on local climbing, see Leigh N. Ortenburger's two-volume tome, *A Complete Guide to the Teton Range* (Palo Alto, CA: self-published).

GRAND TETON PRACTICALITIES

Entrance to Grand Teton National Park costs $10 per vehicle or $4 for individuals entering by bicycle, foot, motorcycle, snowmobile, or bus. The entrance pass covers both Grand Teton and Yellowstone national parks and is good for seven days. If you're planning to be here longer or to make additional visits, get an annual pass covering both parks for $15, or the Golden Eagle Passport, which includes all national parks, for $25 a year. The Golden Age Passport is free to anyone over 62, as is the Golden Access Passport for disabled individuals. Both of these also give you a 50% reduction in camping fees. Call 733-2880 for additional park information.

Lodging

Several places provide comfortable lodging in and around Grand Teton National Park, or you can stay in nearby Jackson. See the accommodations charts for specifics. Togwotee Mountain Lodge, just below Togwotee Pass, is a favorite place for horseback rides and pack trips, while winter turns it into a center for snowmobiling and cross-country skiing. Flagg Ranch is a jumping-off point for winter snowcoach or snowmobile trips into Yellowstone National Park.

Camping

Grand Teton National Park has five different campgrounds. The largest—and last to fill—is Gros Ventre Campground near the town of Kelly. The most scenic location—and quickest to fill—is Jenny Lake Campground. Accommodations at all park campgrounds are on a first-come, first-served basis, and reservations are not available. See the charts (pp. 276-277) for listings of public campgrounds and private RV parks in the Jackson Hole area. All the public campgrounds are closed in winter, but limited RV parking ($5; with restrooms and water) is available near the Colter Bay Visitor Center. Showers are available at Colter Bay.

Food And Services

The little settlement called Moose has a couple of businesses. An old favorite is **Dornans'**, tel. 733-2415, offering very reasonable meals during the summer, including all-you-can-eat breakfasts ($4.50) and chuckwagon dinners ($9). Next door is **Mountain Bike Outfitters**, tel. 733-3314, where you can rent bikes, and **Moosely Seconds**, tel. 733-7176, offering good deals on hiking and climbing gear. Across the way is **Moose Village Store**, tel. 733-3471, with groceries and spirits (best selection of wine and beer in Jackson Hole), and canoes for rent.

Colter Bay General Store, tel. 733-2811,

GRAND TETON NATIONAL PARK AREA ACCOMMODATIONS

LODGE	LOCATION	PHONE	RATES	FEATURES
Buffalo Valley Ranch	Moran	739-9477	$25	rustic cabins
Hatchet Motel	eight miles east of Moran Jct.	543-3413	$47 s, $52 d	AAA-approved, very nice, open mid-May to early Sept.
Colter Bay Village	Jackson Lake	543-2855 (800) 628-9988	$25+ $19+	rustic cabins tent cabins AAA-approved, open mid-May to early Oct.
Flying Heart Ranch	Moran	733-6452	$55-125	open June-Sept., 3 night minimum
Signal Mountain Lodge	Jackson Lake	543-2831	$60+ s or d	AAA-approved, cottages with kitchens, open mid-May to mid-Oct.
Flagg Ranch	Rockefeller Parkway	733-8761 (800) 443-2311	$75 s or d	motel rooms and cabins, open mid-May to mid-Oct. and mid-Dec. to mid-March
Togwotee Mountain Lodge	16 miles east of Moran Jct.	543-2847 (800) 543-2847	$65+ s, $73+ d	AAA-approved, sauna, whirlpools, open mid-June to early Oct. and mid-Dec. to early April
Jackson Lake Lodge	Jackson Lake	543-2855 (800) 628-9988	$92+ s, $100+ d	AAA-approved, pool, late May to mid-Sept.
Dornan's Spur Ranch	Moose	733-2522	$100+	new cabins
Slide Lake Cabins	Kelly	733-9061	$190	cabins sleep up to 8
Jenny Lake Lodge	Jenny Lake	733-4647 (800) 628-9988	$225+ s, $280+ d	AAA-approved, very nice cabins, includes breakfast and dinner, open June to late Sept.

also has a good choice of groceries and supplies. In summer, smaller general stores can be found at Signal Mountain, Flagg Ranch, and Jenny Lake. The stores at Moose and Flagg Ranch are open year-round. Summertime restaurants are at Signal Mountain, Flagg Ranch, Jenny Lake, Jackson Lake Lodge, and Colter Bay. All of these locations except Jenny Lake also have gift shops. Horseback rides are available at Jackson Lake Lodge, Jenny Lake, and Colter Bay. See p. 287 for info on transportation and tours of Grand Teton and Yellowstone. Post offices are located at Colter Bay (summer only), Moran, Moose Junction, and Kelly. **Grand Teton Lodge Company**, tel. 733-2811 or (800) 628-9988, offers twice-daily summer shuttle buses connecting Jackson Hole Airport with Jackson Lake Lodge and Colter Bay Village for $10 OW/$15 RT.

Boating

Canoeists will discover several excellent places to paddle within Grand Teton, particularly the Snake River Oxbow Bend and String and Leigh lakes. Boaters within Grand Teton will need to purchase a permit ($10 for motorboats and $5 for other craft). Motorboats are only allowed on Jackson Lake, Jenny Lake (7½-horsepower max), and Phelps Lake. Windsurfing water-skiing, and sailing are permitted on Jackson Lake. For info on floating the Snake River through the park, see "River Rafting," pp. 281-282. Marinas are located at Colter Bay, tel. 543-2811, Signal Mountain, tel. 733-5470, and Leeks Marina, tel. 543-2494. Rent motorboats, rowboats, and canoes, or hire a guide to take you to the hot fishing spots. Scenic boat cruises ($7.50 and up) are available at Colter Bay Marina, including a variety of cruise-and-dine trips. For more on

fishing and river rafting within the park, see the appropriate sections under "Jackson."

Information Centers

Visitors receive a copy of *Teewinot,* the park newspaper, at the entrance stations. It lists park facilities and services, along with interpretive programs, nature walks, and other activities. Family favorites for generations have been the evening campfire programs at the outdoor amphitheaters. Grand Teton National Park headquarters are located in the settlement of Moose near the southern end of the park. **Moose Visitor Center**, tel. 733-2880, is open daily (except Christmas) 8-4:30 year-round. **Colter Bay Visitor Center**, tel. 543-2467, is open daily 8-5 from mid-May through September. Both centers are open later—generally till 7 p.m.—in midsummer. **Grand Teton Natural History Association** operates bookstores in the visitor centers and provides a mail-order service for books about the park. For a catalog, contact them at P.O. Drawer 170, Moose, WY 83012.

BRIDGER-TETON NATIONAL FOREST

Bridger-Teton ("the B-T") National Forest is the second largest in the lower 48, stretching southward for 135 miles from the Yellowstone border and covering 3.4 million acres. Portions of the forest are described elsewhere; see "Bridger Wilderness," pp. 241-244, and "Greys River Loop Road," p. 164. In Jackson Hole, the two areas of most interest for recreation are the Teton Wilderness and the Gros Ventre Wilderness. Because of its extensive wilderness areas, the B-T has more outfitters than any other national forest. Much of the remaining land managed by the Forest Service is multiple-use, meaning lots of logging, cattle grazing, and oil and gas leasing. The latter has become one of the hottest political issues, since the Forest Service has attempted to open 95% of all non-wilderness lands to oil and gas exploration work, including areas around scenic Togwotee Pass. In 40 years of such exploration, only two commercially viable sites have been found on the B-T. Conservationists fear that if oil is found, the Forest Service will waive its no-surface-occupancy standards to allow development.

The Bridger-Teton National Forest **visitor center** in Jackson, tel. 739-5500, is next to the office at 340 N. Cache. Summer hours are Mon.-Fri. 8-5:30 and Sat. 8-4:30. The rest of the year it is open Mon.-Fri. 8-4:30. If you're planning a trip into surrounding Forest Service lands, be sure to stop by to pick up the forest map ($2) and to ask for other publications on camping and sights. Ranger stations are in Jackson at 140 E. Broadway, tel. 733-4755, and nine miles east of Moran Junction, tel. 543-2386.

TETON WILDERNESS

The Teton Wilderness covers 585,468 acres of mountain country and is bordered to the north by Yellowstone National Park, to the west by Grand Teton National Park, and to the east by the Washakie Wilderness. Established as a primitive area in 1934, it was declared one of the nation's first wilderness areas upon passage of the 1964 Wilderness Act. The Teton Wilderness offers a diverse mixture of rolling lands carpeted with lodgepole pine, spacious grassy meadows, roaring rivers, and dramatic mountains. Elevations range from 7,500 feet to the 12,165-foot summit of Younts Peak. The Continental Divide slices across the wilderness, with headwaters of the Yellowstone River draining the eastern half and headwaters of the Buffalo and Snake rivers flowing down the western side.

One of the most unusual places within Teton Wilderness is **Two Ocean Creek**, where a creek abruptly splits at a rock, the two branches never to rejoin. One branch becomes Atlantic Creek, and its waters eventually reach the Atlantic Ocean, while the other becomes Pacific Creek and its waters flow to the Snake River, the Columbia River, and thence into the Pacific Ocean! Mountain man Osborne Russell described this phenomenon in 1835:

On the South side about midway of the prarie stands a high snowy peak from whence issues a Stream of water which after entering the plain it divides equally one half running West and other East thus bidding adieu to each other one bound for the Pacific and the other for the Atlantic ocean. Here a trout of 12 inches in length may cross the mountains in safety. Poets have sung of the "meeting of the waters" and fish climbing cataracts but the "parting of the waters and fish crossing mountains" I believe remains unsung yet by all except the solitary Trapper who sits under the shade of a spreading pine whistling blank-verse and beating time to the tune with a whip on his trap sack whilst musing on the parting advice of these waters.

Two natural events have had a major effect on the Teton Wilderness. On July 21, 1987, a world-record high-elevation tornado created a massive blowdown of trees around the Enos Lake area. The blowdown covered 10,000 acres, and trails are only now being rebuilt through this incredible jackstraw pile. (Since this is a wilderness area, chainsaws cannot be used.) In 1988, extreme drought conditions led to a series of major fires in Yellowstone and surrounding areas. Within the Teton Wilderness, the Huck and Mink creek fires burned (in varying degrees of severity) approximately 200,000 acres. Over half of the wilderness remained untouched. Don't let these incidents dissuade you from visiting; this is still a marvelous and little-used area. Herds of elk can be seen grazing in alpine areas, and the Thorofare country abutting Yellowstone National Park is considered the most remote place in the lower 48. This is prime grizzly habitat, so be very cautious at all times. Poles have been placed at most campsites for hanging food. Local Forest Service offices have brochures showing the locations of these poles.

Access

Three primary trailheads provide access to the Teton Wilderness: Pacific Creek on the southwestern end, Turpin Meadow on the Buffalo Fork River, and Brooks Lake just east of the Continental Divide. Campgrounds are at each of these trailheads. Teton Wilderness is a favorite of Wyoming people, particularly those with horses, and in the fall, elk hunters come here from across the nation. Distances are so great that few backpackers head into this wilderness area. No permits are needed, but it's a good idea to stop in at the **Blackrock Ranger Station**, tel. 543-2386, nine miles east of Moran Junction on US 26-287, for topographic maps and info on current trail conditions, bear problems, and regulations, along with a list of outfitters offering horse trips. Unfortunately, the Forest Service and USGS maps fail to show the many trails built and maintained (or not maintained) by private outfitters. They can make hiking confusing. A few of the many possible hikes are described below.

Whetstone Creek

Whetstone Creek Trail begins at the Pacific Creek Trailhead, located on the southwest side of Teton Wilderness. An enjoyable 20-mile roundtrip hike leaves the trailhead and follows Pacific Creek for 1 1/2 miles before splitting left to follow Whetstone Creek. Bear left again when the trail splits another three miles upstream and continue through a series of small meadows to the junction with Pilgrim Creek Trail. Turn right here and follow this two more miles to Coulter Creek Trail, climbing up Coulter Creek to scenic Coulter Basin, and then dropping down along the East Fork of Whetstone Creek. This rejoins the Whetstone Creek Trail and returns you to the trailhead, passing many attractive small meadows along the way. The upper half of this loop hike was burned in 1988, and some areas were heavily scorched, while others are quite patchy. Flowers are abundant in the burned areas, and this is important elk habitat.

South Fork To Soda Fork
A fine loop hike leaves Turpin Meadow and follows South Buffalo Fork River to South Fork Falls. Just above this, a trail splits off and climbs to Nowlin Meadow (excellent views of Smokehouse Mountain) and then down to Soda Fork River, where it joins the Soda Fork Trail. Follow this trail back downstream to huge Soda Fork Meadow (a good place to see moose and occasionally grizzlies) and then back to Turpin Meadow, a distance of approximately 23 miles roundtrip. A fascinating side trip from this route would be to head up the Soda Fork into the alpine at Crater Lake, a six-mile hike above the Nowlin Meadows-Soda Fork trail junction. The outlet stream at Crater Lake disappears into a gaping hole, emerging as a large creek two miles below at Big Springs. It's an incredible sight.

Cub Creek Area
The Brooks Lake area just east of Togwotee Pass is a very popular summertime camping and fishing place with magnificent views. Brooks Lake Trail follows the western shore of Brooks Lake and continues past Upper Brooks Lakes to Bear Cub Pass. From here, the trail drops down to Cub Creek, where several good campsites can be found. A long and very scenic loop can be made by following the trail up Cub Creek into the alpine country and then back down along the South Buffalo Fork River to Lower Pendergraft Meadow. From here, take Cub Creek Trail back up along Cub Creek to Bear Cub Pass and back out to Brooks Lake. Get a topographic map before heading into this remote country. Total distance is approximately 33 miles roundtrip.

GROS VENTRE WILDERNESS

The 287,000-acre Gros Ventre Wilderness was established in 1984 and covers the mountain country just east of Jackson Hole. This range trends mainly in a northwest-southeast direction and is probably best known for Sleeping Indian Mountain (maps now call it Sheep Mountain), the distinctive rocky summit visible from Jackson Hole. Although there are densely forested areas at lower elevations, the central portion of the wilderness lies above timberline, with many peaks topping 10,000 feet. Tallest is Doubletop Peak at 11,682 feet. The Tetons are visible from almost any high point in the Gros Ventre, and meadows line the lower-elevation streams. Elk, mule deer, bighorn sheep, moose, and black bears are found here, and a few grizzlies have been reported. The Forest Service office in Jackson has more info on the wilderness, including brief trail descriptions and maps.

Access And Trails
A number of roads provide good access to the Gros Ventre Wilderness: Gros Ventre River Rd. on the northern border, Flat Creek, Curtis Canyon, and Cache Creek roads on the western margin, and Granite Creek Rd. to the south. Note that hikes beginning or ending in the Granite Creek area have the added advantage of nearby Granite Hot Springs, a great place to soak tired muscles. (See p. 284 and p. 294 for more on the hot springs.)

An enjoyable two-day trip begins at **Jackpine Creek Trailhead** on Granite Creek Rd., 35 miles southeast of Jackson. Follow Jackpine Creek Trail up to Shoal Lake and then loop back down via the Swift Creek Trail. The distance is approximately 16 miles roundtrip but involves gaining and then losing 4,000 feet of elevation. Another good hike is to follow **Highline Trail** from the Granite Creek area across to Cache Creek, a distance of 16 miles. This route passes just below a row of high and rugged mountains, but since it isn't a loop route, you'll need to hitchhike or arrange a car shuttle. Plan on three days for this scenic hike. A third hike begins at the **Goosewing Ranger Station**, located 12 miles east of Slide Lake on Gros Ventre River Road. Take the trail from here to Two Echo Park, a fine camping spot, and then continue up to Six Lakes. You can return via the same trail or take the Crystal Creek Trail back to Red Rock Ranch and hitch back to Goosewing. The trail distance is approximately 23 miles roundtrip.

TARGHEE NATIONAL FOREST

The 1.8 million-acre Targhee National Forest extends along the western face of the Tetons and then south and west into Idaho. Much of the forest is heavily logged, but two wilderness areas protect most of the Wyoming portion of the Targhee.

JEDEDIAH SMITH WILDERNESS

The 116,535-acre Jedediah Smith Wilderness lies on the west side of the Teton Range, facing Idaho but lying entirely within Wyoming. Access is primarily from the Idaho side, although trails breach the mountain passes at various points, making it possible to enter from Grand Teton National Park. This area was not declared a wilderness until 1984. A second wilderness area, the 10,820-acre **Winegar Hole Wilderness** (pronounced WINE-a-gur), lies along the southern border of Yellowstone National Park. Grizzlies love this country, but hikers will find it uninteresting and without trails. In contrast, the Jedediah Smith Wilderness contains nearly 300 miles of paths, along with some incredible high-mountain scenery.

A number of roads (most are gravel) lead up from the Driggs and Victor areas into the Tetons. Get a map ($2) showing wilderness trails and access points from Targhee National Forest ranger station in Driggs, Idaho, tel. (208) 354-2431, or from the Forest Service offices in Jackson. (Driggs is also home to the delightfully amusing Spud Drive-In, here since 1953.) Be sure to camp at least 200 feet from lakes and 50 feet away from streams. If you plan to cross into Grand Teton National Park from the west side, be sure you have a camping permit in advance.

Hidden Corral Basin

Located at the northern end of the wilderness, Hidden Corral Basin provides a fine loop hike. Locals (primarily horse parties) crowd this area on late summer weekends. Get to the trailhead by driving north from Tetonia on Idaho 32 to Lamont, where you turn north on a gravel road. (The Tetonia area—Pierre's Hole—offers outstanding views of the Tetons, particularly at sunset. The three dominant peaks are more obvious from this side.) Follow it a mile and then turn right (east) onto Coyote Meadows Road. The trailhead is approximately 10 miles up, where the road dead-ends. An eight-mile trail parallels South Bitch Creek (the name Bitch Creek comes from the French word for a female deer, *biche*) to Hidden Corral, where you may see moose. Be sure to bring a fishing pole to try for the cutthroats.

Above Hidden Corral, you can make a pleasant loop back by turning north onto the trail to Nord Pass and then dropping down along the Carrot Ridge and Conant Basin trails to Bitch Creek Trail and then on to Coyote Meadows, a distance of 21 miles roundtrip. Note that this is grizzly country, so be sure to hang all food. By the way, Hidden Corral received its name in the outlaw days, when rustlers would steal horses in Idaho, change the brands, and then hold them in this natural corral until the branding wounds healed. The horses were then sold to Wyoming ranchers. Owen Wister's *The Virginian* describes a pursuit of horse thieves through Bitch Creek country.

Alaska Basin

The most popular hiking trail in the Jedediah Smith begins at Teton Canyon Campground ($5) and leads up into the flower-bedecked meadows of Alaska Basin. Great country, but don't expect a true wilderness experience with so many other hikers. Get to the campground by following the Grand Targhee Ski Area signs east from Driggs, Idaho. A gravel road splits off to the right approximately six miles beyond the little settlement of Alta. Follow it to the campground. (If you miss the turn, you'll end up at the ski area.) For an enjoyable loop, follow Alaska Basin Trail up the canyon to Basin Lakes and then head southwest along the Teton Crest Trail to the Teton Shelf Trail. Follow this back to its junction with the Alaska Basin Trail, dropping down the Devils Stairs—a series of very steep switchbacks. You can then take the Alaska Basin Trail back to Teton Campground, a roundtrip distance of approximately 19 miles. You could also use these trails to access the high peaks of the Tetons or to cross the mountains into Death Canyon within Grand Teton National Park (permit required). Campfires and horse camping are not allowed in Alaska Basin.

Moose Meadows

For a somewhat less crowded hiking experience, check out the Moose Meadows area on the southern end of the Jedediah Smith Wilderness. Get to the trailhead by going three miles southeast of Victor on State 22. Turn north to Moose Creek Rd. and follow it to the trailhead at

Nordwall Campground. The trail parallels Moose Creek to Moose Meadows, a good place to camp. You'll need to ford the creek twice, so this is best hiked in late summer. At the meadows, the trail dead-ends into Teton Crest Trail, providing access to Grand Teton National Park through some gorgeous alpine country. A nice loop can be made by heading south along this trail to flower-covered Coal Creek Meadows. A trail leads from here past 10,068-foot Taylor Mountain (an easy side trip with magnificent views), down to Taylor Basin, through lodgepole forests, and then back to your starting point. The distance for this loop hike is 15 miles roundtrip.

YELLOWSTONE NATIONAL PARK

Mention the words "national park" and an almost Pavlovian response comes to mind: Yellowstone. The geysers, canyons, and bears of Yellowstone National Park are so intertwined in our collective consciousness that even our cartoons use the park as a model: Jellystone Park where Yogi and Boo Boo are constantly out to thwart the rangers. Yellowstone brings out the child in everyone.

Open almost any chamber of commerce's brochure in the northern Rockies and you're bound to find a claim that their town lies "on the way to Yellowstone." Although one begins to question some of these claims, the attempted link with the park is understandable, for if your town is on the way to Yellowstone, it has at least one thing in its favor. On a map, Yellowstone appears as a gigantic box wedged so tightly against the northwest corner of Wyoming that it squeezes over into Montana and Idaho. The park reaches 63 by 54 miles across and covers 2.2 million acres, making it the largest national park in the lower 48 states. The UN has declared Yellowstone both a World Biosphere Reserve and a World Heritage Site.

The Setting
Yellowstone evokes a torrent of emotions in anyone with a knowledge of and a concern for the natural world. Here was the birthplace of the national-park movement, a place so unusual that those who first wandered through were afraid to tell others lest they be labeled liars. In the Yellowstone backcountry, one can still walk for days without seeing more than a handful of other hardy hikers, and the wildlife, geysers, and canyons continue to bring smiles to the faces of young and old alike. Americans love Yellowstone, the nation's crown jewel. One source estimates that nearly a third of the U.S. population has visited the park, and each year almost three million roll through the gates.

More than any other national park, Yellowstone seems to provide the oddities of nature, creating, as historian Aubrey L. Haines noted, "a false impression that the park is only a colossal, steam-operated freak show." During midsummer, a trip into Yellowstone can be something less than a natural experience. Thousands of behemoth land yachts clog the potholed roads and crowd the parking lots. Throngs of visitors circle Old Faithful Geyser, waiting for an eruption, while dozens of others cluster around bewildered elk to get photos for their scrapbooks.

Although less than three percent of the park is developed, Yellowstone contains more than 2,000 buildings of various types, ranging from graceful historic hotels to one-hour photo shops. In some spots, these developments have grown to the point that the natural world seems simply a backdrop to the human world that pulls visitors in to buy T-shirts or to watch park slide shows on geysers or wildlife.

From day one, Yellowstone National Park was set up for what Edward Abbey called "industrial tourism." The park came into being in part because of a railroad promoter who hoped to gain from its development and grew to maturity on a diet of roads, hotels, and curio shops. Finally, in the 1960s and '70s, America began to take a second look at this heritage and to ask questions about what mattered more: providing a public playground or preserving an area that is unique on this planet. The inherent conflict between the need for public facilities and services in Yellowstone and the survival of a functioning ecosystem has come to the fore in recent years in such issues as wolf reintroduction, grizzly management, and fire suppression.

GEOLOGY

Yellowstone is perhaps the world's preeminent place to view geological processes, for here the forces that elsewhere lie deep within the earth seem close enough to touch. The forces are palpable not only in the geysers and hot springs, but also in the lake that fills part of an enormous caldera, the earthquakes that shake the land, the evidence of massive glaciation, and the deeply eroded Grand Canyon of the Yellowstone.

VOLCANISM

The geologic history of Yellowstone centers around volcanism. The Absaroka Mountains along the park's eastern border were created by volcanic activity some 50 million years ago, but the park itself was most influenced by three violent explosions. Molten lava pushing from below bulged the land upward into an enormous dome. Eventually, this pressure became too great, sending ash and rock blasting from fissures around the dome's margins. Afterward, the dome began to reform as more magma was forced in. This process has been repeated three times over the last two million years, with the last eruption approximately 600,000 years ago. The magnitude of this most recent event is beyond the realm of imagination: 240 cubic miles of ash were blasted into the atmosphere! This eruption—perhaps the largest ever to occur on earth—ejected 20 times more material than the massive Krakatoa eruption of 1883, an explosion heard 3,000 miles away! Undoubtedly, ash from the eruption affected the global climate for years to follow.

After this eruption, the magma chamber collapsed into a gigantic, smoldering pit reaching 28 by 47 miles across and perhaps several thousand feet deep. Over time, additional molten rock pushed up from underneath and flowed as thick lava over the land. Two resurgent domes—near Old Faithful and just north of Yellowstone Lake—are still rising at nearly an inch per year. The one north of Yellowstone Lake is raising the lake's outlet and causing the water level to increase at an inch a year, flooding trees along the margins. Yellowstone's volcanism is far from dead, and scientists believe another eruption is possible or even likely, though nobody knows just when it might occur.

Yellowstone is one of the hottest places on the planet; Firehole Basin has underground temperatures 700 times the global average. Geologists now believe that the source of this heat (and of the volcanism) is an enormous plume of superheated magma just below the surface. The earth's crust is gradually moving over this plume—sort of like somebody pulling a piece of cloth across a candle. The plume has gradually shifted to the northeast over the millennia, leaving behind such places as Craters of the Moon in Idaho. (A similar situation is believed to exist in the chain of Hawaiian Islands.)

GEYSERS

Yellowstone is famous for geysers, and geyser-gazers will not be disappointed. At least 60% of the world's geysers are in the park, easily the largest and most diverse collection of geysers in existence! Yellowstone's more than 300 geysers are spread over nine different basins, the largest being Upper Geyser Basin.

Geysers need three essentials to exist: water, heat, and fractured rock. The water comes from snow and rain falling on this high plateau, while the heat comes from the molten rock close to the earth's surface. Massive pressures from below have created a ring of fractures around the edge of Yellowstone's caldera.

How They Work

Geysers operate because cold, dense water sinks while less-dense hot water rises. The periodic eruption of geysers is due to constrictions in the underground channels that prevent an adequate heat exchange with the surface. Precipitation slowly moves into the earth, eventually contacting the molten rock. Because of high pressures at these depths, water can reach extreme temperatures without boiling (as in a pressure cooker). As this superheated water rises back toward the surface, it emerges in hot springs, fumaroles, mudpots, or geysers. The most spectacular of these phenomena are geysers. Two general types of geysers exist in Yellowstone. Fountain geysers (such as Great Fountain Geyser) explode from pools of water and tend to spray water more widely, while cone-type geysers (such as Old Faithful) jet out of nozzle-like formations.

In a geyser, steam bubbles upward from the superheated source of water and expands as it rises. These bubbles block the plumbing system, keeping hot water from reaching the surface. Eventually, however, pressure from the bubbles begins to force the cooler water out of the vent. This initial release triggers a more violent reaction as the sudden lessening of pressure allows the entire column to begin boiling, sending up the quantities of steam and water for which geysers are known. Once the eruption has emptied the plumbing system, water gradually seeps back into the chambers to begin the process anew. Some of Yellowstone's geysers have enormous underground caverns that fill with water; in its rare eruptions, massive Steamboat Geyser can blast a million gallons of water into the air!

Preserving The Geysers

Unfortunately, some of Yellowstone's geysers have been lost because of human stupidity or vandalism. At one time, it was considered great sport to stuff logs, rocks, and even chairs into the geysers for a little added show. Others poured chemicals into them to make them play. As a result of such actions, some geysers have been severely damaged or destroyed, while a number of hot springs have become collection points for coins, rocks, sticks, and trash. It shouldn't be necessary to point out that such actions ruin these thermal areas for everyone.

OTHER GEOTHERMAL ACTIVITY

Although geysers are Yellowstone's best-known features, they make up only a tiny fraction of perhaps 10,000 thermal features in the park. **Hot springs** appear where water can reach the ground surface relatively easily, allowing for a dissipation of the heat that builds up in the chambers of geysers. When less groundwater is present, you may find **mud pots** (also called paint pots), while the driest shoot only steam through **fumaroles** or steam vents. Probably the best examples of these different forms are at Fountain Paint Pot in Lower Geyser Basin, where geysers and hot springs are found in the wetter lower areas while the drier areas' paint pots and fumaroles sit atop a small hill.

The colors in Yellowstone's hot springs come from a variety of sources, including algae and bacteria as well as various minerals, particularly sulfur, iron oxides, and arsenic sulfide. The algae and bacteria are highly temperature-specific and help to create the distinct bands of colors around many hot springs. Interestingly, many of these algal species are found only in hot springs, though they exist around the world. Above 190° F, even these hot-water bacteria and algae cannot survive, so the hottest springs may appear a deep blue due to the water's ability to absorb all wavelengths of light except blue, which is reflected back into our eyes.

Terms

A couple of other terms are worth learning before heading out to see the sights of Yellowstone. **Sinter** (also called geyserite) is a chemical composed primarily of silica. The silica is dissolved by hot water deep underground and brought to the surface in geysers or hot springs.

At the surface the water evaporates, leaving behind the light gray sinter, which can create large mounds (to 30 feet high) around the older geysers. The rate of accumulation is very slow, and some of the park's geysers have obviously been active for many thousands of years. The other chemical that is sometimes deposited around Yellowstone's hot springs and geysers is **travertine**, consisting of calcium carbonate that was dissolved underground. See "Mammoth Hot Springs" (below) for more on this process.

A Note Of Warning

The surface around many of the hot springs and geysers is surprisingly thin, and people have been killed by falling through into the boiling water. Stay on the boardwalks in developed areas, and use extreme caution around backcountry thermal features.

FLORA AND FAUNA

THE YELLOWSTONE ECOSYSTEM

For most of its existence, Yellowstone has been regarded as an island of nature surrounded by a world of human development. Unfortunately, this attitude has led to all sorts of problems. Despite its size, Yellowstone alone is not large enough to support a viable population of all the animals that once existed within its borders. In recent years, there have been increasing calls to treat the park as part of the larger Greater Yellowstone Ecosystem—14 million acres of land at the juncture of Wyoming, Montana, and Idaho. Within surrounding lands, conflicts between development and preservation are even more obvious than within the park itself. Logging is one of the most obvious of these, and along the park's western border aerial photos reveal a perfectly straight line, with lodgepole trees on the park side and enormous clearcuts on the Forest Service side. One of these was the largest timber sale ever made outside of Alaska! Add to this encroachments in the form of housing developments, oil and gas drilling, mining activities, and even a grizzly bear theme park, and the future looks difficult for the Yellowstone ecosys-

tem. Despite all these impacts, Yellowstone remains one of the largest intact temperate-zone ecosystems on the planet.

PLANTS

Yellowstone National Park is primarily a series of high plateaus ranging 7,500-8,500 feet in elevation. Surrounding this gently rolling expanse are the Absaroka Mountains along the east side and the Gallatin Range in the northeast corner. Elevations are lowest along the northern end of the park, where the Yellowstone River and other streams cut through. Here one finds open country with sagebrush, grasses, and shrubs, along with patches of aspen and Douglas fir. Farther south on the central plateaus are found the extensive lodgepole-pine forests that cover 60% of the park.

At higher and cooler elevations, lodgepole forests grade into groves of Engelmann spruce and subalpine fir, and eventually into stands of whitebark pine—an important food source for grizzlies. At timberline (approximately 10,000 feet), even these trees give way, and only low-growing forbs, grasses, and shrubs survive. Not

> *At ths place there is also large numbers of hot Springs some of which have formed cones of limestone 20 feet high of a Snowy whiteness which make a splendid appearance standing among the ever green pines Some of the lower peaks are very serviceable to the hunter in preparing his dinner when hungry for here his kettle is always ready and boiling his meat being suspended in the water by a string is soon prepared for his meal wihout further trouble . . . Standing upon an eminence and superficially viewing these natural monuments one is half inclined to believe himself in the neighborhood of the ruins of some ancients City whose temples had been constructed of the whitest marble.*
>
> —*Mountain man Osborne Russell, describing the Firehole River area in 1839*

all areas follow this simple elevational gradient, however. The park contains extensive wet meadow areas in the Bechler and upper Yellowstone River areas. Other broad openings are found along the Gardner River, in Pelican Valley, and in Hayden Valley.

WILDLIFE

Yellowstone is world famous for its wildlife and provides a marvelous natural setting in which to view bison, elk, moose, coyotes, antelope, bighorn sheep, and other animals. One of the easiest ways to find wildlife is by simply watching for the brake lights, the cars pulled half off the road, and the cameras all pointed in one direction. Inevitably, you'll find an elk or a bison placidly munching away, oblivious to the chaos that surrounds it.

Because of the constant parade of visitors and the lack of hunting, many of Yellowstone's animals appear to almost ignore the presence of people, and it isn't uncommon to see visitors approach them without respecting the animal's need for space. Although they may appear tame, these really are wild animals, and attacks are not

uncommon. Those quiet bison can suddenly erupt with an enormous ferocity if provoked by photographers who come too close. Stay at least 25 yards away from bison and elk and at least 100 yards away from bears.

The Park Service has a free brochure showing where you're most likely to see wildlife in Yellowstone. Get it at any visitor center. The best time to view wildlife is generally in the early morning and evening hours. Mosquitoes are a special treat and can be found almost anywhere in Yellowstone before mid-August. Fall is the best time to avoid these friendly critters.

Trumpeter swans—beautiful white birds with eight-foot wingspans—are a fairly common sight in Yellowstone, particularly on the Madison and Yellowstone rivers. Many trumpeter swans winter in the hot-springs area. Another large white bird is the awkward-looking and bulbous-billed white pelican, common on Yellowstone Lake. Bald eagles and osprey have also managed comebacks in recent years and are seen along the Yellowstone River.

Killing The Predators
Wildlife have always been one of the big drawing cards at Yellowstone, and early on there were constant charges of mass slaughter by poachers and market hunters. It was not until 1894 that Congress passed the Lacey Act, finally making it illegal to hunt within the park. Unfortunately, predators such as wolves, coyotes, mountain lions, and wolverines were regarded as despoilers of the elk, deer, and moose, and became fair targets for poisoning and shooting by early park managers. The campaign proved all too successful, decimating the wolf and mountain-lion populations. One consequence of this is that bison and elk numbers have grown artificially high within Yellowstone. (Other reasons for this over-population of grazing animals include artificial feeding in Jackson Hole and inadequate hunting restrictions.)

Bears
During the park's early years, bears were commonly viewed as either pets or nuisances. Cubs were tethered to poles out front of the hotels, while other bears fed on the garbage piles that grew up around the hotels and camps. Older folks still recall the bear feeding grounds at the

garbage dumps, where visitors might see 50 bears pawing through the garbage. These feeding shows continued until 1941, but it wasn't until 1970 that the park's open-pit dumps were finally sealed off and the garbage cans bear-proofed. Unfortunately, rather than gradually reducing the food available at the dumps to wean bears from the sites, they were abruptly shut down. The dumps had artificially maintained bear populations above their natural levels, and their closure brought almost immediate consequences; over the next few years at least 50 grizzlies died in confrontations with humans in the park or surrounding areas. Fortunately, the population appears to have finally begun to recover.

There are believed to be 200 grizzlies in the greater Yellowstone ecosystem, fewer than in the 1960s when many lived on garbage dumps and campers' coolers, but more than in the early '80s. Both black and grizzly bears are found throughout Yellowstone, but the days of bear jams along the park roads are past, since rangers actively work to prevent bears from becoming habituated to people. Most bears have returned to their more natural ways of living, although problems still crop up with bears wandering through campgrounds in search of food. You're more likely to encounter a bear in the backcountry areas. Some places—especially around the north end of Yellowstone Lake in Pelican Valley—are off-limits to hiking much of the year for this reason.

One unusual aspect of the Yellowstone grizzlies was just discovered in recent years—the surprising importance of moths as a food source. Millions of army cutworm moths congregate on Yellowstone's high alpine slopes during the summer, when they feed on nectar from the abundant flowers. Bears are attracted to this food source because of the insect's high fat content and its abundance. Researchers have sometimes seen two dozen bears feeding on a single slope!

Bison

When Yellowstone was established in 1872, perhaps 1,000 mountain (wood) bison ranged across this high plateau. Sport and meat hunting—legal until 1894—along with later poaching reduced the population, and by 1902, perhaps only 25 remained. That year, plains bison were brought in from private ranches in Montana and Texas to help restore the Yellowstone herd, and today there are around 2,600 buffalo in the park. Unfortunately, interbreeding between the mountain and plains bison means that the animals in Yellowstone today are genetically different from the original inhabitants.

In 1985, Yellowstone's bison began wandering north into the Gardiner area for the winter. Ranchers feared that the bison could spread the disease brucellosis to their cattle, causing cows to abort calves. A highly controversial "hunt" during the late 1980s let Montana hunters shoot bison when they wandered outside the park. Today the culling is done by state game wardens, but the population is still artificially high. (Ironically, the more numerous elk also carry brucellosis. Although they are hunted, nobody seems anxious to kill all the elk that wander across Yellowstone's borders.)

Wolves

One of the easiest ways to start a bar fight at a town adjoining Yellowstone is to bring up the subject of wolves. Ranchers are fearful of them; environmentalists view them as one of the "missing links" in the Yellowstone ecosystem. Despite their reputation, wolves do not attack humans. They can, however, have an effect on elk, deer, and other ungulates by thinning out their populations. Many of the animals taken are the weak, sick, or old—the easiest to chase down. Without wolves and other predators in Yellowstone, the elk population has grown well above its natural level, throwing the entire system out of balance.

Wolves once ranged across North America, but are now found only in Canada, Alaska, northern Minnesota, Isle Royale, and Glacier National Park. For many years, wolves (along with mountain lions and coyotes) were regarded as unwanted predators in Yellowstone, and both the Army and the Park Service did their best to poison or shoot any that could be found. By 1940, the wolf was probably gone from Yellowstone, though a few turned up briefly again in the early 1970s. With a more enlightened attitude in recent years, ecologists and conservationists began pushing for the reintroduction of wolves to Yellowstone, considered one of the few remaining areas in the Lower 48 that could support a viable wolf population.

Opponents of wolf reintroduction (especially Wyoming's senators, Malcolm Wallop and Alan Simpson) have fought these efforts, despite support from a majority of people in Wyoming, Montana, and Idaho. Opponents of wolf reintroduction even succeeded in muzzling the Park Service's educational programs on wolves and blocking them from even mentioning wolf reintroduction in park newsletters! Despite studies that point to negligible economic losses in Minnesota where wolves and cattle coexist, Yellowstone-area ranchers are nervous. A final environmental impact report is expected to be released soon, and there are now hopes that the cry of the wolf will again be heard within the Yellowstone wilderness.

Yellowstone National Park has a rich and fascinating history that reaches back for thousands of years of settlement. The most thorough source for history is *The Yellowstone Story,* an excellent two-volume set by former park historian Aubrey L. Haines.

PARK HISTORY

SHEEPEATER INDIANS

Yellowstone has been inhabited by people for at least 11,000 years, although the tribes changed over the centuries. By the mid-19th century, the country was surrounded by Blackfeet to the north, Crow to the east, and Shoshone and Bannock to the south and west. These tribes all traveled through Yellowstone and hunted here periodically, but only the Sheepeater Indians actually lived on this high plateau. The Sheepeater were of Shoshone stock, a simple and timid people who hunted bighorn sheep (hence the name) but also depended on other animals, fish, roots, and berries. They built temporary shelters called wickiups made of aspen poles covered with pine boughs, a few of which still exist in Yellowstone. Because they did not have horses, the Sheepeaters used dog travois to carry their few possessions from camp to camp. Summers were spent in high alpine meadows and along passes where they hunted migrating game animals or gathered roots and berries. They wintered in protected canyons.

The Sheepeaters were smaller than other Indians and have achieved an aura of mystery since so little is known of their way of living. Yellowstone was at the heart of their territory, but with the arrival of whites came devastating diseases, particularly smallpox. The survivors joined their Shoshone brothers on the Wind River Reservation or the Bannock Reservation in Idaho. The last of the tribe left Yellowstone in the 1870s.

FUR TRAPPERS

The word "Yellowstone" appears to have come from the Sioux Indians who called the river "Mi tse a-da-zi," a word French-Canadian trappers translated into "Rive des Roche Jaune"—literally, "Yellow Rock River." The Indians called it this because of the yellowish bluffs along the river mouth (not, as some claim, because of the colorful Grand Canyon of the Yellowstone). The term "Yellow Stone" was first used on a map made in 1798. When the Lewis and Clark Expedition traveled through the country north of Yellowstone in 1804, the Indians told them tales of this mysterious place: "There is frequently heard a loud noise like thunder, which makes the earth tremble, they state that they seldom go there because children Cannot sleep—and Conceive it possessed of spirits, who were adverse that men Should be near them." (This certainly was not the attitude of all the native peoples, for the park had long been inhabited.) The first white man to come through Yellowstone was John Colter, a former member of the Lewis and Clark Expedition who wandered through the region in the winter of 1807-08. A map based on Colter's recollections shows Yellowstone Lake ("Eustis Lake"), along with an area of "Hot Spring Brimstone."

As fur trappers spread through the Rockies in the 1820s and '30s, many discovered the geysers and hot springs of Yellowstone, and stories quickly spread around the rendezvous fires. The word of the trappers was passed on to later settlers and explorers, but not entirely believed.

Sheepeater Indian in wickiup

After all, mountain man Jim Bridger described not just petrified trees, but petrified birds singing petrified songs! His tales of a river that "ran so fast that it became hot on the bottom" could well have referred to the Firehole River. When Bridger tried to lead a party of military explorers into Yellowstone, they were stymied by deep snows. Still, the word gradually got out that something very strange could be found in this part of the mountains. Little remains today from the mountain-men era, although in 1880, the letters "J.O.R. Aug. 19, 1819" were found carved in a tree near the Upper Falls of the Yellowstone, and later a cache of iron beaver traps similar to those used by the Hudson's Bay Company was discovered near Obsidian Cliff.

EXPEDITIONS

National attention finally came to Yellowstone with a series of three expeditions to check out the wild claims of local prospectors. In 1869, David E. Folsom, Charles W. Cook, and William Peterson headed south from Bozeman, finding the Grand Canyon, Lake Yellowstone, and the geyser basins. When a friend pressured them to submit a description of their travels for publication, the *New York Tribune* refused to publish it, noting that it "had a reputation that they could not risk with such unreliable material."

Their adventures led another group of explorers into Yellowstone the following year, but this time money was the motive. Jay Cooke's Northern Pacific Railroad needed investors for a planned route across Montana. A good public-relations campaign was the first step, and it happened to coincide with the visit of a former Montana tax collector named Nathaniel P. Langford who had heard of the discoveries of Folsom, Cook, and Peterson. The collection of 19 soldiers and civilians headed out in August of 1870 under Gen. Henry D. Washburn. They were thrilled by what they discovered and proceeded to name the geysers—Old Faithful, Castle, Giant, Grotto, Giantess—names that became permanently attached to them. The joy of the trip was marred when one man—Truman Everts—became separated from the others and then lost his horse. He was not found until nearly a month later, by which time he weighed just 50 pounds. Evert's rescuer did not even recognize him as human. He survived and recovered.

With the return of the Washburn Expedition, national newspapers and magazines finally began to pay attention to Yellowstone, and Langford began lecturing in the East on what they had found. One of those listening was Dr. Ferdinand V. Hayden, director of the U.S. Geological Survey. Hayden asked Congress to fund an official investigation. With the help of Representatives James G. Blaine (coincidentally a supporter of the Northern Pacific Railroad) and conservationist Henry M. Dawes, Congress appropriated $40,000 for an exploration of "The sources of the Missouri and Yellowstone Rivers." Thus began the most famous and influential trip into Yellowstone, the 1871 Hayden Expedition. The troop included 34 men, an escort of cavalry, plus painter Thomas Moran and photographer William H. Jackson.

ESTABLISHING THE PARK

When Hayden returned to Washington to prepare his report, he found a letter from railroad

THE NEZ PERCÉ WAR

One of the saddest episodes in the history of Yellowstone took place in 1877 and involved the Nez Percé (pronounced nay-PUR-say) Indians of Oregon's Wallowa Valley. When the government tried to force the people of Chief White Bird and Chief Joseph onto an Idaho reservation so that white ranchers could have their lands, they stubbornly refused. A few drunk young men killed four whites, and subsequent raids led to the deaths of at least 14 more. The Army retaliated but was turned back by the Nez Percé, Rather than face government reinforcements, more than 1,000 Nez Percé began an 1,800-mile flight in a desperate bid to reach Canada. A series of running battles followed as the Indians managed to confound the inept Army using their geographic knowledge and battle skills. The Nez Percé entered Yellowstone from the west, and a few hotheads immediately attacked vacationing tourists and prospectors. Two whites were killed in the park, while others were kidnapped and one man nearly died from his wounds.

The Nez Percé exited Yellowstone two weeks after they arrived, narrowly missing an encounter with their implacable foe, Gen. William T. Sherman, who just happened to be vacationing in Yellowstone at the time. East of the park, the Indians plotted a masterful escape from two columns of Army forces, feinting a move down the Shoshone River and then heading north along a route that left their pursuers gasping in amazement—straight up the narrow Clarks Fork Canyon, "where rocks on each side came so near together that two horses abreast could hardly pass." Finally, less than 40 miles from the international border with Canada, the Army caught up with the Nez Percé, and after a fierce battle the tribe was forced to surrender (although 300 did make good their escape).

Chief Joseph's haunting words still echo through the years: "Hear me, my chiefs, I am tired; my heart is sick and sad. From where the sun now stands, I will fight no more forever." Despite promises that they would be allowed to return home, the Nez Percé were hustled onto a reservation in Oklahoma, while whites remained on their ancestral lands. Chief Joseph died in 1904, reportedly of a broken heart. Yellowstone's Nez Percé Creek, which feeds the Firehole River, is named for this desperate bid for freedom.

Chief Joseph in October 1887 immediately after his surrender at Bear Paw Mountain, Montana

promoter Jay Cooke. In the letter, Cooke proposed that "Congress pass a bill reserving the Great Geyser Basin as a public park forever—just as it has reserved that far inferior wonder the Yosemite valley and big trees." In an amazingly short time, a bill was introduced to set aside the land, and Hayden rushed to arrange a display in the Capitol rotunda of geological specimens, sketches by Moran, and the photos by Jackson. The bill easily passed both houses of Congress and was signed into law on March 1, 1872, by President Ulysses S. Grant. The first national park had come into existence, a culmination not just of the discoveries in Yellowstone, but also of a growing appreciation for preserving the wonders of the natural world. (Yosemite had actually been established earlier, but as a state park.)

Congress saw no need to set aside money for this new creation, since it seemed to be doing fine already. Besides, it was thought that Jay Cooke's new railroad would soon arrive, making it easy for thousands of vacationers to explore Yellowstone. In turn, concessionaires would build roads and hotels and pay the government franchise fees. The park was placed under the control of the Secretary of the Interior, with Nathaniel P. Langford as its unpaid superintendent. Meanwhile, the planned railroad fizzled when Jay Cooke & Co. declared bankruptcy, precipitating the Panic of 1873.

ROADS AND RAILROADS

Because of the difficult access, fewer than 500 people came in each of Yellowstone's first few years as a park, most to soak in tubs at Mammoth Hot Springs. Not a few decided to take home souvenirs, bringing pickax and shovel for that purpose. Meanwhile, hunters—including some working for the Mammoth Hotel—began shooting the park's abundant game. Two brothers who had a ranch just north of the park killed 2,000 elk in a single year. Superintendent Langford did little to stop the slaughter, only bothering to visit the park twice. Finally, in 1877, the Secretary of the Interior fired him, putting Philetus W. Norris in charge instead. Norris proved a good choice, despite a knack for applying his name to everything in sight. (Most of his attempts at immortality have been replaced by other titles, but Norris Geyser Basin, Norris Rd., and even the town of Norris, Michigan remain.)

Norris oversaw construction of the first major road in Yellowstone, a rough 60-mile route built in just 30 days to connect Upper Geyser Basin with Mammoth and the western entrance. All of this was precipitated by the raids of the Nez Percé Indians earlier that summer and threats that the Bannock Indians would strike next. In addition, Norris began, but never completed, the Queen's Laundry, a bathhouse that is considered the first government building built for the public in any national park. The log walls are still visible in a meadow near Lower Geyser Basin.

By 1882, Norris had managed to alienate the company that helped found the park: the North-

ern Pacific Railroad. The company announced plans to build a railroad line to the geysers and construct a large hotel, "being assured by the Government of a monopoly therein." Norris's opposition led to his being fired and replaced by railroad man Patrick H. Conger. Soon, however, the scheme began to unravel. The Yellowstone Park Improvement Company—whose vice-president happened to be construction superintendent for the Northern Pacific's branch line into Gardiner—had planned not just a lodging monopoly, but also a monopoly on all transportation, timber rights, and ranching privileges in the park. Later it was discovered that the company had contracted for 20,000 pounds of venison (killed in the park) to feed the construction crews. As one newspaper writer commented, "It is a 'Park Improvement Company' doing this, and I suppose they consider it an improvement to rid the park, as far as possible, of game."

Finally, in 1884 Congress acted by limiting the land that could be leased—thus effectively ending the railroad's plans—and adding funding to hire 10 assistants to patrol Yellowstone. Unfortunately, they neglected to include any penalties for the poachers and despoilers other than expulsion, so even the few assistants who did decent work found the culprits quickly returning. The problems were myriad. Cooke City miners were fishing with spears, seine nets, and even dynamite. Guides were throwing rocks into the geysers, squatters had ensconced themselves on prime land in Lamar Valley, and visitors were leaving fires unattended and breaking off specimens from the geysers.

Superintendent Conger was later replaced by Robert E. Carpenter, a man about whom historian Hiram Chittenden noted, "In his opinion, the Park was created to be an instrument of profit to those who were shrewd enough to grasp the opportunity." Carpenter lobbied Congress to remove lands from the park so that the Northern Pacific could construct a railroad along the Yellowstone River to Cooke City. In return, friends promised to locate claims in his name along the route so that he too might profit from the venture. The land grab fell apart when the Senate vetoed the move, and Carpenter was summarily removed from office. Not long thereafter, Congress flatly refused to fund the civilian administration of Yellowstone, and the Secretary of the Interior was forced to call in the military in 1886. It proved a fortuitous step.

THE ARMY YEARS

The Army finally brought a semblance of order, eliminating the political appointees who viewed Yellowstone as a place to get rich. That first year, a temporary fort—Camp Sheridan—was thrown up and a troop of soldiers arrived, but it wasn't until 1891 that work began on a permanent Fort Yellowstone at Mammoth. By 1904, the fort consisted of some 26 buildings, housing 120 men. The soldiers had clear objectives—protecting wildlife (or at least bison and elk) from poachers, fighting fires, stopping vandalism, and generally achieving order out of chaos. These goals were accomplished with a fervor that gained widespread respect, and in a way that would later influence the organization of the National Park Service. One of the major accomplishments of the soldiers was completion of the Grand Loop Road, which passes most of Yellowstone's attractions. The basic pattern was completed by 1905.

Fort Yellowstone was a favorite station for soldiers, and it was considered something of an honor to be sent to such a setting. The life of the soldiers was not always easy, however, and a number died in the bitter winters or in accidents. A series of 16 soldier stations—actually little more than large cabins—was established around the park, and each was manned year-round, usually by four soldiers.

Before the arrival of cars, many visitors to Yellowstone were wealthy people from the east coast or Europe intent upon doing the grand tour of western sights. The railroads (Northern Pacific to the north, Union Pacific to the west, and the Burlington to the east) deposited them near park borders, where they were met by carriages, Tallyhos (26-passenger stagecoaches), and surreys. In 1915, there were some 3,000 horses in use within the park! Most "dudes" paid approximately $50 for a six-day tour that included transportation, meals, and lodging at the hotels. They paid another $2.50

for the privilege of sailing across Lake Yellowstone on the steamship *Zillah*. By contrast, another group, the "sagebrushers," came to Yellowstone in fewer numbers, arriving in their own wagons or hiring a coach to transport them between the "Wylie Way" campgrounds. These seasonal tent camps were scattered around the park, providing an inexpensive ($35 for a seven-day tour) way to see the sights. Even as early as 1908, Yellowstone was being seen by 18,000 visitors a year.

The Northern Pacific was still intent upon carving Yellowstone into a money-making resort, even going so far as to propose an electric railroad, to be powered by a dam at the falls of the Yellowstone River. Fortunately, equally powerful forces—notably Gen. Phillip Sheridan and naturalist Joseph Bird Grinnell—saw through their designs and thwarted each attempt to bring railroads into Yellowstone. Still the Northern Pacific's interests were represented by its indirect control of many of Yellowstone's hotels, stagecoaches, wagons, and other vehicles used to transport tourists.

All this changed when the first car was allowed through the gate on Aug. 1, 1915. (Entrance fees were a surprisingly stiff $5 for single-seat vehicles and $7.50 for five-passenger cars.) Almost immediately, it became clear that horses and cars could not mix, and motor buses replaced the old coaches. From then on, the park would be increasingly a place for "autoists." Interestingly, within a year the park would come under the jurisdiction of the newly created National Park Service.

THE PARK SERVICE TAKES OVER

After years of Army control, supporters of a separate National Park Service finally had their way in 1916. The congressional act created a dual role for the new park system: to "conserve the scenery" and to "provide for the enjoyment of the same," a contradictory mandate that would later lead to all sorts of conflicts. The first couple of years were tenuous, as management flip-flopped between the Army and civilians, with the final changeover coming in 1918, thus ending three decades of military supervision. The manage-

continued on p. 330

THE YELLOWSTONE FIRES OF 1988

The summer of 1988 will long be remembered as the year when Yellowstone National Park was "destroyed" by fire. TV reporters flocked to the park, pronouncing the death of America's most famous national wonder as they stood in front of trees turned into towering torches and 30,000-foot clouds of black smoke. Newspaper headlines screamed, "Park Sizzles," "Winds Whip Fiery Frenzy Out of Control," and "Firestorms Blacken Yellowstone." Residents of nearby towns complained of lost tourism dollars, choking smoke, and intentionally lit backfires that threatened their homes and businesses; Wyoming politicians berated the Park Service's "Let Burn" policy; President Reagan expressed astonishment that fires were ever allowed to burn in the national parks (a policy that had been in place for 16 years). Perhaps the most enduring image is from a forest that had been blown down by tornado-force winds in 1984 and then burned by the wind-whipped fires of 1988. The media ate it up, with one headline reading, Total Destruction: Intense Heat and Flames from the Fires in Yellowstone Left Nothing but Powdered Ash and Charcoal Near Norris Junction. Unfortunately, the real story behind the fires of '88 was lost in this media feeding frenzy.

A Century Of Change

In reality, these fires were not unprecedented; we were just fortunate enough to witness one of the incredible spectacles of nature that may not occur again for another 300 years. When Yellowstone National Park was established in 1872, most of the land was carpeted with a mixture of variously aged lodgepole-pine stands established following a series of large fires. Fewer large fires, partly due to unusually moist summer weather conditions, and partly because of a fire-suppression policy that was in effect until 1972, meant that by the 1980s a third of the park's lodgepole stands were more than 200 years old. Yellowstone was "ripe to burn."

Since the early 1950s, Smokey the Bear drummed an incessant message: "Only You Can Prevent Forest Fires." Forest fires were viewed as dangerous, destructive forces that had to be stopped to protect our valuable public lands. Unfortunately, this immensely effective and generally valid ad campaign convinced the public that all fires were bad. Ecological research has shown not only that this is wrong, but that putting out all fires can sometimes create conditions far more dangerous than if fires had been allowed to burn in the first place. Fire, like the other processes that have affected Yellowstone—cataclysmic volcanic explosions, geothermal activity, and massive glaciation—is neither good nor evil. It is simply a part of the natural world that national parks are attempting to preserve. Unfortunately, national parks are no longer surrounded by similarly undeveloped land, so when fires burned in Yellowstone and surrounding Forest Service lands they also affected the surrounding towns and the people who make a living from tourism or logging.

Fire In Lodgepole Forests

Fire has played an important role in lodgepole-pine forests for thousands if not millions of years, and as a result, the trees have evolved an unusual adaptation. Some of the cones are serotinous, with a resin that melts under the heat of forest fires. The parent trees are killed, but a new generation is guaranteed by the thousands of pine seeds (20 seeds per square foot) that are released to the bare,

Yellowstone fire

BOB RACE

continued

nutrient-rich soil underneath the blackened overstory. Within five years the landscape is dotted with thousands of young pines, competing with a verdant cover of grasses and flowers.

Although some animals are killed in the fires (including, in 1988, 257 elk out of a Yellowstone population of 30,000, and others die from a lack of food immediately after a fire, the early decades following a fire create conditions that are unusually rich for many animals. Wildlife diversity in lodgepole forests reaches a peak within the first 25 years as woodpeckers, mountain bluebirds, and other birds feed on insects in the dead trees, while elk and bears graze on the lush grasses.

As the forest ages, a dense stand of trees forms, keeping light from reaching the forest floor and making it difficult for understory plants to survive. These trees eventually thin themselves out, creating openings in the forest, but after 200-300 years without fire the lodgepole forests become a tangle of fallen trees that are difficult to walk through, are of limited value to many animals, and burn easily. They also become susceptible to attacks by bark beetles, such as those that killed thousands of acres of trees in Yellowstone during the 1980s, creating even more potential fire fuel.

Yellowstone In 1988

Yellowstone's 1988 fires were due not just to the heavy fuel loading from aging forests, but also to weather conditions that were the driest and windiest on record. The winter of 1987-88 had been a mild one, and by spring there was a moderate to severe drought in the park, lessened only by above-normal rainfall in April and May. Since 1972, when Yellowstone Park officials first began allowing certain lightning fires to burn in backcountry areas, the acreage burned totaled less than two percent of the park. (Mistakenly called a "let burn" policy, the natural fire program actually involved close monitoring of these lightning-ignited fires to determine when and if a fire should be suppressed. All human-caused fires were immediately suppressed, along with any that threatened property or life.)

When the first lightning fires of the 1988 season began in late May, those in the backcountry areas were allowed to burn, as fire management officials anticipated normal summer weather conditions. Many went out on their own, but when June and July came and the rains failed to materialize, the fires began to spread rapidly. Alarmed park officials declared them wildfires and sent crews to attempt to put them out. (Ironically, the largest fire, the North Fork/Wolf Lake Complex, was started by humans, and although firefighters immediately attacked the blaze, it consumed more than 500,000 acres.) As the summer progressed, more and more firefighters were called in, eventually totaling over 25,000 personnel, at a cost exceeding $120 million. Firefighters managed to protect many park buildings but had little effect on the forest fires themselves. Experts say that conditions in the summer of 1988 were so severe that even if all the natural fires had been immediately fought, it may have made little difference. Yellowstone has experienced these massive fires in the past and will again in the future, no matter what humans do.

Out Of Control

Firefighters found the weather worsening with each passing hour. Winds blew steadily at 20-40 miles an hour, and gusts to 70 mph threw firebrands two miles in front of the firefront, across firelines, roads, and even the Lewis River Canyon. Fuel moisture in the large logs approached that of kiln-dried wood. By mid-August, more than 25 fires were burning simultaneously all over the park and surrounding national forests, with many joining together to create massive complexes such as the Clover-Mist Fire, the Snake River Complex, and the North Fork/Wolf Lake Complex. On a single day—September 7—more than 100,000 acres burned, and 20 buildings in Old Faithful were torched (out of more than 400). The fires seemed poised to consume the remainder of Yellowstone, but four days later the season's first snow carpeted the park. Within a few days firefighters had the upper hand.

A Transformed Landscape

More than 793,000 acres (36% of the park) had been burned by the fires, along with another 600,000 acres on adjacent Forest Service lands. Of the park total, 41% were canopy fires in which all the trees were killed, and another 35% were a mixture of ground fires and canopy fires. The remainder were lighter burns. The fires are out and the land is slowly recovering, but there continue to be many questions asked about what-ifs and what-might-havebeens. The park's natural-fire program was replaced after the fires by a somewhat more conservative version.

Visitors to Yellowstone today will see enormous expanses of blackened trees in some parts of the park, while in other areas they find a complex

continued

mosaic of burned and unburned forest land. Once you grow accustomed to the burned areas and understand that they are a part of the natural process, they actually add interest to the park. Get out of your car and walk through a blackened area and you'll discover dense carpets of lodgepole seedlings, along with impressive displays of wild-flowers, forbs, and grasses. Vistas that were long blocked by dense forests are now more open. The Park Service has placed informative signboards at seven sites around Yellowstone, describing the fires and the changes they brought about, and has a special display and film on the fires at the Grant Village Visitor Center.

ment of Yellowstone fell on the shoulders of two men, Horace M. Albright and his mentor, Stephen Mather, both of whom had been heavily involved in lobbying to create the new agency. Mather became the Park Service's first director, while Albright served as superintendent at Yellowstone and later stepped into Mather's shoes to head the agency.

Albright quickly upgraded facilities to meet the influx of motorists who demanded more rustic camping facilities, but also cabins, lodges, cafeterias, and bathhouses. Forty-six camps were constructed (only 12 survive today), fulfilling Albright's dream of "a motorist's paradise." The focus of the new Park Service was clearly on visitation rather than preservation. Albright assembled a first-rate force of park rangers and instituted the environmental education programs that have been the agency's hallmark ever since.

As the automobile took over Yellowstone, the railroads gradually lost their sway. The last passenger train to the park's gateway towns stopped in 1961. In the 1950s, the Park Service initiated "Mission 66," a decade-long project to upgrade facilities and add more lodging. By the late '60s, a growing appreciation for the natural world was shifting public opinion away from such developments, and the 1973 master plan scaled back proposed developments. In recent years such issues as wolf reintroduction, grizzly management, winter use, and the fires of 1988 have attracted widespread attention.

TOURING YELLOWSTONE

Yellowstone is perhaps the most accessible national park. Nearly all the famous sights are within a couple hundred feet of the Grand Loop Rd., a 142-mile figure-eight through the middle of the park. For all too many visitors, Yellowstone becomes a checklist of places to visit, geysers to watch, and animals to see. The Park Service has done its part by putting signs and labels on everything, right down to the smallest hot springs. All this tends to inspire an attitude that treats this great national park as a drive-through zoo where the animals come out to perform, and the geyser eruptions are predicted so everyone can be there on time. If you're one of this crowd, give yourself a giant kick in the rear and take a walk, even if it is just around Upper Geyser Basin where you see something beyond Old Faithful. Whatever you do, *don't* see Yellowstone at 45 miles an hour; that's like seeing the Louvre from a passing train.

The following loop tour of Yellowstone begins in the south and traces a clockwise path around the Grand Loop (with side trips). Although it is possible to follow this sequence (or some variation) the entire distance, a far better way to learn about Yellowstone is to stop for a while in the places that are the most interesting to you and really explore them, rather than trying to see everything in a cursory way. If you have the time, the entire park is well worth visiting, but if you have only a day or two, pick a couple of spots and see them right. Be sure to at least spend time at Grand Canyon of the Yellowstone and Norris Geyser Basin. And don't just check out the views everyone else sees; find a nearby trail and do a little exploring on your own. If you are planning a trip to the area, try to set aside a bare minimum of three days in Yellowstone.

SOUTH ENTRANCE ROAD

The South Entrance Station consists of several new log structures, right along the Snake River. Just 1½ miles beyond the entrance is an easily missed turnout where you can walk down to 30-foot-high **Moose Falls.** Beyond this, the road climbs up a long, gentle ramp to Pitchstone Plateau, passing green forests of lodgepole pine. Stop at a turnout to look back at the majestic Tetons. Abruptly, this gentle country is broken by the edge of **Lewis River Canyon,** with rhyolite walls that drop 600 feet on either side. Anyone who has not been to Yellowstone since the fires of 1988 will be shocked by the scene here—blackened remains of trees seem to extend in all directions. The Snake River Complex of fires joined together to leap a quarter-mile across this canyon, revealing the futility of bulldozer-cut firebreaks in trying to halt an inferno under the high wind conditions and severe drought that existed.

The road parallels the river for the next seven miles. Nearly everyone stops at 37-foot-high **Lewis Falls.** Camping is available at the south end of **Lewis Lake.** (The lake, falls, river, and canyon are all named for the Lewis and Clark Expedition's Meriwether Lewis.) Lewis Lake is the park's third-largest body of water (after Yellowstone and Shoshone lakes) and is popular with boaters and anglers. The clear waters contain brown trout and Mackinaw. Approximately four miles north of Lewis Lake, the highway tops the Continental Divide, but the point (7,988 feet above sea level) is not particularly noticeable. This is one of three such traverses roads make within Yellowstone.

Lewis Lake Hikes

Two trailheads are a mile north of Lewis Lake, providing access east to Heart Lake and west to Shoshone Lake through country burned in the fires of 1988. The four-mile-long **Dogshead Trail** offers a direct route to Shoshone Lake, while the **Lewis Channel Trail** takes the scenic trek via the Lewis River channel that connects Shoshone and Lewis lakes. It's seven miles to Shoshone Lake on this path. The path is popular with anglers who come to the channel for brown and cutthroat trout during the fall spawning season. The trail to Heart Lake begins on the opposite side of the road and south a few hundred feet. See "Into the Backcountry" (p. 353) for hikes in the Heart Lake and Shoshone Lake areas. Canoeists sometimes paddle across Lewis Lake and then portage to Shoshone Lake.

Grant Village

The newest Yellowstone development is Grant Village, built to replace facilities at Fishing Bridge, an area of vital grizzly habitat. Unfortunately, instead of one bad development, Yellowstone now has two; Fishing Bridge still exists (although some of the buildings are gone). Grant Village was completed in the 1980s, but unlike some of the more historic places, where a natural rusticity prevailed, Grant Village has less charm than most K marts and absolutely no sense of organization. A steakhouse restaurant juts out along the shore of Yellowstone Lake, and the Grant Village Hotel forms a chintzy condo backdrop. Other facilities include a campground, a store, a gas station, and a post office. Much of the area around here was consumed in the 1988 Snake River Fire; it unfortunately missed this scar on the Yellowstone landscape. **Grant Village Visitor Center** is open 9-5 from late May to late September, with extended midsummer hours. Inside, find informative exhibits on the fires of 1988, along with a Kodak-sponsored slide show and an excellent film on the fires. Call 344-7381, ext. 6602, for more information.

West Thumb

If you look at a map of Yellowstone Lake, it's possible to imagine the lake as a giant hand with three mangled fingers heading south and a gnarled thumb extending west. Thus the name, West Thumb. This portion of Yellowstone Lake is the deepest (to 390 feet) and is actually a caldera that filled with water after erupting 200,000 years ago. There is still considerable heat just below the surface, as revealed by **West Thumb Geyser Basin.** A short loop trail leads through the steaming hot springs and pools. Just offshore is **Fishing Cone Geyser,** where tourists once caught fish and then plopped them in the cone to be cooked. The water is no longer hot enough for this stunt, and besides, it's illegal.

WEST THUMB TO UPPER GEYSER BASIN

Heading west from West Thumb, the highway climbs over the Continental Divide twice. Most of these forests escaped the 1988 fires. A couple miles beyond the unmarked eastern crossing is a turnout at **Shoshone Point** where you catch glimpses of Shoshone Lake and the Tetons. In 1914, highwayman Ed Trafton held up 15 stagecoaches as they passed by this point carrying tourists. He got away with $915.35 in cash and $130 in jewelry but made the mistake of allowing his photo to be taken in the process. He was caught the following year and spent five years in Leavenworth. When he died, a letter in his pocket claimed that he had been Owen Wister's model for the Virginian. Others suspected that he was more likely to have been Wister's model for the villain, Trampas.

DeLacy Creek Trail provides access to Shoshone Lake and begins at the picnic area between the two passes. It's three miles to the lake, which is circled by more trails. The western crossing of the Continental Divide is at **Isa Lake,** a tiny pond that empties into both the Atlantic and Pacific oceans through its two outlet streams. This is Craig Pass.

Approximately 14 miles beyond West Thumb, pull off to see the Firehole River as it drops over **Kepler Cascades.** Just to the east, a wide and partly paved trail (actually an old road) leads 2$1/2$ miles to **Lone Star Geyser.** This is a popular route for bikes in the summer and skiers in the winter. (No bike traffic beyond the geyser, however.) Lone Star Geyser erupts every three hours from a distinctive nine-foot-high cone, with eruptions generally reaching 45 feet and lasting for 30 minutes. Hikers can also get to Lone Star via the Howard Eaton Trail out of Old Faithful. For a longer hike, you can continue south from Lone Star on **Shoshone Lake Trail** to Shoshone Lake, eight fairly easy miles from the main road. See "Into the Backcountry," p. 353, for other Shoshone Lake hikes.

UPPER GEYSER BASIN

TO FAIRY FALLS TRAILHEAD

TO BISCUIT BASIN & MYSTIC FALLS

MORNING GLORY POOL

RIVERSIDE GEYSER

GROTTO GEYSER

GIANT GEYSER

DAISY GEYSER

CHROMATIC POOL

PUNCH BOWL SPRING

BEAUTY POOL

SOLITARY GEYSER

TO MADISON JCT.

FIREHOLE RIVER

GRAND GEYSER

OBSERVATION POINT

CRESTED POOL

CASTLE GEYSER

LION GEYSER

GEYSER HILL

GIANTESS GEYSER

BEEHIVE GEYSER

CHINESE SPRING

OLD FAITHFUL

OLD FAITHFUL LODGE

SERVICE STATION

STORE

OLD FAITHFUL INN

VISITOR CENTER

TRAIL TO MALLARD LAKE

RANGER STATION

PHOTO STORE

SERVICE STATION

BLACK SAND BASIN

CLINIC

SNOW LODGE

STORE

IRON CREEK

POST OFFICE

0   0.2mi
0   0.2km

HOWARD EATON TRAIL

TO WEST THUMB

© MOON PUBLICATIONS, INC.

UPPER GEYSER BASIN

As you approach Old Faithful from either direction, the two-lane road suddenly widens into four, and you are confronted with what has to be one of the only cloverleafs in the entire national-park system. Welcome to Upper Geyser Basin, home of Old Faithful, some 400 buildings of all sizes, and a small town's worth of people. For many folks, this is the heart of Yellowstone, and a visit to the park without seeing Old Faithful is like a baseball game without the national an-

them. If you came to Yellowstone to see the wonders of nature, you're going to see more than your share here, but you'll probably have to share your share with hundreds of other folks. Fortunately, this area contains the largest concentration of geysers in the world, and the adventurous will even discover places where almost nobody ever visits. But be very careful, the crust can be dangerously thin around some of the hot springs and geysers, and people have been badly scalded and even killed by missteps. Stay on the boardwalks.

Old Faithful

The one sight seen by everyone who comes to Yellowstone is Old Faithful Geyser, easily the most visited geyser in the world. Its fame is second only to that of Iceland's Geysir (meaning "gusher" in Icelandic). Old Faithful is neither the tallest nor the most frequent geyser in Yellowstone, but it always provides a good show, is highly accessible, and is relatively predictable. Eruptions reach an average of 130 feet in the air. Contrary to the rumors, Old Faithful never erupted "every hour on the hour," but for many years its periodicity was around 64 minutes. It seems to have slowed down in recent years and is now averaging around 75-90 minutes. In general, the longer the length of the eruption, the longer the interval till the next eruption. Check at the visitor center for the latest prognostications.

An almost level paved path circles Old Faithful, providing many different angles from which to view the eruptions, although none of these is particularly close to the geyser. Along the north side is **Chinese Spring**, named in 1885 for a short-lived laundry operation. Apparently, the washman had filled the spring with clothes and soap, not knowing that soap can cause geysers to erupt. One newspaper correspondent claimed—though the tale obviously suffered from embellishment and racism—that,

The soap awakened the imprisoned giant; with a roar that made the earth tremble, and a shriek of a steam whistle, a cloud of steam and a column of boiling water shot up into the air a hundred feet, carrying soap, raiment, tent and Chinaman along with the rush, and dropping them at various intervals along the way.

Old Faithful provides a textbook example of geyser activity. The first signs of life are when water begins to splash out of the vent in what is called preplay. This splashing can last up to 20 minutes, but it's generally only a couple minutes before the real thing. The water quickly spears into the sky, reaching 100-180 feet for two to five minutes before rapidly dropping down. During a typical eruption, between 3,700 and 8,400 gallons of water are sent skyward.

On any given summer day, the scene at Old Faithful is almost comical. Just before the predicted eruption time, the benches encircling the south and east sides are jammed with hundreds of people waiting expectantly for the geyser to erupt, and with each tentative spray the camera shutters begin to click. Listen closely, and you'll hear half the languages of Europe and Asia. Once the action is over, there is a mad rush back into the visitor center, the stores, and Old Faithful Inn, and within a few minutes the benches are again empty. A story is told of two concessionaire employees who once decided to have fun at Old Faithful by placing a large crank atop a box and putting the contraption near the geyser. When they knew it was ready to erupt, they ran out and turned the crank just as Old Faithful shot into the air. Their employer and the park failed to see the humor in the prank. Both were fired.

Geyser Hill Area

Upper Geyser Basin is laced with paved trails that lead to dozens of nearby geysers and hot springs. The easiest path loops around Geyser Hill, just across the Firehole River from Old Faithful (see the "Upper Geyser Basin" map). Here are 40 different geysers. Check at the visitor center to get an idea of current activity, and while there, pick up the Upper Geyser Basin map (25 cents) which describes most of them. Several geysers are particularly noteworthy. When it plays, **Beehive Geyser** (it has a tall, beehive-shaped cone) vents water as high as 200 feet into the air. Such eruptions may be up to 10 days apart, however. **Lion Geyser Group** consists of four different interconnected geysers with varying periods of activity. Listen for the roaring sound when Lion is ready to erupt. **Giantess Geyser** is active only a few times a year, but the eruptions are spectacularly powerful, sending water 100-200 feet skyward. **Doublet Pool** is a strikingly beautiful deep blue pool that is a favorite of photographers. Not far away is **Sponge Geyser,** which rockets water up to 229 millimeters into the air (nine inches). It's considered the smallest named geyser in Yellowstone, a title achieved by sending up a spurt of water big enough to be mopped up by a sponge.

The two-mile-long **Observation Point Loop Trail** splits off shortly after you cross the bridge on the way to Geyser Hill and climbs to an excellent overlook where you can watch eruptions of Old Faithful. This is also a good place to view

> *From the surface of a rocky plain or table, burst forth columns of water of various dimensions, projected high in the air, accompanied by loud explosions, and sulphurous vapors, which were highly disagreeable to the smell . . . The largest of these wonderful fountains, projects a column of boiling water several feet in diameter, to the height of more than one hundred and fifty feet . . . After having witnessed three of them, I ventured near enough to put my hand into the water of its basin, but withdrew it instantly, for the heat of the water in this immense couldron, was altogether to great for comfort, and the agitation of the water, disagreeable effluvium continually exuding, and the hollow unearthly rumbling under the rock on which I stood, so ill accorded with my notions of personal safety, that I retreated back precipitately to a respectful distance.*
>
> —*Angus Ferris*
> *(Yellowstone's first "tourist") in 1833*

the effects of the 1988 North Fork Fire. Another easy trail splits off from this path to **Solitary Geyser**—actually just a pool that periodically burps four-foot splashes of hot water. This is not a natural geyser. In 1915, the hot spring here was tapped to provide water for Old Faithful Geyser Bath, a concession that lasted until 1950. The lowering of the water level in the pool completely changed the plumbing system of the hot springs and turned it into a geyser that at one time shot 25 feet in the air. The system still hasn't recovered, although water levels have been restored for more than 40 years.

More Geyser Gazin'

Another easy, paved path follows the Firehole River downstream, looping back along the other side for a total distance of three miles. Other trails head off from this loop to the Fairy Falls Trailhead, Biscuit Basin, and Black Sand Basin. The loop is a very popular wintertime ski path, and portions are open to bikes in the summer.

Twelve-foot-high **Castle Geyser** does indeed resemble a ruined old castle. Because of its size and the slow accretion of sinter (silica) to form this cone, it is believed to be somewhere between 5,000 and 50,000 years old. Castle sends up a column of water and steam 90 feet into the air and often erupts every 11 hours or so. Check at the visitor center for current activity.

Daisy Geyser is farther down the path and off to the left. It is usually one of the most predictable of the geysers, erupting to 75 feet approximately every 90 minutes. The water shoots out at a sharp angle and is visible all over the basin, making this a real crowd pleaser. Just east of Daisy is **Radiator Geyser,** which isn't much to look at (eruptions to two feet) but was named when this area was a parking lot and the sudden eruption under a car led people to think its radiator was overheating. **Grotto Geyser** is certainly the weirdest of all the geysers, having formed around a tangle of long-petrified tree stumps. It is in eruption almost half of the time, but most eruptions only reach 10-15 feet.

Look for **Riverside Geyser** across the Firehole from the path and not far below Grotto. This beautiful geyser arches its spray 75 feet over the river and is one of the most predictable, with eruptions approximately every seven hours. The paved trail crosses the river and ends at **Morning Glory Pool.** For many years, the main road passed this colorful pool, and it became something of a wishing well for not just coins but trash, rocks, logs, and other debris. Because of this junk, the pool began to cool, and the beautiful blue color is now tinged by brown and green algae, despite efforts to remove the debris.

Turning back at Morning Glory, re-cross the bridge and head left where the path splits at Grotto Geyser. **Giant Geyser** is on the left along the river. Years may pass between eruptions of Giant—but when it does go, the name rings true, since the water often reaches 200 feet. Cross the river again and pass **Beauty Pool** and **Chromatic Pool,** which are connected below the ground so that one declines as the other rises. Very pretty. **Grand Geyser** is a wonderful sight. The water column erupts in a towering burst of power every 8-10 hours, with a series of bursts lasting 9-16 minutes and reaching up to 200 feet. When Grand isn't playing, watch for eruptions of nearby **Turban** and **Sawmill** geysers. Cross the river again just beyond Grand Geyser and pass **Crested Pool** on your way back to Castle Geyser. The pool contains deep-blue water that is constantly boiling, preventing the survival of algae.

Black Sand Basin
Just a mile west of Old Faithful is Black Sand Basin, a small cluster of geysers and hot springs. Most enjoyable is unpredictable **Cliff Geyser,** which often sends a spray of hot water 15-30 feet over Iron Creek. Three colorful pools are quite interesting in the basin: **Emerald Pool, Rainbow Pool,** and **Sunset Lake. Handkerchief Pool** is now just a small spouter but was famous for many years as a place where visitors could drop a handkerchief in one end and then recover it later at another vent. In 1929, vandals jammed logs in the pool, destroying this little game. The pool was covered by gravel in subsequent eruptions of Rainbow Pool.

Biscuit Basin And Mystic Falls
This basin is named for biscuitlike formations that were found in one of the pools but were destroyed in an eruption following the 1959 Hebgen Lake earthquake. From the parking lot, the trail leads across Firehole River to **Sapphire Pool** and then past **Jewel Geyser,** which typically erupts every 10 minutes to a height of 15-20 feet. The boardwalk follows a short loop through the other sights of Biscuit Basin. From the west end of the boardwalk, a one-mile trail leads to where the Little Firehole River cascades 70 feet over **Mystic Falls.** You can switchback farther up the trail to the top of the falls and then connect with another trail for the loop back to Biscuit Basin (3½ miles RT). This is a very nice short hike and can be lengthened into a trip to **Little Firehole Meadows** and back via the Fairy Creek Trail to Midway Geyser Basin (14 miles RT). Bison are often seen in the meadows.

Old Faithful Inn
Despite its proximity to one of the great sights of the natural world, it is impossible not to love Old Faithful Inn, a place that contains perhaps the most winsome interior of any American building. It is said to be the largest log structure of its kind in existence. Designed by Robert Reamer and built in the winter of 1903-04, the inn has a steeply angled roofline reaching seven stories high, with gables jutting out from the sides and flags flying from the roof. Open the rustic old front door and you enter a world of the past dominated by a massive four-sided stone fireplace (500 tons of native stone were used) and a central space that arches 85 feet overhead. Four overhanging balconies extend above, each bordered by posts made from gnarled lodgepole burls found within the park. Above the fireplace is an enormous clock designed by Reamer and built on the site by a blacksmith. Reamer also designed the two wings that were added in 1913 and 1928.

On warm summer evenings, visitors stand out on the porch where they can watch Old Faithful erupting, while others sit at the old handcrafted tables to write letters as someone plays the piano in the corner. It's enough to warm the heart of even the most cynical visitor. A good restaurant is on the premises, along with a rustic but comfortable bar, a gift shop, and a fast-food eatery. **Chambermaid tours** of Old Faithful Inn are given Thurs.-Mon. between 9:30 a.m. and 3 p.m. Check at the front desk for specifics. Old Faithful Inn closes during the winter months; it would be hard to imagine trying to heat such a chasm when it's 40° below zero outside!

Another building of interest is **Old Faithful Lodge.** Built in 1928, this is the large stone-and-log building just south of the geyser of the same name. The giant fireplace inside is a joy on frosty evenings.

Old Faithful Services
The Park Service's **Old Faithful Visitor Center** is open mid-April through Oct., and mid-Dec. to mid-March. Hours vary throughout the year, but it's generally open daily 9-5 (8-8 in midsummer). Films about Yellowstone are shown throughout the day. The center has a good selection of books, maps, and other publications, and posts predictions for six of the major geysers (including Old Faithful) during the summer. The staff can provide you with all sorts of other info, from where to see bighorn sheep to where to find the restroom. Call 344-7381, ext. 6001, for more information.

Backcountry permits are available from the ranger station, while food, supplies, and post-cards can be purchased at either of the two Hamilton Stores. Old Faithful Inn has a gift shop, a restaurant, a snack bar, a lounge, and an ATM machine, while cafeteria meals are available at Old Faithful Lodge. Other facilities include two gas stations, a post office, a photo shop, and a clinic. See "Yellowstone Practicalities," pp. 358-363, for lodging details. Note that camping is *not* available in the Old Faithful area, and it's illegal to "camp" in the parking lots. The closest campgrounds are Madison (16 miles north) and Grant Village (19 miles southeast).

MIDWAY AND LOWER GEYSER BASINS

Heading north from Upper Geyser Basin, the road follows the Firehole River past Midway and Lower geyser basins, both of which are quite interesting. This stretch of the river is very popular with fly-fishing enthusiasts, and several side roads provide access to a variety of hot springs.

Midway Geyser Basin

Midway is a large and readily accessible geyser basin, with a loop path leading to most of the sights. Climb the hill across the road for fine views of the basin and its colorful pools. **Excelsior Geyser** is actually an enormous hot spring that pours 4,000 gallons per minute of steaming water into the Firehole River. The water is a deep turquoise-blue. During the 1880s, this was a truly spectacular geyser, with explosions that reached 380 feet in the air and were almost as wide. These violent eruptions apparently damaged the plumbing system that fed them, and the geyser was dormant for nearly a century, until smaller eruptions took place in 1985. At 370 feet across, **Grand Prismatic Spring** is Yellowstone's largest hot spring. The brilliant reds and yellows around the edges of the blue pool are from algae and bacteria that can tolerate temperatures of 170° F. There are additional geysers just south of here near a trailhead to Fairy Falls. The first mile of this trail is part of the old Fountain Flat Dr. and is open to bikes.

Firehole Lake Drive

This road (one-way heading north) goes three miles through Lower Geyser Basin, the park's most extensive geyser basin. **Great Fountain Geyser** is truly one of the most spectacular geysers in Yellowstone. Charles Cook of the 1869 Cook-Folsom-Peterson Expedition recalled his impression of the geyser: "We could not contain our enthusiasm; with one accord we all took off our hats and yelled with all our might." Modern-day visitors would not be faulted for reacting similarly.

Great Fountain erupts every 8-12 hours (although it can be irregular) and usually reaches 100 feet. It has been known to blast as high as 230 feet! Eruptions begin approximately an hour after water starts to overflow from the crater

> *At length we came to a boiling Lake about 300 ft in diameter forming nearly a complete circle as we approached on the south side The steam which arose from it was of three distinct Colors from the west side for one third of the diameter it was white, in the middle it was pale red, and the remaining third on the east light sky blue Whether it was something peculiar in the state of the atmosphere the day being cloudy or whether it was some Chemical properties contained in the water which produced this phenomenon I am unable to say and shall leave the explanation to some scientific tourist who may have the Curiosity to visit this place at some future period—The water was of deep indigo blue boiling like an imense caldron running over the white rock which had formed the edges to the height of 4 or 5 feet from the surface of the earth sloping gradually for 60 or 70 feet. What a field of speculation this presents for chemist and geologist.*
>
> *—Mountain man Osborne Russell describing Grand Prismatic Spring in 1839*

and last for 45-60 minutes, consisting of a series of eruptive cycles. Eruption predictions are posted at the geyser. While you're waiting, watch the periodic eruptions of **White Dome Geyser,** just a hundred yards down the road. Because of its massive 30-foot cone, this is believed to be one of the oldest geysers in the park. Eruptions generally occur every 15-30 minutes and spray 30 feet into the air.

Another mile down, the road literally cuts into the mound of **Pink Cone Geyser,** which now erupts every 6-15 hours and reaches a height of 30 feet. The pink color comes from manganese oxide. Just up from here at the bend in the road is **Firehole Lake** which discharges 3,500 gallons of water per minute into Tangled Creek, which then drains across the road into **Hot Lake.** The short **Three Senses Nature Trail** gives blind visitors (and sighted ones too) a chance to touch, smell, and hear the world of the geysers

and hot springs. **Steady Geyser** is unusual in that it forms sinter (silica) deposits as well as travertine (calcium carbonate) deposits. It is located along the edge of Hot Lake and, true to its name, erupts almost continuously, though the height is only five feet. Firehole Lake Dr. continues another mile to its junction with the main road right across from the parking area for Fountain Paint Pot. (In the winter, Firehole Lake Dr. is popular with skiers but is closed to snowmobiles.)

Fountain Paint Pot

Always a favorite of visitors, Fountain Paint Pot seems to have a playfulness about it that belies the immense power just below the surface. Pick up a trail guide (25 cents) as you head up the walkway. During the summer, rangers are often here to offer additional information. **Silex Spring** is off to the right as you walk up the small hill and is colored by different kinds of algae and bacteria. The spring has been known to erupt as a geyser (to 20 feet), but it is currently dormant. The famous **Fountain Paint Pot** is a few steps up the boardwalk and consists of colorful muds that change in consistency throughout the season depending upon soil moisture. The pressure from steam and gasses under the Paint Pot can throw gobs of mud up to 20 feet into the air. Just north of here are fumaroles that spray steam, carbon dioxide, and hydrogen sulfide into the air. Continuing down the boardwalk, you come upon an impressive overlook above a multitude of geysers that change constantly in activity. Some of the largest geysers in the park are here—including Morning Geyser, which erupts to over 150 feet. The most active is **Clepsydra Geyser,** in eruption much of the time. **Fountain Geyser** is usually active every 11 hours or so and can occasionally reach 80 feet. The rest of the loop trail passes dead lodgepole pines that are being petrified as the silica is absorbed, creating a "bobby socks" appearance.

Fountain Flat Drive

Fountain Flat Dr. is an interesting side road that passes through meadows along the Firehole River and provides a good place to see bison and elk. Look for **Ojo Caliente**—a small hot springs with a big odor—right along the edge of the river and just before the bridge. Several more are upstream from here. The paved road ends after three miles at a barricade, but bikes (or skiers and snowmobiles in winter) can continue another two miles to its junction with the main road again. Beautiful 200-foot-high **Fairy Falls** can be reached by hiking the road a mile beyond the barricade, to a junction at the end of the meadow. Here it's another 1½ miles to the falls. This makes a pleasant afternoon walk and can be combined with a scenic loop back along the west edge of the meadow (see map, p. 337) for a RT distance of 6½ miles. A side trip takes you to **Imperial Geyser,** which now shoots water approximately six feet in the air almost continuously.

Firehole Canyon Drive

This one-way road (south only) curves for two miles through Firehole Canyon, where dark rhyolite cliffs rise 800 feet above the river. The road begins just south of Madison Junction and was intensely burned in the 1988 North Fork Fire, giving the canyon's name a dual meaning. **Firehole Falls** is a 40-foot drop that is worth stopping to see, as is **Firehole Cascades** a bit farther up. Kids of all ages enjoy the swimming hole (warmed by hot springs) a short distance up the road.

TO WEST YELLOWSTONE

At Madison Junction, the Gibbon and Firehole rivers join to form the Madison River, a major tributary of the Missouri River. The 14-mile drive from Madison Junction to the West Entrance closely parallels this scenic river, in which geese, ducks, and trumpeter swans are almost always present. Bison and elk are other critters to watch for in the open meadows. The 406,359-acre North Fork Fire of 1988 ripped through most of the Madison River country, so be ready for many blackened trees, but also expect to see many flowers in midsummer. The river is open only to fly-fishing and is considered one of the finest places in the nation to catch trout (though they can be a real challenge to fool). On warm summer evenings, you're likely to see dozens of anglers casting for wily rainbow and brown trout and mountain whitefish. **West Entrance** is the busiest of all the park entry stations, handling roughly half of the 2½ million people who enter

Yellowstone each year. The tourist town of West Yellowstone, Montana (see pp. 363-366), is right outside the boundary.

Madison Canyon is flanked by mountains named for two photographers who had a marked influence on Yellowstone. To the north is 8,257-foot **Mount Jackson** (as in William H. Jackson, whose photos helped bring the area to national attention), while on the south the distinctive peak is 8,235-foot **Mount Haynes,** named for the man who held the park photo concession for nearly four decades. These mountains and the surrounding slopes were created by rhyolite lava flows.

MADISON JUNCTION TO NORRIS

One of the more unique places in Yellowstone is the small **Madison Caldera Arts Center** at Madison Junction. Throughout the summer you'll find a range of artists—including at different times painters, writers, and performers—who help reveal the natural world as a place of visual and sensual beauty. There are free workshops, musical performances, and a broad range of other activities.

Directly behind Madison Junction Campground is 7,560-foot **National Park Mountain,** named in honor of a fabled incident in 1870. Three explorers were gathered around the campfire, discussing the wonders that they had found in this area, when one suggested that rather than letting all these wonders pass into private hands, they should be set aside as a national park. Thus was born the concept that led to the world's first national park. The tale was passed on as the gospel truth for so long that the mountain was named in honor of this evening. Unfortunately, the story was a fabrication. Cynics may read something into the fact that National Park Mountain was torched by the fires of 1988.

North of Madison Junction, the road follows the Gibbon River nearly all of the 14 miles to Norris. It crosses the river five times and hangs right on the edge through Gibbon Canyon. The pretty 84-foot-high **Gibbon Falls** are approximately five miles up the road and are situated right at the edge of the enormous caldera that fills the center of Yellowstone. The 1988 fires consumed most of the trees around the falls. Another five miles beyond this, the road emerges from the canyon into grassy **Gibbon Meadows,** where elk and bison are commonly seen. The prominent peak visible to the north is 10,336-foot Mount Holmes. On the west end of Gibbon Meadows is a barren area that contains **Sylvan Springs Geyser Basin.** No maintained trail leads to this small collection of pools and springs, but hikers sometimes head across the north end of the meadows at the Gibbon River Picnic Area. The path is wet most of the summer.

An easy half-mile trail leads to **Artist Paint Pots,** filled with colorful plopping and steaming mud pots and hot springs. This is a nice place to escape the crowds. The forest was burned in the North Fork Fire, so it's also a good place to see how the lodgepole pine trees are regenerating. Just south of the parking area for Artist Paint Pots is a trail to **Monument Geyser Basin** where there isn't much activity, but the tall sinter cones form all sorts of bizarre shapes, including Thermos Bottle Geyser. The mile-long hike climbs 500 feet and provides good views of the surrounding country. Another attraction is **Chocolate Pots,** found along the highway just north of Gibbon Meadows. The reddish-brown color comes from iron, aluminum, and manganese oxides. Just before you reach Norris, the road crosses through the appropriately named **Elk Park.**

NORRIS GEYSER BASIN

Although Old Faithful is more famous, many visitors to Yellowstone find Norris Geyser Basin more interesting. Norris sits atop the junction of several major fault lines, providing conduits for heat from the molten lava below. Because of this, Norris is considered the hottest geyser basin in North America, if not the world; a scientific team found temperatures of 401° F at just 265 feet underground and was forced to quit drilling when the pressure threatened to destroy its drilling rig! Because of considerable sulfur (and hence sulfuric acid) in the springs and geysers, the water at Norris is quite acidic; a majority of the world's acid geysers are here.

The acidic water kills lodgepole trees in the basin, creating an open, nearly barren place. Norris Basin has been around at least 115,000 years, making it the oldest of any of Yellowstone's active geyser basins. It is a constantly changing place, with small geysers seeming to come and go on an almost daily basis.

The paved trail from the oft-crowded parking area leads to **Norris Museum,** built of stone in 1929-30. The small museum houses exhibit panels on hot springs and geothermal activity and is generally open daily 9-5 (8-9 in midsummer) mid-May through September. Pick up a brochure (25 cents) describing the various features at Norris. Ranger-led walks are given most days. From the museum, the Norris Basin spreads both north and south, with two rather different trails to hike. Take the time to walk along both; you won't regret it. The Norris Campground is only a quarter-mile from the geyser basin.

Porcelain Basin

Just behind the museum is an overlook that provides a fascinating view of Porcelain Basin. The path drops down into the basin, passing steam vents, hot pools, and small geysers along the way, including **Dark Cavern Geyser,** which erupts several times an hour to 20 feet. **Whirligig Geyser** is another one that is often active, spraying a fan of water. (Watch your glasses and camera lenses in the steam, since silica deposits can be very hard to remove.) For an enjoyable short walk, follow the boardwalk around the mile-long loop. Stop to admire the bright colors in the steaming water, indicators of iron, arsenic, and other elements, along with algae and cyanobacteria.

Back Basin

A mile-long loop trail takes you to the sights within the Back Basin, south of the museum. Before heading out, check at the museum for the latest on geyser activity. Most people follow the path in a clockwise direction, coming first to **Emerald Spring,** a beautiful green pool with acidic water just below boiling. A little ways farther down the path is **Steamboat Geyser.** Wait a few minutes and you're likely to see one of its minor eruptions, which may reach 40 feet. But on occasion, Steamboat erupts with a fury that is hard to believe, blasting 380 feet into the air—three times the height of Old Faithful—making this the world's tallest geyser. Eruptions can last up to 20 minutes, enough time to pour out a million gallons of water! They have been heard up to 14 miles away. Steamboat's unforgettable eruptions cannot be predicted; a 50-year span once passed between eruptions, while at other times they may occur several times a year.

The path splits just below Steamboat and on the right is **Cistern Spring,** whose deep blue waters are constantly building deposits of sinter (a grey silica deposit) and have flooded the nearby lodgepole-pine forests, killing the trees. If you turn left where the trail splits, you come next to **Echinus Geyser,** a personal favorite. (The name—Greek for "spiny"—comes from the sea-urchin-like pebbles around the geyser; they are a result of sinter accumulation.) Echinus erupts every 35-75 minutes, so be sure to check at the museum to see when it last played. Watch the pool closely, since explosions of steam and water generally begin once it has filled, with acidic water (pH 3.5) reaching 60-125 feet. Unlike Old Faithful, this is one geyser where you can get up close and personal. Bench-sitters are likely to get wet, although the water is not hot enough to burn. Continue along this trail to see many more hot springs and steam vents. **Porkchop Geyser** was in continuous eruption for several years, but in 1989 it self-destructed in an explosion, leaving behind a bubbling hot spring.

NORRIS JUNCTION TO CANYON

The dozen miles from Norris Geyser Basin to Canyon cut across the center of the park on the high Solfatara Plateau. This stretch of road is best known for what looks like a scene from an atomic blast, with the blackened remains of a forest seemingly blown down by the ferocity of the 1988 North Fork Fire. This is the place the news media focused on after the fires, making it appear as if it were typical of the park as a whole. In reality, the lodgepole pines were all uprooted in a wild 1984 windstorm that flattened many miles of forest both here and farther south in the Teton Wilderness. The dead trees dried out over the next four years, and when the wind-whipped fires arrived, they went up in a holo-

caust. In 50 years, this may well be a meadow. **Virginia Cascades Rd.** is a 2½-mile-long, one-way road that circles around this blow-down area and provides a view of the 60-foot-tall Virginia Cascade of the Gibbon River. Back on the main highway heading east, keep your eyes open for elk and bison as the road approaches Canyon. Also note the thick, young forest of lodgepole pines that was established after a fire burned through in 1955.

NORRIS JUNCTION TO MAMMOTH

The park road between Norris and Mammoth Hot Springs provides a number of interesting sights, although much of this country burned in the 1988 North Fork Fire. Just beyond the highway junction is the **Norris Soldier Station,** built by the Army in 1908 and one of just three still standing in the park. It now houses the **Museum of the National Park Ranger,** with displays on the history of park rangers. The museum is open daily 9-6 in the summer. Just up the road is **Frying Pan Spring** (named for its shape), where the water is actually not that hot. The bubbles are from pungent-smelling hydrogen sulfide gas. **Roaring Mountain** is a bleak, steaming mountainside four miles north of Norris. In 1902, the mountain erupted into activity with fumaroles that made a roar audible at great distances. It is far less active today.

Stop at **Obsidian Cliff** to see the black glassy rocks formed when lava cooled very rapidly. One mountain man (not, as many sources claim, Jim Bridger) told tales of "Glass Mountain" where his shots at an elk kept missing. When he got closer, he found he had actually been firing at a clear mountain of glass. The elk was 25 miles away, but the mountain was acting as a telescope to make the animal appear close. Obsidian Cliff was an important source of rock that Indians used in making arrowheads and other tools. Obsidian points made from this rock have even been found in the Ohio River Valley. North of here the countryside opens up along Obsidian Creek at **Willow Park,** one of the best places to see moose, especially in the fall.

Approximately 13 miles north of Norris, the road passes Indian Creek Campground and the basalt columns of **Sheepeater Cliffs,** named for the Indian inhabitants of these mountains. North of this, the country opens into Gardners Hole, where you get a fine gander at 10,992-foot Electric Peak, nine miles to the northwest. At **Golden Gate** the road suddenly enters a narrow defile, through which flows Glen Creek. Stop to look over the edge of **Rustic Falls** and to note how the road is cantilevered over the cliff edge. Acrophobics should *not* stop here. Instead, have someone else drive, close your eyes, and say three Hail Marys.

Bunsen Peak is the 8,564-foot volcanic cone that is visible just south of Mammoth. Any chemistry student will recognize the name, for Robert W. Bunsen not only first explained the action of geysers, but he also invented the Bunsen burner. Bunsen Peak looks like a chemistry experiment run amuck. The North Fork Fire of 1988 swept through this area in a patchy mosaic, leaving long strips of unburned trees next to those that are now just blackened telephone poles. Trails lead up to the top of Bunsen Peak from both the east and west sides. The west trail (two miles) begins at the entrance to **Bunsen Peak Rd.**, located just south of Rustic Falls. This rough and *very* steep one-way dirt road (six miles) circles around the east side of the mountain. It's closed to trailers and RVs. The road begins a quarter-mile south of Golden Gate (see map, p. 343). From the road you are treated to views of 150-foot-high **Osprey Falls.** A trail to the falls was wiped out by a landslide; hopefully it will be rebuilt in the near future. This side road is well off the beaten track, but scenic.

If you take the steep main road rather than the Bunsen Peak Rd., you will soon come to the **Hoodoos,** a fascinating jumble of travertine boulders leaning in all directions. The rocks were created by hot springs thousands of years ago and toppled from the east face of Terrace Mountain. Just before Mammoth, you'll see the turnoff for Upper Terrace Dr. on the left. This half-mile loop road provides access to the upper end of Mammoth Hot Springs.

MAMMOTH HOT SPRINGS VICINITY

Mammoth Hot Springs lies near the northern border of Yellowstone, and contains park headquarters, a variety of other facilities, and colorful hot springs. The Mammoth area is an important wintering area for elk, antelope, deer, and bison. During the fall, a bull elk and his harem can be seen wandering across the green lawns while lesser males bugle challenges from behind the buildings. The bugling can keep you awake at night if you're staying in the Mammoth Hotel. The town of Gardiner, Montana, is just five miles away.

Origins
Mammoth Hot Springs consists of a series of multihued terraces down which hot, mineral-laden water trickles. This water originates as snow and rain that falls on the surrounding country, although some is believed to come from the Norris area, 20 miles to the south. As it passes through the earth, the water comes in contact with volcanic magma containing massive amounts of carbon dioxide, which is absorbed by the water to form carbonic acid. The now-acidic water passes through and dissolves the region's sedimentary limestone, and the calcium carbonate remains in solution until it reaches the surface at Mammoth. Once at the surface, the carbon dioxide begins to escape into the atmosphere, reducing the acidity and causing the lime to precipitate out, forming the travertine terraces that are so prominent here. As the water flows over small obstructions, more carbon dioxide is released, causing accumulations that eventually grow into the lips that surround the terrace pools. The accumulation of travertine (calcium carbonate) is astounding: more than two tons a day at Mammoth Hot Springs. Some terraces grow by eight inches a year. The first explorers were fascinated by these terraces; mountain man Jim Bridger noted that they made for delightful baths. A later operation—long since ended—coated knickknacks by dipping them in the hot springs!

The springs are constantly changing as underground passages are blocked by limestone deposits, forcing the water into new directions. As a result, old dried-out terraces stand on all sides as new ones grow each day. Areas that were active just a few years ago may now be simply gray masses of crumbling travertine rock. One of the most interesting aspects of the hot springs here are the colors, results of the many different species of algae and bacteria that live in the water. Various factors, including temperature and acidity, affect the survival of different species, with bright yellow algae in the hottest areas, while cooler waters are colored orange and brown by other algae.

Visiting The Springs

Mammoth Hot Springs covers a steep hillside and consists of a series of colorful springs in various stages of development or decay. Road access is either from below or above (Upper Terrace Dr.), with a boardwalk/staircase connecting the two. Pick up a Park Service brochure (25 cents) for more on the springs. The most interesting of the springs are **Minerva Terrace** and **Canary Spring.** Cleopatra and Angel terraces, which were active in the 1930s, are now simply a bland mass of gray rock. At the bottom of Mammoth Hot Springs and off to the right

side is a 37-foot-tall mass of travertine known as **Liberty Cap** for its faint similarity to the caps worn by Revolutionary War soldiers. The spring that created this no longer flows.

Directly across the road is **Opal Terrace,** one of the most active of all the springs. It began flowing in 1926 and has continued to expand over the years until it now threatens the lush lawns of a house built in 1908 and designed by Robert Reamer (of Old Faithful Inn fame). All the water flowing out of Mammoth terraces quickly disappears into underground caverns. In front of the Mammoth Hotel are two sinkholes from which steam often rises. Caverns above the terraces were once open to the public, but later were closed when it became apparent that they contained poisonous gasses. Dead birds are sometimes found around one of the small pools in this area, appropriately named Poison Spring.

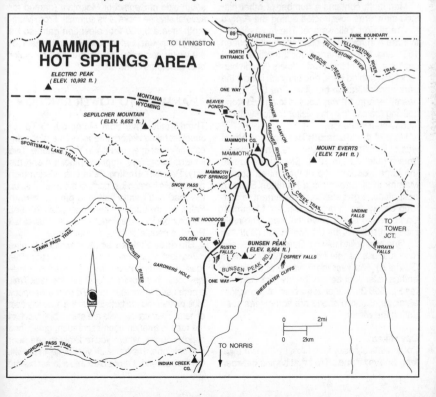

MAMMOTH HOT SPRINGS AREA

Buildings

Albright Visitor Center is named for the first National Park Service superintendent at Yellowstone, Horace Albright, and is housed in the Army's old Bachelor Officers' Quarters. Open daily 9-5 year-round, with extended hours in midsummer. Call 344-7381, ext. 2357, for more information. Inside, find an information desk, racks of books, films, and videos about the park, and frequent ranger-led walks to surrounding sights. Spread over the two floors are various exhibits, but the real treats are the works of two artists who had major hands in bringing Yellowstone's magnificent scenery to public attention. Twenty-three of painter Thomas Moran's famous Yellowstone watercolors line the walls. Equally impressive are 26 classic photographs taken by William H. Jackson in the 1871 Hayden Survey, including one of Thomas Moran at Mammoth Hot Springs.

Mammoth contains a number of other historic structures constructed during the Army's tenure at Fort Yellowstone. The most distinctive are a in row of six buildings built between 1891 and 1909—quarters for the officers and captains. Most of the grunt soldiers lived in barracks just behind here, one of which is now the park administration building. The U.S. Engineers Department was housed in an odd stone building (across from the visitor center) with obvious Asian influences.

Most of the **Mammoth Hot Springs Hotel** was built in 1937, although one wing survives from a hotel built in 1911. Step inside to see the large wooden map of the United States. Mammoth also features a Hamilton Store, a post office, a gas station, a restaurant, a fast-food eatery, and horseback rides. Mammoth Campground is just down the road. The main road north follows the Gardner River. (Both this and the misspelled town of Gardiner are named for a ruthless trapper from the 1820s, Johnson Gardner.) The river is a favorite of fly-fishing enthusiasts. Just before the town of Gardiner (see p. 366-367), look for a herd of pronghorn antelope. Bighorn sheep are sometimes seen during the winter.

Day Hikes

For a relatively easy loop hike, try the five-mile-long **Beaver Ponds Trail** that begins between Liberty Cap and the stone house. It gains 500 feet in elevation, passing through spruce and fir forests along the way and ending at several small ponds. The path then drops down to join the old Gardiner Rd., which you can follow back to Mammoth. This trail provides a good opportunity to see mule deer, antelope, and moose, but is best hiked in the spring or fall when temperatures are cooler. Black bears are sometimes seen along the way, so be sure to make noise while you walk. (See p. 38 for more on bear safety.)

A longer (12 miles RT) hike is the **Sepulcher Mountain Trail**, which climbs to the top of this 9,652-foot peak just northwest of Mammoth. There are several possible routes to the top, and any of these can be combined into a very nice loop hike. One of these begins at the same place as the Beaver Ponds Trail. You'll find many flowers in the expansive meadows on the south side of Sepulcher Mountain (named for several strange rocks at its summit). From Mammoth, it is a 3,400-foot elevation gain, so be ready to sweat. Before heading out, check at the visitor center to see if there are any major bear problems in the area.

MAMMOTH TO TOWER JUNCTION

The 18-mile drive from Mammoth to Tower Junction takes visitors through some of the driest and most open country in Yellowstone. Two waterfalls provide stopping places along the way. Beautiful **Undine Falls** is a 60-foot-high double falls located just north of the road. Just up the road is a gentle half-mile path to **Wraith Falls**, where Lupine Creek cascades 90 feet. Look for ducks and trumpeter swans in **Blacktail Pond**, a couple of miles farther east.

Blacktail Plateau Dr., approximately nine miles east of Mammoth, turns off from the main road. The rough seven-mile dirt road is a one-way route that loosely follows the Bannock Trail, a path used from 1838 to 1878 by the Bannock tribe on their way to buffalo-hunting grounds east of here. Their travois trails are still visible. Much of the road is through open sagebrush, grass, and aspen country, where you're likely to see deer and antelope. The trees are very pretty in the fall. On the east end, it drops back into a forest burned by a severe crown fire in 1988. Look for aspen and lodgepole seedlings among the abundant summertime flowers.

The Park Service has developed a 2/3-mile boardwalk **Children's Fire Trail** approximately six miles east of Mammoth Hot Springs. Trailside exhibits describe the natural world. A half-mile beyond where Blacktail Plateau Dr. rejoins the main road is the turnoff to the **petrified tree.** The 20-foot-tall stump of an ancient redwood tree (50 million years old) stands behind iron bars. A second petrified tree that used to stand nearby was stolen piece by piece over the years by thoughtless tourists. The **Tower Ranger Station,** originally occupied by the U.S. Army, is just before Tower Junction where the road splits, leading to either Northeast Entrance Road or Canyon.

NORTHEAST ENTRANCE ROAD

Of the five primary entryways into Yellowstone, Northeast Entrance is the least traveled, making this a nice place to escape the hordes in midsummer. It is also one of the few places in Yellowstone where one sees tall mountains. The road heads east from Tower Junction and immediately enters **Lamar Valley,** an area of grass and sage along the sinuous Lamar River. Osborne Russell, who trapped this country in the 1830s, described it with affection:

We descended the stream about 15 mls thro. the dense forest and at length came to a beautiful valley about 8 Mls. long and 3 or 4 wide surrounded by dark and lofty mountains. The stream after running thro. the center in a NW direction rushed down a tremendous canyon of basaltic rock apparently just wide enough to admit its waters. The banks of the stream in the valley were low and skirted in many places with beautiful Cotton wood groves. Here we found a few Snake indians comprising 6 men 7 women and 8 or 10 children who were the only Inhabitants of this lonely and secluded spot. They were all neatly clothed in dressed deer and Sheep skins of the best quality and seemed to be perfectly contented and happy. . . . We stopped

at this place and for my own part I almost wished I could spend the remainder of my days in a place like this where happiness and contentment seemed to rein in wild romantic splendor surrounded by majestic battlements which seemed to support the heavens and shut out all hostile intruders. . . . There is something in the wild romantic scenery of this valley which I cannot . . . describe; but the impressions made upon my mind while gazing from a high eminence on the surrounding landscape one evening as the sun was gently gliding behind the western mountain and casting its gigantic shadows across the vale were such as time can never efface from my memory.

This is still one of the best places in Yellowstone to view bison. Elk and mule deer are also commonly seen. The valley contains a number of small ponds created when the retreating glaciers left large blocks of ice that formed "kettles." Erratic glacial boulders are scattered along the way. There are campgrounds at Slough Creek and Pebble Creek. They are the last to fill in the park, but even these fill quickly in July and August. Very good fishing in Slough Creek.

Yellowstone Institute

The nonprofit Yellowstone Institute is housed within Lamar Valley's historic Buffalo Ranch, where turn-of-the-century efforts were made to protect and breed bison. Plains bison were brought here and kept in pens at night and herded during the day. After 1915, they were allowed to roam freely during the summer, although all the park's bison were rounded up and driven here for the winters. After 1938, the roundups ended, but hay was fed them every winter in Lamar Valley. Finally in 1952, even this was halted.

Yellowstone Institute offers 75 different environmental classes between May and mid-Sept., with most lasting two to five days. The courses cover the spectrum from alpine ecology to backcountry skiing. Participants stay in primitive cabins at the ranch and cook meals in the kitchen. The Institute is funded in part by the Yellowstone Association, and discounts are available to Association members. For a brochure, write

Yellowstone Institute, Box 117, Yellowstone National Park, WY 82190; tel. 344-7381.

Specimen Ridge

Just east of Yellowstone Institute is a turnout across from Specimen Ridge, where explorers discovered the standing trunks of petrified trees that had been buried in volcanic ash and mudflows some 50 million years ago. Over the centuries, the trunks literally turned to stone as silica entered the wood. The process was repeated again and again over the centuries as new forests gradually developed atop the volcanic deposits, only to be buried by later flows. Scientists have found 27 different forests on top of each other, containing walnut, magnolia, oaks, redwood, and maple—evidence that the climate was once more like that of today's central states. Erosion eventually revealed the trees, many of which are still standing. This is one of the largest areas of petrified trees known to exist.

There is no trail to the petrified forest, but during the summer, rangers lead hikes into the area. Check at the Mammoth Visitor Center for upcoming treks. Mark Marschall's *Yellowstone Trails* provides a description of the 1½-mile route, if you want to try it on your own. A lesser-known petrified forest in the northwest corner of Yellowstone is accessible via US 191.

Northeast Entrance

At the east end of Lamar Valley, US 212 continues northeast up Soda Butte Creek and between the steep rocky cliffs of Barronette Peak (10,404 feet) and Abiathar Peak (10,928 feet). Stop at **Soda Butte,** where you'll find a small travertine mound similar to those at Mammoth. Although the springs are no longer very active, the air still reeks of hydrogen sulfide, the "rotten egg" gas. South of Soda Butte and several miles up a backcountry trail is **Wahb Springs,** found within Death Gulch. Here poisonous gases are emitted from the ground, killing animals in the vicinity. Early explorers reported finding dead bears who had wandered into the area and had been overcome by the fumes.

Above Pebble Creek Campground, the road squeezes through chilly **Icebox Canyon** and into the lodgepole-pine forests. It follows the creek all the way to the edge of the park, crossing into Montana two miles before the park border. The **Northeast Entrance Station** is a classic log building built in 1935 and designated a National Historic Landmark. The twin towns of Silver Gate and Cooke City (see pp. 367-369) are just up the road.

TOWER JUNCTION TO CANYON

Right at the junction of the roads to Canyon, Mammoth, and Lamar Valley is **Roosevelt Lodge,** built in 1920 and named for President Theodore Roosevelt, who camped a few miles south of here when he visited in 1903. President Roosevelt remained a lifelong supporter of Yellowstone and helped push through legislation that clamped down upon the rampant destruction of its wildlife. The Roosevelt area is a favorite of families, many of whom return each year. It has the rough-edged flavor of a hunting lodge and a peacefulness that you won't find at Old Faithful. Inside the lodge are two giant stone fireplaces. Lodging, food, a gift shop, and horseback rides are available.

Stop at the overlook to **Calcite Springs,** two miles southeast of the junction, where a walkway provides dramatic views into the canyon, with steaming geothermal activity far below. The cliff faces contain a wide strip of columnar basalt, some of which overhangs the highway just south of here.

At **Tower Fall,** Tower Creek plummets 132 feet before joining the Yellowstone River. The towerlike black rocks of the area are made of basalt, a volcanic material. Nearby are a campground and a Hamilton Store. Tower Fall overlook is just a couple hundred paved feet from the parking area, or you can follow the path a half mile down the switchbacks to the canyon bottom, where the vista is far more impressive and a rainbow is sometimes visible. Be prepared to get wet in the spray. A ford of the Yellowstone River—used by Bannock Indians in the 19th century—is just a quarter-mile away. For more than a hundred years, a huge boulder stood atop Tower Fall; the water and gravity finally won in 1986.

Continuing south, the road climbs along Antelope Creek and eventually switchbacks up the aptly named Mae West Curve. The North Fork fire swept through this country in 1988, leaving a blackened forest but abundant summertime flowers and verdant grasses. A popular trail to **Mt. Washburn** splits off just above Mae's curves, and you can drive up the first mile on old Chittenden Road. Park your car and hike the remaining three miles to the top. This is one of the nicest day-hikes in the park, providing a fine opportunity to see and photograph bighorn sheep. Many wildflowers bloom in midsummer, and hikers discover fantastic vistas from the lookout tower on top. Another popular three-mile trail up Mt. Washburn begins at the Dunraven Pass Picnic Area.

Dunraven Pass (8,859 feet) is named for the Earl of Dunraven, who visited the park in 1874, and whose widely read book *The Great Divide* brought Yellowstone to the attention of wealthy European travelers. This is the highest point along any park road. Look for whitebark pines near the road, and be sure to stop just south of here for a view across to the distant Grand Canyon of the Yellowstone.

GRAND CANYON OF THE YELLOWSTONE

Yellowstone is best known for its geysers and animals, but for many, the Grand Canyon is its most memorable feature. The 20-mile-long canyon is 4,000 feet across, with colorful yellow, pink, orange, and buff cliffs that drop as much as 1,200 feet on either side. The river itself tumbles abruptly over two massive waterfalls, sending up a roar audible for miles along the rims. Grand Canyon is accessible by road from both the north and south sides, with equally amazing views. The lodgepole forests around here escaped the fires of 1988.

Carving A Canyon

After the massive volcanic eruptions some 600,000 years ago, rhyolite lava flows came through what is now the Grand Canyon. The flows eventually cooled, but geothermal activity within the rhyolite weakened the rock with hot steam and gasses, making it susceptible to erosion. Over the centuries, a series of glaciers blocked water upstream and then allowed the water in this lake to empty suddenly when they retreated. The weakened rhyolite was easily eroded by these floods of water and glacial debris, thus revealing pastel yellow and red canyon walls colored by the thermal activities. The **Lower Falls** are at the edge of the thermal basin, above rock that was not weakened by geothermal activity. The **Upper Falls** are at a contact point between hard rhyolite that does not erode easily and a band of rhyolite that contains more easily eroded volcanic glass. Today, the canyon is eroding more slowly, having increased in depth only 50 feet over the last 10,000 years.

Canyon Village

Canyon Village on the north rim is a forgettable shopping mall in the wilderness, complete with various stores and eating places, a post office, a gas station, cabins, and a campground (RVs only). Horseback rides are available nearby. **Canyon Visitor Center** includes exhibits on the geology and natural history of the area, along with films and slide shows. Hours are generally 8-7 in midsummer and 9-5 during the spring and fall. It is open mid-May to late September. Call 344-7381, ext. 6205, for more information.

North Rim Vistas

A one-way road takes visitors to a series of extremely popular overlooks along the north rim. Farthest east is **Inspiration Point,** where the views of the Canyon and Lower Falls are, well, inspirational. **North Rim Trail** leads along the rim from Inspiration Point up to Chittenden Bridge, three miles away. Some sections of this scenic and nearly level path are paved. Just a couple hundred feet up from Inspiration Point, be sure to look for the 500-ton boulder left behind 15,000 years ago by the retreating glaciers. It originated at least 15 miles north of here and was carried south atop the moving river of ice. The five-mile-long **Seven Mile Hole Trail** takes off near this boulder, providing fantastic views for the first mile or so, minus the crowds at Inspiration Point. Look for **Silver Cord Cascade,** a thin ribbon of water dropping over the opposite wall of the canyon, but be careful not to go too

close to the very loose edge. It's a long way down! The trail switchbacks steeply down to the Yellowstone River, passing odoriferous thermal areas en route. Many anglers come to Seven Mile Hole (it's seven miles downriver from Lower Falls), while others come to relax along the river. Save your energy for the strenuous 1,400-foot climb back up.

The one-way road continues westward to overlooks at **Grandview** and **Lookout Point.** From Lookout Point, a half-mile trail drops several hundred feet to **Red Rock Point** for a closer view of Lower Falls. Farthest west along the one-way North Rim Rd. is the trail to the **Brink of the Lower Falls.** It's half a mile long and paved, descending 600 feet to a viewing area where you can peer over the 308-foot precipice (twice the height of Niagara Falls). Not recommended for anyone suffering from vertigo. Just south of where the one-way road rejoins the main highway is a turnoff to the **Brink of the Upper Falls,** where a short walk takes you to an over-the-edge view of the 109-foot-high Upper Falls.

A party of prospectors wandered north into this country in 1867, following the Yellowstone downriver without suspecting the canyon below. A. Bart Henderson wrote in his diary of strolling down the river and being

very much surprised to see the water disappear from my sight. I walked out on a rock & made two steps at the same time, one forward, the other backward, for I had unawares as it were, looked down into the depth or bowels of the earth, into which the Yellow plunged as if to cool the infernal region that lay under all this wonderful country of lava and boiling springs.

South Rim Vistas

The south rim is lined with more dramatic views into Grand Canyon. Cross the Chittenden Bridge over the Yellowstone River (otters are sometimes seen playing in the river below) and continue a half-mile to Uncle Tom's parking area, where a short trail leads to views of the Upper Falls and Crystal Falls. More unusual is **Uncle Tom's Trail,** which descends 500 feet to Lower Falls. The trail is partly paved, but steep, and includes 328 metal steps before you get to the bottom. Good exercise if you're in shape. It was named for "Uncle" Tom Richardson who, with the help of wooden ladders and ropes, led paying tourists to the base of the falls around the turn of the century. Because there was no bridge, Uncle Tom also rowed his guests across the river near the present Chittenden Bridge. After his permit was revoked in 1903, visitors had to make do on their own.

A mile beyond Uncle Tom's parking area, the road ends at the parking area for **Artist Point,** the most famous of all Grand Canyon viewpoints. A short paved path leads to an astounding point where one can look upriver to the Lower Falls or down the opposite direction into the canyon. Look for thermal activity far below. The point is apparently where artist Thomas Moran painted a number of his famous watercolors. **South Rim Trail** begins at the Chittenden Bridge and follows along the rim to Artist Point (two miles), providing more viewpoints along the way. The least-traveled part of this trail continues eastward another 1½ miles to Sublime Point, with many fine looks into the canyon. Watch for loose rocks on the edge; it's a long way down!

CANYON TO LAKE JUNCTION

Hayden Valley

Just a few miles south of Canyon, the country abruptly opens into beautiful Hayden Valley, named for Ferdinand V. Hayden, leader of the 1871 expedition into Yellowstone. Reaching eight miles across, this relatively level part of the park was once occupied by an arm of Yellowstone Lake. The sediments left behind by the lake, along with glacial till, do not hold sufficient water to support trees. As a result, the area is occupied primarily by grasses, forbs, and sage. This is one of the best areas in the park to see wildlife, especially bison and elk. The Yellowstone River wanders across Hayden Valley, while streams enter from various sides. The waterways are excellent places to look for Canada geese, trumpeter swans, pelicans, and many kinds of ducks. Although they are less common, grizzly bears sometimes can be found feeding in the eastern end of the valley. Because of the bears, hikers need to be especially cautious when tramping through the grasses and shrubs, where it is easy to surprise a bear or to be likewise surprised. On the north end of Hayden Valley, the road crosses **Alum Creek,** named for the highly alkaline water that could make anything shrink. In the horse-and-buggy days, Yellowstone wags claimed that a man had forded the creek with a team of horses and a wagon, but came out the other side with four Shetland ponies pulling a basket!

Mud Volcano Area

Shortly after the road climbs south out of Hayden Valley, it passes one of the most interesting of Yellowstone's many thermal basins. On the east side of the road, a turnout overlooks **Sulphur Caldron,** where a highly acidic pool is filled with sulfur-tinted waters and the air is filled with the odor of hydrogen sulfide gas. Directly across the road is the Mud Volcano area, where a ⅔-mile loop trail provides what could be a tour through a very bad case of heartburn. Pick up a Park Service brochure (25 cents) from the box for descriptions of all the bizarre features. The area is in a constant state of flux as springs dry up or begin overflowing, killing trees in their path. One of the most interesting features is **Black Dragons Caldron,** where an explosive spring blasts constantly through a mass of seething black mud. The wildest place at Mud Volcano is **Dragon's Mouth,** which the Park Service notes is named for "the rhythmic belching of steam and the flashing tongue of water as it strikes out from the cavernous opening." Easy to imagine the fires of hell not far below this. The waters are 180° F. During the winter months, the Mud Volcano area is a good place to see elk or bison.

Along The Yellowstone

South of Mud Volcano, the road parallels the Yellowstone River. At **LeHardy Rapids** a boardwalk provides an overlook where early summer visitors see blush-red spawning cutthroats. In late summer, this part of the Yellowstone River is a very popular fly-fishing spot—some call it the finest stream cutthroat fishing in the world—and a good place to view ducks and swans. Earlier in the year, it's open only to the bears that gorge on the cutthroats. By the way, the Yellowstone River is the longest free-flowing (undammed) river in the Lower 48 states.

YELLOWSTONE LAKE

When first-time visitors see Yellowstone Lake, they are stunned by its magnitude. The statistics are impressive: 110 miles of shoreline, 20 miles north to south and 14 miles east to west, with an average depth of 139 feet and a maximum depth of 390 feet. This is North America's largest mountain lake. Yellowstone Lake can seem a sheet of glass laid to the horizon, and then just a half-hour later, a roiling ocean of whitecaps and wind-whipped waves. The changeable waters can be dangerous to those in canoes or small boats; a number of people have drowned. The water is covered by ice at least half of the year, and breakup does not come until late May or early June. Even in summer, water temperatures are often only in the 40s. David Folsom, who was part of an exploration party traveling through the area in 1869, described Yellowstone Lake as an

inland sea, its crystal waves dancing and sparkling in the sunlight as if laughing with joy for their wild freedom. It is a scene of transcendent beauty which has been viewed by few white men, and we felt glad to have looked upon it before its primeval solitude should be broken by the crowds of pleasure seekers which at no distant day will throng its shores.

Fishing Bridge

The area around famous Fishing Bridge (built in 1937) was for many years a favorite place to catch cutthroat trout. Unfortunately, these same fish are a major food source for grizzlies, and this area is considered some of the most important bear habitat in Yellowstone. Conflicts between bears and humans led to the death of 16 grizzlies here. To help restore grizzly populations, the Park Service banned fishing from Fishing Bridge in 1973 and tried to move the developments to the Grant Village area. Lobbying by folks from Cody (worried lest they lose some of the tourist traffic) has kept some of the facilities at Fishing Bridge from closing. Remaining facilities include an RV park run by TW Recreational Services, a Hamilton Store, and a gas station. **Fishing Bridge Visitor Center** has ex-

hibits of Yellowstone birds and animals and geology and is open daily 9-5 Memorial Day-Labor Day, with extended hours in midsummer. Call 344-7381, ext. 6150, for more information. A nice loop path is the **Elephant Back Mountain Trail,** which begins a mile south of Fishing Bridge Junction. This four-mile (RT) trail climbs 800 feet, providing panoramic views across Yellowstone Lake and into Pelican Valley.

Lake Yellowstone Hotel

Lake Hotel, the oldest extant park hostelry, was built in 1889-91 by the Northern Pacific Railroad and originally consisted of a simple boxlike structure facing onto Yellowstone Lake. The hotel was sold to Harry Child in 1901, and two years later Robert Reamer—the architect who designed Old Faithful Inn—was given free reign to transform this into a more attractive place, with distinctive Ionic columns added out front. It is the second-largest wooden-framed building in North America and requires 500 gallons of white paint each year to keep it in shape. During the 1960s and '70s the hotel fell into disrepair under the management of General Host Corporation. Finally, in disgust, the Park Service bought out the concession and leased it to TW Recreational Services, which has managed it since. Major renovations in the 1980s transformed the dowdy old structure into a luxurious grand hotel with much of the charm it had when President Calvin Coolidge stayed here in the 1920s. Today, Lake Hotel is one of the nicest lodging places in the park, with fine vistas out over the lake and comfortable quarters. Relax with a drink in the sunlit Sun Room.

Be sure to take a walk along the lakeshore out front of the hotel, where the Absaroka Range forms a backdrop far to the east. The highest mountain is Avalanche Peak (10,566 feet). Almost due south is the 10,308-foot summit of Mt. Sheridan, named for Gen. Philip Sheridan, a longtime supporter of expanding the park to include the Tetons. Watch for the big white pelicans catching fish on the lake. Just east of Yellowstone Hotel is the **Lake Ranger Station,** built in 1922 and on the National Register of Historic Places. Inside the octagonal main room is a massive fireplace, exposed log rafters, and rustic light fixtures. Not far away is **Lake Lodge,** another rustic log structure.

Inside is a reasonably priced cafeteria, while out back are row upon row of very plain cabins. A Hamilton Store stands nearby.

To West Thumb

The highway south from Lake Junction to West Thumb follows the lakeshore nearly the entire distance. A campground and a boat harbor are at **Bridge Bay,** along with a ranger station and a marina store. Immediately south of Bridge Bay is a turnoff to **Natural Bridge.** The mile-long road ends at a 59-foot-high natural span carved by the waters of Bridge Creek. Hikers will discover a three-mile trail that leaves from the campground and climbs to the rock bridge. Back on the main road, keep your eyes open for Canada geese and trumpeter swans as you drive south. **Gull Point Drive,** a two-mile-long side road, offers views of **Stevenson Island** just offshore, while farther south, **Frank Island** and tiny **Dot Island** become visible. The small **Potts Hot Springs Basin** just north of West Thumb is named for fur trapper Daniel T. Potts, one of the first white men to explore the Yellowstone country.

EAST ENTRANCE ROAD

Heading east from Fishing Bridge, the road follows the shore of Yellowstone Lake, passing country that escaped the fires of 1988. Three miles east of the bridge are Indian Pond and the trailhead for **Storm Point Trail,** a pleasant three-mile hike (RT). This loop trail is essentially level and goes past a large colony of yellow-bellied marmots before reaching Storm Point, where waves pound against the rocks. The trail is often closed because of grizzlies. North of here, the Pelican Valley is considered even more important grizzly habitat and is closed to all overnight camping or travel between 7 p.m. and 9 a.m. Even daytime use is not allowed during early summer. Before venturing out on the Storm Point Trail or in Pelican Valley, check at the Lake Ranger Station for bear info.

At **Steamboat Point** the road swings out along the shore, providing excellent views across the lake, along with a noisy fumarole. For an even better view (don't miss this one!), take the **Lake Butte Overlook** road, which continues one mile to a small parking area a thousand feet above the lake. This is a fine place to watch sunsets and to get a feeling for the enormity of Yellowstone Lake. Back on the main highway and heading east, Yellowstone Lake is soon behind you and visible in only a few spots as the road climbs gradually, passing scenic **Sylvan Lake,** a nice place for picnics. Just up the road is tiny Eleanor Lake (little more than a puddle) and the trail to 10,566-foot **Avalanche Peak.** This two-mile-long unmarked trail begins across the road on the east side of the creek and climbs steeply. It emerges from the forest halfway up, with the top gained via a scree slope. At the summit, you can see most of the peaks in the Absarokas, along with the Tetons, 70 miles away.

Immediately east of Eleanor Lake, the main road climbs to 8,541-foot **Sylvan Pass,** flanked by Hoyt Peak on the north and Top Notch Peak to the south. Steep scree slopes drop down both sides. East of Sylvan Pass, the road drops quickly along Middle Creek (a tributary of the Shoshone River), providing good views to the south of Mounts Langford and Doane. **East Entrance Ranger Station** was built by the Army in 1904. For many years, the road leading up to Sylvan Pass from the east took drivers across Corkscrew Bridge, a bridge that literally looped over itself as the road climbed steeply up the narrow valley. For more on the scenic country east of here, see "Wapiti Valley" (p. 374) in the "Bighorn Basin" chapter. The road leads to Cody.

INTO THE BACKCOUNTRY

The vast majority of Yellowstone visitors act as though they were chained to their cars with a hundred-yard tether; if they get out farther than that they might miss some other sight down the road. For the two percent or so who *do* abandon their cars, Yellowstone has much to offer beyond the spectacular geysers and canyons for which it is famous. Although many parts of the Yellowstone backcountry are heavily visited, regulations keep the sense of wildness intact by separating campsites and limiting the number of hikers. And if you head out early or late in the season, you'll discover solitude just a few miles from the traffic jams.

Much of Yellowstone consists of rolling lodgepole (or burned lodgepole) forests. With a few exceptions, anyone looking for dramatic alpine scenery would probably be better off heading to Grand Teton National Park or the Wind River Mountains. Despite this, the backcountry is enjoyable to walk through, and many trails lead to waterfalls, geysers, and hot springs. Besides, this is one of the finest places in America to view wildlife—including grizzlies—in a natural setting. Before August, when they start to die down, you should also be ready for the ubiquitous mosquitoes.

Rules And Regulations

A backcountry-use permit (free) is required of each overnight party and is available only in person at the various ranger stations within 48 hours of your hike. You'll need to specify exactly where you plan to camp each night and will be given a lengthy rundown of what to expect and precautions to take. In many parts of the park, hikers stay at campsites with pit toilets, fire rings, and bear poles. Bear management areas have special regulations that may include seasonal restrictions, day-use only, or minimum group sizes. Wood fires are not allowed in many areas, so be sure to have a gas stove for cooking. Pets are not allowed on the trails within Yellowstone, and special rules apply for those coming in with horses.

For a description of backcountry rules and suggestions for hiking and horse-packing, pick up a copy of the free park brochure *Beyond Road's End* at any ranger station. Those interested in horse-packing or llama trips should contact the park for a list of some 35 different outfitters authorized to operate in Yellowstone. They offer everythin from day-trips to week-long adventures deep into the backcountry.

More Info

I have selected a few two-to-four-day backcountry hikes covering various parts of Yellowstone. The park has over 1,200 miles of trails, so this is obviously a tiny sampling of the various hiking options. In addition, a number of day hikes are described above in conjunction with adjacent sights (such as Mt. Washburn trails in the "Tower Junction to Canyon" section and Mystic Falls in the "Upper Geyser Basin" section). A fine small guide to park trails is *Hiking the Yellowstone Backcountry,* by Orville E. Bach, Jr. (San Francisco: Sierra Club Books), but your best bet (extensively updated since the 1988 fires) is Mark C. Marschall's excellent *Yellowstone Trails,* published by the Yellowstone Association. The best topographic park map is produced by **Earthwalk Press,** 2239 Union St., Eureka, CA 95501. It includes all the major trails and shows the severity of burn from the 1988 fires, a considerable help when planning hiking trips. Get this map, as well as detailed topographic maps, from the Mammoth and Old Faithful visitor centers.

NORTH YELLOWSTONE TRAILS

Sportsman Lake Trail

The land west of Mammoth is some of the most rugged in Yellowstone, with a number of peaks topping 10,000 feet. Several trails cut westward across this country, one of the most interesting being the Sportsman Lake Trail (see maps on pages 317 and 343). It begins at Glen Creek Trailhead, five miles south of Mammoth, and follows Glen Creek for four miles before dropping into the Gardner River drainage. You'll need to ford the river twice; before late summer it can be dangerously deep, so do this hike later in the season. A spur trail makes it possible to climb **Electric Peak**, the 10,992-foot rocky summit just north of here; see Marschall's *Yellowstone Trails* for specifics. Beyond the river fords, the main trail climbs to Electric Divide and then drops to Sportsman Lake. West of here the trail splits and you can either continue to the right and reach US 191 (total distance 24 miles) or follow the Fan Creek and Fawn Pass trails back to the Mammoth area (approximately 40 miles RT). Warning: This country overflows with grizzly activity, and parties of four or more are required for travel here. Off-trail travel is prohibited.

Pebble Creek Trail

This 12-mile-long path cuts through a part of Yellowstone that is far away from the geysers and canyons for which the park is famous. The crowds don't come here, but the country is some of the nicest mountain scenery in the park. Pebble Creek Trail connects with the Northeast Entrance road at both ends, making access easy (see map, p. 317). You can start from either end, but if you begin from the Warm Creek Picnic area (1½ miles west of the entrance station), it's all downhill after the first steep climb. Best time to hike this trail is in late summer when the water levels are down (there are two fords) and the mosquitoes have abated. Lots of alpine flowers and grand mountain scenery along the way. Halfway down the valley, **Bliss Pass Trail** splits westward and crosses Pebble Creek (quite deep till late summer) before climbing 1,400 feet to the pass and then dropping down 2,700 feet to **Slough Creek Trail**. The latter takes you into Slough Creek Campground.

SOUTH YELLOWSTONE TRAILS

Shoshone Lake

Shoshone Lake—the largest lake in the lower 48 without direct road access—is probably the most visited part of Yellowstone's backcountry. Although its shoreline is dotted with more than 20 campsites, nearly every site fills up on midsummer nights. Access to Shoshone Lake is primarily from trailheads along the South Entrance Rd. and the road between West Thumb

and Old Faithful. Paths circle Shoshone Lake, although they are away from the shoreline much of the distance. You may see moose or elk along the way. On the west end of the lake, hikers are delighted to find **Shoshone Geyser Basin**, an area filled with small geysers, beautiful pools, and bubbling mudpots. **Minute Man Geyser** is the most notable one here, with a distinctive five-foot-tall cone and eruptions 10-40 feet into the air. Befitting its name, it often erupts every one to three minutes.

Heart Lake

The Heart Lake area is another extremely popular backcountry (and day-hiking) area, offering easy access along with all sorts of sights: a pretty lake, hot springs, and impressive mountain vistas. **Heart Lake Trail** begins just north of Lewis Lake and six miles south of Grant Village. The trail is fairly easy, climbing slowly for the first 5½ miles and then dropping down the other side to Heart Lake (2½ more miles) along the severely burned Witch Creek drainage. This creek is fed almost entirely by the hot springs and geysers scattered along it.

At Heart Lake Ranger Station the trail splits. Turning right, hike a half-mile to the **Mt. Sheridan Trail**, which heads west, climbing 2,850 vertical feet in a distance of 3½ miles. A fire lookout at the summit provides views across Yellowstone Lake and south to the Tetons. At the base of Mt. Sheridan and just to the north is another small thermal area that contains **Rustic Geyser** (eruptions to 50 feet every half-hour or so, but irregular) and **Columbia Pool**, among other attractions. Be very careful when walking here due to the overhanging rim at the pool edge. Although many people simply hike to Heart Lake for an overnight trip, there are many longer hikes one could take out of here. A complete loop around the lake is approximately 33 miles RT but requires two river fords that are at least to your knees in late July. Check with the rangers for current conditions. The Heart Lake area is prime grizzly habitat and is usually closed until the first of July. Do not take chances in this country.

Bechler River

The southwest portion of Yellowstone is known as Cascade Corner, a reference to its many tall

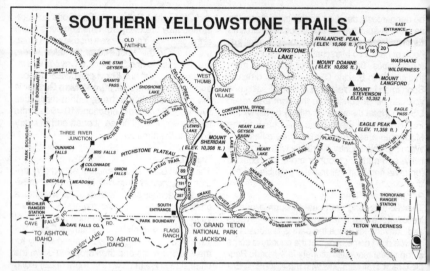

SOUTHERN YELLOWSTONE TRAILS

waterfalls; more than half of the park's falls are here. This country escaped the fires of 1988. Primary access is from either the Bechler Ranger Station (pronounced BECK-ler) or the Cave Falls Trailhead, both of which are well off the beaten path and must be reached via the Cave Falls Rd. from the Idaho side. It's 26 miles in from Ashton, Idaho, the last 10 of this on a gravel road. (Grassy Lake Rd. provides a narrow and rough connection from Flagg Ranch to Ashton.) All hikers must register at the Bechler Ranger Station, even if they are heading out from Cave Falls Trailhead (three miles farther down the road). Cave Falls itself is a very wide, but not particularly tall, drop along the Falls River. It's named for a cave on the west end of the waterfall. The Forest Service has a campground ($5) here.

A maze of trails cuts across the Bechler country, leading to the many waterfalls and other attractions. One very popular hike goes from Bechler Ranger Station to the Old Faithful area (or vice versa), a distance of 32 miles. From Bechler, the trail cuts across the expansive Bechler Meadows and then up narrow Bechler Canyon, passing Colonnade, Ouzel, and Iris falls along the way. Many people stop overnight in Three River Junction before punching on up to the Continental Divide. Beyond this, the trail

cuts above Shoshone Lake and on to Lone Star Geyser and the trailhead at Kepler Cascades. It's best to hike this route in late summer or early fall after the meadows have dried out a bit and the mosquitoes are down to a dull roar. Midsummer finds standing water and the ever-friendly leaches, although it is possible to skirt around the meadows.

The Thorofare

If any part of Yellowstone deserves the title untamed wilderness, it has to be the Thorofare. Situated along Two Ocean Plateau and cut through by the upper Yellowstone River, this broad expanse of unroaded country reaches from Yellowstone Lake into the Teton Wilderness south of the park. This is some of the most remote country in the lower 48—more than 30 miles in any direction from the nearest road. Because of the distances involved, it's best to traverse the Thorofare via horseback. Access is from the Heart Lake area, via the Thorofare Trail, or from the Teton Wilderness. The **Thorofare Trail** begins at Nine-Mile Trailhead on the East Entrance Rd. and hugs the shore of Yellowstone Lake for the first 17 miles. This stretch was spared from the fires of 1988 and provides some incredible opportunities for sunsets over the lake. Canoeists sometimes paddle along the lakeshore and camp. Because of grizzly activity, off-trail travel is prohibited until mid-August, and you need to be very cautious along streams, where bears may be fishing for spawning cutthroats. Longer trips are also possible, but they require deep fords and may not even be possible till late summer. Check at the Lake Ranger Station for current conditions.

WINTER IN YELLOWSTONE

During Yellowstone's first 75 years as a park, winter visitation was almost unknown. The only people in the park were winterkeepers who spent months at a time with no contact with the world outside. This began to change in 1949, when snow-plane tours were first offered from the West Entrance. The planes could only hold two people—the driver and a passenger—so visitation barely topped 30 people that winter. In 1955, snowcoaches were permitted to come into Yellowstone, and more than 500 people arrived that winter, though few stayed overnight. The first snowmobiles arrived in 1964, when they were still a novelty. With the increasing interest in cross-country skiing and snowmobiling, the park opened Old Faithful Snow Lodge in the winter of 1971-72, and since then, winter use has rocketed five-fold; today, over 100,000 people visit Yellowstone Park each winter. On busy days, more than a thousand snowmobiles roar into the park through the West Yellowstone gate. While these numbers pale in comparison to summer visitation, there is growing concern that skiers and snowmobilers could adversely affect the park's wildlife at a time when they are already under great stress.

Approximately 60% of Yellowstone's winter use consists of people who come in on quick day-tours of the park via snowmobile and then spend the night back in one of the gateway towns. To see Yellowstone right, however, it's best to spend more time, either snow camping or staying at Mammoth or Old Faithful. Winter transforms Yellowstone into an extraordinarily beautiful place where the fires and brimstone of hell meet the bitter cold and snow of winter. The snow often averages four feet in depth but can exceed 10 feet on mountain passes. The snow is usually quite dry, although late in the season conditions deteriorate as temperatures rise. Early in the winter or after major storms, backcountry skiing can be very difficult due to the deep powder. Temperatures generally fall in the 10-30° F range during the day, while nights frequently dip well below zero. (The record is -66° F, recorded on Feb. 9, 1933.) Winds can make these temperatures feel even colder, so visitors should come prepared for extreme conditions.

The thermal basins are a real winter treat. Hot springs that are simply colorful pools in

YELLOWSTONE NATIONAL PARK

the Schwatcha Winter Expedition (U.S. Army) of 1887 at Obsidian Cliff summer send up billows of steam in the winter, coating the nearby trees with thick layers of ice turning them into "ghost trees." The geysers put on astounding displays as boiling water meets frigid air; steam from Old Faithful can tower 1,000 feet into the air! Bison and elk gather around the hot springs, soaking up the heat and searching for dried grasses, while eagles are often seen flying over the heated waters of Firehole River. The bison are perhaps the most interesting to watch, as they swing their enormous heads from side to side to shovel snow off the grass. Grand Canyon of the Yellowstone is another place transformed by the snow and cold. Although the water still flows, the falls are surrounded by a tall cone of ice, while the canyon walls lie under deep snow.

Roads

Most of Yellowstone's roads officially close to cars when the first heavy snows block the passes, and by the first of November things are generally shut down all over, except for the 56 miles between Mammoth and Cooke City. Roads don't open for cars again until May, and sometimes not until early June. The roads are open to snowmobiles and snowcoaches from mid-Dec. to mid-March. The rest of the winter you'll only find skiers and park personnel on the snow-covered roads. During the winter, the most popular (and crowded) times to visit Yellowstone are around Christmas and New Year's and over the Presidents' Day weekend in February. If you plan to arrive at these times, make reservations six months to a year in advance. The rest of the winter, you should probably reserve at least three months ahead.

Accommodations And Services

During the winter, only two places offer lodging inside the park. **Mammoth Hotel** is the only one accessible by road, while **Old Faithful Snow Lodge and Cabins** provide accommodations and a proximity to many miles of skiing trails. See the lodging chart for rates. Mammoth also offers two- and six-night package trips in the winter months. Each has a restaurant, a lounge, and a gift shop. For a fee, Mammoth also offers a variety of special events, along with ice skating and hot tubs. **Warming huts** are located at Madison, Canyon, West Thumb, Fishing Bridge, and Mammoth Terraces. All are open 24 hours and contain restrooms and snack machines. Those at Mammoth and Canyon also have snack bars offering hot chili or soup. The Mammoth general store is open for groceries and supplies, but supplies are not available at Old Faithful.

Only the Mammoth and Old Faithful visitor centers are open during the winter. Free ranger-led activities include ski tours, snowshoe hikes, snowmobile tours, films, slide shows, and walks. Check the winter edition of *Yellowstone Today* for details. The only wintertime campground is at Mammoth, where temperatures are milder and there is less snow. **Karst Stage**, tel. (406) 586-8567, has daily bus service from Bozeman, Montana, to Mammoth and West Yellowstone in the winter.

Snowcoaches

The easiest and most fun way to get into Yellowstone in the winter is on the ungainly snowcoaches, machines that look like something the Norwegian Army might have used during WW II. Most were actually made by a Canadian company, Bombidier. The windows fog up (hence the spray bottles of antifreeze), and they can be noisy. Despite their ancient condition and Spartan interior, these beasts still work well and can carry 10 passengers along with gear (two suitcases pp) and skis. The more modern ones (Hagglunds) based at Mammoth are actually not nearly as comfortable as the older models on the bumpy snowpacked roads, and the separate back compartment makes communication with the driver/guide difficult.

A variety of snowcoach tours are available through **TW Recreational Services**, Yellowstone National Park, WY 82190, tel. 344-7311. Roundtrip rates to Old Faithful Snow Lodge are: $61 from Flagg Ranch (where the plowing ends just south of Yellowstone), $53 from West Yellowstone, and $59 from Mammoth. An excellent all-day tour of the south loop is $61 from Old Faithful. See below for combination snow-coach and cross-country-skiing trips. For any of these trips, be sure to make reservations well in advance. During the winter, **Gray Line**, tel. 733-4325 or (800) 443-6133, has daily bus runs from Jackson to Flagg Ranch for $25 OW, arriving in time to meet the snowcoach departures for Yellowstone.

Yellowstone Alpen Guides, Box 518, West Yellowstone, MT 59758, tel. (406) 646-9591, offers a variety of snowcoach day-trips from West Yellowstone into the park. **Yellowstone Expeditions**, tel. (406) 646-9333 or (800) 728-9333, in West Yellowstone runs some of the strangest vehicles in the park, converted vans jacked up above tracks and skis. Excellent four-to-five-day tours ($95 pp/day) include housing in yurts at Canyon, as well as food, lodging, and ski guides. Add in $60 for roundtrip snowcoach fare to the park. Recommended.

Cross-country Skiing

Skis provide the finest way to see Yellowstone in the winter. Rent them at shops in Jackson, Cody, West Yellowstone, Gardiner, and Pahaska, or in the park at Old Faithful and Mammoth. (Snowshoes can also be rented and ski waxes are available at Mammoth and Old Faithful.) The Old Faithful area is the center for skiing within Yellowstone, with trails circling the Upper Geyser Basin and leading to nearby sights. Similar ski trails (marked but not groomed) can be found in the Tower Fall, Canyon, and Mammoth areas. Get free ski-trail maps at the visitor centers.

Skiers sometimes assume that they can't possibly cause problems for Yellowstone's wildlife, but studies show that elk and bison often move away from skiers, which forces the animals to expend energy they need to survive through the bitterly cold winters. It's best to stay on the trails and to keep from skiing into areas where elk or bison may be disturbed by your presence.

TW Recreational Services, tel. 344-7311, operates **skier shuttles** ($7-9 RT) from Mammoth to Tower Junction, Blacktail Plateau, and the Swan Lake Flats and Indian Creek areas. A similar skier shuttle (via snowcoach) is available from Old Faithful to Fairy Falls or the Continental Divide area for $7. The latter is a one-way service that allows you to ski back to the lodge. A variety of other guided snowcoach-and-ski trips are also available, including a Canyon ski tour ($79 RT) and a Lower Geyser Basin afternoon ski tour ($22). Park naturalists sometimes lead ski trips from Old Faithful to nearby sights.

Yellowstone's roads are heavily traveled by snowmobiles and snowcoaches, making for all sorts of potential conflicts. Be sure to keep to the right while skiing. If you're planning a longer backcountry trip, pick up a use permit at one of the ranger stations. A thorough understanding of winter camping and survival is imperative before you head out on any overnight trip. For more on skiing and winter visitation in the park, get the small booklet *Winter at Old Faithful,* by Frank Balthis, Steve Bogen, and Fred Hirschmann (Yellowstone: Firehole Press). It's available in the Old Faithful Visitor Center.

Snowmobiles

Winter snowmobile use in Yellowstone has risen in recent years, and it isn't uncommon to meet long lines of machines ripping down the roads at any time of the day, disrupting Yellowstone's pristine winter silence with their noise and smoke. Despite the fact that the five national forests surrounding Yellowstone have many hundreds of miles of groomed trails, along with thousands of square miles of terrain open to the machines, Yellowstone's 180 miles of roads have become the focus of this mechanized winter onslaught. Environmentalists fear that the problems will worsen if the proposed Continental Divide Snowmobile Trail is opened through Grand Teton National Park, thus attracting even more 'bilers.

If you really must come into Yellowstone by snowmobile, please show a few courtesies and precautions. In particular, stay on the roads and stay well away from the bison and elk that are commonly found along or on the roads. This is a stressful time of the year for them already, without being harassed by a steady stream of machines. If skiers are on the road, slow down and give them a wide berth as you pass. The speed limit (45 mph) is enforced, and one of the most bizarre Yellowstone sights is a park ranger waiting in a speed trap with his radar gun, ready to catch speeding sleds. Park rangers lead 1½-hour snowmobile tours from the Canyon Warming Hut on weekends.

Snowmobiles are available for rent from all four sides of the park, with West Yellowstone being the most popular entry point. They can also be rented at Mammoth and Old Faithful within the park. Contact the chambers of commerce in West Yellowstone, Jackson, Cody, or Gardiner for a listing of companies. Snowmobiles generally cost $100-140/day, with the lowest rates generally out of West Yellowstone. Snowmobile suits run another $10-12/day. Most 'bilers join guided tours through the park. Gas can be purchased at Mammoth, Canyon, and Old Faithful.

YELLOWSTONE PRACTICALITIES

Entrance to Yellowstone costs $10 per vehicle or $4 for individuals entering by bicycle, foot, motorcycle, snowmobile, or bus. The pass covers both Yellowstone and Grand Teton national parks and is good for seven days. If you're planning to be here longer or to make more visits, get an annual pass covering both parks for $15, or the Golden Eagle Passport, which is good for all national parks, for $25 a year. The Golden Age Passport is free to anyone over 62, as is the Golden Access Passport for disabled individuals. Both of these also give you 50% reductions in camping fees.

Upon entering the park, you'll receive a Yellowstone map, along with a copy of *Yellowstone Today,* a quarterly newspaper that describes facilities and services and provides camping, fishing, and backcountry information. This is the best source for up-to-date park information. It's also packed with enough warnings to scare off a platoon of Marines. Examples include cautions against falling trees, letting your children wander, bathing in thermal pools (infections and/or amoebic meningitis), unpredictable wildlife, frost heaves, bicycling, rock climbing, scalding water, driving while intoxicated, theft, and crossing streams. And, oh yes, "swimming is generally discouraged." (Maybe they should just close Yellowstone entirely!) If you're planning a trip to Yellowstone, write the park and request a copy of another free publication, *Yellowstone Guide.* The address is: Yellowstone National Park, WY 82190, tel. 344-7381.

Visitor Centers
The Park Service maintains visitor centers in five different places: Mammoth Hot Springs, Old Faithful, Canyon, Fishing Bridge, and Grant Village. All of these places sell maps and natural-history books covering the park and surrounding areas. The hours and seasons are listed in "Touring Yellowstone" (above). Park interpreters (most folks call them rangers, but the real rangers actually do more law enforcement than education) offer slide shows, films, hikes, kids programs, campfire talks, and other activities at the various campgrounds and visitor centers. These are always favorites of visitors, and on summer days you can choose from any one of more than two-dozen different Yellowstone activities. For a complete listing of the many daily events, stop by a visitor center to pick up a copy of *Discover Yellowstone* (50 cents).

Yellowstone Association
Founded in 1933, the Yellowstone Association is a nonprofit organization that serves an educational and scientific role in the park by producing books and pamphlets, helping fund the Yellowstone Institute, and assisting in the visitor centers. Members receive a 15% discount on books. Contact them for membership information ($25 and up), along with a listing of Yellowstone books, at Box 117, Yellowstone National Park, WY 82190, tel. 344-7381, ext. 2349.

GETTING AROUND

The speed limit on all park roads is 45 mph, and it is strictly enforced, although during the summer you're not likely to approach this speed, since long lines of traffic form behind monstrous RVs. Most roads in Yellowstone close with the first heavy snows, generally around Nov. 1, and open again around May 1. They reopen in sections, with the roads connecting Mammoth to West Yellowstone opening first, and Dunraven Pass being plowed last. Only the road between Mammoth and Cooke City is kept plowed all winter long. If you're planning a trip early or late in the season, call the park (tel. 344-7381) for current road conditions.

Buses And Tours

During the summer, most people come into Yellowstone in private cars or RVs, but there *are* other ways of getting around. **Karst Stage,** tel. (406) 586-8567, has summertime buses (Tues., Thurs., and Fri.) that stop in West Yellowstone, Montana, Old Faithful, and Mammoth, continuing on to Gardiner and Bozeman, Montana.

TW Recreational Services, tel. 344-7311, offers full-day bus tours from Canyon Lodge, Lake Hotel, Old Faithful Inn, Fishing Bridge RV Park, and Grant Village. Tours of either the upper or lower loops run approximately $23 adults or $11 for kids. A longer "Grand Loop" tour (not recommended unless you're into sensory overload) is $23 from Mammoth.

Similar loop tours ($30) are available out of West Yellowstone, Montana, from **Gray Line,** tel. (406) 646-9374, or **Yellowstone Tours,** tel. (406) 646-7337. More Yellowstone tours out of Cody ($41) aboard **Powder River Tours,** tel. 587-5544 or (800) 442-3682; and Jackson ($36) aboard **Gray Line,** tel. 733-4325 or (800) 443-6133. Gray Line also has one-way service between Yellowstone and Jackson for $25 in either direction (but reserve ahead).

FACILITIES AND SERVICES

Shopping And Gifts

Nearly every road junction in Yellowstone has some sort of general store, gas station, gift shop, or other facility. **Hamilton Stores** are the most interesting, since they tend to be located in rustic old log structures and staffed by friendly retired folks and fresh college kids. All the standard tourist supplies and paraphernalia can be found, along with groceries, camping equipment, books, and fishing supplies. You'll find jewelry, pottery, and other Native American items at the **Indian Handicrafts Shop** within Old Faithful Inn.

Food

Restaurants are located at Mammoth Hot Springs, Lake Hotel, Old Faithful Inn, Old Faithful Snow Lodge, Grant Village, Roosevelt Lodge, and Canyon Lodge, offering reasonably priced and reasonably good meals. The chocolate pecan pie at Mammoth Hot Springs is noteworthy. Dinner reservations are required at all of these except Canyon Lodge and Old Faithful Snow Lodge. Roosevelt Lodge offers an "Old West" barbecue dinner, while cafeteria food can be found at Lake Lodge, Old Faithful Lodge, and Canyon Lodge. Get box lunches from any of these places. In addition, fast-food eateries (not the chains) and/or delis are found at Mammoth, Old Faithful, Lake, and Canyon. General stores with at least some groceries are at Mammoth, Canyon, Old Faithful, Grant Village, and Lake; the biggest selection is at Canyon General Store.

Other Services

Medical facilities include clinics at Old Faithful and Mammoth Hot Springs and a small hospital at Lake. Check at any visitor center for a schedule of church services. Foreign currency can be exchanged at front desks in the various park hotels, and you'll discover an ATM machine (Cirrus and Plus networks) in Old Faithful Inn. For a complete directory of the many other Yellowstone visitor services—including one-hour film processing—see *Yellowstone Today,* which you get upon entering the park.

CAMPGROUNDS

Tent camping in Yellowstone's early days left a bit to be desired. One 1884 tourist noted that during the height of the summer season, "the principle upon which the beds are populated is said to be the addition of visitors so long as they may arrive, or until the occupants 'go for their guns.' The plan is simple, and relieves the authorities of responsibility." It's still crowded in the park, but generally not this bad! Camping is available at a dozen sites scattered along the road network. Bridge Bay RV Park can be reserved up to eight weeks in advance between mid-June and Labor Day by calling Mistix at (800) 365-2267. Reserve spaces at Fishing

YELLOWSTONE CAMPGROUNDS

CAMPGROUND	APPROXIMATE SEASON	FEE	FEATURES
Bridge Bay	May 22-Sept. 14	$10	fills early, reservable
Canyon Village	June 5-Sept. 8	$8	fills early, hard-sided RVs only, showers
Fishing Bridge	May 22-Sept. 7	$18	fills early, RVs only, showers
Grant Village	June 22-Oct. 12	$8	fills early, showers
Indian Creek	June 5-Sept. 14	$6	
Lewis Lake	June 12-Nov. 1	$6	fills early
Madison	May 1-Nov. 1	$8	fills early, dump station
Mammoth	Year-round	$8	
Norris	May 15-Sept. 28	$8	fills early
Pebble Creek	June 12-Sept. 8	$6	
Slough Creek	May 22-Nov. 1	$6	
Tower Fall	May 22-Sept. 14	$6	fills early

Bridge RV park by calling TW Recreational Services at 344-7311. All other campgrounds in Yellowstone are on a first-come, first-served basis. Only Mammoth Campground remains open year-round. Roadside or parking lot camping is not allowed, and rangers *do* enforce this prohibition.

During peak season, all campsites in Yellowstone fill *before noon,* so get there early! The busiest weekends are—not surprisingly—around July 4 and Labor Day. Yellowstone's most popular campgrounds fill up even in late fall and early summer. When everything else is full, folks head to campgrounds on surrounding Forest Service lands or to motels in the gateway towns. See "Shoshone National Forest" (p. 373) for areas east of Yellowstone and "Jackson Hole Campgrounds" (p. 276) for areas to the south. Other campgrounds (both public and private) are described under the various park gateways—Cody, Jackson, Dubois, West Yellowstone, Gardiner, Silver Gate, and Cooke City. The farther you get from Yellowstone, the more likely you are to find space. Campers will be happy to know that showers are available at Old Faithful Lodge, Grant Village Campground, Lake Lodge, Fishing Bridge, RV Park, and Canyon Village Campground.

HOTELS AND CABINS

At the turn of the century, most visitors to Yellowstone stayed in park hotels rather than roughing it on the ground. Three of these wonderful old lodging places remain: Old Faithful Inn, Lake Yellowstone Hotel, and Mammoth Hot Springs Hotel. They are also remarkably inexpensive; see the accommodations chart for specifics. (Hot tip: the best views of Old Faithful are from Old Faithful Inn suites 176 and 177.)

TW Recreational Services, tel. 344-7311, is the official concessionaire for lodging. In addition to the three hotels, they operate everything from very plain cabins to comfortable motel rooms. Most of these are open early June to mid-September. During the winter, only Mammoth Hot Springs Hotel and the Old Faithful Snow Lodge are open. Try to book rooms at least six months ahead. Many more motel rooms are available in the towns that surround the park.

Following a fine old Yellowstone tradition, none of these rooms have phones, radios, or TVs. What they do offer is the chance to relax in comfortable accommodations and explore the magical world outside.

YELLOWSTONE ACCOMMODATIONS

Note: These rates are for one or two people. Extra persons are $7 each; children under 12 stay free. The less expensive rooms and cabins generally have bathrooms nearby, but not in the rooms. Call TW Recreational Services at 344-7311 for reservations.

LOCATION	HOTEL ROOMS	CABINS	APPROXIMATE SEASON
Canyon Lodge Cabins		$43-72	June 12-Aug. 31
Grant Village		$56-60	June 1-Sept. 27
Lake Lodge Cabins		$39-72	June 8-Sept. 13
Lake Yellowstone Hotel and Cabins	$66-260	$49	May 18-Sept. 27
Mammoth Hot Springs Hotel and Cabins	$35-150 $36-150	$24-49	May 22-Sept. 20 Dec. 19-Feb. 28
Old Faithful Inn	$35-170		May 8-Oct. 11
Old Faithful Lodge Cabins	$19-31		May 22-Sept. 13
Old Faithful Snow Lodge and Cabins	$35 $36-82	$49-72 $55-72	May 16-Oct. 11 Dec. 16-Mar. 14
Roosevelt Lodge Cabins		$19-49	June 6-Aug. 31

FISHING

In the early years of the park, fish from Yellowstone Lake were a specialty at the various hotels, and because there was no limit on the take, up to 7,500 pounds of fish were caught each year. By the 1970s, Yellowstone Lake had been devastated by overfishing, and new regulations were needed. Beginning in 1973, bait fishing was banned, Fishing Bridge was closed to anglers, and catch-and-release rules were put into place. Because of these regulations, Yellowstone National Park has achieved an almost mythical status when it comes to fishing—the average cutthroat caught in Yellowstone Lake measures 18 inches. Increased fish populations have also been a boon for wildlife, especially grizzlies, bald eagles, and osprey. The most commonly caught fish in Yellowstone are cutthroat, rainbow, brown, and brook trout, and mountain whitefish. Grayling are found in the Madison, Firehole, and Gallatin rivers, while lake trout swim in Shoshone, Lewis, Heart, and Grebe lakes. Above the falls on the Yellowstone River (and in Yellowstone Lake), the only trout is the native cutthroat. The best Yellowstone Lake fishing is from boats rather than from the shoreline. There are several good books on fishing the waters of Yellowstone; see the Booklist for specifics.

Fishing Regs

In most parts of Yellowstone, the fishing season extends Memorial Day through October, but check the regulations for specifics. Anglers don't need a state fishing license but must obtain a free permit from Yellowstone National Park, available from any visitor center or ranger station. Note that some waters are closed to fishing entirely, often to prevent conflicts with bears. Only artificial lures are allowed, lead is not allowed, and a catch-and-release policy (with exceptions) is in effect for cutthroat and rainbow trout and grayling. Many of the fish are caught over and over again; a typical fish may be caught 45 times in its life! Barbless hooks are preferable for catch-and-release fishing, since they cause less damage and are easier to remove.

BICYCLING

One of the finest ways to see Yellowstone is by bicycle. Unfortunately, Yellowstone's roads tend to be narrow and have little or no shoulders, making for dangerous conditions. These problems are exacerbated early in the year by high snowbanks, so bikes are not allowed on some roads. Call 344-7381 for current road conditions. Some stretches—especially the roads over Dunraven Pass and between Madison and Norris—are filled with potholes. If you're planning a cycling trip through Yellowstone, be sure to wear a helmet and high-visibility clothing. A bike mirror also helps.

The best times to ride are in the morning before traffic thickens or late in the afternoon before the light begins to fade. The best roads to ride (less traffic and better visibility and shoulders) are the Northeast Entrance Rd. (Tower to Cooke City), Canyon to Lake, and Lake to Grant Village. There are a couple of short bike/hiking trails in the Old Faithful and Midway Geyser Basin areas, but the other roads are all open to cars. Bikes are not allowed on backcountry trails. For more on cycling in the park, get Gene Colling's *The Bicyclist's Guide to Yellowstone National Park,* (Helena, Montana: Falcon Press).

OTHER RECREATION

During the summer months TW Recreational Services, tel. 344-7311, offers a variety of recreational opportunities in Yellowstone. **Horseback rides** are available at Mammoth Hot Springs, Canyon Lodge, and Roosevelt Lodge for $11/hour. Roosevelt also has daily **stagecoach rides** ($6 adults or $5 kids) and old-west dinner cookouts combined with a stage or horseback ride for $25-36 adults or $17-28 kids. Get tickets from any hotel or lodge in the park. Bridge Bay Marina runs hour-long scenic **boat tours** of Yellowstone Lake ($7 adults or $4 children), **motorboat rentals** ($20/hour), as well as **guided fishing trips** ($35-50/hour for up to six people). Rent rowboats for $19/day.

If you're bringing your own boat or canoe to Yellowstone, pick up a park permit ($10 for motorized and $5 for nonmotorized vessels) at the Lake Ranger Station or Grant Village Visitor Center. All streams are closed to watercraft with the exception of the Lewis River between Shoshone and Lewis lakes. Motorboats are allowed only on Lewis Lake and parts of Yellowstone Lake.

Many people are disappointed to discover that there are no places in Yellowstone where you can soak in the hot springs. Not only is this illegal, but it can be dangerous, since temperatures often approach boiling, and bathers can cause severe damage to these surprisingly fragile natural wonders. Legal bathing pools are found in cold-water streams that have hot springs feeding into them. You're not allowed to enter the source pool or stream itself. Locations of these legal bathing streams are not publicized.

GREATER YELLOWSTONE COALITION

The most important environmental group involved with protecting Yellowstone and the surrounding public lands from development is the Greater Yellowstone Coalition. This private nonprofit organization is involved in all sorts of controversies within the 10-million-acre Greater Yellowstone Ecosystem—from wolf reintroduction to timber harvesting and mineral development. It represents some 4,000 members and publishes a quarterly newsletter detailing various issues. Membership costs $25 and up; write GYC, Box 1874, Bozeman, MT 59771, tel. (406) 586-1593.

WORKING IN YELLOWSTONE

During the summer months, Yellowstone National Park provides several thousand jobs for both young and old. Most of these are with the concessionaires, but the Park Service also hires a cadre of park rangers, interpretive staff, maintenance workers, and backcountry rangers. Get applications from: National Park Service, Seasonal Employment Unit, 18th and C St. NW, Room 2229, Washington, D.C. 20240. In addition, volunteer jobs are available in Yellowstone through the **Student Conservation Association** at Box 550C, Charlestown, NH 03603. For both paid and volunteer positions, you need to apply early, before mid-January. Paid Park Service positions require U.S. citizenship.

Hamilton Stores is the oldest privately owned concession in the entire national park system, having been around since 1915. Contact the company in the winter months at: Personnel Dept., Hamilton Stores Inc., 1709 W. College St., Bozeman, MT 59715, tel. (406) 587-2208, or in summer at Box 250, West Yellowstone, MT 59758, tel. (406) 646-7325. **TW Recreational Services** (once a division of TWA, but now owned by Canteen Corporation) is in charge of lodging, restaurants, bus tours, boat rentals, horse rides, and similar services. It hires more than 2,000 people each summer. For more info, write TW Recreational Services, Human Resources Dept., Yellowstone National Park, WY 82190, tel. 344-7901. Many of the employees of these companies are either college students (who live in dorm-style accommodations) or retired folks (who live in their RVs). Don't expect high pay; entry positions start around $4.25 an hour, with meals and lodging deducted from this. It's best to apply early in the year for summer jobs. The more competitive winter positions often go to those with previous work experience in the park.

GATEWAY TOWNS

Yellowstone National Park is most commonly entered via one of several Wyoming or Montana towns. The Wyoming entry points—Cody, Dubois, and Jackson—are described in other chapters. The four towns listed below are in Montana but lie just across the border and are important gateways into the park. Note that the area code for all these Montana towns is 406.

WEST YELLOWSTONE

West Yellowstone, Montana, is the definitive western tourist town. With a year-round population of only 800 (twice that in the summer) but more than 45 motels, it's pretty easy to see what makes the cash registers ring. The West Entrance gate—most popular of all Yellowstone entrances—lies just a couple hundred feet away. The town looks nicer than it did a few years back but still isn't particularly noteworthy. Motels, restaurants, T-shirt stores, and gift shops crowd the streets.

West Yellowstone is surrounded by the Gallatin (GAL-a-tin) National Forest, with Targhee National Forest only a few miles to the south. "West," as the town is known locally, began in 1908 when the first Union Pacific Yellowstone Special rolled into town from Salt Lake City. From here, stagecoaches took tourists into the park. The historic stone depot and a neighboring dining hall still stand, although the last passengers stepped off the train in 1959. Hamilton Stores—one of the primary Yellowstone concessionaires—has its summer offices in West Yellowstone.

Sights
Museum of the Yellowstone, tel. 646-7814, is a stone-and-log structure located right along the main highway into the park. Entrance is $4 for adults, $3 for seniors, students, and kids, and $10 for families. Kids under nine get in free. It is open daily 8 a.m.-10 p.m. May-Oct. and has a good collection of regional books for sale. The museum houses excellent displays on black and grizzly bears, an extensive Plains Indian collection, mountain-men and U.S. cavalry artifacts, an exhibit on the Yellowstone fires of 1988, and various videos. The grand old park bus parked out front was last used in 1959.

Right next door is another wonderful stone structure (built in 1925) that served until the late 1950s as an elegant Union Pacific Dining Lodge. It now houses the **International Fly Fishing Center,** tel. 646-9541, a free museum run by the Federation of Fly Fishers. Open summers only, daily 11-8. The building has a spacious dining hall containing an enormous fireplace, a 45-foot-tall vaulted ceiling, and handmade light fixtures. Displays cover the art of fly tying and aquatic insects. An aquarium contains baby trout, and an art gallery features paintings of fish and fishing (of course). Out back, find a fly-casting pond where you can practice. Local fly-fishing shops offer classes, and free casting lessons are given on Saturday and Sunday evenings. They even supply the rods. For $20 a year, you can join the organization that sponsors this. There are five different **fly-fishing shops** in town, a reflection of the sport's importance in Yellowstone. See the chamber of commerce for a list.

Family-run **Eagle's Store,** on the corner of Canyon and Yellowstone, tel. 646-9300, is well worth a stop. Built in the 1920s, this historic log building contains all the standard tourist knick-knacks, along with quality western clothing and a delightful old-fashioned soda fountain (summer only).

New to West Yellowstone is **Grizzly Park,** a controversial wildlife theme park that will supposedly replicate grizzly- and black-bear habitats. We're talking about a $28 million project covering 87 acres and housing—in addition to the bears—an IMAX theater, a museum, a resort hotel, a gift shop, two restaurants, and two fast-food places. Yellowstone National Park officials are not pleased at the prospect of such a massive development within a few hundred feet of their border. Park Service Director James Ridenour noted, "Putting a grizzly park on the edge of Yellowstone is like putting a roller rink next to the Sistine Chapel!" The first stage—including several bears—opens in 1993.

Hostel

Budget travelers will be happy to discover the **West Yellowstone International Hostel** (not affiliated with AYH) in the historic Madison Hotel, 139 Yellowstone Ave., tel. 646-7745. Built in 1912 and on the National Register of Historic Places, the hostel has a rustic downstairs lobby but no kitchen. Very friendly owner. Rates are $14 pp ($15 for non-hostel members) in dorm rooms or $33 d and up for a private hotel room. It's open late May through mid-Oct. only, but almost always has space. No smoking.

Motels

The proximity to Yellowstone makes the town of West Yellowstone an exceptionally popular stopping place for vacationers in both summer and winter. It is also a fairly pricey place to stay, with most rooms costing $50 and up during the peak summer season. Every street is lined with motels, so I won't try to list all of them, but if you're a member of AAA, check their *TourBook,* which includes at least 18 of the best. (Rates are often substantially lower for AAA members, too.) Be aware that during the summer everything fills up by early afternoon, so get there early or make advance reservations. To be certain of a place in July and August, make reservations by April! The chamber of commerce's free brochure lists the West Yellowstone motels. Make reservations for any of them by calling (800) 521-5241 (summer only).

Two recommended budget-end places are **Al's Westward Ho Motel,** 16 Boundary St., tel. 646-7331, where rooms are $34 s or d and up, (kitchenettes $3 more), and **Alpine Motel,** 120 Madison Ave., tel. 646-7544, where rooms start at $32 s or d. Both these are open May-Oct. only. For inexpensive year-round lodging, head to **Lazy G Motel,** 123 Hayden, tel. 646-7586, where nice rooms start for $35 s or d. Excellent new accommodations can be found at **Brandin' Iron Motel,** 201 Canyon St., tel. 646-9411 or (800) 231-5991. Rooms start for $52 s or $61 d, with access to whirlpools and a hot tub.

The fanciest lodging in West Yellowstone is the block-long **Stage Coach Inn,** 209 Madison Ave., tel. 646-7381 or (800) 842-2882, owned by Hamilton Stores. Rooms start for $63 s or $69 d in the old wing and include access to a sauna and hot tubs. The impressive lobby is a treat. If you're willing to drive the extra seven miles west of town, **Lionshead Super 8 Lodge,** tel. 646-9584 or (800) 843-1991, has quality rooms, a very nice country setting, and a sauna and hot tub. Rooms start at $48 s or $51 d. It's very popular with the retirement crowd who park RVs in the "campground" for $15.

Families may prefer renting a furnished condo from **Yellowstone Townhouses** on Horse Rd., tel. 646-9331, or **Geyser Apartments,** 318 Geyser St., tel. 646-7518. Two-bedroom units go for around $65 per night including a kitchen. **Sportsman's High Bed & Breakfast,** 750 Deer St., tel. 646-7865, is in an attractive home eight miles west of town. Very nice accommodations and a big breakfast cost $70 s or $75 d. Another nice B&B is **Rainbow Point Inn,** along Hebgen Lake, tel. 646-7848.

Camping

The closest public camping (RVs only) is at **Baker's Hole** ($7; open late May to mid-Sept.), three miles north of West Yellowstone. Tent campers will need to go to **Hebgen Lake,** eight miles north of town, where five different camping areas are strung westward along the lake; the farthest is 23 miles from West Yellowstone. Rates range from free (at the undeveloped sites) to $7 a night, and reservations (additional $6) can be made by calling (800) 282-2267. The Forest Service also maintains three public-use cabins ($20/night) in the country around here; check at the ranger station for details.

West Yellowstone has at least half a dozen different private campgrounds, but most of these are just RV parking lots. The nicest are **Rustic RV Campground,** 634 US 20, tel. 646-7387, and **Wagon Wheel RV Park,** 408 Gibbon Ave., tel. 646-7872. Expect to pay around $12 for tents or $15 for RVs at either place. Noncampers can shower for $3. Both campgrounds are open mid-April to mid-October. **Canyon Street Laundromat,** 312 Canyon, tel. 646-9649, also has hot showers for $1.

Food

West Yellowstone has quite a number of good eateries. For breakfast, both **Running Bear Pancake House,** 538 Madison Ave., tel. 646-7703, and **Jedediah's House of Sourdough,** 315 Madison, tel. 646-7656, are good. Be ready for a long wait during peak summer season. Another decent breakfast place is **Silver Spur Cafe,** 111 Canyon St., tel. 646-9400. **Ernie's Bighorn Deli,** 406 Highway Ave., tel. 646-9467, makes unbeatable sandwiches. **Coachman Restaurant,** downstairs in the Stage Coach Inn, 209 Madison Ave., tel. 646-7381, has a good salad bar and the best local pizzas. **Gusher Pizza and Sandwich Shoppe,** Madison and Dunraven, tel. 646-9050, has all-you-can-eat spaghetti dinners on Wednesday nights. Pig out cheaply at tiny **Thiem's Cafe,** 38 Canyon, tel. 646-9462, where the chicken soup and homemade biscuits are local favorites. For a treat, head to **Arrowleaf Ice Cream Parlor,** 29 Canyon St., tel. 646-9776, home of "2001 flavors." **Totem Restaurant,** 115

Canyon St., tel. 646-7630, has the best prime rib in town. Fine German cooking at **Alice's Restaurant,** seven miles west of town, tel. 646-7296, where the fresh rainbow trout is a specialty. Get delicious gourmet coffee and fresh baked goods—including monster cinnamon rolls—at **Nancy P's,** 29 Canyon St., tel. 646-9737. It's open summers only.

Entertainment

During the summer, two places offer melodramas in town: **Musical Moose Playhouse,** 124 Madison Ave., tel. 646-9710, and **Playmill Theatre,** 29 Madison Ave., tel. 646-7757. For C&W and rock bands, try **Stage Coach Inn,** 209 Madison Ave., tel. 646-7381, or **The Ranch Lounge,** 235 Canyon, tel. 646-7388. For something different, **Lionshead Super 8 Lodge,** seven miles west of town, tel. 646-9584, offers square dancing with callers from all over the nation and even provides the outfits.

Summer Recreation

Llamas of West Yellowstone, tel. 646-9605, has guided day treks into Yellowstone. Horseback trail rides and western cookouts are available at **Parade Rest Guest Ranch,** eight miles north of town, tel. 646-7217, and from **Diamond P Ranch,** approximately 14 miles west of town, tel. 646-7246. Unguided horse rentals are also available at **Lone Rider Stable,** eight miles west of town, tel. 646-7900. Rent mountain bikes from **Yellowstone Bicycles,** 132 Madison Ave., tel. 646-7815.

Winter Sports

West Yellowstone is infamous for its bitterly cold winters—the thermometer can drop to 50 degrees below zero. Fortunately, it doesn't always stay there, and by March the days have often warmed to a balmy 20 degrees above. In November, West becomes a national center for cross-country skiers, with the U.S. Nordic and biathlon ski teams training here. Both the 25-km Rendezvous Trail and the 10-km Riverside Trail take off right from town. The streets are snowpacked and can be skied in winter. In mid-March the **Yellowstone Rendezvous,** a nationally known Nordic ski race, attracts hundreds of participants. There are many more places for flat tracking or telemarking in adjacent Yellowstone National Park and the Gallatin and Targhee national forests. Rent skinny skis at **Bud Lilly's Trout Shop,** 39 Madison Ave., tel. 646-7801, or **Madison River Outfitters,** 117 Canyon St., tel. 646-9644.

The chamber of commerce trumpets West as "snowmobile capital of the world," and each day between November and late March, hundreds of 'bilers show up to roar through Yellowstone's entrance or across thousands of acres of adjacent Forest Service lands. At least half a dozen different tour and snowmobile rental companies operate out of West Yellowstone. Rentals run $70-100/day (tours more expensive); see the chamber of commerce for a list. Hundreds more folks bring in their own "crotch rockets" to ride on Yellowstone National Park roads and across Gallatin and Targhee national forest lands. The chamber has a map of trails. The **World Snowmobile Expo** is held here the third weekend in March and includes races, demos, and other activities.

Information And Services

The **West Yellowstone Chamber of Commerce office** is at the corner of Canyon St. and Yellowstone Ave., tel. 646-7701. Open daily 8-5 in summer, and Mon.-Fri. 8-5 in winter. The **Hebgen Lake Ranger District Office** is just north of town on US 191-287, tel. 646-7369. Get maps of Gallatin National Forest and info on the **Madison River Canyon** where a magnitude-7.1 earthquake hit in 1959. It caused a massive landslide that killed 28 people, created Quake Lake, and caused cracks in Hebgen Dam. The quake also dramatically affected Yellowstone's geysers and hot springs. The site of the slide is approximately 20 miles north and west of West Yellowstone on US 287. It is marked with various signs.

Books

The Book Peddler, 106 Canyon St., tel. 646-9358 or (800) 253-2855, is an attractive bookstore with many Montana, Wyoming, and Yellowstone titles. Sip a cup of espresso while you read. **Bookworm Books,** 14 Canyon, tel. 646-9736, is another large bookshop with both new and used titles. Open till midnight in the summer! The local **library,** tel. 646-9017, next to the Fly Fishers Museum, is open Mon.-Saturday.

Tours And Transportation

Two companies offer all-day tours of Yellowstone from June through September: **Gray Line,** 633 Madison Ave., tel. 646-9374 and **Yellowstone Tours,** 214 Madison, tel. 646-7337. Choose from either the "upper loop" or the "lower loop" for $30 ($15 for kids). Gray Line also has Quake Lake and Jackson Hole tours out of West Yellowstone. If you want to overnight in the park, check with **Karst Stage,** 127 Yellowstone Ave., tel. 586-8567 (Bozeman phone number). They have summertime buses (Tues., Thurs., and Fri.) that stop in Old Faithful and Mammoth, continuing on to Bozeman, Montana. At Old Faithful, you can also connect with Gray Line, which has one-way service to Jackson (reserve ahead). **Greyhound Bus,** 127 Yellowstone Ave., tel. 646-7666, has daily summertime runs between Bozeman and Salt Lake City, with a stop in West Yellowstone.

Sky West Airlines, tel. (800) 453-9417, has summer-only service to West Yellowstone airport from Salt Lake City. During the winter, the closest airports are in Bozeman or Jackson Hole. Rental cars are available through **Budget,** tel. (800) 527-0700; **Big Sky Car Rentals,** tel. (800) 426-7669; and **Payless,** tel. (800) 729-5377. Big Sky has the cheapest rates: $30/day.

GARDINER

The little tourism town of Gardiner, Montana (pop. 600) lies barely outside Yellowstone's northwest entrance and three miles from the Wyoming line. The Yellowstone River slices right through town. Park headquarters at Mammoth Hot Springs is just five miles away, and the large warehouses of park concessionaire TW Recreational Services dominate the vicinity. Gardiner is the only year-round entrance to Yellowstone, and the Absaroka-Beartooth Wilderness lies just north of here. Also nearby is the 33,000-acre ranch of the Church Universal and Triumphant (CUT). Led by Elizabeth Clare Prophet, CUT has been involved in all sorts of end-of-the-world fantasies and has built bomb-shelter developments within grizzly-bear habitat (one shelter can house 756 people), stockpiled weapons, constructed fences that block elk migrations, and proposed for geothermal projects that could affect Yellowstone's hot springs. (There have been Congressional proposals to halt all geothermal development within 15 miles of Yellowstone.) CUT is not exactly popular with the townsfolk of Gardiner.

Gardiner was founded in 1883 when the Northern Pacific Railroad extended a line to the edge of Yellowstone, making it the first major entryway into the park. A reporter of that era described Gardiner as having "200 hardy souls, with 6 restaurants, 1 billiard hall, 2 dance halls, 4 houses of ill-fame, 1 milk man and 21 saloons." Today, the most distinctive structure in town is the monumental stone park entryway—similar to France's arc de Triomphe—that was for many years the primary entry point into Yellowstone. Built in 1903, **Roosevelt Arch** was dedicated by President Theodore Roosevelt, a man regarded by many as Yellowstone's patron saint. A tablet above the keystone is inscribed, "For the Benefit and Enjoyment of the People." (The arch was actually built to offset the park visitors' initial disappointment at finding the rather uninteresting country in this part of Yellowstone!)

Accommodations

Gardiner has 10 different lodging places; see the chart for specifics. Nicest of all—if you have the bucks—is **Yellowstone Inn B&B**, an attractive stone-walled house (built in 1903) that has been beautifully restored. Public camping is available within Yellowstone at **Mammoth Campground** ($7) or on Gallatin National Forest in the undeveloped **Eagle Creek Recreation Area** (free), two miles northeast of Gardiner on Jardine Road. Park RVs at **Yellowstone Village North Motel**, tel. 848-7417, or at **Rocky Mountain Campground**, tel. 848-7251, for $16 ($12 for tents). Showers for noncampers cost $3.50. Both are open year-round. Campsites are also available at **Yellowstone RV Park**, tel. 848-7251, open June-October, on the north end of town. Tents cost $12, RVs $16, and showers for noncampers run $2.

Food And Entertainment

Bear Country has a popular breakfast buffet for $5. **K Bar Club,** tel. 848-9995, doesn't look like much either outside or inside, but the from-scratch pizzas are very good in this locals' hangout. **Town Cafe,** tel. 848-7322, has sandwiches,

burgers, and a big salad bar. Better food upstairs in the Town Loft (summer only), where you can enjoy the vistas while you eat. **Sawtooth Deli,** tel. 848-7600, has sandwiches and soups (summer only). **Yellowstone Mine Restaurant** in the Best Western, tel. 848-7336, offers very good, but overpriced, meals. The most distinctive food in town is, surprisingly, at **Corral Drive Inn,** tel. 848-7627, where Helen and her sons serve up the biggest, juiciest, and messiest (get a handful of napkins) hamburgers anywhere around. Look for live bands in the **Two Bit Saloon** or the **Blue Goose Tavern.**

Other Practicalities

The big annual event in town is the **Gardiner Rodeo,** which comes around in mid-June. During the summer, **Yellowstone Raft Company,** tel. 848-7777, offers half-day ($27 adults, or $15 for kids) and full-day ($53 adults, or $35 for kids) whitewater-rafting trips down the Yellowstone beginning in Gardiner. Guided fishing trips are also available ($225/day for two people). **Yellowstone Mt. Bike** next to Sawtooth Deli, tel. 848-7600, rents bikes for $20/day in the summer. **Wilderness Connection,** tel. 848-7287, has horseback trips into Yellowstone. In winter, rent cross-country skis at **Trailhead Sporting Goods,** tel. 848-7712, or **Park's Fly Shop,** tel. 848-7314.

No chamber of commerce office in Gardiner, but local info is available at a bulletin board in the center of town. The **Gardiner District Office** of Gallatin National Forest, tel. 848-7375, has maps and info on the 930,584-acre **Absaroka-Beartooth Wilderness.** The portion around Gardiner is lower in elevation and covered with forests, while farther east are the alpine peaks of the Beartooth Mountains. In the summer **Karst Stage,** tel. 586-8567, has Mon., Wed., and Fri. bus service from Bozeman to Gardiner and on to Mammoth, Old Faithful, and West Yellowstone. On Tues., Thurs., and Sat. the buses run north from Gardiner to Bozeman.

SILVER GATE AND COOKE CITY

A couple of miles after you exit Yellowstone's northeast corner along US 212, the road widens slightly to pass through the historic gold-mining

GARDINER ACCOMMODATIONS

MOTEL	TELEPHONE	RATES	FEATURES
Gardiner Town Motel	848-7322	$28 s, $32 d	see rooms first
Mile Hi Motel	848-7544	$38+ s or d	open May to mid-Oct.
Absaroka Lodge	848-7414 (800) 755-7414	$40 s or d	AAA-approved, immaculate, overlooks Yellowstone River
Jim Bridger Court	848-7371	$40 $60	cabins, kitchenettes
Yellowstone River Motel	848-7303	$45 s or d	AAA-approved
Flamingo Motor Lodge	848-7536	$45 s, $50 d	AAA-approved
Blue Haven Motel	848-7719	$45 s or d $55/cabin	kitchenettes
Yellowstone Village North Motel	848-7417 (800) 228-8158	$54 s or d	AAA-approved, pool, sauna
Super 8 Motel	848-7401 (800) 800-8000	$60 s or d	
Westernaire Motel	848-7397	$60 s, $67 d	very nice
West Yellowstone Inn B&B	848-7000	$64+ s or d	beautiful historic inn
Best Western by Mammoth Hot Springs	848-7311 (800) 829-9080	$65+ s or d	AAA-approved, saunas, whirlpool

towns of Silver Gate and Cooke City (originally called Shoofly), Montana. The towns are just a couple miles apart and almost within spitting distance of the Wyoming line. The area code (406) for Silver Gate and Cooke City is larger than the total population of both settlements! Most establishments are built of log, befitting the mining heritage, and evidence of the old mines abounds. Noranda Minerals Corp., a Canadian-based mining company, has proposed development of a major gold, silver, and copper mine just north of Cooke City. Needless to say, the mine proposal has stirred up a hornet's nest of controversy.

For the present, both towns depend almost entirely on tourism and are crowded during the peak summer season. Cooke City looks pretty spiffy now with a gaudy new paint job on the bars and shops, funded in part by slot-machine gambling. Because the road is plowed all the way into Cooke City, this is a popular winter staging area for snowmobilers heading into the Beartooth Mountains. The Beartooth Hwy.

across 10,947-foot Beartooth Pass is closed by the first of November (often earlier) and doesn't open again until June.

The country around both Silver Gate and Cooke City was torched in the Storm Creek Fire in 1988, leaving charred hills just a couple hundred feet to the north and prompting alterations in the road signs to read "Cooked City." The **Absaroka-Beartooth Wilderness** is accessible directly north of Cooke City or from various other points to the east along the gorgeous Beartooth Highway. One of the more unusual sights is **Grasshopper Glacier,** eight miles north of Cooke City, and four thousand feet higher. It's accessible by car and foot. The glacier contains the remains of a swarm of locusts that were apparently caught in a snowstorm while flying over the mountains. (See "Bighorn Basin," p. 376 for more on the wilderness.) Pilot and Index peaks are the prominent rocky spires visible along the highway east of Cooke City. Dramatic Abiathar Peak juts out just south of Silver Gate.

COOKE CITY AND SILVER GATE ACCOMMODATIONS

MOTEL	TELEPHONE	RATES	FEATURES
High Country Motel	838-2272	$34+ s or d	kitchenettes $44
Alpine Motel	838-2262	$35+ s or d	
Betty's Cabins	838-2268	$35+ s or d	kitchenettes $40+
Antlers Lodge	838-2432	$35+ s or d	cabins, kitchens, sauna, hot tub, open May-Oct.
Hoosier's Motel	838-2241	$36+ s or d	AAA-approved, open mid-May to Nov.
Parkview Cabins	838-2371	$37 s or d	cabins, kitchenettes, open May 15-Oct. 15
Pine Edge Cabins	838-2222	$37+ s or d	cabins with kitchenettes, open mid-May to mid-Oct.
Grizzly Lodges	838-2219	$40+ s or d	kitchenettes, sauna, hot tub, open May-Oct.
Bearclaw Cabins	838-2336	$40+ s, $45+ d	cabins
All Seasons Hotel	838-2251	$40+ s, $45 d	AAA-approved, pool, whirlpool
Elk Horn Lodge	838-2332	$45 s, $50 d	kitchenettes, cabins, or motel rooms

Practicalities

See the chart above for cabins and motel rooms in Cooke City and Silver Gate. Heading east from Cooke City, you'll find four Forest Service campgrounds ($5; open July-early Sept.) within seven miles. The closest—Soda Butte—is just a half-mile up the road.

Joan and Bill's Restaurant, tel. 838-2280, serves excellent family-style food, along with justly famous homemade pies and huge cinnamon rolls. Get here early to avoid the long lines. **Beartooth Cafe** makes good sandwiches and all-American dinners. Good pizza is available at **Miner's Saloon.** Get groceries in the old red **Cooke City General Store,** built in 1886, tel. 838-2234 (open summers only), or in Silver Gate at **Summit Provisions,** tel. 838-2248.

Drinking appears to be the most popular local sport, but several local places occasionally have live music on weekends. Try **Miner's Saloon, Elkhorn Saloon,** or **Hoosiers** for a start. **All Seasons Inn and Casino,** tel. 838-2251, is the largest place in either town. They also rent snowmobiles in the winter.

BIGHORN BASIN

Bighorn Basin is an enormous intermountain desertscape, reaching almost 100 miles north to south and 50 miles east to west. Mountain ranges rim the basin—the Absarokas rise as a western border, the Owl Creek Mountains line the southern horizon, and the snowcapped Big Horns gleam in the east. The basin's rolling desert hills are topped with oil pumpjacks, and the wind blows incessantly. Cactus and sagebrush struggle up through a hardened surface of small rocks, while rugged badland buttes rise above dry creekbeds. The countryside looks like southern Nevada.

Much of the basin gets less than 10 inches of precipitation per year; in some places just half that amount falls, and even in midwinter there isn't much snow on the ground. Three lazy rivers—Bighorn, Greybull, and Shoshone—create long green corridors through this desolation, offering oases in the dry desert country. Because of the lack of water, this was one of the last parts of Wyoming to be settled, and most of the towns did not spring up until the 1890s, when passage of the Carey Act brought a flood of irrigation speculators, investors, and farm-

ers. Canals have created wide swatches of irrigated green around the towns and along the rivers. Much of this water comes from the Buffalo Bill Reservoir just west of Cody and a series of canals supplying water to sugar-beet and barley farms along the Bighorn and Greybull rivers.

In the early part of this century boom times came to the basin with discoveries of oil and natural gas at Grass Creek and Byron. Along with cattle and sheep ranching (important since the 1880s), these industries still dominate the economy of Bighorn Basin. To most tourists, the basin (with the exception of Cody) is a place to get through on the way to Yellowstone or the Black Hills. Locals, however, call it a retirement haven, offering as proof the dry, sunny climate (more than 300 days of sun per year), relatively mild winters, cheap housing, low crime rate, and proximity to the recreational wonderlands of Yellowstone and the Absaroka and Big Horn mountains. (In case you're confused, the word "Bighorn" is used for the national forest, river, canyon, and the basin, while "Big Horn" is for the mountain range, town, and county.)

SHOSHONE NATIONAL FOREST

Shoshone National Forest encompasses 2.4 million acres and extends along a 180-mile strip from the Montana border to the Wind River Mountains. Sagebrush dominates at the lowest elevations, but as you climb, lodgepole, Douglas fir, Engelmann spruce, and subalpine fir cover the slopes. Above 10,000 feet, the land opens into alpine vegetation and barren rocky peaks. The supervisor's office is in Cody at 225

W. Yellowstone Ave., tel. 527-6241, with ranger stations in Cody, Dubois, Powell, Meeteetse, and Lander. Forest maps ($2) are available at any of these locations.

More than half the forest lies inside wilderness boundaries; the Absaroka-Beartooth, North Absaroka, and Washakie wilderness areas cover much of the country east of Yellowstone National Park, while the Wind River Mountains

TO RED LODGE

MONTANA
WYOMING

COOKE CITY

TO TOWER JUNCTION

ABSAROKA - BEARTOOTH
WILDERNESS

CLAY BUTTE
LOOKOUT

BEARTOOTH
LOOP TRAIL

120

NORTHERN SHOSHONE NATIONAL FOREST

NORTH ABSAROKA WILDERNESS

WINDY MTN.

SUNLIGHT
BASIN

296

DEAD
INDIAN
PASS

HEART MTN.

ALT.
14

YELLOWSTONE NATIONAL PARK

WINDY MT. TRAIL

SUNLIGHT
RANGER
STATION

DEAD INDIAN TRAIL

CAMP MONACO

PAHASKA SUNLIGHT TRAIL

WAPITI
RANGER
STATION

CODY

14

16
20

TO YELLOWSTONE
LAKE

14
16
20

PAHASKA

WAPITI

CEDAR MTN.

SLEEPING GIANT
SKI AREA

EAGLE CREEK TRAIL

KITTY CREEK TRAIL

BUFFALO BILL
RESERVOIR

THOROFARE TRAIL

OPEN CREEK TRAIL

ELK FORK TRAIL

291

SHOSHONE
NATIONAL
FOREST

DEER CREEK TRAIL

DEER CREEK CG

SOUTH FORK RD.

120

CONTINENTAL DIVIDE

THOROFARE PLATEAU

WASHAKIE
WILDERNESS

JACK CREEK
TRAILHEAD

TO MEETEETSE

WOOD RIVER RD.

ABSAROKA
RANGE

BROWN MT. CG

WOOD RIVER CG

TO GRAND TETON
NATIONAL PARK

SOUTH FORK TRAIL

WIGGINS FORK TRAIL

26

287

TOGWOTEE PASS

PINNACLE
BUTTES

BROOKS LAKE

DOUBLE
CABIN CG

WASHAKIE
NEEDLES

N

DUBOIS

0   10mi

0   10km

© MOON PUBLICATIONS, INC

WAPITI VALLEY LODGES

The lodges are arranged by their distance from Yellowstone's East Entrance on US 14-16-20. (Subtract these numbers from 52 to determine the mileage from Cody.) All of these offer horseback rides and other activities. Many also offer weekly dude ranch accommodations.

LODGE	PHONE	MILES FROM YELLOWSTONE	RATES	FEATURES
Pahaska Tepee	527-7701 (800) 628-7791	2	$60+ s or d	cabins, historic place, closed Oct. and Nov.
Shoshone Lodge	587-4044	4	$42+ s, $50+ d	AAA-approved, cabins, open May-Oct.
Goff Creek Lodge	587-3753	11	$60+ s or d	AAA-approved, cabins, open May to mid-Oct.
Elephant Head Lodge	587-3980	12	$50+ s or d	cabins, open May to mid-Oct.
Absaroka Mountain Lodge	587-3963	13	$46+ s, $56+ d	AAA-approved, cabins, open May to mid-Nov.
Bill Cody's Ranch Resort	587-6271	27	$100 s or d	AAA-approved, cabins, hot tub, open year-round
Lodge at June Creek	587-2143	28	$65+ s or d	cabins, open mid-May to mid-Nov.
Mountain View Lodge	587-2081	29	$55 s or d $50 s or d	cabins motel
Wise Choice Motel	587-5004	30	$34 s, $36 d	AAA-approved, motel, jacuzzi, open mid-April to mid-Nov.
Half Mile Creek Ranch	587-9513	31	$60 s or d	whirlpool, open year-round
Yellowstone Valley Inn	587-3961 (800) 234-2902	34	$54 s or d	AAA-approved, motel, pool, open May-Oct.
Trout Creek Inn	587-6288 (800) 341-8000	37	$46 s, $50 d	AAA-approved, motel, pool

contain the Fitzpatrick and Popo Agie wildernesses. (See pp. 244-246 for the latter two.) More than 1,500 miles of trails offer hiking and horseback access to much of this country. Shoshone has more than 50 campgrounds, with most costing $5 per night during the summer. Once the water has been shut off for the winter months (generally Oct.-April) you can camp for free but will have to haul out your own trash. Space is generally available even at the busiest times of year. In addition, dispersed camping is possible throughout the forest, with the exception of heavily traveled US 14-16-20,

where you must be a half-mile from the road.

Black bears roam throughout the forest (though encounters are uncommon), and grizzlies are found within the northern portions, including the North Absaroka and Washakie wilderness areas. Be sure to take the necessary bear precautions anywhere in the backcountry. Bears also sometimes wander into campgrounds along US 14-16-20 near Yellowstone National Park. Actually, you are more likely to encounter mosquitoes, deer flies, and horse flies in midsummer; be sure to bring insect repellent.

History

Shoshone National Forest is America's oldest. On March 30, 1891, President Benjamin Harrison signed a proclamation creating Yellowstone Timber Reserve adjacent to Yellowstone National Park. At first this title meant very little, but in 1902, President Theodore Roosevelt appointed rancher and artist A.A. Anderson to control grazing and logging and catch poachers. His strong management almost got him lynched. Three years later, under Gifford Pinchot, the forest reserves were transferred to the Department of Agriculture and renamed national forests. Part of the credit for the surprising expanse of wilderness areas on the Shoshone goes to Buffalo Bill. By bringing people into the area to hunt, fish, and explore, he helped create what one author called a "dude's forest." In addition, the Buffalo Bill Dam (which he vociferously supported) prevented logs from being sent down the North Fork of the Shoshone River and thus reduced logging's importance to the local economy.

WAPITI VALLEY

Wapiti Valley provides one of the most popular and scenic routes into or out of Yellowstone National Park. President Theodore Roosevelt came here often and called it "the most scenic 50 miles in the U.S." Along US 14-16-20 are numerous lodges and resorts, private summer homes, Forest Service campgrounds, and hiking trails. The fishing is great in the North Fork of the Shoshone River, which the road parallels for the entire 52 miles from Yellowstone to Cody. After Sylvan Pass, the highway drops through high forests and past an array of volcanic pinnacles and cliffs as the country becomes drier and more open. Cottonwoods line the gradually widening river, and Douglas firs intermix with sage, grass, and rock at lower elevations. Two wilderness areas border the highway, North Absaroka and Washakie (see below), with trailheads scattered all along the valley. Many mountain resorts and dude ranches line the road between Yellowstone and Cody; most offer both food and lodging in a rustic but scenic setting, and all have horseback rides. Eleven different Forest Service campgrounds ($5) provide more rustic living along the North Fork.

Pahaska Tepee

Pahaska Tepee (pronounced pa-HAZ-ka) is just 2½ miles from Yellowstone's East Entrance and was built around the turn of the century to house Buffalo Bill's guests and others on their way to the park. (Pahaska was Buffalo Bill's nickname, a Crow Indian word meaning "Long Hair.") Come winter, Pahaska Tepee is a very popular place to rent snowmobiles and cross-country skis for trips into Yellowstone. The road is not plowed beyond Pahaska. The ski center here has 12 km of groomed ski trails ($2), covering a widely varied terrain. Buffalo Bill's original lodge is a two-story log building with many of the original furnishings still intact, including an old buffalo skull over the stone fireplace. The lodge is no longer used and is in need of repairs, but it's open for tours during the summer. On one of Buffalo Bill's many hunting treks with European royalty, he led the Prince of Monaco into the North Fork country. **Camp Monaco,** 15 miles up the Pahaska-Sunlight Trail from Pahaska Tepee, was named in his honor. Unfortunately, the old aspen tree inscribed with the words "Camp Monoco" was killed when the Clover-Mist Fire burned through here in 1988.

Down The Road

Sleeping Giant Ski Area, a small family area four miles from Yellowstone's East Gate, has been undergoing renovations but should be open by late 1993. For more info, call 587-4044. Below Sleeping Giant, the road passes by a whole series of delightfully weird volcanic rock formations. Signs point out several of the most obvious. Stop at a rock memorial to 15 firefighters who were killed in the Blackwater Fire of 1937. The picnic area here has a special pond for handicapped anglers. Eight miles farther is the historic **Wapiti Ranger Station.** Built in 1903, it was the nation's first Forest Service ranger station. A summer-only **visitor center** has a short video on grizzlies. Three campgrounds are nearby.

Next up is a parking area at **Holy City,** an impressive group of dark red volcanic rocks with the Shoshone River cutting away at their base. Try to pick out Anvil Rock, Goose Rock, and Slipper Rock here. The highway leaves Shoshone National Forest and then passes the scattered settlement called **Wapiti**—an Indian word mean-

(previous page) Killpecker Dunes, near Farson; (this page top left) aspen, near Pinedale; (top right) Cascade Creek, Grand Teton; (bottom) Sacajawea Cemetery, Fort Washakie (photos by Don Pitcher) ing "elk"—20 miles east of Cody. As you might guess, a large elk herd winters in this valley. An unusual volcanic-rock ridge near here is locally called Chinese Wall. The eastern half of the road between Cody and Yellowstone passes the northern shore of Buffalo Bill Reservoir, cutting through three tunnels along the way.

BUFFALO BILL RESERVOIR

Located six miles west of Cody on US 14-16-20, Buffalo Bill Reservoir is a very popular place for local boaters and fishermen. **Buffalo Bill State Park,** tel. 587-9227, encompasses the reservoir of the same name and includes a campground ($4; open May to mid-September). A brand new **visitor center** atop Buffalo Bill Dam has interesting historical displays and impressive views into the canyon, which drops 350 feet below you. Be sure to take the time to walk across the dam. Fishing is good for rainbow, cutthroat, brown, and Mackinaw trout. The lake also offers some of the finest windsurfing conditions anywhere; *Outside Magazine* rated it one of the country's 10 best spots. (You'll need a dry suit till mid-June.)

History
In 1899, Buffalo Bill Cody acquired the rights to build canals and irrigate some 60,000 acres of land near the new town of Cody. With passage of the Reclamation Act of 1902, the project was taken over by the Reclamation Service and an enormous concrete-arch dam was added to provide water. The 328-foot-high dam was begun in 1904 and required five long years to finish. It cost nearly $1 million and, when finally completed, it was the tallest dam in the world. Seven men died along the way—including a chief engineer—and the first two contractors were forced into bankruptcy as a result of bad weather, floods, engineering difficulties, and labor strife. A lack of sand and crushed gravel forced them to manufacture it from granite, and 200-pound boulders were hand-placed into the concrete to save having to crush more gravel.

Originally named Shoshone Dam, the impoundment was renamed in honor of Buffalo Bill in 1946. A hydroelectric plant and a 25-foot addition to the top were completed in 1991,

bringing the total dam height to 353 feet and increasing water storage by 50 percent. The dam irrigates more than 93,000 downstream acres through the Shoshone Reclamation Project, making it one of the only Wyoming irrigation schemes that really benefited the state's farmers to a large extent.

SUNLIGHT BASIN

State 296, popularly known as Sunlight Basin Rd., is now officially called Chief Joseph Scenic Highway. The road has approximately 20 miles of gravel, but the paved portions get longer every year, and it should be entirely paved by late 1994. It remains open year-round, providing access for snowmobilers to Beartooth Pass. The road begins 17 miles north of Cody along State 120, with Heart Mountain prominent to the southeast, and climbs sharply up from the dry east side, passing a red butte en route to **Dead Indian Pass.** The pass was supposedly named for an incident during an 1878 fight between Bannocks and the U.S. Army. After the battle, Crow scouts found a wounded Bannock here and killed him, burying the body under a pile of rocks. Other tales claim that the name came from the body of an Indian propped up as a ruse to trick the Army during Chief Joseph's attempted escape to Canada in 1877. Chief Joseph *did* lead the Nez Percé through this country, avoiding the cavalry by heading up Clarks Fork Canyon, a route the Army had considered impassable. An overlook on top of Dead Indian Pass provides extraordinary panoramic vistas of the rugged mountains and valleys. The river forms a boundary between the volcanic Absarokas to the south and the granitic Beartooth Mountains to the north.

West of the overlook, the road switchbacks down hairpin turns into remote and beautiful Sunlight Basin, where it turns to pavement again. A gravel side road leads seven miles to **Sunlight Ranger Station,** built in 1936 by the CCC. This is some of the finest elk winter range anywhere and the home for a number of scenic old guest ranches. Back on the main road, a bridge (highest in Wyoming) spans deep, cliff-walled **Sunlight Gorge.** Sorry, no bungee jumping allowed. The highway then continues northwest past Cathedral Cliffs and through the scenic ranching and timbering valley of the Clarks Fork, with views into the 1,200-foot-deep gorge. Part of the area burned by the 1988 Clover-Mist Fire is visible near Crandall Guard Station. This area contains the only large herd of mountain goats in Wyoming. Eventually you reach the junction with US 212, the Beartooth Hwy. (see below for a description of this beautiful route).

Recreation

Three campgrounds ($5) are found along Chief Joseph Scenic Highway. **Dead Indian Trail** (just uphill from Dead Indian Campground) goes two miles to a fine overlook into Clarks Fork Canyon. Also of interest is **Windy Mountain Trail**, which climbs 10,262-foot Windy Mountain. It starts at Reef Creek Campground and is approximately seven miles one-way, gaining 3,700 feet in elevation. Windy Mountain can also be climbed from the other side near the Sunlight Ranger Station. Trailheads to the North Absaroka Wilderness are at the Crandall Guard Station (interesting old log buildings) and beyond the Sunlight Ranger Station on Forest Rd. 101.

Clarks Fork of the Yellowstone River (named for William Clark of the Lewis and Clark expedition) is Wyoming's only designated Wild and Scenic River. Experienced kayakers will find a couple of great stretches of class-IV-V whitewater in the upper Clarks Fork, but use considerable caution, since there are several big drops. Be sure to pull out before dangerous Box Canyon, considered unrunnable. More Class-IV waters are farther down the river. Check with the Forest Service for specifics.

BEARTOOTH MOUNTAINS

Spectacular Beartooth Scenic Byway (US 212) connects Cooke City and Yellowstone National Park with the historic mining town of Red Lodge, Montana. Along the way, it passes through the Beartooth Mountains on a road built by the CCC in the 1930s. A small corner (23,750 out of a total of 945,334 acres) of the **Absaroka-Beartooth Wilderness** lies in Wyoming north of the highway, with the rest right across the Montana border. Some have called this the most scenic route in America. If you like alpine country, hundreds of small lakes, and towering rocky spires, you're gonna love this drive. Be sure to take a few casts for the brook, cutthroat, and rainbow trout in the lakes and streams.

The road sails across a high plateau and then over Beartooth Pass, 10,947 feet above the sea, the highest highway pass in Wyoming and one of the highest in America. As the road crosses into Montana, it passes the Beartooth Mts. and begins a rapid elevator ride down folded ribbon curves into Red Lodge. On top, keep your eyes open for moose, mule deer, mountain goats, bighorn sheep, marmots, and pikas. Be ready for strange weather at this elevation, including snow at any time of year. The highway is closed with the first heavy snows (generally in September) and doesn't open till June.

Recreation

Lots to see and do in the Beartooths. Majestic rock faces rise in all directions, the most obvious being Beartooth Mt., Pilot Peak, and Index Peak. Twenty-three miles east from Cooke City is the turnoff to an old fire lookout tower at **Clay Butte** (three miles off the main road). Although no longer used, the tower offers a chance to see even more of the surrounding countryside. There are four developed campgrounds ($5) along this stretch of State 212, with more once you drop into Montana. **Beartooth Lake** and **Island Lake campgrounds** border on alpine lakes with marvelous cross-country hiking opportunities all around. (Be sure to bring a compass and topo map, plus warm clothes.) The trees are whitebark pine and Engelmann spruce. **Top-of-the-World Store** (gas, food, and limited accommodations) lies between the two campgrounds along the highway. A nice 11-mile loop hike leaves Island Lake and climbs up past several lakes before circling back. **Beartooth Loop National Recreation Trail** is a popular hiking path just two miles east of Beartooth Pass. This 15-mile loop traverses alpine tundra and passes several lakes and a century-old log stockade of unknown origins.

NORTH ABSAROKA WILDERNESS

The 350,488-acre North Absaroka Wilderness is one of the lesser-known wild places in Wyoming.

The wilderness abuts Yellowstone National Park to the west and is bordered by the Sunlight Basin and Beartooth highways to the north and US 14-16-20 to the south. North Absaroka Wilderness is primarily used by hunters who arrive on horseback. The few hikers tend to be quite experienced with backcountry travel and willing to tolerate the lack of trail signs and the steep and frequently washed-out paths. Much of the wilderness is relatively inaccessible, and snow may be present on passes until mid-July. Ask at the ranger stations for current trail conditions, and be sure to get topographic maps before heading out. Large populations of grizzly and black bears, bighorn sheep, moose, and elk are found in the Absaroka Mountains, and golden eagles are a common sight. The tough landscape is of volcanic origin, and the topsoil erodes easily, turning mountain creeks into churning rivers of mud after heavy summer rainstorms.

Hikes

The enormous 1988 Clover-Mist Fire that began in Yellowstone burned through a large portion of the North Absaroka Wilderness, so be prepared for blackened forests. Pick up a map of burned areas from the Forest Service in Cody if you want to avoid these areas. Probably the most popular wilderness path is **Pahaska-Sunlight Trail,** an 18-mile-long trek that begins at Pahaska Campground on US 14-16-20 and heads north through historic Camp Monaco to Sunlight Basin. Another popular path is the 25-mile-long **Big Creek-Dead Indian Trail** across the eastern (unburned) portion of the wilderness. At opposite ends are the Dead Indian trailhead and the Big Creek trailhead. This is not a loop route, so you'll need to either hike out and back the same route or arrange transportation to and from the trailheads.

WASHAKIE WILDERNESS

Covering 704,529 acres, Washakie Wilderness is one of the largest chunks of wild land in Wyoming. Named for Shoshone Chief Washakie, it lies between US 14-16-20 (the road connecting Yellowstone and Cody) and US 26-287 (to the Dubois area). To the west

are Yellowstone National Park and Teton Wilderness. The Washakie is a land of deep, narrow valleys, mountains of highly erodible volcanic material, and steplike buttes. The mountains—a few top 13,000 feet—are part of the Absaroka Range. About half of the land is forested. One of the unique features of Washakie Wilderness is a petrified forest, a reminder of the region's volcanic past.

Hikes

There are numerous trails through the Washakie Wilderness, but most require that you either return the same way or end at a location far from your starting point. Several trails extend into Yellowstone National Park and are popular for extended horse-packing trips. The most popular Washakie Wilderness trails lead from US 14-16-20 in Wapiti Valley. Most folks use them for short day-hikes or horseback rides rather than attempting longer backcountry treks.

Kitty Creek Trail leaves from the Kitty Creek summer-home area, nine miles east of Yellowstone. Low-clearance vehicles need to be parked along the highway. The trail follows the creek past two large scenic meadows to Flora Lake, 6½ miles away and 2,500 feet higher. This is the shortest hike in the area and one of the most popular.

The 21-mile-long **Elk Fork Trail** starts at Elk Fork Campground and crosses Elk Creek several times en route to remote Rampart Pass at nearly 11,000 feet. It is steep and rocky in the higher elevations. West of the Continental Divide you enter the Teton Wilderness. For the really ambitious, the Open Creek and Thorofare trails continue on into Yellowstone National Park.

Deer Creek Trail departs from the free Deer Creek Campground, 42 miles southwest of Cody on State 291 (South Fork Road). The trail switchbacks very steeply uphill at first and after two miles reaches an attractive waterfall. Continue another eight miles from here to the Continental Divide and the Thorofare portion of the Teton Wilderness. This is probably the quickest route into this remote country and is popular with both horse-packers and hikers.

South Fork Trail takes off from the South Fork Guard Station across the creek from Deer Creek Campground. (Take a signed spur road to get there.) It climbs up along South Fork Creek to Shoshone Pass on the Continental Divide (9,858 feet). From here you can continue on a number of trails to the south, rambling over three more passes to eventually reach Double Cabin Campground, 27 miles north of Dubois. Another long hike into Washakie Wilderness leaves from this campground and follows the **Wiggins Fork Trail** up into a connecting series of paths: Absaroka, Nine Mile, East Fork, and Bug Creek trails. It ends back at Double Cabin Campground. Total length is 60 miles. Along the way you're likely to see hundreds of elk in the high country as well as bighorn sheep. You won't see many other hikers.

CODY

The city of Cody (pop. 8,000) marks the transition point between the forested mountains of northwest Wyoming and the barren deserts of Bighorn Basin. It's a favorite stopping place for Yellowstone tourists. The park is just 52 miles due west, and other magnificent country spreads in all directions—the Beartooth Mountains and Sunlight Basin to the north, and the Absaroka Range and Wapiti Valley to the west and south. Established as an agricultural and tourism center, Cody retains both roles today, though tourism seems to be gaining in importance with each passing year. The town is one of the few places in Wyoming that continued to grow through the 1980s; only Jackson Hole exceeds Cody as a center for tourism. Not surprisingly, both are gateways to the two national parks that dominate northwest Wyoming.

Cody itself has a number of attractions, including the justly famous Buffalo Bill Historical Center, Trail Town, and other local sights. The Shoshone River flows right through town, providing scenic float trips. Lots of events crowd the summer calendar, from nightly rodeos to parades and powwows; biggest of all is the annual Cody Stampede in July. The town also takes pride in a long list of artists that includes Charles Cary Rumsey and Harry Jackson. Famed abstract expressionist Jackson Pollock was born here but achieved his reputation in New York and never returned to his birthplace.

History

Just west of Cody are the Absaroka Mountains (pronounced ab-SOR-ka), named for the Native Americans who first lived here. They called themselves the Absaroka, or "Children of the Large Beaked Bird." Whites interpreted this as *crow,* and they have been called Crow Indians ever since. Explorer John Colter passed through this region in 1808 while recruiting Indians to supply beaver furs. When Colter returned to the semblance of civilization called Fort Manual Lisa, everyone laughed at his tales of a spectacular geothermal area along the Stinkingwater River. Soon everyone was calling it "Colter's Hell." But the geysers were real; they still steam along the Shoshone (formerly the Stinkingwater) just west of present-day Cody. Other mountain men came later, followed by miners who found copper and sulfur in Sunlight Basin. The first real settler in the area was a Prussian, Otto Franc, who developed a large cattle spread.

In 1895, William F. "Buffalo Bill" Cody and two partners began plans for the Shoshone Land and Irrigation Company, with headquarters along the Shoshone River just west of the present city of Cody. Cody had spent much time in the Bighorn Basin, guiding parties of wealthy sportsmen and exploring the country, and was convinced that a combination of tourism and irrigated farming could transform this desert land. At the urging of Buffalo Bill, the Chicago, Burlington, & Quincy Railroad arrived in 1901, bringing in thousands of tourists who continued west up Shoshone Canyon to Yellowstone by stagecoach. Oil was first discovered near Cody in 1904, and Park County is now the second-largest oil producer in the state. Marathon Oil Company has its Rocky Mountain headquarters in Cody and is one of the town's largest employers. Also important are a wallboard manufacturing plant, a lumber mill, and a producer of ranch products.

BUFFALO BILL HISTORICAL CENTER

Each year, more than a quarter of a million people visit Cody's main attraction, the Buffalo Bill

CODY

Historical Center. This is the largest and most impressive museum in Wyoming and the finest western museum in the world. Author James Michener labeled it "one of the top four museums in America." The collection focuses on the western frontier and includes thousands of artifacts and works of art spread through more than 237,000 square feet of space. The center actually houses four separate museums, as well as a research library, the boyhood home of Buffalo Bill, and two sculpture gardens.

The original Buffalo Bill Museum opened in 1927 in what is now the chamber of commerce log cabin. The Whitney Gallery of Western Art formed a nucleus for the current complex, opening in 1959. Later additions included the Buffalo Bill Museum, the Plains Indian Museum, and the Cody Firearms Museum (completed in 1991). Other facilities at the Buffalo Bill Historical Center include a large gift shop/bookstore, a snack bar, and a downstairs exhibition space. The **Harold McCracken Research Library** has thousands of historical photos and books, including more than 300 volumes about Buffalo Bill, mostly dime novels and comic books. Check the calendar of events at the historical center for activities ranging from historical talks to cowboy singing (see "Events," below). Of note is the **Summer Institute in Western American Studies,** an in-depth two-week history course offered by the Historical Center.

The complex is open daily 7 a.m.-10 p.m. June-August; daily 8-8 in May and September; and daily 8-5 in October. April hours are Tues.-Sun. 8-5, while March and Nov. hours are Tues.-Sun. 10-3. The museum is closed Dec.-February. A two-day admission pass costs $7 for adults, $6 for seniors, $4 for students, and $2 for children ages 6-12. Children under 6 are admitted free. Excellent recorded audio tours of all three galleries are just $2. Call 587-4771 or (800) 227-8483 for more information.

Outside

Before heading inside, stop to view **Buffalo Bill's boyhood home,** a tiny yellow building built in 1841 by Isaac Cody. The house stood in LaClarie, Iowa for almost a century. In 1933 it was sawn in half, loaded on two railcars, and hauled to Cody to be reassembled and refurbished. The house is on your left as you face the museum. Flanking the museum on the opposite side is *The Scout,* a dramatic larger-than-life statue of a larger-than-life character, Buffalo Bill. This huge bronze piece was created by New York sculptress Gertrude Vanderbilt Whitney and was unveiled in 1924. Her family later donated 40 acres of surrounding land to the Buffalo Bill Museum. Directly in front of the historical center are three colorfully painted **tipis,** a treat for kids.

Buffalo Bill Museum

The Buffalo Bill Museum is a real joy in which the life of Buffalo Bill Cody is briefly sketched. The museum features all sorts of memorabilia from Buffalo Bill's Wild West Show, including the famous Deadwood Stage, silver-laden saddles, enormous posters, furniture, guns, wagons, and clothing. Be sure to look for "Lucretia Borgia," the Springfield rifle that helped William Cody gain his nickname. Also here are some of the gifts given to Buffalo Bill by European heads of state (including a fur carriage robe from Czar Alexander II), and by Wild Bill Hickok and Sitting Bull. Original film footage from the Wild West Show runs continuously, offering a fascinating and sometimes unintentionally comical glimpse into the past. Amazingly choreographed marching soldiers, fake Indian battles, and bucking broncos make it easy to see how the Wild West Show could have inspired Western movies. Downstairs from the Buffalo Bill Museum are changing exhibits.

Whitney Gallery Of Western Art

The Whitney Gallery contains a stunning collection of masterworks by such Western artists and sculptors as Charles Russell, Frederic Remington, Carl Bodmer, George Catlin, Thomas Moran, Albert Bierstadt, Alfred Jacob Miller, Edgar Paxson, N.C. Wyeth, and others. The studios of Frederic Remington and W.H.D. Koerner have been re-created, and Gertrude Vanderbilt Whitney's *The Scout* is visible from a large window on the north end. The collections of both "cowboy artist" Charles Russell and Frederic Remington—best known for his paintings of battles during the Indian wars—are the most complete here; the museum has more than a hundred of each man's paintings. There are even a few contemporary works on display.

Next to the Whitney Gallery is **Joseph Henry Sharp Garden,** where you'll find the "Absarokee Hut" filled with the painter's paraphenalia.

Cody Firearms Museum

The new Cody Firearms Museum contains one of the most comprehensive collections of American firearms in the world, including everything from 16th-century matchlocks to self-loading semiautomatic pistols. Start your visit by viewing "Lock, Stock, & Barrel," a 10-minute video program that describes the history of guns and how they work; it's interesting even for those who are not gun fanatics. In fact, the entire firearms collection is remarkably informative and well worth taking time to view.

The museum now contains more than 5,000 weapons, but these aren't just rows of guns in glass cases. Some of the more unusual weapons include a 10-shot repeating flintlock rifle made for the New York Militia around 1825 and a double-barrel knife-pistol. There are all sorts of displays to explore, including a colonial gun shop, a western stage station, a turn-of-the-century firearms factory, and a truly extraordinary collection of embellished arms. One of the most lavish is an intricately carved flintlock sporting carbine presented by Empress Elizabeth I of Russia to King Louis XV of France. The Boone and Crockett Club's collection of trophy animal heads is here, including an elephant-sized moose. All told, more implements of destruction than you're likely to see at an NRA convention.

Plains Indian Museum

The largest exhibition space in the historical center encloses the Plains Indian Museum, with items from the Sioux, Cheyenne, Blackfeet, Crow, Arapaho, Shoshone, and Gros Ventre tribes. At first it may seem incongruous that a museum featuring the man once called the "youngest Indian slayer of the plains" should include so much about the culture of Indians, but Cody's later maturity forced him to the realization that Indians had been severely mistreated and that their culture was of great value. His Wild West Shows re-created some semblance of that lost society, if only for show. Some of the more important items here were given to Buffalo Bill by various Indian performers over the

years, and the collection of artifacts is now one of the finest in America. Included are an extraordinary painted buffalo robe from 1890 that depicts the Battle of Little Big Horn, elaborately decorated baby carriers, ghost-dance dresses, leather garments, war bonnets, medicine pipes, and even a Pawnee grizzly-claw necklace. The moccasin collection fills an entire wall, and one room holds a Sioux camp as it might have appeared in the 1880s.

OTHER SIGHTS

Trail Town

Point your horses toward the mountains and head 'em two miles west of town to a unique collection of historic buildings at Trail Town, tel. 587-5302. The site is open daily 8 a.m.-8 p.m., mid-May to mid-Sept. only; $3 entrance (free for kids under 12). This was the original location of "Cody City" in 1895. Trail Town is the creation of Bob and Terry Edgar. (In 1957 Bob Edgar discovered Mummy Cave—one of the most important archaeological finds in the west.) The Edgars bought the old Arland and Corbett trading post that had stood here since the 1880s and began dragging in other historic Wyoming cabins. Some were transported whole, while others were disassembled and then put back together at Trail Town. Twenty-two buildings, dating from 1879 to 1901, and 100 wagons are currently on the site.

For those who love history, Trail Town is an incredible treasure trove without the fancy gift shops and commercial junk that tag along with most such endeavors. This is the real thing, low-key and genuine. Probably the most famous building here is a cabin from the Hole-in-the-Wall country that Butch Cassidy and the Sundance Kid used as a rendezvous spot. Also at Trail Town is the oldest saloon from this part of Wyoming, complete with bullet holes in the door, and a cabin where Jim White—one of the most famous buffalo hunters—was murdered in 1879. The log home of Crow Indian scout Curley stands along main street too. (Curley was the only one of Gen. Custer's command that escaped alive from the Battle of the Little Big Horn.) Inside the old Burlington Store are a black hearse, arrowheads, a cradleboard, and items

CODY ACCOMMODATIONS

MOTEL	ADDRESS	TELEPHONE	RATES	FEATURES
Pawnee Hotel	1032 12 St.	587-2239	$24 s, $28+ d	
Gateway Motel	203 Yellowstone	587-2561	$30 s, $35 d	kitchenettes, cabins, open April-Oct.
4 Bar Motel	1213 17th St.	587-2084	$30+ s, $35+ d	kitchenettes, very plain
Holiday Motel	1807 Sheridan Ave.	587-4258	$35 s, $38 d	AAA-approved
Uptown Motel	1562 Sheridan Ave.	587-4245	$35 s, $40 d	kitchenettes
7 K's Motel	232 Yellowstone	587-5890 (800) 223-9204	$36 s, $42 d	pool, open May-Sept.
Rainbow Park Motel	1136 17th St.	587-6251	$36 s, $39 d	AAA-approved, kitchenettes $8 extra
Wigwam Motel	1701 Alger Ave.	587-3861	$40 s or d	kitchenettes
Skyline Motor Inn	1919 17th St.	587-4201 (800) 843-8809	$42 s, $48 d	AAA-approved, pool
Super 8 Motel	730 Yellowstone	527-6214 (800) 800-8000	$43 s, $55 d	AAA-approved
Big Bear Motel	139 Yellowstone	587-3117	$44 s or d	AAA-approved, pool
Cedar Mountain Lodge	1192 Sheridan Ave.	587-2248	$45 s or d	open May-Sept.
Western 6 Gun Motel	433 Yellowstone	587-4835	$45 s, $50 d	open May-Dec.
Irma Hotel	1192 Sheridan Ave.	587-4221	$45 s, $51 d $72 s, $78 d	motel rooms historic hotel rooms
Buffalo Bill Village	1701 Sheridan Ave.	587-5544 (800) 527-5544	$48 s, $54 d	pool, kitchenettes, cabins, open May-Sept.
Carriage House Motel	1816 8th St.	587-2572	$49+ s or d	open April.-Sept.
Frontier Motel	US 14-16-20 E	527-7119	$50 s, $52 d	kitchenettes $12 extra
Colonial Inn	720 Yellowstone	587-4208	$55 s or d	pool, open May to mid-Oct.
Cody Motor Lodge	1455 Sheridan Ave.	527-6291	$56 s, $64 d	
Kelly Inn	2513 Greybull Hwy.	527-5505 (800) 635-3559	$59 s, $74 d	AAA-approved, sauna, whirlpool, exercise room
Wind Chimes Cottage B&B	1501 Beck Ave.	527-5310	$60 s, $65+ d	full breakfast
Best Western Sunrise	1407 8th St.	587-5566 (800) 528-1234	$63 s or d	pool, open May-Oct.
Lockhart Bed & Breakfast Inn	109 Yellowstone	587-6074	$65+ s or d	AAA-approved, historic home
Best Western Sunset	1601 8th St.	587-4265 (800) 528-1234	$65+ s, $67+ d	pool, very nice
Parson's Pillow B&B	1202 14th Ave.	587-2382 (800) 377-2348	$65+ s or d	historic church building full breakfast
Comfort Inn	1601 Sheridan Ave.	587-5556 (800) 221-2222	$90 s, $96 d	pool
Holiday Inn	1701 Sheridan Ave.	587-5555 (800) 465-4329	$93 s, $99 d	AAA-approved, pool
Cody's Victorian Guest House,	1519 Beck Ave.	587-6460	$150+	furnished house sleeps six

from fur traders. The bodies of buffalo hunter Jim White, Belle Drewry ("The Woman in Blue"), and several other historic figures have been reinterred in a small graveyard at Trail Town. Most famous is **John "Liver Eating" Johnson,** the mountain man portrayed by Robert Redford in the film *Jeremiah Johnson.* (Redford was here for the reburial in 1974.) A memorial to explorers John Colter and Jim Bridger stands near the graveyard. Trail Town provides a fine low-key contrast to the glitzier Buffalo Bill Historical Center.

Irma Hotel

Pick up a copy of the **Cody Historic Walking Tour** ($1) at the visitor center. It offers an informative introduction to local buildings and their history. One of the most interesting is the Irma Hotel, named for Buffalo Bill Cody's daughter. It was built in 1902 to house tourists arriving by train and was one of three way stations to Yellowstone built by Cody. For many years this was one of the finest hotels in Wyoming. The luxurious saloon still has a $100,000 French-made cherrywood bar given to Buffalo Bill by Queen Victoria. Many famous people have gathered here over the years. The Irma Hotel puts on a free **"gunfight"** on the front porch at 7 p.m. Wed., Thurs., and Fri. evenings during the summer. Kids like to pose for photos atop the **stuffed bull** here.

Et Cetera

Another lodging place with a famous past is the **Lockhart Bed & Breakfast Inn,** 109 W. Yellowstone, tel. 587-6074, once the home of novelist and flamboyant newspaper editor Caroline Lockhart (see p. 415). The **Foundation for North American Wild Sheep** has its national headquarters at 720 Allen Ave., tel. 527-6261 (just south of Buffalo Bill Historical Center). Open Mon.-Fri. 8-5, this nonprofit corporation works to preserve and reestablish wild sheep populations. The videos and sculpture garden here are worth a look.

Cedar Mountain, the 7,889-foot-tall summit overlooking Cody from the west, is where Buffalo Bill had wanted to be buried. A winding 4WD trail climbs to the top, making a fine mountain-bike ride if you don't mind the 2,800-foot elevation gain. Also here is **Spirit Mountain Cave,**

one of the first national monuments ever designated (1909). A lack of interest caused the designation to be withdrawn, but the caverns are still on public land. Spelunkers can get permission to enter from the BLM office in Cody.

East of Cody near Beck Lane is the **Wyoming Vietnam Veterans Memorial,** a black granite memorial modelled after the one in Washington. It contains the names of 137 Wyoming men killed or missing in action. The **Cody Wildlife Exhibit,** 433 Yellowstone Hwy., tel. 587-2804, has a rather nice display of more than 400 mounted American and African wildlife specimens. All sorts of record-sized critters, from a 17-foot-tall giraffe to a 2,800-pound buffalo. Admission costs $2 ($1 for kids).

If you're really desperate for something to do, visit the **Cody Mural** on the domed ceiling of the LDS church at 1719 Wyoming Ave., tel. 587-3290. Tours are available Mon.-Fri. 9-9 during the summer. No, it isn't the Sistine Chapel. The mural (painted in 1951) offers a rosy-tinted version of Mormon Church history.

ACCOMMODATIONS

Motels And Hotels

The tourist town of Cody is jam-packed with lodging facilities, but be ready to pay more than in just about any place in Wyoming except Jackson Hole. Budget accommodations are nonexistent during the summer, though rates plummet with the first cold nights of fall. A youth hostel is definitely needed! Most of the year, lodging in Cody is not a problem as long as you check in before 4 p.m.; but during July and August you should reserve a week ahead, and even longer for Cody Stampede (early July). See the chart for rates at Cody's motels and hotels. Mountain lodges are listed in the section on Shoshone National Forest (p. 373), and the chamber of commerce has a listing of more than 20 guest ranches in the area.

Campgrounds

The closest public campground ($4) is 11 miles west in Buffalo Bill State Park. Find many more campgrounds ($5) in Shoshone National Forest, but the nearest is 28 miles west of town. There are six different private RV park/camp-

BUFFALO BILL CODY

For many people today, the name "Buffalo Bill" brings to mind a man who helped slaughter the vast herds of wild bison. But William F. Cody cannot be so easily pigeonholed, for here was one of the most remarkable men of his or any other era, a man who almost single-handedly established the aura of the wild west. More than 800 books—many of them the dimestore novels that thrilled generations of youngsters—have been written about Cody. In many of these, the truth was stretched far beyond any semblance of reality, but the real life of William Cody contains so many adventures and plot twists that it seems hard to believe one person could have done so much.

Young Cody

Born to an Iowa farm family in 1846, William Cody started life like many others of his era. His parents moved to Kansas when he was six, but soon his abolitionist father, Isaac Cody, became embroiled in arguments with the many slaveholders. While defending his views at a public meeting, Isaac Cody was stabbed in the back and fled for his life. When a mob learned of his father's whereabouts, the eight-year-old Will Cody rode on his first venture through enemy lines, galloping 35 miles to warn of the impending attack. Three years later, when Isaac Cody died from complications of the stabbing, 11-year-old Will Cody became the family's breadwinner. There were four other children to feed. Will quickly joined the company of Alexander Majors, running dispatches between his Army supply wagons, with his $40/month wages going to his mother. In Cody's autobiography, he claimed to have killed his first Indian on this trip, an action that gave him the then-enviable title "youngest Indian slayer of the plains."

On his first long wagon trek west, the Army supply wagons were attacked by Mormon zealots who took all the weapons and horses, forcing Cody to walk much of the thousand miles back to his Kansas home. It was apparently on this walk that Cody met Wild Bill Hickok. At Wyoming's Fort Laramie, young Will sat in awe as famed scouts Jim Bridger and Kit Carson reminisced about their adventures. The experience was a turning point in Cody's life; he resolved to one day become a scout. Cody's next job offered excellent training: riding for the Pony Express. At just 15 years of age he already was one of the finest riders in the west and a crack shot with a rifle. On one of his Pony Express rides Cody covered a total of 320 miles in just 21 hours and 40 minutes, the longest Pony Express ride ever. The Civil War had begun, and at age 18 Cody joined the Seventh Kansas Regiment, serving as a scout and spy for the Union Army.

After the Civil War, Will Cody tried his hand at the hotel business then briefly joined Gen. George Custer as a scout before returning to Kansas to do a little land speculation along the route of the newly built railroad. He and a partner bought land and laid out a town that they named Rome. For a time it boomed, but when a man came to Rome and offered Cody the chance to own a small part of Cody's own town, he laughed at the offer, not knowing that the offer came from the president of the railroad's townsite company. Three days later the entire town of Rome—including all its buildings—was moved east to a new location at a site selected by the railroad company. Cody had laughed at the wrong man.

Buffalo Hunter And Scout

In 1867, Cody found work hunting buffalo to supply fresh meat for the railroad construction crews, a job that soon made him famous as "Buffalo Bill" and paid a hefty $500 per month. With 75 million bison spread from northern Canada to Mexico, and herds so vast that they took many days to pass one point, it seemed impossible that they could ever be killed off. Cody was one of the best hunters in the west; in just eight months, he slaughtered 4,280 buffalo, often saving transportation by driving the herd toward the camp, and dropping them within sight of the workers. Cody's name lives on in the jingle: "Buffalo Bill, Buffalo Bill; never missed and never will; always aims and shoots to kill; and the company pays his buffalo bill . . . ."

After this stint, Cody finally got the job he wanted, chief scout for the U.S. Army in the west, a job packed with excitement and danger. Conflicts with Indians had reached a fever pitch as more and more whites moved into the last Indian strongholds. Cody worked as scout for Gen. Philip Sheridan, providing information on movements of the Indians, leading troops in pursuit of the warriors, and joining in the battles, including one in which he supposedly killed Chief Tall Bull. His men considered Buffalo Bill good luck, since he managed to keep them out of ambushes.

continued

Buffalo Bill with Indian children, 1913—this photo was probably taken during the filming of The Indian Wars.

During the Indian campaigns, the writer/preacher/scoundrel Ned Buntline began writing of Cody's exploits for various New York papers, giving Buffalo Bill his first taste of national acclaim. Soon Buntline had cranked out several romantic novels loosely based on Cody's adventures. America had a new national hero. European and Eastern gentry began asking Cody to guide them on buffalo hunts. On the trips, Cody referred to them as "dudes" and to his camps as "dude ranches," perhaps the first time anyone had used the terms for the hunters. One of Wyoming's most unusual businesses had begun. Cody's incredible knowledge of the land and hunting impressed the men, but they were stunned to also discover in him a natural showman. In 1872, the Grand Duke Alexis of Russia came to the U.S. and was guided by Cody on a hunt that made national headlines and brought even more fame to the 26-year-old Buffalo Bill. On a trip to New York in 1872, Cody met Buntline again and watched a wildly distorted theater production called *Buffalo Bill*. Amazingly, Cody adjusted quickly to the new surroundings. Dressed in the finest silk clothes, but with his long scout's hair under a Western hat, Cody suddenly entered the world of high society.

In a short while, Cody was on the stage himself, performing with Ned Buntline and fellow scout Texas Jack in a play called *Scouts of the Plains*. Although meant to be serious, the acting of all three proved so atrocious that the play had audiences rolling in the aisles with laughter. A New York reviewer called the play "so wonderfully bad it was almost good. The whole performance was so far aside of human experience, so wonderful in its daring feebleness, that no ordinary intellect is capable of comprehending it." Audiences packed the theaters for weeks on end. But then, suddenly, Cody was called back to the west, for the Sioux were again on the warpath.

Shortly after Cody had returned to guide Gen. Eugene Carr's forces, they learned of the massacre of Custer's men at the Battle of the Little Big Horn. In revenge, Carr's men set out to pursue Indians along the border between Nebraska and Wyoming. Under Cody's guidance, they surprised a group of warriors at War Bonnet Creek. Cody shot the chief, Yellow Hand, and immediately scalped him, raising the scalp above his head with the cry "first scalp for Custer!" (Cody later claimed that he scalped the chief because he was wearing an American flag as a loincloth and had a lock of yellow hair from a white woman's scalp pinned to his clothing.) The Sioux immediately fled. If Cody had been famous before, this event propelled him to even more acclaim. It

continued

became the grist for countless dimestore novels and was embellished in so many ways over the years that the true story will never be known.

The Wild West Show

Buffalo Bill's days in the real wild west were over, and he returned to staging shows, eventually starting his famed wild-west extravaganza. This was unlike anything ever done before, an outdoor circus that seemed to transport all who watched to the frontier. One newspaper remarked that Cody had "out-Barnumed Barnum." There were buffalo stampedes, cowboy bronc riding, Indian camps, a Deadwood stage and outlaws, crack shooting by Annie Oakley, and of course, Buffalo Bill. At its peak in the late 1890s, the show made Cody more than a million dollars in profit each year.

Amazingly, Sitting Bull and Buffalo Bill became good friends. Cody, who had earlier bragged of his many Indian killings, changed his attitude, eventually saying, "In nine cases out of 10 when there is trouble between white men and Indians, it will be found that the white man is responsible." Meanwhile, Cody's other attitudes continued to evolve. He criticized the buffalo hidehunters of the 1870s and 1880s for their reckless slaughter, and later became an ardent supporter of game preserves and limitations on hunting seasons.

The Wild West Show became one of the most popular events anywhere in America and Europe, attracting crowds of up to 40,000 people. Queen Victoria was a special fan (although rumors of an affair are probably false). At the peak of his fame around the turn of the century, Buffalo Bill was arguably the world's best-known man. Cody, however, continued to drink heavily, and on one day, an obviously drunk Buffalo Bill insisted that his cowboys ride a massive and dangerous bison, named Monarch, in the entourage. When they refused in front of thousands of spectators, Cody himself climbed on top and was immediately thrown to the ground. He spent the next two weeks in a hospital. For the next decade the show continued to tour, gradually losing its appeal as other forms of entertainment came along, especially movies. Cody used his money to buy the 40,000-acre TE Ranch in northwestern Wyoming near Yellowstone National Park. For him the Bighorn Basin was paradise. The town that he helped establish here was named Cody in his honor, and he backed the massive Shoshone irrigation project.

A Sad Farewell

Unfortunately, Buffalo Bill could not save money. He was a notorious soft touch and would give money to almost anyone who asked. As his fortune slipped away and his show became more dated, Cody was finally forced to join up with H.H. Tammen, the crooked owner of the *Denver Post*. Tammen used the aging Cody's fame to attract people to his own circus. He forced Cody's Wild West Show into bankruptcy in 1913, selling off all the incredible collection of historical artifacts that had been amassed over the years and leaving workers to find their own way home. Buffalo Bill was heartbroken but, still trusting Tammen, agreed to join his circus almost as a sideshow act.

Three years later, Cody died while visiting his sister in Denver and was buried on Lookout Mountain near Denver. Cody had wanted to be buried on Cedar Mountain above the town of Cody, but even this wish was denied by Tammen, who apparently paid Cody's widow Louisa $10,000 for the privilege of choosing the burial site (and to use the funeral parade to the burial site as an advertisement for his circus troop). When rumors came that folks from Wyoming intended to dig up Cody's body and take it back to its rightful burial place, Tammen had tons of concrete dumped on top of the grave.

Despite the tragic ending to Buffalo Bill's life, there are few individuals who could have lived such a diverse and adventure-filled life and who could count so many people as friends, from the lowliest beggar to the richest king. Cody's life spanned one of the most remarkable eras in American history, and his impact on American culture is still felt today, not just in the image of the west that he created and that lives on in hundreds of Western movies, but also in the Boy Scouts (an organization inspired partly by his exploits), the city of Cody, and even in the dude ranches that dot Wyoming.

Late in life, Cody was asked how he wanted to be remembered. He replied:

I don't want to die and have people say "Oh, there goes another old showman." When I die I want the people of Wyoming who are living on the land that has been made fertile by my work and expenditure to remember me. I would like people to say, "This is the man who opened up Wyoming to the best of civilization."

grounds in Cody. The best are: **Ponderosa Campground,** 1815 eighth St., tel. 587-9203, where tent sites are $12 and RVs $18; and **7 K's RV Park,** 232 Yellowstone Ave., tel. 587-2532, where tent sites cost $13 and RV sites run $16. Both of these have shade trees. **Cody KOA,** two miles east on US 14-16-20, tel. 587-2369, opened in 1964 as the first franchised KOA. Tent sites cost $13, RVs $17. Other places are **Buffalo Bill Village Campground,** 1701 Sheridan Ave., tel. 587-5544 or (800) 527-5544 (tents $10, RVs $15); **Gateway Campground,** 203 Yellowstone Ave., tel. 587-2561 (tents $9, RVs $12); **Parkway Village** 132 W. Yellowstone, tel. 527-5927, and **Cody Campground,** 415 Yellowstone Ave., tel. 587-9730 (no tents, RVs $15); Camp Cody is open year-round; others are generally open May to mid-October. Non-campers can take showers ($3) at Gateway Campground, 7 K's, or Ponderosa Campground.

FOOD

Because Cody is a tourist town, it comes as no surprise to find many fine places to eat, covering the spectrum from buffalo burgers to Cajun cooking.

Breakfast And Lunch

A good breakfast-and-lunch place is **RJ's Cafe,** 148 W. Yellowstone, tel. 527-4420. Big portions and reasonable prices too. **Maxwell's,** 1256 Sheridan Ave., tel. 527-7749, serves homemade lunches, including pizza, pasta, and salads. **Patsy Ann's Pastry & Ladle,** 1243 Beck Ave., tel. 527-6297, creates good sandwiches, soups, and pastries. **Silver Dollar Bar & Grill,** 1313 Sheridan Ave., tel. 587-3554, makes the best hamburgers and other cowboy grub in town, served in a "kick-ass" western atmosphere. Guaranteed to fill you up. **Pizza on the Run,** 1453 Sheridan Ave., tel. 587-5550, sells hot slices for $1.50.

Dinner

Proud Cut Saloon, 1227 Sheridan Ave., tel. 587-7343, is an old-time Wyoming bar offering unusual sandwiches at lunchtime and outstanding steak and prime rib for dinner. **Maggie's Supper Club,** 1901 Mountain View Rd.,

tel. 527-5001, is another favorite steak-and-seafood place. It features Irish specials. **Louisiana Cajun Seafood,** 1905 Sheridan Ave., tel. 587-2118, is one of the most distinctive local restaurants. The seafood is air freighted from Louisiana and cooked over a hickory BBQ. Good food and friendly service. The nightly smorgasbord at **Eugene's,** 875 Sheridan Ave., tel. 587-2989, is a good deal and popular with families. **irma Hotel,** 1192 Sheridan Ave., tel. 587-4221, is a longtime favorite for lunch and dinner and has a big salad bar.

International Eats

Outstanding Northern Italian cuisine at **Franca's,** 1374 Rumsey Ave., tel. 587-5354. The menu changes through the week, with a fixed-price dinner each evening ($20-25). Try the house specialty: Tortelloni Verdi al Mascarpone. Completely authentic, right down to the chef. **Tag's on 10th,** 937 Sheridan Ave., tel. 587-4971, offers homestyle "West-Mex" cooking, reasonable prices, and a pleasant atmosphere. **La Comida,** 1385 Sheridan Ave., tel. 587-9556, has very good Mexican food for reasonable prices. For Chinese food, visit **Hong Kong Restaurant,** 1244 Sheridan Ave., tel. 587-6420.

Grocers And Bakeries

Cody's grocers include an **IGA** at 1526 Rumsey, tel. 587-6289, and **Blair's Market** at 1825 17th, tel. 587-6721. For natural foods and Wyoming-made gifts, head to **Whole Foods Trading Co.,** 1243 Rumsey, tel. 587-3213. **The Town Bakery,** 1191 Sheridan Ave., tel. 527-5040, bakes breads, cookies, and turnovers. It's a nice place for sub sandwiches and soups. More baked goods and fresh coffee at **Honey Buns & Sweetie Pies,** 917 12th St., tel. 587-5330.

EVENTS AND ENTERTAINMENT

Cody calls itself "Rodeo Capital of the World" and packs the calendar with nightly summertime rodeos, plus the famous Cody Stampede. The rodeo grounds are a mile west of town on US 14-16-20.

Cody Nite Rodeo

Almost everyone who passes through Cody between June and August makes sure to attend one of the evening rodeos. After more than 50 years of operation, the Cody Nite Rodeo is still one of the best in a state filled with rodeos. A favorite is always the calf scramble, starring kids from the stands. The best performances are on Friday and Saturday nights, when you'll see events sanctioned by the Professional Rodeo Cowboys Association (PRCA). The show begins at 8:30 p.m. Tickets cost $6 for adults and $3.50 for children; call 587-5155 for ticket information.

Cody Stampede

Independence Day sets the stage for Cody's main event, the Cody Stampede, held July 2-4. Established in 1922, the Stampede attracts thousands of visitors from all over the nation. Parade fans are treated to one each morning (including a kiddies parade), with dozens of marching bands, mountain men, vintage autos, floats, cowboys, and tons of free candy. Special PRCA rodeo performances, a street dance, art shows, running events, fireworks, and a carnival complete the schedule.

More Events

The Cowboy Antiques and Collectibles Show in mid-June offers the chance for collectors to purchase quality old cowboy gear. It is considered the finest such event in the nation. To get a flavor of the mountain-man era, be sure to attend a performance of Ballad of the West, a dramatic musical held six nights a week in July and August. The story is based upon the life of Jim Bridger and features 15 actors and singers. Well worth seeing. Cowboy Songs and Range Ballads is a unique western musical festival held in early April. You'll hear true cowboy music (not C&W), along with poetry and stories from cowboys, ranchers, and folklorists.

Frontier Festival, held each June at the Buffalo Bill Historical Center, is a celebration of the many skills that were needed to survive on the frontier. Included are demonstrations of horsepacking, hide tanning, gunsmithing, rawhide braiding, weaving, and other homegrown talents. Various contests, musical performances, and booths make this an enjoyable and popular event.

Held on the Robbie Powwow Garden in front of the Buffalo Bill Historical Center in late June, the Plains Indian Powwow attracts several hundred participants from all over the Rockies and Canada. It includes day-long singing and dancing in tribal regalia, along with various dance competitions. Visitors can purchase Indian arts and crafts and taste Indian tacos and fry bread. The Yellowstone Jazz Festival in mid-July attracts both regional and national jazz groups, and Roamin' Wyoming Rally in late August draws some 2,000 motorcycle riders for five days of bike judging, trade shows, and other activities.

Nightlife

Cassie's, 214 Yellowstone Ave., tel. 527-5500, offers Wednesday-night country-swing dance lessons and C&W tunes nightly through the summer. Hang around the bar long enough and you can join in that old Cassie's favorite, barroom brawling. Silver Dollar Bar, 1313 Sheridan Ave., tel. 587-3554, sometimes has rock or jazz bands on the "beach" next door. Maggie's Supper Club, 1901 Mountain View Rd., tel. 527-5001, has Guiness and Harps on tap and dart boards. Park Drive In, on the east end of Big Horn Dr., tel. 587-2712, is one of the few drive-in theaters left in Wyoming.

RECREATION

River Rafting

One of the most popular summertime activities in Cody is floating the class-I and -II Shoshone River. Beware, however, that even with these mild conditions, you should plan on getting soaked in the rapids. Prices vary depending upon the trip length and whether it includes lunch, but expect around $16 ($13 for kids) for a six-mile run (1½ hours) or $22 ($18 for kids) for a 13-mile (three-hour) float. For details, contact Wyoming River Trips, 1701 Sheridan Ave., tel. 587-6661, or River Runners, 1491 Sheridan Ave., tel. 527-7238.

If you want to try rafting or kayaking on your own, there are several miles of very technical class-IV water with some class-V drops below the dam and above DeMaris Springs. Above the dam are stretches of class-I and -II water with good access from the main highway. Ask locally for flow conditions before heading out, since snow melt and dam releases can dramatically affect water levels. The rafting companies offer half-day whitewater trips down the North Fork above the reservoir for $35 pp. These trips only run mid-May to early July, when the water level is high.

Most folks put in three miles west of Cody off Demaris Street. Just upstream from the put-in point is DeMaris Springs, a part of **"Colter's Hell."** The area was once far more active, with hot springs bubbling out of the river and sulfurous smoke rising all around. People actually died from the poisonous gas. Today the geothermal activity has lessened, but the air still smells of sulfur and small hot springs color the cliff faces. Miners worked over nearby hillsides in search of sulfur; the diggings are still apparent. Pretty obvious why they first called this the Stinkingwater River.

Trail Rides

Horseback rides are available from **Gateway Motel and Campground,** 203 Yellowstone, tel. 587-2561. The chamber of commerce office has a complete listing of more than 60 outfitters and guides in the Cody area.

More Recreation

Rent mountain bikes from **Olde Faithful Bicycle,** 1362 Sheridan Ave., tel. 527-5110. Swim at the **outdoor pool,** 1240 Beck Ave., tel. 587-5254, for 75 cents (kids 50 cents), or the **Stock Natorium,** Ninth St. and Beck Ave., for 50 cents. The 18-hole **Olive-Glenn Golf and Country Club,** 802 Meadow Lane, tel. 587-5688, is a PGA championship course. They also have an indoor pool (tel. 587-5551) for lap swimming. Call 587-9306 for information on day-long van tours of beautiful **Sunlight Basin.**

OTHER PRACTICALITIES

Art

Big Horn Gallery, 1167 Sheridan Ave., tel. 587-6762, contains a wide selection of western and wildlife art prints and paintings. If you're a serious art patron, make an appointment to view the bronze pieces of nationally renowned sculptor **Harry Jackson** at his private studio. Call 587-5508 for details, but be ready to part with a hundred thou or so. **Shoshone River Pottery,** 1725 E. Sheridan, offers a wide choice of pottery. Next to the chamber of commerce office is the **Cody Country Art League,** tel. 587-3597, with a variety of paintings, sculptures, and crafts for sale, plus workshops and judged art shows. The **Buffalo Bill Art Show & Sale** in mid-September is the biggest art event of the year. It features exhibitions, a symposium, receptions, and an auction.

Shopping

Corral West Ranchwear, 1202 Sheridan Ave., tel. 587-2122, has a large collection of big-game heads and a couple of stuffed nine-foot-tall bears. **North Fork Anglers,** 973 Sheridan Ave., tel. 527-7274, has anything you might need for fly-fishing, including professional fishing guides and fly-tying clinics. Get camping and hiking supplies at **War Surplus** (there always does seem to be a surplus of wars, so you might as well buy a couple while you're in town), 130 N. Bent, tel. 754-2694. Topo maps can be found at **Cody Newstand,** 1121 13th St., tel. 587-2843.

Books

Park County Library, 1057 Sheridan Ave., tel. 587-6204, is open Mon.-Fri. 10-5:30, Sat. 10-1, plus Mon. and Thurs. 7-9 p.m. New books are available at **Cody Newstand,** 1121 13th St., tel. 587-2843, and **The Thistle,** 1243 Rumsey, tel. 587-6635. **Wyoming Well Book Exchange and Oilfield Supply,** 2220 Big Horn Ave., tel. 587-4249, is the oddest combination in town: bodice-buster novels and oil equipment!

Information And Services

The **Cody Country Chamber of Commerce,** 836 Sheridan Ave., tel. 587-2297, is open Mon.-Sat. 8-7 and Sun. 10-3 during the summer, and Mon.-Fri. 8-5 the rest of the year. This log building housed the original Buffalo Bill Museum from 1927 to 1969 and was built as a replica of Cody's TE Ranch. It is on the National Register of Historic Places. While here, be sure to pick up the free *Cody Country Summer Guide* for up-to-date regional information.

The BLM's **Cody Resources Office** is at 1002 Blackburn Ave., tel. 587-2216. The Forest Service has two local offices: the **Shoshone National Forest Supervisor's Office** at 225

W. Yellowstone Ave., tel. 527-6241, and the **Wapiti Ranger District Office** at 203 W. Yellowstone, tel. 527-6921.

Transportation
Yellowstone Regional Airport is just east of town on US 14-16-20. **Continental Express,** tel. (800) 525-0280, has year-round service to Denver, and **United Express,** tel. (800) 241-6522, connects with Denver during the summer. Rent cars at the airport from **Avis,** tel. (800) 331-1212, **Hertz,** tel. (800) 654-3131, or **Rent-A-**

Wreck, tel. 587-4993 or (800) 535-1391.

In the summer, daily lower loop tours of Yellowstone National Park ($41) are available through **Powder River Tours** at Buffalo Bill Village, 1701 Sheridan Ave., tel. 587-5544 or (800) 442-3682. You can stay overnight in Yellowstone and return on a later bus for no extra charge, or transfer to Gray Line and Karst Stage buses en route to Jackson, West Yellowstone, or Gardiner. **Cody Bus Lines,** 1928 Big Horn Ave., tel. 587-4181 or (800) 733-2304, has daily bus service to Powell as well as Billings, Montana.

CODY VICINITY

HEART MOUNTAIN

Halfway between Cody and Powell is Heart Mountain, so named because its twin summits faintly resemble the traditional valentine. The mountain is visible for many miles in all directions. Geologists scratch their heads over this seemingly upside-down mountain. The Heart Mountain detachment fault stretches for over a hundred miles, cutting southwest from near Cooke City, Montana. To the east are enormous blocks of land that have slid onto the tops of more recent deposits, reversing the normal situation in which older rocks lie beneath more recent ones. Scientists know that these limestone and dolomite blocks moved around 45 to 50 million years ago but none have been able to adequately explain how entire mountains, including Heart Mountain, could have slid for dozens of miles.

HEART MOUNTAIN RELOCATION CENTER

For Americans of Japanese ancestry, Heart Mountain might as well have been called Broken Heart Mountain. After the Japanese attack on Pearl Harbor in 1941, Japanese-Americans found their patriotism under increasing suspicion, and the following spring, President Roosevelt signed an executive order establishing the War Relocation Authority to move them away from the coasts. The authority built 10 re-

mote "relocation centers" to imprison anyone of Japanese ancestry, including one just east of Heart Mountain that housed nearly 11,000 Japanese-Americans (two-thirds of them born in America). The camp became Wyoming's third-largest settlement. It took just 62 days to complete the 468 barracks, 40 laundry-toilet buildings, Buddhist and Christian churches, high school, fire station, recreation hall, power station, mess hall, hospital, sewage plant, administrative offices, and numerous other structures. (No environmental-impact reports on this baby!) Barbed wire surrounded the perimeter, and military police manned nine guard towers with high-beam searchlights and machine guns.

Camp Life
Most of the Japanese-Americans took the forced relocation with remarkable aplomb, realizing the futility of any escape attempt. It almost seemed the patriotic thing to do; "shikata-ga-nai" (or "I guess it cannot be helped") became the accepted phrase. Although life in the camp maintained a sense of normalcy—some kids came to enjoy their peaceful high-school years and the picnics in Yellowstone—it was far from idyllic. Three or four people were jammed into each room, furniture was minimal, people had to share communal bathhouses, and the winter winds blew through the uninsulated tar-paper buildings. Wyoming folks resented the Japanese-Americans but appreciated the cheap farm labor while their sons were off fighting the Germans and Japanese.

After The War

With the war's end in 1945, the camp was closed and the internees were given $25 and a one-way bus ticket home (or rather to what remained; many found their homes ransacked). Over the next four years the 740 acres of land was opened to homesteading, with the barracks being sold at two for $1. Most ended up as temporary homes for the new settlers. None of the Japanese-American interns remained in the area, and most have little desire to even visit what seemed such a desolate, godforsaken place. They would rather try to forget.

The Camp Today

Today the only reminders of the camp are three buildings, the largest being the old hospital heating plant with its tall brick chimney. A couple of plaques mark the site of Heart Mountain Relocation Center, one noting the more than 600 men who left the camp to join the U.S. Army in Europe. Twenty-one internees and a camp teacher died.

The site is 11 miles east of Cody on US 14A. Barley fields now surround the former camp, while Heart Mountain stands guard over the western flank. The nonprofit **Heart Mountain Relocation Center Memorial Association,** Box 774, Ralston, WY 82440, works to preserve the memory of this painful era. Efforts are underway to preserve the remaining buildings and to open a visitor center and museum.

EAST TO POWELL

The historic Eagles Nest Stage Station stands east of the relocation camp as you head toward Powell. The log cabins and barns were built a century ago by the Lanchbury family, who homesteaded here. Their ranch served as a stage station midway between Meeteetse (then the largest town in Bighorn Basin) and Red Lodge, Montana. Today, a fifth generation of the Lanchburys lives in the restored buildings of historic Eagles Nest. If you're looking for trivia, stop in the tiny settlement of **Ralston** to see the railroad bridge over a highway bridge, atop a creek. This odd collection made it into "Ripley's Believe It or Not!"

MEETEETSE

Along the western edge of Bighorn Basin is a charming little ranching center called Meeteetse (pop. 370). The name is a Crow Indian word meaning "Meeting Place of the Chiefs." The Absarokas rise gently to the south and west of Meeteetse, and the Greybull River flows right through town, cottonwood trees on either side. To the north, the highway crosses a rolling land of sage and greasewood, while to the south are rugged badlands. The town has wooden sidewalks and hitching rails, cattle drives right down Main St., and not just one, but three free museums.

History

One of the oldest towns in Bighorn Basin, Meeteetse was first settled in the early 1880s by homesteaders and wealthy European cattle barons. By 1890 it was the largest community in the basin. Several original buildings are still standing, including the **Meeteetse Mercantile,** built in 1899 and still stocked with everything you might need to survive. The last wild black-footed ferrets (see p. 75) were discovered just a dozen miles to the west at the famed Pitchfork Ranch. They were captured in 1987 after an outbreak of canine distemper threatened to kill all the remaining wild ferrets.

Museums

Town Hall Museum, built in 1900, is filled with cowboy paraphernalia of all sorts, along with a nice collection of old china dolls and historic photographs. It's open Sun. 1-4 and Mon.-Sat. 11-5 during the summer, or by appointment at other times, tel. 868-2423. More historical items are at **Meeteetse Archives,** located in the old Hogg, Cheeseman, and MacDonald's Bank (1901). Hours here are Mon.-Fri. 10-4. The new **Charles Belden Western Photography Museum** is open daily 8-8 in summer and Mon.-Fri. 8-5 in winter. Inside are a number of famous cowboy photographs that Charles Belden took at the 30,000-acre Pitchfork Ranch in the 1930s and '40s. Well worth a look.

Accommodations

Oasis Motel, 1702 State St., tel. 868-2551, has cabins for $25 s or $29 d, along with campsites for $7 and RV spots for $10; open June-October. **Vision Quest Motel,** 2207 State St., tel. 868-2512, charges $30 s or d. **High Island Guest Ranch** in Hamilton Dome, tel. 867-2374, provides a chance to take part in cattle drives and other cowpoke adventures on a working ranch. Visits by the week only.

Other Practicalities

Elkhorn Bar has the best local burgers and is a meeting spot for local folks, especially on weekend evenings when country bands play. **Outlaw Cafe** at the Cowboy Bar also has good food and old photos from early-day Meeteetse. Be sure to ask the bartender at the Cowboy for the "true" origins of the word Meeteetse. More food next door at **Lucille's Cafe,** tel. 868-9909. The **Forest Service District Office** is at 2044 State St., tel. 868-2379. The town **swimming pool** is in the high school. Come to Meeteetse on **Labor Day weekend** for a small town parade, country rodeo, barbecue, street dance, and crafts fair. Great fun.

MEETEETSE AREA

The excellent **Wood River Valley Ski Touring Park** (free) is 22 miles southwest of town on Wood River Road. Meeteetse Recreation District, tel. 868-2603, runs the park and provides ski rentals in town. The cross-country ski area includes 25 km of groomed trails, wonderful mountain scenery, a warming hut, and an overnight tent with wood stove ($15 per group per night; reserve ahead). It's open daily through the winter.

The drive up Wood River Rd. is also enjoyable at other times of the year, providing the chance to see moose and elk in the bottomlands. Two free Forest Service **campgrounds** (open June-Nov.) are available near the end of the road. From here you can hike into the Washakie Wilderness along any of several different trails.

A 4WD road continues on to **Kirwin,** a turn-of-the-century gold- and copper-mining town. The long-abandoned town was recently given to the Forest Service by the Mellon Foundation. It is a fascinating place to explore, with an old hotel, several cabins, and a mine shafthouse. A summer home was being built near here for Amelia Earhart shortly before her 1934 disappearance during an around-the-world flight. The cabin was never finished.

Another historic place—**Palatte Ranch**—is at the end of a gravel road paralleling the Greybull River. The ranch was once owned by A.A. Anderson, first superintendent of the Yellowstone Timber Reserve (now Shoshone National Forest). The Anderson lodge is on the National Historic Register and is undergoing restoration by the Forest Service.

Legend Rock Petroglyph Site

One of the finest sites for Indian rock art in all Wyoming lies between Meeteetse and Thermopolis in the foothills of the Owl Creek Mountains. Head 31 miles southeast of Meeteetse on US 120 (or 21 miles northwest of Thermopolis) and turn right at the Hamilton Dome Road (if you're coming from Thermopolis, turn left at the second Hamilton Dome turnoff). After five miles, turn right onto the gravel Cottonwood Creek Road. Continue two miles to the second cattle guard and follow the road a short distance to a parking area in front of a gate. The petroglyphs are a quarter-mile walk down from here. (If you want to drive down the hill, borrow the key from the Hot Springs State Park office in Thermopolis, tel. 864-2176.) The total distance from Hwy. 120 to the petroglyph site is eight miles.

At least 283 petroglyphs have been found on the nearby sandstone cliffs, covering a variety of styles. There are deer, bison, elk, various human figures, and even a "flying" rabbit. Owl Creek flows not far away, and oil pumpjacks dot the nearby hills (Hamilton Dome is one of the most important oil fields in Bighorn Basin). The rock art is believed to have been associated with shamanism and ritual healing and may date back 2,000 years.

West of Legend Rock is **Anchor Dam,** a major engineering blunder. The dam has never held much water, despite repeated attempts to seal the lake bottom at a cost of millions of dollars; the water simply seeps into the porous limestone beneath.

Northwest of Meeteetse is another important Indian site, the **Great Arrow,** a 58-foot-long arrow made from rocks and placed atop a long hogback ridge. It points toward the Medicine Wheel (see pp. 423-424) in the Big Horn Mountains, 70 miles to the northeast. Its age is unknown.

POWELL

One of the nicest settlements in Bighorn Basin is Powell (pop. 5,300), a farming, oil, and college town halfway between Cody and Lovell. Sugar beets, malting barley (grown for Coors and Anheuser-Busch), and dry beans are the primary crops produced here. Because they are harvested at different times of the year, many farmers grow all three. The big elevators of Powell Bean Growers Association and Baker Bean & Feed border the railroad tracks on the south edge of town. A dozen miles to the north is the giant Elk Basin oil field. First discovered in 1915, it had 150 wells pumping more than 4,200 barrels a day within five years. The field has proven a major factor in the growth of the northern Bighorn Basin. Although production is gradually declining as the supply is exhausted, modern recovery techniques pushed pumping over 11,000 barrels per day in the 1980s. The U.S. Air Force also maintains a radar installation just west of Powell.

The Early Years
Powell was named for John Wesley Powell (1834-1902), the famed one-armed explorer of the Colorado River and an early director of the U.S. Geological Survey. His 1889 report on the agricultural potential of western desert lands had declared the value of irrigation in "reclaiming" these areas through dams and canal systems funded by the government. One of the earliest of these was the mammoth Shoshone Project, involving Buffalo Bill Dam and a series of canals to feed water to the fields along the Shoshone River. Powell is right at the center of all this irrigation, and homesteaders flocked here in the first two decades of this century. The town sprang up at a campsite used by workers on the Shoshone Project. With the arrival of the Chicago, Burlington, and Quincy Railroad (now part of Burlington Northern), Powell became an agricultural shipping point.

Earl Durand
Folks still talk about "Tarzan of the Tetons," a local kid gone bad. Earl Durand was a crack shot and a mountain man of sorts. He had once traveled by horse and foot to Mexico, and he bragged that he could survive on practically anything, even raw bobcat meat. Durand hated being cooped up inside buildings, so when he was arrested for poaching in 1939, he escaped the Cody jail. Five people died in the shooting rampage that followed, and the murders attracted intense national attention. The climax came when Durand robbed a Powell bank and suddenly found himself surrounded. A 17-year-old kid shot, but didn't kill, Durand as he came out of the bank with a screen of hostages. Sensing the futility of the situation, he went back inside and committed suicide. Powell's Homesteader Museum has lots of old newspaper clippings on this sad story, and the incident inspired a minor 1974 movie that starred Slim Pickens, Peter Haskell, and Martin Sheen, *The Legend of Earl Durand*. The story still touches raw nerves in Powell, even after more than 50 years.

Sights
The free **Homesteader Museum,** on the corner of First and Clark streets, tel. 754-9481, is open Tues.-Fri. 1-5 May-Sept., and Fri. and Sat. 10-12 and 1-5 the rest of the year. The museum captures the hardscrabble life of turn-of-the-century homesteaders in the northern Bighorn Basin. You'll find interesting old photographs, a beautiful collection of dryhead agate, and some Indian artifacts. The grotesque elk chairs and furniture in the back corner are unique, to say the least. Lots more junk to check out. Be sure to take the time to watch the videotape detailing the history of the nearby Heart Mountain Relocation Center (see above). An adjacent building is filled with horse-drawn machines and old tractors, while outside are a caboose and various pieces of old farm equipment.

Founded in 1946, **Northwest College** is one of the state's top junior colleges. The 95-acre campus is quite attractive, with modern brick buildings and fluorescent green lawns (at least in the summer). Two-thirds of the students live on campus, but the school does offer evening classes in the surrounding towns. Northwest is a cultural and social center for Powell and the area, bringing a variety of theater productions and entertainment, plus art exhibits at the **Northwest Gallery** (open Mon.-Fri. 8-5 Sept.-May). For information on Northwest, call 754-6111 or (800) 442-2946.

Accommodations

See the chart for a list of local motels. **Park County Fairgrounds,** tel. 754-5421, has RV sites ($10) and shower facilities. RVers park for free at the highway rest area in the 57-acre **Homesteader Park** on the east end of town.

You can pitch a tent on the grass here, but the sprinklers go on at night.

Food

At the top of the Powell food chain is **Munchies,** 333 E. Second, tel. 754-2683, where you'll find good breakfasts, authentic Mexican food, burgers, and homemade pies. Highly recommended. **Skyline Family Dining,** 141 E. Coulter, tel. 754-2772, is very popular with locals for breakfast. Try the chicken-fried steak for dinner. **Powell Drug,** 140 N. Bent, tel. 754-2031, has an old-fashioned soda fountain where the root beer floats and malts still attract kids. **Hansel & Gretel's,** 113 S. Bent, tel. 754-2191, makes good

© MOON PUBLICATIONS, INC.

spaghetti, soups, and sandwiches. Be sure to order a slice of homemade pie for dessert. **Pizza on the Run,** 215 E. First, tel. 754-5720, is the local pizza joint. **Gallaigoss Steak House,** 337 E. Second., tel. 754-2243, is the carnivore place in town, with delicious steaks and BBQ chicken. Easily the least expensive meal deal in Powell is at the **Student Union Cafeteria** on the Northwest College campus. Get groceries at **Blair's Market,** 210 S. Douglas, tel. 754-3122, or **Food Basket IGA,** 421 E. First, tel. 754-3602.

Entertainment

Since this is a college town, you can always find live music on weekends. Try **The Timbers,** 1017 US 14A, tel. 754-9581, or **Bent Street Station,** 117 S. Bent, tel. 754-3384, for rock or country tunes. **American Legion** on E. First, tel. 754-3411, sometimes has C&W bands. Northwest College's **Pub** in the Student Union Building is a popular student hangout before 10 p.m.

Events

Powell's big annual event, **Homesteader Days,** arrives on the last weekend of June. There are frontier demonstrations, crafts for sale, races, contests, picnics, music, dancing, an antique-car show, and lots of other activities. This is followed in late July by the **Park County Fair,** with parades, horseshoe-pitching contests, 4-H shows, a demolition derby, tractor pulls, a horse pull, dancing, headline acts, and a carnival. The **Yellowstone Jazz Festival** in mid-July has performances in both Cody and Powell. The **Tour of Heart Mountain** bike race circles the mountain in a 100-mile marathon. **Sheepman's Holiday** in late October features sheep events of all sorts, including sheepdog trials. If you happen to be in the area in early December, stop by for **Country Christmas,** a three-day festivity with a variety of activities and craft exhibits, plus a live nativity scene.

Recreation

Attractive **Homesteader Park** has a number of modern recreation facilities, including a kids'll-love-it green frog slide at the wading pool. In winter, there is a free ice arena here with skate rentals and a warming hut. The public **swimming pool** ($1) is in the high school. A nine-hole municipal **golf course** is five miles east of

Powell, tel. 754-3039. **Larsen's Bikes,** 255 E. Second St., tel. 754-5481 or (800) 325-7653, may have mountain bikes for rent.

Shopping

Mountain Man Moccasin Co., 265 N. Bent, tel. 754-9779 or (800) 734-9779, makes quality leather moccasins of deerskin or elk leather. Powell Office Supply is at the same address and sells books and topographic maps. More books for sale at the **Northwest College Bookstore,** tel. 754-6308.

Information And Services

The **Powell Valley Chamber of Commerce,** 111 S. Day, tel. 754-3494 or (800) 325-4278 (outside Wyoming), is open Mon.-Fri. 8:30-4:30. The modern **Powell Public Library,** 217 E. Third, tel. 754-2261, is open Mon.-Fri. 10-5:30, Mon. and Thurs. 7-9 p.m., and Sat. 10-1. **John Hinckley Memorial Library** on the Northwest College campus, tel. 754-6207, is open Sun. 2-10, Mon.-Thurs. 7:45 a.m.-10 p.m., Fri. 7:45-5, and Sat. 11-4. (No, it isn't named for the man who shot former President Reagan.) The **Shoshone National Forest District Office** is 2 1/2 miles west of town, tel. 754-2407. **Cody Bus Lines,** tel. (800) 733-2304, has daily bus service to Cody as well as Billings, Montana.

EAST TO LOVELL

A tangle of roads wanders through the country between Lovell and Powell, tying together a cluster of small agriculture and oil settlements established by Mormon emigrants. **Cowley** (pop. 480) has a number of impressive old sandstone buildings. Ancient Indian petroglyphs can be found north of town in Blue Wash. The Cowley rodeo comes in July. **Byron** (pop. 470) has quite a few old log buildings and is surrounded by dairy farms. Check out the "roadkill" menu at **Half Fast Diner** in Byron. Just two miles south of the Montana border on US 310 lies **Frannie** (pop. 150), straddling the line between Park and Big Horn counties. Residents say it's "The Biggest Little Town in Wyoming because it takes two counties to hold the people." Stop by **Frannie Tack Shop,** tel. 548-2344 or (800) 552-8836, to see the saddles or to get repairs on

POWELL & LOVELL ACCOMMODATIONS

MOTEL	ADDRESS	TELEPHONE	RATES	NOTES
POWELL MOTELS				
Best Choice Motel	337 E. Second St.	754-2243	$28 s or d	
Lamplighter Inn	234 First St.	754-2226	$28 s, $32 d	
Park Motel	737 E. Second St.	754-2233	$34 s, $37 d	kitchenettes
Super 8 Motel	845 E. Coulter	754-7231 (800) 800-8000	$38 s, $42 d	
King's Inn (Best Western)	777 E. Second St.	754-5117 (800) 528-1234	$59 s or d	AAA-approved, pool, steam baths
LOVELL MOTELS				
Uptown Motel	43 E. Main	548-2741 (800) 457-5490	$21 s, $25 d	continental breakfast
Horseshoe Bend Motel	375 E. Main St.	548-2221	$27 s, $30 d	AAA-approved, pool, kitchenettes
Cattleman Motel	470 Montana Ave.	548-2296	$27 s, $30 d	AAA-approved
Super 8 Motel	595 E. Main St.	548-2725 (800) 800-8000	$33 s, $37 d	

canvas or leather items. In **Deaver** (pop. 200), be sure to drop in at the unusual **Showboat Dinner Theatre,** tel. 664-2504, for live music and dramas with your dinner. The dot of a place called **Garland** (pop. 50) has a wonderful old schoolhouse (now used as a church) built in the early 1900s.

Just east of Lovell, the pungent odors of sulfur and oil hang in the air, and the dry badlands are punctuated by oil pumpjacks. More than 117 million barrels of oil and 13 million cubic feet of gas have been produced in the Byron Oil Field since its discovery in 1918. The other business here is farming. Much of this desert land is now under irrigation, and the lush green farmlands are filled with sugar beets, beans, malting barley, alfalfa, and corn. A sign along Hwy. 14A notes the **Sidon Canal,** built in 1900 by Mormon settlers of the Bighorn Basin. The 37-mile-long canal was entirely self-financed with land donated by the government and transports water from the Shoshone River to 20,000 acres of farm land. Mormons claim that "Prayer Rock," a large impediment to the canal's construction, was miraculously split as a result of their supplications.

LOVELL

The sleepy little burg of Lovell (pop. 2,100; pronounced LOVE-ul) calls itself the "City of Roses," a title that comes from Dr. William Horsley, who lived here from 1924 till his death in 1971. Horsley loved roses and, in the course of a lifetime of cultivating them, became one of the nation's foremost rose authorities. The "Rose Doctor's" enthusiasm rubbed off on others, and today gardens all over town are packed with roses. Oil fields crowd around Lovell, and a Georgia Pacific wallboard plant and two bentonite plants are substantial local employers, but farming is king. The Western Sugar factory stands on the edge of town, providing jobs for workers and a market for local farmers who contract with the plant to grow sugar beets. In late fall, huge mounds of straw-covered beets pile up beside the factory and the rancid/sweet odor of cooking beets fills the air. Stray beets, spilled from overloaded farm trucks, lie along the highway for miles. Lovell doesn't offer much for tourists, but the surrounding country includes Bighorn National Recreation Area and the Big Horn Mountains. A state-run fish rearing station at Tillett Springs, 17 miles north of Lovell, raises cutthroat and rainbow trout.

Like most towns in the northern Bighorn Basin, Lovell is dominated by Mormons. An enormous brick LDS church fills an entire block along the main drag. Although Lovell has wide, clean streets, the downtown has quite a few empty storefronts.

History

The town of Lovell has its roots in the enormous ML Ranch, founded in 1880 by Anthony L. Mason and Henry Clay Lovell (see p. 400 for more on this ranch). In 1900, Mormon settlers moved to the remote Bighorn Basin (partly to escape prosecution for polygamy), working on the Burlington Railroad and developing irrigation projects. The area boomed with the discovery of natural gas and the opening of various factories. A few years later, German emigrants provided labor for the farm fields and then settled down to acquire their own land. Yellowtail Dam on the Bighorn River was built in 1965, and the surrounding land became a national recreation area the following year.

Lovell claims to have the lowest crime rate in Wyoming, but nowhere in the tourist brochures do they mention the history of two of its most prominent doctors. A few years before his 1971 death, Dr. William Horsley, the famed "Rose Doctor," was forced to resign from the local hospital following a series of homosexual incidents with boys. But another respected physician, Dr. John Story, gained considerably more notoriety for his actions. Story arrived in 1958 to practice general medicine, joining the local Baptist church and becoming a strong conservative community leader. Unfortunately, over the next 25 years he also raped or molested dozens (some say hundreds) of women and girls in his office. A combination of strict Mormon upbringing, sexual ignorance, shame, and fear prevented them from talking, and the few who did speak up were called liars. Finally, in 1983, the charges began to surface. The trial turned Lovell inside out. Despite intense pressure from local and state politicians (then-Governor Herschler called the victims' testimony "hogwash"), Story was convicted in April 1985 of several rape charges and is currently serving a 20-year sentence in the Wyoming State Penitentiary. Jack Olson's harrowing book, *Doc*, describes this sorry chapter in recent Wyoming history. It is perhaps fitting that Lovell will be the site of a new state prison.

Accommodations

See the chart for a listing of local motels. The **TX Ranch,** a 10,000-acre cattle ranch, offers a unique chance to take part in ranch life. It isn't a dude ranch, and visitors end up joining in cattle drives, branding calves, and doing roundups. Call (406) 484-2583 for details.

The best campsites in the Lovell area lie within nearby Bighorn Canyon National Recreation Area (see below). In town, camp for free (including showers) at **Lovell Camper Park** on Quebec Ave. north of Main Street. It's a quiet place surrounded by cottonwoods. RVers can pay to stay at **Camp Big Horn RV Park,** 595 E. Main St., tel. 548-2725.

Food

Rose Bowl Cafe, 483 Shoshone Ave., tel. 548-7121, is popular for breakfast and lunch; try one of their huge cinnamon rolls. For pizzas, head to **Pizza on the Run,** 214 Main St., tel. 548-2206. **Grandma's,** 443 E. Main, tel. 548-7134, offers fast food. The nicest local eatery is **Big Horn Restaurant,** 605 E. Main St., tel. 548-6811, where locals and visitors come for a dinner out or to enjoy a leisurely breakfast. Get groceries and deli food at **Red Apple Supermarket,** 9 E. Main St., tel. 548-9907. While there, take a gander at the War Memorial.

Information And Services

For local info, head to the new **Lovell Information Center,** 287 E. Main, tel. 548-7552. Hours are Mon.-Fri. 8-1 and 1-5. There's a big indoor **pool,** along with other recreation facilities, on the southwest end of town. The **Medicine Wheel Ranger District** of Bighorn National Forest office is at 604 E. Main, tel. 548-6541. Stop here for information on the Medicine Wheel. Rent cars from **Murphey Ford,** 80 E. Main, tel. 548-6546.

The big annual event in Lovell is **Mustang Days,** held the last full week in June. Activities include parades, fireworks, barbecues, and a rodeo.

BIGHORN CANYON NATIONAL RECREATION AREA

Just east of Lovell is one of America's lesser-known but most stunning sights, Bighorn Canyon. Over the eons, the Bighorn River has slowly carved out a 2,200-foot-deep chasm through the desert country. Since 1965, when the 525-foot-tall Yellowtail Dam was completed, the canyon has lain under a deep blanket of water, water that provides 250,000 kilowatts of electricity for the western U.S., and that irrigates thousands of acres of Montana farmland. The dam itself is—as the raven flies—more than 20 miles north of the Wyoming-Montana border, but its impact reaches 70 river miles upstream, creating Bighorn Lake. The upper reaches of the lake are shallow and often go dry by late summer.

The Setting

The 120,000-acre Bighorn Canyon National Recreation Area (no charge) is managed by the National Park Service. Separate facilities on both ends of the recreation area are linked by a circuitous 180-mile route that takes you through Billings. For this reason, most road-bound visitors come to either the Montana side or the Wyoming side, but not both. Boaters can traverse the entire reach of the canyon.

Attractions accessible only from Montana include the dam itself (daily tours available through the summer), tel. (406) 666-2358, the nearby

Fort Smith Visitor Center, tel. (406) 666-2339, a short nature trail, and the site of two Bozeman Trail features: Fort C.F. Smith and the Hayfield Fight (both on private land).

From the Wyoming side, things are considerably more interesting, even though some of the sights actually lie across the Montana border. A paved road extends for 27 miles along the western side of the recreation area, with a rough dirt road continuing 15 more miles to the Crow Indian Reservation. Along the way are a couple of campgrounds, the historic Bad Pass Trail, two old ranches, magnificent Devil Canyon, and a good chance to see bighorn sheep and wild horses. The road cuts through impressive red-and-gray badlands carpeted by juniper, sagebrush, and mountain mahogany.

SIGHTS

Devil Canyon Area

The pièce de résistance of Bighorn National Recreation Area is **Devil Canyon,** at the confluence of the Bighorn River and Porcupine Creek. From the overlook, the earth drops suddenly away. More than a thousand feet below, motorboats look like miniature toys in a bathtub. A real treat in the canyon is the chance to

see **bighorn sheep** up close. Although the more impressive rams tend to hang out in remote parts of the Pryor Mountains most of the year, ewes and lambs can be seen along the road between Horseshoe Bend and Devil Canyon Overlook. The rams are more likely to be seen during the Nov.-Dec. rutting season.

Precipitous Bighorn Canyon was known as **Bad Pass** by the Indians. The trail they used to reach the buffalo herds followed the canyon rim for many miles, marked by rock cairns. Some of these cairns are still visible between Devil Canyon Overlook and Barry's Landing, as are some of the caves where Indians wintered near the canyon bottoms.

Before it was dammed, the river offered a torrent of rushing rapids and falls, with jagged rocks waiting to punch holes in any boat, and a canyon so deep that the sun only reached the bottom for a brief period each day. In 1825, the famed mountain man and guide Jim Bridger decided to take a wooden raft down the canyon to see if it could provide a way to ship furs back east. It was a feat that was not matched for over a century, when a motorboat finally ran the wild currents.

Hillsboro

The ghost settlement of **Hillsboro** is about a mile above Barry's Landing and is accessible only by foot. Established around the turn of the century by a self-proclaimed physician, Grosverner William Barry, the site was originally a gold-mining center. When that didn't pan out, Barry turned to dude ranching, promoting his ranch as a place where guests could cruise through Bighorn Canyon on motorboats or ride English Hackney horses. The dude ranch flourished until the 1930s, but the collection of antique furniture and paintings was destroyed by a fire in the winter of 1947-48. Still standing are the old post office and various cabins.

ML Ranch

The great ML Ranch was founded in 1880 by Anthony L. Mason and Henry Clay Lovell. Lovell trailed herds of cattle up from Kansas to this newly opened country, building his main headquarters along the Bighorn River, just east of the community that was later named for him. The vast unfenced ranch became known as the

"Big Outfit" and employed hundreds of cow hands. Grazed by 25,000 cattle, it stretched from Thermopolis all the way to the Crow Reservation in Montana, 90 miles away.

Most of the buildings from the old ML Ranch are now gone, but you can still visit the restored bunkhouse, blacksmith shop, and two cabins. Most interesting is the bunkhouse, actually three cabins connected by dogtrots (covered breezeways). The end cabins acted as sleeping quarters, while the middle one was a cook shack and mess hall. Get here by heading east from Lovell across the bridge over Bighorn Reservoir. A sign points out the ranch. Check at the visitor center for tours.

Other Sights

Adjacent to the recreation area is the 19,424-acre **Yellowtail Wildlife Habitat Management Unit,** a popular place for hunters and birdwatchers. Many dirt roads and trails crisscross the area, and wildlife of all types abounds. During fall migration, the wetlands here are jammed with up to 10,000 ducks. Get a map of the roads and trails of Yellowtail at the Bighorn Visitor Center.

Caves create a latticework under portions of the recreation area. On the east side of Bighorn Lake is **Bighorn Caverns.** Access is limited to experienced spelunkers and requires 4WD vehicles; get the gate key and directions at the Bighorn Visitor Center. This cave links with **Horsethief Cave** several miles north. Although closed to the public, **Natural Trap Cave** is of biological value. Located 35 miles northeast of Lovell, a 12-by-15-foot opening drops into the 65-foot-deep cavern. Over the centuries many animals—from prehistoric horses to rabbits—have fallen in.

PRACTICALITIES

Camping

There are three campgrounds in the southern half of Bighorn Canyon. Folks in RVs park at **Horseshoe Bend** ($4). It has water and toilets, but just one lone tree for shade, making this a rather bleak place for anyone in a tent. The drive in to Horseshoe Bend passes lovely red sandstone badlands. **Barry's Landing Camp-**

ground is much nicer (and also much smaller). No charge, but bring your own water. Firewood is usually available at both of these places. In addition, you can pitch a tent at the free **Medicine Creek Campground**, though you'll need to hike in on a two-mile dirt road or come in by boat. Backcountry camping is available throughout the southern end of the recreation area, but be sure to get a permit at the visitor center first. Also be sure to avoid trespassing on the nearby Crow Indian Reservation.

Hiking

Although there are only a few trails in Bighorn Canyon, the open badland country makes hiking relatively easy. Best times are in the fall or in Feb. and March when temperatures are milder and you're less likely to meet a rattler. Prairie rattlesnakes and black-widow spiders are both common in this desert country, so be aware, especially when exploring old buildings.

Crooked Creek Nature Trail, a short path with self-guiding brochures, takes off from the Horseshoe Bend campground. A two-mile trail (actually an old prospecting road) follows the canyon rim from Barry's Landing to the Medicine Creek Campground. You can also hike the mile-long dirt path to **Hillsboro** and the 2 1/2-mile road to the **Lockhart Ranch** (the road can be driven in high-clearance cars). Ask at the visitor center for other interesting places to hike in Bighorn Canyon.

On The Water

Most visitors come to Bighorn Canyon to play on the water. You'll see lots of people tooling around in powerful boats, towing water-skiers, trolling for fish, or windsurfing. Fishing is the biggest attraction, with walleye, rainbow, and brown trout, yellow perch, ling, crappie, and catfish commonly caught. Note that because the lake straddles the state line, you need to purchase fishing licenses for both Wyoming and Montana if you plan on cruising around the lake. Launch ramps are at Barry's Landing and Horseshoe Bend, plus several other sites at the north end of the lake. Swimmers hang out at the Horseshoe Bend swim beach, the only place with a lifeguard (Fri.-Tues. in the summer).

Horseshoe Bend Marina, tel. 548-7766, is open daily in summer and rents boats, inner tubes, air mattresses, and water-skis. You can buy food and beer here as well. Ok-A-Beh Boater Service on the Montana end has limited supplies. For something different, try a boat tour of the canyon by **S-S Enterprises**, tel. 548-6418. Available mid-June to mid-Sept. only, these 1 1/2-hour trips provide glimpses of the magnificent canyon walls from below. Led by experienced guides, they cost $13 for adults, $10 for seniors, $9 for students, and $5 for children under five. Bring your camera!

Information

For a good orientation to the area, stop by **Bighorn Canyon Visitor Center,** tel. 548-2251, just east of Lovell along US 14A. It's open daily 8-6 in the summer, or daily 8-5 the rest of the year (except Thanksgiving, Christmas, and New Year's Day). Opened in 1977, this solar-heated center is an attraction in itself; 70% of its heat comes directly from the sun. Inside are a three-dimensional relief map of the canyon, displays on local animals, books and topo maps for sale, plus a 14-minute movie on Bighorn Canyon. The visitor center also loans out free 45-minute cassette tapes (and recorders) that provide an informative tour of Bighorn Canyon. Check the notice board for other talks or hikes in the recreation area, including the weekend **campfire programs** at Horseshoe Bend Campground (summer only). Summertime canoe tours of the canyon may be available; call a week ahead for specifics. Be sure to pick up a copy of *Canyon Echoes,* the free visitor guide with current information. Ranger stations are found at Horseshoe Bend and Layout Creek. The **Ewing-Snell Historical Site** at Layout Creek has a recently restored one-room schoolhouse.

PRYOR MOUNTAIN WILD HORSE RANGE

Bordering on the western side of Bighorn Canyon is 47,000 acres of rugged country set aside in 1968 as the nation's first wild-horse preserve. (Two other wild-horse ranges now exist in Nevada and Colorado, and there are another 3,000 wild horses in the Red Desert of southwestern Wyoming.) Managed by the BLM, Pryor Mountain's desert country contains three herds totaling more than 100 wild horses. Many of them remain out of sight in remote box canyons, but you're likely to see some relatively tame ones along the road between Horseshoe Bend and Layout Creek Ranger Station, especially during cooler parts of the year.

Most "wild horses" of the West are of mixed origins. Some are primarily domestic horses that were released into the wild by local ranchers, while others can trace at least some of their bloodlines to Spanish mustangs brought to the New World in the 16th century. Recent studies of wild horses found that the mustangs at Pryor Mountain are the most strongly Spanish of any feral horse herd in America, with little intermixing from more recent breeds. This purity is exhibit-

ed in the distinctive colors that include roan, sorrel, black, blue, tan, and grulla. Most have dark manes and tails.

Prior to protection of the wild horses, many were rounded up for use on ranches or for the glue factory. After 1971, when it became illegal to harass or kill wild horses, their numbers began to grow rapidly. Each year's colt crop increases the herd by 20%, creating conflicts with deer, elk, and antelope. Today, the BLM controls numbers through its adopt-a-horse program, removing 20 to 30 horses a year from Pryor Mountain and offering them to the public. For details on acquiring a wild horse, contact the BLM at 810 E. Main St. Billings, MT 59105, tel. (406) 657-6262.

> *Winter looks like a fictional place, an elaborate simplicity, a Nabokovian invention of rarefied detail. Winds howl all night and day, pushing litters of storm fronts from the Beartooth to the Big Horn Mountains. When it lets up, the mountains disappear. The hayfield that runs east from my house ends in a curl of clouds that have fallen like sails luffing from sky to ground. Snow returns across the field to me, and the cows, dusted with white, look like snowcapped continents drifting.*
>
> —Gretel Ehrlich in *The Solace of Open Spaces*

GREYBULL

For travelers en route to Yellowstone, the crossroads town of Greybull (pop. 1,800) is a splotch of irrigated green surrounded by desert country. Greybull lies at the junction of Shell Creek and the Bighorn River, and at the intersection of US highways 14 and 16-20. As such, it is both an agricultural center and a commercial center. Most of the town lies along the western shore of the river, behind a long levee; barren rocky bluffs line the opposite bank. There are bentonite-processing plants just north of town, oil pumpjacks farther afield, and irrigated farms along the river. Tip: If you are heading west to Cody and Yellowstone, fill up your tank here. Gas prices get progressively more expensive as you approach the mountains.

History
The land around Greybull was first settled in the 1880s by stockmen, with several hundred Mormon homesteaders moving in a decade later to dig irrigation ditches and establish the minuscule farming settlements of **Burlington** and **Otto** north of the Greybull River. Nearby **Emblem** was established by 600 German farmers in the late 1890s. A diversion of the Greybull River was begun in 1895, the first reclamation project under the Carey Act. Originally Germania, the town's name was changed to Emblem (a reference to the American flag) during the anti-German hysteria of WW I.

The name Greybull comes from a huge albino buffalo that once roamed this country. The animal was sacred to the Indians, who noted it on pictographs that are still visible on the sandstone bluffs that line the river. The town is a creation of the Burlington Railroad in 1909-10, but much of its growth has been fueled by oil and gas developments in the surrounding country. Completion of US 14 across the Big Horn Mountains in the 1930s brought tourists and led to Greybull's development as a way station for folks heading east to the Black Hills or west to Yellowstone.

Sights
The free **Greybull Museum** is in the same build-ing as the library (325 Greybull Ave., tel. 765-2444) and is open Mon.-Fri. 10-8 and Sat. 10-6 in the summer, and Mon.-Sat. 2-5 in the winter. It houses agate collections and polished petrified-wood pieces, plus a fine fossil collection that includes one of the largest fossil ammonites ever found. Also here are various Native American items, guns, and historical artifacts. Find an attractive flower garden in the shape of the Wyoming state flag at the west end of Greybull Avenue. The **Greybull Livestock Auction** is held north of town every Friday. And if you are really bored, head to the city park to find picnic tables, a jogging track, and the chimney of the first house built in Greybull.

Five miles northeast of Greybull is **Devil's Kitchen,** a fascinating arroyo filled with brilliantly colored badlands and many fossils. Get a map from the chamber of commerce and follow it closely; the last turnoff is easy to miss. **Sheep Mountain,** a 15-mile long hogback of eroded land just north of Greybull, is a favorite of geologists, who marvel at this fossil-packed anticline. Photographers love the vivid reds, browns, and yellows of this desert landscape.

Big Horn County Airport is just north of town. No commercial service, but this is an interesting place to see a couple dozen aging military planes—including C-140s and PB4Ys. Some date back to WW II. Several of the Royal Canadian Air Force's old B-29s are being cannibalized for parts by Hawkins & Powers Aviation, a major charter company that uses B-29s to drop fire retardant on forest fires. An airplane museum may be opening here soon.

PRACTICALITIES

Accommodations
See the chart on p. 405 for a listing of local motels. **Green Oasis RV Park,** 540 N. 12th Ave., tel. 765-2524, has tent sites for $8 and RV sites for $11. Showers for noncampers cost $2. It's open May-October. **Greybull KOA,** 333 N. Second Ave., tel. 765-2555, charges $13 for tent sites and $17 for RVs. Showers cost $3 for

noncampers. It's open mid-April through Oct., and has trees and a pool.

Restaurants And Bars

MJ's Cafe in the KOA, 333 N. Second Ave., tel. 765-2555, is easily the most popular local eatery. Good food at a good price, and in quantity. Locals drop by for breakfast, for the lunchtime salad bar, and to enjoy prime-rib specials on the weekend. **Lisa's Restaurant,** 200 Greybull Ave., tel. 765-4765, serves both Mexican and American fare and fills up most evenings. **Parker Cafe,** 536 Greybull Ave., tel. 765-2152, has working-class food at reasonable prices, while **Wheels Inn Restaurant,** 1336 N. Sixth Ave., tel. 765-2456, is open all day and serves up standard American fare. (It's said to be the only 24-hour restaurant between Casper and Billings.) **Pizza on the Run,** 427 Greybull Ave., tel. 765-4454, has pizza by the slice or by the pie. Drive up to the **Dairy Freez,** 601 N. Sixth Ave., tel. 765-4718, for fast food. Get groceries at **Ron's Thriftway,** 909 N. Sixth, tel. 765-2890, and fresh-baked goods from **Millie's Bake Shop,** 620 First Ave., tel. 765-2473.

Entertainment And Events

For live music, head to **Smokehouse Saloon,** 562 Greybull Ave., tel. 765-2232; **Hanging Tree Lounge,** 1040 N Sixth Ave., tel. 765-9986 (rock), or **Silver Spur,** 445 Greybull Ave., tel. 765-2300. Greybull's big annual event is **Days of '49** (1949, that is), held the second weekend in June. There's a top-notch rodeo, plus a parade, a barbecue, dancing, and a demolition derby.

Information And Services

The **Greybull Chamber of Commerce** office (tel. 765-2100) is next to the library at 325 Greybull Avenue. It's open daily 9-5 in the summer, or Mon.-Fri. 9-2 and Sat. 9:30-noon the rest of the year. Ask here for directions to the Native American pictograph of an albino bison, after which the town is named. They can also provide information on the major dinosaur digs (*Allosaurus, Diplodocus,* and *Stegosaurus)* taking place just north of town, and maps of the 4WD roads on Sheep Mountain.

Two other places may be of interest: **Greybull Wildlife Museum,** 420 Greybull Ave., has a small collection of stuffed critters, while the big

Probst Western Store, 547 Greybull Ave., tel. 765-2171, has a fine selection of cowboy hats, boots, and western clothes.

The Forest Service's **Paintrock Ranger Station** is at 1220 N. Eighth St., tel. 765-4435. **Greybull Public Library,** 325 Greybull Ave., tel. 765-2551, is open Mon. 12-7 and Tues.-Thurs. 12-6. A marvelous old log building, built in the 1920s, houses the **Greybull Roller Rink** (527 S. First Ave., tel. 765-2761; the cost is $2 per skate). Swim at the **pool** across from the high school on Sixth Ave. for $1.25 (children 50¢). **Powder River Transportation,** tel. (800) 442-3682, has daily bus service from Greybull to Billings, Montana, and eastern Wyoming. Buses stop in front of the chamber of commerce.

GREYBULL VICINITY

Basin

South of Greybull, the highway parallels the Bighorn River. Sharp bluffs rise along the eastern side of the river, while cottonwoods and willows crowd the banks. Heading away from the broad river valley, the endless hills are covered with dry grass, sage, and greasewood. It's a plain-Jane, arid landscape. Eight miles away lies the pleasant town of Basin (pop. 1,200). After a stretch of rough going in which it seemed on its way to extinction, Basin has bounced back somewhat. The town putters along on its title as Big Horn County seat, an impressive state retirement center, plus a couple of publishing-related businesses.

Basin is a relaxing place to retire after a long day of driving. Established in 1896, the town has always been an agricultural center, with both farming and ranching in the surrounding land. In 1897, a bitter custody battle for the county seat split voters between Basin City, as it was then known, and the older town of Otto. Basin City won by 38 votes.

Practicalities: Free **camping** in the town park, but you'll have to pitch tents on the dirt. The **Lilac Motel,** 710 W. C St., tel. 568-3355, has a quiet location and kindly owner. Rates are just $21 s or $26 d. Decent breakfasts at **Big B Restaurant,** 602 S. Fourth St., tel. 568-2246, and very good steak and seafood at **Outpost Lounge,** 151 N. Fourth St., tel. 568-2134.

GREYBULL AND WORLAND ACCOMMODATIONS

MOTEL	ADDRESS	TELEPHONE	RATES	NOTES
GREYBULL MOTELS				
Antler Motel	1116 N. Sixth Ave.	765-4404	$25 s, $27 d	AAA-approved, kitchenettes, open April-Oct.
Wheels Inn Motel	1324 N. Sixth Ave.	765-2105	$25 s, $28 d	
Sage Motel	1135 N. Sixth Ave.	765-4443	$27 s or d	AAA-approved
Three Chief Motel	625 N. Sixth Ave.	765-4626	$28 s or d	
K-Bar Motel	300 Greybull Ave.	765-4426	$28+ s or d	AAA-approved,
Yellowstone Motel	247 Greybull Ave.	765-4456 (800) 456-4155	$30+ s, $34+ d	AAA-approved, pool
WORLAND MOTELS				
Pawnee Motel	1735 Big Horn	347-3206	$24 s, $35 d	
Town & Country Motel	1021 Russell St.	347-3249	$26 s, $30 d	
Sun Valley Motel	500 N. Tenth St.	347-4251	$30 s, $34+ d	AAA-approved, very nice
Town House Motor Inn	119 N. Tenth St.	347-2426	$30 s, $37+ d	
Super 8 Motel	2500 Big Horn	347-9236 (800) 800-8000	$36 s, $41 d	AAA-approved
Settler's Inn Best Western	2200 Big Horn	347-8201 (800) 528-1234	$38+ s, $44+ d	AAA-approved

Also try **Mom's Cafe,** 257 N. Fourth, tel. 568-3301. **Big Horn County Library,** 103 W. C St., tel. 568-2388, is open Mon.-Fri. 10-5 and Sat. 9-12. There is an outdoor **swimming pool** at the high school. **Stockman's Bar,** 105 S. Fourth St., tel. 568-9942, has live country music a couple of times a month. Each August, Basin hosts the **Big Horn County Fair and Bean Festival** (pretty strange combination!) with livestock judging, a rodeo, a barbecue, and other activities.

Shell And Manderson
Shell Valley is farming and ranching country, its lush irrigated hay fields contrasting sharply with the arid landscape to the west. Tiny **Shell** has a country store/bar. Be sure to stop at the **Old Stone School** here, built in 1903 and used as a one-room school until the early 1950s. It is now run as an excellent little art gallery, bookstore, and information center, tel. 765-4384.

Kedesh Ranch, three miles east of Shell on US 14, tel. 765-2791, has log cabins with fine views, open June-October. Guests enjoy a quiet rural setting at **Clucas Ranch B&B,** just east of Shell, tel. 765-2946. Horseback riding is also available here.

State 789 heads south from Basin to **Manderson** (pop. 80), where you'll find a small country store and cafe. South of Manderson the road splits and continues on both sides of Bighorn River to Worland. The main road (on the east side of the river) plays tag with the irrigation ditch much of the way, passing eroded desert bluffs to the east and flat farm country closer to the river. A thin strip of trees runs right down the middle; in fall they look like skeletons against the skyline. Lots of barley, sugar-beet, and hay fields.

Medicine Lodge State Park
Twenty-one miles east of Manderson on State

31 is the ranching center called **Hyattville,** really not much more than a wide spot in the road. Stay here at **Paint Rock Inn,** tel. 469-2339 for $10 s or $20 d. Campers can use the showers for $2.

Get to Medicine Lodge State Park by heading north out of town and turning right onto Cold Springs Road. After four miles, turn left again at the Medicine Lodge sign and follow the gravel road 1¹/2 miles to the park. The main attraction is a 750-foot-long low cliff that served as a backdrop to 10,000 years of Native American settlements. The cliff is covered with dozens of petroglyphs. A small log **visitor center** (tel. 469-2234)—built almost a century ago as a cowboy bunkhouse—is open summers Mon.-Fri. 8-5 and Sat.-Sun. 9-8. Inside are displays on the area's incredibly rich archaeological history. Beginning in 1973, researchers uncovered some 60 cultural levels and thousands of artifacts and

bones here. It's considered one of the most significant archaeological sites in the west. Ask at the visitor center to pick fruit from the old apple trees next door. A ³/4-mile **nature trail** begins nearby, and the old 4WD roads make for fine mountain biking. Just a few hundred feet away is a very pleasant creekside **campground** (free) with restrooms and water. Good fishing for brown trout in the creek.

Staying on Cold Springs Rd.—instead of turning off to Medicine Lodge State Park—takes you 15 miles to Paint Rocks Lakes, a jumping-off point for Cloud Peak Wilderness (see pp. 424-426). North of Hyattville is another place of interest to folks willing to do a bit of adventuring, **Trapper Canyon.** Located on public land, the canyon has colorful walls rising 1,200 feet above Trapper Creek. Access is pretty tough and requires 4WD vehicles; check with the Forest Service office in Greybull for details.

WORLAND

The prosperous farming town of Worland (pop. 5,700) depends upon a mixture of agriculture (primarily malt barley and sugar beets), sheep and cattle ranching, oil production, and manufacturing. Sheep glean plowed fields near town, and the Holly Sugar Company's plant on the southwest edge of Worland provides economic stability, keeping more than 15,000 acres in beets. Also important is a major aluminum-can factory that produces three million cans a day and a Pepsi bottling plant that fills many of these. The town itself has a pleasant Midwestern feel, with nightly baseball games through the summer, tree-bordered streets and simple homes in the center, and suburban ranch-style homes spreading across the surrounding countryside. The slow Bighorn River twists its way along the edge of Worland, but just a few miles farther west is desert country with dry rocky buttes, sagebrush, and sheep.

History

Worland is named for Charlie "Dad" Worland, one of the first homesteaders in this part of the Bighorn Basin and the manager of a stage station and saloon built along the old Bridger Trail in 1900. It wasn't much to look at—a cave dug

into the riverbank, with log walls out front. His bar quickly acquired the title, "The Hole-in-the-Wall." A cigar box just behind the bar served as the local bank, and anyone needing money could borrow it and leave behind an I.O.U. Other folks settled around Dad Worland, and A.G. Rupp added a general store nearby, also built into the side of the bank to save precious timber. Ray Pendergraft in *Washakie: A Wyoming County History,* relates the following story about early-day Worland:

Once a compactly-built man rode into the settlement, refreshed himself at Worland's saloon, then went on to Rupps for some supplies. On one wall of the store was a poster, complete with a picture. It read, "$5,000 Reward, Dead or Alive Robert Leroy Parker, alias Butch Cassidy." The visitor examined it. "It's not a very good likeness," he told Rupp. Rupp examined the poster, looked at the man, and readily agreed. "You don't want it up there do you, Mr. Rupp?" the man politely asked. "No, I don't," replied Mr. Rupp. "I'll take it down for you," the man said, did so and went on about his selection of supplies.

(this page top left) hot-air ballooning over Riverton; (top right) ranch near Recluse; (bottom) Wind River Mountains, east of Dubois; (following page) Lookout Lake, Snowy Range (photos by Don Pitcher)

Originally located on the western side of the Bighorn River, Worland moved to the other side after the Chicago, Burlington, and Quincy Railroad announced plans to build along the east bank. The nucleus of Worland, 10 buildings, was slid across the river on the ice during the winter of 1905-06. The following year, construction was finished on the 54-mile-long Big Horn irrigation canal, opening some 30,000 acres to agriculture. It had been begun almost 20 years earlier. A new sugar-beet-processing plant in 1917 attracted more farmers and workers from the Midwest, along with many Germans and Ukrainians. The discovery of oil in the Hidden Dome field in that same year brought boom times as speculators flooded the area. Oil and agriculture, especially sugar beets, have remained important ever since, although oil production has declined since the 1950s as the fields are pumped out.

Sights

The **Washakie County Museum and Cultural Center,** 1115 Obie Sue Ave., tel. 347-4102, is housed in an old LDS church and is open Mon.-Fri. 10-5 and Sun. 2-4 in the summer, Mon.-Fri. 10-5 the rest of the year. Inside this spacious multiroom museum are Native American artifacts from cave sites near Ten Sleep, a re-creation of the A.G. Rupp Store, old photos, an array of cowboy and ranch equipment and other historical items, plus a fine geology and fossil collection. Kids will enjoy the hands-on exhibits such as the corn sheller and grinder. Local art shows and traveling exhibits can also be found here.

Next to the County Court House at the corner of Big Horn Ave. and 10th St. is a fountain fed by a 4,330-foot-deep **artesian well** located 23 miles north of Worland. The well flows at an impressive 14,000 gallons per minute, and with sufficient pressure to push water all the way to Worland. Also on the courthouse grounds is an incredibly ugly 15-foot-tall **Indian statue** carved out of wood by Peter Toth and placed here in 1980. **Pioneer Square,** just across the road, has interesting metal sculptures depicting pioneer settlers.

West of Worland in the Painted Desert, you'll find some of the most interesting badland country in Wyoming. Of particular note are the **Gooseberry Badlands** on BLM land near Squaw Teats and off State 431. Plenty of eroded country to explore, including arches and a variety of bizarrely carved shapes. Stop by the BLM office for directions.

Accommodations

See the chart for a complete listing of local lodging places. No public campgrounds near Worland (although you can pitch a tent on nearby BLM lands), but the private **Worland Campground,** 2401 Big Horn Ave., tel. 347-2329, has shady tent sites for $11, RV spaces for $16. Showers for noncampers cost $4. It's open April-October.

Food

Maggie's Cafe, 541 Big Horn Ave., tel. 347-3354, has very reasonable breakfasts and lunches, including homemade soups and breads. Things can get pretty chaotic at times. Get good breakfasts and lunchtime sandwiches (homemade bread) at **The Office,** 1515 Big Horn Ave., tel. 347-8171. Excellent salads and specials too. **Ranchito Mexican Food,** 1010 Big Horn Ave., tel. 347-8501, serves authentic south-of-the-border fare. Recommended. **Pizza Hut,** 1927 Big Horn Ave., tel. 347-2434, and **Pizza on the Run,** 1214 Big Horn Ave., tel. 347-2453, are the local pizza joints. **Antone's Supper Club,** three miles east of town on US 16, tel. 347-2301, has great deals on sirloin steaks and a Wednesday-night smorgasbord. **Harry's Steak House,** 1620 Big Horn Ave., tel. 347-9261, is the fanciest place in town and grills the best steaks. Another option is the **Elks Club,** 604 Coburn Ave., tel. 347-4401, where the service tends to be slow, but you get all-American food for a reasonable price.

Stop by **Rolling Pin Bakery,** 105 N. 15th St., tel. 347-2763, for fresh breads, cookies, and donuts. **Jon's IGA Foodliner,** 221 N. 10th St., tel. 347-3628, or the **Worland Thriftway,** 420 N. 10th St., tel. 347-9820, are the places to go for groceries. Jon's also has a deli.

Events And Entertainment

The big annual event in town is the **Washakie County Fair** in mid-August. The two-day **Sauger Derby** is a popular fishing event held in the Big Horn River each March. **The Other Room,** 1515 Big Horn Ave., tel. 347-8171, has rock or country bands most weekends, or try **RJ's Saloon,** 607 Big Horn Ave., tel. 347-8891. **Little Chicago,** 629 Big Horn Ave., tel. 347-6135, is another popular bar.

Information And Services

The **Worland Chamber of Commerce** office, tel. 347-3226, sits in front of the county courthouse at 120 N. 10th St. and stays open Mon.-Fri. 8-12 and 1-5. **Washakie County Library,** 1019 Coburn Ave., tel. 347-2231, is open Mon.-Fri. 8-5 with evening hours (7-9 p.m.) on Tues. and Thursday. The **Bighorn National Forest Tensleep Ranger Station** is at 2009 Big Horn Ave., tel. 347-8291, and the **BLM Worland District Office** is at 101 S. 23rd St., tel. 347-9871.

There is a public swimming **pool** ($1.50) at the high school, 1706 Washakie Ave., tel. 347-4113, and an 18-hole **Municipal Golf Course,** tel. 347-2695, next to the airport. Roller skate at **Wheels Skate Palace,** 1115 Big Horn Ave., tel. 347-8808.

Transportation

Powder River Transportation, tel. (800) 442-3682, has daily bus service to Billings, Montana, as well as eastern Wyoming. The airport is two miles south of town and is served by **United Express,** tel. (800) 241-6522, with daily flights to Cody, Riverton, and Denver. Rent cars from **Big Horn Chevrolet,** 545 N. 10th Ave., tel. 347-4229, **Worland Ford,** 500 Big Horn Ave., tel. 347-4236, or **Western Motors,** 910 Pullman Ave., tel. 347-2441.

TEN SLEEP

Ten Sleep (pop. 300) has one of the most picturesque settings in all Wyoming. The drive in from Worland offers a traipse across dry desert badlands crowded with oil pumpjacks and then up into rolling grass-and-sagebrush country with the tree-covered Big Horn Mountains marking the distant horizon. Great views from atop the long hills, before the road descends sharply into a lush green valley cut through by Nowood and Tensleep creeks. Because of its mountain valley location, the town of Ten Sleep offers an escape from the oppressive summer heat of Bighorn Basin. This verdant valley is one of the few places in Wyoming where apple, peach, and pear trees grow. Rustic log buildings fill this tiny ranching and tourism center. Take away the cars and the asphalt and it's easy to imagine Ten Sleep as the location for some Hollywood film about the Green Valley.

The name Ten Sleep comes from the Sioux Indians, who frequently stopped in this valley during their travels between a permanent camp along the Clarks Fork River in Montana and another one along the Platte River. Halfway between the two was Ten Sleeps, so-named because they measured distances in the number of nights it took to get to a place. The town of Ten Sleep was established as a trading center for the Scottish and Irish sheepmen who came here in the 1890s.

Sights

The main sights in Ten Sleep are the comfortable, slow-paced town itself and its pretty setting. **Pioneer Museum** behind the Flagstaff Cafe has local artifacts and is open daily in the summer. An old sheriff wagon sits along the main street, ready to haul off the bad guys. Ask locally for directions to the Native American pictographs on the Walt Patch Ranch. Drop into the **Ten Sleep Saloon,** tel. 366-9208, or the **Big Horn Bar,** tel. 366-9222, for a cold one with local ranchers. Ten Sleep Saloon has a bar inlaid with 5,052 pennies and 233 nickels; the bartender claims that they started out with inlaid silver dollars, but this is all they had left after the taxes!

Accommodations And Camping

Pitch your tent at **Flagstaff Camp,** tel. 366-2250, for $8 ($14 for RVs); open May-October. **Flagstaff Motel,** tel. 366-2330, on the other end of town, charges $28 s or $30 d. **Circle S Motel,** tel. 366-2320, has rooms for $22 s or $24 d and an overnight camping area ($8 for RVs or $3.50 pp for tents). If you're camping elsewhere, take showers at the laundromat here for $2.50. The nicest local lodging place is **Valley Motel,** tel. 366-2321, where rooms cost $25 s or $32 d. You can also stay at any of a dozen campgrounds ($5-7) in Bighorn National Forest east of town.

Food

Head to **Flagstaff Cafe,** tel. 366-2330, for great breakfasts, burgers, and steaks. The other local eatery is **Mountain Man Cafe,** housed in a building built in 1914. It still has the original tin ceiling. **Dirty Sally's,** tel. 366-2319, has a soda fountain and gift shop. Quite a lot of fruit grows in the country around town; ask locally to see who might have some for sale. There's usually a bowl of fresh fruit at the **Senior Center,** tel. 366-2210, which acts as the local information center. Hours are Mon.-Fri. 7-3 year-round. Stop by on Wed. nights to join in the bingo games. **Ten Sleep Mercantile** sells groceries.

Events

Come to Ten Sleep on the **Fourth of July** for a very popular rodeo, parade, and dance. **Ten Sleep Celebration Days** (second weekend in July) brings a junior rodeo, an ice-cream social, races, and family events of all types. On Labor Day the town comes alive with a unique **quadrathon** for women (horse riding, cycling, running, and canoeing).

Tensleep Canyon

A couple of miles east of town, US 16 passes the entrance to a 6,000-acre nature preserve managed by **The Nature Conservancy.** This is a nice place for day hikes. Facilities include an environmental education center as well as

THE TEN SLEEP RAID

Cattlemen have always viewed sheep with disdain, regarding them as despoilers of the range, "locusts with hooves," or "range maggots." Cattle reached Wyoming's grazing lands first, and when sheep began to arrive in large numbers around the turn of the century, the cattle owners fought back with intimidation and violence. In many places, the cattlemen declared a "dead line," and any sheep or sheepherder that crossed the line risked being killed. (One such line existed in Jackson Hole; even today the county has just 300 sheep, versus 12,000 cattle.) Despite these threats, sheep ranching was simply too lucrative to pass up; by 1889 Bighorn Basin was overrun with more than 387,000 sheep, versus fewer than 22,000 cattle.

Perhaps 10,000 sheep throughout the state were killed by cattlemen; some flocks were driven over cliffs, others were dynamited or attacked by dogs, while thousands more died from gunshots. Many of Wyoming's sheepherders were viciously attacked, and at least 16 were murdered. The most notorious of all these incidents took place along Spring Creek near Ten Sleep in 1909. Joe Emge, a hotheaded cattleman turned sheepman, announced plans to trail his sheep across the dead line set up in the Nowater Creek area. One April night, just after the sheep had reached the grazing grounds, at least half a dozen masked men burst into the camp, murdering Emge, his partner, and a herder. Their wagons were then set afire and many sheep were shot, and the attackers disappeared into the night, leaving a grisly scene to be discovered the next morning.

The investigation pointed directly at local cattlemen, and after testifying before a grand jury, one of the suspected raiders was found dead; officially it was called suicide, but it appeared he had been waylaid by others seeking to silence anyone who might tell the truth. Eventually, two men broke the silence and fingered five others, including several prominent ranchers. All five were convicted, spending from three years to life in prison for the murders. Like the Johnson County War two decades earlier, this incident helped turn many people against the cattlemen. Sheep continued to grow in importance for a while, with Wyoming becoming the largest wool-producing state, but overgrazing, the severe winter of 1911-12, and the removal of a wool tariff the following year led to a long decline. Wyoming is still the third-largest wool producer in America.

wall tents where you can camp for a fee. Shortly beyond this, the highway climbs up spectacular Tensleep Canyon toward 9,666-foot Powder River Pass in the Big Horn Mountains. **Wigwam Fish Rearing Station,** run by the Wyoming Game and Fish Dept., is five miles east of town. Another five miles up is the turnoff to **Ten Sleep Fish Hatchery.** Both of these are open daily. See p. 418 for more on this route.

THERMOPOLIS

The town of Thermopolis (pop. 3,300) lies on the southern edge of the Bighorn Basin, surrounded by the Owl Creek Mountains. It's one of two towns in Wyoming established around hot springs; the other is Saratoga. The name Thermopolis comes from the words *thermae* (Latin for "hot springs") and *polis* (Greek for "city"). It is a fitting title, since the world's largest hot springs are the centerpiece of Thermopolis. Hot Springs State Park is right in town, encompassing both a wonderful public bathhouse and several commercial endeavors. The economy of Thermopolis was for a long while dependent upon oil and ranching, but tourism has become increasingly important. Travelers find ample reasons to stop here.

History

Thermopolis came into existence with the 1896 purchase of Big Springs from the Shoshones and Arapahos. Streets were laid out wide enough for a 16-mule team to turn around in the middle of the block, something still obvious today, though you don't often see mule teams on the streets. Because of their medicinal value, the hot springs attracted many people, and the town became a health center, particularly for those suffering from arthritis and polio. Not much timber around here, so the first lodging place was the Sage Brush Hotel, made from a wooden frame laced with sagebrush and covered with a thatched roof of more sage.

HOT SPRINGS STATE PARK

History

Shoshone legends tell of a young warrior and his lover who were standing in the Wind River Canyon when an eagle feather—earned in battles with the enemy—blew out of the warrior's hair and wafted down the canyon. They raced after it, finding it floating in an enormous hot spring with steam gushing from its mouth. The springs were a gift from the Great Spirit.

Originally a part of Wind River Reservation, Big Springs and 10 square miles of surrounding land were sold to the U.S. government in 1896 for the bargain-basement price of $60,000. The treaty was signed by Shoshone Chief Washakie and Arapaho Chief Sharp Nose. Washakie stipulated that some of the water must remain free to all people, and that a campground be set aside for Indians: "I, Washakie, chief of Shoshones, freely give to the great white father these waters, belov'd by my people; that all may receive that great blessing of bodily health in the bathing." Thus was established Wyoming's first state park. (See "Events," below, for the annual Gift of the Waters Pageant.)

Today the park is the third most popular attraction in Wyoming; only Yellowstone and Grand Teton national parks attract more visitors. The park includes a variety of facilities: a state-run bathhouse, two commercial establishments, a senior center, a rehabilitation center, and even a small herd of buffalo. Adjacent are the Plaza Inn and Holiday Inn spa facilities.

Big Springs

Big Springs flows approximately 2,575 gallons per minute at 135° F and is considered the largest hot springs in the world. The springs are located at the base of a small butte; just in case there might be some confusion, someone has placed white rocks along the hillside, spelling out "World's Largest Mineral Hot Spring." A number of cooling ponds spread out in front of the springs, dropping water over terraces of lime and gypsum to the Bighorn River. (Because of the hot water, this stretch of the Bighorn River remains open through the winter, attracting ducks and other birds.) The cooling ponds are very colorful, with algae and minerals (particularly calcium carbonate, bicarbonate, sulfate, and sodium) adding splashes of reds, greens, browns, and yellows. A concrete path winds around the terraces and along the river, leading to a scenic **swinging bridge.** Many people drink the mineral-rich water, claiming an array of medicinal benefits.

State Bath House

For an incredibly relaxing soak, be sure to visit the very nice **State Bath House,** tel. 864-3765, open Mon.-Sat. 8-6 and Sun. noon-6. No entry charge, and the facilities are always exceptionally clean, with lockers to store your clothes. Rent towels (50 cents) and swimsuits (75 cents) here as well. There are private tubs in the locker rooms (where you can temper the mineral water with cooler water), a central indoor pool, and an outdoor soaking pool (open May-Sept. only). The pools are wheelchair accessible. Attendants make sure folks don't stay in the hot water for more than 20 minutes, since the heat can be weakening. This is not a place to clean up, and no soap is allowed, even in the showers.

Other Park Attractions

Hot Springs Water Park, tel. 864-9250, in the white dome building next to the State Bath House, has two pools, a 272-foot long water slide, a steam room, a sauna, and a mineral spa. Adults pay $5, kids $3, and seniors $4. It's open 9-9 daily.

Even bigger is **Star Plunge,** tel. 864-3771, also in the state park, with two long water slides and two spacious pools, a steam room, a jacuzzi, and tanning booths. The 500-foot-long outdoor slide is one of the three longest in the nation. Entrance to Star Plunge costs $5 for adults, $4 for kids. Towels, swimsuits, and inner tubes can also be rented. The state's largest outdoor mineral pool at Fountain of Youth RV Park is described below.

Also on the grounds of the state park are **Gottsche Rehabilitation Center**—an outpatient treatment facility established in 1959 to make use of the medicinal properties of the hot springs—**Big Horn Basin Children's Center** for handicapped kids, and a **Wyoming Pioneer Home** for the elderly. A small **museum** in the basement of the Pioneer Home features arrowheads, baskets, and other Native American artifacts, as well as antiques from nearby ranches. A statue commemorating Chief Washakie's "gift of the smoking waters" stands in front of the home. Washakie would be proud of all the good his gift has done.

In addition to facilities associated with the hot springs, the park includes shady picnic tables and playgrounds. A rough trail cuts to the top of **Monument Hill**, right behind Big Springs. The northeast portion of Hot Springs State Park includes a pasture where a herd of 20 or so **buffalo** roam. A loop road through the pasture gives you a chance to drive by. They are fed daily at 8:30 a.m.

MUSEUM

The free **Hot Springs Historical Museum** calls itself "one of the best small museums in the country" and lives up to this billing with an impressive collection of old photos, wagons, Native American artifacts, and much more. Located at 700 Broadway, tel. 864-5183, the museum is open daily 8-6 in summer, and daily 8-5 the rest of the year. Entrance costs $2 for adults, $2.50 for seniors, $1 for ages 10-17, $5 for families. Kids under 10 get in free.

The museum sprawls through two floors of the main building and across the street to include an agriculture building, an old schoolhouse, a petroleum building, and a caboose. The main museum houses various displays of frontier life: a newspaper shop, a dentist's office (complete with frightening tools), a blacksmith shop, and a general store. The cherrywood bar from the Hole-in-the-Wall Saloon is particularly popular; here members of the famous outlaw gang tipped their glasses with sympathetic locals.

The Indian artifact collection downstairs is very impressive, not just because of the thousands of arrowheads, but also because it includes an elk hide painted by Shoshone Chief Washakie. Outside, the 1920 Middleton Schoolhouse comes complete with old desks; check out the amusing letters from present-day school children. Kids of all ages love traipsing through the old Burlington caboose and trying to figure how the agriculture building's amazing 1926 Case threshing machine worked. The petroleum building houses exhibits on drilling and refining oil, including old gusher photos and a gigantic power unit once used to pump oil before the arrival of electric pumps.

PRACTICALITIES

Motels And Hotels

Because of the popularity of Thermopolis during the summer, it's a good idea to reserve ahead (or check in during the afternoon) to be assured of a place. See the chart for specific motel and hotel rates. The fanciest lodging in town is **Holiday Inn,** located right in Hot Springs State Park. It's very popular with busloads of blue-haired Grey Line tourists and includes racquetball courts, a weight room, a swimming pool, a hot mineral jacuzzi, soaking tubs, saunas, massages, and more. Most of these cost extra. The walls are lined with big-game trophy mounts and skins, along with pictures of great white hunters standing over their deceased quarry. Owner Jim Mills killed most of the animals hanging around here. (It's either appealing or appalling, depending upon your perspective.)

Directly across from the elaborate Holiday Inn is **Plaza Inn,** a funky old hotel where Marvin and Nancy Jacobs greet everyone with down-to-earth hospitality. Plaza Inn also houses an **International Youth Hostel** ($10 pp) with a communal kitchen and no curfew. Built in 1918, the old-fashioned hotel is a what-you-see-is-what-you-get place. This is not one of those elaborate country inns, just an affordable, friendly place with lots of character. Try an hour-long steam bath, mineral soak, and blanket wrap for just $7.50, or an hour-long massage with acupressure for just $30. A new cafe is expected to open here.

THERMOPOLIS ACCOMMODATIONS

MOTEL	ADDRESS	TELEPHONE	RATES	FEATURES
Plaza Inn	Hot Springs Park	864-2251	$15+ s, $25+ d $10 pp	massage, mineral bath, youth hostel
Bah-Gue-Wana Motel	401 Park St.	864-3119	$20 s, $26 d	kitchenettes
El Rancho Motel	924 Shoshoni Rd.	864-2341	$25+ s, $34+ d	AAA-approved
Coachman Inn	US 20 South	864-3141	$28 s, $34 d	
Rainbow Motel	408 Park St.	864-2129 (800) 554-8815	$32 s or d	kitchenettes $4 extra
Wind River Motel	501 S. Sixth	864-2325	$35 s, $39 d	
Cactus Inn	US 20 South	864-3155	$35 s, $45 d	kitchenettes $10 extra
Roundtop Mt. Motel	412 N. Sixth	864-3126 (800) 310-3126	$35 s, $39 d $39+ s, $42+ d	motel rooms cabins with kitchenettes, very nice
Moonlighter Motel (Best Western)	600 Broadway	864-2321 (800) 528-1234	$40+ s, $43+ d	AAA-approved, pool
Holiday Inn	Hot Springs Park	864-3131 (800) 465-4329	$51+ s, $57+ d	AAA-approved, pool, jacuzzi, sauna, exercise facility

Campgrounds

The closest public camping is a dozen miles south in Wind River Canyon (see below). **Fountain of Youth RV Park,** two miles north of Thermopolis on US 20, tel. 864-9977, boasts Wyoming's largest mineral swimming pool, fed by what was intended to be an oil well. In 1918, C.F. Cross began drilling, but instead of hitting oil, he struck hot mineral water, blowing the pipe casing out of the ground. Eventually a small travertine cone formed around the old casing. The "Sacajawea" well still flows 1.3 million gallons per day. Not surprisingly, this is a very popular place with the "snowbird" RV crowd. The Labor Day breakfast in the pool is a favorite event. Open March-Oct., it costs $15 for RVs. **Grandview RV Park,** 122 US 20 S, tel. 864-3463, has tent spaces for $11 and RV sites for $13. Showers for noncampers cost $3. Open mid-March to mid-October. **Latchstring Campground,** on the south edge of town, tel. 864-5262, charges $10 for tents and $14 for RVs, and showers cost $3 for noncampers; open April-September.

Food

Very good breakfasts and senior citizen's specials at **Log Cabin Cafe,** 706 S. Sixth, 864-9219. The best lunches and dinners in Thermop can be found at **Pumpernick's,** 512 Broadway, tel. 864-5151. Try their pita-pocket sandwiches for lunch or the homemade desserts. **Manhattan Cafe,** 526 Broadway, tel. 864-2501, has spicy BBQ beef rib and excellent malts. Decent pizzas and pasta at **Tony's Pizza** , 530 Arapahoe, tel. 864-5546.

Legion Supper Club, at the golf course on Airport Hill, tel. 864-3918, is the local steak-and-seafood spot. Pricey, but good. **The Safari Club,** in the Holiday Inn, tel. 864-3131, has reasonably priced buffet breakfasts and dinners. Interesting atmosphere, but variable food. Get groceries at **Consumers' Thriftway,** 600 S. Sixth, tel. 864-3112, or **Don's IGA,** 225 S. Fourth, tel. 864-5576. Don's also has a small deli and bakery.

Entertainment

The main entertainment in Thermopolis comes in the various water parks at Hot Springs State

Park. **Mac's Bar,** 506 Broadway, tel. 864-3763, has live music on the weekends, and the **Safari Club** at the Holiday Inn sometimes has a band.

Events

Buffalo Field Days comes to Thermopolis in late July with live music, storytelling, dancing, a black-powder shoot, and delicious buffalo stew. The **Gift of the Waters Pageant**—held the first weekend in August at Hot Springs State Park—commemorates the transfer of Big Springs to the federal government in 1896. The pageant has been presented every summer since 1950, with a cast that includes both local residents and Shoshones from the Wind River Reservation in full regalia. A tipi camp is set up near the hot springs for the festivities. Other events during Gift of the Waters include Native American dancing and a parade. **Hot Springs County Fair** is also held in early Aug., with rodeos and various agricultural and ranching shows.

A unique way to discover the old West is the **Outlaw Trail Ride** in mid-August. This six-day, 100-mile trip follows the "Outlaw Trail" from the Hole-in-the-Wall country of Butch Cassidy and the Sundance Kid to Thermopolis. You'll need to bring your own horse, bedroll, and gear, but meals are provided for a fee. There is a limit of 100 riders. Call (800) 443-6235 for information on this fascinating not-for-profit adventure.

Recreation

Most of the playing takes place around the many pools in Thermopolis, including those in the state park (described above), but there are other things to do as well. Rent clunker **bikes** from the Holiday Inn, tel. 864-3131. The nine-hole **Legion Golf Course,** tel. 864-5294, is on Airport Hill north of town. **Roundtop Mountain,** the distinctive butte that dominates the Thermopolis area, is an enjoyable but fairly steep hike. Take Seventh St. to Airport Hill and turn on the first left. After the cemetery, turn right onto a gravel road that takes you to the trailhead.

Shopping

For a good selection of books and tapes, stop by **The Wherehouse,** 107 N. Fifth St., tel. 864-5702. **Hole-in-the-Wall Gallery,** 105 N. Fifth St., tel. 864-2208, sells limited-edition prints and

CAROLINE LOCKHART

The West overflows with famous men, and women sometimes get unjustly shunted aside in the accolades. One of the most interesting was Caroline Lockhart (1871-1962), a woman who began her career as an actress but turned quickly to journalism. Using the pen name "Suzette," she became one of the country's first woman newspaper reporters, a job that led her into all sorts of adventures, from entering a circus cage with a lion that had killed his trainer the previous day to testing the Boston Fire Department's new fire nets by jumping out of a fourth-story hotel window. When she heard of a "Home for Intemperate Women" where the women were being severely mistreated, Caroline decided to investigate by posing as a derelict. She got her story all right, but it took considerable convincing from her editor to get her out. "Release!" shouted the matron running the house, "We can't! She's not cured yet." One of her most lasting impacts was the creation of Mother's Day. Although the idea was that of Anna Jarvis, it was Caroline Lockhart who made it a reality by tirelessly pushing the idea in the newspapers.

In 1904, Miss Lockhart took a bold step. After an interview with Buffalo Bill Cody in the town named for him, she decided to move to Wyoming. She purchased the local newspaper, the *Cody Enterprise,* and quickly made a name for herself as a crusader against prohibition and against "game hogs." She founded the Cody Stampede, the big annual event in Bighorn Basin, and later wrote several novels about the West, including *The Lady Doc,* a book that managed to ruffle local feathers with its too-close-to-the-truth descriptions of real-life Cody people. Lockhart's witty, humorous, and insightful writing gained her a national reputation.

In 1924, she sold the *Cody Enterprise* and bought a 7,000-acre ranch in the country along the Bighorn River north of Lovell, dividing her time between her Cody home (now the Lockhart Bed and Breakfast) and her ranch. She died at the age of 92. Today her old ranch lies within Bighorn Canyon National Recreation Area.

original paintings, and **Domhoff's Pottery Studio,** north of Thermopolis, tel. 864-3710, offers some of the finest pottery in Bighorn Basin.

Information And Services
The **Thermopolis Chamber of Commerce** office, 220 Park St., tel. 864-3192 or (800) 786-6772, is right at the entrance to Hot Springs State Park. Hours are daily 9-5. Just behind the chamber office is an impressive travertine cone,

created when workers put in a vent pipe. A summer-only **Welcome Wagon** is on the corner of Sixth and Broadway. While you are at the visitor center, ask about getting a gate key to access the Legend Rock pictographs. **Hot Springs County Library,** 344 Arapahoe St., tel. 864-3104, is open Mon.-Fri. 9-5. Laundromats don't normally merit mention, but it is hard to omit a place with a name like **Wishy Washy Laundromat** on 630 Shoshone.

WIND RIVER CANYON

South of Thermopolis, the highway cuts across lush irrigated farm fields. Turn around and you'll see the steep slopes of Roundtop Mountain dominating the vistas. The highway bridges the Bighorn River and then, four miles south of town, abruptly enters magnificent Wind River Canyon. At this point the river's name changes just as abruptly. Lewis and Clark had named it the Bighorn River; Crow Indians the Wind River. Early explorers somehow concluded that they were two separate waterways, and in the confusion Wind River Canyon became the Wedding of the Waters. Above this point the river is called Wind River, while below, it is the Bighorn River. A bit confusing.

Floating And Fishing
Many people float the Bighorn River, putting in at the Wedding of the Waters and taking out in Thermopolis. It's an enjoyable, leisurely drift with nice scenery and excellent fishing for rainbow trout (average size 15 inches) along the way. A special permit (available at *Coast to Coast* in Thermopolis) is required to fish in the canyon above Wedding of the Waters, since it is part of the Wind River Indian Reservation. **Wind River Canyon Whitewater,** tel. 864-9343, leads exciting river trips through the canyon during the summer. Fishing and float trips down the Bighorn are offered by **Wind River Canyon**

Outfitters, Sixth and Richards, tel. 864-3617. They also provide horseback and 4WD tours of the high country.

Geologic History Lesson
The drive through Wind River Canyon is one of the most dramatic in Wyoming, with US 20 clinging to the eastern bank of the river and canyon walls rising up to 2,500 feet overhead. Tracks of the Burlington Northern Railroad (built in 1913) parallel the river on the other side, threading in and out of several tunnels. This place is a geologist's wet dream, slicing through rocks that grow progressively older as you continue south, with the oldest dating back to the Precambrian era, 2.7 billion years ago. A succession of roadside signs notes the various geologic formations, and the Thermopolis Chamber of Commerce can provide you with a descriptive log of the canyon's complex geology. At the upper end, the road quickly climbs past Boysen Dam and into the open country of Boysen State Park (see p. 211). Within the canyon are two attractive **campgrounds,** Upper and Lower Wind River State Parks ($4). The river flows right alongside, and there are many big old cottonwoods, but highway noise may keep you awake. Free tours of **Boysen Powerplant,** tel. 864-3772, are available Mon.-Fri. 8-4.

POWDER RIVER COUNTRY

Powder River country is the most historically interesting part of a state overflowing with history. For the Indians who made this their home, the basin was paradise, a place of massive bison herds and abundant forage for horses. Because of this richness, the area became a confrontation point between various Indian tribes and later between Indians and invading whites along the Bozeman Trail. Still later, the clashes were among the whites: cattlemen versus homesteaders, and outlaws against lawmen. Today, the clashes have faded into memory, but the rich country remains. Coal, cattle, and sheep rule.

The Powder River Basin stretches from the crest of the Big Horn Mountains to the Black Hills and then south to Casper. The three largest settlements—Gillette, Sheridan, and Buffalo—dominate the region's economy. Sheridan and Buffalo provide gateways to the magnificent Big Horn Mountains, a recreation paradise capped by barren alpine peaks. Rolling grassland predominates across Powder River Basin, accented by steep-sided buttes and lush riversides. The land is grazed extensively by cattle and sheep, though alfalfa and wheat are grown in many places. Oil and coal resources are vital to the economy of the Powder River Basin, especially around Gillette, making this the most important energy region in Wyoming. Despite the many large coal mines, the land remains relatively untouched. Nearly everyone chooses to live in the cities and smaller settlements, leaving enormous open expanses of land.

BIG HORN MOUNTAINS

Sandwiched between two broad basins—Bighorn to the west and Powder River to the east—are the majestic Big Horn Mountains. To the early explorers this 70-mile-long range was the Shining Mountains, a name inspired by its snowcapped peaks, some topping 13,000 feet. The Indians called it "Ahsahta," meaning "The Big Horns," after the Rocky Mountain bighorn sheep found here. Eventually, whites applied the name to all sorts of places in the region. The mountain country here is carpeted primarily with lodgepole and ponderosa pine, along with Engelmann spruce and subalpine fir at higher elevations. While much of the country here is not as rugged as the mountains on the western border of Wyoming, the Big Horns do contain many rocky peaks above 9,000 feet, with 13,175-foot Cloud Peak crowning the skyline. Hundreds of small lakes reflect this dramatic scenery within the Cloud Peak Wilderness.

Nearly all of these mountains lie within **Bighorn National Forest**, a million-acre chunk of public land set aside by President Grover Cleveland in 1897. Forest headquarters is in Sheridan at 1969 S. Sheridan Ave., tel. 672-0751, with additional district offices in Lovell (tel. 548-6514), Worland (tel. 347-8291), Buffalo (tel. 684-7981), and Greybull (tel. 765-4435). Any of these can provide detailed forest maps ($4) and a listing of local outfitters. **Mountainworks Adventures**, tel. 655-9000 or (800) 869-9056, leads a full range of custom backpacking and rock-climbing trips in the Big Horns.

This is multiple-use country, with logging, grazing, and recreation the primary attractions. Commercial logging has gone on within the forest for almost a century, and old tie flumes are still visible near Dayton. At one time, vast numbers of sheep grazed the Big Horns, totaling perhaps half a million. More than 50,000 sheep and 30,000 cattle still graze in these mountains, and sheepherder camps are common sights in the high meadows.

Most visitors simply drive through the Big Horns on one of the three scenic highways, but the country is well worth stopping to savor, especially if you're a fan of waterfalls. There are many campgrounds, over 630 miles of hiking trails, and good fishing for rainbow, cutthroat, brook, and brown trout. Come winter, this is a popular destination for snowmobilers as well as cross-country and downhill skiers. Quite a bit of wildlife to see here, too. Bighorn sheep have been reintroduced to the area and now number around seventy. No grizzlies, but there are quite a few black bears in these mountains. Also look for mule and white-tailed deer, elk, and moose. (The moose are not native here; they were transplanted from Jackson Hole in 1948.)

CRUISIN' THROUGH

Three paved highways cut across the Big Horn Mountains, providing popular connections between Yellowstone and the Black Hills. US 14 and 16 are both kept plowed through the winter, while US 14A generally closes Nov.-May. All three have National Scenic Byway status—that becomes more obvious with each mile traveled.

Highway 16

US 16 climbs across the southern end of the range from Ten Sleep to Buffalo. More than a dozen Forest Service campgrounds line the route. This was the original "Black and Yellow Trail," first proposed in 1912 as a link between Chicago, the Black Hills, and Yellowstone. The first caravan of automobiles made it over the old sheepwagon track in the following year, reaching Yellowstone after 18 hard days on the road. By the 1920s, the highway was marked by poles with alternating black and yellow bands. For many years, this was the main route to Yellowstone. East from Ten Sleep, US 16 parallels cottonwood-lined Tensleep Creek, climbing past impressive red and yellow cliffs. A cross and marker commemorate Gilbert Leigh, an English nobleman who fell to his death while hunting here in 1884. Eventually the switchbacks take you up to **Meadowlark Lake**, a popular winter destination for both cross-country skiers and 'bilers. The dirt road to **High Park**

POWDER RIVER COUNTRY

© MOON PUBLICATIONS, INC.

Lookout Tower is two miles east of here. Look for flower-bedecked **St. Christopher's Chapel of the Big Horns** as this side road climbs to the fire tower (not in use). Great views from the top. East of here, the road winds over Powder River Pass, providing breathtaking views into Cloud Peak Wilderness.

Highway 14

US 14 offers an equally impressive passage over the Big Horns between Greybull and Dayton. Above the dot of a town called Shell, the road passes a remarkably phallic rocky butte then catches Shell Creek, winding with it through the deep red rocks of Shell Canyon, past Shell Falls and the Antelope Butte Ski Area before topping out at Granite Pass. At 120-foot-high **Shell Falls**, approximately eight miles east of Shell on US 14, you'll find a visitor center and several short walking trails with interpretive signs. Douglas fir and limber pine grow nearby. Keep your eyes open for water ouzels, the gray, water-loving birds that often nest beneath waterfalls. (By the way, all these "Shells" are named for the fossil invertebrate shells that are common in the rocks.) After joining up with US 14A at Burgess Junction, the road continues to Twin Buttes, Sibley Lake, and the amusing jumble of rocks called Fallen City, before zigzagging sharply down to Tongue River Canyon and the town of Dayton. A new Forest Service **visitor center** is located a few miles east of Burgess Junction near Twin Buttes.

Highway 14A

US 14A (officially this is Alternate US 14) was completely rebuilt in the 1980s. Engineers like this road, modeled after similar routes in the Alps. It's said to be the most expensive stretch of road built in America. Locals claim the "A" in US 14A stands for adventure, and with three different runaway truck ramps and 10% grades on some stretches, it's easy to see why. The climb to the top is *very* long and steep, but the views make the tough climb worthwhile. US 14A rises over the Big Horns from Lovell to Burgess Junction, where it meets up with US 14. Along the way you're treated to miles of open sage-and-grass country with timbered islands on Bald and Little Bald mountains, spectacular Bucking Mule Falls, and the famous Medicine Wheel. Watch for moose and deer in the meadows near Burgess Junction.

An enjoyable side loop is **Burgess Rd.** (Forest Rd. 15). The gravel road starts at Burgess Junction and continues approximately 20 miles to a junction with US 14A near Bald Mountain. Along the way are fine opportunities to view deer and elk, and a grand vista from Burgess Road Overlook into the Lake Creek country.

PRACTICALITIES

Camping

With 35 different campgrounds ($5-7), you should have no trouble finding places to commune with nature. Most are above 5,000 feet in elevation, making for welcome escapes from summertime heat. Reservations ($7 extra) are available for the most popular ones through MISTIX, tel. (800) 283-2267. During weekends in July and August, campgrounds along the main roads are frequently filled (get there before 2 p.m.), but harder-to-reach campgrounds usually have space. The BLM's Five Springs Campground (free) is just off US 14A on the western border of the national forest. Scenic **Five Springs Falls** is nearby. In addition to the official campgrounds, you can

> *The Crow country is a good country; the Great Spirit has put it in exactly the right place. It is good for horses —and what is a country without horses? On the Columbia, the people are poor and dirty; they paddle about in canoes and eat fish. On the Missouri the water is muddy and bad. To the north of the Crow country it is too cold, and to the south it is too hot. The Crow country is just right. The water is clear and sweet. There are plenty of buffalo, elk, deer, antelope, and mountain sheep. It is the best wintering place in the world and has plenty of game. Is it any wonder that the Crows have fought long and hard to defend this country, which we love so much?*
>
> —Crow Chief Arapooish, describing the Powder River Basin.

camp anywhere in the forest for free, as long as you are a half-mile off the main highways.

Lodging And Food

Scattered throughout the Big Horns are six mountain lodges, all of which have bars and restaurants. **Bear Lodge**, at Burgess Junction, tel. 655-2444, occasionally has live country music on weekends; they offer motel rooms ($35 s or d) and bring-your-own-linen rustic cabins ($18 for up to four, plus $3 for showers). If you're staying elsewhere, take a shower for $4. The bar is a great place to shoot a game of pool, and the gift shop has a few groceries. Bear Lodge is open year-round.

Arrowhead Lodge, tel. 655-2388 or 672-4111, four miles east of Burgess Junction on US 14, has rustic cabins with kitchenettes starting for $24 s or d, and motel rooms starting for $33 s or d. It's open year-round. If you aren't staying here you can use the showers for $2. RVs can park for $9 a night. Be sure to check out the ceiling in the bar.

Deer Haven Lodge, 18 miles east of Ten Sleep on US 16, tel. 366-2449, has rustic cabins starting for $17 s or $20 d, and motel rooms for $32 s or d. **Meadowlark Resort**, 30 miles east of Ten Sleep along US 16, tel. 366-2449, has rustic cabins ($24), cottages ($38 and up), and motel rooms ($34). Drop in on Sunday for an all-you-can-eat buffet. Meadowlark also rents boats for the lake and offers snowmobile tours in winter. Rent horses at nearby Willow Park. **Lodge in the Pines**, 14 miles west of Buffalo on US 16, tel. 686-4620, has cabins of all types for $22-50. Kids and seniors can throw in a line at the fishing pond. **South Fork Inn**, 16 miles west of Buffalo on US 16, tel. 684-9609, also has a wide variety of cabins for $35-75. They also rent mountain bikes, and offer horseback rides. It's open mid-May to mid-Sept. only.

Skiing And Snowmobiling

The Big Horns provide some of the finest snow in Wyoming, with groomed cross-country ski trails at Sibley Lake, Willow Park, and Pole Creek. The rest of the forest makes for outstanding skiing most of the winter, but you'll need to break your own trail. Snowmobilers will find trails all over the forest; get a route map from Forest Service offices. **Meadowlark Resort**, tel. 366-2424, offers guided snowmobile tours. **High Country Adventures**, tel. 664-2241, has rustic winter cabins with ski or snowmobile access.

Antelope Butte Ski Area, tel. 672-0369, is a small family ski area located 60 miles west of Sheridan and 35 miles east of Greybull on US 16, with a chair lift and platter. The vertical rise is 1,000 feet from a base elevation of 8,400 feet. It's open Fri., Sat., Sun., and holidays 9:30-4, mid-Nov. through March. Lift tickets cost $18 for adults, $12 for ages 6-15, and free for young-uns. Rent skis, boots, and poles here for just $12, or take lessons from the ski school. The lodge has light meals.

High Park Ski Area, 35 miles east of Ten Sleep on US 16, tel. 347-4480, is another small ski area with two platter lifts covering a 620-foot vertical rise. It's open mid-Dec. to early April, with lifts running Fri., Sat., and Sun. 10-4. Get food, drinks, and ski rentals at the base lodge. Tickets cost $12 adults, $9 students, and $6 under age 12. Half-day prices are $2 less.

Hikes And Sights

Plenty to see and do in the Big Horns, including Medicine Wheel and the Cloud Peak Wilderness (described separately below). Several trails take off from Sheep Mountain Rd., on US 14A, approximately 30 miles east of Lovell and three miles east of the turnoff to Medicine Wheel. **Littlehorn Trail** parallels the Little Bighorn River for 18 miles. Along the way you'll see 1,600-foot canyon faces and water fountaining off the limestone cliffs of Leaky Mountain. The trailhead is two miles up Sheep Mountain Road (see map, p. 422). A half-mile farther up the road is the trailhead for **Porcupine Falls**, a 200-foot-tall cascade accessed by a half-mile path. Along the way the trail passes a 1930s-era gold mine. Much of the area here was burned in a 1988 forest fire.

One of the not-to-be-missed places in the Big Horns is spectacular **Bucking Mule Falls**, a 600-foot cascade dropping into Devil Canyon. The trailhead for Bucking Mule Falls is 11 miles off US 14A on Sheep Mountain Rd., and the waterfall is a three-mile RT hike. You can also do an 11-mile loop hike by following the trail to the falls and then continuing south to Porcupine Campground.

The trailhead for **Tongue River Canyon** is 3½ miles southwest of Dayton to the end of Tongue Canyon Road. This loop trail climbs up the canyon and then back again for a total of 14 miles, offering glimpses of the old McShane brothers' tie flume—built in 1894 and stretching for 26 miles—the fast-flowing blue-ribbon fishing stream (cutthroat, rainbow, brook, and German brown trout), and canyon walls reaching a thousand feet into the air. Ambitious hikers may want to continue all the way to Burgess Junction. Locals float down parts of the river during the spring, when water levels are high.

Tongue River Cave is near the trailhead. With well over a mile of passages, it's one of the most popular caves in Wyoming but has been considerably vandalized. Because of its size, inexperienced spelunkers can become lost, so it's wise to ask locally for someone willing to act as a guide. More than 100 other caves honeycomb this country; see the Forest Service for locations and precautions. Their Sheridan office also has a helpful brochure listing other local hikes.

An enjoyable waterfall is **Big Goose Falls**. Follow Forest Rd. 26 (it starts approximately five miles south of Burgess Junction on US 14) to Big Goose Ranger Station, continuing on from there via Forest Rd. 296 to the end. The falls are about five miles below the ranger station, along the East Fork of Big Goose Creek. They include plunge pools and water-sculpted rocks.

One of the most interesting drives in the Big Horns slices through **Crazy Woman Canyon**. The canyon is named for either (take your pick) an Indian squaw who went insane while living alone in her tipi here or a white woman who, after her wagon train had been brutally attacked by Indians, became demented and wandered away, never to be seen again. Not exactly a soothing name for emigrants on the old Bozeman Trail! Nevertheless, the canyon cut by cascading Crazy Woman Creek is a stunning one, with steep cliffs on both sides. A gravel road (no trailers or RVs) heads down the canyon from Crazy Woman Campground (25 miles west of Buffalo on US 16). You can follow the road all

MEDICINE WHEEL AREA

BUCKING MULE FALLS

BIGHORN NATIONAL FOREST

PORCUPINE FALLS

DUNCUM MT.
(ELEV. 9,830 ft.)

PORCUPINE CG

MEDICINE WHEEL

MEDICINE WHEEL RANGER STATION

FIVE SPRINGS CG

MEDICINE MT.

BALD MT. CITY
(SITE)

TO LOVELL

BALD MOUNTAIN CG

BALD MT.
(ELEV. 10,042 ft.)

TO BURGESS JUNCTION

ALT. 14

0   2mi

0   2km

© MOON PUBLICATIONS, INC.

the way to the mouth of the canyon and then on to State 196. **Crazy Woman Canyon Tours**, tel. 684-5446, offers 4WD treks into this country.

MEDICINE WHEEL

High atop a windswept mountain plateau sits one of the best-known and least-understood archaeological sites in America, the Medicine Wheel. Measuring 80 feet across, this uneven "wagon wheel" of stones seems ready to roll over the nearby slopes. Twenty-eight rock spokes radiate out from a central hub, with six smaller rock cairns scattered around the rim. A variety of lesser-known rock structures surround the Medicine Wheel on nearby slopes, including an arrow that points southwest to another "wheel" near Meeteetse (70 miles away), a large rectangle of stones, and more than 50 tipi rings. An ancient cairn-marked travois trail continues northwest from Medicine Wheel over the Big Horn Mountains.

Origins And Purpose

Medicine Wheel's origins are hidden in the depths of time. White prospectors from the nearby gold-mining camp of Bald Mountain City (now entirely gone) discovered the Medicine Wheel around 1885. Carbon-14 dating of wood fragments found in one of the cairns gave a date of A.D. 1760, and today's best guess is that these limestone rocks were placed here sometime between A.D. 1200 and 1700.

medicine wheel

Prevailing theories about the purpose behind the Medicine Wheel fall into two schools: it was either an astronomical observatory or a site for sacred ceremonies. One of the most interesting theories was suggested by astronomer John Eddy in a 1977 *National Geographic* article. He noted that the 28 spokes are equal to the number of days in the lunar month and that two of the cairns served as horizon markers for sunrise and sunset, with the other four cairns marking the rising of three of the brightest stars. These could have signaled the summer solstice. Interestingly, similar alignments occur on a stone wheel in Saskatchewan, Canada.

Other scientists counter that the Indians would have little reason to care exactly when summer solstice occurred, since they were not farmers, and that the rocks probably served some religious function. These researchers point out the striking similarities between the wheel and medicine lodges used during Cheyenne and Sioux sun-dance ceremonies—both have 28 spokes. The first published report (1885) described the Medicine Wheel as consisting of a central hub with spokes leading to stone huts: "It is said that these smaller huts were, during religious ceremonies, occupied by medicine men of different tribes, while the larger hut in the center was supposed to be the abode of Manitour." Various later reports attributed it to the Crow, Sheepeater, Arapaho, or Cheyenne tribes.

Regardless of its origins or earliest uses, the Medicine Wheel *was* used in historical times—and is still used today—as a place for prayer and vision quests. Chief Joseph of the Nez Percé fasted here, and Shoshone Chief Washakie was said to have gained his "medicine" here. Because of the Medicine Wheel's location and the importance of ceremony in Native American life, it certainly was a sacred site, whether or not it served any astronomical function. Its origins and original purpose will remain shrouded in the unknowable past.

Visiting Medicine Wheel

The gravel road into Medicine Wheel (well marked) turns off US 14A approximately 27 miles east of Lovell. The wheel is three miles in, past an FAA radar dome built on nearby Medicine Mountain; an incredibly disturbing structure to find near such a significant Native

American site. (It's used to monitor air traffic in a three-state area.) The road to Medicine Wheel is usually covered with snow until late June, but you can walk in to the site. A wire fence surrounding the wheel is frequently festooned with strips of cloth, feathers, bells, herbs, flowers, and other offerings left behind by Indians who come here on personal vision quests and other sacred ceremonies. They are particularly evident following solstices and equinoxes. Respect the importance of this religious site by not disturbing these items.

It is obvious why this mountain was chosen for the Medicine Wheel. The surrounding open country has scattered pine, juniper, and spruce, and the ridge drops off a 150-foot precipice just 50 feet away. From its 9,956-foot elevation, a vast panorama stretches to include the Bighorn Basin, the Wind River, the Absaroka Range, and the Pryor Mountains. Medicine Wheel is also a good place to look for hawks wheeling through the sky, especially red-taileds and kestrels.

CLOUD PEAK WILDERNESS

Although maintained as a primitive area since 1932, the 195,500-acre Cloud Peak Wilderness did not receive official wilderness status until 1984. It's named for 13,175-foot **Cloud Peak**, a rocky mountain visible for a hundred miles in all directions. At one time this entire range was glaciated, and reminders abound in the sharpened peaks, broad U-shaped valleys, and multitude of lakes in glacial tarns. There are even a few small patches of glacial ice. The Big Horns still get plenty of snow, leaving many hiking trails in the high country blocked until July. One oddly named mountain in the wilderness is **Bomber Peak**, just south of Cloud Peak. An Air Force B-17 bomber crashed here in 1943, killing all 10 men on board. It was not found for two years.

With more than 100 miles of trails and thousands of acres more above timberline, there are abundant hiking and horse-packing opportunities throughout Cloud Peak. Backcountry permits are not required, but you should fill out the registration cards at trailheads. Be sure to camp at least 100 feet from water sources and trails, and hang all food out of reach of black bears. Use existing campsites whenever possible to lessen your impact. The Forest Service produces a free map/guide to the wilderness area that lists additional precautions. For complete trail and historical info on the wilderness, request a copy of Kenneth Melius's book, *Cloud Peak Wilderness Area* (Tensleep Publications, Box 925, Aberdeen, SD 57401). *The Hiker's Guide to Wyoming,* by Bill Hunger, also features several hikes within Cloud Peak Wilderness. Be sure to get topographic maps before heading out. Check with the Forest Service offices in Sheridan, Buffalo, Lovell, Greybull, or Worland for a list of local outfitters. For something different, **Cloud Peak Llama Treks** in Story, tel. 683-2732, or **Great Western Outfitters** in Big Horn, tel. 674-4006, both offer backcountry llama trips.

Access into Cloud Peak Wilderness is via several entry roads along US 16 on the southern border, and from the north (US 14) at Cross Creek and Ranger Creek campgrounds and Twin Lakes Picnic Ground. Other entrance points surround Cloud Peak, but many require long hikes up 4WD roads to get to the wilderness boundary.

Trails

The **Stull Lakes-Coney Lake Trail** is one of the shortest and most popular hikes into the lake country of Cloud Peak. It climbs three miles from the Twin Lakes Picnic Ground, passing Stull Lake and ending in the alpine country surrounding Coney Lake. Watch for elk and deer in late summer.

An excellent 21-mile loop hike begins at **Lower Paintrock Lake Trailhead** on the west side of the wilderness. This route provides a wide variety of country, from dense timber to rocky mountain passes and small glaciers. The path climbs to a trail junction 1 1/2 miles west of Cliff Lake. From here, turn left and follow the trail to Geneva Pass (10,300 feet). The trail drops down to Lake Geneva and then follows East Fork Creek to the junction with the Edelman Trail. This path leads over Edelman Pass, around Emerald Lake, and then back down to the Edelman Trailhead, just 1 1/2 miles by road from your starting point. There are all sorts of other hikes and side trips in this area.

CLOUD PEAK
WILDERNESS AREA

Another long loop trip takes you to **Lake Solitude**. Begin at the Paint Rock Trailhead, located approximately 10 miles north of Meadowlark Lake. Take the road to Tyrell Ranger Station and turn left after a mile, continuing up the rough gravel road to the trailhead. The trail climbs to Lily Lake—which is filled with water lilies—and then up a steep valley to Mistymoon Lake. Beyond this you can either return the same route or follow the trail down Paint Rock Creek to Lake Solitude and Grace Lake. Past Grace Lake, the route splits at Long Park where a trail takes you back to Lily Lake and the trailhead. The loop is approximately 16 miles roundtrip.

The easiest route to the top of **Cloud Peak** takes off from Mistymoon Lake; see above for access to this lake. Plan on a strenuous 10 hours for the 11-mile climb up and back. This is not a developed trail and will require considerable rock hopping, but the spectacularly desolate scenery makes it all worthwhile. Be prepared for sudden weather changes, and carry an ice ax into August. The final stretch is marked by rock cairns. For detailed route instructions up Cloud Peak, get a topographic map and a copy of Bill Hunter's trail guide.

The **Elk Lake Loop** (19 miles RT) begins at Hunter Corrals Trailhead on the southeast side of the wilderness. Follow the old jeep trail to Soldier Park, a scenic grassy meadow. Turn north at the trail junction and follow the path to Elk Lake. Along the way are some outstanding views across the alpine terrain to Cloud Peak. Turn left at Elk Lake, up over a pass, then down the other side to Soldier Park and back to the trailhead.

SHERIDAN

The attractive, vibrant town of Sheridan (pop. 14,000) has plenty to see, several fine restaurants, great country in the nearby Big Horn Mountains, and a genuine sense of history. At just 3,745 feet above sea level, it has the lowest elevation of any Wyoming town, making for hot summers. The country around Sheridan was settled by a broad mixture of Europeans, including everyone from British lords to Polish coal miners. Their heritage carries on in such events as weekly polo matches at the oldest polo field in the nation (see p. 435) and an annual polka festival.

History

Sheridan, like other towns in the Powder River Basin, was built on coal, cattle, farming, and the railroad. In 1882, John D. Loucks took a liking to the country here and decided to establish a town, drawing up a plat on a piece of brown wrapping paper. He named the new place for his commanding officer during the Civil War, Gen. Philip Sheridan, and immediately set about getting others to come. For several years Sheridan competed with nearby Big Horn City for the county seat, a title that ensured survival. Finally, in 1885, Sheridan promoters offered cowboys at the fall roundup free lots in the town. When most accepted, Sheridan finally had enough folks to incorporate. Almost overnight (literally in some cases) businesses in Big Horn City moved to Sheridan, sometimes bringing buildings along too.

When the Burlington and Missouri Railroad reached Sheridan in 1892, the town suddenly changed. Now ranchers could get their cattle to market more easily and visitors could stay in the sumptuous Sheridan Inn. Dryland farming became more profitable as investors built large grain mills and a sugar-processing plant. The first underground coal mines opened in 1883, but it was not until 1903 that the Burlington Railroad began using the coal in its engines. For the next several decades these "black diamonds" were mainstays of the local economy. Sheridan soon had 1,500 people, wooden sidewalks, 30 saloons, six churches, and two opera houses. Small mining towns—Dietz, Acme, Kooi, Model, Riverside, and Carneyville —opened in the surrounding countryside, worked by thousands of European emigrants; newspapers often featured ads in both Polish and English. Electric streetcars were added in 1911, with frequent interurban service to the surrounding coal mines.

World War II brought prosperity, as local mines operated at full tilt and new technology allowed construction of the first open-pit mine.

SHERIDAN

After the war, however, trains shifted to diesel and homes began burning the less-polluting natural gas, so that by 1953 the last of the old coal towns had died. With increasing demand for western coal in the 1970s, Sheridan's population again boomed. Recent years have seen the closing of some nearby strip mines, with many workers now crossing the Montana border to work in the Decker and Spring Creek strip mines there, although a long strike in the Decker mine has split the community. Sheridan now depends upon a mixture of mining, ranching, government jobs, and tourism.

SIGHTS

Trail End Historic Center

Located on spacious grounds overlooking Sheridan, Trail End Historic Center, 400 E. Clarendon Ave., tel. 674-4589, is the city's best-known attraction. Managed by the state, it's open daily 9-5 (Wed. till 9 p.m.) June-Aug.; daily 2-5 in the fall and spring; and closed Dec. 15-Mar. 15. No charge. This was the home of John B. Kendrick, a wealthy rancher and powerful Democratic politician. Born in Texas in 1857, Kendrick was raised as an orphan. He became a ranchhand by age 15 and, after trailing cattle north to Wyoming, fell in love with the country and took a job as a ranch foreman.

Over the years Kendrick acquired more than 200,000 acres of land in Wyoming and Montana, grazed by tens of thousands of his cattle. He personally financed local homesteaders, friends, former employees, and relatives. Politics beckoned once Kendrick was firmly established as a rancher and businessman, and he served first as governor, then as a U.S. senator until his death in 1933. One paper called him "the craftiest politician the state has ever produced." Kendrick helped expose the Teapot Dome Scandal and gained funding for the massive Kendrick Project, a series of dams and irrigation canals on the North Platte River.

Shortly before entering politics, Kendrick selected the site for his end-of-the-trail mansion, high atop a hill overlooking Sheridan. Begun in 1908, Trail End took five years to complete and served primarily as a summer home since politics kept Kendrick away the rest of the year. The

mansion is in the Flemish Revival style, with curvilinear gables on the third-floor windows, a red-tile roof, hardwood floors, mahogany walls, and exposed-beam ceilings. Many of the sumptuous original furnishings (including a 25-foot-long Kurdistan rug) are inside. Look for photos of several of Kendrick's ranches upstairs.

The house cost $165,000 in an era when typical homes went for less than $1,000. Its 18 rooms include a third-floor ballroom with a loft where musicians could play without interfering with the dancers below. Heating Trail End sometimes required up to a ton of coal each day! Out back is a sod-roofed **log cabin** that was reconstructed and moved onto the grounds in recent years. Built in 1878, this historic structure served at various times as Sheridan's first post office, school, store, law office, and bank!

Sheridan Inn

Built in 1893, Sheridan Inn was considered by many to be the finest hotel between Chicago and San Francisco. Visitors included presidents Theodore Roosevelt, Taft, and Hoover, along with other celebrities such as Will Rogers and Ernest Hemingway. Architect Thomas Kimball modeled the Inn after a Scottish hunting lodge, with dormer windows on all 62 rooms; "Ripley's Believe it or Not!" labeled it "The House of 69 Gables," a name that has stuck through the years. Inside, carpenters added hand-hewn ponderosa pine beams, three large cobblestone fireplaces, the Buffalo Bill Bar (imported from England), elegant oak furnishings, and the first electric lights in Sheridan. Colonel William F. Cody (Buffalo Bill) led the grand march for the first dance on opening night. Later, Cody was a part owner of the hotel and used the veranda to audition performers for his Wild West Show. It was operated as a hotel until 1965 and later as a restaurant and bar.

Located on the corner of Fifth St. and Broadway, the Inn is on the National Register of Historic Places and is now being restored by a local nonprofit group. Admission is $3 for adults, $2 for seniors, and free for children under 12. Visitors are treated to a 45-minute guided tour of this fascinating old building. If Anna Lawrence is around when you visit, be sure to ask her about working here as a girl. Hours are daily 9-8 in the summer, or Mon.-Fri. 9-5 and Sun. 9-4 the rest of the year. Tall cottonwoods guard the front, and the huge porch wraps around the sides. Try counting the gables to see if you can find all 69 of them.

Fort Mackenzie

Built in 1902, Fort Mackenzie never really served much of a military function. Pushed through Congress by Wyoming's powerful Senator Francis E. Warren, the fort was ostensibly built as a base to put down any Indian uprising on nearby reservations. (The last major Indian battles had been 20 years earlier.) It was named for Gen. Ranald S. Mackenzie, a veteran of the Civil War and various Indian battles. Over the decades, the size of the fort shrank from 6,280 acres to 342 acres, and the last troops departed during WW I. In 1922, it became a 339-bed hospital for mentally ill vets. You're welcome to walk around the grounds and admire the old brick buildings, but check in at the administration building first.

King's Saddlery

Well worth a stop is King's Saddlery, 184 N. Main, tel. 672-2702, a Sheridan-area fixture for almost 50 years. When you step inside the doors the smell of leather is almost overwhelming. The long, narrow shop has handmade saddles, leatherwork, ropes, spurs, chaps, belt buckles, cowboy hats, and various other tack for horses. Be sure to take a look at the miles of rope in the back room; many top rodeo cowboys drop by for their lariats.

A free **Western Museum** in the back has hundreds of gorgeous saddles—some from before the Civil War—along with rifles, spurs, chaps, tools, and several wagons. Also here is an impressive collection of Indian artifacts. King's Saddlery is fittingly named: both Queen Elizabeth and the king of Saudi Arabia have visited, and ex-Prez Reagan has one of their leather belts. King's Saddlery is open Mon.-Sat. 8-5.

Sheridan County Library

Sheridan's excellent library at 320 N. Brooks, tel. 674-8585, is open Mon.-Thurs. 9-9 and Fri.-Sat. 9-6. One section encloses a small collection of Indian artifacts and items from early settlers. The Wyoming Room has an extensive collection of old books, maps, and paintings, including a mural of the Wagon Box Fight (see p. 439); upstairs are more historical exhibits and current artwork, plus a model of the Medicine Wheel. Also on the walls of the library are 11 paintings by Bill Gollings (1878-1932), a self-taught, but accomplished, cowboy artist.

Other Sights

A historic marker on the corner of West Dow and Alger streets commemorates **Gen. Crook's campsite.** In 1876 he camped here at the junction of Big and Little Goose creeks with 1,325 men and 1,900 pack animals after being forced to a stalemate by Sioux and Crow warriors on the Rosebud River. The fight took place just eight days before Custer would die at nearby Little Big Horn.

Directly across from the Sheridan Inn is the old red Sheridan **train depot,** built in 1892 and now housing a restaurant. Nearby is a huge Chicago, Burlington, and Quincy Railroad **locomotive.** Downtown on Third and Gould streets is one of Sheridan's **streetcars** from the early 1900s. History and architectural buffs should pick up a copy of the guide to Sheridan's **Main Street Historic District** at the visitor center. One of the buildings included—the **Mint Bar,** 151 N. Main, tel. 674-9696—offers a genuine taste of the west. Cartoonist Linda Barry's description of the Mint says it all: "Stuffed animal heads galore. Taxidermied fish galore. Burlwood carpentry galore."

PRACTICALITIES

Motels And Dude Ranches

Most of Sheridan's motels lie along Coffeen Ave. and Main Street. See the chart for specific rates. The **Mill Inn Motel** is unique in that it is located within a historic flour mill. (Sort of adds a new meaning to the term "hitting the sack.") A warning on one place: the Super 8 is next to a very smelly stockyard.

Sheridan is surrounded by several classic dude ranches. The first in the area was run by the Hilman family, who took in their first paying dudes in 1889. It operated until the 1930s. The famous **Eaton's Guest Ranch,** 18 miles west of Sheridan, tel. 655-9285, is one of the oldest and best-known dude ranches in America. The three Eaton brothers—Howard, Alden, and Willis—began ranching in North Dakota in the late 1800s but soon found themselves overwhelmed by visiting friends from the east. Eventually one offered to pay, and thus was born the dude ranch. At first these "dudes" (a term that both Buffalo Bill and Howard Eaton took credit for first using in this context) stayed wherever they could find space, eating the cowboy's grub and joining in on chores. In 1904, the brothers bought a ranch along Wyoming's Wolf Creek that would eventually grow to 7,000 acres. Today the ranch accommodates 125 dudes in modernized guest cabins. Two other fine local dude ranches are **Spear-O-Wigwam Dude Ranch,** tel. 674-4496, begun in 1923 by Virginia and Willis Spear, and **Masters Ranches** in Ranchester, tel. 655-2386.

Camping

Camp for free in town at **Washington Park,** close to Little Goose Creek but also along the busy main drag (one night only—water sprinklers enforce this every afternoon, so get your tent down in time!). Many more campgrounds ($5-7) are within nearby Bighorn National Forest; see above for details. **Bighorn Mountain KOA,** 63 Decker Rd., tel. 674-8766, has quiet tent sites for $11 and RV sites for $14. Noncampers may shower for $3.25 (before 4 p.m. only). It's open May-early October.

Food

Sheridan has a broad choice of eateries, from two-bit greasy spoons to gourmet restaurants. The **Silver Spur,** 832 N. Main, tel. 672-2749, only serves breakfast and lunch, but it has the best down-home cowboy food in town. Reasonable prices, too. **Ritz Sporting Goods,** 135 N. Main, tel. 674-4101, is home to the local coffee klatch most mornings and has a lunch counter for burgers. **Brown Drug,** 55 N. Main, tel. 672-2620, has an old-time soda fountain. It's been here since 1905.

Sheridan's finest lunches and dinners are found at **Ciao,** 120 N. Main, tel. 672-2838. Wonderful pastas, salads, desserts, and fresh-baked breads. Get here early for lunch to avoid the lines, and make reservations for dinner. This is the only place east of Jackson Hole where you're likely to find riddiccio on the menu! The other truly noteworthy local restaurant is **Golden Steer Restaurant,** 2071 N. Main, tel. 674-9334, where you'll find consistently good steaks.

Bazels Restaurant, 748 N. Main, tel. 672-7183, serves all-American fries and shakes in an infectiously fun '50s diner atmosphere, but the best local burgers can be found at **Dairy Queen,** 544 N. Main, tel. 674-9379. Try **California Zephyr Restaurant,** across from the Sheridan Inn, for steak sandwiches and Mexican dishes, but the quality can be hit-or-miss. **Alger St. Cafe,** in the historic Cady building (5 E. Alger), is a relaxing place with gourmet lunches and dinners. This is a fine place for a leisurely Sunday brunch.

Little Big Men Pizza, 1424 Coffeen Ave., tel. 672-9877, serves reasonable pizza, burger, and salad meal deals, but **Ole's Pizza,** in the mall next to the Holiday Inn, tel. 672-3636, is better. Their BBQ ribs are an even better bet. Fill up on

SHERIDAN ACCOMMODATIONS

MOTEL	ADDRESS	TELEPHONE	RATES	FEATURES
Parkway Motel	2112 Coffeen Ave.	672-7259	$24+ s, $26+ d	kitchenettes $30
Stage Stop Motel	2167 N. Main	672-3459	$26 s, $30 d	
Alamo Motel	1326 N. Main	672-2455	$26 s, $30 d	
Guest House Motel	2007 N. Main	674-7496 (800) 341-8000	$26 s, $32 d	AAA-approved, pool
Rock Trim Motel	449 Coffeen Ave.	672-2464	$26+ s or d	AAA-approved
Sundown Motel	1704 N. Main	672-2439	$28 s, $34 d	pool
Energy Inn	580 E. Fifth St.	672-9757	$28 s, $38 d	jacuzzi
Rancher Motel	1552 Coffeen Ave.	672-2428	$30 s, $36 d	jacuzzi, sauna
Mill Inn Motel	2161 Coffeen Ave.	672-6401	$30 s, $33 d	AAA-approved
Holiday Lodge	625 Coffeen Ave.	672-2407	$32 s, $36 d	pool, kitchenettes
X-L Motel	402 N. Main	674-6458	$32 s, $38 d	
Trails End Motel	2125 N. Main	672-2477	$42+ s or d	AAA-approved, pool
Super 8 Motel	2435 N. Main	672-9725 (800) 800-8000	$46 s or d	
Sheridan Center Motor Inn (Best Western)	609 N. Main	674-7421 (800) 528-1234	$46 s, $54 d	pool, sauna, jacuzzi, continental breakfast
Holiday Inn	1809 Sugarland Dr. (800) 465-4329	672-8931	$69+ s, $77+ d	AAA-approved, pool, sauna, whirlpool, exercise room

barbecued buffalo during the evening chuck-wagons at **Bighorn Mountain KOA,** 63 Decker Rd., tel. 674-8766. **A. E. Suk,** 2004 N. Main, tel. 672-0357, has a Chinese, Korean, and Japanese buffet lunch every day, and the cheapest breakfasts going. You won't go away hungry here. More Chinese cookery at **Golden China Restaurant** in the T&C Shopping Center at Brundage and Coffeen, tel. 674-7181.

In addition to the standard mega-marts (Safeway, Decker's Market, Warehouse Foods, and Buttery Foods) in Sheridan, you'll find holistic groceries at **Nanci's Natural Foods,** 38 S. Main, tel. 674-8344. Get pastries and espresso coffees at **Cappuccino Cowboy,** 109 N. Main. (Pretty hard to imagine a cowboy sipping espresso coffee!)

Entertainment
During the summer months, **WYO Theater,** 42 N. Main, tel. 672-9084, has live melodramas five nights a week, and the Kendrick Park bandshell is home to free Tues. night **concerts in the park.** The bands range from polka to jazz. **Carriage House Theater** at Trail End, tel. 672-9886, presents plays throughout the year. Ask at the visitor center about the annual **Shakespeare in the Park** performance put on by a Missoula-based troupe.

Enjoy live rock 'n' roll on weekends at **LBM Pizza,** 1424 Coffeen Ave., tel. 672-9877, or watch sports on their big-screen TV. **Golden Steer,** 2071 N. Main, tel. 674-9334, often has golden oldies from the '50s, while the **Brass Banjo** at the Holiday Inn, 1809 Sugarland Dr., tel. 672-8931, has recorded dance tunes most nights and rock on weekends. Another place to check is **California Zephyr Lounge.**

Events
The **Sheridan Wyo Rodeo** comes around in July each year, bringing with it not just profes-

sional rodeo cowboys at the "world's largest one go-round rodeo," but also a parade down Main St., a pancake breakfast, the Wyoming Chili Cook-off, C&W bands, and street dances. In early August, visit the **Sheridan County Fair,** followed by the **Sheridan County Rodeo** later in the month. This rodeo is for the younger set and even includes stick-horse races for those under age four! **Big Horn Mountain Polka Days** is a fun early-September event that attracts hundreds of polka enthusiasts. Oom-pa-pa! During the winter, **"Chariot Races"** are held at the Soldier Creek Complex on Fifth Street.

Recreation

Kendrick City Park has a small game preserve with various native critters such as bison and elk. Swim at the **outdoor swimming pool** (summer only) in the park, and feel like a kid again on the 90-foot-long waterslide. There's another pool at the **YMCA,** 417 N. Jefferson, tel. 674-7488, plus racquetball and tennis courts and weight machines.

Big Horn Mountain Sports, 334 N. Main St., tel. 672-6866, has a good choice of camping, backpacking, skiing, topographic maps, and windsurfing equipment. Much of this gear can also be rented. They teach classes in skiing, kayaking, windsurfing, fly-tying, fly-fishing, and rock climbing. **Ritz Sporting Goods,** 135 N. Main, tel. 674-4101, also sells a range of camping and outdoor supplies. **Fly Shop of the Big Horns,** 377 Coffeen Ave., tel. 672-5866, has classes in fly-casting and fly-tying and offers guided fishing trips on the Big Horn and Platte rivers. Rent float tubes and fins here. Golfers will want to try out the 18-hole **Kendrick Golf Course,** three miles west of town, tel. 674-8148. For something really different, try an hour-long sailplane ride ($50) from **Sheridan Soaring,** tel. 672-5277.

Shopping

You'll find a fine selection of Wyoming titles at **The Book Shop,** 122 N. Main, tel. 672-6505, and **Sheridan Stationery,** 206 N. Main, tel. 672-8080. The Book Shop also has monthly poetry readings and other literary events. See **Wyoming Gifts and Imports,** 227 N. Main,

tel. 672-8569, for a large local choice of made-in-Wyoming gifts and souvenirs. Several Sheridan art galleries are worth a peek, including **Side Street Gallery,** tel. 672-6561, and **Gallery 348,** tel. 672-6120, in the Best Out West Mall at 109 N. Main, along with **Golden Crown Art Gallery,** 50 N. Main, tel. 674-7676. **Custom Cowboy Shop,** 321 N. Main, tel. 672-7733, has quality boots, hats, saddles, and tack. See also King's Saddlery, described above.

Information And Services

The **Sheridan Visitor Center/State Information Center,** tel. 672-2485, is located in the rest area at the Fifth St. exit of I-90. Inside are various historical displays and a 3-D map, plus a panoramic view of the Big Horns from the windows. The center is open daily 8-8 June-Aug., and Mon.-Fri. 8-5 in winter. A small kiosk visitor center in Washington Park opens during the summer. The **Wyoming Game & Fish Department Visitor Center** (tel. 672-2790) is directly across the road and contains a number of informative wildlife and fish displays. Hours here are Mon.-Fri. 8-5. Pick up a copy of their *Campbell County Wildlife and Natural History Loop Tours* to learn more.

The **Bighorn National Forest Supervisors Office** is at 1969 S. Sheridan Ave., tel. 672-0751. Get forest maps and info here. **Sheridan College,** tel. 674-6446, a 2,000-student, two-year school just south of Sheridan, is one of the largest in the state. Founded in 1948, it offers degrees in both academic and technical fields. The **Special Collections** room of the college library (tel. 674-6446) has a variety of Indian artifacts, including vests, moccasins, pipes, and weapons.

Transportation

Sheridan airport is just southwest of town. Both **Continental Express,** tel. (800) 525-0280, and **United Express,** tel. (800) 631-1500, have daily flights to Denver. **Powder River Transportation,** 580 E. Fifth, tel. 674-6188 or (800) 442-3682, has daily bus service to Billings, Montana, and most towns in eastern Wyoming. Rent cars from **Avis,** tel. (800) 331-1212, at the airport or **Sheridan Motor,** 1766 Coffeen Ave., tel. 672-3411.

SHERIDAN VICINITY

RANCHESTER

The little village of Ranchester (pop. 680) calls itself "The town where the handshake's stronger and the smile lasts longer." Seems true enough. Stay at the clean and friendly **Ranchester Motel,** tel. 655-2212 or (800) 341-8000, for $30 s or $32 d. Head to **BJ Pizza** for genuine homemade pizzas. Other good places are **Ranch House Restaurant,** tel. 655-9527, for family fare and **Magnum Restaurant,** tel. 655-9634, for steaks. **DD's Bar & Lounge,** tel. 655-9818, has live music on weekends. Get groceries at **Buckhorn Groceries,** tel. 655-9766. Children will enjoy the kid-designed wooden playground of forts and slides at the elementary school. **Ranchester Days** in early August features a horseshoe tournament, arts-and-crafts booths, and a street dance.

Historic Sights
Connor Battlefield State Historic Site is right in Ranchester city park. It's a very pleasant place with picnic tables, free camping, and tall cottonwood trees along the Tongue River (so named because of a tonguelike rock along a tributary). Good fishing for brown trout. A cable footbridge leads across the river. Despite this bucolic setting, the park has a gruesome history, representing one of the worst massacres in the Powder River Basin. It was the year 1865, a time of hit-and-run battles throughout the plains set off by the massacre of Cheyenne at Sand Creek in Colorado, but continued by dozens of Indian attacks upon settlers and emigrants. Red Cloud had just struck against Platte Bridge Station (see "Casper," pp. 183-184) a few weeks before, killing 28 men, and the Army was anxious to avenge that raid and attacks along the Bozeman Trail.

Gen. Patrick E. Connor—a proponent of the shoot-first, ask-questions-later school of military diplomacy—attacked Indian villages throughout the West, killing 200 Shoshone in a Utah attack in 1863 and then rampaging through Nevada and Idaho. Connor's 1865 expedition to the Powder River included nearly a thousand soldiers, plus 179 Pawnee and Winnebago scouts. Most of the effort was a failure, as Indians kept ahead of the ponderous military wagons, but on August 29 they came upon Chief Black Bear's Arapaho village along the Tongue River. Connor ordered his men, "You will not receive overtures of peace or submission from the Indians, but will attack and kill every male Indian over 12 years of age." In a pell-mell rush, Connor's men slaughtered 63 men, women, and children, destroyed 250 lodges along with much of their winter supplies, and captured more than 1,100 ponies. Eight troopers died. It never was ascertained whether the Arapaho they encountered were the same ones who had been attacking along the Bozeman Trail. The expedition ended when the government realized the expedition was costing over a million dollars a month for transportation alone. A chastened Connor stashed his supplies at Fort Connor (later renamed Fort Reno) and returned to Fort Laramie.

Four miles west of here on US 14, another monument marks the **Sawyer Fight.** Here, two days after Connor attacked the Arapaho along the Tongue River, they retaliated against a 100-man roadbuilding expedition led by Col. James Sawyer. Three of his men were killed and the rest were pinned down for nearly two weeks before finally being rescued by Gen. Connor's troops.

DAYTON

The little settlement of Dayton (pop. 560) has a number of attractions. The log cabin studio of water colorist **Hans Kleiber** (1887-1966) now serves as a combination museum and visitor center. Kleiber was known as "Artist of the Big Horns," and his works are internationally collected today. Inside are his press, art books, and several of his etchings. The museum is open daily in the summer. Dayton's old **bell tower,** built in 1910 to warn of fires, is now in the city park.

Accommodations

Foothills Campground and Motel, tel. 655-2547, has cabins for $20 s or d (kitchenettes $4 more). Camp along the river here for $8 (showers 25 cents extra) or park RVs for $13. Noncampers can shower up for $1. The campground is open mid-April through October. Lodging is also available at **Double Rafter Ranch** near the Montana state line, tel. 655-9362. Bed-and-breakfast accommodations cost $75 for a family of four; horseback rides are available.

Food And Shopping

Dayton Mercantile, tel. 655-2214, was built in 1898 and is now run as a gift shop and restaurant by the exuberantly friendly owner, Isabel Le Beau. The interior is filled with local handicrafts and jewelry. The cafe here features homemade sandwiches, soups, breads, and especially good pies. Try a sarsaparilla float. There are family-style dinners on Fri. and Sat. nights during the summer. Out back is a small gallery of western art in the old icehouse. Meals are also available at **Hitching Post Cafe,** tel. 655-9054.

Humphrey's Blacksmithing, tel. 655-9744, has various hand-forged ironware for sale. **Summerhouse Books,** tel. 655-2367 (summers only or by appointment), has both new and used books for sale. At the **Packstring Gallery,** tel. 655-2350, Mike Flanagan creates traditional western bronze works, including a sculpture in the governor's mansion.

Events And Recreation

Dayton Days, held the last weekend in July, has the usual country favorites, including a parade, food and craft booths, and a street dance. Fishermen will find blue-ribbon trout fishing along the Tongue River. Dayton also has an outdoor **swimming pool** open June-August. The nine-hole **Horseshoe Mountain Golf Course** in Dayton includes some unique hazards: horse-hoof-sized potholes.

EAST OF SHERIDAN

Some of the prettiest plains country in Wyoming lies along US 14, a quiet, scenic road that curls through mile after mile of ranch land and winter wheat. The road heads southeast from

Sheridan, gradually narrowing as it climbs through rugged hills and down a long green valley filled with fine ranches and modern homes.

Ucross

At the crossroads called Ucross, a huge red barn (Big Red) dominates the view. The ranch is headquarters for the nonprofit Ucross Foundation, tel. 737-2291, an important artist retreat sponsored by grants from Apache Oil. Selected artists enjoy a two-to-eight week residency program that includes individual work spaces and royal-treatment living accommodations. It's all to give time for artists to focus on ideas, theories, and works. Also here are a conference center and a restaurant, along with a summer camp for young Wyoming writers.

The **art gallery** at Ucross is open Sun. 12:30-5:30 and Mon.-Fri. 8:30-4:30 and contains rotating exhibits throughout the summer. Big Red was headquarters for the enormous Pratt and Ferris Cattle Co., a spread that extended 35 miles along Clear Creek. At one time, more than 35,000 calves were branded each fall, and the huge barn could hold 30 teams of horses. The "U Cross" was their brand. Ucross is also home to a luxurious (and pricey) resort, **Ucross Guest Ranch,** tel. 737-2281. Make reservations for a gourmet meal here. If you're in the area around **July Fourth,** stick around for food, games, live music, and a spectacular fireworks display.

The 20 miles east from Ucross are some of the most distinctive in Wyoming. The road parallels cottonwood-bordered Clear Creek, winding its way down the grassy hillsides. The Big Horn Mountains form a dramatic western backdrop, while large ranches dot the countryside with stone buildings and spreading old trees. It's easy to see why the Sioux fought so hard to keep this country out of white hands! The highway crosses the Powder River at the little settlement called Arvada and then heads east to Spotted Horse.

Spotted Horse

At Spotted Horse—named for a minor Cheyenne chief—the combination country store/gas station/saloon/cafe is worth a stop, if only to hang out with locals in the five-stool bar. Hard times show in the faces of local ranchers. During the 1930s, tourists en route to Yellowstone posed on a stuffed bucking bronc in the back paddock, but once I-90 was completed, business plummeted. The area's economy has suffered a long decline, and other tiny burgs nearby—Recluse, Arvada, Clearmont, and Leiter—appear on their ways to extinction. In between Clearmont and Leiter is the **RBL Bison Ranch,** tel. 758-4387, where tours are available Mon. and Thurs. for $3 pp. This is a great chance to see buffalo "up close and personal."

Beyond Spotted Horse, the highway curves southeast toward the coal mines of Gillette. The red scoria rock of the highway points through summer-green grass. (Also called clinker, this rock was created when coal burned underground, baking adjacent shale and sandstone to a bright red. Similar red roads exist all over Powder River Basin.) Old windmills pump water for cattle and sheep. From atop the hills a landscape of fences, phone lines, plowed fields, bales of hay, and horses spread out in all directions. The sun darts between cottonball clouds as a lone cyclist pumps up the road, swerving around the smashed jackrabbits and passed by pickup trucks with gun racks and tipped-back cowboy hats. This is the true west, not the cutesified west for the tourists. Red-sided buttes rise above the rolling plains. The new ranch houses—trailer homes—stand next to aging farmsteads and collapsed log cabins; imported pickups are in the driveway and satellite dishes are out front. If you like grass and sky, brilliant starry nights, antelope, haystacks, and oil wells, you'll love this place. Stop for a while and listen to the silence, broken only by the meadowlarks and the wind. God's country.

SOUTH OF SHERIDAN

Although I-90 cuts south of Sheridan toward Buffalo, US 87 offers a much more interesting route, taking you through rolling ranch country and past cottonwood-lined draws. Along the way are the little settlements of Big Horn and Story and the historically rich country around old Fort Phil Kearny and the Bozeman Trail.

Big Horn

Tiny Big Horn was founded in 1879 by O.P. Hanna (local Indians called him "Big Spit," be-

cause of his tobacco chewing), a ceaseless promoter who sent glowing accounts of "Big Horn City" to various newspapers. Unfortunately, a reporter decided to investigate and found the town consisted primarily of a few outlaws, including "Big Nose" George Parrott and Frank James (of the James Gang). A few homesteaders and settlers did come, however, so by 1884 Big Horn City had a hotel, three stores, two blacksmith shops, three saloons, a newspaper, a school, a church, and even a college. Over the years, most of the businesses moved to Sheridan, but still here is the **Big Horn Mercantile,** built in 1882 and considered the oldest business in northern Wyoming. Take a look inside for the photo of Queen Elizabeth, who visited here in 1984. (The area has a prominent British heritage.) From the same era is **Bozeman Trail Inn,** tel. 672-9288, where you'll find one of the oldest bars in Wyoming.

Bozeman Trail Museum is housed in a historic blacksmith shop dating from 1881. Open Sat. and Sun. 11-8 June-Aug. (by appointment at other times), it has various local memorabilia, old photos of the town, and a small gift shop. The ceiling is "branded" with local cattle brands. No charge. The town park next door makes a pleasant picnic spot. **Spahn's Bed & Breakfast,** tel. 674-8150, has lodge rooms as well as cabins with great views across Powder River Basin. Rates are $60 s or d. The **State Bird Farm,** tel. 674-7701, on Bird Farm Rd. raises more than 10,000 pheasants each year. These birds are released around Wyoming shortly before the fall hunting season and just in time to get shot as "wild game." The farm also has show birds, including over a dozen species of pheasants, as well as peacocks, turkey, chukkar, and guinea hens.

Certainly the last thing one might expect to find in Big Horn is a polo field, but the English tradition lives on at **Big Horn Equestrian Center,** south of town on Bird Farm Road. Polo games are held on Sundays during the summer. These are informal events with changing teams and players of varying abilities. Steeplechase events are another summertime feature. The ranch is owned by Malcnlm Wallop, one of Wyoming's U.S. senators and the grandson of Sir Oliver H. Wallop, seventh earl of Portsmouth (who served in the Wyoming Legislature before returning to England to sit in the British House of Lords). Oliver Wallop and the two Moncrieffe brothers (see below) bought western horses for the British Army during the Boer War, shipping 20,000 of them overseas. To test the ponies, the British purchasing officer would ride them the length of a polo field. Malcolm Moncrieffe trained a team on this field, later competing with them in England. Thus began what is believed to be the oldest polo field in America.

The biggest annual event in Big Horn is the **Cowboy Round-Up** held in mid-June. It features polo matches, stock-dog trials, music, storytelling, crafts demonstrations, and more.

Bradford Brinton Memorial Museum

In 1892, two Scottish brothers, William and Malcolm Moncrieffe, built a spacious two-story ranch house along Little Goose Creek. It became headquarters for their Quarter Circle A Ranch. A businessman and lover of the west, Bradford Brinton bought the ranch in 1923 and enlarged the home to 20 rooms, furnishing it with fine furniture and lining the walls with his art collection. After his death in 1936, the house was owned by his sister. Her will established it as a museum in honor of Bradford Brinton, which it has been since her death in 1960. The museum, tel. 672-3173, is open daily 9:30-5 from May 15 to Labor Day (closed the rest of the year) and has guided tours. Entrance costs $3 pp, or $5 for families. Step inside to taste the genteel life and to view works by some of the west's best-known artists, many of whom were friends of Bradford Brinton. The collection includes over 600 works by such artists as John James Audubon, Hans Kleiber, Charles M. Russell, Frederic Remington, and Will Gollings. Also here are various Indian handicrafts, books, and historic documents. Horses are still raised on the 600-acre ranch, and the rural setting is most enjoyable: mountains rise on two sides and big old cottonwoods border the drive. Get here by heading five miles west on State 335 from the junction with US 87. Follow the signs.

Story

The town of Story (pop. 650) is surprisingly different from nearby Sheridan and Buffalo. The road winds more than a thousand feet above the valley floor to the pine-covered slopes of the Big Horns. Locals and visitors come up to escape the hot summer air, enjoy the restaurants, and look for deer, elk, moose, and wild turkeys. Story is the site of "Piney Island," a stand of timber used to build nearby Fort Phil Kearny in 1866. It was named for Nelson Story, the first man to trail cattle north across Powder River Basin. **Story Fish Hatchery,** established in 1907, raises trout for Wyoming lakes and streams. It's open daily 7 a.m. till dark; tel. 683-2234.

Lodore Supper Club and Lounge, tel. 683-2355, first opened in 1919, is a very popular steak, seafood, and Mexican restaurant with live country music on summer weekends. For good fish and chips, and a menu that covers the spectrum from frog legs to enchiladas, head to **Tunnel Inn,** tel. 683-9921. **Wagon Box Inn,** tel. 683-2444, has cozy cabins starting for $35 and bunkhouse accommodations for $15 s or $25 d, including a sauna and a jacuzzi. Showers for those not staying here are $3. It's wise to reserve rooms ahead of time during the peak summer season. On weekend nights, folks come here for live music and tasty Mexican dishes.

Ed and Sali Smyth's **Line Camp Gallery** on Rosebud Lane, tel. 683-2213, exhibits fine western artwork. **Piney Creek Pottery,** across from Tunnel Inn, tel. 683-2181, sells pottery and other artwork. Check with **North Piney Horse Corral,** tel. 683-2838, for trail rides and pack trips.

THE BLOODY BOZEMAN

The discovery of gold in Montana during the 1860s started an avalanche of miners and businessmen. The fastest route to the Virginia City goldfields headed northwest from Bridger's Ferry (near present-day Douglas, Wyoming), through the Powder River Basin, and then west across Montana. One of the pioneers who scouted and constantly promoted the "Montana Road" was John M. Bozeman (as in Bozeman, Montana). Before being killed by Indians on the Yellowstone River in 1867, he led several groups up the Bozeman Trail, as the route became known. Hundreds of others would die along Bozeman's route to the goldfields. Guide Jim Bridger knew that the Sioux would never stand for whites in their Powder River country—a place they had recently wrested from the Crows, Shoshone, and Arapaho. Instead, he recommended a different route that would cut west of the Big Horn Mountains. Unfortunately, Bridger's advice went unheeded, and as attacks on emigrant wagon trains increased in 1864, so did pressure to protect them from the Sioux. Appeals to Washington brought military assistance in the form of forts filled with soldiers and cavalry. Parallels between the events that followed and America's experience in Vietnam—from the guerrilla warfare to the hurried exit of U.S. troops at the end of the conflict—are disconcertingly similar.

Red Cloud's War

The first salvo by the Army came in Gen. Connor's savage wanderings through the Powder River in 1865 (see "Ranchester," above). The following year, while treaty negotiations were being held at Fort Laramie, Col. Henry B. Carrington and a battalion of infantry marched in heading to the Bozeman Trail, where they planned to construct new forts. Red Cloud, a fiery military leader of the Oglala Sioux, grew more and more angry, shouting,

> *Great Father sends us presents and wants new road, but White Chief goes with soldier, to steal road before Indian says yes or no. . . . White man lies and steals. My lodges were many, but now they are few. The white man wants all. The white man must fight, and the Indian will die where his fathers died.*

The treaty was signed by older chiefs and the "Laramie Loafers," who hung around the fort, but not by Red Cloud. He and his warriors stormed out, arriving at Powder River ahead of Col. Carrington.

Carrington was a strange man to direct this massive undertaking. A political appointee with no battlefield experience—let alone experience with guerrilla warfare—he approached the task of building forts and protecting travelers along the Bozeman Trail with a take-no-chances attitude that rankled his trigger-happy men. (The troupe left Nebraska with a 30-piece brass band, carriages, and comfortable furnishings, gaining the name "Carrington's Overland Circus.")

Once finally in the Powder River country, Carrington split his men into three groups, stationing some at Fort Reno near present-day Buffalo (begun the previous year by Gen. Connor), and sending others to build Fort C.F. Smith in Montana. These way stations were to provide military escorts for travelers and a haven from Indian attacks. Instead, they themselves came under attack, and Carrington's men nearly became prisoners inside them.

Fort Phil Kearny

In the heart of the Powder River country, Carrington found what seemed a perfect site for a fort along Little Piney Creek: good water, grass so thick that horses could barely walk through it, and timber close at hand. His guide, the famed Jim Bridger, pushed instead for a site farther north, and away from the center of Sioux country. To Bridger, these "damn paper collar soldiers" seemed bound and determined to get killed. The new garrison—named Fort Phil Kearny for a Civil War general—measured 600 by 800 feet, entirely enclosed by a heavy log

Fort Phil Kearny

stockade. It was big enough for 1,000 men, though it never housed nearly that many. Both Indian attackers and its white defenders came to view this as the west's most hated fort. From the very first day, Carrington found himself harassed by the Sioux; by mid-December, more than 50 raids on the troops and civilians had left 17 military men and 58 civilians dead. Many of the horses and mules were stolen in the raids, and more than 700 cattle were lost when the Indians created a stampede by driving a herd of buffalo into them. With winter setting in, food and ammunition shortages made conditions worse, and even the nightly band concerts could not maintain morale. Jim Bridger revealed something of even greater concern after one of his scouting trips:

Crow chiefs report that it took a half a day's ride to go through the villages of the war parties on Tongue River. The Sioux chiefs said they would not touch the new fort on Powder River [Fort Reno] but would destroy the two new forts, in their hunting grounds, meaning Phil Kearny and C. F. Smith.

Fetterman Fight

Again and again, the Sioux tempted soldiers into traps, drawing them away with attacks on the vital wood wagons (more than 12,000 logs were used to build the fort) and those cutting hay, or by stealing stock and then attacking the pursuers. Carrington's caution caused dissension in the ranks, and when a new company of cavalry arrived, led by Capt. William J. Fetterman, the dissension edged on open revolt. Fetterman, like Gen. George A. Custer, had achieved fame for his bravery during the Civil War. And, like Custer, he would meet an early death. Fetterman viewed the Sioux with reckless disdain, claiming, "I can take 80 men and go to Tongue River through all the Sioux forces." Jim Bridger responded to this boast with, "Your men who fought down South are crazy! They don't know anything about fighting Indians."

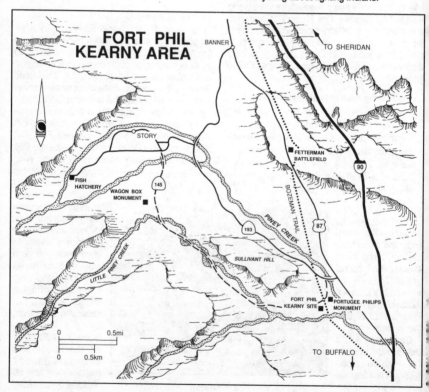

On the morning of December 21, 1866, Indians attacked a wood train, and a force of cavalry and infantrymen under Capt. Fetterman was sent out. Disobeying orders from Col. Carrington, Fetterman responded to taunts by Sioux decoys (including young Crazy Horse) by following them into an ambush. Perhaps 2,000 warriors of Red Cloud, High Back Bone, Red Leaf, and Little Wolf suddenly appeared in the tall grass. Within a half-hour, all 81 soldiers had been killed. It was, until Custer's last stand a decade later, the worst annihilation of any American force. Carrington had lost his most experienced fighters. Perhaps 30 Sioux died in the raid. Troops sent out to investigate what had happened found the frozen bodies horribly mutilated. They buried the men in a mass grave.

After the Fetterman Fight, just 119 soldiers remained to guard against several thousand Sioux. Fearing further attacks (which never came), Carrington put the fort on full alert and sent messengers to Fort Laramie in a desperate bid for help. John "Portugee" Phillips made the 236-mile ride in four nights of hard riding, struggling through subzero temperatures and blinding blizzards and traveling at night to avoid Indian attacks. In a scene straight out of a Hollywood movie, Phillips staggered into a gala Christmas night ball with the stunning news. His horse collapsed and died. Because of bad weather, help did not reach Fort Phil Kearny for another two weeks. Col. Carrington was sent in humiliation to Nebraska, and it took many years to clear his name.

Wagon Box Fight
The tables were turned in the Wagon Box Fight. Woodcutters took the running gear off their wagons to haul logs back to the fort and arranged the wagon boxes into a makeshift fortress filled with ammunition and supplies in case of attack. The attack came on August 2, 1867, when Red Cloud's 3,000 warriors suddenly surrounded 32 woodchoppers and soldiers led by Capt. James Powell. Unbeknownst to Red Cloud, they were armed with new Springfield rifles that could fire up to 20 rounds per minute. Expecting the soldiers to take time to reload, Red Cloud sent waves of men, only to meet a withering gunfire each time. Finally, after six hours of this, soldiers from Fort Phil Kearny arrived with their howitzer, sending

the Sioux fleeing. Four soldiers died in the Wagon Box Fight, while estimates of Indian casualties range from six to over a thousand. (Sioux warriors removed their dead after a battle, making it impossible to know how many had been killed.)

The Fighting Ends
By late 1867, public sentiment had moved against the Army's invasion of Sioux country, and the Bozeman Trail had become an anachronism, with miners heading to Montana via steamboat up the Missouri River. Besides, the Union Pacific Railroad was well on its way across Wyoming, and the diversion was no longer needed. (Some historians believe this was the primary reason for the forts being built in the first place.) In 1868, the three Bozeman Trail forts were all abandoned. As the soldiers left Fort Phil Kearny, they turned back to see smoke on the horizon. The Sioux were burning it to the ground. Thus ended, at least temporarily, one of the most senseless conflicts in American history. Red Cloud finally returned to Fort Laramie to sign the treaty, having (he thought) forced the government to leave Powder River to the Sioux. Actually the treaty was ambiguous and contradictory, giving them rights to hunt buffalo on the Powder River, but saying they would have to live on reservations in Dakota Territory. Six years later, the country would again boil over when another gold rush—this time in the Black Hills—brought Gen. Custer north to fight the Sioux.

The Bozeman Trail Today
The site of **Fort Phil Kearny** is now a National Historic Landmark and is managed by the Wyoming Division of Parks and Cultural Resources. Entrance costs $1 pp (free under age 18). There isn't a lot to see of the old fort itself, though three small archaeological excavations reveal the charred remains of foundations. Various signs mark building locations, the cemetery, and the Bozeman Trail. A fine small **museum** (tel. 684-7629) is open daily 8-6 from mid-May through Sept., and Wed.-Sun. noon-4 during fall and spring. It is closed Dec.-March. Inside, find an excellent model of the fort, videos about the Bozeman Trail and Ft. Phil Kearny, and displays on Indian life. The fort is 17 miles north of Buffalo and 21 miles south of Sheridan off I-90 (take exit 44). Portugee

Phillips' ride is noted by a pyramid-shaped monument not far away. In midsummer, **Bozeman Trail Days** at Fort Phil Kearny brings archaeological tours of the fort and nearby battlegrounds, living history presentations, concerts, a chuckwagon BBQ, and more.

Ruts from the Bozeman Trail are still visible along much of its path, and the battle sites are all marked with monuments of various sorts. Get to the site of the **Wagon Box Fight** by heading a mile south from Story on a rutted dirt road (not recommended for RVs). The **Fetterman Fight** is marked by a stone obelisk on the hilltop where the final stand was made. A three-quarter-mile interpretive trail leads visitors through the battlefield.

THE JOHNSON COUNTY WAR

Wyoming's history is one of constant conflict between white emigrants and Indians, between Chinese and white miners, between big ranchers and homesteaders, and between sheepherders and cattlemen. The Powder River had more than its share of confrontation; one of the most notorious was the so-called Johnson County War of 1892. (The 1980 box office flop *Heaven's Gate*—reportedly the most expensive film ever produced—was based on this conflict.)

Barons And Grangers

The first white settlers in the Powder River Basin were the "cattle barons," men who owned enormous herds of cattle but who generally resided on the land only part of the year. During the 1880s, more and more homesteaders ("grangers") began to settle here, fencing their spreads and gradually forcing the large cow outfits onto less and less land. The barons tried to force homesteaders off the land, and several Johnson County grangers were found face-down in gullies, shot in the back. Homesteaders retaliated by appropriating cattle that wandered onto their land, while outlaws made off with other stock.

As rustling increased along the Powder River, the big ranchers found little sympathy in nearby Buffalo. Local juries, either sympathetic with or intimidated by cattle rustlers, failed to convict men who were caught, and even the Buffalo sheriff, "Red" Angus, was accused of being in cahoots with rustlers. The cattle barons feared for their lives. The small ranchers and homesteaders in the largest town north of the Platte River—Buffalo—were soon openly at odds with the absentee cattle barons based in the largest town south of the Platte—Cheyenne.

The Invasion

In 1892, the small Johnson County ranchers organized their own roundup, an action that proved too much for the powerful Wyoming Stock Growers Association. In a secret meeting, the Association proposed a military coup d'état. On April 6, two days after their annual meeting in Cheyenne, a train headed for Douglas with 25 hired Texas gunmen (mostly ex-sheriffs and ex-U.S. marshals) along with an equal number of Wyoming men. With them was a hit list of 70 suspected rustlers. Cutting the telegraph lines to keep advance word from reaching folks in Johnson County and traveling in darkened railway cars, the "Invaders" headed north, stopping the train near Casper and continuing on by horseback.

They first came to the KC Ranch—actually just a couple of cabins—and discovered two of the most notorious rustlers holed up inside, Nate Champion and Nick Ray. In the day-long shoot-out that followed, Ray died quickly, but Champion managed to hold off the Invaders until dusk when they finally torched the cabin and shot him as he ran for safety. A blood-stained diary found on Champion described his last hours. It ended: "Shooting again. I think they will fire the house this time. It's not night yet. The house is all fired. Goodbye, boys, if I never see you again. Nathan D. Champion."

After this initial success, the Invaders headed on to the friendly TA Ranch, 30 miles north, to rest up for their planned siege of Buffalo. But word got out, and the Invaders suddenly found themselves under attack by a mob of 200 well-armed grangers and rustlers led by Sheriff Red Angus (who was on the hit list). In the shootout that followed, two Texans died. The tables had been turned, and the desperate Invaders faced almost certain annihilation. Meanwhile, word had gotten out to Acting Governor Amos W. Barber (a supporter of the Invaders), who cabled President Harrison for help. Troops from nearby Fort McKinney arrived before the townsfolk could attack with their tanklike wagon and dynamite bombs. Newspapers around the nation castigated the cattle barons for their effrontery; the *Laramie Sentinel* noted, "of all the fool things the stock association ever did this takes the cake."

Justice Denied

The events that followed made a mockery of the legal system. After being rescued by Army troops, the Invaders were taken to Cheyenne to stand trial. Not surprisingly, two trappers who had happened upon the raid at the KC Ranch mysteriously disappeared until the trial was over, leaving no witnesses for the prosecution. Everyone pleaded not guilty, but when the judge discovered that Johnson County was unable to pay for the prisoners' room and board, he ordered them all released on their own recognizance. After being paid by the Barons, the hired Texas gunmen immediately skipped town, never to be seen again. The Wyoming men involved in the raid were released when Johnson County had no more money to prosecute. Many of Wyoming's most prominent citizens—including Acting Governor Barber and senators Carey and Warren—would later be implicated as supporters of the raid. Johnson County would take years to settle down after the battles of 1892, and for a while the big cattlemen lived in fear for their lives.

museum one of the finest in Wyoming. The museum occupies two downtown buildings. Out front are several wagons, including the de rigueur sheepherder wagon. The front building contains historic photos, a model of Fort Phil Kearny, a video about Bomber Mountain, and other items.

Inside the main building are two floors; downstairs is the standard collection of old junk (including a piece of coral from Maui!), but upstairs is a treasure trove of unusual items, including one of the largest collections of Indian artifacts in Wyoming. Featured are detailed dioramas and displays of items found at various local battle sites: the Wagon Box Fight, the Johnson County War, and the Fetterman Fight. Most touching is the flattened horn of bugler Adolph Metzger, who was the last to die at the Fetterman Fight. The note here says his body was the only one the Indians did not mutilate after the massacre; instead covering it with a buffalo robe out of respect for his valor. Other stories say that after trying to fight off the warriors with his hands and bugle, he was taken captive and tortured to death at the Sioux camp.

Scattered around the room are other surprises: a pair of Cheyenne medicine rattles used in the Dance of Victory after Custer's defeat at Little Big Horn, an arrowhead that belonged to Red Cloud, a cartridge belt made by mountain man Jim Bridger, and the outlaw Tom Horn's spurs and a bridle he braided while awaiting execution. Ask the folks at the museum to point out a rifle probably used by the cavalry at Little Big Horn and a shell from Custer's handgun. Look around and you'll find even more surprises at this most impressive small museum. The museum, on the corner of Main and Fort streets, tel. 684-9331, costs $2 (free under age 18). A small gift shop sells historical books and old Wyoming license plates. During June, July, and August, it is open daily 9-8. The rest of the summer (May 15-31 and Sept.-Oct. 15) it is open Mon.-Fri. 9-5. At other times of the year, stop by the chamber of commerce for access information.

> *Three years ago a guileless tenderfoot came into Wyoming, leading a single Texas steer and carrying a branding iron; now he is the opulent possessor of six hundred head of fine cattle—the ostensible progeny of that one steer. . . . A poor boy can in a few years, with an ordinary Texas steer and a branding iron, get together a band of cattle that would surprise those who figure simply on the ordinary rate of increase. Men soon learn that it is possible and even frequent for a cow wearing a "Z" brand to be the fond and loving mother of a calf wearing the "X" brand, and vice versa. Sometimes a calf will develop a brand that has never been in the family before.*
>
> *—19th-century humorist Bill Nye*

Petrified Forest

One of the more unusual local sights is a petrified forest on BLM land, seven miles south of Buffalo. Take the Red Hills exit from I-90 and follow the road another seven miles to Dry Creek Petrified Forest. An easy three-quarter-mile trail loops through the hot sagebrush country, with markers along the way describing the geologic history. Some 60 million years ago, this was a swampy plain, dominated by towering metasequoia trees. You can still count the growth rings on the petrified stumps, some of which are over four feet in diameter and 60 million years old.

Other Sights

Willow Grove Cemetery on the south end of town is an interesting place to explore. Here you will find the graves of rustlers Nate Champion and Nick Ray, Sheriff "Red" Angus, homesteader John Tisdale, and others involved in the Johnson County Wars. Injured or aged veterans live on the grounds of the **Veterans' Home** (old Fort McKinney), two miles west of Buffalo on US 16. Of the original fort, only an old cavalry stable and the post hospital building are still standing. Check in at the office (tel. 684-5511) before sightseeing.

Children (and those who never really grew up) will love the antique **Carousel Park,** tel. 684-7033, on the east end of town behind Col. Bozeman's Restaurant. This is the only carousel in Wyoming and is open daily in the summer and on winter holidays. Just $1 a ride. Included are a dozen custom-carved Wyoming bucking horses. Also here is a Ferris wheel and a mini golf course. The **Occidental Hotel,** 10 N. Main St., was the place where Owen Wister's Virginian "got his man." The hotel is not in business but is open for self-guided tours during the summer. The chamber of commerce has a walking tour of Buffalo's other historic buildings.

The Johnson County War helped dissuade the Chicago, Burlington, and Quincy Railroad from coming through Buffalo, and for many years Buffalo remained America's largest inland city without a railway. Eventually a spur line was built, connecting Buffalo to Clearmont. Locals called it BC & BM (Buffalo-Clearmont and Back, Maybe). Even it was abandoned in 1946 due to competition from trucking companies. Wyoming Railroad's **Engine 105** now rusts in the city park.

PRACTICALITIES

Motels
There's plenty of comfortable and friendly motels to choose from in Buffalo, but it's a good idea to reserve well ahead for accommodations during midsummer, when tourists flood the area. See the chart for rates. Be forewarned that these prices may rise precipitously during the peak season, and you may have to pay up to $60 a night.

Camping
There's free camping at **Lake DeSmet,** eight miles north of town, but the sites can get steaming hot. Mostly for the RV crowd. Other nearby public campgrounds ($5) are in Bighorn National Forest, approximately 15 miles west of Buffalo on US 16. **Big Horn Mt. Campground** (a.k.a. Cross C Campground), two miles west on US 16, tel. 684-2307, has tent spaces for $10, RV sites for $16. Showers for noncampers cost $3; open year-round. The friendly folks at **Indian Campground,** on US 16 east of town, tel. 684-9601 or (800) 524-4224, charge $13 for tents and $16 for RVs in shady spots. Showers for noncampers run $3.50. It's open April-October. Farther out on US 16 is **Deer Park Campground,** tel. 684-5722 or (800) 222-9960, where sites cost $13 for tents or $16 for RVs. They also serve meals and have a pool and spa, plus a pleasant creekside trail. The evening ice-cream socials are a favorite. It's open May to mid-October.

Food
For breakfast, eat with the truckers at **Kozy Korner** on west US 16, tel. 684-7397, or go to the homey **Busy Bee,** 2 N. Main, tel. 684-7544 (here since 1928). The Busy Bee sits right along Clear Creek, and on summer mornings the benches out front are often crowded with folks waiting to get in. Inside seating is atop stools around a central grill. **Donut Shop,** 386 N. Main, tel. 684-5446, is another local favorite for breakfast. **The Breadboard,** 57 S. Main, tel. 684-2318, has decent sub sandwiches, soups, and spicy chili for lunch. **Outback Deli,** 215 N. Main, tel. 684-7617, also makes sandwiches, soups, and salads. **Seney's Rexall Drug,** 38 S. Main, tel. 684-7182, houses an old-fashioned soda fountain.

The best local dinner place is **Stagecoach Inn,** 845 Fort St., tel. 684-2507, where the prices are reasonable and the portions substantial. The chicken pot pie special (served on Mon., Tues., and Thurs. nights) is recommended. Get frozen yogurt and pizzas at **Pizza Spot,** 401 Fort, tel. 684-7607; look for the polka dots. A popular family dining place with a good salad bar is **Cross Roads Inn,** on US 16 east, tel. 684-2256. **Col. Bozeman's,** 675 E. Hart, tel. 684-5555, serves buffalo steaks. Their Friday night "popcorn shrimp" is a favorite. When folks are looking for an enjoyable evening away from town, they drive to **Pines Lodge,** 14 miles west, tel. 686-4620, or **South Fork Inn,** 17 miles west of Buffalo, tel. 684-9609. Each place has a bar and lounge, along with a standard supper-club menu. Best place for fast food (excellent hickory-smoked fried chicken and ribs) is **Dash Inn,** 620 E. Hart, tel. 684-7930. Get groceries at **Jon's IGA** and **DJ's Thriftway.**

Entertainment
Buffalo has three places to go for live C&W tunes most weekends: **Cross Roads Inn,** (HoJo Inn), tel. 684-2256; **Century Club,** 14 S. Main, tel. 684-2821; and **21 Club,** 4 S. Main, tel. 684-7332.

BUFFALO ACCOMMODATIONS

MOTEL	ADDRESS	TELEPHONE	RATES	FEATURES
Big Horn Motel	209 N. Main St.	684-7611	$25 s, $27 d	kitchenettes, continental breakfast open April-Oct.
Mountain View Motel	585 Fort St.	684-2881	$26 s, $30 d	cabins
Canyon Motel	997 Fort St.	684-2957 (800) 231-0742	$27 s, $30+ d	AAA-approved, kitchenettes $3 extra
Pistol Pete's Motel	800 N. Main St.	684-7453	$28 s or d	open May-Oct.
Buffalo Motel	350 N. Main St.	684-2225	$28 s, $32 d	kitchenettes $48
Arrowhead Motel	749 Fort St.	684-9453	$29+ s, $32+ d	AAA-approved, kitchenettes $5 extra
Z-Bar Motel	626 Fort St.	684-5535 (800) 341-8000	$30 s, $34 d	AAA-approved, kitchenettes
Mansion House Motel	313 N. Main St.	684-2218	$31 s, $38 d	AAA-approved, historic building
Wyoming Motel (Budget Host)	US 16 at I-25	685-5505 (800) 666-5505	$32+ s or d	AAA-approved, pool, kitchens
Blue Gables Motel	662 N. Main St.	684-2574	$38 s or d	pool, cabins, very clean
This Olde House B&B	365 N. Main	684-5930	$40 s, $50 d	historic home, full country breakfast
Super 8 Motel	US 16 at I-25	684-2531 (800) 800-8000	$43 s, $48 d	AAA-approved
Econo Lodge	US 16 East	684-2219 (800) 553-2666	$46 s, $51 d	AAA-approved
Klondike Ranch	15 miles SW	684-2390	$55+ s or d	cabins with kitchenettes, working ranch
HoJo Inn (Howard Johnson's)	US 16 West	684-2256 (800) 852-2302	$59 s, $65 d	AAA-approved, pool

Events

Powder River Roundup Days in early July features a unique rodeo, in which teams compete instead of individuals. The big event each year is the **Johnson County Fair and Rodeo,** held in early August. In March, the **Pole Creek Cross-Country Ski Challenge** attracts racers from near and far. Other events include a **Horseshoe Tournament** in late June and a big **Christmas Parade** on the first Sat. in December.

Recreation

The huge **outdoor swimming pool** (free!) in Washington Park is the largest in the Rocky Mountains. It has swimming lanes, two diving boards, and a shallow end for tots. Hours are 11-7 daily during the summer. This is a great place to play on a hot day. Inside the modern **YMCA,** 101 Klondike Dr., tel. 684-9558, you'll find a pool, a jacuzzi, a weight room, and racquetball and handball courts for just $3. Buffalo has a popular **walking path** that makes for a pleasant afternoon stroll or bike ride. It follows Clear Creek all the way to the foot of the mountains and is paved to the edge of town. Buffalo's 18-hole **municipal golf course,** northwest of town, tel. 684-5266, is one of the finest in Wyoming. One hole features a 90-foot vertical drop over 140 yards.

Shopping

Buffalo has two good fishing shops: **Just Gone Fishing,** 777 Fort St., tel. 684-2755, and **The Sports Lure,** 66 S. Main, tel. 684-7682. The latter also sells hiking, skiing, and backpacking gear, as well as topo maps. If you think you're starting to see spots, you may be at **Alabam's Polka Dot Spot,** 421 Fort St., tel. 684-7452, a shop geared to hunters and anglers. Pretty strange. The factory outlet for **Big Horn Threads,** 1040 Fort St., tel. 684-5684, sells locally sewn packs and bags of all sorts, from soft luggage to snowboard covers. Also in Buffalo, at 68 S. Main, is Sagewood, tel. 684-2788, an "earth-friendly" store that sells nature T-shirts, books, and rainforest products. **Home Spun Creations,** 5 N. Lobban Ave., tel. 684-5916, sells items from local artisans. **Town Saddlery,** US 16 east, tel. 684-2759, has custom-made tack and saddles.

Information And Services

The **Buffalo Chamber of Commerce** office, 55 N. Main St., tel. 684-5544 or (800) 227-5122, is open 8-7 daily in summer, and Mon.-Fri. 8-5 at other times. The new **Johnson County Public Library,** at the intersection of Adams and Lott streets, tel. 684-7888, is open Mon. 1-8, Tues.-Thurs. 10-8, and Fri.-Sat. 10-5. Head to **The Office,** 33 N. Main, tel. 684-2215, to buy guidebooks and volumes of western history. The **Buffalo Ranger District Office** of Bighorn National Forest is at 300 Spruce, tel. 684-7981, while the **Bureau of Land Management Office** is located at 189 N. Cedar, tel. 684-5586.

Transportation

Powder River Bus Lines, tel. (800) 442-3682, connects Buffalo with Gillette, Sheridan, and Casper. Buses stop at the Bighorn Travel Plaza. Rent bikes from **Indian Campground,** on US 16 east of town, tel. 684-9601. Get rental cars at **Northside Car Sales** (Avis), north of Buffalo, tel. 684-5136. The airport in Buffalo does not have scheduled service. Therefore, it was quite a surprise one day in 1979 when a Western Airlines 737 carrying 94 passengers mistakenly landed in Buffalo instead of Sheridan. The pilot has since been "honored" by the celebration of Buffalo's Lowell Ferguson Day (July 31).

BUFFALO VICINITY

LAKE DESMET

Eight miles north of Buffalo is Lake DeSmet, a deep natural lake surrounded by open-range country. A stone **monument** to the Belgian Jesuit missionary, Father Pierre Jean DeSmet (1801-73), stands along the western shore. DeSmet was one of the few 19th-century men who maintained lifelong friendships with both Indians and whites. The Plains Indians called him "Black Robe" and trusted him with various peacemaking roles at Fort Laramie. The Indians viewed the lake named for DeSmet with suspicion, as did early settlers who told of sea monsters and mermaids that came out at night from a seemingly bottomless body of water. When first found by DeSmet in 1851, it was a salten lake—the second largest in the west (after Great Salt Lake)—but dams and dikes have increased its size and decreased its salinity. Today, it's a popular place for local boaters. Try your luck at catching one of the mermaids, but you're more likely to pull in a big rainbow trout. Also here are brown trout, crappie, yellow perch, and rock bass. **Lake DeSmet Fishing Derby** is held each Memorial Day weekend.

There is free **camping** just south of the Father DeSmet monument. Volleyball nets, picnic tables, and outhouses, but no shade or water. **Lake Stop Resort,** tel. 684-9051, rents boats and has a cafe, a bait shop, and cabins. Also here—so the sign claims—is the "world's smallest bar." Just north of the lake is a bed of coal that, in some places, is more than 200 feet thick—second in thickness only to one in Manchuria. No wonder Texaco owns most of the land around Lake DeSmet!

KAYCEE

The town of Kaycee (pop. 260) is named for the nearby KC Ranch and serves as a bentonite, oil, and ranching center. Get on the side roads in spring or fall and you're likely to find yourself behind huge flocks of sheep being herded into or out of the Big Horn Mountains.

Frewen Castle

When the Powder River country was opened to white settlers in the late 1870s, it quickly attracted ranchers and farmers of all types, from homesteaders trying to prove up their 160 acres to wealthy international investors. Two of the most interesting were the English brothers Moreton and Richard Frewen, relatives of Sir Winston Churchill. Coming originally to hunt buffalo, the two saw the lush Powder River area and decided to invest in cattle. Near present-day Kaycee, they erected an elaborate two-story log house, filling it with furniture and fixtures from England, even adding an incredible luxury, a telephone. Frewen Castle, as it was soon called, became the center of an enormous spread with at least 60,000 cattle.

Their kingdom attracted English hunting parties and became something of an unofficial dude

THE WILD BUNCH

Glorified in the 1969 Oscar-winning film *Butch Cassidy and the Sundance Kid*, the Wild Bunch is one of the most famous of all Western outlaw gangs. The Wild Bunch consisted of a constantly changing membership that was held together by two friends, Robert Parker (Butch Cassidy) and Harry Longabaugh (the Sundance Kid). In 1884, Parker, then a teenager, met up with a local ranch hand and part-time cattle rustler named Mike Cassidy. Rebelling against a strict Mormon upbringing, Parker picked up a few of the master's tricks before getting caught and told to move on. But when he left Utah for Colorado and Wyoming, he took with him his mentor's name, Cassidy. (The "Butch" came later when he worked in several Rock Springs butcher shops.) Linking up with other outlaws, Cassidy held up the San Miguel Valley Bank of Telluride and then drifted back to horse stealing in Wyoming. Several years later, those horses landed him in the Wyoming State Prison in Laramie. Cassidy was pardoned by the governor after 18 months, reportedly after agreeing not to pursue that line of work in Wyoming anymore. (Other places were fair game, however.)

The Gang

If anything, prison made Cassidy more determined than ever to outwit the lawmen. Joining up with Harry Longabaugh—who picked up his Sundance Kid sobriquet while serving time in the Sundance, Wyoming, jail for horse thievery—and Harvey Logan (Kid Curry)—a deadly and fearless Montana fugitive—Cassidy assembled a rogues' gallery of rustlers, drifters, killers, and wanted men soon known as the Wild Bunch. They operated from remote hidden canyons in the west, especially Brown's Park in western Colorado, Bighorn Canyon in Montana, Wyoming's Wind River Valley, and the famous Hole-in-the-Wall southwest of Buffalo, Wyoming—places where entire herds of stolen cattle could be hidden, and where the finest horses could be trained for quick getaways.

The Wild Bunch achieved a measure of respect from local ranchers who bought horses and cattle at low prices and found ready workers when the outlaws needed to rest up awhile. For many, Cassidy seemed a modern-day Robin Hood, taking from the rich railroads, banks, mines, and cattle barons, while leaving the small folks alone. To this day, locals in Kaycee, Wyoming still talk fondly of the affable Butch Cassidy.

The gang's activities reached a peak in the late 1890s, with bank robberies in Utah, South Dakota, and Idaho (the latter to pay for a lawyer to clear a gang member on a murder charge). Cassidy—breaking his promise to Wyoming's governor—also led a train robbery in Wilcox, Wyoming, that netted $50,000, but only after he'd blown up the safe with 10 pounds of dynamite, sending money and banknotes in all directions. Within hours, a sheriff's posse was in hot pursuit, and in a gun battle near Casper the sheriff was killed. Somehow, the Wild Bunch managed to slip through the posse's lines for a clean getaway.

In 1900, they struck another Union Pacific train near Tipton, Wyoming. Amazingly, the same express messenger was present for both robberies; the first time he had refused to open the railcar door and was literally blown out with explosives. The second time the conductor persuaded him to open the door. Perhaps he knew that the safe held only $54; the train carrying $100,000 worth of gold had passed just a few hours before. Then the Wild Bunch was off to Nevada, where a bank holdup netted them a cool $32,000. After a fling at Fanny Porter's Sporting House in San Antonio, the gang members bought some new hats at a Fort Worth haberdasher and, dressed as dudes, posed for the famous group portrait later used by Pinkerton detectives. Cassidy and two other gang members tried their hands once more at train robbery in 1901, taking at least $40,000 from the dynamited safe in Montana. The law was closing in, however. Of the gang members who stayed behind, all but one died a violent death. For Butch Cassidy and the Sundance Kid, the future lay in South America.

Gringos

In 1901, a trio headed for Argentina: Butch Cassidy, the Sundance Kid, and Etta Place—a strikingly beautiful woman whom Sundance apparently met in Fanny Porter's Sporting House. (Butch later called her "a fine housekeeper, but a whore at heart.") There they settled with their ill-gotten wealth to a quiet life of ranching, traveling occasionally to Buenos Aires, where they stayed in the finest hotels and dressed in formal clothes, befitting their new role as bourgeois American settlers. But even in South America, Pinkerton detectives managed to pick up their trail and, sensing this, the three decided to try their skills in virgin territory. They robbed three banks in Argentina and a train in Bolivia before Etta Place came down with acute appendicitis. A hurried trip took the trio back to the States, but in Denver, where the operation was performed, the Sundance Kid got in trouble for getting drunk and shooting up his hotel room. Rather than face the law, he fled to New York, where he and Cassidy again boarded a steamer bound for Argentina. Etta remained behind.

The two outlaws now worked part-time at a Peruvian gold mine, using the work as a cover for their periodic forays into banks, trains, and stores in search of money. For many years it was believed that Butch Cassidy and the Sundance Kid died in a blaze of gunfire at a remote village on the Bolivian-Argentine border in 1909. Today, however, it appears that Cassidy escaped (and perhaps the Kid as well), using his reported death as a convenient opportunity to change his ways. According to Larry Pointer's *In Search of Butch Cassidy,* Cassidy later fought with Pancho Villa in the Mexican Revolution, met Wyatt Earp in Alaska, and settled down to running a Spokane machine shop, living under the name of William T. Phillips until his death from cancer in 1937. Several Wyoming residents, old friends of the famous outlaw, met him in Lander and Riverton on several occasions before his death. Cassidy reportedly spent considerable time in a fruitless effort to recover buried loot that he had stashed near Mary's Lake in the Wind River Mountains. Today, the Butch and Sundance legends keep growing. Stop by the towns of Rock Springs, Lander, Laramie, Worland, Dubois, or Kaycee and you'll be regaled with more tales of their exploits.

The Wild Bunch: Harry Longabaugh (Sundance Kid), Bill Carver, Ben Kilpatrick, Harvey Logan (Kid Curry), and George Parker (Butch Cassidy).

ranch. (To keep their ladies in the proper spirit, the Frewens set up relay stations to bring hothouse flowers from Denver on galloping horses.) The Frewens' Powder River Cattle Company, Ltd., attracted investments from the British royal family and various lords before reality struck. The cattle did not do as well as expected, competition from surrounding ranchers and rustlers cut into profits, and the disastrous winter of 1886-87 forced the company to the brink of bankruptcy. The Frewens and many other "cattle barons" never really recovered. Today almost nothing remains of Frewen Castle.

Sights

Hoofprints of the Past Museum in Kaycee is open daily May 15-Nov. 15 and contains items from early settlers, outlaws, and the cattle wars. Look for the wooden potato planter inside. Just south of Kaycee, a marker describes the killing of rustlers Nate Champion and Nick Ray in the Johnson County War of 1892 (see p. 443). The old **KC Ranch house,** where the two were killed by the Invaders, stood here. The **TA Ranch,** where the Invaders holed up after raiding the KC Ranch, is approximately 30 miles north of here along State 87. Bullet holes are still visible in many of the ranch buildings. It is now run as a guest ranch (tel. 684-5833).

Ten miles east of Kaycee on State 192 is a marker noting the first buildings in northern Wyoming, constructed in 1834 by Portuguese trapper Antonio Montero. The log stockade and trading post (known as the **Portuguese Houses**) were abandoned around 1839, and nothing remains on the site. The site of old **Fort Reno** (1865-68) is in the same general vicinity; ask in Kaycee for directions. A monument marks the place, and various remains are still present from this little-known fort.

Practicalities

There are two friendly motels where you can stay in Kaycee: **Siesta Motel,** tel. 738-2291, for $20 s or $24 d, and **Cassidy Inn Motel,** tel. 738-2250, for $23 s or $28 d. Free **camping** in the town park. Both the **Feed Rack Restaurant** and **Country Inn** offer good all-American food. Events in Kaycee include the **Sheepherders Rodeo and Dog Trials** in mid-July

and the **Deke Latham Memorial PRCA Rodeo** in early September. If you're around in mid-June, ask about the annual wagon-train trip through Hole-in-the-Wall country.

HOLE-IN-THE-WALL COUNTRY

Outlaw Country

The remote country used by the Wild Bunch and other outlaws lies some 30 miles west of Kaycee. Get here by following State 190 for 20 miles to where the pavement ends. At the road junction—maps call this Barnum, but there is no town here—is a side road leading to Blue Creek Ranch (private), land once homesteaded by Butch Cassidy and the Sundance Kid. Surrounding you are gorgeous red-walled canyons rising above the Middle Fork of the Powder River. Its waters provide a fine place to fish for rainbow, brook, and brown trout.

Turning right (north) leads you to the Kenny Graves ranch, tel. 738-2319, where **bed and breakfast** accommodations are available. The Graves family offers tours of **Dull Knife Battlefield** and other Hole-in-the-Wall area sights for a fee. The battlefield is named for an incident that took place in 1876 when Gen. Crook's soldiers surprised Dull Knife's band of Northern Cheyenne in this remote valley. The attack killed at least 40 Cheyenne and ended what was viewed by whites as a campaign of terror on settlers. (Indians viewed their raids as retaliation for invading their last stronghold.)

To reach other area sites, turn left (south) on the graded gravel road that parallels the river. Follow the road five miles (past the Bar C Ranch) and bear right at the signed 4WD side road to Outlaw Caves. Beyond the intersection, the road is really only passable in high-clearance vehicles, not 4WD Subarus. You may be better walking in or riding a mountain bike. The road crosses a 3/4-mile long stretch of prehistoric **rock cairns** and then tops a knoll. Stop here for impressive views of Hole-in-the-Wall and the country behind it. **Outlaw Cave Campground** (free but no water) is two miles beyond this.

From the campground a quarter-mile path drops 660 feet down to two caves used by the

Wild Bunch and other outlaws. One of the caves is little more than a depression in the rocks, while the other is room-sized. A corral reputedly used by rustlers is still here. Take your fishing pole down to try for trout. On the other side of the road and up another third of a mile is **Rock Art Cave.** The cave (actually just overhanging rock) contains some of the most unusual Indian rock art in Wyoming, including a large warrior figure, bear claws, and shield designs. A major buffalo jump site (where Indians hunted buffalo by driving them over a cliff) is nearby, along with many tipi rings. The BLM office in Buffalo (tel. 684-5586) can provide a useful map and road log of the Outlaw Caves/Hole-in-the-Wall country.

Hole-in-the-Wall

The wealthy Frewen brothers who ranched here in the 19th century named this country after London's Hole-in-the-Wall Tavern. The "Hole" lies at the end of a steep "V" in the red cliffs bordering Buffalo Creek. It was accessed via a narrow trail that cut up the talus slope and into a funnel-shaped opening that could be blocked with a triangular boulder. The setting was perfect for rustling and as a hideout from the law, especially for such gangs as the Wild Bunch. The cliff was easy to defend and offered a vantage point where sentries could warn of approaching lawmen. Hole-in-the-Wall itself is on public land (BLM), but much of the surrounding land belongs to ranchers who guard their privacy closely and do not allow access. There are ongoing efforts to gain easements to this famous but almost-unseen place.

Bear Track Outfitters in Buffalo, tel. 684-2528, and **Kenny Graves,** tel. 738-2319, both offer tours of Hole-in-the-Wall country. **Historic Trail Expeditions,** tel. 266-4868, also leads a week-long cattle drive into this country. A unique way to discover the old west is the **Outlaw Trail Ride** in mid-August. This week-long trip takes horse riders from the Hole-in-the-Wall country to Thermopolis. You'll need to bring your own horse, bedroll, and gear, but meals are provided for a fee. There is a limit of 100 riders. Call (800) 443-6235 for information on this fascinating not-for-profit adventure.

GILLETTE

Campbell County proclaims itself "Energy Capital of the United States," a title gained by producing more coal and oil than any other county in Wyoming. There are more than 188 oil fields, yielding over 25 million barrels per year, while 16 giant strip mines shovel up an eighth of the total U.S. production of coal. At the center of all this is Gillette (pop. 18,000), Wyoming's fourth-largest city. Gillette isn't known as a tourist destination, and its neighborhoods and shopping malls are indistinguishable from those of a thousand other homogenized American cities. Gillette is a young town; the median age in 1980 was less than 27 years. Interpret this your own way: Gillette actually has an E-Z Street! (By the way, despite the lack of any connection to the shaving company, Gillette is jokingly called "Razor City.")

The Past

When you drive into Gillette, the sense of history that permeates much of Wyoming quickly gives way to the raucous present. History is decidedly not Gillette's strong suit, even though the town is nearly a century old. When the Burlington and Missouri route to Sheridan was being planned, it was originally set to go south of the present location, but an astute surveyor, Edward Gillette, discovered a route farther north that saved construction of 30 bridges. Initially, the new company-platted town was to be called "Donkey Town" for its proximity to Donkey Creek, but instead it was named for Gillette. (Edward Gillette later served a term in Washington as a congressman from Wyoming, but preferred to live in the more scenic town of Sheridan than in his namesake.) The railroad reached Gillette in 1891, and the town was incorporated the following year. It became a shipping point for local ranchers and homesteaders, growing slowly over the decades.

The Present

Since the late 1960s, Gillette has ridden an enormous growth rocket, powered first by oil, then by coal. Gillette's oil boom really began in the fall of 1967, when a drilling company hit an oil gusher that ignited an enormous fire. Fire-fighter Red Adair was called in to extinguish the flames, attracting worldwide attention. Not surprisingly, Hollywood soon followed—John Wayne's *Hell Fighters* was based on the events. Other oil companies flooded the area with exploratory rigs, and almost overnight, Gillette grew from a sleepy cow town to a major energy center. A frantic scramble for the almighty dollar ensued, with real-estate values quadrupling between 1966 and 1970.

Unlike the rest of Wyoming, where the oil boom of the '70s was quickly followed by the bust of the '80s, Gillette caught the coal wave just as the oil tide was heading back out to sea. With enormous reserves of low-sulfur coal throughout the surrounding countryside, Campbell County quickly became a major player on the energy scene. The population nearly tripled in the decade of the '80s. Today, Gillette is the modern version of middle America—shopping malls, spreading suburbia, used-car lots, and fast-food joints. Author Wallace Stegner's description of a California town could fit just as well here: "But mostly it is Main Street, Anywhere, a set used over and over in a hundred B movies, a stroboscopic image pulsing to reassure us by subliminal tricks that though we are nowhere, we are at home."

Sights

The fine **Rockpile Museum,** on US 14-16, tel. 682-5723, is open Tues.-Sun. 10-8, May 15-Oct. 15. The rest of the year the hours are Tues.-Sat. 10-4 and Sun. 12-4. Out front is a minor local landmark that gives the museum its name. This spacious, free museum contains sheep wagons, a horse-drawn hearse (originally from Montana; its first eight customers died from gunshots), and other wagons, along with a blacksmith shop, an impressive arrowhead collection, and dozens of elaborate spurs and old rifles. A big board contains a directory of several hundred brands. Be sure to check out the floating rocks from Lake DeSmet. Out front is a tiny one-room schoolhouse that could have served double duty as a doghouse. The metal building next door has some very strange sandstone rocks.

The new **Campbell County Public Library,** 2101 Four J Rd., tel. 682-3223, is one of the finest in the state. Besides a large collection of books about Wyoming, it houses a remarkable collection of art, including paintings by Hans Kleiber, Gene Kloss, and Conrad Schwiering. Out front are life-sized bronze statues of cowboys and horses. Library hours are Sun. 1-5, Mon.-Thurs. 9-9 and Fri.-Sat. 9-5. Between Sept. and May, it's also open Sun. 1-5. A branch library at 412 S. Gillette Ave. is open Mon.-Fri. 1-5 and Sat. 9-noon. The **planetarium,** 1000 W. Lakeview Rd., has free programs on Mon. nights; call 687-7616 for details.

Camplex, a large and modern multi-events center east of town on Garner Lake Rd., contains an art gallery with changing exhibits, plus a beautiful 960-seat theater for concerts. Out front of Camplex is an odd collection of items from the past and present. You'll discover turn-of-the-century log cabins and an old locomotive just a few feet away from a drilling rig and an enormous coal-hauling truck. Kids are guaranteed to have fun in the gargantuan tires.

GILLETTE ACCOMMODATIONS

MOTEL	ADDRESS	TELEPHONE	RATES	FEATURES
Motel 6	2105 Rodgers Dr.	686-8600	$22 s, $26 d	whirlpool, sauna
Arrowhead Motel	202 Emerson Ave.	686-0909 (800) 227-8483	$26+ s, $29+ d	kitchenettes $40+
Thrifty Inn	1002 E. Second St.	682-2616	$27+ s, $29+ d	
Mustang Motel	922 E. Third	682-4784	$28 s, $32 d	kitchen available
High Plains Lodge	109 N. US 14-16	686-1989	$29 s or d	
Rolling Hills Motel	409 Butler Spaeth Rd.	682-4757	$33 s, $38 d	
Super 8 Motel	208 S. Decker Ct.	682-8078 (800) 800-8000	$38 s, $41 d	AAA-approved
Days Inn	910 E. Boxelder Rd.	682-3999 (800) 325-2525	$38 s, $42 d	AAA-approved
Rodeway Inn	1020 E. US 14-16	682-5111 (800) 221-2222	$44+ s, $50+ d	AAA-approved, pool, sauna
Sands Motor Lodge (Best Western)	608 E. Second St.	682-9341 (800) 528-1234	$45+ s, $49+ d	AAA-approved, pool
Holiday Inn	2009 S. Douglas Hwy.	686-3000 (800) 465-4329	$48 s, $56 d	AAA-approved, pool, sauna, exercise room
Tower West Lodge (Best Western)	109 N. US 14-16	686-2210 (800) 528-1234	$52 s, $58 d	AAA-approved, pool, whirlpool, sauna, hot tub, weight room

STRIP MINING

Coal mining has been an important part of the Campbell County economy for many years. The first mines were underground, but once the technology developed to remove the overlying soil, strip mining became feasible. Today, 16 Campbell County strip mines are scattered along an enormous coal seam that is five miles wide, over 50 miles long, and up to 100 feet thick, enough to last hundreds of years. If Campbell County were a nation, it would rank fourth in the world in coal reserves, behind the U.S., Russia, and China! Most of the mines are owned by giant multinational energy companies such as Exxon (Caballo and Rawhide), Amax (Belle Ayr), Kerr-McGee (Jacobs Ranch), and ARCO (Black Thunder and Coal Creek). All of these mines are quite new, the oldest (Belle Ayr) opened in 1973. Cranking out over 30 million tons per year, the Black Thunder Mine just east of Wright is the largest coal mine in America.

Digging The Coal

Powder River Basin mines are heavily mechanized operations with relatively few employees; despite massive increases in production, the number of employees continues to drop. Mining coal here is a relatively simple process, made easier by the use of machinery and blasting equipment that are some-

thing beyond gargantuan; all the vehicles seem to be on steroids. Imagine a truck that carries 240 tons of coal (that's 2½ railroad coal cars worth) and is powered by a 2,200-horsepower engine. Then try changing a flat when the tire stands 11 feet tall and weighs four tons! Even this behemoth is dwarfed by the dragline used at the Black Thunder Coal Mine. Its 300-foot boom pulls in a 90-cubic-yard bucket (a typical dump truck holds 12 cubic yards). Powered by electricity, the 3,600-ton machine waddles along like a duck, dragging its power line behind. After blasting loosens the overburden, it is stripped away and dumped into waiting trucks. (Topsoil is stored for use in later reclamation.) Below this overburden lies the deep black coal seam that must be drilled and blasted. Electric shovels scoop up the loosened coal and dump it into the trucks for delivery to crushing and storage facilities. The entire scale of the operation comes into focus by watching as mile-long, 100-car trains move constantly through the loading facility. Up to 12 trains can be loaded in a day—over 130,000 tons.

Environmental Impacts

The strip mining of coal has always been a controversial subject, with environmentalists concerned over the impacts from burning coal in an era of acid

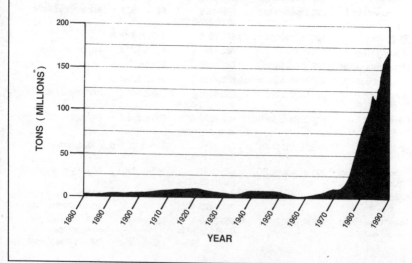

rain, global warming, and escalating atmospheric carbon dioxide. They also question whether reclamation will really work on Wyoming's arid lands. The other impacts from mining are equally important: access roads divide up antelope and deer habitat, subdivisions for the workers spread out over the countryside, and wells draw down the water table. Mining companies, however, point with pride to herds of antelope grazing near the coal mines and believe that the land can be restored after the coal is gone.

A visit to the coal mines is an eye-opening odyssey into the Super Bowl of strip mining. No matter what you think about strip mining, a tour of the mines is well worth taking, if only to see the enormous equipment and to ponder what burning all this coal will do to the environment. Free summertime tours of several local mines are available. The Gillette Chamber of Commerce has an up-to-date listing, but two-hour weekday tours are generally available at **Amax,** tel. 687-3200, **Black Thunder Mine,** tel. 939-1300, and **Wyodak Mine** (east of Gillette), tel. 686-1248. Wyodak is the oldest mine in

Powder River Basin, and it feeds the world's largest air-cooled power plant (also on the site). A highway overlook of the mine is nearby.

Accommodations
See the chart for lodging at any of a dozen different motels and hotels. Campers and RVers will enjoy **Crazy Woman Campground,** 1001 W. Second St., tel. 682-3665. It's a pleasant place with genuine shade trees, a rarity in Wyoming's private campgrounds. Also here is a spa, a pool, and bike rentals. Rates start at $8 for tents, $14 for RVs. Showers for noncampers cost $4. The rather bleak **High Plains Campground,** tel. 687-7339, is next to Camplex on the east side of town.

Food
Gillette has a number of interesting eateries. The best breakfast can be found at **Flying J Restaurant,** 1810 S. Douglas Hwy., tel. 686-0077. **Bazels Restaurant,** 408 S. Douglas Hwy., tel. 686-5149, has a retro-'50s diner-style decor, good breakfasts, and substantial portions. Also try **Granny's Kitchen,** 413 S. Douglas Hwy., tel. 682-4181, or 1414 W. US 14-16, tel. 687-1200, for breakfast or lunch.

Peking House Restaurant, 2701 S. Douglas Hwy., tel. 682-7868, is one of the finest Chinese restaurants in Wyoming. Come here at lunchtime for buffet specials. Get pizza and pasta at **Ole's Pizza Parlor,** 114 N. US 14-16, tel. 682-8484. **Mona's Cafe,** 403 El Camino Dr., tel. 686-6506, makes great breakfasts and Mexican food, or try **Aunt Chilotta Tacos,** 400 W. Second, tel. 682-0610. The big salad bar/dessert bar at **Golden Corral,** 2700 S. Douglas Hwy., tel. 682-9130, makes for a bargain meal.

Bailey's Bar & Grill, 301 S. Gillette Ave., tel. 686-7667, is a fine place for homemade lunches and dinner specialities such as chicken-fried steak, burgers, or Mexican fare. Great finger food, too. The award-winning **Prime Rib Restaurant,** 1205 S. Douglas Hwy., tel. 682-2944, is another very good place for prime rib, steak, and seafood. Last, but not least, **Boot Hill Nightclub,** 910 N. Gurley Ave., tel. 682-1600, offers unbeatably priced nightly specials, including a $6 top sirloin steak. Get groceries from any of the big chains: Albertson's, Buttery, Decker's, and IGA.

Entertainment
Head to Gillette City Park on Thursday nights in June and July for the **Concerts in the Park** series. Music ranges from bluegrass to classical.

The state's largest dance hall is **Boot Hill Nightclub,** at 910 N. Gurley Ave., tel. 682-1600. It's a popular place to dance the night away to country music seven nights a week. Top-40 and oldies bands play most nights at **Tower West Lodge,** 109 N. US 14-16, tel. 686-2210. **Kicks Lounge** in the Holiday Inn at 2009 S. Douglas Hwy., tel. 686-3000, is the place to go for rock and pop tunes six nights a week. **Prime Rib Restaurant,** 1205 S. Douglas Hwy., tel. 682-2944, also has live entertainment. **Mingles,** 2209 S. Douglas Hwy., tel. 686-1222, has half-a-dozen pool tables, a big-screen TV, and periodic comedy nights.

Events

Gillette's **Fourth of July** celebration is the biggest in northeastern Wyoming. In addition to an impressive fireworks show, you'll discover a pancake breakfast, a parade, mud volleyball, firehose water fights, and even a Ping-Pong drop (a Ping-Pong drop?). **Festival in the Park** brings a full day of musical entertainment at Camplex Park each August. The **Campbell County Fair** each August includes livestock judging, arts-and-crafts exhibits, and all the old favorites. **Camplex,** a large and modern multi-events center east of town on Garner Lake Rd., frequently has concerts, cattle shows, rodeos, conventions, and other events. During the summer there are rodeos almost every weekend, the biggest being the **National Old Timers Rodeo** in late May and the **PRCA Rodeo** in late July and early August. The highlight of the PRCA Rodeo is the camel (!) race. **Pari-mutuel horse racing** takes place in July at Energy Downs, next to Camplex.

Recreation

Gillette has outstanding recreation facilities. **Campbell County Recreation Center,** 1000 S. Douglas Hwy., tel. 682-5470, houses an indoor pool with a diving well, a 383-foot waterslide (summer only), plus weight rooms, racquetball and squash courts, a gym, and a sauna. The cost is just $2 per swim ($1 for kids). No charge for seniors. Free summertime swimming at the pool in **City Park** at Gillette and 10th, tel. 682-1962. There is also a brand new **Aquatic Center** at S. Gillette and 10th, tel. 682-1962, for competitive swimming events. Roller skaters

will enjoy **Razor City Skateland,** 885 Hannum Rd., tel. 682-3529. Golfers head to **Bell Nob Golf Links,** 1316 Overdale Dr., tel. 686-7069, or **Gillette Golf Course,** 1800 Country Club Rd., tel. 686-4744. **Big Horn Mountain Sports** in Powder Basin Mall, tel. 687-1422, has a full range of outdoor gear.

Information And Services

A summer-only **Information Center,** tel. (800) 544-6136, is next to the Flying J Truckstop at Exit 126. It's open daily 9-6 May to mid-October. The **Gillette Chamber of Commerce,** 314 S. Gillette Ave., tel. 682-3673, is open year-round Mon.-Fri. 9-5. Get books at **Daniels Books,** 320 S. Gillette Ave., tel. 682-8266. Gillette has the state's fastest-growing junior college (over 900 students), the **Gillette Campus** of Northern Wyoming Community College. Located at 720 W. Eighth St., tel. 686-0254, the campus offers a range of classes and degree programs, from business to mining.

Transportation

Powder River Transportation, 1700 E. US 14-16, tel. 674-6188 or (800) 442-3682, has daily bus service to most other eastern Wyoming towns, as well as Billings, Montana, and Rapid City, South Dakota. (Look for the big Petrolane propane tank to find this easy-to-miss bus station.) The airport is five miles north of Gillette. Both **United Express,** tel. (800) 631-1500, and **Rocky Mountain Air (Continental),** tel. (800) 525-0280, have daily commuter service to Denver and Sheridan. Rent cars from **AA Car Rental,** tel. 686-8250; **Bill Barth Chrysler,** tel. 687-0499; **U-Save Rental,** tel. 682-5809; **Avis Rent-A-Car,** tel. 682-8588; or **Hertz Rent A Car,** tel. 686-0550. **Yellow Checker Cab,** tel. 686-4090, is the local taxi company.

HEADING SOUTH

Two roads point south from Gillette; State 50 is the more remote and would make a fine bike route. This distinctive red highway was built from scoria. The drive south from Gillette along State 59 takes you into the heart of the mixed-grass prairie, with oil pumpjacks, windmills, enormous bales of hay, and thousands of cattle and sheep. Tumbleweeds are plastered against the barbed-wire fences and abandoned farm equipment rusts on hilltops. Amax's Belle Ayr mine stands on the eastern horizon a dozen miles south of town, with flat-topped mesas and nipple-shaped buttes adding a little spice to the scenery. Far to the west, the Big Horn Mountains rise from the plains. Be sure to pause for a look at the grasses—blue grama is especially pretty when seen up close.

Durham Buffalo Ranch

Approximately 30 miles south of Gillette is Durham Buffalo Ranch, the largest private buffalo herd in existence. The Flocchini family owns a 55,000-acre spread here and is dedicated to returning the land to its original state when bison and other native animals dominated the prairie landscape. Watch for some of the 3,500 head of buffalo along the highway. Herds more than 1,000 times this size once roamed across this land; this is a rare opportunity to see bison today in a relatively natural setting. Call 939-1271 for tour information (groups only).

Wright

Wyoming's newest town is Wright, right in the center of America's largest low-sulfur coal deposit. Established in 1976, Wright quickly grew to some 1,600 residents. Modern schools, a small shopping mall, and five churches popped up, along with trailer courts and suburban split-level homes on curving streets. Funded partly by Atlantic Richfield Company (ARCO), Wright was built to house workers for nearby coal mines. Pretty weird place. Imagine an enclave of middle-class America plunked down in a setting straight out of *High Plains Drifter*. A small **museum,** tel. 464-1222, houses local items. The library is inside the mall. Wright also has a fine recreation center (tel. 464-0198) with an indoor heated pool and gym. Get buffalo burgers at **Reno Junction Cafe,** tel. 939-1298.

The annual event here is **Wright Days,** held each Aug. with the standard games, parades, and the obligatory rodeo. Gigantic coal strip mines surround Wright; all of them use Paul Bunyan-scale equipment and skeleton crews of employees. Much of this is public land belonging to Thunder Basin National Grassland, meaning enormous revenues for the federal government, along with severance taxes for the state of Wyoming. The coal trains seem to never end. Stop on the railroad overpass near the dot of a settlement called Bill and you'll see a hundred cars of coal pass every couple of minutes, with empty trains waiting on the sidings. Most of this coal is on its way to electric-generating plants in Texas and the Midwest.

THE BLACK HILLS

Northeast Wyoming feels quite unlike any other part of the state. South Dakota's Black Hills roll across an arbitrary state line into Wyoming, while the Belle Fourche River (pronounced bell-FOORSH; the name is from the French for "Beautiful Fork," of the Missouri River) drifts through these hills, heading northeast and then cutting a sudden right angle to the southeast and across the state line. Cattle graze in rich pastures along the river. Nearby, one of the most stunning of all sights—Devils Tower—seems almost alive in its abrupt rise from the surrounding land. South of the Black Hills in Weston County, the country quickly opens into the mixed-grass prairie of the plains. This out-of-the-way part of Wyoming is truly a special place. It's no wonder that the Sioux considered the Black Hills home for the Great Spirit.

Only 13,000 people live in Crook and Weston counties, scattered on rural ranches or in the small settlements of Sundance and Hulett in the midst of Wyoming's Black Hills, plus Newcastle, Moorcroft, and Upton along the southern edge. Cattle grazing, bentonite mining, oil wells, and logging provide the jobs.

The Land

The Black Hills stretch in a long ellipse, 125 miles north to south and 65 miles across, rising 3,000 to 4,000 feet above the surrounding plains. South Dakota's Harney Peak, at 7,242 feet, is the tallest mountain in the Black Hills; in fact, it's the tallest peak between the South Dakota/Wyoming line and the Atlantic Ocean. The most famous attraction in this part of Wyoming is Devils Tower, but the Black Hills north of Sundance are captivating, especially in the spring and fall. Most visitors who come to northeast Wyoming do so as part of a trip that includes Yellowstone and various South Dakota sights, including Mt. Rushmore and Deadwood.

From a distance, the dark green carpet of ponderosa pine darkens the hills; hence the Sioux name Paha Sapa, meaning "Hills that are Black." The Black Hills are a blend of open meadows, rocky hills crowded with forests of pine and aspen, and valleys lined with bur oak. This is one of the few places you're likely to see native oak trees in Wyoming.

White-tailed deer are abundant throughout the Black Hills, while herds of elk are found southeast of Sundance. Merriam's turkeys are another common sight all through this country. Introduced from New Mexico in 1948, they are now the most widespread game-bird species in northeast Wyoming.

NEWCASTLE

Newcastle (pop. 3,000) sits at the junction of several major roads, acting as a gateway to the Black Hills. Like much of northeast Wyoming, the town's economy is a mixture of energy, ranching, and logging. Every half-hour, day and night, traffic backs up on the railroad tracks across Main St., waiting as a hundred soot-black coal cars rumble past, bound for mid-western power plants. A Newcastle refinery produces jet fuel for South Dakota's giant Ellsworth Air Force Base, and a natural-gas processing plant sits 25 miles south of town in the midst of the Finn-Shurley fields. Large ranches encompass the town, dotted with oil pumpjacks, windmills, and Herefords. Piles of fresh-cut ponderosa pine surround Newcastle's big sawmill.

THE BLACK HILLS

© MOON PUBLICATIONS, INC.

HISTORY

The first white settlement of the Newcastle area came in 1875, when Professor Walter P. Jenney and Lt. Col. R.I. Dodge led 432 soldiers and an army of mining engineers, scientists, and map-makers to a base camp along Beaver Creek. They built the Jenny Stockade, which became a stage station and distribution point along the Cheyenne-Deadwood Trail. Many of the west's most famous characters stopped by en route to Deadwood, including Wild Bill Hickok, Calamity Jane, and Wyatt Earp.

Tubb Town

In 1888, the Chicago, Burlington, and Quincy Railroad announced plans to construct tracks across northeast Wyoming and into Montana. Speculators established Tubb Town, a ram-shackle collection of saloons and hotels along the proposed railroad route. (All visitors were required to pay a toll upon entrance: "set 'em up for the bunch.") The party didn't last long; when the Burlington Railroad decided instead to build a town at present-day Newcastle, Tubb Town faded into history. At Whoopup Canyon (so named because the spring floods came "a-whoopin' through"), a railroad worker attempted to pry the cap off a 25-pound can of black powder. After struggling without success, he decided to try a more forceful approach—using a pickax to punch a hole in the lid. His coworkers found little left to bury.

The Cambria Mines

Coal was discovered in Cambria Canyon in the 1880s, and the coal-mining town of Cambria popped up almost overnight. It became a model community, with a water system, modern homes, three churches, electric lights, and some of the safest underground mines in the nation. Alcohol was banned, along with bawdy entertainment. At its peak more than 1,500 people lived in Cambria, but when the coal ran out in 1928, the mines were forced to close.

The discovery of coal at Cambria led the Burlington Railroad to establish a townsite as near the mouth of Cambria Canyon as possible, with a spur to the four mines. It was called Newcastle, after the English coal port of Newcastle-upon-Tyne. At first, the wide-open frontier town of Newcastle contrasted sharply with quiet, sedate Cambria. When the new mayor, Frank Mondell (who had established the Cambria mines), decided to get rid of 20 of Newcastle's undesirables, a local hotel owner—fearing that he would lose most of his business—shot the mayor. Mondell (who later served for 26 years as Wyoming's lone congressional representative) carried the bullet in his spine the rest of his life.

After the Cambria mines closed, the town of Newcastle faded, but with the discovery of huge oil deposits nearby in the 1950s, it again boomed. By the mid-'50s more than 25,000 people crowded the surrounding countryside. A bust soon followed, only to be repeated by a similar cycle in the 1970s. Now Newcastle perks along on an economy of equal parts oil, coal, logging, and ranching. Folks from Nebraska or Kansas would feel right at home among the quiet streets, staid older homes, pickup trucks, and freight trains.

SIGHTS

Anna Miller Museum

The Newcastle museum at Delaware St. and US 16, tel. 746-4188, is open Mon.-Fri. 9-5. It's housed in the old National Guard Cavalry Barn, a stone structure built in the 1930s by the WPA. Inside is the typical collection of local paraphernalia: items from the Cambria mines, a horse-drawn hearse, a noose (not, however, the one that vigilantes used to hang murderer Diamond Slim Clifton from the Newcastle railroad trestle), a model of the giant KB&C ranch, and even a six-legged lamb and a two-headed Hereford calf as a sideshow. Be sure to try a couple of cranks on the old carnival noisemaker. (Trivial tip: Anna Miller, for whom the museum was named, was a local school superintendent whose husband, Sheriff Billy Miller, was the last white man to die in a battle with the Indians. He was killed in 1903.)

Outside the museum is a furnished one-room schoolhouse built in 1890, along with the **Stockade cabin** (built in 1875), the oldest building in the Black Hills. Ask at the museum for directions to the Cheyenne-Deadwood Trail

The coal-mining town of Cambria was considered a model community in its time.

ANNA MILLER MUSEUM

NEWCASTLE

TO CAMBRIA INN,
LEAD, & DEADWOOD

BURLINGTON NORTHERN RAILROAD

OLD U.S. 85

LIBRARY
POST OFFICE

HORTON
HOUSE
B & B

PINES MOTEL

16

SUPREME
MOTEL

CORRAL REST
CAMPGROUND

CARTER AVE.

SUNDOWNER
INN MOTEL

WAKEFIELD

SENECA AVE.

WENTWORTH ST.

MORGAN'S
MOTEL

S. SPOKANE AVE.

85

TO UPTON &
MOORCROFT

5th AVE.

4th AVE.

FOREST HILL WAY

3rd AVE.

2nd AVE.

ROADSIDE
MOTEL

WEST MAIN ST.

S. SUMMIT AVE.

S. SONORA AVE.

DELAWARE

MUSEUM

FOUNTAIN INN/
RV PARK

BLM OFFICE

REFINERY

HILL ST.

CHAMBER OF
COMMERCE

16

16

FOREST SERVICE OFFICE
STARDUST MOTEL

TO
ACCIDENTIAL OIL AND
MT. RUSHMORE

STAMPEDE AVE.

WESTON COUNTY
FAIRGROUNDS

FAYE AVE.

HILLTOP
MOTEL

SAGE MOTEL

S. SUMMIT AVE.

SAWMILL

TO LUSK

SCALE NOT AVAILABLE

MOON

© MOON PUBLICATIONS, INC.

ruts and an Indian petroglyph site in Whoopup Canyon.

Accidental Oil Company

Certainly the most amusing sight around Newcastle is the kitschy Accidental Oil Company. In 1966 (around the time Jed Clampett of television's "Beverly Hillbillies" was "shootin' at some food, and up from the ground came a bubbling crude—oil that is, black gold, Texas tea . . ."), Newcastle rancher Al Smith decided to dig a hole to see how far down it was to oil. Using a pick and shovel, and later dynamite, he reached oil at 21 feet. The "world's only hand-dug oil well" is now a small run-down tourist trap along US 16, four miles east of Newcastle. Outside are steam-powered oil rigs and antique pumps. An old oil-storage tank encloses a gift shop, and you can walk down to view the oil-bearing rock under black light. Pure Americana. Accidental Oil, tel. 746-2042, is open daily 9-6 in summer, or Mon.-Sat. 9-6 the rest of the year; entrance costs $3 for adults or $2 for kids.

PRACTICALITIES

Accommodations

There are nearly a dozen different places to stay in Newcastle (see chart), but of particular note is the historic and antique-filled **Flying V Cambria Inn.** You can pitch a tent for free anywhere on nearby public lands within both Thunder Basin National Grassland (see p. 174-176) and Black Hills National Forest (see p. 468). The closest public campground ($7) is across the South Dakota border at **Jewel Cave National Monument,** 25 miles east of Newcastle. Back in Newcastle, **Corral Rest RV Camp,** 2206 W. Main, tel. 746-2007, has tent sites for $8 and RV sites for $11; open mid-April to mid-November. Showers for noncampers cost $2. **Crystal Park Campground,** 3 Seminoe Ave., tel. 746-4426, is open year-round, with tent sites for $9 and RV sites for $13. Showers for noncampers are $2. Neither of these places is particularly appealing. **Fountain Inn,** 3 Seminoe

NEWCASTLE ACCOMMODATIONS

MOTEL	ADDRESS	TELEPHONE	RATES	FEATURES
Stardust Motel	833 S. Summit	746-4719	$18 s, $24 d	see rooms first
Supreme Motel	2503 W. Main	746-2734	$24 s or d	
Hilltop Motel	1121 S. Summit	746-4494	$25 s, $28 d	kitchenettes $45
Pines Motel	248 E. Wentworth	746-4334	$25 s, $28 d	kitchenettes $45, quiet location
Roadside Motel	1605 W. Main St.	746-9640	$26 s, $30 d	
Sage Motel	1227 S. Summit	746-2724	$29 s or d	AAA-approved
Horton House B&B	17 S. Summit	746-4366	$45+ s or d	historic home, full breakfast
Morgan's Motel	205 S. Spokane	746-2715	$30 s or d	open April-Oct., quiet location
Flying V Cambria Inn	eight miles north	746-2096	$39 s, $53 d	B&B, historic place, open May-Sept.
Sundowner Inn Motel	451 W. Main	746-2796	$46 s or d	pool, jaccuzzi
Fountain Inn	3 Seminoe Ave.	746-4426 (800) 882-8858	$52+ s, $58+ d	AAA-approved, pool

Ave., tel. (800) 882-8858, has an elaborate amusement park with a water slide, a pond for swimming and paddle boats, a roller-skating rink, a merry-go-round, and a video arcade.

Food

For excellent breakfasts, head to **Old Mill Inn,** 500 W. Main, tel. 746-4608, housed in the old Toomey's Flour Mill. They also have a salad bar and all-American dinners. The **Slatewood Inn,** 66 Old US 85, tel. 746-4686, is one of the best steak-and-prime-rib establishments in this part of Wyoming. On Wed. nights, they offer a reasonable BBQ-rib all-you-can-eat special. For fast food and sit-down meals in a friendly diner setting, head to **Hi-16 Drive In,** 2951 W. Main, tel. 746-4055. **Howdy Drive In,** 834 S. Summit, tel. 746-2176, is one fast-food place that actually delivers to your doorstep. Historic **Flying V Cambria Inn,** eight miles north of town on US 85, tel. 746-2096, offers a special Italian night on Thurs.; huge two-pound steaks and fresh fish at other times. Big portions and great food in a nostalgic setting. Get groceries at

Decker's Food Center, 709 W. Main, tel. 746-2779, or **Safeway,** 622 W. Main, tel. 746-3511. Decker's has a good bakery.

The best meal deals (and entertainment) in the area are across the South Dakota line. Deadwood's newly legal gambling casinos have all sorts of discount come-ons, including $6 steak dinners. This is where Newcastle folks go for an evening out.

Entertainment And Events

Head to the **Gay Nineties Lamplighter** for C&W or rock tunes. The **Buckhorn Bar and Grill,** tel. 746-3675, 25 miles north of Newcastle on US 85, is a favorite spot for both travelers and locals. Good food and live C&W music. The big local event is the **Weston County Fair,** held in early August each year. You're likely to find a **rodeo** going on at the fairgrounds most summer weekends.

Information And Services

The **Newcastle Chamber of Commerce** at the intersection of US 16 and 85, tel. 746-2739, is open Mon.-Sat. 9-5. **Weston County Library,** 23 W. Main, tel. 746-2206, is open Mon.-Wed. and Fri. noon-5, Thurs. noon-8, and Sat. 9-1. Swim at the high school **pool,** 15 Stampede, tel. 746-2713. Try your fishing skills at **LAK Lake** east of town (named for the Lake, Allenton, and King ranch here), or play a few rounds of

golf at **Newcastle Country Club,** 2302 W. Main, tel. 746-2639. The **Bureau of Land Management** office is at 1101 Washington, tel. 746-4453, and the **Forest Service Office** is at 640 S. Summit Ave., tel. 746-2783. There is no bus or plane service into Newcastle.

NEWCASTLE VICINITY

Heading North

North of Newcastle, US 85 climbs quickly into the pine-covered Black Hills, providing wide vistas over the town and across the open plains to the south. Eight miles north of Newcastle is **Flying V Cambria Inn,** constructed in 1928 as a memorial to the Cambria miners and completed just months before the mines closed down for good. It is listed on the National Register of Historic Places. The ghost town of Cambria is on private land nearby.

Another nine miles north is **Red Butte,** a steep-sided sandstone peak rising right along the road like a miniature Devils Tower. A local landmark, it was used by both Indians and early whites as a lookout. Beyond this, the land begins to open up into an undulating grassy terrain with rich red-black soil. Just a couple more miles up the road is a combination store, cafe (try the chili), and post office at **Four Corners.** The "world's most desolate pay phone" stands alone in front of the store. The graveled Mallo Rd. heads east from Four Corners, offering a colorful fall drive as the aspens turn a brilliant yellow.

Not far away is the site of the 1878 Canyon Springs robbery on the old Cheyenne-Deadwood Stage Route. A passenger and an outlaw died in the shootout, and at least $20,000 (some accounts claim up to $140,000) in gold was taken and buried nearby. Many years later, a local farmer digging potatoes near Red Butte apparently found some of the loot. Packing up his family, he split town without a word.

Heading South

South of Newcastle, US 85 is an arrow aimed at the horizon, pointing across the almost-flat landscape of grass, wind, and antelope. A few bottomland trees line the creeks, and the Cheyenne River etches a narrow line through the land,

nearly dry in the late-summer heat. This is the heart of the great mixed-grass prairie that borders eastern Wyoming, reaching into adjacent Nebraska and south into Colorado.

UPTON

On the edge of Upton (pop. 980), a sign makes no bones about where you are: the "Best Town on Earth!" Who am I to argue? Like its neighbors—Osage and Newcastle—Upton lies right along the edge of the Black Hills, with ponderosa pines topping the ridge to the north (appropriately named Pine Ridge), and open-range country spreading to the south. The Chicago, Burlington, and Quincy Railroad established a depot here in 1892, and railroad tracks now form Upton's southern border. Beyond this, State 116 climbs over gentle grassy hills through the heart of Thunder Basin National Grassland. It's a high-plains landscape filled with windmills and scattered ranches and grazed by sheep, cattle, antelope, and mule deer. The sky completely dominates the landscape, sending giant white thunderheads over the plains. Upton's limited economy is dependent upon American Colloid's bentonite mine, local ranchers, oil pumping, and coal mining in nearby Campbell County.

Practicalities

If you don't mind in-town, no-shade camping, pitch a tent next to the **Country Market Conoco,** tel. 468-2551, for $4 a night, $10 for RVs. Stay at **Upton Motel,** tel. 468-9282, for $20 s or $25 d (with kitchenettes), or the somewhat nicer **Weston Inn Motel,** tel. 468-2401, for $29 s or $31 d.

Doug's Place and **Western Bar & Cafe** are both popular eating spots, and **Upton Drug,**

tel. 468-2770, has an old-fashioned soda fountain. Get groceries at **Joe's Super Valu.** The **library,** tel. 468-2324, Pine and Fourth streets, is open Mon.-Fri. 1-5 and Wed. 6-9.

OSAGE

Located halfway between Newcastle and Upton, tiny Osage (pop. 300) has a bar, a gas station, and a general store, but not much else to show for having once been the center of the oil industry in northeast Wyoming. In 1920, a huge oil gusher turned the surrounding country into a madhouse of oil prospectors and turned Osage into a tent city of 1,500 people. When the boom inevitably turned to bust, only a core of folks remained in what is now a railroad way station.

MOORCROFT

Moorcroft (pop. 770) is a nondescript ranching and oil-field town perched within a few miles of popular Keyhole Reservoir. It isn't particularly attractive, but it will do as a stop on the way to somewhere else. Because the famed Texas Trail passed through Moorcroft, it became an important cattle town. Up until the end of WW II, it served as the largest cattle shipping point along the entire Chicago, Burlington, and Quincy Railroad. The local historical stopping place is **Helen Robinson Zimmerschied Western-Texas Trail Museum,** at 200 S. Bighorn, tel. 756-9300. The name is almost bigger than the museum's collection of local items! Inside you can watch local artisans at the pedal loom and spinning wheel. Outside are a tipi and a sheep wagon. The main summertime event is **Moorcroft Jubilee Days** in early July.

Practicalities

Lodging is available at **Wyoming Motel,** 111 W. Converse, tel. 756-3452, for $26 s or $30 d,

and **Moorcroft Motel,** 214 Yellowstone Ave., tel. 756-3411, where rooms with kitchenettes go for $28 s or $38 d. The nicest place in town is **Cozy Motel,** 219 W. Converse, tel. 756-3486, where rooms are $39 s or $49 d. The **Yellow Rose,** 116 S. Bighorn, tel. 756-3727, is a very good place for breakfasts and may be serving other meals as well. Families like **Donna's Diner,** 203 W. Converse, tel. 756-3422. Moorcroft's **library,** 105 E. Converse, tel. 756-3232, is open Mon. noon-7 and Tues.-Fri. 10-5. **Lee's Books & Videos,** 108 N. Big Horn, tel. 756-3520, sells books on Wyoming. Check at the **Town Hall,** 104 N. Big Horn, tel. 756-3526, for more about the moors and mores of Moorcroft.

KEYHOLE STATE PARK

Keyhole State Park, tel. 756-3596, surrounds Keyhole Reservoir, a 14,720-acre warm-water lake that backs up water from the Belle Fourche River. (The name comes from the keyhole brand, used by a local ranch.) The dam was built in 1952 by the Bureau of Reclamation and supplies irrigation water for South Dakota farmers. Recent drought years have left a bathtubring effect, particularly in late fall. Most of the visitors are locals, but it's an okay place to camp. Pine trees crowd hills to the east, while grass and sage grow around the reservoir's western shore. Anglers angle for the biggest walleye and northern pike in the state; birdwatchers watch for Merriam's turkeys and white pelicans; and snowmobilers 'bile around in winter. **Camping** costs $4 at seven different state campgrounds along the lake's east and south shores. Nicest are Pats Point and Pronghorn campgrounds. Get to Keyhole State Park from I-90 by taking the Pine Ridge exit and continuing eight miles north. A swimming beach is here, plus a motel, a cafe, and a marina (tel. 756-9529) with supplies and boat rentals.

SUNDANCE

The quiet country town of Sundance (pop. 1,100) nestles at the foot of Sundance Mountain. The mountain—"Temple of the Sioux"—rises a thousand feet above the town and was an important sacred spot to the various tribes who claimed this land. Sun dances were performed at its base each year. Sundance got its start in 1879, when rancher Albert Hoge set up a trading post. The town grew slowly until the 1950s, when Sundance Air Base arrived. Since its closing, the town of Sundance has settled into middle age, with the old standbys of ranching and logging as economic mainstays, though tourism is increasingly important.

SIGHTS

Crook County Museum

The local museum, tel. 283-3666, is located in the basement of the Crook County Courthouse on Cleveland Street. Hours are Mon.-Fri. 9-8 and Sat. 9-4:30 in the summer, and Mon.-Fri. 9-12 and 1-5 the rest of the year. Inside are the usual collection of local paraphernalia, such as arrowheads, "period" rooms, wooden wheelchairs, bison skulls, and cowboy gear. There is also a model of Devils Tower. More interesting are the momentos from Harry Longabough's visit to the town. Better known as the **"Sundance Kid,"** (see "The Wild Bunch," p. 448), Longabough spent 18 months in Sundance's Crook County Jail for horse stealing before being pardoned by the governor in 1889. The museum has the criminal bar docket signed by Longabough during his trial and furnishings from the original courthouse. A replica (built in 1983) of the jail that once housed the Sundance Kid stands beside the old stone high school.

Around Sundance

Access to 5,829-foot **Sundance Mountain** is via a dirt road that heads east from State 116, about a half mile south of town. An enjoyable trail leads to the top, gaining 800 feet in elevation along the way. From the top, you're treated with views of the nearby Black Hills and, on clear days, even the Big Horn Mountains, 180 miles west. Ask at the visitor center for access information.

Three miles west of the small settlement of **Beulah** (on the South Dakota border, 18 miles east of Sundance) is the **Vore Buffalo Jump,** where Indians drove hundreds of bison into a pit between A.D. 800 and 1600. No developments here. Reader Johan Bakker suggests a side-trip south from Beulah:

Get an excellent feel for the Black Hills canyon country by driving from Beulah to Buckhorn. Take Sand Creek Rd. south from the freeway at Beulah, and you can drive for about 30 miles through the canyons, through the deserted mining town of Mosekee, to Buckhorn on US 85. This road is passable in good weather in a regular auto, but in the spring and fall you may need a 4WD. (Road is closed during winter.) As a bonus, the private homes in Sand Hill Country Club and the state fish hatchery at Ranch "A" provide an excellent deer sanctuary, and especially in fall and early winter, many hundreds of deer may be observed from the road. These include some awesome trophy animals—needless to say, hunting is forbidden.

Eleven miles south of Sundance on State 116 is **Inyan Kara Mountain** (an Indian name meaning "Stone-made Peak"), a 6,368-foot summit that dominates the surrounding country. In 1874, Gen. George A. Custer led a large scientific expedition through this region en route to the Black Hills. Among others, Custer climbed the mountain, carving "G. Custer '74" on a rock near the summit. The inscribed rock is still here, though access to the mountain may be restricted by surrounding ranchers. Ask at the information center or museum for access info.

PRACTICALITIES

Accommodations

Visitors will find four places to stay in Sundance. Least expensive, but very nice, is **Bear Lodge Motel,** 218 Cleveland, tel. 283-1611 or (800) 341-8000, with rooms for $38 s or $40 d and a whirlpool. **Arrowhead Motel,** right next door at 214 Cleveland, tel. 283-3307 or (800) 456-6016, charges $38 s or d, and **Deane's Pine View Motel,** 117 N. Eighth St., tel. 283-2262, has cabins for $45 s or d, with kitchenettes for $50; open April-November. The town's fanciest lodging is **Apache Motel (Best Western),** 121 S. Sixth, tel. 283-2173 or (800) 528-1234. Rates start at $64 s or d. It has a pool, a sauna, and a whirlpool. Located between Sundance and Keyhole Reservoir, **Hawken Guest Ranch,** tel. 756-9319 or (800) 544-4309, offers a variety of lodging options, from bed and breakfast to tipi camping. Another interesting and authentic place to stay is **Canfield Ranch,** tel. 283-2062.

Camping

The Forest Service's fine **Reuter Campground** ($5) is just four miles northwest of Sundance. See "Black Hills National Forest" and "Devils Tower National Forest" (below) for other public campgrounds. The private **Mountain View**

SUN DANCES

The most spectacular of all Plains Indians religious ceremonies was the sun dance. An annual event, it frequently attracted hundreds or even thousands of tribal onlookers, serving not simply as an important religious service but also as a social and political rally. Native American legends say that it originated centuries ago, when a hunter was

approached by a buffalo who suddenly spoke to him, offering a cure for sickness. Much later, an eagle came to another young man in a dream, prescribing the complete ceremony. The name sun dance is something of a misnomer, since it was not a worship of the sun but a highly involved ceremony representing the creation of life and the triumph of good over evil. The specifics varied somewhat between the tribes. A common Native American term for it is "Thirsting Dance," referring to the long periods of dancing without water.

The sun dance was always held in late spring or early summer and led by a young man who spent considerable time learning the complex ceremonial steps from a priest. If he passed the test, the pledger gained immense status in the village as a fearless leader. The festivities lasted up to two weeks, with the main ceremony an intense four-day event. Central to the sun dance were an eagle representation (air), a buffalo head (earth), and a pole connecting the two, signifying the sacred Tree of Life. The ceremony took place in a lodge, generally built around a central pole that was forked at the top. After the sacred cottonwood tree had been selected by a scouting party, warriors attacked the tree in a furious charge. If it withstood this symbolic battle, the tree was cut down by a respected tribal woman and carried to the sundance site where it was carefully erected. A bundle of brush (to represent an eagle or thunderbird nest) and a buffalo head were placed in the fork of the pole. Twelve other poles (the number varied with different tribes) were erected around the central one, with cross beams to the center. (Missionaries would later claim these represented Jesus and the 12 apostles.) Brush was then laced around the outside to provide partial shade, and a buffalo-skull altar was erected at the center of the structure.

BOB RACE

Campground, tel. 283-2270, 1¹/₂ miles east of town, has tent sites for $12, RV spaces for $15, and tipis for $15 d.

Food
Good burgers and other American food at **Higbee's Cafe,** 101 N. Third, tel. 283-2165. It is open for breakfast and lunch daily and has Wed.-evening specials. For breakfast, head to **Log Cabin,** 1620 Cleveland. **Aro Restaurant,** 307 Cleveland, tel. 283-2000, has homemade soups, a salad bar, and the best food in town. Get fast food at **Mountain View Drive-In** west of town, tel. 283-2205, and groceries from **Decker's Food Center,** 106 N. Seventh, tel. 283-3155.

Information And Services
The **Sundance Information Center,** in the rest area at Exit 189 off I-90, tel. 283-2440, is open daily 8-7 May-Sept., daily 8-5 in Oct., and closed

---

Supplicants spent four days without food or water, dancing, praying, blowing on eagle-bone whistles, staring at the buffalo head, at the sun, or at a sacred doll, as they waited for a vision of power. In most tribes, the sun dance also involved self-mutilation. Assistants commonly cut small pieces of skin from the candidates' arms and shoulders as a blood sacrifice to the Great Spirit. (Before the battle at Little Big Horn, Sitting Bull sacrificed 100 pieces of flesh in a sun-dance ceremony, after which a vision told him of the coming destruction of Gen. Custer and his men.) Torture commonly went even further, as assistants cut slices into the back or chest of the dancers and slid bone skewers into the muscle. Thongs would be attached between the skewers and the central pole, while other skewers held heavy buffalo skulls to be dragged behind. The candidates would lean back until the ropes were taunt, jerking as they danced. Eventually the skin and muscle ripped loose and the dancers collapsed on the ground. In some tribes, the dancers were actually lifted off the ground by these tethers.

Whites found the sun dance's torture difficult to understand, and thought even less of the sexual aspects of the ceremony (such as the parading of a giant phallus). When the Indians were forced to reservations, the sun dance was outlawed, but some tribes continued to practice it secretly. Finally, in the late 1920s, the government relented, and a more sedate version of the sun dance was resurrected. The traditional blood sacrifice still exists among some tribes, but not in Wyoming. Today, the sun dance is performed in separate ceremonies by both the Shoshone and the Arapaho on the Wind River Reservation. Visitors may watch but cannot take photos or recordings.

The sun dance is now performed primarily as a thanksgiving ceremony, to cure disease, and to pray for the coming year. After several days of preparation, the main ceremony lasts for four days. Without food or water, the dancers move into a trance state that brings visions and power. One authority describes dancers seeing the buffalo head shaking and steam coming out of its nostrils as the power is imparted. On the fourth day, a bucket of water is passed around to signal the end of the sun dance, and that evening more dancing and feasting complete the ceremony.

BOB RACE

the rest of the year. The new **Crook County Library,** tel. 283-1006, is open Mon. 11-8 and Tues.-Fri. 11-5:30. Swim or take a shower at the grade school **pool,** tel. 283-2133, for $2; open June-Sept. only. **Country Cottage,** on Cleveland, tel. 283-2450, has locally made gifts as well as frozen yogurt. **Powder River Transportation,** tel. (800) 442-3682, has daily service to Gillette, along with Deadwood and Rapid City, South Dakota. The main event in Sundance is the **Crook County Fair and Rodeo,** which comes to town in early August.

BLACK HILLS NATIONAL FOREST

Black Hills National Forest lies primarily within South Dakota, reaching across the state line around Sundance. It was established in 1897 by President Grover Cleveland, after a series of large forest fires had focused attention on the need to protect the timber resource. The Forest Service's very first commercial timber sale was held within the Black Hills, and the area is still a supplier for lumber mills in Hulett and Newcastle. Nearby, South Dakota's Black Hills maintain a wide range of justifiably famous sites: the Homestake Gold Mine at Lead, historic Deadwood (now a gambler's mecca), Jewel and Wind caves, Mt. Rushmore, and an enormous bison herd in Custer State Park. Black Hills National Forest offices are in Sundance, tel. 283-1361, and Newcastle, tel. 746-2783. Pick up a forest map ($3), along with information on camping and sights in the area.

Camping

Three year-round campgrounds lie within the Wyoming portion of the forest. **Reuter Campground** ($5) is five miles northwest of Sundance, while **Cook Lake Campground** ($5-7) is 16 miles north of Sundance on a tiny forest pond. There's free camping at **Bearlodge Campground**, seven miles west of Aladdin on State 24. You can also camp for free on Forest Service land throughout the Black Hills. Over on the South Dakota side of the line, you'll find more than two dozen additional Forest Service campgrounds; call (800) 283-2267 for reservations (extra charge).

Scenic Drives

Many gravel roads wind up through the forested hills, and fall colors are brilliant along the aspen-lined stretches of the road just south of Cook Lake. A considerable amount of logging is going on within the ponderosa pine forests here, but it is selective logging, not clearcutting, and hence not as visible. Be sure to stop at **Warren Peak Lookout,** eight miles north of Sundance. The road is paved to this point, and you can climb the tower for a magnificent vista and a chance to visit folks at one of the few active fire lookouts remaining in Wyoming. **Grand Canyon Creek,** located southwest of Sundance along County Rd. 141, offers a long, scenic route into the hills of South Dakota, but be ready for 25 miles of gravel road. There are no hiking trails in the Wyoming portion of Black Hills National Forest.

ALADDIN AND VICINITY

Aladdin (pop. 10) was established in the 1870s to supply coal for gold smelters in Lead and Deadwood, South Dakota. During Prohibition, these mines housed moonshine stills. At 3,740 feet, it's the lowest settlement in Wyoming. Don't blink or you'll miss it, but if you do blink, turn around and stop for a visit. Aladdin is dominated by the fluorescent red **Aladdin Store,** built in 1890 and operated continuously ever since. Out front is a "liar's bench" for local storytellers; inside is a potbelly stove and an ancient post office with the original boxes. Worth a visit for a taste of unspoiled Americana. A small **museum** is upstairs. Free RV camping in the lot beside the store, or stay at **Aladdin Hotel,** tel. 896-4317, where rooms go for $20 s or $25 d. It's open May-December. A cafe that serves up all-American grub is next door, and across the street is a shady town park. The "Aladdin Arena" is home to an annual **Bronc Match and Horseshow** each August.

Ten miles northeast of Aladdin is the **lowest point in Wyoming**. From here, the Belle Fourche River drops only another 3,125 feet on its several-thousand-mile descent to the sea via the Missouri and Mississippi rivers. Just east of Aladdin is the **Tipple Mine Historical Site,** with restored coal-loading chutes and other facilities. Approximately two miles east of Aladdin is a historical marker noting the still-visible tracks left by the party of 110 wagons, 2,000 animals, and 1,000 men led by Gen. George A. Custer in the summer of 1874. Despite the Treaty of 1868 that reaffirmed this as Sioux Indian land, Custer's geologists, scouts, miners, and engineers had come to explore the Black Hills and to investigate the rumors of gold. Gold was indeed found by Custer's miners, and when word got out, the rush was on. Custer's own rush to judgment at Montana's Little Big Horn had also begun. He and all 268 of his men would die there just two years later.

On the other side of Aladdin, State 24 follows Beaver Creek past 150-foot-tall sandstone cliffs, ridge-top pines, and valley-bottom oaks. Old farmsteads appear, surrounded by fields filled with huge pyramidlike hay piles. The dot of a place called **Alva** (pop. 50) has a few old homes in the midst of the Bear Lodge Mountains, but nothing in the way of services. West of Alva the road climbs up into rolling grassy hills with trees in the draws and cattle grazing along the Belle Fourche River.

HULETT AND VICINITY

The tiny logging and ranching town of Hulett (pop. 430) lies right along the Belle Fourche River. Two lumber mills saw up timber from the adjacent Black Hills National Forest. The side of **Hulett National Bank** has burned-in brands from local cattle ranchers.

Practicalities
For food in Hulett, try **Hulett Cafe, Ponderosa Cafe,** or **Little Wrangler Cafe**. Two places to stay in town are: **Pioneer Motel**, tel. 467-5656, $29 s or $39 d, and **Hulett Motel**, tel. 467-5220, $24 s or $28 d. Park RVs at **S-A RV Camp** for $10. Showers are just 25 cents. It's open May-November. The library is in the high school. For entertainment, most evenings you'll find folks at the horseshoe pit next to the hardware store, or head to **Rodeo Saloon** or **Ponderosa Bar** for a beer with the locals. The big annual event is **Loggers and Ranchers Play Days**, held each September. Horse shows, cookouts, and old farm machinery are on display, along with down-home neighborliness. A couple of miles west of Hulett, you'll see bison grazing at a private ranch, while magnificent Devils Tower looms on the horizon.

West and then south from Hulett is the tiny town of **Oshoto** (a Native American word meaning "Bad Weather"), accessible only via gravel roads. The Brislawn Cayuse Ranch near Oshoto is one of the last places in America to have pure-blooded Spanish Mustangs, tough, small horses that were the pride of the wild west. The nearly extinct mule-footed Spanish pigs (say what?) are also here.

Alzada And Colony
North from Hulett, State 112 heads to the Montana border settlement of Alzada, cutting across land not unlike the foothills of California's Sierra Nevada. Cottonwoods and oaks fill the draws, and grassy meadows alternate with tree-topped hills. Very scenic, with an abundance of white-tailed deer all the way. The road doesn't really go anywhere most tourists are heading; because of this, it is perfect for cyclists and anyone with an explorer's streak. From Alzada, US 212 cuts southeast across Wyoming and to the South Dakota town of Belle Fourche. Along the way it passes a couple of bentonite mines in the grass-and-sage country around the nothing settlement called Colony. Antelope and cattle abound. Talk about confusion: since there is no post office in Colony, Wyoming, locals have South Dakota addresses on a Montana delivery route!

DEVILS TOWER NATIONAL MONUMENT

Devils Tower is a strange otherworldly apparition that rises some 1,267 feet above the surrounding plains. It is fitting that such a place was used as the contact point for aliens and earthlings in the 1977 film, *Close Encounters of the Third Kind.* The flat-topped tower of rock seems to push out of the earth like an enormous sawed-off stump from Paul Bunyan's forest. From a distance the tower looks as if it had been scratched by some giant beast, with parallel gouges running up the sides. Up closer, the gouges turn into enormous columns of rock molded into four-, five-, and six-sided shapes. In the setting sun, Devils Tower glows a golden red long after the surrounding hills no longer reflect the sun's rays, and as night comes on, the stars and moon outline its bold shape against the horizon. The tower is surrounded by ponderosa pine and bur-oak forests, while the winding Belle Fourche River flows less than a mile away. A large colony of **black-tailed prairie dogs** exists along the river just inside the park, and you're likely to also see white-tailed deer feeding in the meadows. On top, the tower is a relatively flat oval that reaches approximately 300 by 180 feet.

THE LEGEND OF BEAR LODGE

The place we call Devils Tower was known to the Kiowa Indians as Mato Tipila, meaning "Bear Lodge." Many tales are told about the origins of this mystical place, but the best-known is that of the Kiowa. Once upon a time, the people camped along a stream that had many bears. Seven sisters and their brother were playing nearby when the boy suddenly turned into a ferocious bear and began chasing the girls. In desperation, the girls climbed on a small rock and prayed, "Rock, take pity on us—rock, save us!" The rock started to grow, pushing them higher and higher as the bear clawed at the sides, trying to get them. Eventually the seven girls were pushed upward into the sky, forming the points of the Big Dipper. The gouges from the bear remain today on the sides of Bear Lodge.

Geology

Geologists argue over two similar theories for the creation of Devils Tower; most accepted is that it formed as the core of an ancient volcano. Some 60 million years ago, a mass of molten magma was forced up through the overlying sedimentary rocks. As it cooled and contracted, vertical fractures formed in the magma, creating long columnar joints—the "scratches" up the side of Devils Tower today. (Some of these columns are as much as 14 feet in diameter!) Eventually, the nearby Belle Fourche River eroded away the surrounding sedimentary rock, leaving the ancient volcanic neck exposed to the elements. Surrounding the 1,000-foot-wide base of Devils Tower is a mass of talus from fallen pieces of columns, but erosion of this very hard igneous rock is almost imperceptible. The four prominent peaks of the **Missouri Buttes**, located four miles northwest of Devils Tower, were formed in the same manner. At 500 to 800 feet in height, they are not as dramatic and lie outside the national monument's boundaries.

HISTORY

Devils Tower was known to Native Americans by a variety of names, most commonly as Bear Lodge, Tree Lodge, or Bear's Tipi. Fur trappers and early explorers certainly knew of the existence of Bear Lodge, but it wasn't until 1857 that any note of it was made—an exploration party led by Lt. G.K. Warren saw the rock from a distance. In 1875, Col. Richard I. Dodge finally led a U.S. Geological Survey party to the formation. Dodge somehow came up with the name Devils Tower, claiming that the Native Americans called it "Bad God's Tower." Despite protests that "Bear Lodge" had long been the aboriginal name, the label Devils Tower stuck.

Establishing The Monument
After the Indians had been driven from their traditional homeland in the 1870s, northeast Wyoming was opened to settlement by whites. Most lands were available to the homesteaders, but

the General Land Office prevented developers from gaining this freak of geology. Wyoming already had America's first national park in Yellowstone, and soon support grew to make the tower a park. After years of effort, President Theodore Roosevelt proclaimed Devils Tower the country's first national monument in 1906. Unfortunately, the final monument was only 1,153 acres in size, excluding the Missouri Buttes.

The First Climb
In the early years of Devils Tower National Monument the area served as a popular spot for picnics and camping, especially on the Fourth of July, when Independence Day celebrations attracted settlers from the entire region. The most famous of all these came in 1893. Handbills announced that the previously unclimbable tower would be scaled, and "On July 4th, 1893, Old Glory will be flung to the breeze from the top of the Tower, 800 feet from the ground by Wm. Rogers." The stunt was well planned. Several days before, two local ranchers, William Rogers and Willard Ripley, drove wooden pegs into a long crack that led to the top, tying the pegs together with strips of wood to make a ladder. They hauled a 12-foot flagpole to the top and returned on July 4 to scale the ladder in front of 800 people. Once on top (it took an hour to climb), Rogers unfurled a flag, but a gust of wind blew it off. Wives of the promoters tore it up

DEVILS TOWER

DEVILS TOWER NAT'L MONUMENT

JOYNER RIDGE TRAIL

RED BEDS TRAIL

TOWER TRAIL

VISITOR CENTER

▲ DEVILS TOWER
ELEV. 5,117 ft.

ENTRANCE STATION

POST OFFICE

PRAIRIE DOG COLONY

SOUTH SIDE TRAIL

VALLEY VIEW TRAIL

TO HULETT

24

PARK HEADQUARTERS

CAMPGROUND

BELLE FOURCHE RIVER

TO MOORCROFT & SUNDANCE

0   0.5mi

0   0.5km

and sold the pieces as souvenirs (stripes cost 25 cents, while stars went for 50 cents). The climb had been a smashing success.

On July 4, 1895, Mrs. Rogers became the first woman to climb the ladder to the top of Devils Tower, and many other adventurous folks followed over the next several decades. The ladder was last climbed in 1927, but pieces of it are still visible today along the southeast side of the Tower. (An iron stairway to the top, proposed by Wyoming's Congressman Mondell as a tourist attraction, was never built.)

Developing The Tower
For many years, Devils Tower remained undeveloped, and it was not until 1928 that a bridge was built across the Belle Fourche River to the site. During the Depression era, the CCC constructed a log visitor center, new roads, trails, picnic areas, and a campground. Visitation increased as access became easier and more families gained automobiles. One of the strangest events came in 1941, when George Hopkins—one of the top skydivers in the world—parachuted out of a plane to the top of Devils Tower as a publicity stunt. He had planned to descend on a 1,000 foot rope, but the rope landed on the side of the tower, leaving him stranded on top. Newspapers all over the country headlined his plight. Food and blankets were dropped to him, and for the next six days he spent a lonely vigil on top, waiting to be rescued. Finally, Jack Durrance, a mountain climber who had scaled Devils Tower three years before, arrived to lead seven other climbers to the top and to help Hopkins down. Many years later, in 1976, *Close Encounters of the Third Kind* was filmed here. Several hundred locals appeared in the crowd scenes. When the movie was released the following year, tourism here suddenly hit the stars.

Climbing The Tower
Although Devils Tower was first climbed in 1893 on a wooden ladder, the first ascent using modern rock-climbing techniques was not until 1937. Led by Fritz Wiessner, three New York City climbers made it to the top in a little under five hours. Over the years, as climbing technology has improved and as more people have been attracted to the sport, Devils Tower has become

LANDSCAPE 60 MILLION YEARS AGO

SEDIMENTARY ROCK

MAGMA

PARTIALLY ERODED LANDSCAPE

VOLCANIC NECK

SEDIMENTARY ROCK

DEVILS TOWER

PRESENT DAY LANDSCAPE

SEDIMENTARY ROCK

BOB RACE

one of the favorite climbing spots in the nation. During the summer you're bound to meet several dozen climbers heading for the base of the tower each morning. More than 25,000 people have reached the top, and the figure grows by at least 2,000 each year.

For information on the various routes (at least 120 have been climbed), pick up one of the small technical guides in the visitor center, or get *Devils Tower National Monument—A Climber's Guide,* by Steve Gardiner and Dick Guilmette (Seattle: The Mountaineers). Displays in the visitor center and at a kiosk out front describe climbing routes and techniques. Climbing demonstrations are given here each day during the summer. If you're planning to climb Devils Tower, be sure to register at the visitor center.

If you want to climb Devils Tower but lack the skills or equipment, there are several options. **Andy Petefish** is in the area much of the summer and leads climbs. A two-day climbing class and ascent costs around $190 including equipment. For details, stop by Devils Tower Trading Post, or call 467-5555. **Jackson Hole Mountain Guides**, 165 N. Glenwood, Jackson, WY 83001, tel. 733-4979, also leads guided trips to the top of Devils Tower.

Hiking Trails

Four different trails loop through this small national monument, providing fine views of the tower and surrounding country. Most popular is the 1½-mile **Tower Trail** that circles the tower. It is an easy, paved path with periodic openings offering impressive views of the tower, along with side paths to see the nearby Missouri Buttes and Belle Fourche River. Be sure to look through the peep sight to find the old wooden ladder that once went all the way to the top of Devils Tower.

Red Beds/South Side Trail is a three-mile dirt path that also takes off near the visitor center but makes a longer (and less crowded) loop around the tower. Along the way you get nice views of the Belle Fourche River and the Red Beds, iron-stained bluffs near the river. A 30-minute side loop, **Valley View Trail,** takes you to the prairie-dog town and the Belle Fourche River. The finest views of Devils Tower can be had from the **Joyner Ridge Trail,** a 1½-mile path. Views from this hilltop trail are unforgettable, especially at sunrise or sunset.

PRACTICALITIES

Access And Information

Devils Tower is 33 miles northeast of Moorcroft. You enter the park from State 24, seven miles north of its junction with US 14. Entrance fees are $4 for vehicles or $1 for hikers or cyclists; the passes are good for seven days. Annual passes to the monument cost $10, or purchase the Golden Eagle Pass ($25), which lets you in all national parks and monuments. Seniors get in free with a Golden Age Pass. The monument is open year-round, although most of the over-300,000 annual visitors arrive during the summer.

Beyond the entrance station, it is approximately three miles along a paved road to the base of the tower, where you'll find a pleasant old log **visitor center** (tel. 467-5501) and a parking lot that overflows on sunny summer days with rock climbers and gawkers. The center is open daily 8 a.m.-7:45 p.m. from mid-June to Labor Day, and daily 8 a.m. -4:45 p.m. the rest of the year. Inside you can watch a six-minute film on the history of Devils Tower, look at ecological displays and photos showing the dozens of climbing routes, or buy books on local lore. Nightly **campfire programs** are held at the amphitheater in the campground during the summer, with the standard Park Service fare of talks, tunes, and transparencies. Ask at the visitor center for tonight's activities.

Camping And Food

The Park Service maintains a fine **campground** ($6; open May-Oct.) a half-mile inside the entrance. In midsummer, get a space at the campground in the morning to be sure of having a spot. Just outside the monument are two private campgrounds. The friendlier of the two is **Devils Tower KOA**, tel. 467-5395, where sites cost $14 for tents or $18 for RVs, including pool access; open May-September. Rent mountain bikes, horses, and even binoculars here. And if you haven't seen it before, they show *Close Encounters* on the video.

Most folks stock up on food in nearby towns, but if you want a meal out, **Mateo Village**, tel. 756-3201, also at the park entrance gate, has meals including prime rib and seafood.

If the reader thinks he is done, now, and that this book has no moral to it, he is in error. The moral of it is this: If you are of any account, stay at home and make your way by faithful diligence; but if you are "no account," go away from home, and then you will have to work, whether you want to or not. Thus you become a blessing to your friends by ceasing to be a nuisance to them—if the people you go among suffer by the operation.

—Mark Twain in Roughing It

BOOKLIST

DESCRIPTION AND TRAVEL

Anderson, Susan. *Living in Wyoming: Settling for More.* Oakland, CA: Rockridge Press, 1990. A witty and insightful book about the people of Wyoming. Outstanding photos by Zbigniew Bzdak.

Burt, Nathaniel. *Wyoming.* Oakland, CA: Compass American Guides, 1990. Provides a tour of Wyoming and its historical attractions. Photography by Don Pitcher.

Ehrlich, Gretel. *The Solace of Open Spaces.* New York, NY: Viking Penguin Inc., 1985. A stunningly beautiful collection of observations and stories about ranch life in Wyoming from one of America's finest writers.

Kelsey, Joe. *Wyoming's Wind River Range.* Helena, MT: American Geographic Publishing, 1988. A profusely illustrated and well-written book about Wyoming's finest hiking country.

Lewis, Dan. *8,000 Miles of Dirt: A Backroad Travel Guide to Wyoming.* Casper, WY: Hawks Book Co., 1992. Describes dozens of the state's most enjoyable backroads in a folksy but not always informative manner. (Example: The chapter on the Outlaw Cave drive doesn't bother to mention its most famous inhabitant, Butch Cassidy!)

Mealey, Catherine E. *The Best of Wyoming.* Laramie, WY: Meadowlark Press, 1990. Contains brief county-by-county descriptions of the state's attractions.

Pence, Mary Lou, and Lola M. Homsher. *The Ghost Towns of Wyoming.* New York, NY: Hastings House, 1956. Describes the state's many historic towns that are slowly fading into the landscape.

Perry, John, and Jane Greverus Perry. *The Sierra Club Guide to the Natural Areas of Idaho, Montana, and Wyoming.* San Francisco, CA: Sierra Club Books, 1988. Information on national parks, national forests, wilderness areas, state parks, wildlife refuges, and other natural areas. Of limited usefulness except as a general description.

Roberts, Philip J., David L. Roberts, and Steven L. Roberts. *Wyoming Almanac.* Laramie, WY: Skyline West Press, 1989. Packed with 376 pages of Wyoming trivia, including such things as the Wyoming man who invented a cattle guard for use on railroad tracks and Wyoming news stories on CBS Evening News between 1977 and 1988. Hard to plow through it all (no index), but there are some real gems buried in this avalanche of facts.

Skinner, Holly L. *Only the River Runs Easy: A Historical Portrait of the Upper Green River Valley.* Boulder, CO: Pruett Publishing Co., 1985. An attractive and lovingly written history of the Upper Green River. Excellent.

Stienstra, Tom. *Rocky Mountain Camping.* San Francisco, CA: Foghorn Press, 1989. Describes over 1,200 public and private campgrounds in Wyoming, Colorado, and Montana.

Urbanek, Mae. *Wyoming Place Names.* Missoula, MT: Mountain Press Publishing Co., 1988. An excellent sourcebook for the names of everything from Abiathar Peak to the town of Zenith.

Williamson, Chilton, Jr. *Roughnecking It.* New York, NY: Simon and Schuster, 1982. A funny, insightful, and disturbing portrait of Wyoming during the oil-boom years of the the early 1980s. Gonzo journalism at its best.

Works Projects Administration. *Wyoming: A Guide to its History, Highways, and People.* Lincoln, NE: University of Nebraska Press, 1981. Reprint of a depression-era guide to Wyoming (originally printed in 1940), this classic guide still makes fascinating reading.

Wyoming Department of Administration and Fiscal Control. *Wyoming Data Handbook.* Cheyenne, WY: Wyoming Department of Administration and Fiscal Control. A free annual publication jammed with all sorts of technical information about Wyoming. Helpful for folks writing guides to Wyoming.

Wyoming Recreation Commission. *Wyoming: A Guide to Historic Sites.* Basin, WY: Big Horn Publishers, 1988. An excellent collection of descriptions of more than 300 historic sites in Wyoming.

GEOLOGY, GEOGRAPHY, AND WEATHER

Blackstone, D. L., Jr. *Traveler's Guide to the Geology of Wyoming.* Laramie, WY: Geological Survey of Wyoming, 1988. An excellent overview of Wyoming's geological history and how to see it through today's landscapes.

Brown, Robert Harold. *Wyoming: A Geography.* Boulder, CO: Westview Press, 1980. All sorts of interesting info about Wyoming, from political party affiliations to Indian handicrafts.

Largeson, David R., and Darwin R. Spearing. *Roadside Geology of Wyoming.* Missoula, MT: Mountain Press Publishing Co., 1988. Wyoming is perhaps the most geologically interesting of any state. This is an invaluable road guide for anyone wanting to know more geology without resorting to dense textbooks.

McPhee, John. *Rising from the Plains.* New York, NY: The Noonday Press, 1986. A delightful intertwining of the story of Wyoming's complex geology and the life of its preeminent geologist, David Love.

FICTION

Ehrlich, Gretel. *Heart Mountain.* New York, NY: Viking Penguin Inc., 1988. A touching novel about life in the Heart Mountain Relocation Camp near Cody, forced home for hundreds of Japanese-Americans during WW II.

Nye, Bill. *Bill Nye's Western Humor.* Lincoln, NE: University of Nebraska Press, 1968. A collection of delightfully wry essays by one of America's best-known 19th-century humorists.

Wister, Owen. *The Virginian.* Originally published in 1902 and now available from various publishers. The classic Western novel that established the cowboy hero and the lure of Wyoming.

BIOGRAPHY

Alter, Cecil. J. *Jim Bridger.* Norman, OK: University of Oklahoma Press, 1962. The incredible story of the most famous of all mountain men.

Anonymous. *The Sweet Smell of Sagebrush: A Prisoner's Diary 1903-1912.* Rawlins, WY: Friends of the Old Penitentiary, 1990. This wonderful small volume contains the writings of an "anonymous" criminal (John Kirby) who served four terms in the Rawlins penitentiary for horse stealing and other crimes. It not only provides descriptions of his many escapades outside the law but also opens a window on the criminal mind.

Olsen, Jack. *Doc: The Rape of the Town of Lovell.* New York, NY: Atheneum, 1989. The true, but hard-to-believe story of a respected physician who raped dozens of women in this small, religious town.

Pointer, Larry. *In Search of Butch Cassidy.* Norman, OK: University of Oklahoma Press, 1977. A thoroughly researched book that seems to show that Butch Cassidy's death in South America was a ruse, and that he died much later in Seattle.

Sell, Henry Blackman, and Victor Weybright. *Buffalo Bill and the Wild West.* Basin, WY: Big Horn Books, 1979. The authors attempt to sort the incredible true story of William Cody from the legends created by decades of tall tales. Nicely illustrated.

Woods, L. Milton. *Moreton Frewen's Western Adventures.* Boulder, CO: Roberts Rinehart, Inc., 1986. The strange tale of a wealthy British adventurer who made and lost his (and other folks') fortunes in Wyoming.

HIKING AND CLIMBING

Note: See also Jackson Hole and Grand Teton National Park *and* Yellowstone National Park *(below).*

Bach, Orville E., Jr. *Hiking the Yellowstone Backcountry.* San Francisco, CA: Sierra Club Books, 1979. A pocket-sized volume with descriptions of the park's trails.

Gardiner, Steve, and Dick Guilmette. *Devils Tower National Monument—A Climber's Guide.* Seattle, WA: The Mountaineers, 1986. A detailed guide to one of the most varied and enjoyable rock faces in Wyoming.

Hunger, Bill. *The Hiker's Guide to Wyoming.* Helena, MT: Falcon Press, 1992. A fine, detailed book that describes 75 different hikes in all parts of the state.

Kelsey, Joe. *Climbing and Hiking in the Wind River Mountains.* San Francisco, CA: Sierra Club Books, 1980. The definitive guide to climbing and hiking in the Winds.

Melius, Kenneth W., ed. *Cloud Peak Primitive Area: Trail Guide, History, and Photo Odyssey.* Aberdeen, SD: Melius Petterson Publications, 1984. A fine, complete guide to trails, history, and the environment of the Big Horn's dramatic wilderness country.

Mitchell, Finis. *Wind River Trails.* Salt Lake City, UT: Wasatch Publications, 1975. A folksy, inexpensive guide by a man who has hiked this country since 1909.

HISTORY

Baber, D. F. *The Longest Rope.* Caldwell, ID: The Caxton Printers, Ltd., 1953. The fascinating story of the Johnson County War as told by William Walker, only surviving "rustler" witness of the siege at KC Ranch.

Bille, Ed. *Early Days at Salt Creek and Teapot Dome.* Casper, WY: Mountain States Lithographing Co., 1978. The story of oil boom-times in Wyoming's most famous oil fields. Many fine old photos.

Burt, Struthers. *Powder River: Let 'er Buck.* New York, NY: Rinehart, 1938. A classic book on this famous part of Wyoming, by one of the finest writers to come out of the state.

Cheyenne Centennial Committee. *The Magic City on the Plains: Cheyenne 1867-1967.* Cheyenne, WY: Cheyenne Centennial Committee, 1967. A comprehensive history of Cheyenne.

Combs, Barry B. *Westward to Promontory: Building the Union Pacific Across the Plains and Mountains.* New York, NY: Crown Publishers, 1986. How the west was really won. Includes a wonderful collection of historic photos by Andrew J. Russell.

DeVoto, Bernard. *Across the Wide Missouri.* New York, NY: Houghton Mifflin Co., 1947. The Rocky Mountain fur trade and how it shaped American culture. A classic.

Edgar, Bob, and Jack Turnell. *Brand of a Legend.* Greybull, WY: Wolverine Gallery, 1978. The story of one of Wyoming's most famous ranches, the Pitchfork. Includes many of Charles Belden's wonderful old photographs.

Gowans, Fred R., and Eugene E. Campbell. *Fort Bridger, Island in the Wilderness.* Provo,

UT: Brigham Young University Press, 1975. An excellent book about the first way station specifically built to serve immigrants on the Oregon Trail.

Gowans, Fred R. *Rocky Mountain Rendezvous: A History of the Fur Trade Rendezvous 1825-1840.* Layton, UT: Peregrine Smith Books, 1985. Describes each of the rendezvous in detail.

Gunderson, Mary Alice. *Devils Tower: Stories in Stone.* Glendo, WY: High Plains Press, 1988. A small book on the history of Devils Tower National Monument.

Haines, Aubrey L. *Journal of a Trapper: Osborne Russell.* Lincoln, NE: University of Nebraska Press, 1955. The fascinating first-person account of a fur trapper from 1834-43. A classic and surprisingly well-written book.

Hanesworth, Robert D. *Daddy of 'em All; The Story of Cheyenne Frontier Days.* Cheyenne, WY: Flintlock Publishing Co., 1967. Stories and photos from the early days of Cheyenne's Frontier Days celebration.

Hedgpeth, Don. *Spurs Were A-Jinglin'.* Cody, WY: Northland Press, 1975. Brief text follows the excellent photos by Charles J. Belden of cowboys and ranching in the early parts of this century.

Hill, William E. *The Oregon Trail: Yesterday and Today.* Caldwell, ID: The Caxton Printers, 1986. A historical and pictorial trek along the path of the pioneers. Includes diaries, old photos, and museums along the Oregon Trail.

Homsher, Lola M., ed. *South Pass, 1868; James Chisholm's Journal of the Wyoming Gold Rush.* Lincoln, NE: University of Nebraska Press, 1960. Tales of life in the gold-mining town of South Pass shortly after the first wave of boomers had left. Very interesting.

Junge, Mark. *Wyoming: A Pictorial History.* Norfolk, NE: The Donning Co., 1989. A gorgeous coffee-table book filled with historic black-and-white photos from throughout Wyoming.

Kahin, Sharon, and Laurie Rufe. *In the Shadows of the Rockies: A Photographic History of the Pioneer Experience in Wyoming's Big Horn Basin.* Powell, WY: Northwest Community College, 1983. Outstanding photos and interesting historical quotes on the Big Horn Basin.

Larson, T. A. *History of Wyoming.* 2nd ed. Lincoln, NE: University of Nebraska Press, 1978. The definitive tome (663 pages worth) on Wyoming's history, with an emphasis on politics and development rather than on outlaws and Indian wars.

Lavender, David. *Fort Laramie and the Changing Frontier.* Washington, D.C.: U.S. Department of the Interior, National Park Service, 1983. An interesting little book filled with the history of the people who made Fort Laramie a primary center of trade and war in the west. Excellent illustrations too.

Mead, Jean. *Casper Country.* Boulder, CO: Pruett Publishing Co., 1987. A profusely illustrated history of Casper.

Mercer, Asa Shinn. *Banditti of the Plains;* or, *The Cattlemen's Invasion of Wyoming in 1892: the Crowning Infamy of the Ages.* Norman, OK: University of Oklahoma Press, 1954. A reprint of a classic book about the Johnson County War.

Mothershead, Harmon Ross. *The Swan Land and Cattle Company, Ltd.* Norman, OK: University of Oklahoma Press, 1971. The story of the most famous of all Wyoming ranches, the million-acre spread begun by Alexander Swan in 1883.

Munkres, Robert L. *Saleratus and Sagebrush: The Oregon Trail Through Wyoming.* Cheyenne, WY: Wyoming State Archives and Historical Department, 1974. This interesting small book offers eyewitness accounts from many travelers along the Oregon Trail.

Murray, Robert A. *The Bozeman Trail: Highway of History.* Boulder, CO: Pruett Publishing Company, 1988. An attractively illustrated history of the west's most violent trail.

Osgood, Ernest Staples. *The Day of the Cattleman.* Chicago, IL: University of Chicago Press, 1929. An authoritative history of the 50 years when cowboys and cattle barons ruled Wyoming and Montana.

Parkman, Francis. *The Oregon Trail.* Boston, MA: Little, Brown and Co., 1886. A classic first-person account of the great westward migration.

Pinkerton, Joan Tregs. *Knights of the Broadax.* Caldwell, ID: The Caxton Printers, Inc., 1981. An account of the life of the tie hacks in the upper Wind River country.

Rhode, Robert B. *Booms & Busts on Bitter Creek: A History of Rock Springs, Wyoming.* Boulder, CO: Pruett Publishing Co., 1987. A fine history of one of Wyoming's most turbulent cities.

Sandoval, Judith Hancock. *Historic Ranches of Wyoming.* Casper, WY: Mountain States Lithographing, 1986. Details nearly a hundred of the state's classic old ranches.

Spring, Agnes Wright. *The Cheyenne and Black Hills Stage and Express Routes.* Lincoln, NE: University of Nebraska Press, 1948. Tales from the early days of eastern Wyoming.

Thompson, George A. *Throw Down the Box!* Salt Lake City, UT: Dream Garden Press, 1989. A book about the Gilmer and Salisbury stagecoaches, including one of the line's branches, the famous Cheyenne and Black Hills stage line.

Thybony, Scott, Robert G. Rosenberg, and Elizabeth Mullett Rosenberg. *The Medicine Bows: Wyoming's Mountain Country.* Caldwell, ID: The Caxton Printers, Ltd., 1985. An outstanding historical account of the Indians, explorers, miners, and tie hacks who called this scenic part of Wyoming home.

Twain, Mark. *Roughing It.* First published in 1872, this is one of the classics in American literature. Samuel Clemens's witty descriptions of the old west seem ageless.

NATIVE AMERICANS

Clark, Ella E., and Margot Edmonds. *Sacagawea of the Lewis and Clark Expedition.* Berkeley, CA: University of California Press, 1979. A fascinating investigation into the truth behind one of the best known women in Wyoming history. Bursts a few bubbles.

Frison, George C. *Prehistoric Hunters of the High Plains.* New York, NY: Academic Press, 1978. The authoritative source on the earliest inhabitants of Wyoming.

Hendry, Mary Helen. *Indian Rock Art in Wyoming.* Lincoln, NE: Augstams Printing, 1983. Descriptions of rock-art sites in the state. Her ages for the rock art are too recent, and she intentionally omits locations.

Lowie, Robert. *Indians of the Plains.* New York, NY: The Natural History Press, 1954. Famed anthropologist Robert Lowie presents a detailed picture of life on the plains before the arrival of whites.

Nadeau, Remi. *Fort Laramie and the Sioux Indians.* Englewood Cliffs, NJ: Prentice-Hall Inc., 1967. A thorough historical account of the impact of Fort Laramie on the high plains Indians.

Trenholm, Virginia Cole, and Maurine Carley. *The Shoshonis: Sentinels of the Rockies.* Norman, OK: University of Oklahoma Press, 1964. The history of Chief Washakie and the Shoshone tribe.

Trenholm, Virginia Cole. *The Arapahoes, Our People.* Norman, OK: University of Oklahoma Press, 1970. The history of this important Wyoming tribe, from prehistory to their forced relocation to the Wind River Reservation.

Urbanek, Mae. *Chief Washakie*. Boulder, CO: Johnson Publishing Co., 1971. The fascinating story of the chief who led the Shoshone people for 60 years, always remaining a friend of whites.

Utley, Robert M. *The Indian Frontier of the American West 1846-1890*. Albuquerque, NM: University of New Mexico Press, 1984. An even-handed portrayal of a half-century of conflict between Indians and whites.

NATURAL HISTORY

Note: See also Jackson Hole and Grand Teton National Park *and* Yellowstone National Park *(below).*

Blair, Neal. *The History of Wildlife Management in Wyoming*. Cheyenne, WY: Wyoming Game and Fish, 1987. A large, detailed book covering the time from when the bison blackened the plains to the present.

Clark, Tim W., and Mark R. Stromberg. *Mammals in Wyoming*. Lawrence, KS: University of Kansas Museum of Natural History, 1987. The definitive guide to 117 native or naturalized Wyoming mammals: their identification, distribution, biology, and ecology.

Craighead, Frank J. *Track of the Grizzly*. San Francisco, CA: Sierra Club Books, 1979. The life of grizzlies in Yellowstone, by one of the most famous bear researchers.

Crowe, Douglas M. *Furbearers of Wyoming*. Cheyenne, WY: Wyoming Department of Game and Fish, 1986. A small book describing the state's fur-coated critters, with distribution maps.

Dorn, Robert D. *Vascular Plants of Wyoming*. Cheyenne, WY: Mountain West Publishing Company, 1988. The authoritative key to Wyoming plants; a dense book with few illustrations. For botanists.

Petersen, David. *Among the Elk*. Flagstaff, AZ: Northland Publishing, 1988. The story of wapiti, with outstanding photos by Alan D. Carey.

JACKSON HOLE AND GRAND TETON NATIONAL PARK

Betts, Robert B. *Along the Ramparts of the Tetons; the Saga of Jackson Hole, Wyoming*. Boulder, CO: Colorado Associated University Press, 1978. A substantial, detailed, and beautifully written book about Jackson Hole's fascinating history.

Burt, Nathaniel. *Jackson Hole Journal*. Norman, OK: University of Oklahoma Press, 1983. Tales of growing up as a dude in Jackson Hole. Contains some very amusing stories.

Carrighar, Sally. *One Day at Teton Marsh*. Lincoln, NE: University of Nebraska Press, 1979. A classic natural history of life in a Jackson Hole marsh. Made into a movie by Walt Disney.

Clark, Tim W. *Ecology of Jackson Hole, Wyoming: A Primer*. Salt Lake City, UT: Paragon Press, 1981. An excellent scientific introduction to ecological interrelationships within Jackson Hole.

Harry, Bryan. *Teton Trails*. Moose, WY: Grand Teton Natural History Association, 1987. An inexpensive small guide to the hiking trails of Grand Teton National Park.

Hayden, Elizabeth Wied, and Cynthia Nielsen. *Origins, A Guide to the Place Names of Grand Teton National Park and the Surrounding Area*. Moose, WY: Grand Teton Natural History Association, 1988. A guide to the obscure sources for place names in Grand Teton.

Huidekoper, Virginia. *The Early Days in Jackson Hole*. Boulder, CO: Colorado Associated University Press, 1978. Filled with over 100 photos from old-time Jackson Hole.

Johnsgard, Paul A. *Teton Wildlife*. Boulder, CO: Colorado Associated University Press, 1982. A descriptive book by a noted naturalist from the University of Nebraska.

Lawrence, Paul. *Hiking the Teton Backcountry*. San Francisco, CA: Sierra Club Books, 1979. Outdated, but still useful, guide to trails in Grand Teton National Park.

Love, J.D., and John C. Reed, Jr. *Creation of the Teton Landscape: the Geologic Story of Grand Teton National Park*. Moose, WY: Grand Teton Natural History Association, 1971. A small but authoritatively detailed guide to the geology of Jackson Hole and the Tetons.

Murie, Margaret, and Olaus Murie. *Wapiti Wilderness*. Boulder, CO: Colorado Associated University Press, 1985. The lives of two of America's most-loved conservationists in Jackson Hole, and their work with elk.

Ortenburger, Leigh N., and Reynold G. Jackson. *A Complete Guide to the Teton Range*. Palo Alto, CA: self-published, 1990. A very thorough two-volume climbing guide.

Petzoldt, Paul. *Petzoldt's Teton Trails*. Salt Lake City, UT: Wasatch Publishers, Inc., 1976. An enjoyable small hiking guide by one of the grand old men of mountain climbing.

Raynes, Bert. *Birds of Grand Teton National Park and the Surrounding Area*. Moose, WY: Grand Teton Natural History Association, 1984. A guide to local birds.

Righter, Robert W. *Crucible for Conservation: The Creation of Grand Teton National Park*. Boulder, CO: Colorado Associated University Press, 1982. The story of how the Tetons were spared through a half-century battle.

Ringholz, Raye C. *Little Town Blues: Voices from the Changing West*. Salt Lake City, UT: Gibbs-Smith Publisher, 1992. This important small book visits several small towns in the west—including Jackson, Wyoming—where the rural qualities and beauty that attract visitors are being innundated by tourism and development. It offers a cautionary note on the consequences of unbridled growth.

Thompson, Edith M., and William Leigh Thompson. *Beaver Dick: The Honor and the Heartbreak*. Laramie, WY: Jelm Mountain Press, 1982. A touching historical biography of Beaver Dick Leigh, one of the first white men to settle in Jackson Hole.

U.S. Department of the Interior, National Park Service. *Grand Teton: Official National Park Handbook*. Washington, D.C.: National Park Service, 1984. An attractive small book about the park and its history.

YELLOWSTONE NATIONAL PARK

Back, Orville E. *Hiking the Yellowstone Back Country*. San Francisco, CA: Sierra Club Books, 1979. A pocket-sized guide to hikes in the park.

Balthis, Frank, Steve Bogen, and Fred Hirschmann. *Winter at Old Faithful*. Yellowstone, WY: Firehole Press, 1980. A thin guide to the natural history of Yellowstone and how to see it on cross-country skis.

Bartlett, Richard A. *Yellowstone: A Wilderness Besieged*. Tuscon, AZ: University of Arizona Press, 1985. The history of Yellowstone and the fight to prevent its destruction by railroad magnates, concessionaires, and others.

Bryan, Scott. T. *The Geysers of Yellowstone*. Boulder, CO: Colorado Associated University Press, 1979. A complete and detailed guide to more than 400 geysers and other geothermal features in Yellowstone.

Charlton, Robert E. *Yellowstone Fishing Guide: A Comprehensive Guide to Fishing the Lakes and Streams Located in Yellowstone National Park*. Portland, OR: Flying Pencil Publications, 1990. A detailed guide to fishing in the park. Leaves no trickle unfished.

Chase, Alston. *Playing God in Yellowstone: The Destruction of America's First National Park*. Boston, MA: Atlantic Monthly Press, 1986. A long tirade against everything the

Park Service has ever done in Yellowstone. Disturbing to read and with many valid criticisms, but so one-sided that it is difficult to sort truth from opinion. Read this and *Wildlife in Transition* for two sides of the issues.

Colling, Gene. *The Bicyclist's Guide to Yellowstone National Park.* Helena, MT: Falcon Press Publishing Co., 1984. Includes maps and all you need to know about cycling in America's oldest park.

Fritz, William J. *Roadside Geology of the Yellowstone Country.* Missoula, MT: Mountain Press Publishing Co., 1985. All the park roads are covered in this easy-to-follow Yellowstone geology primer.

Haines, Aubrey L. *The Yellowstone Story: A History of Our First National Park.* Yellowstone Library and Museum Association, 1977. A definitive two-volume history of the park. Volume one (history up to the park's establishment) is the most interesting.

Hirschmann, Fred. *Yellowstone.* Portland, OR: Graphic Arts Center Publishing, 1982. Exceptional photography.

Janetski, Joel C. *Indians of Yellowstone Park.* Salt Lake City, UT: University of Utah Press, 1987. A general overview of the earliest settlers in Yellowstone and later conflicts with incoming whites.

Krakell, Dean, II. *Downriver: A Yellowstone Journey.* San Francisco, CA: Sierra Club Books, 1987. A extraordinarily moving journey down the magnificent Yellowstone River.

Marschall, Mark C. *Yellowstone Trails: A Hiking Guide.* Yellowstone National Park, WY: The Yellowstone Association, 1990. An excellent, up-to-date, and detailed guidebook to the park's 1000 miles of hiking trails.

McEneaney, Terry. *Birds of Yellowstone.* Boulder, CO: Roberts Rinehart, 1988. A guide to Yellowstone birds and where to find them.

McNulty, Tim (text), and Pat O'Hara (photos). *Yellowstone National Park: Land of Fire and Falling Water.* San Rafael, CA: Woodlands Press, 1986. A coffee-table book of luscious pictures from the park.

Reese, Rick. *Greater Yellowstone: The National Park and Adjacent Wildlands.* Helena, MT: Montana Magazine, 1984. An attractive book with considerable information on ecological conditions in one of the lower 48's largest intact ecosystems.

Schmidt, Jeremy, and Steven Fuller. *Yellowstone Grand Teton Road Guide.* Jackson, WY: Free Wheeling Travel Guides, 1990. A nicely done pocket-sized guide to the roads of the two parks, with accurate, up-to-date information. Easily the best road guide available.

Schreier, Carl, ed. *Yellowstone: Selected Photographs 1870-1960.* Moose, WY: Homestead Publishing, 1989. An outstanding collection of historic photographs from the park.

Schreier, Carl. *Yellowstone's Geysers, Hot Springs and Fumaroles.* Moose, WY: Homestead Publishing, 1987. An attractive small book filled with color photos and brief descriptions.

Scott, Douglas M. and Suvi A. Scott. *Wildlife of Yellowstone and Grand Teton National Parks.* Salt Lake City, UT: Wheelwright Press, Ltd., 1988. A brief descriptive guide to Yellowstone and Grand Teton critters.

Shaw, Richard J. *Plants of Yellowstone and Grand Teton National Parks.* Salt Lake City, UT: Wheelwright Press, 1981. Photos and descriptions of the most commonly found plants in the park.

Varley, John D. *Freshwater Wilderness: Yellowstone Fishes and Their World.* Yellowstone Library and Museum Association, 1983. A lovely book for anglers and those interested in fish.

, Lee H. *Yellowstone Place Names*.
, MT: Montana Historical Society Press,
1988. For the Trivial Pursuit enthusiast; detailed descriptions of every possible name from every possible obscure corner of Yellowstone.

Wuerthner, George. *Yellowstone and the Fires of Change*. Salt Lake City, UT: Haggis House Publications, 1988. Good photos and an ecological look at the fires make this perhaps the best book about the fires of '88.

INDEX

Page numbers in **boldface** indicate the primary reference. *Italicized* page numbers indicate information in captions, callouts, charts, illustrations, or maps.

ABOUT THE AUTHOR

Born in Atlanta, Georgia, Don Pitcher grew up all over the East Coast—from Florida to Maine. He moved west to attend college and immediately fell in love with the wide open spaces of the American West. Don holds a bachelor's degree in Biology from Pacific Union College and a master's degree in Wildland Resource Science from the University of California, Berkeley. Once out of school, he traveled north to Alaska to work for the Park Service, Forest Service, and Alaska Department of Fish and Game. In 1989, he headed to Wyoming's Teton Wilderness to take part in a grizzly bear habitat study. Don remained in Wyoming to research and write this guide and to photograph a second book. He now lives in Alaska but criss-crossed 4,000 miles of Wyoming roads to thoroughly research this new edition.

Trained as an ecologist, Don Pitcher's love of travel led him to work on various guidebooks as both a writer and photographer. He is coauthor of *Alaska-Yukon Handbook* (Moon Publications) and the author of *Berkeley Inside/Out* (Heyday Books). His photographs have appeared in many books, calendars, magazines, and other publications, most notably in *Wyoming* (Compass American Guides).

MOON HANDBOOKS—THE IDEAL TRAVELING COMPANIONS

Open a Moon Handbook and you're opening your eyes and heart to the world. Thoughtful, sensitive, and provocative, Moon Handbooks encourage an intimate understanding of a region, from its culture and history to essential practicalities. Fun to read and packed with valuable information on accommodations, dining, recreation, plus indispensable travel tips, detailed maps, charts, illustrations, photos, glossaries, and indexes, Moon Handbooks are ideal traveling companions: informative, entertaining, and highly practical.

To locate the bookstore nearest you that carries Moon Travel Handbooks or to order directly from Moon Publications, call: (800) 345-5473, Monday-Friday, 9 a.m.-5 p.m. PST.

THE PACIFIC/ASIA SERIES

BALI HANDBOOK   by Bill Dalton
Detailed travel information on the most famous island in the world. 428 pages.   **$12.95**

BANGKOK HANDBOOK   by Michael Buckley
Your tour guide through this exotic and dynamic city reveals the affordable and accessible possibilities. Thai phrasebook. 214 pages.   **$10.95**

BLUEPRINT FOR PARADISE: How to Live on a Tropic Island   by Ross Norgrove
This one-of-a-kind guide has everything you need to know about moving to and living comfortably on a tropical island. 212 pages.   **$14.95**

FIJI ISLANDS HANDBOOK   by David Stanley
The first and still the best source of information on travel around this 322-island archipelago. Fijian glossary. 198 pages.   **$11.95**

INDONESIA HANDBOOK   by Bill Dalton
This one-volume encyclopedia explores island by island the many facets of this sprawling, kaleidoscopic island nation. Extensive Indonesian vocabulary. 1,000 pages.   **$19.95**

MICRONESIA HANDBOOK: Guide to the Caroline, Gilbert, Mariana, and Marshall Islands
by David Stanley
Micronesia Handbook guides you on a real Pacific adventure all your own. 345 pages.   **$11.95**

NEW ZEALAND HANDBOOK   by Jane King
Introduces you to the people, places, history, and culture of this extraordinary land. 571 pages.
$18.95

OUTBACK AUSTRALIA HANDBOOK   by Marael Johnson
Australia is an endlessly fascinating, vast land, and *Outback Australia Handbook* explores the cities and towns, sheep stations, and wilderness areas of the Northern Territory, Western Australia, and South Australia. Full of travel tips and cultural information for adventuring, relaxing, or just getting away from it all. 355 pages.   **$15.95**

PHILIPPINES HANDBOOK by Peter Harper and Evelyn Peplow
Crammed with detailed information, *Philippines Handbook* equips the escapist, hedonist, or business traveler with thorough coverage of the Philippines's colorful history, landscapes, and culture. 587 pages. **$12.95**

SOUTHEAST ASIA HANDBOOK by Carl Parkes
Helps the enlightened traveler discover the real Southeast Asia. 873 pages. **$16.95**

SOUTH KOREA HANDBOOK by Robert Nilsen
Whether you're visiting on business or searching for adventure, *South Korea Handbook* is an invaluable companion. Korean glossary with useful notes on speaking and reading the language. 548 pages. **$14.95**

SOUTH PACIFIC HANDBOOK by David Stanley
The original comprehensive guide to the 16 territories in the South Pacific. 740 pages. **$19.95**

TAHITI-POLYNESIA HANDBOOK by David Stanley
All five French-Polynesian archipelagoes are covered in this comprehensive guide by Oceania's best-known travel writer. 235 pages. **$11.95**

THAILAND HANDBOOK by Carl Parkes
Presents the richest source of information on travel in Thailand. 568 pages. **$16.95**

THE HAWAIIAN SERIES

BIG ISLAND OF HAWAII HANDBOOK by J.D. Bisignani
An entertaining yet informative text packed with insider tips on accommodations, dining, sports and outdoor activities, natural attractions, and must-see sights. 347 pages. **$11.95**

HAWAII HANDBOOK by J.D. Bisignani
Winner of the 1989 Hawaii Visitors Bureau's Best Guide Award and the Grand Award for Excellence in Travel Journalism, this guide takes you beyond the glitz and high-priced hype and leads you to a genuine Hawaiian experience. Covers all 8 Hawaiian Islands. 879 pages. **$15.95**

KAUAI HANDBOOK by J.D. Bisignani
Kauai Handbook is the perfect antidote to the workaday world. Hawaiian and pidgin glossaries. 236 pages. **$9.95**

MAUI HANDBOOK by J.D. Bisignani
"No fool-'round" advice on accommodations, eateries, and recreation, plus a comprehensive introduction to island ways, geography, and history. Hawaiian and pidgin glossaries. 350 pages. **$11.95**

OAHU HANDBOOK by J.D. Bisignani
A handy guide to Honolulu, renowned surfing beaches, and Oahu's countless other diversions. Hawaiian and pidgin glossaries. 354 pages. **$11.95**

THE AMERICAS SERIES

ALASKA-YUKON HANDBOOK by Deke Castleman and Don Pitcher
Get the inside story, with plenty of well-seasoned advice to help you cover more miles on less money. 384 pages. **$13.95**

ARIZONA TRAVELER'S HANDBOOK by Bill Weir
This meticulously researched guide contains everything necessary to make Arizona accessible and enjoyable. 505 pages. **$14.95**

BAJA HANDBOOK by Joe Cummings
A comprehensive guide with all the travel information and background on the land, history, and culture of this untamed thousand-mile-long peninsula. 356 pages. **$13.95**

BELIZE HANDBOOK by Chicki Mallan
Complete with detailed maps, practical information, and an overview of the area's flamboyant history, culture, and geographical features, *Belize Handbook* is the only comprehensive guide of its kind to this spectacular region. 212 pages. **$13.95**

BRITISH COLUMBIA HANDBOOK by Jane King
With an emphasis on outdoor adventures, this guide covers mainland British Columbia, Vancouver Island, the Queen Charlotte Islands, and the Canadian Rockies. 381 pages.
$13.95

CANCUN HANDBOOK by Chicki Mallan
Covers the city's luxury scene as well as more modest attractions, plus many side trips to unspoiled beaches and Mayan ruins. Spanish glossary. 257 pages. **$12.95**

CATALINA ISLAND HANDBOOK: A Guide to California's Channel Islands
by Chicki Mallan
A complete guide to these remarkable islands, from the windy solitude of the Channel Islands National Marine Sanctuary to bustling Avalon. 245 pages. **$10.95**

COLORADO HANDBOOK by Stephen Metzger
Essential details to the all-season possibilities in Colorado fill this guide. Practical travel tips combine with recreation—skiing, nightlife, and wilderness exploration—plus entertaining essays. 422 pages. **$15.95**

IDAHO HANDBOOK by Bill Loftus
A year-round guide to everything in this outdoor wonderland, from whitewater adventures to rural hideaways. 275 pages. **$12.95**

JAMAICA HANDBOOK by Karl Luntta
From the sun and surf of Montego Bay and Ocho Rios to the cool slopes of the Blue Mountains, author Karl Luntta offers island-seekers a perceptive, personal view of Jamaica. 213 pages.
$12.95

MONTANA HANDBOOK by W.C. McRae and Judy Jewell
The wild West is yours with this extensive guide to the Treasure State, complete with travel practicalities, history, and lively essays on Montana life. 393 pages. **$13.95**

NEVADA HANDBOOK   by Deke Castleman
Nevada Handbook puts the Silver State into perspective and makes it manageable and affordable. 400 pages.   **$14.95**

NEW MEXICO HANDBOOK   by Stephen Metzger
A close-up and complete look at every aspect of this wondrous state. 375 pages.   **$13.95**

NORTHERN CALIFORNIA HANDBOOK   by Kim Weir
An outstanding companion for imaginative travel in the territory north of the Tehachapis. 759 pages.   **$16.95**

OREGON HANDBOOK   by Stuart Warren and Ted Long Ishikawa
Brimming with travel practicalities and insider views on Oregon's history, culture, arts, and activities. 422 pages.   **$12.95**

TEXAS HANDBOOK   by Joe Cummings
Seasoned travel writer Joe Cummings brings an insider's perspective to his home state. 483 pages.   **$13.95**

UTAH HANDBOOK   by Bill Weir
Weir gives you all the carefully researched facts and background to make your visit a success. 445 pages.   **$14.95**

WASHINGTON HANDBOOK   by Dianne J. Boulerice Lyons and Archie Satterfield
Covers sights, shopping, services, transportation, and outdoor recreation, with complete listings for restaurants and accommodations. 433 pages.   **$13.95**

WYOMING HANDBOOK   by Don Pitcher
All you need to know to open the doors to this wide and wild state. 495 pages.   **$14.95**

YUCATAN HANDBOOK   by Chicki Mallan
All the information you'll need to guide you into every corner of this exotic land. Mayan and Spanish glossaries. 391 pages.   **$14.95**

THE INTERNATIONAL SERIES

EGYPT HANDBOOK   by Kathy Hansen
An invaluable resource for intelligent travel in Egypt. Arabic glossary. 510 pages.   **$18.95**

MOSCOW-ST. PETERSBURG HANDBOOK   by Masha Nordbye
Provides the visitor with an extensive introduction to the history, culture, and people of these two great cities, as well as practical information on where to stay, eat, and shop. 205 pages.   **$13.95**

NEPAL HANDBOOK   by Kerry Moran
Whether you're planning a week in Kathmandu or months out on the trail, *Nepal Handbook* will take you into the heart of this Himalayan jewel. 378 pages.   **$12.95**

NEPALI AAMA by Broughton Coburn
A delightful photo-journey into the life of a Gurung tribeswoman of Central Nepal. Having lived with Aama (translated, "mother") for two years, first as an outsider and later as an adopted member of the family, Coburn presents an intimate glimpse into a culture alive with humor, folklore, religion, and ancient rituals. 165 pages. **$13.95**

PAKISTAN HANDBOOK by Isobel Shaw
For armchair travelers and trekkers alike, the most detailed and authoritative guide to Pakistan ever published. Urdu glossary. 478 pages. **$15.95**

STAYING HEALTHY IN ASIA, AFRICA, AND LATIN AMERICA
by Dirk G. Schroeder, Sc D, MPH
Don't leave home without it! Besides providing a complete overview of the health problems that exist in these areas, this book will help you determine which immunizations you'll need beforehand, what medications to take with you, and how to recognize and treat infections and diseases. Includes extensively illustrated first-aid information and precautions for heat, cold, and high altitude. 200 pages. **$10.95**

**New travel handbooks may be available that are not on this list.
To find out more about current or upcoming titles,
call us toll-free at (800) 345-5473.**

TRAVEL MATTERS

Travel Matters is Moon Publications' biannual newsletter. It provides today's traveler with timely, informative travel news and articles.

You'll find resourceful coverage on:

‣ **Money**—What does it cost? Is it worth it?

• **Low impact travel**—tread lightly travel tips

• **Special interest travel**—cultural tours, environmental excursions, outdoor recreation, adventure treks, and more

• **Travel styles**—families, seniors, disabled travelers, package and theme tours

• **Consumer reviews**—books, language aids, travel gadgets, products, and services

• **Facts and opinions**—reader's letters and Moon Handbook author news

• **Moon Handbook booklist**—the latest titles and editions, and where and how to purchase them

To receive a free copy of *Travel Matters*, write Moon Publications Inc., P.O. Box 3040, Chico, CA 95927-3040, or call toll-free (800) 345-5473.

IMPORTANT ORDERING INFORMATION

FOR FASTER SERVICE: Call to locate the bookstore nearest you that carries Moon Travel Handbooks or order directly from Moon Publications:

(800) 345-5473 • **Monday-Friday** • **9 a.m.-5 p.m. PST** • fax **(916) 345-6751**

PRICES: All prices are subject to change. We always ship the most current edition. We will let you know if there is a price increase on the book you ordered.

SHIPPING & HANDLING OPTIONS: 1) Domestic UPS or USPS first class (allow 10 working days for delivery): $3.50 for the first item, 50 cents for each additional item.

Exceptions:
 • **Moonbelt** shipping is $1.50 for one, 50 cents for each additional belt.
 • Add $2.00 for same-day handling.
 • UPS 2nd Day Air or Printed Airmail requires a special quote.
 • International Surface Bookrate (8-12 weeks delivery):
   $3.00 for the first item, $1.00 for each additional item. Note: Moon Publications cannot guarantee international surface bookrate shipping.

FOREIGN ORDERS: All orders that originate outside the U.S.A. must be paid for with either an International Money Order or a check in U.S. currency drawn on a major U.S. bank based in the U.S.A.

TELEPHONE ORDERS: We accept Visa or MasterCard payments. Minimum order is US$15.00. Call in your order: (800) 345-5473, 9 a.m.-5 p.m. Pacific Standard Time.

MOONBELTS

Made of heavy-duty Cordura nylon, the Moonbelt offers maximum protection for your money and important papers. This all-weather pouch slips under your shirt or waistband, rendering it virtually undetectable and inaccessible to pickpockets. One-inch-wide nylon webbing, heavy-duty zipper, one-inch quick-release buckle. Accommodates traveler's checks, passport, cash, photos. Size 5 x 9 inches. Black.   **$8.95**

ORDER FORM

Be sure to call (800) 345-5473 for current prices and editions or for the name of the bookstore
nearest you that carries Moon Travel Handbooks • 9 a.m.–5 p.m. PST
(See important ordering information on preceding page)

Name: _____ Date: _____

Street: _____.

City: _____ Daytime Phone: _____

State or Country: _____ Zip Code: _____

QUANTITY	TITLE	PRICE

Taxable Total_____

Sales Tax (7.25%) for California Residents_____

Shipping & Handling_____

TOTAL_____

Ship: ☐ UPS (no PO Boxes)   ☐ 1st class   ☐ International surface mail

Ship to: ☐ address above   ☐ other _____

_____

Make checks payable to: **MOON PUBLICATIONS, INC.** P.O. Box 3040, Chico, CA 95927-3040
U.S.A. We accept Visa and MasterCard. **To Order**: Call in your Visa or MasterCard number, or send
a written order with your Visa or MasterCard number and expiration date clearly written.

Card Number: ☐ **Visa**   ☐ **MasterCard**

☐ ☐ ☐ ☐ ☐ ☐ ☐ ☐ ☐ ☐ ☐ ☐ ☐ ☐ ☐ ☐

Exact Name on Card: _____

expiration date:_____

signature_____

SP/93

WHERE TO BUY THIS BOOK

BOOKSTORES AND LIBRARIES:
Moon Publications Handbooks are sold worldwide. Please write our sales manager for a list of wholesalers and distributors in your area that stock our travel handbooks.

TRAVELERS:
We would like to have Moon Publications Handbooks available throughout the world. Please ask your bookstore to write or call us for ordering information. If your bookstore will not order our guides for you, please write or call for a free catalog.

MOON PUBLICATIONS, INC.
P.O. BOX 3040
CHICO, CA 95927-3040 U.S.A.
TEL: (800) 345-5473
FAX: (916) 345-6751

THE METRIC SYSTEM

1 inch = 2.54 centimeters (cm)
1 foot = .304 meters (m)
1 mile = 1.6093 kilometers (km)
1 km = .6124 miles
1 fathom = 1.8288 m
1 chain = 20.1168 m
1 furlong = 201.168 m
1 acre = .4047 hectares
1 sq km = 100 hectares
1 sq mile = 2.59 square km
1 ounce = 28.35 grams
1 pound = .4536 kilograms
1 short ton = .90718 metric ton
1 short ton = 2000 pounds
1 long ton = 1.016 metric tons
1 long ton = 2240 pounds
1 metric ton = 1000 kilograms
1 quart = .94635 liters
1 US gallon = 3.7854 liters
1 Imperial gallon = 4.5459 liters
1 nautical mile = 1.852 km

To compute centigrade temperatures, subtract 32 from Fahrenheit and divide by 1.8. To go the other way, multiply centigrade by 1.8 and add 32.